T5-CCJ-878

2000 DOCUMENTS SUPPLEMENT TO

NAFTA

A PROBLEM–ORIENTED COURSEBOOK

By

Ralph H. Folsom
Professor of Law
University of San Diego

Michael Wallace Gordon
Professor of Law
University of Florida

David Lopez
Professor of Law
St. Mary's University, San Antonio

AMERICAN CASEBOOK SERIES®

WEST GROUP

ST. PAUL, MINN., 2000

American Casebook Series, and the West Group symbol
are registered trademarks used herein under license.

COPYRIGHT © 2000 By WEST GROUP
                610 Opperman Drive
                P.O. Box 64526
                St. Paul, MN 55164–0526
                1–800–328–9352

All rights reserved
Printed in the United States of America

ISBN 0–314–23968–5

 TEXT IS PRINTED ON 10% POST
CONSUMER RECYCLED PAPER

Preface

The 2000 edition of this Documents Supplement is designed to accompany the first edition of our West Group problem-oriented coursebook, The Law of the NAFTA (2000). Nearly every problem in the cousebook in some way involves the application of documentary law. The Supplement provides primary legal authority indispensable to the resolution of the many issues raised in each problem.

This Documents Supplement includes most of the NAFTA and its annexes, plus numerous related documents, such as the procedural rules and codes of conduct for dispute resolution panels. Annexes to specific articles of the NAFTA, and the Environmental and Labor Side Agreements, have been placed at the end of each specific article, rather than all together at the end of the Document. Several of the Documents are edited to provide those portions of each law which are necessary to discussing the issues raised in each problem.

Your suggestions as to what might be added to the next edition of this Supplement, as well as to the coursebook, are most welcome.

RALPH H. FOLSOM
San Diego, California

MICHAEL WALLACE GORDON
Gainesville, Florida

DAVID LOPEZ
San Antonio, Texas

December, 1999

*

Table of Contents

*

2000 DOCUMENTS SUPPLEMENT TO

NAFTA

A PROBLEM–ORIENTED COURSEBOOK

*

A. THE BASIC AGREEMENT—THE NORTH AMERICAN FREE TRADE AGREEMENT

DOCUMENT 1

NORTH AMERICAN FREE TRADE AGREEMENT BETWEEN THE GOVERNMENT OF THE UNITED STATES OF AMERICA, THE GOVERNMENT OF CANADA AND THE GOVERNMENT OF THE UNITED MEXICAN STATES

Table of Contents

PREAMBLE

PART ONE. GENERAL

PART TWO. TRADE IN GOODS

PART EIGHT. OTHER PROVISIONS

PREAMBLE

The Government of the United States of America, the Government of Canada and the Government of the United Mexican States, resolved to: STRENGTHEN the special bonds of friendship and cooperation among their nations; CONTRIBUTE to the harmonious development and expansion of world trade and provide a catalyst to broader international cooperation; CREATE an expanded and secure market for the goods and services produced in their territories; REDUCE distortions to trade; ESTABLISH clear and mutually advantageous rules governing their trade; ENSURE a predictable commercial framework for business planning and investment; BUILD on their respective rights and obligations under the General Agreement on Tariffs and Trade and other multilateral and bilateral instruments of cooperation; ENHANCE the competitiveness of their firms in global markets; FOSTER creativity and innovation, and promote trade in goods and services that are the subject of intellectual property rights; CREATE new employment opportunities and improve working conditions and living standards in their respective territories; UNDERTAKE each of the preceding in a manner consistent with environmental protection and conservation; PRESERVE their flexibility to safeguard the public welfare; PROMOTE sustainable development; STRENGTHEN the development and enforcement of environmental laws and regulations; and PROTECT, enhance and enforce basic workers' rights;

HAVE AGREED as follows:

Part One
GENERAL

Chapter One

OBJECTIVES

Article 101: Establishment of the Free Trade Area

The Parties to this Agreement, consistent with Article XXIV of the General Agreement on Tariffs and Trade, hereby establish a free trade area.

Article 102: Objectives

1. The objectives of this Agreement, as elaborated more specifically through its principles and rules, including national treatment, most-favored-nation treatment and transparency, are to:

(a) eliminate barriers to trade in, and facilitate the cross-border movement of, goods and services between the territories of the Parties;

(b) promote conditions of fair competition in the free trade area;

(c) increase substantially investment opportunities in the territories of the Parties;

(d) provide adequate and effective protection and enforcement of intellectual property rights in each Party's territory;

(e) create effective procedures for the implementation and application of this Agreement, for its joint administration and for the resolution of disputes; and

(f) establish a framework for further trilateral, regional and multilateral cooperation to expand and enhance the benefits of this Agreement.

2. The Parties shall interpret and apply the provisions of this Agreement in the light of its objectives set out in paragraph 1 and in accordance with applicable rules of international law.

Article 103: Relation to Other Agreements

1. The Parties affirm their existing rights and obligations with respect to each other under the General Agreement on Tariffs and Trade and other agreements to which such Parties are party.

2. In the event of any inconsistency between this Agreement and such other agreements, this Agreement shall prevail to the extent of the inconsistency, except as otherwise provided in this Agreement.

Article 104: Relation to Environmental and Conservation Agreements

1. In the event of any inconsistency between this Agreement and the specific trade obligations set out in:

(a) the Convention on International Trade in Endangered Species of Wild Fauna and Flora, done at Washington, March 3, 1973, as amended June 22, 1979,

(b) the Montreal Protocol on Substances that Deplete the Ozone Layer, done at Montreal, September 16, 1987, as amended June 29, 1990,

(c) the Basel Convention on the Control of Transboundary Movements of Hazardous Wastes and Their Disposal, done at Basel, March 22, 1989, on its entry into force for Canada, Mexico and the United States, or

(d) the agreements set out in Annex 104.1,such obligations shall prevail to the extent of the inconsistency, provided that where a Party has a choice among equally effective and reasonably available means of complying with such obligations, the Party chooses the alternative that is the least inconsistent with the other provisions of this Agreement.

2. The Parties may agree in writing to modify Annex 104.1 to include any amendment to an agreement referred to in paragraph 1, and any other environmental or conservation agreement.

Annex 104.1

Bilateral and Other Environmental and Conservation Agreements

1. The Agreement Between the Government of Canada and the Government of the United States of America Concerning the Transboundary Movement of Hazardous Waste, signed at Ottawa, October 28, 1986.

2. The Agreement Between the United States of America and the United Mexican States on Cooperation for the Protection and Improvement of the Environment in the Border Area, signed at La Paz, Baja California Sur, August 14, 1983.

Article 105: Extent of Obligations

The Parties shall ensure that all necessary measures are taken in order to give effect to the provisions of this Agreement, including their observance, except as otherwise provided in this Agreement, by state and provincial governments.

Chapter Two

GENERAL DEFINITIONS

Article 201: Definitions of General Application

1. For purposes of this Agreement, unless otherwise specified:

Commission means the Free Trade Commission established under Article 2001(1) (The Free Trade Commission);

Customs Valuation Code means the Agreement on Implementation of Article VII of the General Agreement on Tariffs and Trade, including its interpretative notes;

days means calendar days, including weekends and holidays;

enterprise means any entity constituted or organized under applicable law, whether or not for profit, and whether privately-owned or governmentally-owned, including any corporation, trust, partnership, sole proprietorship, joint venture or other association;

enterprise of a Party means an enterprise constituted or organized under the law of a Party;

existing means in effect on the date of entry into force of this Agreement;

Generally Accepted Accounting Principles means the recognized consensus or substantial authoritative support in the territory of a Party with respect to the recording of revenues, expenses, costs, assets and liabilities, disclosure of information and preparation of financial statements. These standards may be broad guidelines of general application as well as detailed standards, practices and procedures;

goods of a Party means domestic products as these are understood in the General Agreement on Tariffs and Trade or such goods as the Parties may agree, and includes originating goods of that Party;

Harmonized System (HS) means the Harmonized Commodity Description and Coding System, and its legal notes and rules, as adopted and implemented by the Parties in their respective tariff laws;

measure includes any law, regulation, procedure, requirement or practice;

national means a natural person who is a citizen or permanent resident of a Party and any other natural person referred to in Annex 201.1;

originating means qualifying under the rules of origin set out in Chapter Four (Rules of Origin);

person means a natural person or an enterprise;

person of a Party means a national, or an enterprise of a Party;

Secretariat means the Secretariat established under Article 2002(1) (The Secretariat);

state enterprise means an enterprise that is owned, or controlled through ownership interests, by a Party; and

territory means for a Party the territory of that Party as set out in Annex 201.1.

2.   For purposes of this Agreement, unless otherwise specified, a reference to a state or province includes local governments of that state or province.

Annex 201.1

Country–Specific Definitions

For purposes of this Agreement, unless otherwise specified:

national also includes: (a) with respect to Mexico, a national or a citizen according to Articles 30 and 34, respectively, of the Mexican Constitution; and (b) with respect to the United States, "national of the United States" as defined in the existing provisions of the Immigration and Nationality Act;

territory means: (a) with respect to Canada, the territory to which its customs laws apply, including any areas beyond the territorial seas of Canada within which, in accordance with international law and its domestic law, Canada may exercise rights with respect to the seabed and subsoil and their natural resources; (b) with respect to Mexico, (i) the states of the Federation and the Federal District, (ii) the islands, including the reefs and keys, in adjacent seas, (iii) the islands of Guadalupe and Revillagigedo situated in the Pacific Ocean, (iv) the continental shelf and the submarine shelf of such islands, keys and reefs, (v) the waters of the territorial seas, in accordance with international law, and its interior maritime waters, (vi) the space located above the national territory, in accordance with international law, and (vii) any areas beyond the territorial seas of Mexico within which, in accordance with international law, including the United Nations Convention on the Law of the Sea, and its domestic law, Mexico may exercise rights with respect to the seabed and subsoil and their natural resources; and (c) with respect to the United States, (i) the customs territory of the United

States, which includes the 50 states, the District of Columbia and Puerto
Rico, (ii) the foreign trade zones located in the United States and Puerto
Rico, and (iii) any areas beyond the territorial seas of the United States
within which, in accordance with international law and its domestic law,
the United States may exercise rights with respect to the seabed and
subsoil and their natural resources.

Part Two
TRADE IN GOODS

Chapter Three

NATIONAL TREATMENT AND MARKET ACCESS FOR GOODS

Article 300: Scope and Coverage

This Chapter applies to trade in goods of a Party, including: (a) goods covered by Annex 300–A (Trade and Investment in the Automotive Sector), (b) goods covered by Annex 300–B (Textile and Apparel Goods), and (c) goods covered by another Chapter in this Part, except as provided in such Annex or Chapter.

Section A—National Treatment

Article 301: National Treatment

1. Each Party shall accord national treatment to the goods of another Party in accordance with Article III of the General Agreement on Tariffs and Trade (GATT), including its interpretative notes, and to this end Article III of the GATT and its interpretative notes, or any equivalent provision of a successor agreement to which all Parties are party, are incorporated into and made part of this Agreement.

2. The provisions of paragraph 1 regarding national treatment shall mean, with respect to a state or province, treatment no less favorable than the most favorable treatment accorded by such state or province to any like, directly competitive or substitutable goods, as the case may be, of the Party of which it forms a part.

3. Paragraphs 1 and 2 do not apply to the measures set out in Annex 301.3.

Annex 301.3

Exceptions to Articles 301 and 309

Section A—Canadian Measures

1. Articles 301 and 309 shall not apply to controls by Canada on the export of logs of all species.

2.   Articles 301 and 309 shall not apply to controls by Canada on the export of unprocessed fish pursuant to the following existing statutes, as amended as of August 12, 1992: (a) New Brunswick Fish Processing Act, R.S.N.B. c. F–18.01 (1982), and Fisheries Development Act, S.N.B. c. F–15.1 (1977); (b) Newfoundland Fish Inspection Act, R.S.N.1990, c. F–12; (c) Nova Scotia Fisheries Act, S.N.S.1977, c. 9; (d) Prince Edward Island Fish Inspection Act, R.S.P.E.I.1988, c. F–13; and (e) Quebec Marine Products Processing Act, No. 38, S.Q.1987, c. 51.

3.   Articles 301 and 309 shall not apply to: (a) except as provided in Annex 300–A, Appendix 300–A.1, paragraph 4, measures by Canada respecting the importation of any goods enumerated or referred to in Schedule VII of the Customs Tariff, R.S.C.1985, c. 41 (3rd Supp.), as amended, (b) measures by Canada respecting the exportation of liquor for delivery into any country into which the importation of liquor is prohibited by law under the existing provisions of the Export Act, R.S.C.1985, c. E–18, as amended, (c) measures by Canada respecting preferential rates for certain freight traffic under the existing provisions of the Maritime Freight Rate Act, R.S.C.1985, c. M–1, as amended, (d) Canadian excise duties on absolute alcohol used in manufacturing under the existing provisions of the Excise Act, R.S.C.1985, c. E–14, as amended, and (e) measures by Canada prohibiting the use of foreign or non-duty paid ships in the coasting trade of Canada unless granted a license under the Coasting Trade Act, S.C.1992, c. 31, to the extent that such provisions were mandatory legislation at the time of Canada's accession to the GATT and have not been amended so as to decrease their conformity with the GATT.

4.   Articles 301 and 309 shall not apply to quantitative import restrictions on goods that originate in the territory of the United States, considering operations performed in, or materials obtained from, Mexico as if they were performed in, or obtained from, a non-Party, and that are indicated by asterisks in Chapter 89 in Annex 401.2 (Tariff Schedule of Canada) of the Canada–United States Free Trade Agreement for as long as the measures taken under the Merchant Marine Act of 1920, 46 App. U.S.C. § 883, and the Merchant Marine Act of 1936, 46 App. U.S.C. §§ 1171, 1176, 1241 and 1241o, apply with quantitative effect to comparable Canadian origin goods sold or offered for sale into the U.S. market.

5.   Articles 301 and 309 shall not apply to: (a) the continuation or prompt renewal of a non-conforming provision of any statute referred to in paragraph 2 or 3; and (b) the amendment to a non-conforming provision of any statute referred to in paragraph 2 or 3 to the extent that the amendment does not decrease the conformity of the provision with Articles 301 and 309.

Section B—Mexican Measures

1.   Articles 301 and 309 shall not apply to controls by Mexico on the export of logs of all species.

2.   Articles 301 and 309 shall not apply to: (a) measures under the existing provisions of Articles 192 through 194 of the General Ways of Communication Act ("Ley de Vias Generales de Communicacion") reserving exclusively to Mexican vessels all services and operations not authorized for foreign vessels and empowering the Mexican Ministry of Communications and Transportation to deny foreign vessels the right to perform authorized services if their country of origin does not grant reciprocal rights to Mexican vessels; and (b) export permit measures applied to goods for exportation to another Party that are subject to quantitative restrictions or tariff rate quotas adopted or maintained by that other Party.

3.   Articles 301 and 309 shall not apply to: (a) the continuation or prompt renewal of a non-conforming provision of the statute referred to in paragraph 2(a); and (b) the amendment to a non-conforming provision of the statute referred to in paragraph 2(a) to the extent that the amendment does not decrease the conformity of the provision with Articles 301 and 309.

4.   (a) Notwithstanding Article 309, for the first 10 years after the date of entry into force of this Agreement, Mexico may adopt or maintain prohibitions or restrictions on the importation of used goods provided for in the items, as of August 12, 1992, in the Tariff Schedule of the General Import Duty Act (Tarifa de la "Ley del Impuesto General de Importacion") set out below: * * *

(b) Notwithstanding subparagraph (a), Mexico shall not prohibit or restrict the importation, on a temporary basis, of used goods provided for in the items set out in subparagraph (c) for the provision of a cross-border service subject to Chapter Twelve (Cross–Border Trade in Services) or the performance of a contract subject to Chapter Ten (Government Procurement), provided that the imported goods (i) are necessary to the provision of the cross-border service or the performance of the contract awarded to a supplier of another Party, (ii) are used solely by or under the supervision of the service provider or the supplier performing the contract, (iii) are not sold, leased or loaned while in the territory of Mexico, (iv) are imported in no greater quantity than is necessary for the provision of the service or the performance of the contract, (v) are re-exported promptly on completion of the service or the contract, and (vi) comply with other applicable requirements on the importation of such goods to the extent they are not inconsistent with this Agreement.

(c) Subparagraph (b) applies to used goods provided for in the following items: * * *

Section C—U.S. Measures

1.   Articles 301 and 309 shall not apply to controls by the United States on the export of logs of all species.

2.   Articles 301 and 309 shall not apply to: (a) taxes on imported perfume containing distilled spirits under existing provisions of sections 5001(a)(3) and 5007(b)(2) of the Internal Revenue Code of 1986, 26

U.S.C. §§ 5001(a)(3) and 5007(b)(2), and (b) measures under existing provisions of the Merchant Marine Act of 1920, 46 App.U.S.C. § 883; the Passenger Vessel Act, 46 App.U.S.C. §§ 289, 292 and 316; and 46 U.S.C. § 12108, to the extent that such measures were mandatory legislation at the time of the United States' accession to the GATT and have not been amended so as to decrease their conformity with the GATT.

3.   Articles 301 and 309 shall not apply to: (a) the continuation or prompt renewal of a non-conforming provision of any statute referred to in paragraph 2; and (b) the amendment to a non-conforming provision of any statute referred to in paragraph 2 to the extent that the amendment does not decrease the conformity of the provision with Articles 301 and 309.

Section B—Tariffs

Article 302: Tariff Elimination

1.   Except as otherwise provided in this Agreement, no Party may increase any existing customs duty, or adopt any customs duty, on an originating good.

2.   Except as otherwise provided in this Agreement, each Party shall progressively eliminate its customs duties on originating goods in accordance with its Schedule to Annex 302.2.

3.   On the request of any Party, the Parties shall consult to consider accelerating the elimination of customs duties set out in their Schedules. An agreement between two or more Parties to accelerate the elimination of a customs duty on a good shall supersede any duty rate or staging category determined pursuant to their Schedules for such good when approved by each such Party in accordance with its applicable legal procedures.

4.   Each Party may adopt or maintain import measures to allocate in-quota imports made pursuant to a tariff rate quota set out in Annex 302.2, provided that such measures do not have trade restrictive effects on imports additional to those caused by the imposition of the tariff rate quota.

5.   On written request of any Party, a Party applying or intending to apply measures pursuant to paragraph 4 shall consult to review the administration of those measures.

Annex 302.2

Tariff Elimination

1.   Except as otherwise provided in a Party's Schedule attached to this Annex, the following staging categories apply to the elimination of customs duties by each Party pursuant to Article 302(2): (a) duties on goods provided for in the items in staging category A in a Party's Schedule shall be eliminated entirely and such goods shall be duty-free, effective January 1, 1994; (b) duties on goods provided for in the items in

staging category B in a Party's Schedule shall be removed in five equal annual stages beginning on January 1, 1994, and such goods shall be duty-free, effective January 1, 1998; (c) duties on goods provided for in the items in staging category C in a Party's Schedule shall be removed in 10 equal annual stages beginning on January 1, 1994, and such goods shall be duty-free, effective January 1, 2003; (d) duties on goods provided for in the items in staging category C+ in a Party's Schedule shall be removed in 15 equal annual stages beginning on January 1, 1994, and such goods shall be duty-free, effective January 1, 2008; and (e) goods provided for in the items in staging category D in a Party's Schedule shall continue to receive duty-free treatment.

2. The base rate of customs duty and staging category for determining the interim rate of customs duty at each stage of reduction for an item are indicated for the item in each Party's Schedule attached to this Annex. These rates generally reflect the rate of duty in effect on July 1, 1991, including rates under the U.S. Generalized System of Preferences and the General Preferential Tariff of Canada.

3. For the purpose of the elimination of customs duties in accordance with Article 302, interim staged rates shall be rounded down, except as set out in each Party's Schedule attached to this Annex, at least to the nearest tenth of a percentage point or, if the rate of duty is expressed in monetary units, at least to the nearest .001 of the official monetary unit of the Party.

4. Canada shall apply a rate of customs duty no higher than the rate applicable under the staging category set out for an item in Annex 401.2, as amended, of the Canada–United States Free Trade Agreement, which Annex is hereby incorporated into and made a part of this Agreement, to an originating good provided that: (a) notwithstanding any provision in Chapter Four, in determining whether such good is an originating good, operations performed in or materials obtained from Mexico are considered as if they were performed in or obtained from a non-Party; and (b) any processing that occurs in Mexico after the good would qualify as an originating good in accordance with subparagraph (a) does not increase the transaction value of the good by greater than seven percent.

5. Canada shall apply a rate of customs duty no higher than the rate applicable under the staging category set out for an item in Column I of its Schedule to this Annex to an originating good provided that: (a) notwithstanding any provision in Chapter Four, in determining whether such good is an originating good, operations performed in or materials obtained from the United States are considered as if they were performed in or obtained from a non-Party; and (b) any processing that occurs in the United States after the good would qualify as an originating good in accordance with subparagraph (a) does not increase the transaction value of the good by greater than seven percent.

6. Canada shall apply to an originating good to which neither paragraph 4 nor 5 applies a rate of customs duty no higher than the rate

indicated for its corresponding item in Column II of its Schedule to this Annex. The rate of customs duty in Column II for such good shall be: (a) in each year of the staging category indicated in Column I, the higher of (i) the rate of customs duty under the staging category set out for the item in Annex 401.2, as amended, of the Canada–United States Free Trade Agreement, and (ii) the General Preferential Tariff rate of customs duty for the item applied on July 1, 1991, reduced in accordance with the applicable staging category set out for the item in Column I of its Schedule to this Annex; or (b) where specified in Column II of its Schedule to this Annex, the most-favored-nation rate of customs duty for the item applied on July 1, 1991, reduced in accordance with the applicable staging category set out for the item in Column I of its Schedule to this Annex, or reduced in accordance with the applicable staging category otherwise indicated.

7. Paragraphs 4 through 6 and 10 through 13 shall not apply to textile and apparel goods identified in Appendix 1.1 of Annex 300–B (Textiles and Apparel Goods).

8. Paragraphs 4, 5 and 6 shall not apply to agricultural goods as defined in Article 708. For these goods, Canada shall apply the rate applicable under the staging category set out for an item in Annex 401.2, as amended, of the Canada–United States Free Trade Agreement to an originating good when the good qualifies to be marked as a good of the United States pursuant to Annex 311, without regard to whether the good is marked. When an originating good qualifies to be marked as a good of Mexico, pursuant to Annex 311, whether or not the good is marked, Canada shall apply the rate applicable under the staging category set out for an item in Column I of its Schedule to this Annex.

9. As between the United States and Canada, Article 401(7) and (8) of the Canada–United States Free Trade Agreement is hereby incorporated and made a part of this Annex. The term "goods originating in the territory of the United States of America" in Article 401(7) of that agreement shall be determined in accordance with paragraph 4 of this Annex. The term "goods originating in the territory of Canada" in Article 401(8) of that agreement shall be determined in accordance with paragraph 12 of this Annex.

10. Mexico shall apply a rate of customs duty no higher than the rate applicable under the staging category set out for an item in Column I of its Schedule to this Annex to an originating good when the good qualifies to be marked as a good of the United States, pursuant to Annex 311, without regard to whether the good is marked.

11. Mexico shall apply a rate of customs duty no higher than the rate applicable under the staging category set out for an item in Column II of its Schedule to this Annex to an originating good when the good qualifies to be marked as a good of Canada, pursuant to Annex 311, without regard to whether the good is marked.

12. The United States shall apply a rate of customs duty no higher than the rate applicable under the staging category set out for an item in

Annex 401.2, as amended, of the Canada–United States Free Trade Agreement to an originating good when the good qualifies to be marked as a good of Canada pursuant to Annex 311, without regard to whether the good is marked.

13. The United States shall apply a rate of customs duty no higher than the rate applicable under the staging category set out for an item in its Schedule to this Annex to an originating good when the good qualifies to be marked as a good of Mexico pursuant to Annex 311, whether or not the good is marked.

[The schedules of Canada, Mexico and the United States are omitted]

Article 303: Restriction on Drawback and Duty Deferral Programs

1. Except as otherwise provided in this Article, no Party may refund the amount of customs duties paid, or waive or reduce the amount of customs duties owed, on a good imported into its territory, on condition that the good is: (a) subsequently exported to the territory of another Party, (b) used as a material in the production of another good that is subsequently exported to the territory of another Party, or (c) substituted by an identical or similar good used as a material in the production of another good that is subsequently exported to the territory of another Party, in an amount that exceeds the lesser of the total amount of customs duties paid or owed on the good on importation into its territory and the total amount of customs duties paid to another Party on the good that has been subsequently exported to the territory of that other Party.

2. No Party may, on condition of export, refund, waive or reduce: (a) an antidumping or countervailing duty that is applied pursuant to a Party's domestic law and that is not applied inconsistently with Chapter Nineteen (Review and Dispute Settlement in Antidumping and Countervailing Duty Matters); (b) a premium offered or collected on an imported good arising out of any tendering system in respect of the administration of quantitative import restrictions, tariff rate quotas or tariff preference levels; (c) a fee applied pursuant to section 22 of the U.S. Agricultural Adjustment Act, subject to Chapter Seven (Agriculture and Sanitary and Phytosanitary Measures); or (d) customs duties paid or owed on a good imported into its territory and substituted by an identical or similar good that is subsequently exported to the territory of another Party.

3. Where a good is imported into the territory of a Party pursuant to a duty deferral program and is subsequently exported to the territory of another Party, or is used as a material in the production of another good that is subsequently exported to the territory of another Party, or is substituted by an identical or similar good used as a material in the production of another good that is subsequently exported to the territory of another Party, the Party from whose territory the good is exported:

(a) shall assess the customs duties as if the exported good had been withdrawn for domestic consumption; and (b) may waive or reduce such customs duties to the extent permitted under paragraph 1.

4.   In determining the amount of customs duties that may be refunded, waived or reduced pursuant to paragraph 1 on a good imported into its territory, each Party shall require presentation of satisfactory evidence of the amount of customs duties paid to another Party on the good that has been subsequently exported to the territory of that other Party.

5.   Where satisfactory evidence of the customs duties paid to the Party to which a good is subsequently exported under a duty deferral program described in paragraph 3 is not presented within 60 days after the date of exportation, the Party from whose territory the good was exported: (a) shall collect customs duties as if the exported good had been withdrawn for domestic consumption; and (b) may refund such customs duties to the extent permitted under paragraph 1 on the timely presentation of such evidence under its laws and regulations.

6.   This Article does not apply to: (a) a good entered under bond for transportation and exportation to the territory of another Party; (b) a good exported to the territory of another Party in the same condition as when imported into the territory of the Party from which the good was exported (processes such as testing, cleaning, repacking or inspecting the good, or preserving it in its same condition, shall not be considered to change a good's condition). Except as provided in Annex 703.2, Section A, paragraph 12, where such a good has been commingled with fungible goods and exported in the same condition, its origin for purposes of this subparagraph may be determined on the basis of the inventory methods provided for in the Uniform Regulations established under Article 511 (Uniform Regulations); (c) a good imported into the territory of a Party that is deemed to be exported from its territory, or used as a material in the production of another good that is deemed to be exported to the territory of another Party, or is substituted by an identical or similar good used as a material in the production of another good that is deemed to be exported to the territory of another Party, by reason of (i) delivery to a duty-free shop, (ii) delivery for ship's stores or supplies for ships or aircraft, or (iii) delivery for use in joint undertakings of two or more of the Parties and that will subsequently become the property of the Party into whose territory the good was deemed to be exported; (d) a refund of customs duties by a Party on a particular good imported into its territory and subsequently exported to the territory of another Party, where that refund is granted by reason of the failure of such good to conform to sample or specification, or by reason of the shipment of such good without the consent of the consignee; (e) an originating good that is imported into the territory of a Party and is subsequently exported to the territory of another Party, or used as a material in the production of another good that is subsequently exported to the territory of another Party, or is substituted by an identical or similar good used as a material

in the production of another good that is subsequently exported to the territory of another Party; or (f) a good set out in Annex 303.6.

7. Except for paragraph 2(d), this Article shall apply as of the date set out in each Party's Section of Annex 303.7.

8. Notwithstanding any other provision of this Article and except as specifically provided in Annex 303.8, no Party may refund the amount of customs duties paid, or waive or reduce the amount of customs duties owed, on a non-originating good provided for in item 8540.11.aa (color cathode-ray television picture tubes, including video monitor tubes, with a diagonal exceeding 14 inches) or 8540.11.cc (color cathode-ray television picture tubes for high definition television, with a diagonal exceeding 14 inches) that is imported into the Party's territory and subsequently exported to the territory of another Party, or is used as a material in the production of another good that is subsequently exported to the territory of another Party, or is substituted by an identical or similar good used as a material in the production of another good that is subsequently exported to the territory of another Party.

9. For purposes of this Article:

customs duties are the customs duties that would be applicable to a good entered for consumption in the customs territory of a Party if the good were not exported to the territory of another party;

identical or similar goods means "identical or similar goods" as defined in Article 415 (Rules of Origin—Definitions);

material means "material" as defined in Article 415; and

used means "used" as defined in Article 415.

10. For purposes of this Article:

Where a good referred to by a tariff item number in this Article is described in parentheses following the tariff item number, the description is provided for purposes of reference only.

Annex 303.6

Goods Not Subject to Article 303

1. For exports from the territory of the United States to the territory of Canada or Mexico, a good provided for in U.S. tariff item 1701.11.02 that is imported into the territory of the United States and used as a material in the production of, or substituted by an identical or similar good used as a material in the production of, a good provided for in Canadian tariff item 1701.99.00 or Mexican tariff items 1701.99.01 and 1701.99.99 (refined sugar) is not subject to Article 303.

2. For trade between Canada and the United States the following are not subject to Article 303: (a) imported citrus products; (b) an imported good used as a material in the production of, or substituted by an identical or similar good used as a material in the production of, a good provided for in U.S. items 5811.00.20 (quilted cotton piece goods), 5811.00.30 (quilted man-made piece goods) or 6307.90.99 (furniture

moving pads), or Canadian items 5811.00.10 (quilted cotton piece goods), 5811.00.20 (quilted man-made piece goods) or 6307.90.30 (furniture moving pads), that are subject to the most-favored-nation rate of duty when exported to the territory of the other Party; and (c) an imported good used as a material in the production of, or substituted by an identical or similar good used as a material in the production of, apparel that is subject to the most-favored-nation rate of duty when exported to the territory of the other Party.

Annex 303.7

Effective Dates for the Application of Article 303

Section A—Canada

For Canada, Article 303 shall apply to a good imported into the territory of Canada that is: (a) subsequently exported to the territory of the United States on or after January 1, 1996, or subsequently exported to the territory of Mexico on or after January 1, 2001; (b) used as a material in the production of another good that is subsequently exported to the territory of the United States on or after January 1, 1996, or used as a material in the production of another good that is subsequently exported to the territory of Mexico on or after January 1, 2001; or (c) substituted by an identical or similar good used as a material in the production of another good that is subsequently exported to the territory of the United States on or after January 1, 1996, or substituted by an identical or similar good used as a material in the production of another good that is subsequently exported to the territory of Mexico on or after January 1, 2001.

Section B—Mexico

For Mexico, Article 303 shall apply to a good imported into the territory of Mexico that is: (a) subsequently exported to the territory of another Party on or after January 1, 2001; (b) used as a material in the production of another good that is subsequently exported to the territory of another Party on or after January 1, 2001; or (c) substituted by an identical or similar good used as a material in the production of another good that is subsequently exported to the territory of another Party on or after January 1, 2001.

Section C—United States

For the United States, Article 303 shall apply to a good imported into the territory of the United States that is: (a) subsequently exported to the territory of Canada on or after January 1, 1996, or subsequently exported to the territory of Mexico on or after January 1, 2001; (b) used as a material in the production of another good that is subsequently exported to the territory of Canada on or after January 1, 1996, or used as a material in the production of another good that is subsequently exported to the territory of Mexico on or after January 1, 2001; or (c) substituted by an identical or similar good used as a material in the production of another good subsequently exported to the territory of Canada on or after January 1, 1996, or substituted by an identical or similar good used as a material in the production of another good subsequently exported to the territory of Mexico on or after January 1, 2001.

Annex 303.8

Exception to Article 303(8) for Certain Color Cathode–Ray Television Picture Tubes—Mexico * * *

Article 304: Waiver of Customs Duties

1. Except as set out in Annex 304.1, no Party may adopt any new waiver of customs duties, or expand with respect to existing recipients or extend to any new recipient the application of an existing waiver of customs duties, where the waiver is conditioned, explicitly or implicitly, on the fulfillment of a performance requirement.

2. Except as set out in Annex 304.2, no Party may, explicitly or implicitly, condition on the fulfillment of a performance requirement the continuation of any existing waiver of customs duties.

3. If a waiver or a combination of waivers of customs duties granted by a Party with respect to goods for commercial use by a designated person can be shown by another Party to have an adverse impact on the commercial interests of a person of that Party, or of a person owned or controlled by a person of that Party that is located in the territory of the Party granting the waiver, or on the other Party's economy, the Party granting the waiver shall either cease to grant it or make it generally available to any importer.

4. This Article shall not apply to measures subject to Article 303.

Annex 304.1

Exceptions for Existing Waiver Measures

Article 304(1) shall not apply in respect of existing Mexican waivers of customs duties, except that Mexico shall not: (a) increase the ratio of customs duties waived to customs duties owed relative to the performance required under any such waiver; or (b) add any type of imported good to those qualifying on July 1, 1991, in respect of any waiver of customs duties in effect on that date.

Annex 304.2

Continuation of Existing Waivers of Customs Duties

For purposes of Article 304(2): (a) as between Canada and Mexico, Canada may condition on the fulfillment of a performance requirement the waiver of customs duties under any measure in effect on or before January 1, 1989, on any goods entered or withdrawn from warehouse for consumption before January 1, 1998; (b) as between Canada and the

United States, Article 405 of the Canada–United States Free Trade Agreement is hereby incorporated and made a part of this Annex solely with respect to measures adopted by Canada or the United States prior to the date of entry into force of this Agreement; (c) Mexico may condition on the fulfillment of a performance requirement the waiver of customs duties under any measure in effect on July 1, 1991, on any goods entered or withdrawn from warehouse for consumption before January 1, 2001; and (d) Canada may grant waivers of customs duties as set out in Annex 300–A (Trade and Investment in the Automotive Sector).

Article 305: Temporary Admission of Goods

1.   Each Party shall grant duty-free temporary admission for: (a) professional equipment necessary for carrying out the business activity, trade or profession of a business person who qualifies for temporary entry pursuant to Chapter Sixteen (Temporary Entry for Business Persons), (b) equipment for the press or for sound or television broadcasting and cinematographic equipment, (c) goods imported for sports purposes and goods intended for display or demonstration, and (d) commercial samples and advertising films, imported from the territory of another Party, regardless of their origin and regardless of whether like, directly competitive or substitutable goods are available in the territory of the Party.

2.   Except as otherwise provided in this Agreement, no Party may condition the duty-free temporary admission of a good referred to in paragraph 1(a), (b) or (c), other than to require that such good: (a) be imported by a national or resident of another Party who seeks temporary entry; (b) be used solely by or under the personal supervision of such person in the exercise of the business activity, trade or profession of that person; (c) not be sold or leased while in its territory; (d) be accompanied by a bond in an amount no greater than 110 percent of the charges that would otherwise be owed on entry or final importation, or by another form of security, releasable on exportation of the good, except that a bond for customs duties shall not be required for an originating good; (e) be capable of identification when exported; (f) be exported on the departure of that person or within such other period of time as is reasonably related to the purpose of the temporary admission; and (g) be imported in no greater quantity than is reasonable for its intended use.

3.   Except as otherwise provided in this Agreement, no Party may condition the duty-free temporary admission of a good referred to in paragraph 1(d), other than to require that such good: (a) be imported solely for the solicitation of orders for goods, or services provided from the territory, of another Party or non-Party; (b) not be sold, leased or put to any use other than exhibition or demonstration while in its territory; (c) be capable of identification when exported; (d) be exported within such period as is reasonably related to the purpose of the

temporary admission; and (e) be imported in no greater quantity than is reasonable for its intended use.

4.   A Party may impose the customs duty and any other charge on a good temporarily admitted duty-free under paragraph 1 that would be owed on entry or final importation of such good if any condition that the Party imposes under paragraph 2 or 3 has not been fulfilled.

5.   Subject to Chapters Eleven (Investment) and Twelve (Cross–Border Trade in Services): (a) each Party shall allow a vehicle or container used in international traffic that enters its territory from the territory of another Party to exit its territory on any route that is reasonably related to the economic and prompt departure of such vehicle or container; (b) no Party may require any bond or impose any penalty or charge solely by reason of any difference between the port of entry and the port of departure of a vehicle or container; (c) no Party may condition the release of any obligation, including any bond, that it imposes in respect of the entry of a vehicle or container into its territory on its exit through any particular port of departure; and (d) no Party may require that the vehicle or carrier bringing a container from the territory of another Party into its territory be the same vehicle or carrier that takes such container to the territory of another Party.

6.   For purposes of paragraph 5, "vehicle" means a truck, a truck tractor, tractor, trailer unit or trailer, a locomotive, or a railway car or other railroad equipment.

Article 306: Duty–Free Entry of Certain Commercial Samples and Printed Advertising Materials

Each Party shall grant duty-free entry to commercial samples of negligible value, and to printed advertising materials, imported from the territory of another Party, regardless of their origin, but may require that: (a) such samples be imported solely for the solicitation of orders for goods, or services provided from the territory, of another Party or non-Party; or (b) such advertising materials be imported in packets that each contain no more than one copy of each such material and that neither such materials nor packets form part of a larger consignment.

Article 307: Goods Re–Entered After Repair or Alteration

1.   Except as set out in Annex 307.1, no Party may apply a customs duty to a good, regardless of its origin, that re-enters its territory after that good has been exported from its territory to the territory of another Party for repair or alteration, regardless of whether such repair or alteration could be performed in its territory.

2.   Notwithstanding Article 303, no Party may apply a customs duty to a good, regardless of its origin, imported temporarily from the territory of another Party for repair or alteration.

3. Annex 307.3 applies to the Parties specified in that Annex respecting the repair and rebuilding of vessels.

Annex 307.1

Goods Re-entered After Repair or Alteration

Section A—Canada

Canada may impose customs duties on goods, regardless of their origin, that re-enter its territory after such goods have been exported from its territory to the territory of another Party for repair or alteration as follows: (a) for goods set out in Section D that re-enter its territory from the territory of Mexico, Canada shall apply to the value of the repair or alteration of such goods the rate of customs duty for such goods applicable under its Schedule to Annex 302.2; (b) for goods other than those set out in Section D that re-enter its territory from the territory of the United States or Mexico, other than goods repaired or altered pursuant to a warranty, Canada shall apply to the value of the repair or alteration of such goods the rate of customs duty for such goods applicable under the Tariff Schedule of Canada attached to Annex 401.2 of the Canada–United States Free Trade Agreement, as incorporated into Annex 302.2 of this Agreement; and (c) for goods set out in Section D that re-enter its territory from the territory of the United States, Canada shall apply to the value of the repair or alteration of such goods the rate of customs duty for such goods applicable under its Schedule attached to Annex 401.2 of the Canada–United States Free Trade Agreement, as incorporated into Annex 302.2 of this Agreement.

Section B—Mexico

Mexico may impose customs duties on goods set out in Section D, regardless of their origin, that re-enter its territory after such goods have been exported from its territory to the territory of another Party for repair or alteration, by applying to the value of the repair or alteration of those goods the rate of customs duty for such goods that would apply if such goods were included in staging category B in Mexico's Schedule to Annex 302.2.

Section C—United States

1. The United States may impose customs duties on: (a) goods set out in Section D, or (b) goods that are not set out in Section D and that are not repaired or altered pursuant to a warranty, regardless of their origin, that re-enter its territory after such goods have been exported from its territory to the territory of Canada for repair or alteration, by applying to the value of the repair or alteration of such goods the rate of customs duty applicable under the Canada–United States Free Trade Agreement, as incorporated into Annex 302.2 of this Agreement.

2. The United States may impose customs duties on goods set out in Section D, regardless of their origin, that re-enter its territory after such goods have been exported from its territory to the territory of

Mexico for repair or alteration, by applying to the value of the repair or alteration of such goods a rate of customs duty of 50 percent reduced in five equal annual stages beginning on January 1, 1994, and the value of such repair or alteration shall be duty-free on January 1, 1998.

Section D—List of Goods

Any vessel, including the following goods, documented by a Party under its law to engage in foreign or coastwise trade, or a vessel intended to be employed in such trade: (a) cruise ships, excursion boats, ferry-boats, cargo ships, barges and similar vessels for the transport of persons or goods, including (i) tankers, (ii) refrigerated vessels, other than tankers, and (iii) other vessels for the transport of goods and other vessels for the transport of both persons and goods, including open vessels; (b) fishing vessels, including factory ships and other vessels for processing or preserving fishery products of a registered length not exceeding 30.5m; (c) light-vessels, fire-floats, dredgers, floating cranes, and other vessels the navigability of which is subsidiary to their main function, floating docks, floating or submersible drilling or production platforms; and drilling ships, drilling barges and floating drilling rigs; and (d) tugboats.

Annex 307.3

Repair and Rebuilding of Vessels
United States

For the purpose of increasing transparency regarding the types of repairs that may be performed in shipyards outside the territory of the United States that do not result in any loss of privileges for such vessel to: (a) remain eligible to engage in coastwise trade or to access U.S. fisheries, (b) transport U.S. government cargo, or (c) participate in U.S. assistance programs, including the "operating difference subsidy," the United States shall, (d) provide written clarification no later than July 1, 1993, to the other Parties of current U.S. Customs and Coast Guard practices that constitute, and differentiate between, the repair and the rebuilding of vessels, including clarifications with respect to "jumboizing", vessel conversions and casualty repairs, and (e) begin a process, no later than the date of entry into force of this Agreement, to define the terms "repairs" and "rebuilding" under U.S. maritime law, including the Merchant Marine Act of 1920, 46 App.U.S.C. § 883, and the Merchant Marine Act of 1936, 46 App.U.S.C. §§ 1171, 1176, 1241 and 1241o.

Article 308: Most–Favored–Nation Rates of Duty on Certain Goods

1.   Annex 308.1 applies to certain automatic data processing goods and their parts.

2.   Annex 308.2 applies to certain color television tubes.

3.   Each Party shall accord most-favored-nation duty-free treatment to any local area network apparatus imported into its territory, and shall consult in accordance with Annex 308.3.

Annex 308.1 Most–Favored–Nation Rates of Duty on Certain
Automatic Data Processing Goods and Their Parts

Section A—General Provisions

1. Each Party shall reduce its most-favored-nation rate of duty
applicable to a good provided for under the tariff provisions set out in
Tables 308.1.1 and 308.1.2 in Section B to the rate set out therein, to the
lowest rate agreed by any Party in the Uruguay Round of Multilateral
Trade Negotiations, or to such reduced rate as the Parties may agree, in
accordance with the schedule set out in Section B, or with such accelerated schedule as the Parties may agree.

2. Notwithstanding Chapter Four (Rules of Origin), when the
most-favored-nation rate of duty applicable to a good provided for under
the tariff provisions set out in Table 308.1.1 in Section B conforms with
the rate established under paragraph 1, each Party shall consider the
good, when imported into its territory from the territory of another
Party, to be an originating good.

3. A Party may reduce in advance of the schedule set out in Table
308.1.1 or Table 308.1.2 in Section B, or of such accelerated schedule as
the Parties may agree, its most-favored-nation rate of duty applicable to
any good provided for under the tariff provisions set out therein, to the
lowest rate agreed by any Party in the Uruguay Round of Multilateral
Trade Negotiations, or the rate set out in Table 308.1.1 or 308.1.2, or to
such reduced rate as the Parties may agree.

4. For greater certainty, most-favored-nation rate of duty does not
include any other concessionary rate of duty.

Section B—Rates of Duty and Schedule for Reduction

* * *

Annex 308.2

Most–Favored–Nation Rates of Duty on Certain Color Cathode–Ray
Television Picture Tubes

1. Any Party considering the reduction of its most-favored-nation
rate of customs duty for goods provided for in item 8540.11.aa (color
cathode-ray television picture tubes, including video monitor cathode-ray
tubes, with a diagonal exceeding 14 inches) or 8540.11.cc (color cathode-
ray television picture tubes for high definition television, with a diagonal
exceeding 14 inches) during the first 10 years after the date of entry into
force of this Agreement shall consult with the other Parties in advance
of such reduction.

2. If any other Party objects in writing to such reduction, other
than a reduction in the Uruguay Round of Multilateral Trade Negotiations, and the Party proceeds with the reduction, any objecting Party
may raise its applicable rate of duty on originating goods provided for in
the corresponding tariff item set out in its Schedule to Annex 302.2, up

to the applicable rate of duty as if such good had been placed in staging category C for purpose of tariff elimination.

Annex 308.3

Most–Favored–Nation Duty–Free Treatment
of Local Area Network Apparatus

To facilitate the operation of Article 308(3), the Parties shall consult regarding the tariff classification of local area network apparatus and shall endeavor to agree, no later than January 1, 1994, on the classification of such goods in each Party's tariff schedule.

Section C—Non–Tariff Measures

Article 309: Import and Export Restrictions

1. Except as otherwise provided in this Agreement, no Party may adopt or maintain any prohibition or restriction on the importation of any good of another Party or on the exportation or sale for export of any good destined for the territory of another Party, except in accordance with Article XI of the GATT, including its interpretative notes, and to this end Article XI of the GATT and its interpretative notes, or any equivalent provision of a successor agreement to which all Parties are party, are incorporated into and made a part of this Agreement.

2. The Parties understand that the GATT rights and obligations incorporated by paragraph 1 prohibit, in any circumstances in which any other form of restriction is prohibited, export price requirements and, except as permitted in enforcement of countervailing and antidumping orders and undertakings, import price requirements.

3. In the event that a Party adopts or maintains a prohibition or restriction on the importation from or exportation to a non-Party of a good, nothing in this Agreement shall be construed to prevent the Party from: (a) limiting or prohibiting the importation from the territory of another Party of such good of that non-Party; or (b) requiring as a condition of export of such good of the Party to the territory of another Party, that the good not be re-exported to the non-Party, directly or indirectly, without being consumed in the territory of the other Party.

4. In the event that a Party adopts or maintains a prohibition or restriction on the importation of a good from a non-Party, the Parties, on request of any Party, shall consult with a view to avoiding undue interference with or distortion of pricing, marketing and distribution arrangements in another Party.

5. Paragraphs 1 through 4 shall not apply to the measures set out in Annex 301.3.

Article 310: Customs User Fees

1. No Party may adopt any customs user fee of the type referred to in Annex 310.1 for originating goods.

2. The Parties specified in Annex 310.1 may maintain existing such fees in accordance with that Annex.

Annex 310.1

Existing Customs User Fees
Section A—Mexico

Mexico shall not increase its customs processing fee ("derechos de tramite aduanero") on originating goods, and shall eliminate such fee on originating goods by June 30, 1999.

Section B—United States

1. The United States shall not increase its merchandise processing fee and shall eliminate such fee according to the schedule set out in Article 403 of the Canada–United States Free Trade Agreement on originating goods where those goods qualify to be marked as goods of Canada pursuant to Annex 311, without regard to whether the goods are marked.

2. The United States shall not increase its merchandise processing fee and shall eliminate such fee by June 30, 1999, on originating goods where those goods qualify to be marked as goods of Mexico pursuant to Annex 311, without regard to whether the goods are marked.

Article 311: Country of Origin Marking

Annex 311 applies to measures relating to country of origin marking.

Annex 311

Country of Origin Marking

1. The Parties shall establish by January 1, 1994, rules for determining whether a good is a good of a Party ("Marking Rules") for purposes of this Annex, Annex 300–B and Annex 302.2, and for such other purposes as the Parties may agree.

2. Each Party may require that a good of another Party, as determined in accordance with the Marking Rules, bear a country of origin marking, when imported into its territory, that indicates to the ultimate purchaser of that good the name of its country of origin.

3. Each Party shall permit the country of origin marking of a good of another Party to be indicated in English, French or Spanish, except that a Party may, as part of its general consumer information measures, require that an imported good be marked with its country of origin in the same manner as prescribed for goods of that Party.

4. Each Party shall, in adopting, maintaining and applying any measure relating to country of origin marking, minimize the difficulties, costs and inconveniences that the measure may cause to the commerce and industry of the other Parties.

5.   Each Party shall: (a) accept any reasonable method of marking of a good of another Party, including the use of stickers, labels, tags or paint, that ensures that the marking is conspicuous, legible and sufficiently permanent; (b) exempt from a country of origin marking requirement a good of another Party that (i) is incapable of being marked, (ii) cannot be marked prior to exportation to the territory of another Party without causing injury to the goods, (iii) cannot be marked except at a cost that is substantial in relation to its customs value so as to discourage its exportation to the territory of the Party, (iv) cannot be marked without materially impairing its function or substantially detracting from its appearance, (v) is in a container that is marked in a manner that will reasonably indicate the good's origin to the ultimate purchaser, (vi) is a crude substance, (vii) is imported for use by the importer and is not intended for sale in the form in which it was imported, (viii) is to undergo production in the territory of the importing Party by the importer, or on its behalf, in a manner that would result in the good becoming a good of the importing Party under the Marking Rules, (ix) by reason of its character, or the circumstances of its importation, the ultimate purchaser would reasonably know its country of origin even though it is not marked, (x) was produced more than 20 years prior to its importation, (xi) was imported without the required marking and cannot be marked after its importation except at a cost that would be substantial in relation to its customs value, provided that the failure to mark the good before importation was not for the purpose of avoiding compliance with the requirement, (xii) for purposes of temporary duty-free admission, is in transit or in bond or otherwise under customs administration control, (xiii) is an original work of art, or (xiv) is provided for in subheading 6904.10, or heading 8541 or 8542.

6.   Except for a good described in subparagraphs 5(b)(vi), (vii), (viii), (ix), (x), (xii), (xiii) and (xiv), a Party may provide that, wherever a good is exempted under subparagraph 5(b), its outermost usual container shall be marked so as to indicate the country of origin of the good it contains.

7.   Each Party shall provide that: (a) a usual container imported empty, whether or not disposable, shall not be required to be marked with its own country of origin, but the container in which it is imported may be required to be marked with the country of origin of its contents; and (b) a usual container imported filled, whether or not disposable, (i) shall not be required to be marked with its own country of origin, but (ii) may be required to be marked with the country of origin of its contents, unless the contents are marked with their country of origin and the container can be readily opened for inspection of the contents, or the marking of the contents is clearly visible through the container.

8.   Each Party shall, wherever administratively practicable, permit an importer to mark a good of a Party subsequent to importation but prior to release of the good from customs control or custody, unless there have been repeated violations of the country of origin marking requirements of the Party by the same importer and that importer has been

previously notified in writing that such good is required to be marked prior to importation.

9. Each Party shall provide that, except with respect to importers that have been notified under paragraph 8, no special duty or penalty shall be imposed for failure to comply with country of origin marking requirements of that Party, unless the good is removed from customs custody or control without being properly marked, or a deceptive marking has been used.

10. The Parties shall cooperate and consult on matters related to this Annex, including additional exemptions from a country of origin marking requirement, in accordance with Article 513 (Customs Procedures—Working Group and Customs Subgroup).

11. For purposes of this Annex:

conspicuous means capable of being easily seen with normal handling of the good or container;

customs value means the value of a good for purposes of levying duties of customs on an imported good;

legible means capable of being easily read;

sufficiently permanent means capable of remaining in place until the good reaches the ultimate purchaser, unless deliberately removed;

the form in which it was imported means the condition of the good before it has undergone one of the changes in tariff classification described in the Marking Rules;

ultimate purchaser means the last person in the territory of an importing Party that purchases the good in the form in which it was imported; such purchaser need not be the last person that will use the good; and

usual container means the container in which a good will ordinarily reach its ultimate purchaser.

Article 312: Wine and Distilled Spirits

1. No Party may adopt or maintain any measure requiring that distilled spirits imported from the territory of another Party for bottling be blended with any distilled spirits of the Party.

2. Annex 312.2 applies to other measures relating to wine and distilled spirits.

Annex 312.2

Wine and Distilled Spirits

Section A—Canada and the United States

As between Canada and the United States, any measure related to the internal sale and distribution of wine and distilled spirits, other than a measure covered by Article 312(1) or 313, shall be governed under this

Agreement exclusively in accordance with the relevant provisions of the Canada–United States Free Trade Agreement, which for this purpose are hereby incorporated into and made a part of this Agreement.

Section B—Canada and Mexico

As between Canada and Mexico:

1. Except as provided in paragraphs 3 through 6, in respect of any measure related to the internal sale and distribution of wine and distilled spirits, Article 301 shall not apply to: (a) a non-conforming provision of any existing measure; (b) the continuation or prompt renewal of a non-conforming provision of any existing measure; or (c) an amendment to a non-conforming provision of any existing measure to the extent that the amendment does not decrease its conformity with Article 301.

2. The Party asserting that paragraph 1 applies to one of its measures shall have the burden of establishing the validity of such assertion.

3. (a) Any measure related to the listing of wine and distilled spirits of the other Party shall: (i) conform with Article 301, (ii) be transparent, non-discriminatory and provide for prompt decision on any listing application, prompt written notification of such decision to the applicant and, in the case of a negative decision, provide for a statement of the reason for refusal, (iii) establish administrative appeal procedures for listing decisions that provide for prompt, fair and objective rulings, (iv) be based on normal commercial considerations, (v) not create disguised barriers to trade, and (vi) be published and made generally available to persons of the other Party. (b) Notwithstanding paragraph 3(a) and Article 301, and provided that listing measures of British Columbia otherwise conform with paragraph 3(a) and Article 301, automatic listing measures in the province of British Columbia may be maintained provided they apply only to existing estate wineries producing less than 30,000 gallons of wine annually and meeting the existing content rule.

4. (a) Where the distributor is a public entity, the entity may charge the actual cost-of-service differential between wine or distilled spirits of the other Party and domestic wine or distilled spirits. Any such differential shall not exceed the actual amount by which the audited cost of service for the wine or distilled spirits of the exporting Party exceeds the audited cost of service for the wine or distilled spirits of the importing Party. (b) Notwithstanding Article 301, Article I (Definitions) except for the definition of "distilled spirits", Article IV.3 (Wine), and Annexes A, B, and C, of the Agreement between Canada and the European Economic Community concerning Trade and Commerce in Alcoholic Beverages, dated February 28, 1989, shall apply with such changes as the circumstances may require. (c) All discriminatory mark-ups on distilled spirits shall be eliminated immediately on the date of entry into force of this Agreement. Cost-of-service differential mark-ups

as described in subparagraph (a) shall be permitted. (d) Any other discriminatory pricing measure shall be eliminated on the date of entry into force of this Agreement.

5. (a) Any measure related to distribution of wine or distilled spirits of the other Party shall conform with Article 301. (b) Notwithstanding subparagraph (a), and provided that distribution measures otherwise ensure conformity with Article 301, a Party may (i) maintain or introduce a measure limiting on-premise sales by a winery or distillery to those wines or distilled spirits produced on its premises, and (ii) maintain a measure requiring existing private wine store outlets in the provinces of Ontario and British Columbia to discriminate in favor of wine of those provinces to a degree no greater than the discrimination required by such existing measure. (c) Nothing in this Agreement shall prohibit the Province of Quebec from requiring that any wine sold in grocery stores in Quebec be bottled in Quebec, provided that alternative outlets are provided in Quebec for the sale of wine of the other Party, whether or not such wine is bottled in Quebec.

6. Unless otherwise specifically provided in this Annex, the Parties retain their rights and obligations under the GATT and agreements negotiated under the GATT.

7. For purposes of this Annex:

wine includes wine and wine-containing beverages.

Article 313: Distinctive Products

Annex 313 applies to standards and labeling of the distinctive products set out in that Annex.

Annex 313

Distinctive Products

1. Canada and Mexico shall recognize Bourbon Whiskey and Tennessee Whiskey, which is a straight Bourbon Whiskey authorized to be produced only in the State of Tennessee, as distinctive products of the United States. Accordingly, Canada and Mexico shall not permit the sale of any product as Bourbon Whiskey or Tennessee Whiskey, unless it has been manufactured in the United States in accordance with the laws and regulations of the United States governing the manufacture of Bourbon Whiskey and Tennessee Whiskey.

2. Mexico and the United States shall recognize Canadian Whisky as a distinctive product of Canada. Accordingly, Mexico and the United States shall not permit the sale of any product as Canadian Whisky, unless it has been manufactured in Canada in accordance with the laws and regulations of Canada governing the manufacture of Canadian Whisky for consumption in Canada.

3. Canada and the United States shall recognize Tequila and Mezcal as distinctive products of Mexico. Accordingly, Canada and the

United States shall not permit the sale of any product as Tequila or Mezcal, unless it has been manufactured in Mexico in accordance with the laws and regulations of Mexico governing the manufacture of Tequila and Mezcal. This provision shall apply to Mezcal, either on the date of entry into force of this Agreement, or 90 days after the date when the official standard for this product is made obligatory by the Government of Mexico, whichever is later.

Article 314: Export Taxes

Except as set out in Annex 314, no Party may adopt or maintain any duty, tax or other charge on the export of any good to the territory of another Party, unless such duty, tax or charge is adopted or maintained on: (a) exports of any such good to the territory of all other Parties; and (b) any such good when destined for domestic consumption.

Annex 314

Export Taxes

Mexico

1.   Mexico may adopt or maintain a duty, tax or other charge on the export of those basic foodstuffs set out in paragraph 4, on their ingredients or on the goods from which such foodstuffs are derived, if such duty, tax or other charge is adopted or maintained on the export of such goods to the territory of all other Parties, and is used: (a) to limit to domestic consumers the benefits of a domestic food assistance program with respect to such foodstuff; or (b) to ensure the availability of sufficient quantities of such foodstuff to domestic consumers or of sufficient quantities of its ingredients, or of the goods from which such foodstuffs are derived, to a domestic processing industry, when the domestic price of such foodstuff is held below the world price as part of a governmental stabilization plan, provided that such duty, tax, or other charge (i) does not operate to increase the protection afforded to such domestic industry, and (ii) is maintained only for such period of time as is necessary to maintain the integrity of the stabilization plan.

2.   Notwithstanding paragraph 1, Mexico may adopt or maintain a duty, tax or other charge on the export of any foodstuff to the territory of another Party if such duty, tax or other charge is temporarily applied to relieve critical shortages of that foodstuff. For purposes of this paragraph, "temporarily" means up to one year, or such longer period as the Parties may agree.

3.   Mexico may maintain its existing tax on the export of goods provided for under tariff item 4001.30.02 of the Tariff Schedule of the General Export Duty Act ("Tarifa de la Ley del Impuesto General de Exportacion") for up to 10 years after the date of entry into force of this Agreement.

4.   For purposes of paragraph 1, "basic foodstuffs" means: * * *

Article 315: Other Export Measures

1.   Except as set out in Annex 315, a Party may adopt or maintain a restriction otherwise justified under Articles XI:2(a) or XX(g), (i) or (j) of the GATT with respect to the export of a good of the Party to the territory of another Party, only if: (a) the restriction does not reduce the proportion of the total export shipments of the specific good made available to that other Party relative to the total supply of that good of the Party maintaining the restriction as compared to the proportion prevailing in the most recent 36–month period for which data are available prior to the imposition of the measure, or in such other representative period on which the Parties may agree; (b) the Party does not impose a higher price for exports of a good to that other Party than the price charged for such good when consumed domestically, by means of any measure, such as licenses, fees, taxation and minimum price requirements. The foregoing provision does not apply to a higher price that may result from a measure taken pursuant to subparagraph (a) that only restricts the volume of exports; and (c) the restriction does not require the disruption of normal channels of supply to that other Party or normal proportions among specific goods or categories of goods supplied to that other Party.

2.   The Parties shall cooperate in the maintenance and development of effective controls on the export of each other's goods to a non-Party in implementing this Article.

Annex 315

Other Export Measures

Article 315 shall not apply as between Mexico and the other Parties.

Section D—Consultations

Article 316: Consultations and Committee on Trade in Goods

1.   The Parties hereby establish a Committee on Trade in Goods, comprising representatives of each Party.

2.   The Committee shall meet on the request of any Party or the Commission to consider any matter arising under this Chapter.

3.   The Parties shall convene at least once each year a meeting of their officials responsible for customs, immigration, inspection of food and agricultural products, border inspection facilities, and regulation of transportation for the purpose of addressing issues related to movement of goods through the Parties' ports of entry.

Article 317: Third–Country Dumping

1.   The Parties affirm the importance of cooperation with respect to actions under Article 12 of the Agreement on Implementation of Article VI of the General Agreement on Tariffs and Trade.

2.   Where a Party presents an application to another Party requesting antidumping action on its behalf, those Parties shall consult within 30 days respecting the factual basis of the request, and the requested Party shall give full consideration to the request.

Section E—Definitions

Article 318: Definitions

For purposes of this Chapter:

advertising films means recorded visual media, with or without sound-tracks, consisting essentially of images showing the nature or operation of goods or services offered for sale or lease by a person established or resident in the territory of any Party, provided that the films are of a kind suitable for exhibition to prospective customers but not for broadcast to the general public, and provided that they are imported in packets that each contain no more than one copy of each film and that do not form part of a larger consignment;

commercial samples of negligible value means commercial samples having a value, individually or in the aggregate as shipped, of not more than one U.S. dollar, or the equivalent amount in the currency of another Party, or so marked, torn, perforated or otherwise treated that they are unsuitable for sale or for use except as commercial samples;

consumed means: (a) actually consumed; or (b) further processed or manufactured so as to result in a substantial change in value, form or use of the good or in the production of another good;

customs duty includes any customs or import duty and a charge of any kind imposed in connection with the importation of a good, including any form of surtax or surcharge in connection with such importation, but does not include any: (a) charge equivalent to an internal tax imposed consistently with Article III:2 of the GATT, or any equivalent provision of a successor agreement to which all Parties are party, in respect of like, directly competitive or substitutable goods of the Party, or in respect of goods from which the imported good has been manufactured or produced in whole or in part; (b) antidumping or countervailing duty that is applied pursuant to a Party's domestic law and not applied inconsistently with Chapter Nineteen (Review and Dispute Settlement in Antidumping and Countervailing Duty Matters); (c) fee or other charge in connection with importation commensurate with the cost of services rendered; (d) premium offered or collected on an imported good arising out of any tendering system in respect of the administration of quantitative import restrictions, tariff rate quotas or tariff preference levels; and (e) fee applied pursuant to section 22 of the U.S. Agricultural Adjustment Act, subject to Chapter Seven (Agriculture and Sanitary and Phytosanitary Measures);

distilled spirits include distilled spirits and distilled spirit-containing beverages;

duty deferral program includes measures such as those governing foreign-trade zones, temporary importations under bond, bonded warehouses, "maquiladoras" and inward processing programs;

duty-free means free of customs duty;

goods imported for sports purposes means sports requisites for use in sports contests, demonstrations or training in the territory of the Party into whose territory such goods are imported;

goods intended for display or demonstration includes their component parts, ancillary apparatus and accessories;

item means a tariff classification item at the eight-or 10–digit level set out in a Party's tariff schedule;

local area network apparatus means a good dedicated for use solely or principally to permit the interconnection of automatic data processing machines and units thereof for a network that is used primarily for the sharing of resources such as central processor units, data storage devices and input or output units, including in-line repeaters, converters, concentrators, bridges and routers, and printed circuit assemblies for physical incorporation into automatic data processing machines and units thereof suitable for use solely or principally with a private network, and providing for the transmission, receipt, error-checking, control, signal conversion or correction functions for non-voice data to move through a local area network;

performance requirement means a requirement that: (a) a given level or percentage of goods or services be exported; (b) domestic goods or services of the Party granting a waiver of customs duties be substituted for imported goods or services; (c) a person benefitting from a waiver of customs duties purchase other goods or services in the territory of the Party granting the waiver or accord a preference to domestically produced goods or services; (d) a person benefitting from a waiver of customs duties produce goods or provide services, in the territory of the Party granting the waiver, with a given level or percentage of domestic content; or (e) relates in any way the volume or value of imports to the volume or value of exports or to the amount of foreign exchange inflows;

printed advertising materials means those goods classified in Chapter 49 of the Harmonized System, including brochures, pamphlets, leaflets, trade catalogues, yearbooks published by trade associations, tourist promotional materials and posters, that are used to promote, publicize or advertise a good or service, are essentially intended to advertise a good or service, and are supplied free of charge;

repair or alteration does not include an operation or process that either destroys the essential characteristics of a good or creates a new or commercially different good;

satisfactory evidence means: (a) a receipt, or a copy of a receipt, evidencing payment of customs duties on a particular entry; (b) a copy of the entry document with evidence that it was received by a customs administration; (c) a copy of a final customs duty determination by a customs administration respecting the relevant entry; or (d) any other evidence of payment of customs duties acceptable under the Uniform Regulations established in accordance with Chapter Five (Customs Procedures);

total export shipments means all shipments from total supply to users located in the territory of another Party;

total supply means all shipments, whether intended for domestic or foreign users, from: (a) domestic production; (b) domestic inventory; and (c) other imports as appropriate; and

waiver of customs duties means a measure that waives otherwise applicable customs duties on any good imported from any country, including the territory of another Party.

Chapter Four

RULES OF ORIGIN

Article 401: Originating Goods

Except as otherwise provided in this Chapter, a good shall originate in the territory of a Party where:

(a) the good is wholly obtained or produced entirely in the territory of one or more of the Parties, as defined in Article 415;

(b) each of the non-originating materials used in the production of the good undergoes an applicable change in tariff classification set out in Annex 401 as a result of production occurring entirely in the territory of one or more of the Parties, or the good otherwise satisfies the applicable requirements of that Annex where no change in tariff classification is required, and the good satisfies all other applicable requirements of this Chapter;

(c) the good is produced entirely in the territory of one or more of the Parties exclusively from originating materials; or

(d) except for a good provided for in Chapters 61 through 63 of the Harmonized System, the good is produced entirely in the territory of one or more of the Parties but one or more of the non-originating materials provided for as parts under the Harmonized System that are used in the production of the good does not undergo a change in tariff classification because (i) the good was imported into the territory of a Party in an unassembled or a disassembled form but was classified as an assembled good pursuant to General Rule of Interpretation 2(a) of the Harmonized System, or (ii) the heading for the good provides for and specifically describes both the good itself and its parts and is not further subdivided into subheadings, or the subheading for the good provides for and specifically describes both the good itself and its parts, provided that the regional value content of the good, determined in accordance with Article 402, is not less than 60 percent where the transaction value method is used, or is not less than 50 percent where the net cost method is used, and that the good satisfies all other applicable requirements of this Chapter.

Article 402: Regional Value Content

1. Except as provided in paragraph 5, each Party shall provide that the regional value content of a good shall be calculated, at the choice of the exporter or producer of the good, on the basis of either the transaction value method set out in paragraph 2 or the net cost method set out in paragraph 3.

2. Each Party shall provide that an exporter or producer may calculate the regional value content of a good on the basis of the following transaction value method: $RVC = TV\text{–}VNM \, / \, TV \times 100$ where RVC is the regional value content, expressed as a percentage; TV is the transaction value of the good adjusted to a F.O.B. basis; and VNM is the value of non-originating materials used by the producer in the production of the good.

3. Each Party shall provide that an exporter or producer may calculate the regional value content of a good on the basis of the following net cost method: $RVC = NC\text{–}VNM \, / \, NC \times 100$ where RVC is the regional value content, expressed as a percentage; NC is the net cost of the good; and VNM is the value of non-originating materials used by the producer in the production of the good.

4. Except as provided in Article 403(1) and for a motor vehicle identified in Article 403(2) or a component identified in Annex 403.2, the value of non-originating materials used by the producer in the production of a good shall not, for purposes of calculating the regional value content of the good under paragraph 2 or 3, include the value of non-originating materials used to produce originating materials that are subsequently used in the production of the good.

5. Each Party shall provide that an exporter or producer shall calculate the regional value content of a good solely on the basis of the net cost method set out in paragraph 3 where: (a) there is no transaction value for the good; (b) the transaction value of the good is unacceptable under Article 1 of the Customs Valuation Code; (c) the good is sold by the producer to a related person and the volume, by units of quantity, of sales of identical or similar goods to related persons during the six-month period immediately preceding the month in which the good is sold exceeds 85 percent of the producer's total sales of such goods during that period; (d) the good is (i) a motor vehicle provided for in heading 87.01 or 87.02, subheading 8703.21 through 8703.90, or heading 87.04, 87.05 or 87.06, (ii) identified in Annex 403.1 or 403.2 and is for use in a motor vehicle provided for in heading 87.01 or 87.02, subheading 8703.21 through 8703.90, or heading 87.04, 87.05 or 87.06, (iii) provided for in subheading 6401.10 through 6406.10, or (iv) provided for in tariff item 8469.10.aa (word processing machines); (e) the exporter or producer chooses to accumulate the regional value content of the good in accordance with Article 404; or (f) the good is designated as an intermediate material under paragraph 10 and is subject to a regional value-content requirement.

6.   If an exporter or producer of a good calculates the regional value content of the good on the basis of the transaction value method set out in paragraph 2 and a Party subsequently notifies the exporter or producer, during the course of a verification pursuant to Chapter Five (Customs Procedures), that the transaction value of the good, or the value of any material used in the production of the good, is required to be adjusted or is unacceptable under Article 1 of the Customs Valuation Code, the exporter or producer may then also calculate the regional value content of the good on the basis of the net cost method set out in paragraph 3.

7.   Nothing in paragraph 6 shall be construed to prevent any review or appeal available under Article 510 (Review and Appeal) of an adjustment to or a rejection of: (a) the transaction value of a good; or (b) the value of any material used in the production of a good.

8.   For purposes of calculating the net cost of a good under paragraph 3, the producer of the good may: (a) calculate the total cost incurred with respect to all goods produced by that producer, subtract any sales promotion, marketing and after-sales service costs, royalties, shipping and packing costs, and non-allowable interest costs that are included in the total cost of all such goods, and then reasonably allocate the resulting net cost of those goods to the good, (b) calculate the total cost incurred with respect to all goods produced by that producer, reasonably allocate the total cost to the good, and then subtract any sales promotion, marketing and after-sales service costs, royalties, shipping and packing costs and non-allowable interest costs that are included in the portion of the total cost allocated to the good, or (c) reasonably allocate each cost that forms part of the total cost incurred with respect to the good so that the aggregate of these costs does not include any sales promotion, marketing and after-sales service costs, royalties, shipping and packing costs, and non-allowable interest costs, provided that the allocation of all such costs is consistent with the provisions regarding the reasonable allocation of costs set out in the Uniform Regulations, established under Article 511 (Customs Procedures—Uniform Regulations).

9.   Except as provided in paragraph 11, the value of a material used in the production of a good shall: (a) be the transaction value of the material determined in accordance with Article 1 of the Customs Valuation Code; or (b) in the event that there is no transaction value or the transaction value of the material is unacceptable under Article 1 of the Customs Valuation Code, be determined in accordance with Articles 2 through 7 of the Customs Valuation Code; and (c) where not included under subparagraph (a) or (b), include (i) freight, insurance, packing and all other costs incurred in transporting the material to the location of the producer, (ii) duties, taxes and customs brokerage fees on the material paid in the territory of one or more of the Parties, and (iii) the cost of waste and spoilage resulting from the use of the material in the production of the good, less the value of renewable scrap or by-product.

10.   Except as provided in Article 403(1), any self-produced material, other than a component identified in Annex 403.2, that is used in the production of a good may be designated by the producer of the good as an intermediate material for the purpose of calculating the regional value content of the good under paragraph 2 or 3, provided that where the intermediate material is subject to a regional value-content requirement, no other self-produced material subject to a regional value-content requirement used in the production of that intermediate material may itself be designated by the producer as an intermediate material.

11.   The value of an intermediate material shall be: (a) the total cost incurred with respect to all goods produced by the producer of the good that can be reasonably allocated to that intermediate material; or (b) the aggregate of each cost that forms part of the total cost incurred with respect to that intermediate material that can be reasonably allocated to that intermediate material.

12.   The value of an indirect material shall be based on the Generally Accepted Accounting Principles applicable in the territory of the Party in which the good is produced.

Article 403: Automotive Goods

1.   For purposes of calculating the regional value content under the net cost method set out in Article 402(3) for: (a) a good that is a motor vehicle provided for in tariff item 8702.10.bb or 8702.90.bb (vehicles for the transport of 15 or fewer persons), or subheading 8703.21 through 8703.90, 8704.21 or 8704.31, or (b) a good provided for in the tariff provisions listed in Annex 403.1 where the good is subject to a regional value-content requirement and is for use as original equipment in the production of a good provided for in tariff item 8702.10.bb or 8702.90.bb (vehicles for the transport of 15 or fewer persons), or subheading 8703.21 through 8703.90, 8704.21 or 8704.31, the value of non-originating materials used by the producer in the production of the good shall be the sum of the values of non-originating materials, determined in accordance with Article 402(9) at the time the non-originating materials are received by the first person in the territory of a Party who takes title to them, that are imported from outside the territories of the Parties under the tariff provisions listed in Annex 403.1 and that are used in the production of the good or that are used in the production of any material used in the production of the good.

2.   For purposes of calculating the regional value content under the net cost method set out in Article 402(3) for a good that is a motor vehicle provided for in heading 87.01, tariff item 8702.10.aa or 8702.90.aa (vehicles for the transport of 16 or more persons), subheading 8704.10, 8704.22, 8704.23, 8704.32 or 8704.90, or heading 87.05 or 87.06, or for a component identified in Annex 403.2 for use as original equipment in the production of the motor vehicle, the value of non-originating materials used by the producer in the production of the good shall be the sum of: (a) for each material used by the producer listed in Annex 403.2,

whether or not produced by the producer, at the choice of the producer and determined in accordance with Article 402, either (i) the value of such material that is non-originating, or (ii) the value of non-originating materials used in the production of such material; and (b) the value of any other non-originating material used by the producer that is not listed in Annex 403.2, determined in accordance with Article 402.

3. For purposes of calculating the regional value content of a motor vehicle identified in paragraph 1 or 2, the producer may average its calculation over its fiscal year, using any one of the following categories, on the basis of either all motor vehicles in the category or only those motor vehicles in the category that are exported to the territory of one or more of the other Parties: (a) the same model line of motor vehicles in the same class of vehicles produced in the same plant in the territory of a Party; (b) the same class of motor vehicles produced in the same plant in the territory of a Party; (c) the same model line of motor vehicles produced in the territory of a Party; or (d) if applicable, the basis set out in Annex 403.3.

4. For purposes of calculating the regional value content for any or all goods provided for in a tariff provision listed in Annex 403.1, or a component or material identified in Annex 403.2, produced in the same plant, the producer of the good may: (a) average its calculation (i) over the fiscal year of the motor vehicle producer to whom the good is sold, (ii) over any quarter or month, or (iii) over its fiscal year, if the good is sold as an aftermarket part; (b) calculate the average referred to in subparagraph (a) separately for any or all goods sold to one or more motor vehicle producers; or (c) with respect to any calculation under this paragraph, calculate separately for those goods that are exported to the territory of one or more of the Parties.

5. Notwithstanding Annex 401, and except as provided in paragraph 6, the regional value-content requirement shall be: (a) for a producer's fiscal year beginning on the day closest to January 1, 1998 and thereafter, 56 percent under the net cost method, and for a producer's fiscal year beginning on the day closest to January 1, 2002 and thereafter, 62.5 percent under the net cost method, for (i) a good that is a motor vehicle provided for in tariff item 8702.10.bb or 8702.90.bb (vehicles for the transport of 15 or fewer persons), or subheading 8703.21 through 8703.90, 8704.21 or 8704.31, and (ii) a good provided for in heading 84.07 or 84.08, or subheading 8708.40, that is for use in a motor vehicle identified in subparagraph (a)(i); and (b) for a producer's fiscal year beginning on the day closest to January 1, 1998 and thereafter, 55 percent under the net cost method, and for a producer's fiscal year beginning on the day closest to January 1, 2002 and thereafter, 60 percent under the net cost method, for (i) a good that is a motor vehicle provided for in heading 87.01, tariff item 8702.10.aa or 8702.90.aa (vehicles for the transport of 16 or more persons), 8704.10, 8704.22, 8704.23, 8704.32 or 8704.90, or heading 87.05 or 87.06, (ii) a good provided for in heading 84.07 or 84.08 or subheading 8708.40 that is for use in a motor vehicle identified in subparagraph (b)(i), and (iii) except

for a good identified in subparagraph (a)(ii) or provided for in subheading 8482.10 through 8482.80, 8483.20 or 8483.30, a good identified in Annex 403.1 that is subject to a regional value content requirement and that is for use in a motor vehicle identified in subparagraph (a)(i) or (b)(i).

6. The regional value-content requirement for a motor vehicle identified in Article 403(1) or (2) shall be: (a) 50 percent for five years after the date on which the first motor vehicle prototype is produced in a plant by a motor vehicle assembler, if (i) it is a motor vehicle of a class, or marque, or, except for a motor vehicle identified in Article 403(2), size category and underbody, not previously produced by the motor vehicle assembler in the territory of any of the Parties, (ii) the plant consists of a new building in which the motor vehicle is assembled, and (iii) the plant contains substantially all new machinery that is used in the assembly of the motor vehicle; or (b) 50 percent for two years after the date on which the first motor vehicle prototype is produced at a plant following a refit, if it is a different motor vehicle of a class, or marque, or, except for a motor vehicle identified in Article 403(2), size category and underbody, than was assembled by the motor vehicle assembler in the plant before the refit.

Article 404: Accumulation

1. For purposes of determining whether a good is an originating good, the production of the good in the territory of one or more of the Parties by one or more producers shall, at the choice of the exporter or producer of the good for which preferential tariff treatment is claimed, be considered to have been performed in the territory of any of the Parties by that exporter or producer, provided that: (a) all non-originating materials used in the production of the good undergo an applicable tariff classification change set out in Annex 401, and the good satisfies any applicable regional value-content requirement, entirely in the territory of one or more of the Parties; and (b) the good satisfies all other applicable requirements of this Chapter.

2. For purposes of Article 402(10), the production of a producer that chooses to accumulate its production with that of other producers under paragraph 1 shall be considered to be the production of a single producer.

Article 405: De Minimis

1. Except as provided in paragraphs 3 through 6, a good shall be considered to be an originating good if the value of all non-originating materials used in the production of the good that do not undergo an applicable change in tariff classification set out in Annex 401 is not more than seven percent of the transaction value of the good, adjusted to a F.O.B. basis, or, if the transaction value of the good is unacceptable under Article 1 of the Customs Valuation Code, the value of all such non-

originating materials is not more than seven percent of the total cost of the good, provided that: (a) if the good is subject to a regional value-content requirement, the value of such non-originating materials shall be taken into account in calculating the regional value content of the good; and (b) the good satisfies all other applicable requirements of this Chapter.

2. A good that is otherwise subject to a regional value-content requirement shall not be required to satisfy such requirement if the value of all non-originating materials used in the production of the good is not more than seven percent of the transaction value of the good, adjusted to a F.O.B. basis, or, if the transaction value of the good is unacceptable under Article 1 of the Customs Valuation Code, the value of all non-originating materials is not more than seven percent of the total cost of the good, provided that the good satisfies all other applicable requirements of this Chapter.

3. Paragraph 1 does not apply to: (a) a non-originating material provided for in Chapter 4 of the Harmonized System or tariff item 1901.90.aa (dairy preparations containing over 10 percent by weight of milk solids) that is used in the production of a good provided for in Chapter 4 of the Harmonized System; (b) a non-originating material provided for in Chapter 4 of the Harmonized System or tariff item 1901.90.aa (dairy preparations containing over 10 percent by weight of milk solids) that is used in the production of a good provided for in tariff item 1901.10.aa (infant preparations containing over 10 percent by weight of milk solids), 1901.20.aa (mixes and doughs, containing over 25 percent by weight of butterfat, not put up for retail sale), 1901.90.aa (dairy preparations containing over 10 percent by weight of milk solids), heading 21.05, or tariff item 2106.90.dd (preparations containing over 10 percent by weight of milk solids), 2202.90.cc (beverages containing milk) or 2309.90.aa (animal feeds containing over 10 percent by weight of milk solids); (c) a non-originating material provided for in heading 08.05 or subheading 2009.11 through 2009.30 that is used in the production of a good provided for in subheading 2009.11 through 2009.30 or tariff item 2106.90.bb (concentrated fruit or vegetable juice of any single fruit or vegetable, fortified with minerals or vitamins) or 2202.90.aa (fruit or vegetable juice of any single fruit or vegetable, fortified with minerals or vitamins); (d) a non-originating material provided for in Chapter 9 of the Harmonized System that is used in the production of a good provided for in tariff item 2101.10.aa (instant coffee, not flavored); (e) a non-originating material provided for in Chapter 15 of the Harmonized System that is used in the production of a good provided for in heading 15.01 through 15.08, 15.12, 15.14 or 15.15; (f) a non-originating material provided for in heading 17.01 that is used in the production of a good provided for in heading 17.01 through 17.03; (g) a non-originating material provided for in Chapter 17 of the Harmonized System or heading 18.05 that is used in the production of a good provided for in subheading 1806.10; (h) a non-originating material provided for in heading 22.03 through 22.08 that is used in the production of a good provided for in heading 22.07 through

22.08; (i) a non-originating material used in the production of a good provided for in tariff item 7321.11.aa (gas stove or range), subheading 8415.10, 8415.81 through 8415.83, 8418.10 through 8418.21, 8418.29 through 8418.40, 8421.12, 8422.11, 8450.11 through 8450.20 or 8451.21 through 8451.29, Mexican tariff item 8479.82.aa (trash compactors) or Canadian or U.S. tariff item 8479.89.aa (trash compactors), or tariff item 8516.60.aa (electric stove or range); and (j) a printed circuit assembly that is a non-originating material used in the production of a good where the applicable change in tariff classification for the good, as set out in Annex 401, places restrictions on the use of such non-originating material.

4. Paragraph 1 does not apply to a non-originating single juice ingredient provided for in heading 20.09 that is used in the production of a good provided for in subheading 2009.90, or tariff item 2106.90.cc (concentrated mixtures of fruit or vegetable juice, fortified with minerals or vitamins) or 2202.90.bb (mixtures of fruit or vegetable juices, fortified with minerals or vitamins).

5. Paragraph 1 does not apply to a non-originating material used in the production of a good provided for in Chapter 1 through 27 of the Harmonized System unless the non-originating material is provided for in a different subheading than the good for which origin is being determined under this Article.

6. A good provided for in Chapter 50 through 63 of the Harmonized System that does not originate because certain fibers or yarns used in the production of the component of the good that determines the tariff classification of the good do not undergo an applicable change in tariff classification set out in Annex 401, shall nonetheless be considered to originate if the total weight of all such fibers or yarns in that component is not more than seven percent of the total weight of that component.

Article 406: Fungible Goods and Materials

For purposes of determining whether a good is an originating good: (a) where originating and non-originating fungible materials are used in the production of a good, the determination of whether the materials are originating need not be made through the identification of any specific fungible material, but may be determined on the basis of any of the inventory management methods set out in the Uniform Regulations; and (b) where originating and non-originating fungible goods are commingled and exported in the same form, the determination may be made on the basis of any of the inventory management methods set out in the Uniform Regulations.

Article 407: Accessories, Spare Parts and Tools

Accessories, spare parts or tools delivered with the good that form part of the good's standard accessories, spare parts, or tools, shall be considered as originating if the good originates and shall be disregarded in determining whether all the non-originating materials used in the production of the good undergo the applicable change in tariff classification set out in Annex 401, provided that: (a) the accessories, spare parts or tools are not invoiced separately from the good; (b) the quantities and value of the accessories, spare parts or tools are customary for the good; and (c) if the good is subject to a regional value-content requirement, the value of the accessories, spare parts or tools shall be taken into account as originating or non-originating materials, as the case may be, in calculating the regional value content of the good.

Article 408: Indirect Materials

An indirect material shall be considered to be an originating material without regard to where it is produced.

Article 409: Packaging Materials and Containers for Retail Sale

Packaging materials and containers in which a good is packaged for retail sale shall, if classified with the good, be disregarded in determining whether all the non-originating materials used in the production of the good undergo the applicable change in tariff classification set out in Annex 401, and, if the good is subject to a regional value-content requirement, the value of such packaging materials and containers shall be taken into account as originating or non-originating materials, as the case may be, in calculating the regional value content of the good.

Article 410: Packing Materials and Containers for Shipment

Packing materials and containers in which a good is packed for shipment shall be disregarded in determining whether: (a) the non-originating materials used in the production of the good undergo an applicable change in tariff classification set out in Annex 401; and (b) the good satisfies a regional value-content requirement.

Article 411: Transshipment

A good shall not be considered to be an originating good by reason of having undergone production that satisfies the requirements of Article 401 if, subsequent to that production, the good undergoes further production or any other operation outside the territories of the Parties, other than unloading, reloading or any other operation necessary to preserve it in good condition or to transport the good to the territory of a Party.

Article 412: Non–Qualifying Operations

A good shall not be considered to be an originating good merely by reason of: (a) mere dilution with water or another substance that does not materially alter the characteristics of the good; or (b) any production or pricing practice in respect of which it may be demonstrated, on the basis of a preponderance of evidence, that the object was to circumvent this Chapter.

Article 413: Interpretation and Application

For purposes of this Chapter: (a) the basis for tariff classification in this Chapter is the Harmonized System; (b) where a good referred to by a tariff item number is described in parentheses following the tariff item number, the description is provided for purposes of reference only; (c) where applying Article 401(d), the determination of whether a heading or subheading under the Harmonized System provides for and specifically describes both a good and its parts shall be made on the basis of the nomenclature of the heading or subheading, or the General Rules of Interpretation, the Chapter Notes or the Section Notes of the Harmonized System; (d) in applying the Customs Valuation Code under this Chapter, (i) the principles of the Customs Valuation Code shall apply to domestic transactions, with such modifications as may be required by the circumstances, as would apply to international transactions, (ii) the provisions of this Chapter shall take precedence over the Customs Valuation Code to the extent of any difference, and (iii) the definitions in Article 415 shall take precedence over the definitions in the Customs Valuation Code to the extent of any difference; and (e) all costs referred to in this Chapter shall be recorded and maintained in accordance with the Generally Accepted Accounting Principles applicable in the territory of the Party in which the good is produced.

Article 414: Consultation and Modifications

1. The Parties shall consult regularly to ensure that this Chapter is administered effectively, uniformly and consistently with the spirit and objectives of this Agreement, and shall cooperate in the administration of this Chapter in accordance with Chapter Five.

2. Any Party that considers that this Chapter requires modification to take into account developments in production processes or other matters may submit a proposed modification along with supporting rationale and any studies to the other Parties for consideration and any appropriate action under Chapter Five.

Article 415: Definitions

For purposes of this Chapter:

class of motor vehicles means any one of the following categories of motor vehicles: (a) motor vehicles provided for in subheading 8701.20, tariff item 8702.10.aa or 8702.90.aa (vehicles for the transport of 16 or more persons), subheading 8704.10, 8704.22, 8704.23, 8704.32 or 8704.90, or heading 87.05 or 87.06; (b) motor vehicles provided for in subheading 8701.10 or 8701.30 through 8701.90; (c) motor vehicles provided for in tariff item 8702.10.bb or 8702.90.bb (vehicles for the transport of 15 or fewer persons), or subheading 8704.21 or 8704.31; or (d) motor vehicles provided for in subheading 8703.21 through 8703.90;

F.O.B. means free on board, regardless of the mode of transportation, at the point of direct shipment by the seller to the buyer;

fungible goods or fungible materials means goods or materials that are interchangeable for commercial purposes and whose properties are essentially identical;

goods wholly obtained or produced entirely in the territory of one or more of the Parties means: (a) mineral goods extracted in the territory of one or more of the Parties; (b) vegetable goods, as such goods are defined in the Harmonized System, harvested in the territory of one or more of the Parties; (c) live animals born and raised in the territory of one or more of the Parties; (d) goods obtained from hunting, trapping or fishing in the territory of one or more of the Parties; (e) goods (fish, shellfish and other marine life) taken from the sea by vessels registered or recorded with a Party and flying its flag; (f) goods produced on board factory ships from the goods referred to in subparagraph (e) provided such factory ships are registered or recorded with that Party and fly its flag; (g) goods taken by a Party or a person of a Party from the seabed or beneath the seabed outside territorial waters, provided that a Party has rights to exploit such seabed; (h) goods taken from outer space, provided they are obtained by a Party or a person of a Party and not processed in a non-Party; (i) waste and scrap derived from (i) production in the territory of one or more of the Parties, or (ii) used goods collected in the territory of one or more of the Parties, provided such goods are fit only for the recovery of raw materials; and (j) goods produced in the territory of one or more of the Parties exclusively from goods referred to in subparagraphs (a) through (i), or from their derivatives, at any stage of production;

identical or similar goods means "identical goods" and "similar goods", respectively, as defined in the Customs Valuation Code;

indirect material means a good used in the production, testing or inspection of a good but not physically incorporated into the good, or a good used in the maintenance of buildings or the operation of equipment associated with the production of a good, including: (a) fuel and energy; (b) tools, dies and molds; (c) spare parts and materials used in the maintenance of equipment and buildings; (d) lubricants, greases, compounding materials and other materials used in production or used to operate equipment and buildings; (e) gloves, glasses, footwear, clothing, safety equipment and supplies; (f) equipment, devices, and supplies used for testing or inspecting the goods; (g) catalysts and solvents; and (h) any other goods that are not incorporated into the good but whose use in the production of the good can reasonably be demonstrated to be a part of that production;

intermediate material means a material that is self-produced and used in the production of a good, and designated pursuant to Article 402(10);

marque means the trade name used by a separate marketing division of a motor vehicle assembler;

material means a good that is used in the production of another good, and includes a part or an ingredient;

model line means a group of motor vehicles having the same platform or model name;

motor vehicle assembler means a producer of motor vehicles and any related persons or joint ventures in which the producer participates;

new building means a new construction, including at least the pouring or construction of new foundation and floor, the erection of a new structure and roof, and installation of new plumbing, electrical and other utilities to house a complete vehicle assembly process;

net cost means total cost minus sales promotion, marketing and after-sales service costs, royalties, shipping and packing costs, and non-allowable interest costs that are included in the total cost;

net cost of a good means the net cost that can be reasonably allocated to a good using one of the methods set out in Article 402(8);

non-allowable interest costs means interest costs incurred by a producer that exceed 700 basis points above the applicable federal government interest rate identified in the Uniform Regulations for comparable maturities;

non-originating good or non-originating material means a good or material that does not qualify as originating under this Chapter;

producer means a person who grows, mines, harvests, fishes, traps, hunts, manufactures, processes or assembles a good;

production means growing, mining, harvesting, fishing, trapping, hunting, manufacturing, processing or assembling a good;

reasonably allocate means to apportion in a manner appropriate to the circumstances;

refit means a plant closure, for purposes of plant conversion or retooling, that lasts at least three months;

related person means a person related to another person on the basis that: (a) they are officers or directors of one another's businesses;

(b) they are legally recognized partners in business; (c) they are employer and employee; (d) any person directly or indirectly owns, controls or holds 25 percent or more of the outstanding voting stock or shares of each of them; (e) one of them directly or indirectly controls the other; (f) both of them are directly or indirectly controlled by a third person; or (g) they are members of the same family (members of the same family are natural or adoptive children, brothers, sisters, parents, grandparents, or spouses);

royalties means payments of any kind, including payments under technical assistance or similar agreements, made as consideration for the use or right to use any copyright, literary, artistic, or scientific work, patent, trademark, design, model, plan, secret formula or process, excluding those payments under technical assistance or similar agreements that can be related to specific services such as: (a) personnel training, without regard to where performed; and (b) if performed in the territory of one or more of the Parties, engineering, tooling, die-setting, software design and similar computer services, or other services;

sales promotion, marketing and after-sales service costs means the following costs related to sales promotion, marketing and after-sales service: (a) sales and marketing promotion; media advertising; advertising and market research; promotional and demonstration materials; exhibits; sales conferences, trade shows and conventions; banners; marketing displays; free samples; sales, marketing and after-sales service literature (product brochures, catalogs, technical literature, price lists, service manuals, sales aid information); establishment and protection of logos and trademarks; sponsorships; wholesale and retail restocking charges; entertainment; (b) sales and marketing incentives; consumer, retailer or wholesaler rebates; merchandise incentives; (c) salaries and wages, sales commissions, bonuses, benefits (for example, medical, insurance, pension), travelling and living expenses, membership and professional fees, for sales promotion, marketing and after-sales service personnel; (d) recruiting and training of sales promotion, marketing and after-sales service personnel, and after-sales training of customers' employees, where such costs are identified separately for sales promotion, marketing and after-sales service of goods on the financial statements or cost accounts of the producer; (e) product liability insurance; (f) office supplies for sales promotion, marketing and after-sales service of goods, where such costs are identified separately for sales promotion, marketing and after-sales service of goods on the financial statements or cost accounts of the producer; (g) telephone, mail and other communications, where such costs are identified separately for sales promotion, marketing and after-sales service of goods on the financial statements or cost accounts of the producer; (h) rent and depreciation of sales promotion, marketing and after-sales service offices and distribution centers; (i) property insurance premiums, taxes, cost of utilities, and repair and maintenance of sales promotion, marketing and after-sales service offices and distribution centers, where such costs are identified separately for sales promotion, marketing and after-sales service of goods on the financial statements or cost accounts of the producer; and (j) payments by the producer to other persons for warranty repairs;

self-produced material means a material that is produced by the producer of a good and used in the production of that good;

shipping and packing costs means the costs incurred in packing a good for shipment and shipping the good from the point of direct shipment to the buyer, excluding costs of preparing and packaging the good for retail sale;

size category means for a motor vehicle identified in Article 403(1)(a): (a) 85 or less cubic feet of passenger and luggage interior volume, (b) between 85 and 100 cubic feet of passenger and luggage interior volume, (c) 100 to 110 cubic feet of passenger and luggage interior volume, (d) between 110 and 120 cubic feet of passenger and luggage interior volume, and (e) 120 and more cubic feet of passenger and luggage interior volume;

total cost means all product costs, period costs and other costs incurred in the territory of one or more of the Parties;

transaction value means the price actually paid or payable for a good or material with respect to a transaction of, except for the application of Article 403(1) or 403(2)(a), the producer of the good, adjusted in accordance with the principles of paragraphs 1, 3 and 4 of Article 8 of the Customs Valuation Code, regardless of whether the good or material is sold for export;

used means used or consumed in the production of goods; and

underbody means the floor pan of a motor vehicle.

Chapter Five

CUSTOMS PROCEDURES

Section A—Certification of Origin

Article 501: Certificate of Origin

1. The Parties shall establish by January 1, 1994 a Certificate of Origin for the purpose of certifying that a good being exported from the territory of a Party into the territory of another Party qualifies as an originating good, and may thereafter revise the Certificate by agreement.

2. Each Party may require that a Certificate of Origin for a good imported into its territory be completed in a language required under its law.

3. Each Party shall: (a) require an exporter in its territory to complete and sign a Certificate of Origin for any exportation of a good for which an importer may claim preferential tariff treatment on importation of the good into the territory of another Party; and (b) provide that where an exporter in its territory is not the producer of the good, the exporter may complete and sign a Certificate on the basis of (i) its knowledge of whether the good qualifies as an originating good, (ii) its reasonable reliance on the producer's written representation that the good qualifies as an originating good, or (iii) a completed and signed Certificate for the good voluntarily provided to the exporter by the producer.

4. Nothing in paragraph 3 shall be construed to require a producer to provide a Certificate of Origin to an exporter.

5. Each Party shall provide that a Certificate of Origin that has been completed and signed by an exporter or a producer in the territory of another Party that is applicable to: (a) a single importation of a good into the Party's territory, or (b) multiple importations of identical goods into the Party's territory that occur within a specified period, not exceeding 12 months, set out therein by the exporter or producer, shall be accepted by its customs administration for four years after the date on which the Certificate was signed.

Article 502: Obligations Regarding Importations

1.　Except as otherwise provided in this Chapter, each Party shall require an importer in its territory that claims preferential tariff treatment for a good imported into its territory from the territory of another Party to: (a) make a written declaration, based on a valid Certificate of Origin, that the good qualifies as an originating good; (b) have the Certificate in its possession at the time the declaration is made; (c) provide, on the request of that Party's customs administration, a copy of the Certificate; and (d) promptly make a corrected declaration and pay any duties owing where the importer has reason to believe that a Certificate on which a declaration was based contains information that is not correct.

2.　Each Party shall provide that, where an importer in its territory claims preferential tariff treatment for a good imported into its territory from the territory of another Party: (a) the Party may deny preferential tariff treatment to the good if the importer fails to comply with any requirement under this Chapter; and (b) the importer shall not be subject to penalties for the making of an incorrect declaration, if it voluntarily makes a corrected declaration pursuant to paragraph 1(d).

3.　Each Party shall provide that, where a good would have qualified as an originating good when it was imported into the territory of that Party but no claim for preferential tariff treatment was made at that time, the importer of the good may, no later than one year after the date on which the good was imported, apply for a refund of any excess duties paid as the result of the good not having been accorded preferential tariff treatment, on presentation of: (a) a written declaration that the good qualified as an originating good at the time of importation; (b) a copy of the Certificate of Origin; and (c) such other documentation relating to the importation of the good as that Party may require.

Article 503: Exceptions

Each Party shall provide that a Certificate of Origin shall not be required for: (a) a commercial importation of a good whose value does not exceed US $1,000 or its equivalent amount in the Party's currency, or such higher amount as it may establish, except that it may require that the invoice accompanying the importation include a statement certifying that the good qualifies as an originating good, (b) a non-commercial importation of a good whose value does not exceed US $1,000 or its equivalent amount in the Party's currency, or such higher amount as it may establish, or (c) an importation of a good for which the Party into whose territory the good is imported has waived the requirement for a Certificate of Origin, provided that the importation does not form part of a series of importations that may reasonably be considered to have been undertaken or arranged for the purpose of avoiding the certification requirements of Articles 501 and 502.

Article 504: Obligations Regarding Exportations

1.   Each Party shall provide that: (a) an exporter in its territory, or a producer in its territory that has provided a copy of a Certificate of Origin to that exporter pursuant to Article 501(3)(b)(iii), shall provide a copy of the Certificate to its customs administration on request; and (b) an exporter or a producer in its territory that has completed and signed a Certificate of Origin, and that has reason to believe that the Certificate contains information that is not correct, shall promptly notify in writing all persons to whom the Certificate was given by the exporter or producer of any change that could affect the accuracy or validity of the Certificate.

2.   Each Party: (a) shall provide that a false certification by an exporter or a producer in its territory that a good to be exported to the territory of another Party qualifies as an originating good shall have the same legal consequences, with appropriate modifications, as would apply to an importer in its territory for a contravention of its customs laws and regulations regarding the making of a false statement or representation; and (b) may apply such measures as the circumstances may warrant where an exporter or a producer in its territory fails to comply with any requirement of this Chapter.

3.   No Party may impose penalties on an exporter or a producer in its territory that voluntarily provides written notification pursuant to paragraph (1)(b) with respect to the making of an incorrect certification.

Section B—Administration and Enforcement

Article 505: Records

Each Party shall provide that: (a) an exporter or a producer in its territory that completes and signs a Certificate of Origin shall maintain in its territory, for five years after the date on which the Certificate was signed or for such longer period as the Party may specify, all records relating to the origin of a good for which preferential tariff treatment was claimed in the territory of another Party, including records associated with (i) the purchase of, cost of, value of, and payment for, the good that is exported from its territory, (ii) the purchase of, cost of, value of, and payment for, all materials, including indirect materials, used in the production of the good that is exported from its territory, and (iii) the production of the good in the form in which the good is exported from its territory; and (b) an importer claiming preferential tariff treatment for a good imported into the Party's territory shall maintain in that territory, for five years after the date of importation of the good or for such longer period as the Party may specify, such documentation, including a copy of the Certificate, as the Party may require relating to the importation of the good.

Article 506: Origin Verifications

1. For purposes of determining whether a good imported into its territory from the territory of another Party qualifies as an originating good, a Party may, through its customs administration, conduct a verification solely by means of: (a) written questionnaires to an exporter or a producer in the territory of another Party; (b) visits to the premises of an exporter or a producer in the territory of another Party to review the records referred to in Article 505(a) and observe the facilities used in the production of the good; or (c) such other procedure as the Parties may agree.

2. Prior to conducting a verification visit pursuant to paragraph (1)(b), a Party shall, through its customs administration: (a) deliver a written notification of its intention to conduct the visit to (i) the exporter or producer whose premises are to be visited, (ii) the customs administration of the Party in whose territory the visit is to occur, and (iii) if requested by the Party in whose territory the visit is to occur, the embassy of that Party in the territory of the Party proposing to conduct the visit; and (b) obtain the written consent of the exporter or producer whose premises are to be visited.

3. The notification referred to in paragraph 2 shall include: (a) the identity of the customs administration issuing the notification; (b) the name of the exporter or producer whose premises are to be visited; (c) the date and place of the proposed verification visit; (d) the object and scope of the proposed verification visit, including specific reference to the good that is the subject of the verification; (e) the names and titles of the officials performing the verification visit; and (f) the legal authority for the verification visit.

4. Where an exporter or a producer has not given its written consent to a proposed verification visit within 30 days of receipt of notification pursuant to paragraph 2, the notifying Party may deny preferential tariff treatment to the good that would have been the subject of the visit.

5. Each Party shall provide that, where its customs administration receives notification pursuant to paragraph 2, the customs administration may, within 15 days of receipt of the notification, postpone the proposed verification visit for a period not exceeding 60 days from the date of such receipt, or for such longer period as the Parties may agree.

6. A Party shall not deny preferential tariff treatment to a good based solely on the postponement of a verification visit pursuant to paragraph 5.

7. Each Party shall permit an exporter or a producer whose good is the subject of a verification visit by another Party to designate two observers to be present during the visit, provided that: (a) the observers do not participate in a manner other than as observers; and (b) the

failure of the exporter or producer to designate observers shall not result in the postponement of the visit.

8. Each Party shall, through its customs administration, conduct a verification of a regional value-content requirement in accordance with the Generally Accepted Accounting Principles applied in the territory of the Party from which the good was exported.

9. The Party conducting a verification shall provide the exporter or producer whose good is the subject of the verification with a written determination of whether the good qualifies as an originating good, including findings of fact and the legal basis for the determination.

10. Where verifications by a Party indicate a pattern of conduct by an exporter or a producer of false or unsupported representations that a good imported into its territory qualifies as an originating good, the Party may withhold preferential tariff treatment to identical goods exported or produced by such person until that person establishes compliance with Chapter Four (Rules of Origin).

11. Each Party shall provide that where it determines that a certain good imported into its territory does not qualify as an originating good based on a tariff classification or a value applied by the Party to one or more materials used in the production of the good, which differs from the tariff classification or value applied to the materials by the Party from whose territory the good was exported, the Party's determination shall not become effective until it notifies in writing both the importer of the good and the person that completed and signed the Certificate of Origin for the good of its determination.

12. A Party shall not apply a determination made under paragraph 11 to an importation made before the effective date of the determination where: (a) the customs administration of the Party from whose territory the good was exported has issued an advance ruling under Article 509 or any other ruling on the tariff classification or on the value of such materials, or has given consistent treatment to the entry of the materials under the tariff classification or value at issue, on which a person is entitled to rely; and (b) the advance ruling, other ruling or consistent treatment was given prior to notification of the determination.

13. If a Party denies preferential tariff treatment to a good pursuant to a determination made under paragraph 11, it shall postpone the effective date of the denial for a period not exceeding 90 days where the importer of the good, or the person who completed and signed the Certificate of Origin for the good, demonstrates that it has relied in good faith to its detriment on the tariff classification or value applied to such materials by the customs administration of the Party from whose territory the good was exported.

Article 507: Confidentiality

1. Each Party shall maintain, in accordance with its law, the confidentiality of confidential business information collected pursuant to

this Chapter and shall protect that information from disclosure that could prejudice the competitive position of the persons providing the information.

2. The confidential business information collected pursuant to this Chapter may only be disclosed to those authorities responsible for the administration and enforcement of determinations of origin, and of customs and revenue matters.

Article 508: Penalties

1. Each Party shall maintain measures imposing criminal, civil or administrative penalties for violations of its laws and regulations relating to this Chapter.

2. Nothing in Article 502(2), 504(3) or 506(6) shall be construed to prevent a Party from applying such measures as the circumstances may warrant.

Section C—Advance Rulings

Article 509: Advance Rulings

1. Each Party shall, through its customs administration, provide for the expeditious issuance of written advance rulings, prior to the importation of a good into its territory, to an importer in its territory or an exporter or a producer in the territory of another Party, on the basis of the facts and circumstances presented by such importer, exporter or producer of the good, concerning: (a) whether materials imported from a non-Party used in the production of a good undergo an applicable change in tariff classification set out in Annex 401 as a result of production occurring entirely in the territory of one or more of the Parties; (b) whether a good satisfies a regional value-content requirement under either the transaction value method or the net cost method set out in Chapter Four (Rules of Origin); (c) for the purpose of determining whether a good satisfies a regional value-content requirement under Chapter Four, the appropriate basis or method for value to be applied by an exporter or a producer in the territory of another Party, in accordance with the principles of the Customs Valuation Code, for calculating the transaction value of the good or of the materials used in the production of the good; (d) for the purpose of determining whether a good satisfies a regional value-content requirement under Chapter Four, the appropriate basis or method for reasonably allocating costs, in accordance with the allocation methods set out in the Uniform Regulations, for calculating the net cost of the good or the value of an intermediate material; (e) whether a good qualifies as an originating good under Chapter Four; (f) whether a good that re-enters its territory after the good has been exported from its territory to the territory of another Party for repair or alteration qualifies for duty-free treatment in accordance with Article 307 (Goods Re–Entered after Repair or Altera-

tion); (g) whether the proposed or actual marking of a good satisfies country of origin marking requirements under Article 311 (Country of Origin Marking); (h) whether an originating good qualifies as a good of a Party under Annex 300–B (Textile and Apparel Goods), Annex 302.2 (Tariff Elimination) or Chapter Seven (Agriculture and Sanitary and Phytosanitary Measures); (i) whether a good is a qualifying good under Chapter Seven; or (j) such other matters as the Parties may agree.

2. Each Party shall adopt or maintain procedures for the issuance of advance rulings, including a detailed description of the information reasonably required to process an application for a ruling.

3. Each Party shall provide that its customs administration: (a) may, at any time during the course of an evaluation of an application for an advance ruling, request supplemental information from the person requesting the ruling; (b) shall, after it has obtained all necessary information from the person requesting an advance ruling, issue the ruling within the periods specified in the Uniform Regulations; and (c) shall, where the advance ruling is unfavorable to the person requesting it, provide to that person a full explanation of the reasons for the ruling.

4. Subject to paragraph 6, each Party shall apply an advance ruling to importations into its territory of the good for which the ruling was requested, beginning on the date of its issuance or such later date as may be specified in the ruling.

5. Each Party shall provide to any person requesting an advance ruling the same treatment, including the same interpretation and application of provisions of Chapter Four regarding a determination of origin, as it provided to any other person to whom it issued an advance ruling, provided that the facts and circumstances are identical in all material respects.

6. The issuing Party may modify or revoke an advance ruling: (a) if the ruling is based on an error (i) of fact, (ii) in the tariff classification of a good or a material that is the subject of the ruling, (iii) in the application of a regional value-content requirement under Chapter Four, (iv) in the application of the rules for determining whether a good qualifies as a good of a Party under Annex 300–B, Annex 302.2 or Chapter Seven, (v) in the application of the rules for determining whether a good is a qualifying good under Chapter Seven, or (vi) in the application of the rules for determining whether a good that re-enters its territory after the good has been exported from its territory to the territory of another Party for repair or alteration qualifies for duty-free treatment under Article 307; (b) if the ruling is not in accordance with an interpretation agreed by the Parties regarding Chapter Three (National Treatment and Market Access for Goods) or Chapter Four; (c) if there is a change in the material facts or circumstances on which the ruling is based; (d) to conform with a modification of Chapter Three, Chapter Four, this Chapter, Chapter Seven, the Marking Rules or the Uniform Regulations; or (e) to conform with a judicial decision or a change in its domestic law.

7. Each Party shall provide that any modification or revocation of an advance ruling shall be effective on the date on which the modification or revocation is issued, or on such later date as may be specified therein, and shall not be applied to importations of a good that have occurred prior to that date, unless the person to whom the advance ruling was issued has not acted in accordance with its terms and conditions.

8. Notwithstanding paragraph 7, the issuing Party shall postpone the effective date of such modification or revocation for a period not exceeding 90 days where the person to whom the advance ruling was issued demonstrates that it has relied in good faith to its detriment on that ruling.

9. Each Party shall provide that where its customs administration examines the regional value content of a good for which it has issued an advance ruling pursuant to subparagraph 1(c), (d) or (f), it shall evaluate whether: (a) the exporter or producer has complied with the terms and conditions of the advance ruling; (b) the exporter's or producer's operations are consistent with the material facts and circumstances on which the advance ruling is based; and (c) the supporting data and computations used in applying the basis or method for calculating value or allocating cost were correct in all material respects.

10. Each Party shall provide that where its customs administration determines that any requirement in paragraph 9 has not been satisfied, it may modify or revoke the advance ruling as the circumstances may warrant.

11. Each Party shall provide that, where the person to whom an advance ruling was issued demonstrates that it used reasonable care and acted in good faith in presenting the facts and circumstances on which the ruling was based, and where the customs administration of a Party determines that the ruling was based on incorrect information, the person to whom the ruling was issued shall not be subject to penalties.

12. Each Party shall provide that where it issues an advance ruling to a person that has misrepresented or omitted material facts or circumstances on which the ruling is based or has failed to act in accordance with the terms and conditions of the ruling, the Party may apply such measures as the circumstances may warrant.

Section D—Review and Appeal
of Origin Determinations
and Advance Rulings

Article 510: Review and Appeal

1. Each Party shall grant substantially the same rights of review and appeal of marking determinations of origin, country of origin determinations and advance rulings by its customs administration as it provides to importers in its territory to any person: (a) who completes

and signs a Certificate of Origin for a good that has been the subject of a determination of origin; (b) whose good has been the subject of a country of origin marking determination pursuant to Article 311 (Country of Origin Marking); or (c) who has received an advance ruling pursuant to Article 509(1).

2.   Further to Articles 1804 (Administrative Proceedings) and 1805 (Review and Appeal), each Party shall provide that the rights of review and appeal referred to in paragraph 1 shall include access to: (a) at least one level of administrative review independent of the official or office responsible for the determination under review; and (b) in accordance with its domestic law, judicial or quasi-judicial review of the determination or decision taken at the final level of administrative review.

Section E—Uniform Regulations

Article 511: Uniform Regulations

1.   The Parties shall establish, and implement through their respective laws or regulations by January 1, 1994, Uniform Regulations regarding the interpretation, application and administration of Chapter Four, this Chapter and other matters as may be agreed by the Parties.

2.   Each Party shall implement any modification of or addition to the Uniform Regulations no later than 180 days after the Parties agree on such modification or addition, or such other period as the Parties may agree.

Section F—Cooperation

Article 512: Cooperation

1.   Each Party shall notify the other Parties of the following determinations, measures and rulings, including to the greatest extent practicable those that are prospective in application: (a) a determination of origin issued as the result of a verification conducted pursuant to Article 506(1); (b) a determination of origin that the Party is aware is contrary to (i) a ruling issued by the customs administration of another Party with respect to the tariff classification or value of a good, or of materials used in the production of a good, or the reasonable allocation of costs where calculating the net cost of a good, that is the subject of a determination of origin, or (ii) consistent treatment given by the customs administration of another Party with respect to the tariff classification or value of a good, or of materials used in the production of a good, or the reasonable allocation of costs where calculating the net cost of a good, that is the subject of a determination of origin; (c) a measure establishing or significantly modifying an administrative policy that is likely to affect future determinations of origin, country of origin marking requirements or determinations as to whether a good qualifies as a good of a Party under the Marking Rules; and (d) an advance ruling, or a ruling modifying or revoking an advance ruling, pursuant to Article 509.

2. The Parties shall cooperate: (a) in the enforcement of their respective customs-related laws or regulations implementing this Agreement, and under any customs mutual assistance agreement or other customs-related agreement to which they are party; (b) for purposes of the detection and prevention of unlawful transshipments of textile and apparel goods of a non-Party, in the enforcement of prohibitions or quantitative restrictions, including the verification by a Party, in accordance with the procedures set out in this Chapter, of the capacity for production of goods by an exporter or a producer in the territory of another Party, provided that the customs administration of the Party proposing to conduct the verification, prior to conducting the verification (i) obtains the consent of the Party in whose territory the verification is to occur, and (ii) provides notification to the exporter or producer whose premises are to be visited, except that procedures for notifying the exporter or producer whose premises are to be visited shall be in accordance with such other procedures as the Parties may agree; (c) to the extent practicable and for purposes of facilitating the flow of trade between them, in such customs-related matters as the collection and exchange of statistics regarding the importation and exportation of goods, the harmonization of documentation used in trade, the standardization of data elements, the acceptance of an international data syntax and the exchange of information; and (d) to the extent practicable, in the storage and transmission of customs-related documentation.

Article 513: Working Group and Customs Subgroup

1. The Parties hereby establish a Working Group on Rules of Origin, comprising representatives of each Party, to ensure: (a) the effective implementation and administration of Articles 303 (Restriction on Drawback and Duty Deferral Programs), 308 (Most–Favored–Nation Rates of Duty on Certain Goods) and 311, Chapter Four, this Chapter, the Marking Rules and the Uniform Regulations; and (b) the effective administration of the customs-related aspects of Chapter Three.

2. The Working Group shall meet at least four times each year and on the request of any Party.

3. The Working Group shall: (a) monitor the implementation and administration by the customs administrations of the Parties of Articles 303, 308 and 311, Chapter Four, this Chapter, the Marking Rules and the Uniform Regulations to ensure their uniform interpretation; (b) endeavor to agree, on the request of any Party, on any proposed modification of or addition to Article 303, 308 or 311, Chapter Four, this Chapter, the Marking Rules or the Uniform Regulations; (c) notify the Commission of any agreed modification of or addition to the Uniform Regulations; (d) propose to the Commission any modification of or addition to Article 303, 308 or 311, Chapter Four, this Chapter, the Marking Rules, the Uniform Regulations or any other provision of this Agreement as may be required to conform with any change to the

Harmonized System; and (e) consider any other matter referred to it by a Party or by the Customs Subgroup established under paragraph 6.

4. Each Party shall, to the greatest extent practicable, take all necessary measures to implement any modification of or addition to this Agreement within 180 days of the date on which the Commission agrees on the modification or addition.

5. If the Working Group fails to resolve a matter referred to it pursuant to paragraph 3(e) within 30 days of such referral, any Party may request a meeting of the Commission under Article 2007 (Commission—Good Offices, Conciliation and Mediation).

6. The Working Group shall establish, and monitor the work of, a Customs Subgroup, comprising representatives of each Party. The Subgroup shall meet at least four times each year and on the request of any Party and shall: (a) endeavor to agree on (i) the uniform interpretation, application and administration of Articles 303, 308 and 311, Chapter Four, this Chapter, the Marking Rules and the Uniform Regulations, (ii) tariff classification and valuation matters relating to determinations of origin, (iii) equivalent procedures and criteria for the request, approval, modification, revocation and implementation of advance rulings, (iv) revisions to the Certificate of Origin, (v) any other matter referred to it by a Party, the Working Group or the Committee on Trade in Goods established under Article 316, and (vi) any other customs-related matter arising under this Agreement; (b) consider (i) the harmonization of customs-related automation requirements and documentation, and (ii) proposed customs-related administrative and operational changes that may affect the flow of trade between the Parties' territories; (c) report periodically to the Working Group and notify it of any agreement reached under this paragraph; and (d) refer to the Working Group any matter on which it has been unable to reach agreement within 60 days of referral of the matter to it pursuant to subparagraph (a)(v).

7. Nothing in this Chapter shall be construed to prevent a Party from issuing a determination of origin or an advance ruling relating to a matter under consideration by the Working Group or the Customs Subgroup or from taking such other action as it considers necessary, pending a resolution of the matter under this Agreement.

Article 514: Definitions

For purposes of this Chapter:

commercial importation means the importation of a good into the territory of any Party for the purpose of sale, or any commercial, industrial or other like use;

customs administration means the competent authority that is responsible under the law of a Party for the administration of customs laws and regulations;

determination of origin means a determination as to whether a good qualifies as an originating good in accordance with Chapter Four;

exporter in the territory of a Party means an exporter located in the territory of a Party and an exporter required under this Chapter to maintain records in the territory of that Party regarding exportations of a good;

identical goods means goods that are the same in all respects, including physical characteristics, quality and reputation, irrespective of minor differences in appearance that are not relevant to a determination of origin of those goods under Chapter Four;

importer in the territory of a Party means an importer located in the territory of a Party and an importer required under this Chapter to maintain records in the territory of that Party regarding importations of a good;

intermediate material means "intermediate material" as defined in Article 415;

Marking Rules means "Marking Rules" established under Annex 311;

material means "material" as defined in Article 415;

net cost of a good means "net cost of a good" as defined in Article 415;

preferential tariff treatment means the duty rate applicable to an originating good;

producer means "producer" as defined in Article 415;

production means "production" as defined in Article 415;

transaction value means "transaction value" as defined in Article 415;

Uniform Regulations means "Uniform Regulations" established under Article 511;

used means "used" as defined in Article 415; and

value means value of a good or material for purposes of calculating customs duties or for purposes of applying Chapter Four.

Chapter Six

ENERGY AND BASIC PETROCHEMICALS

Article 601: Principles

1. The Parties confirm their full respect for their Constitutions.

2. The Parties recognize that it is desirable to strengthen the important role that trade in energy and basic petrochemical goods plays in the free trade area and to enhance this role through sustained and gradual liberalization.

3. The Parties recognize the importance of having viable and internationally competitive energy and petrochemical sectors to further their individual national interests.

Article 602: Scope and Coverage

1. This Chapter applies to measures relating to energy and basic petrochemical goods originating in the territories of the Parties and to measures relating to investment and to the cross-border trade in services associated with such goods, as set forth in this Chapter.

2. For purposes of this Chapter, energy and basic petrochemical goods refer to those goods classified under the Harmonized System as: (a) subheading 2612.10; (b) headings 27.01 through 27.06; (c) subheading 2707.50; (d) subheading 2707.99 (only with respect to solvent naphtha, rubber extender oils and carbon black feedstocks); (e) headings 27.08 and 27.09; (f) heading 27.10 (except for normal paraffin mixtures in the range of C sub9 to C sub15); (g) heading 27.11 (except for ethylene, propylene, butylene and butadiene in purities over 50 percent); (h) headings 27.12 through 27.16; (i) subheadings 2844.10 through 2844.50 (only with respect to uranium compounds classified under those sub-headings); (j) subheading 2845.10; and (k) subheading 2901.10 (only with respect to ethane, butanes, pentanes, hexanes, and heptanes).

3. Except as specified in Annex 602.3, energy and petrochemical goods and activities shall be governed by the provisions of this Agreement.

Annex 602.3

Reservations and Special Provisions

Reservations

1. The Mexican State reserves to itself the following strategic activities, including investment in such activities and the provision of services in such activities: (a) exploration and exploitation of crude oil and natural gas; refining or processing of crude oil and natural gas; and production of artificial gas, basic petrochemicals and their feedstocks and pipelines; (b) foreign trade; transportation, storage and distribution, up to and including the first hand sales of the following goods: (i) crude oil, (ii) natural and artificial gas, (iii) goods covered by this Chapter obtained from the refining or processing of crude oil and natural gas, and (iv) basic petrochemicals; (c) the supply of electricity as a public service in Mexico, including, except as provided in paragraph 5, the generation, transmission, transformation, distribution and sale of electricity; and (d) exploration, exploitation and processing of radioactive minerals, the nuclear fuel cycle, the generation of nuclear energy, the transportation and storage of nuclear waste, the use and reprocessing of nuclear fuel and the regulation of their applications for other purposes and the production of heavy water. In the event of an inconsistency between this paragraph and another provision of this Agreement, this paragraph shall prevail to the extent of that inconsistency.

2. Pursuant to Article 1101(2) (Investment—Scope and Coverage), private investment is not permitted in the activities listed in paragraph 1. Chapter Twelve (Cross–Border Trade in Services) shall only apply to activities involving the provision of services covered in paragraph 1 when Mexico permits a contract to be granted in respect of such activities and only to the extent of that contract.

Trade in Natural Gas and Basic Petrochemicals

3. Where end-users and suppliers of natural gas or basic petro-chemical goods consider that cross-border trade in such goods may be in their interests, each Party shall permit such end-users and suppliers, and any state enterprise of that Party as may be required under its domestic law, to negotiate supply contracts.

Each Party shall leave the modalities of the implementation of any such contract to the end-users, suppliers, and any state enterprise of the Party as may be required under its domestic law, which may take the form of individual contracts between the state enterprise and each of the other entities. Such contracts may be subject to regulatory approval.

Performance Clauses

4. Each Party shall allow its state enterprises to negotiate perfor-mance clauses in their service contracts.

Activities and Investment in Electricity Generation Facilities

5. (a) Production for Own Use. An enterprise of another Party may acquire, establish, and/or operate an electrical generating facility in Mexico to meet the enterprise's own supply needs. Electricity generated in excess of such needs must be sold to the Federal Electricity Commission (Comision Federal de Electricidad) (CFE) and CFE shall purchase such electricity under terms and conditions agreed to by CFE and the enterprise. (b) Co-generation. An enterprise of another Party may acquire, establish, and/or operate a co-generation facility in Mexico that generates electricity using heat, steam or other energy sources associated with an industrial process. Owners of the industrial facility need not be the owners of the co-generating facility. Electricity generated in excess of the industrial facility's supply requirements must be sold to CFE and CFE shall purchase such electricity under terms and conditions agreed to by CFE and the enterprise. (c) Independent Power Production. An enterprise of another Party may acquire, establish, and/or operate an electricity generating facility for independent power production (IPP) in Mexico. Electricity generated by such a facility for sale in Mexico shall be sold to CFE and CFE shall purchase such electricity under terms and conditions agreed to by CFE and the enterprise. Where an IPP located in Mexico and an electric utility of another Party consider that cross-border trade in electricity may be in their interests, each relevant Party shall permit these entities and CFE to negotiate terms and conditions of power purchase and power sale contracts. The modalities of implementing such supply contracts are left to the end users, suppliers and CFE and may take the form of individual contracts between CFE and each of the other entities. Each relevant Party shall determine whether such contracts are subject to regulatory approval.

Article 603: Import and Export Restrictions

1. Subject to the further rights and obligations of this Agreement, the Parties incorporate the provisions of the General Agreement on Tariffs and Trade (GATT), with respect to prohibitions or restrictions on trade in energy and basic petrochemical goods. The Parties agree that this language does not incorporate their respective protocols of provisional application to the GATT.

2. The Parties understand that the provisions of the GATT incorporated in paragraph 1 prohibit, in any circumstances in which any other form of quantitative restriction is prohibited, minimum or maximum export-price requirements and, except as permitted in enforcement of countervailing and antidumping orders and undertakings, minimum or maximum import-price requirements.

3. In circumstances where a Party adopts or maintains a restriction on importation from or exportation to a non-Party of an energy or basic petrochemical good, nothing in this Agreement shall be construed to prevent the Party from: (a) limiting or prohibiting the importation from the territory of any Party of such energy or basic petrochemical

good of the non-Party; or (b) requiring as a condition of export of such energy or basic petrochemical good of the Party to the territory of any other Party that the good be consumed within the territory of the other Party.

4. In the event that a Party adopts or maintains a restriction on imports of an energy or basic petrochemical good from non-Party countries, the Parties, on request of any Party, shall consult with a view to avoiding undue interference with or distortion of pricing, marketing and distribution arrangements in another Party.

5. Each Party may administer a system of import and export licensing for energy or basic petrochemical goods provided that such system is operated in a manner consistent with the provisions of this Agreement, including paragraph 1 and Article 1502 (Monopolies and State Enterprises).

6. This Article is subject to the reservations set out in Annex 603.6.

Annex 603.6

Exception to Article 603

For only those goods listed below, Mexico may restrict the granting of import and export licenses for the sole purpose of reserving foreign trade in these goods to itself.

2707.50 Other aromatic hydrocarbon mixtures of which 65 percent or more by volume (including losses) distills at 250 degrees C by the ASTM D 86 method.

2707.99 Rubber extender oils, solvent naphtha and carbon black feedstocks only.

27.09 Petroleum oils and oils obtained from bituminous minerals, crude.

27.10 Aviation gasoline; gasoline and motor fuel blending stocks (except aviation gasoline) and reformates when used as motor fuel blending stocks; kerosene; gas oil and diesel oil; petroleum ether; fuel oil; paraffinic oils other than for lubricating purposes; pentanes; carbon black feedstocks; hexanes; heptanes and naphthas.

27.11 Petroleum gases and other gaseous hydrocarbons other than: ethylene, propylene, butylene and butadiene, in purities over 50 percent.

2712.90 Only paraffin wax containing by weight more than 0.75 percent of oil, in bulk (Mexico classifies these goods under HS 2712.90.02) and only when imported to be used for further refining.

2713.11 Petroleum coke not calcined.

2713.20 Petroleum bitumen (except when used for road surfacing purposes under HS 2713.20.01).

2713.90 Other residues of petroleum oils or of oils obtained from bituminous minerals.

27.14   Bitumen and asphalt, natural; bituminous or oil shale and tar sands, asphaltites and asphaltic rocks (except when used for road surfacing purposes under HS 2714.90.01).

2901.10   Ethane, butanes, pentanes, hexanes, and heptanes only.

Article 604: Export Taxes

No Party may adopt or maintain any duty, tax or other charge on the export of any energy or basic petrochemical good to the territory of another Party, unless such duty, tax or charge is adopted or maintained on: (a) exports of any such good to the territory of all other Parties; and (b) any such good when destined for domestic consumption.

Article 605: Other Export Measures

Subject to Annex 605, a Party may adopt or maintain a restriction otherwise justified under Article XI:2(a) or XX(g), (i) or (j) of the GATT with respect to the export of an energy or basic petrochemical good to the territory of another Party, only if: (a) the restriction does not reduce the proportion of the total export shipments of the specific energy or basic petrochemical good made available to that other Party relative to the total supply of that good of the Party maintaining the restriction as compared to the proportion prevailing in the most recent 36–month period for which data are available prior to the imposition of the measure, or in such other representative period on which the Parties may agree; (b) the Party does not impose a higher price for exports of an energy or basic petrochemical good to that other Party than the price charged for such good when consumed domestically, by means of any measure such as licenses, fees, taxation and minimum price requirements. The foregoing provision does not apply to a higher price that may result from a measure taken pursuant to subparagraph (a) that only restricts the volume of exports; and (c) the restriction does not require the disruption of normal channels of supply to that other Party or normal proportions among specific energy or basic petrochemical goods supplied to that other Party, such as, for example, between crude oil and refined products and among different categories of crude oil and of refined products.

Annex 605

Exception to Article 605

Notwithstanding any other provision of this Chapter, the provisions of Article 605 shall not apply as between the other Parties and Mexico.

Article 606: Energy Regulatory Measures

1.   The Parties recognize that energy regulatory measures are subject to the disciplines of: (a) national treatment, as provided in Article 301; (b) import and export restrictions, as provided in Article 603; and (c) export taxes, as provided in Article 604.

2. Each Party shall seek to ensure that in the application of any energy regulatory measure, energy regulatory bodies within its territory avoid disruption of contractual relationships to the maximum extent practicable, and provide for orderly and equitable implementation appropriate to such measures.

Article 607: National Security Measures

Subject to Annex 607, no Party may adopt or maintain a measure restricting imports of an energy or basic petrochemical good from, or exports of an energy or basic petrochemical good to, another Party under Article XXI of the GATT or under Article 2102 (National Security), except to the extent necessary to: (a) supply a military establishment of a Party or enable fulfillment of a critical defense contract of a Party; (b) respond to a situation of armed conflict involving the Party taking the measure; (c) implement national policies or international agreements relating to the non-proliferation of nuclear weapons or other nuclear explosive devices; or (d) respond to direct threats of disruption in the supply of nuclear materials for defense purposes.

Annex 607

National Security

1. Article 607 shall impose no obligations and confer no rights on Mexico.

2. Article 2102 (National Security) shall apply as between Mexico and the other Parties.

Article 608: Miscellaneous Provisions

1. The Parties agree to allow existing or future incentives for oil and gas exploration, development and related activities in order to maintain the reserve base for these energy resources.

2. Annex 608.2 applies only to the Parties specified in that Annex with respect to other agreements relating to trade in energy goods.

Annex 608.2

Other Agreements

1. Canada and the United States shall act in accordance with the terms of Annexes 902.5 and 905.2 of the Canada–United States Free Trade Agreement, which are hereby incorporated into and made a part of this Agreement for such purpose. This paragraph shall impose no obligations and confer no rights on Mexico.

2. Canada and the United States intend no inconsistency between this Chapter and the Agreement on an International Energy Program (IEP). In the event of any inconsistency between the IEP and this

Chapter, the IEP shall prevail as between Canada and the United States to the extent of that inconsistency.

Article 609: Definitions

For purposes of this Chapter:

consumed means transformed so as to qualify under the rules of origin set out in Chapter Four (Rules of Origin), or actually consumed;

cross-border trade in services means "cross-border trade in services" as defined in Article 1213 (Cross–Border Trade in Services—Definitions);

energy regulatory measure means any measure by federal or sub-federal entities that directly affects the transportation, transmission or distribution, purchase or sale, of an energy or basic petrochemical good;

enterprise means "enterprise" as defined in Article 1139 (Investment—Definitions);

enterprise of a Party means "enterprise of a Party" as defined in Article 1139;

facility for independent power production means a facility that is used for the generation of electric energy exclusively for sale to an electric utility for further resale;

first hand sale refers to the first commercial transaction affecting the good in question;

investment means investment as defined in Article 1139;

restriction means any limitation, whether made effective through quotas, licenses, permits, minimum or maximum price requirements or any other means;

total export shipments means the total shipments from total supply to users located in the territory of the other Party; and

total supply means shipments to domestic users and foreign users from: (a) domestic production; (b) domestic inventory; and (c) other imports, as appropriate.

Chapter Seven

AGRICULTURE AND SANITARY AND PHYTOSANITARY MEASURES

Section A—Agriculture

Article 701: Scope and Coverage

1. This Section applies to measures adopted or maintained by a Party relating to agricultural trade.

2. In the event of any inconsistency between this Section and another provision of this Agreement, this Section shall prevail to the extent of the inconsistency.

Article 702: International Obligations

1. Annex 702.1 applies to the Parties specified in that Annex with respect to agricultural trade under certain agreements between them.

2. Prior to adopting pursuant to an intergovernmental commodity agreement, a measure that may affect trade in an agricultural good between the Parties, the Party proposing to adopt the measure shall consult with the other Parties with a view to avoiding nullification or impairment of a concession granted by that Party in its Schedule to Annex 302.2.

3. Annex 702.3 applies to the Parties specified in that Annex with respect to measures adopted or maintained pursuant to an intergovernmental coffee agreement.

Article 703: Market Access

1. The Parties shall work together to improve access to their respective markets through the reduction or elimination of import barriers to trade between them in agricultural goods.

Customs Duties, Quantitative Restrictions, and Agricultural Grading and Marketing Standards

2. Annex 703.2 applies to the Parties specified in that Annex with respect to customs duties and quantitative restrictions, trade in sugar and syrup goods, and agricultural grading and marketing standards.

Special Safeguard Provisions

3. Each Party may, in accordance with its Schedule to Annex 302.2, adopt or maintain a special safeguard in the form of a tariff rate quota on an agricultural good listed in its Section of Annex 703.3. Notwithstanding Article 302(2), a Party may not apply an over-quota tariff rate under a special safeguard that exceeds the lesser of: (a) the most-favored-nation (MFN) rate as of July 1, 1991; and (b) the prevailing MFN rate.

4. No Party may, with respect to the same good and the same country, at the same time: (a) apply an over-quota tariff rate under paragraph 3; and (b) take an emergency action covered by Chapter Eight (Emergency Action).

Article 704: Domestic Support

The Parties recognize that domestic support measures can be of crucial importance to their agricultural sectors but may also have trade distorting and production effects and that domestic support reduction commitments may result from agricultural multilateral trade negotiations under the General Agreement on Tariffs and Trade (GATT). Accordingly, where a Party supports its agricultural producers, that Party should endeavor to work toward domestic support measures that: (a) have minimal or no trade distorting or production effects; or (b) are exempt from any applicable domestic support reduction commitments that may be negotiated under the GATT. The Parties further recognize that a Party may change its domestic support measures, including those that may be subject to reduction commitments, at the Party's discretion, subject to its rights and obligations under the GATT.

Article 705: Export Subsidies

1. The Parties share the objective of the multilateral elimination of export subsidies for agricultural goods and shall cooperate in an effort to achieve an agreement under the GATT to eliminate those subsidies.

2. The Parties recognize that export subsidies for agricultural goods may prejudice the interests of importing and exporting Parties and, in particular, may disrupt the markets of importing Parties. Accordingly, in addition to the rights and obligations of the Parties specified in Annex 702.1, the Parties affirm that it is inappropriate for a Party to provide an export subsidy for an agricultural good exported to the territory of another Party where there are no other subsidized imports of that good into the territory of that other Party.

3. Except as provided in Annex 702.1, where an exporting Party considers that a non-Party is exporting an agricultural good to the

territory of another Party with the benefit of export subsidies, the importing Party shall, on written request of the exporting Party, consult with the exporting Party with a view to agreeing on specific measures that the importing Party may adopt to counter the effect of any such subsidized imports. If the importing Party adopts the agreed-upon measures, the exporting Party shall refrain from applying, or immediately cease to apply, any export subsidy to exports of such good to the territory of the importing Party.

4. Except as provided in Annex 702.1, an exporting Party shall deliver written notice to the importing Party at least three days, excluding weekends, prior to adopting an export subsidy measure on an agricultural good exported to the territory of another Party. The exporting Party shall consult with the importing Party within 72 hours of receipt of the importing Party's written request, with a view to eliminating the subsidy or minimizing any adverse impact on the market of the importing Party for that good. The importing Party shall, when requesting consultations with the exporting Party, at the same time, deliver written notice to a third Party of the request. A third Party may request to participate in such consultations.

5. Each Party shall take into account the interests of the other Parties in the use of any export subsidy on an agricultural good, recognizing that such subsidies may have prejudicial effects on the interests of the other Parties.

6. The Parties hereby establish a Working Group on Agricultural Subsidies, comprising representatives of each Party, which shall meet at least semi-annually or as the Parties may otherwise agree, to work toward elimination of all export subsidies affecting agricultural trade between the Parties. The functions of the Working Group shall include: (a) monitoring the volume and price of imports into the territory of any Party of agricultural goods that have benefitted from export subsidies; (b) providing a forum for the Parties to develop mutually acceptable criteria and procedures for reaching agreement on the limitation or elimination of export subsidies for imports of agricultural goods into the territories of the Parties; and (c) reporting annually to the Committee on Agricultural Trade, established under Article 706, on the implementation of this Article.

7. Notwithstanding any other provision of this Article: (a) if the importing and exporting Parties agree to an export subsidy for an agricultural good exported to the territory of the importing Party, the exporting Party or Parties may adopt or maintain such subsidy; and (b) each Party retains its rights to apply countervailing duties to subsidized imports of agricultural goods from the territory of a Party or non-Party.

Article 706: Committee on Agricultural Trade

1. The Parties hereby establish a Committee on Agricultural Trade, comprising representatives of each Party.

2.   The Committee's functions shall include: (a) monitoring and promoting cooperation on the implementation and administration of this Section; (b) providing a forum for the Parties to consult on issues related to this Section at least semi-annually and as the Parties may otherwise agree; and (c) reporting annually to the Commission on the implementation of this Section.

Article 707: Advisory Committee on Private Commercial Disputes regarding Agricultural Goods

The Committee shall establish an Advisory Committee on Private Commercial Disputes regarding Agricultural Goods, comprising persons with expertise or experience in the resolution of private commercial disputes in agricultural trade. The Advisory Committee shall report and provide recommendations to the Committee for the development of systems in the territory of each Party to achieve the prompt and effective resolution of such disputes, taking into account any special circumstance, including the perishability of certain agricultural goods.

Article 708: Definitions

For purposes of this Section:

agricultural good means a good provided for in any of the following:

(a) Harmonized System (HS) Chapters 1 through 24 (other than a fish or fish product); or

(b) [HS subheadings 2905.43–.44, 33.01, 35.01–.05, 3809.10, 3823.60, 41.01–.03, 43.01, 50.01–.03, 51.01–.03, 52.01–.03, 53.01, 53.02]

customs duty means "customs duty" as defined in Article 318 (National Treatment and Market Access for Goods—Definitions);

duty-free means "duty-free" as defined in Article 318;

fish or fish product means a fish or crustacean, mollusc or other aquatic invertebrate, marine mammal, or a product thereof provided for in any of the following: [HS Chapter 03; HS heading 05.07, 05.08, 05.09, 05.11; dead animals of Chapter 3; HS heading 15.04, 16.03, 16.04, 16.05, HS subheading 2301.20]

material means "material" as defined in Article 415 (Rules of Origin—Definitions);

over-quota tariff rate means the rate of customs duty to be applied to quantities in excess of the quantity specified under a tariff rate quota;

sugar or syrup good means "sugar or syrup good" as defined in Annex 703.2;

tariff item means a "tariff item" as defined in Annex 401; and

tariff rate quota means a mechanism that provides for the application of a customs duty at a certain rate to imports of a particular good up to a specified quantity (in-quota quantity), and at a different rate to imports of that good that exceed that quantity.

[Annexes to Chapter 7A are omitted]

Section B—Sanitary and Phytosanitary Measures

Article 709: Scope and Coverage

In order to establish a framework of rules and disciplines to guide the development, adoption and enforcement of sanitary and phytosanitary measures, this Section applies to any such measure of a Party that may, directly or indirectly, affect trade between the Parties.

Article 710: Relation to Other Chapters

Articles 301 (National Treatment) and 309 (Import and Export Restrictions), and the provisions of Article XX(b) of the GATT as incorporated into Article 2101(1) (General Exceptions), do not apply to any sanitary or phytosanitary measure.

Article 711: Reliance on Non-governmental Entities

Each Party shall ensure that any non-governmental entity on which it relies in applying a sanitary or phytosanitary measure acts in a manner consistent with this Section.

Article 712: Basic Rights and Obligations

Right to Take Sanitary and Phytosanitary Measures

1. Each Party may, in accordance with this Section, adopt, maintain or apply any sanitary or phytosanitary measure necessary for the protection of human, animal or plant life or health in its territory, including a measure more stringent than an international standard, guideline or recommendation.

Right to Establish Level of Protection

2. Notwithstanding any other provision of this Section, each Party may, in protecting human, animal or plant life or health, establish its appropriate levels of protection in accordance with Article 715.

Scientific Principles

3. Each Party shall ensure that any sanitary or phytosanitary measure that it adopts, maintains or applies is: (a) based on scientific principles, taking into account relevant factors including, where appropriate, different geographic conditions; (b) not maintained where there is no longer a scientific basis for it; and (c) based on a risk assessment, as appropriate to the circumstances.

Non-discriminatory Treatment

4.   Each Party shall ensure that a sanitary or phytosanitary measure that it adopts, maintains or applies does not arbitrarily or unjustifiably discriminate between its goods and like goods of another Party, or between goods of another Party and like goods of any other country, where identical or similar conditions prevail.

Unnecessary Obstacles

5.   Each Party shall ensure that any sanitary or phytosanitary measure that it adopts, maintains or applies is applied only to the extent necessary to achieve its appropriate level of protection, taking into account technical and economic feasibility.

Disguised Restrictions

6.   No Party may adopt, maintain or apply any sanitary or phytosanitary measure with a view to, or with the effect of, creating a disguised restriction on trade between the Parties.

Article 713: International Standards and Standardizing Organizations

1.   Without reducing the level of protection of human, animal or plant life or health, each Party shall use, as a basis for its sanitary and phytosanitary measures, relevant international standards, guidelines or recommendations with the objective, among others, of making its sanitary and phytosanitary measures equivalent or, where appropriate, identical to those of the other Parties.

2.   A Party's sanitary or phytosanitary measure that conforms to a relevant international standard, guideline or recommendation shall be presumed to be consistent with Article 712. A measure that results in a level of sanitary or phytosanitary protection different from that which would be achieved by a measure based on a relevant international standard, guideline or recommendation shall not for that reason alone be presumed to be inconsistent with this Section.

3.   Nothing in Paragraph 1 shall be construed to prevent a Party from adopting, maintaining or applying, in accordance with the other provisions of this Section, a sanitary or phytosanitary measure that is more stringent than the relevant international standard, guideline or recommendation.

4.   Where a Party has reason to believe that a sanitary or phytosanitary measure of another Party is adversely affecting or may adversely affect its exports and the measure is not based on a relevant international standard, guideline or recommendation, it may request, and the other Party shall provide in writing, the reasons for the measure.

5.   Each Party shall, to the greatest extent practicable, participate in relevant international and North American standardizing organizations, including the Codex Alimentarius Commission, the International

Office of Epizootics, the International Plant Protection Convention, and the North American Plant Protection Organization, with a view to promoting the development and periodic review of international standards, guidelines and recommendations.

Article 714: Equivalence

1.   Without reducing the level of protection of human, animal or plant life or health, the Parties shall, to the greatest extent practicable and in accordance with this Section, pursue equivalence of their respective sanitary and phytosanitary measures.

2.   Each importing Party: (a) shall treat a sanitary or phytosanitary measure adopted or maintained by an exporting Party as equivalent to its own where the exporting Party, in cooperation with the importing Party, provides to the importing Party scientific evidence or other information, in accordance with risk assessment methodologies agreed on by those Parties, to demonstrate objectively, subject to subparagraph (b), that the exporting Party's measure achieves the importing Party's appropriate level of protection; (b) may, where it has a scientific basis, determine that the exporting Party's measure does not achieve the importing Party's appropriate level of protection; and (c) shall provide to the exporting Party, on request, its reasons in writing for a determination under subparagraph (b).

3.   For purposes of establishing equivalence, each exporting Party shall, on the request of an importing Party, take such reasonable measures as may be available to it to facilitate access in its territory for inspection, testing and other relevant procedures.

4.   Each Party should, in the development of a sanitary or phytosanitary measure, consider relevant actual or proposed sanitary or phytosanitary measures of the other Parties.

Article 715: Risk Assessment and Appropriate Level of Protection

1.   In conducting a risk assessment, each Party shall take into account: (a) relevant risk assessment techniques and methodologies developed by international or North American standardizing organizations; (b) relevant scientific evidence; (c) relevant processes and production methods; (d) relevant inspection, sampling and testing methods; (e) the prevalence of relevant diseases or pests, including the existence of pest-free or disease-free areas or areas of low pest or disease prevalence; (f) relevant ecological and other environmental conditions; and (g) relevant treatments, such as quarantines.

2.   Further to paragraph 1, each Party shall, in establishing its appropriate level of protection regarding the risk associated with the introduction, establishment or spread of an animal or plant pest or disease, and in assessing the risk, also take into account the following

economic factors, where relevant: (a) loss of production or sales that may result from the pest or disease; (b) costs of control or eradication of the pest or disease in its territory; and (c) the relative cost-effectiveness of alternative approaches to limiting risks.

3. Each Party, in establishing its appropriate level of protection: (a) should take into account the objective of minimizing negative trade effects; and (b) shall, with the objective of achieving consistency in such levels, avoid arbitrary or unjustifiable distinctions in such levels in different circumstances, where such distinctions result in arbitrary or unjustifiable discrimination against a good of another Party or constitute a disguised restriction on trade between the Parties.

4. Notwithstanding paragraphs (1) through (3) and Article 712(3)(c), where a Party conducting a risk assessment determines that available relevant scientific evidence or other information is insufficient to complete the assessment, it may adopt a provisional sanitary or phytosanitary measure on the basis of available relevant information, including from international or North American standardizing organizations and from sanitary or phytosanitary measures of other Parties. The Party shall, within a reasonable period after information sufficient to complete the assessment is presented to it, complete its assessment, review and, where appropriate, revise the provisional measure in the light of the assessment.

5. Where a Party is able to achieve its appropriate level of protection through the phased application of a sanitary or phytosanitary measure, it may, on the request of another Party and in accordance with this Section, allow for such a phased application, or grant specified exceptions for limited periods from the measure, taking into account the requesting Party's export interests.

Article 716: Adaptation to Regional Conditions

1. Each Party shall adapt any of its sanitary or phytosanitary measures relating to the introduction, establishment or spread of an animal or plant pest or disease, to the sanitary or phytosanitary characteristics of the area where a good subject to such a measure is produced and the area in its territory to which the good is destined, taking into account any relevant conditions, including those relating to transportation and handling, between those areas. In assessing such characteristics of an area, including whether an area is, and is likely to remain, a pest-free or disease-free area or an area of low pest or disease prevalence, each Party shall take into account, among other factors: (a) the prevalence of relevant pests or diseases in that area; (b) the existence of eradication or control programs in that area; and (c) any relevant international standard, guideline or recommendation.

2. Further to paragraph 1, each Party shall, in determining whether an area is a pest-free or disease-free area or an area of low pest or disease prevalence, base its determination on factors such as geography,

ecosystems, epidemiological surveillance and the effectiveness of sanitary or phytosanitary controls in that area.

3.   Each importing Party shall recognize that an area in the territory of the exporting Party is, and is likely to remain, a pest-free or disease-free area or an area of low pest or disease prevalence, where the exporting Party provides to the importing Party scientific evidence or other information sufficient to so demonstrate to the satisfaction of the importing Party. For this purpose, each exporting Party shall provide reasonable access in its territory to the importing Party for inspection, testing and other relevant procedures.

4.   Each Party may, in accordance with this Section: (a) adopt, maintain or apply a different risk assessment procedure for a pest-free or disease-free area than for an area of low pest or disease prevalence, or (b) make a different final determination for the disposition of a good produced in a pest-free or disease-free area than for a good produced in an area of low pest or disease prevalence, taking into account any relevant conditions, including those relating to transportation and handling.

5.   Each Party shall, in adopting, maintaining or applying a sanitary or phytosanitary measure relating to the introduction, establishment or spread of an animal or plant pest or disease, accord a good produced in a pest-free or disease-free area in the territory of another Party no less favorable treatment than it accords a good produced in a pest-free or disease-free area, in another country, that poses the same level of risk. The Party shall use equivalent risk assessment techniques to evaluate relevant conditions and controls in the pest-free or disease-free area and in the area surrounding that area and take into account any relevant conditions, including those relating to transportation and handling.

6.   Each importing Party shall pursue an agreement with an exporting Party, on request, on specific requirements the fulfillment of which allows a good produced in an area of low pest or disease prevalence in the territory of an exporting Party to be imported into the territory of the importing Party and achieves the importing Party's appropriate level of protection.

Article 717: Control, Inspection and Approval Procedures

1.   Each Party, with respect to any control or inspection procedure that it conducts: (a) shall initiate and complete the procedure as expeditiously as possible and in no less favorable manner for a good of another Party than for a like good of the Party or of any other country; (b) shall publish the normal processing period for the procedure or communicate the anticipated processing period to the applicant on request; (c) shall ensure that the competent body (i) on receipt of an application, promptly examines the completeness of the documentation and informs the appli-

cant in a precise and complete manner of any deficiency, (ii) transmits to the applicant as soon as possible the results of the procedure in a form that is precise and complete so that the applicant may take any necessary corrective action, (iii) where the application is deficient, proceeds as far as practicable with the procedure if the applicant so requests, and (iv) informs the applicant, on request, of the status of the application and the reasons for any delay; (d) shall limit the information the applicant is required to supply to that necessary for conducting the procedure; (e) shall accord confidential or proprietary information arising from, or supplied in connection with, the procedure conducted for a good of another Party (i) treatment no less favorable than for a good of the Party, and (ii) in any event, treatment that protects the applicant's legitimate commercial interests, to the extent provided under the Party's law; (f) shall limit any requirement regarding individual specimens or samples of a good to that which is reasonable and necessary; (g) should not impose a fee for conducting the procedure that is higher for a good of another Party than is equitable in relation to any such fee it imposes for its like goods or for like goods of any other country, taking into account communication, transportation and other related costs; (h) should use criteria for selecting the location of facilities at which the procedure is conducted that do not cause unnecessary inconvenience to an applicant or its agent; (i) shall provide a mechanism to review complaints concerning the operation of the procedure and to take corrective action when a complaint is justified; (j) should use criteria for selecting samples of goods that do not cause unnecessary inconvenience to an applicant or its agent; and (k) shall limit the procedure, for a good modified subsequent to a determination that the good fulfills the requirements of the applicable sanitary or phytosanitary measure, to that necessary to determine that the good continues to fulfill the requirements of that measure.

2.   Each Party shall apply, with such modifications as may be necessary, paragraphs 1(a) through (i) to its approval procedures.

3.   Where an importing Party's sanitary or phytosanitary measure requires the conduct of a control or inspection procedure at the level of production, an exporting Party shall, on the request of the importing Party, take such reasonable measures as may be available to it to facilitate access in its territory and to provide assistance necessary to facilitate the conduct of the importing Party's control or inspection procedure.

4.   A Party maintaining an approval procedure may require its approval for the use of an additive, or its establishment of a tolerance for a contaminant, in a food, beverage or feedstuff, under that procedure prior to granting access to its domestic market for a food, beverage or feedstuff containing that additive or contaminant. Where such Party so requires, it shall consider using a relevant international standard, guideline or recommendation as the basis for granting access until it completes the procedure.

Article 718: Notification, Publication and Provision of Information

1. Further to Articles 1802 (Publication) and 1803 (Notification and Provision of Information), each Party proposing to adopt or modify a sanitary or phytosanitary measure of general application at the federal level shall: (a) at least 60 days prior to the adoption or modification of the measure, other than a law, publish a notice and notify in writing the other Parties of the proposed measure and provide to the other Parties and publish the full text of the proposed measure, in such a manner as to enable interested persons to become acquainted with the proposed measure; (b) identify in the notice and notification the good to which the measure would apply, and provide a brief description of the objective and reasons for the measure; (c) provide a copy of the proposed measure to any Party or interested person that so requests and, wherever possible, identify any provision that deviates in substance from relevant international standards, guidelines or recommendations; and (d) without discrimination, allow other Parties and interested persons to make comments in writing and shall, on request, discuss the comments and take the comments and the results of the discussions into account.

2. Each Party shall seek, through appropriate measures, to ensure, with respect to a sanitary or phytosanitary measure of a state or provincial government: (a) that, at an early appropriate stage, a notice and notification of the type referred to in paragraph 1(a) and (b) are made prior to their adoption; and (b) observance of paragraph 1(c) and (d).

3. Where a Party considers it necessary to address an urgent problem relating to sanitary or phytosanitary protection, it may omit any step set out in paragraph 1 or 2, provided that, on adoption of a sanitary or phytosanitary measure, it shall: (a) immediately provide to the other Parties a notification of the type referred to in paragraph 1(b), including a brief description of the urgent problem; (b) provide a copy of the measure to any Party or interested person that so requests; and (c) without discrimination, allow other Parties and interested persons to make comments in writing and shall, on request, discuss the comments and take the comments and the results of the discussions into account.

4. Each Party shall, except where necessary to address an urgent problem referred to in paragraph 3, allow a reasonable period between the publication of a sanitary or phytosanitary measure of general application and the date that it becomes effective to allow time for interested persons to adapt to the measure.

5. Each Party shall designate a government authority responsible for the implementation at the federal level of the notification provisions of this Article, and shall notify the other Parties thereof. Where a Party designates two or more government authorities for this purpose, it shall provide to the other Parties complete and unambiguous information on the scope of responsibility of each such authority.

6. Where an importing Party denies entry into its territory of a good of another Party because it does not comply with a sanitary or phytosanitary measure, the importing Party shall provide a written explanation to the exporting Party, on request, that identifies the applicable measure and the reasons that the good is not in compliance.

Article 719: Inquiry Points

1. Each Party shall ensure that there is one inquiry point that is able to answer all reasonable inquiries from other Parties and interested persons, and to provide relevant documents, regarding: (a) any sanitary or phytosanitary measure of general application, including any control or inspection procedure or approval procedure, proposed, adopted or maintained in its territory at the federal, state or provincial government level; (b) the Party's risk assessment procedures and factors it considers in conducting the assessment and in establishing its appropriate levels of protection; (c) the membership and participation of the Party, or its relevant federal, state or provincial government authorities in international and regional sanitary and phytosanitary organizations and systems, and in bilateral and multilateral arrangements within the scope of this Section, and the provisions of those systems and arrangements; and (d) the location of notices published pursuant to this Section or where such information can be obtained.

2. Each Party shall ensure that where copies of documents are requested by another Party or by interested persons in accordance with this Section, they are supplied at the same price, apart from the actual cost of delivery, as the price for domestic purchase.

Article 720: Technical Cooperation

1. Each Party shall, on the request of another Party, facilitate the provision of technical advice, information and assistance, on mutually agreed terms and conditions, to enhance that Party's sanitary and phytosanitary measures and related activities, including research, processing technologies, infrastructure and the establishment of national regulatory bodies. Such assistance may include credits, donations and grants for the acquisition of technical expertise, training and equipment that will facilitate the Party's adjustment to and compliance with a Party's sanitary or phytosanitary measure.

2. Each Party shall, on the request of another Party: (a) provide to that Party information on its technical cooperation programs regarding sanitary or phytosanitary measures relating to specific areas of interest; and (b) consult with the other Party during the development of, or prior to the adoption or change in the application of, any sanitary or phytosanitary measure.

Article 721: Limitations on the Provision of Information

Nothing in this Section shall be construed to require a Party to: (a) communicate, publish texts or provide particulars or copies of documents other than in an official language of the Party; or (b) furnish any information the disclosure of which would impede law enforcement or otherwise be contrary to the public interest or would prejudice the legitimate commercial interests of particular enterprises.

Article 722: Committee on Sanitary and Phytosanitary Measures

1. The Parties hereby establish a Committee on Sanitary and Phytosanitary Measures, comprising representatives of each Party who have responsibility for sanitary and phytosanitary matters.

2. The Committee should facilitate: (a) the enhancement of food safety and improvement of sanitary and phytosanitary conditions in the territories of the Parties; (b) activities of the Parties pursuant to Articles 713 and 714; (c) technical cooperation between the Parties, including cooperation in the development, application and enforcement of sanitary or phytosanitary measures; and (d) consultations on specific matters relating to sanitary or phytosanitary measures.

3. The Committee: (a) shall, to the extent possible, in carrying out its functions, seek the assistance of relevant international and North American standardizing organizations to obtain available scientific and technical advice and minimize duplication of effort; (b) may draw on such experts and expert bodies as it considers appropriate; (c) shall report annually to the Commission on the implementation of this Section; (d) shall meet on the request of any Party and, unless the Parties otherwise agree, at least once each year; and (e) may, as it considers appropriate, establish and determine the scope and mandate of working groups.

Article 723: Technical Consultations

1. A Party may request consultations with another Party on any matter covered by this Section.

2. Each Party should use the good offices of relevant international and North American standardizing organizations, including those referred to in Article 713(5), for advice and assistance on sanitary and phytosanitary matters within their respective mandates.

3. Where a Party requests consultations regarding the application of this Section to a Party's sanitary or phytosanitary measure, and so notifies the Committee, the Committee may facilitate the consultations, if it does not consider the matter itself, by referring the matter for non-binding technical advice or recommendations to a working group, including an ad hoc working group, or to another forum.

4.   The Committee should consider any matter referred to it under paragraph 3 as expeditiously as possible, particularly regarding perishable goods, and promptly forward to the Parties any technical advice or recommendations that it develops or receives concerning the matter. Each Party involved shall provide a written response to the Committee concerning the technical advice or recommendations within such time as the Committee may request.

5.   Where the involved Parties have had recourse to consultations facilitated by the Committee under paragraph 3, the consultations shall, on the agreement of the Parties involved, constitute consultations under Article 2006 (Consultations).

6.   The Parties confirm that a Party asserting that a sanitary or phytosanitary measure of another Party is inconsistent with this Section shall have the burden of establishing the inconsistency.

Article 724: Definitions

For purposes of this Section:

animal includes fish and wild fauna;

appropriate level of protection means the level of protection of human, animal or plant life or health in the territory of a Party that the Party considers appropriate;

approval procedure means any registration, notification or other mandatory administrative procedure for: (a) approving the use of an additive for a stated purpose or under stated conditions, or (b) establishing a tolerance for a stated purpose or under stated conditions for a contaminant, in a food, beverage or feedstuff prior to permitting the use of the additive or the marketing of a food, beverage or feedstuff containing the additive or contaminant;

area means a country, part of a country or all or parts of several countries;

area of low pest or disease prevalence means an area in which a specific pest or disease occurs at low levels;

contaminant includes pesticide and veterinary drug residues and extraneous matter;

control or inspection procedure means any procedure used, directly or indirectly, to determine that a sanitary or phytosanitary measure is fulfilled, including sampling, testing, inspection, evaluation, verification, monitoring, auditing, assurance of conformity, accreditation, registration, certification or other procedure involving the physical examination of a good, of the packaging of a good, or of the equipment or facilities directly related to production, marketing or use of a good, but does not mean an approval procedure;

international standard, guideline or recommendation means a standard, guideline or recommendation: (a) regarding food safety, adopted by the Codex Alimentarius Commission, including one regarding decomposition elaborated by the Codex Committee on Fish and Fishery Products, food additives, contaminants, hygienic practice, and methods of analysis and sampling; (b) regarding animal health and zoonoses, developed under the auspices of the International Office of Epizootics; (c) regarding plant health, developed under the auspices of the Secretariat of the International Plant Protection Convention in cooperation with the North American Plant Protection Organization; or (d) established by or developed under any other international organization agreed on by the Parties;

pest includes a weed;

pest-free or disease-free area means an area in which a specific pest or disease does not occur;

plant includes wild flora;

risk assessment means an evaluation of: (a) the potential for the introduction, establishment or spread of a pest or disease and associated biological and economic consequences; or (b) the potential for adverse effects on human or animal life or health arising from the presence of an additive, contaminant, toxin or disease-causing organism in a food, beverage or feedstuff;

sanitary or phytosanitary measure means a measure that a Party adopts, maintains or applies to: (a) protect animal or plant life or health in its territory from risks arising from the introduction, establishment or spread of a pest or disease, (b) protect human or animal life or health in its territory from risks arising from the presence of an additive, contaminant, toxin or disease-causing organism in a food, beverage or feedstuff, (c) protect human life or health in its territory from risks arising from a disease-causing organism or pest carried by an animal or plant, or a product thereof, or (d) prevent or limit other damage in its territory arising from the introduction, establishment or spread of a pest, including end product criteria; a product-related processing or production method; a testing, inspection, certification or approval procedure; a relevant statistical method; a sampling procedure; a method of risk assessment; a packaging and labelling requirement directly related to food safety; and a quarantine treatment, such as a relevant requirement associated with the transportation of animals or plants or with material necessary for their survival during transportation; and

scientific basis means a reason based on data or information derived using scientific methods.

Chapter Eight

EMERGENCY ACTION

Article 801: Bilateral Actions

1.   Subject to paragraphs 2 through 4 and Annex 801.1, and during the transition period only, if a good originating in the territory of a Party, as a result of the reduction or elimination of a duty provided for in this Agreement, is being imported into the territory of another Party in such increased quantities, in absolute terms, and under such conditions that the imports of the good from that Party alone constitute a substantial cause of serious injury, or threat thereof, to a domestic industry producing a like or directly competitive good, the Party into whose territory the good is being imported may, to the minimum extent necessary to remedy or prevent the injury: (a) suspend the further reduction of any rate of duty provided for under this Agreement on the good; (b) increase the rate of duty on the good to a level not to exceed the lesser of (i) the most-favored-nation (MFN) applied rate of duty in effect at the time the action is taken, and (ii) the MFN applied rate of duty in effect on the day immediately preceding the date of entry into force of this Agreement; or (c) in the case of a duty applied to a good on a seasonal basis, increase the rate of duty to a level not to exceed the MFN applied rate of duty that was in effect on the good for the corresponding season immediately preceding the date of entry into force of this Agreement.

2.   The following conditions and limitations shall apply to a proceeding that may result in emergency action under paragraph 1: (a) a Party shall, without delay, deliver to any Party that may be affected written notice of, and a request for consultations regarding, the institution of a proceeding that could result in emergency action against a good originating in the territory of a Party; (b) any such action shall be initiated no later than one year after the date of institution of the proceeding; (c) no action may be maintained (i) for a period exceeding three years, except where the good against which the action is taken is provided for in the items in staging category C+ of the Schedule to Annex 302.2 of the Party taking the action and that Party determines that the affected industry has undertaken adjustment and requires an

extension of the period of relief, in which case the period of relief may be extended for one year provided that the duty applied during the initial period of relief is substantially reduced at the beginning of the extension period, or (ii) beyond the expiration of the transition period, except with the consent of the Party against whose good the action is taken; (d) no action may be taken by a Party against any particular good originating in the territory of another Party more than once during the transition period; and (e) on the termination of the action, the rate of duty shall be the rate that, according to the Party's Schedule to Annex 302.2 for the staged elimination of the tariff, would have been in effect one year after the initiation of the action, and beginning January 1 of the year following the termination of the action, at the option of the Party that has taken the action (i) the rate of duty shall conform to the applicable rate set out in its Schedule to Annex 302.2, or (ii) the tariff shall be eliminated in equal annual stages ending on the date set out in its Schedule to Annex 302.2 for the elimination of the tariff.

3. A Party may take a bilateral emergency action after the expiration of the transition period to deal with cases of serious injury, or threat thereof, to a domestic industry arising from the operation of this Agreement only with the consent of the Party against whose good the action would be taken.

4. The Party taking an action under this Article shall provide to the Party against whose good the action is taken mutually agreed trade liberalizing compensation in the form of concessions having substantially equivalent trade effects or equivalent to the value of the additional duties expected to result from the action. If the Parties concerned are unable to agree on compensation, the Party against whose good the action is taken may take tariff action having trade effects substantially equivalent to the action taken under this Article. The Party taking the tariff action shall apply the action only for the minimum period necessary to achieve the substantially equivalent effects.

5. This Article does not apply to emergency actions respecting goods covered by Annex 300–B (Textile and Apparel Goods).

Annex 801.1

Bilateral Actions

1. Notwithstanding Article 801, bilateral emergency actions between Canada and the United States on goods originating in the territory of either Party, other than goods covered by Annex 300–B (Textile and Apparel Goods), shall be governed in accordance with the terms of Article 1101 of the Canada–United States Free Trade Agreement, which is hereby incorporated into and made a part of this Agreement for such purpose.

2. For such purposes, "good originating in the territory of one Party" means "good originating in the territory of a Party" as defined in Article 805.

Article 802: Global Actions

1.   Each Party retains its rights and obligations under Article XIX of the GATT or any safeguard agreement pursuant thereto except those regarding compensation or retaliation and exclusion from an action to the extent that such rights or obligations are inconsistent with this Article. Any Party taking an emergency action under Article XIX or any such agreement shall exclude imports of a good from each other Party from the action unless: (a) imports from a Party, considered individually, account for a substantial share of total imports; and (b) imports from a Party, considered individually, or in exceptional circumstances imports from Parties considered collectively, contribute importantly to the serious injury, or threat thereof, caused by imports.

2.   In determining whether: (a) imports from a Party, considered individually, account for a substantial share of total imports, those imports normally shall not be considered to account for a substantial share of total imports if that Party is not among the top five suppliers of the good subject to the proceeding, measured in terms of import share during the most recent three-year period; and (b) imports from a Party or Parties contribute importantly to the serious injury, or threat thereof, the competent investigating authority shall consider such factors as the change in the import share of each Party, and the level and change in the level of imports of each Party. In this regard, imports from a Party normally shall not be deemed to contribute importantly to serious injury, or the threat thereof, if the growth rate of imports from a Party during the period in which the injurious surge in imports occurred is appreciably lower than the growth rate of total imports from all sources over the same period.

3.   A Party taking such action, from which a good from another Party or Parties is initially excluded pursuant to paragraph 1, shall have the right subsequently to include that good from the other Party or Parties in the action in the event that the competent investigating authority determines that a surge in imports of such good from the other Party or Parties undermines the effectiveness of the action.

4.   A Party shall, without delay, deliver written notice to the other Parties of the institution of a proceeding that may result in emergency action under paragraph 1 or 3.

5.   No Party may impose restrictions on a good in an action under paragraph 1 or 3: (a) without delivery of prior written notice to the Commission, and without adequate opportunity for consultation with the Party or Parties against whose good the action is proposed to be taken, as far in advance of taking the action is practicable; and (b) that would have the effect of reducing imports of such good from a Party below the trend of imports of the good from that Party over a recent representative base period with allowance for reasonable growth.

6.   The Party taking an action pursuant to this Article shall provide to the Party or Parties against whose good the action is taken mutually

agreed trade liberalizing compensation in the form of concessions having substantially equivalent trade effects or equivalent to the value of the additional duties expected to result from the action. If the Parties concerned are unable to agree on compensation, the Party against whose good the action is taken may take action having trade effects substantially equivalent to the action taken under paragraph 1 or 3.

Article 803: Administration of Emergency Action Proceedings

1. Each Party shall ensure the consistent, impartial and reasonable administration of its laws, regulations, decisions and rulings governing all emergency action proceedings.

2. Each Party shall entrust determinations of serious injury, or threat thereof, in emergency action proceedings to a competent investigating authority, subject to review by judicial or administrative tribunals, to the extent provided by domestic law. Negative injury determinations shall not be subject to modification, except by such review. The competent investigating authority empowered under domestic law to conduct such proceedings should be provided with the necessary resources to enable it to fulfill its duties.

3. Each Party shall adopt or maintain equitable, timely, transparent and effective procedures for emergency action proceedings, in accordance with the requirements set out in Annex 803.3.

4. This Article does not apply to emergency actions taken under Annex 300–B (Textile and Apparel Goods).

Annex 803.3

Administration of Emergency Action Proceedings

Institution of a Proceeding

1. An emergency action proceeding may be instituted by a petition or complaint by entities specified in domestic law. The entity filing the petition or complaint shall demonstrate that it is representative of the domestic industry producing a good like or directly competitive with the imported good.

2. A Party may institute a proceeding on its own motion or request the competent investigating authority to conduct a proceeding.

Contents of a Petition or Complaint

3. Where the basis for an investigation is a petition or complaint filed by an entity representative of a domestic industry, the petitioning entity shall, in its petition or complaint, provide the following information to the extent that such information is publicly available from governmental or other sources, or best estimates and the basis therefor if such information is not available: (a) product description—the name and description of the imported good concerned, the tariff subheading

under which that good is classified, its current tariff treatment and the name and description of the like or directly competitive domestic good concerned; (b) representativeness—(i) the names and addresses of the entities filing the petition or complaint, and the locations of the establishments in which they produce the domestic good, (ii) the percentage of domestic production of the like or directly competitive good that such entities account for and the basis for claiming that they are representative of an industry, and (iii) the names and locations of all other domestic establishments in which the like or directly competitive good is produced; (c) import data—import data for each of the five most recent full years that form the basis of the claim that the good concerned is being imported in increased quantities, either in absolute terms or relative to domestic production as appropriate; (d) domestic production data—data on total domestic production of the like or directly competitive good for each of the five most recent full years; (e) data showing injury—quantitative and objective data indicating the nature and extent of injury to the concerned industry, such as data showing changes in the level of sales, prices, production, productivity, capacity utilization, market share, profits and losses, and employment; (f) cause of injury—an enumeration and description of the alleged causes of the injury, or threat thereof, and a summary of the basis for the assertion that increased imports, either actual or relative to domestic production, of the imported good are causing or threatening to cause serious injury, supported by pertinent data; and (g) criteria for inclusion—quantitative and objective data indicating the share of imports accounted for by imports from the territory of each other Party and the petitioner's views on the extent to which such imports are contributing importantly to the serious injury, or threat thereof, caused by imports of that good.

4.   Petitions or complaints, except to the extent that they contain confidential business information, shall promptly be made available for public inspection on being filed.

Notice Requirement

5.   On instituting an emergency action proceeding, the competent investigating authority shall publish notice of the institution of the proceeding in the official journal of the Party. The notice shall identify the petitioner or other requester, the imported good that is the subject of the proceeding and its tariff subheading, the nature and timing of the determination to be made, the time and place of the public hearing, dates of deadlines for filing briefs, statements and other documents, the place at which the petition and any other documents filed in the course of the proceeding may be inspected, and the name, address and telephone number of the office to be contacted for more information.

6.   With respect to an emergency action proceeding instituted on the basis of a petition or complaint filed by an entity asserting that it is representative of the domestic industry, the competent investigating authority shall not publish the notice required by paragraph 5 without

first assessing carefully that the petition or complaint meets the requirements of paragraph 3, including representativeness.

Public Hearing

7. In the course of each proceeding, the competent investigating authority shall: (a) hold a public hearing, after providing reasonable notice, to allow all interested parties, and any association whose purpose is to represent the interests of consumers in the territory of the Party instituting the proceeding, to appear in person or by counsel, to present evidence and to be heard on the questions of serious injury, or threat thereof, and the appropriate remedy; and (b) provide an opportunity to all interested parties and any such association appearing at the hearing to cross-question interested parties making presentations at that hearing.

Confidential Information

8. The competent investigating authority shall adopt or maintain procedures for the treatment of confidential information, protected under domestic law, that is provided in the course of a proceeding, including a requirement that interested parties and consumer associations providing such information furnish non-confidential written summaries thereof, or where they indicate that the information cannot be summarized, the reasons why a summary cannot be provided.

Evidence of Injury and Causation

9. In conducting its proceeding the competent investigating authority shall gather, to the best of its ability, all relevant information appropriate to the determination it must make. It shall evaluate all relevant factors of an objective and quantifiable nature having a bearing on the situation of that industry, including the rate and amount of the increase in imports of the good concerned, in absolute and relative terms as appropriate, the share of the domestic market taken by increased imports, and changes in the level of sales, production, productivity, capacity utilization, profits and losses, and employment. In making its determination, the competent investigating authority may also consider other economic factors, such as changes in prices and inventories, and the ability of firms in the industry to generate capital.

10. The competent investigating authority shall not make an affirmative injury determination unless its investigation demonstrates, on the basis of objective evidence, the existence of a clear causal link between increased imports of the good concerned and serious injury, or threat thereof. Where factors other than increased imports are causing injury to the domestic industry at the same time, such injury shall not be attributed to increased imports.

Deliberation and Report

11. Except in critical circumstances and in global actions involving perishable agricultural goods, the competent investigating authority,

before making an affirmative determination in an emergency action proceeding, shall allow sufficient time to gather and consider the relevant information, hold a public hearing and provide an opportunity for all interested parties and consumer associations to prepare and submit their views.

12.   The competent investigating authority shall publish promptly a report, including a summary thereof in the official journal of the Party, setting out its findings and reasoned conclusions on all pertinent issues of law and fact. The report shall describe the imported good and its tariff item number, the standard applied and the finding made. The statement of reasons shall set out the basis for the determination, including a description of: (a) the domestic industry seriously injured or threatened with serious injury; (b) information supporting a finding that imports are increasing, the domestic industry is seriously injured or threatened with serious injury, and increasing imports are causing or threatening serious injury; and (c) if provided for by domestic law, any finding or recommendation regarding the appropriate remedy and the basis therefor.

13.   In its report, the competent investigating authority shall not disclose any confidential information provided pursuant to any undertaking concerning confidential information that may have been made in the course of the proceedings.

Article 804: Dispute Settlement in Emergency Action Matters

No Party may request the establishment of an arbitral panel under Article 2008 (Request for an Arbitral Panel) regarding any proposed emergency action.

Article 805: Definitions

For purposes of this Chapter:

competent investigating authority means the "competent investigating authority" of a Party as defined in Annex 805;

contribute importantly means an important cause, but not necessarily the most important cause;

critical circumstances means circumstances where delay would cause damage that would be difficult to repair;

domestic industry means the producers as a whole of the like or directly competitive good operating in the territory of a Party;

emergency action does not include any emergency action pursuant to a proceeding instituted prior to January 1, 1994;

good originating in the territory of a Party means an originating good, except that in determining the Party in whose territory that good originates, the relevant rules of Annex 302.2 shall apply;

serious injury means a significant overall impairment of a domestic industry;

surge means a significant increase in imports over the trend for a recent representative base period;

threat of serious injury means serious injury that, on the basis of facts and not merely on allegation, conjecture or remote possibility, is clearly imminent; and

transition period means the 10–year period beginning on January 1, 1994, except where the good against which the action is taken is provided for in the items in staging category C+ of the Schedule to Annex 302.2 of the Party taking the action, in which case the transition period shall be the period of staged tariff elimination for that good.

Annex 805

Country–Specific Definitions

For purposes of this Chapter: **competent investigating authority** means: (a) in the case of Canada, the Canadian International Trade Tribunal, or its successor; (b) in the case of Mexico, the designated authority within the Ministry of Trade and Industrial Development ("Secretaria de Comercio y Fomento Industrial"), or its successor; and (c) in the case of the United States, the U.S. International Trade Commission, or its successor.

Part Three

TECHNICAL BARRIERS
TO TRADE

Chapter Nine

STANDARDS–RELATED MEASURES

Article 901: Scope and Coverage

1. This Chapter applies to standards-related measures of a Party, other than those covered by Section B of Chapter Seven (Sanitary and Phytosanitary Measures), that may, directly or indirectly, affect trade in goods or services between the Parties, and to measures of the Parties relating to such measures.

2. Technical specifications prepared by governmental bodies for production or consumption requirements of such bodies shall be governed exclusively by Chapter Ten (Government Procurement).

Article 902: Extent of Obligations

1. Article 105 (Extent of Obligations) does not apply to this Chapter.

2. Each Party shall seek, through appropriate measures, to ensure observance of Articles 904 through 908 by state or provincial governments and by non-governmental standardizing bodies in its territory.

Article 903: Affirmation of Agreement on Technical Barriers to Trade and Other Agreements

Further to Article 103 (Relation to Other Agreements), the Parties affirm with respect to each other their existing rights and obligations relating to standards-related measures under the GATT Agreement on Technical Barriers to Trade and all other international agreements, including environmental and conservation agreements, to which those Parties are party.

Article 904: Basic Rights and Obligations

Right to Take Standards–Related Measures

1. Each Party may, in accordance with this Agreement, adopt, maintain or apply any standards-related measure, including any such

measure relating to safety, the protection of human, animal or plant life or health, the environment or consumers, and any measure to ensure its enforcement or implementation. Such measures include those to prohibit the importation of a good of another Party or the provision of a service by a service provider of another Party that fails to comply with the applicable requirements of those measures or to complete the Party's approval procedures.

Right to Establish Level of Protection

2.   Notwithstanding any other provision of this Chapter, each Party may, in pursuing its legitimate objectives of safety or the protection of human, animal or plant life or health, the environment or consumers, establish the levels of protection that it considers appropriate in accordance with Article 907(2).

Non-discriminatory Treatment

3.   Each Party shall, in respect of its standards-related measures, accord to goods and service providers of another Party: (a) national treatment in accordance with Article 301 (Market Access) or Article 1202 (Cross–Border Trade in Services); and (b) treatment no less favorable than that it accords to like goods, or in like circumstances to service providers, of any other country.

Unnecessary Obstacles

4.   No Party may prepare, adopt, maintain or apply any standards-related measure with a view to or with the effect of creating an unnecessary obstacle to trade between the Parties. An unnecessary obstacle to trade shall not be deemed to be created where: (a) the demonstrable purpose of the measure is to achieve a legitimate objective; and (b) the measure does not operate to exclude goods of another Party that meet that legitimate objective.

Article 905: Use of International Standards

1.   Each Party shall use, as a basis for its standards-related measures, relevant international standards or international standards whose completion is imminent, except where such standards would be an ineffective or inappropriate means to fulfill its legitimate objectives, for example because of fundamental climatic, geographical, technological or infrastructural factors, scientific justification or the level of protection that the Party considers appropriate.

2.   A Party's standards-related measure that conforms to an international standard shall be presumed to be consistent with Article 904(3) and (4).

3.   Nothing in paragraph 1 shall be construed to prevent a Party, in pursuing its legitimate objectives, from adopting, maintaining or applying any standards-related measure that results in a higher level of

protection than would be achieved if the measure were based on the relevant international standard.

Article 906: Compatibility and Equivalence

1. Recognizing the crucial role of standards-related measures in achieving legitimate objectives, the Parties shall, in accordance with this Chapter, work jointly to enhance the level of safety and of protection of human, animal and plant life and health, the environment and consumers.

2. Without reducing the level of safety or of protection of human, animal or plant life or health, the environment or consumers, without prejudice to the rights of any Party under this Chapter, and taking into account international standardization activities, the Parties shall, to the greatest extent practicable, make compatible their respective standards-related measures, so as to facilitate trade in a good or service between the Parties.

3. Further to Articles 902 and 905, a Party shall, on request of another Party, seek, through appropriate measures, to promote the compatibility of a specific standard or conformity assessment procedure that is maintained in its territory with the standards or conformity assessment procedures maintained in the territory of the other Party.

4. Each importing Party shall treat a technical regulation adopted or maintained by an exporting Party as equivalent to its own where the exporting Party, in cooperation with the importing Party, demonstrates to the satisfaction of the importing Party that its technical regulation adequately fulfills the importing Party's legitimate objectives.

5. The importing Party shall provide to the exporting Party, on request, its reasons in writing for not treating a technical regulation as equivalent under paragraph 4.

6. Each Party shall, wherever possible, accept the results of a conformity assessment procedure conducted in the territory of another Party, provided that it is satisfied that the procedure offers an assurance, equivalent to that provided by a procedure it conducts or a procedure conducted in its territory the results of which it accepts, that the relevant good or service complies with the applicable technical regulation or standard adopted or maintained in the Party's territory.

7. Prior to accepting the results of a conformity assessment procedure pursuant to paragraph 6, and to enhance confidence in the continued reliability of each other's conformity assessment results, the Parties may consult on such matters as the technical competence of the conformity assessment bodies involved, including verified compliance with relevant international standards through such means as accreditation.

Article 907: Assessment of Risk

1. A Party may, in pursuing its legitimate objectives, conduct an assessment of risk. In conducting an assessment, a Party may take into

account, among other factors relating to a good or service: (a) available scientific evidence or technical information; (b) intended end uses; (c) processes or production, operating, inspection, sampling or testing methods; or (d) environmental conditions.

2. Where pursuant to Article 904(2) a Party establishes a level of protection that it considers appropriate and conducts an assessment of risk, it should avoid arbitrary or unjustifiable distinctions between similar goods or services in the level of protection it considers appropriate, where the distinctions: (a) result in arbitrary or unjustifiable discrimination against goods or service providers of another Party; (b) constitute a disguised restriction on trade between the Parties; or (c) discriminate between similar goods or services for the same use under the same conditions that pose the same level of risk and provide similar benefits.

3. Where a Party conducting an assessment of risk determines that available scientific evidence or other information is insufficient to complete the assessment, it may adopt a provisional technical regulation on the basis of available relevant information. The Party shall, within a reasonable period after information sufficient to complete the assessment of risk is presented to it, complete its assessment, review and, where appropriate, revise the provisional technical regulation in the light of that assessment.

Article 908: Conformity Assessment

1. The Parties shall, further to Article 906 and recognizing the existence of substantial differences in the structure, organization and operation of conformity assessment procedures in their respective territories, make compatible those procedures to the greatest extent practicable.

2. Recognizing that it should be to the mutual advantage of the Parties concerned and except as set out in Annex 908.2, each Party shall accredit, approve, license or otherwise recognize conformity assessment bodies in the territory of another Party on terms no less favorable than those accorded to conformity assessment bodies in its territory.

3. Each Party shall, with respect to its conformity assessment procedures: (a) not adopt or maintain any such procedure that is stricter, nor apply the procedure more strictly, than necessary to give it confidence that a good or a service conforms with an applicable technical regulation or standard, taking into account the risks that non-conformity would create; (b) initiate and complete the procedure as expeditiously as possible; (c) in accordance with Article 904(3), undertake processing of applications in non-discriminatory order; (d) publish the normal processing period for each such procedure or communicate the anticipated processing period to an applicant on request; (e) ensure that the competent body (i) on receipt of an application, promptly examines the completeness of the documentation and informs the applicant in a precise

and complete manner of any deficiency, (ii) transmits to the applicant as soon as possible the results of the conformity assessment procedure in a form that is precise and complete so that the applicant may take any necessary corrective action, (iii) where the application is deficient, proceeds as far as practicable with the procedure where the applicant so requests, and (iv) informs the applicant, on request, of the status of the application and the reasons for any delay; (f) limit the information the applicant is required to supply to that necessary to conduct the procedure and to determine appropriate fees; (g) accord confidential or proprietary information arising from, or supplied in connection with, the conduct of the procedure for a good of another Party or for a service provided by a person of another Party (i) the same treatment as that for a good of the Party or a service provided by a person of the Party, and (ii) in any event, treatment that protects an applicant's legitimate commercial interests to the extent provided under the Party's law; (h) ensure that any fee it imposes for conducting the procedure is no higher for a good of another Party or a service provider of another Party than is equitable in relation to any such fee imposed for its like goods or service providers or for like goods or service providers of any other country, taking into account communication, transportation and other related costs; (i) ensure that the location of facilities at which a conformity assessment procedure is conducted does not cause unnecessary inconvenience to an applicant or its agent; (j) limit the procedure, for a good or service modified subsequent to a determination that the good or service conforms to the applicable technical regulation or standard, to that necessary to determine that the good or service continues to conform to the technical regulation or standard; and (k) limit any requirement regarding samples of a good to that which is reasonable, and ensure that the selection of samples does not cause unnecessary inconvenience to an applicant or its agent.

4. Each Party shall apply, with such modifications as may be necessary, the relevant provisions of paragraph 3 to its approval procedures.

5. Each Party shall, on request of another Party, take such reasonable measures as may be available to it to facilitate access in its territory for conformity assessment activities.

6. Each Party shall give sympathetic consideration to a request by another Party to negotiate agreements for the mutual recognition of the results of that other Party's conformity assessment procedures.

Annex 908.2

Transitional Rules for Conformity Assessment Procedures

1. Except in respect of governmental conformity assessment bodies, Article 908(2) shall impose no obligation and confer no right on Mexico until four years after the date of entry into force of this Agreement.

2. Where a Party charges a reasonable fee, limited in amount to the approximate cost of the service rendered, to accredit, approve, license or otherwise recognize a conformity assessment body in the territory of another Party, it need not, prior to December 31, 1998 or such earlier date as the Parties may agree, charge such a fee to a conformity assessment body in its territory.

Article 909: Notification, Publication, and Provision of Information

1. Further to Articles 1802 (Publication) and 1803 (Notification and Provision of Information), each Party proposing to adopt or modify a technical regulation shall: (a) at least 60 days prior to the adoption or modification of the measure, other than a law, publish a notice and notify in writing the other Parties of the proposed measure in such a manner as to enable interested persons to become acquainted with the proposed measure, except that in the case of any such measure relating to perishable goods, each Party shall, to the greatest extent practicable, publish the notice and provide the notification at least 30 days prior to the adoption or modification of the measure, but no later than when notification is provided to domestic producers; (b) identify in the notice and notification the good or service to which the measure would apply, and shall provide a brief description of the objective of, and reasons for the measure; (c) provide a copy of the proposed measure to any Party or interested person that so requests, and shall, wherever possible, identify any provision that deviates in substance from relevant international standards; and (d) without discrimination, allow other Parties and interested persons to make comments in writing and shall, on request, discuss the comments and take the comments and the results of the discussions into account.

2. Each Party proposing to adopt or modify a standard or any conformity assessment procedure not otherwise considered to be a technical regulation shall, where an international standard relevant to the proposed measure does not exist or such measure is not substantially the same as an international standard, and where the measure may have a significant effect on the trade of the other Parties: (a) at an early appropriate stage, publish a notice and provide a notification of the type required in paragraph 1(a) and (b); and (b) observe paragraph 1(c) and (d).

3. Each Party shall seek, through appropriate measures, to ensure, with respect to a technical regulation of a state or provincial government other than a local government: (a) that, at an early appropriate stage, a notice and notification of the type required under paragraph 1(a) and (b) are made prior to their adoption; and (b) observance of paragraph 1(c) and (d).

4. Where a Party considers it necessary to address an urgent problem relating to safety or to protection of human, animal or plant life or health, the environment or consumers, it may omit any step set out in

paragraph 1 or 3, provided that on adoption of a standards-related measure it shall: (a) immediately provide to the other Parties a notification of the type required under paragraph 1(b), including a brief description of the urgent problem; (b) provide a copy of the measure to any Party or interested person that so requests; and (c) without discrimination, allow other Parties and interested persons to make comments in writing, and shall, on request, discuss the comments and take the comments and the results of the discussions into account.

5.   Each Party shall, except where necessary to address an urgent problem referred to in paragraph 4, allow a reasonable period between the publication of a standards-related measure and the date that it becomes effective to allow time for interested persons to adapt to the measure.

6.   Where a Party allows non-governmental persons in its territory to be present during the process of development of standards-related measures, it shall also allow non-governmental persons from the territories of the other Parties to be present.

7.   Each Party shall notify the other Parties of the development of, amendment to, or change in the application of its standards-related measures no later than the time at which it notifies non-governmental persons in general or the relevant sector in its territory.

8.   Each Party shall seek, through appropriate measures, to ensure the observance of paragraphs 6 and 7 by a state or provincial government, and by non-governmental standardizing bodies in its territory.

9.   Each Party shall designate by January 1, 1994 a government authority responsible for the implementation at the federal level of the notification provisions of this Article, and shall notify the other Parties thereof. Where a Party designates two or more government authorities for that purpose, it shall provide to the other Parties complete and unambiguous information on the scope of responsibility of each such authority.

Article 910: Inquiry Points

1.   Each Party shall ensure that there is an inquiry point that is able to answer all reasonable inquiries from other Parties and interested persons, and to provide relevant documents regarding: (a) any standards-related measure proposed, adopted or maintained in its territory at the federal, state or provincial government level; (b) the membership and participation of the Party, or its relevant federal, state or provincial government authorities, in international and regional standardizing bodies and conformity assessment systems, and in bilateral and multilateral arrangements regarding standards-related measures, and the provisions of those systems and arrangements; (c) the location of notices published pursuant to Article 909, or where the information can be obtained; (d) the location of the inquiry points referred to in paragraph 3; and (e) the Party's procedures for assessment of risk, and factors it considers in

conducting the assessment and in establishing, pursuant to Article 904(2), the levels of protection that it considers appropriate.

2. Where a Party designates more than one inquiry point, it shall: (a) provide to the other Parties complete and unambiguous information on the scope of responsibility of each inquiry point; and (b) ensure that any inquiry addressed to an incorrect inquiry point is promptly conveyed to the correct inquiry point.

3. Each Party shall take such reasonable measures as may be available to it to ensure that there is at least one inquiry point that is able to answer all reasonable inquiries from other Parties and interested persons and to provide relevant documents or information as to where they can be obtained regarding: (a) any standard or conformity assessment procedure proposed, adopted or maintained by non-governmental standardizing bodies in its territory; and (b) the membership and participation of relevant non-governmental bodies in its territory in international and regional standardizing bodies and conformity assessment systems.

4. Each Party shall ensure that where copies of documents are requested by another Party or by interested persons in accordance with this Chapter, they are supplied at the same price, apart from the actual cost of delivery, as the price for domestic purchase.

Article 911: Technical Cooperation

1. Each Party shall, on request of another Party: (a) provide to that Party technical advice, information and assistance on mutually agreed terms and conditions to enhance that Party's standards-related measures, and related activities, processes and systems; (b) provide to that Party information on its technical cooperation programs regarding standards-related measures relating to specific areas of interest; and (c) consult with that Party during the development of, or prior to the adoption or change in the application of, any standards-related measure.

2. Each Party shall encourage standardizing bodies in its territory to cooperate with the standardizing bodies in the territories of the other Parties in their participation, as appropriate, in standardizing activities, such as through membership in international standardizing bodies.

Article 912: Limitations on the Provision of Information

Nothing in this Chapter shall be construed to require a Party to: (a) communicate, publish texts, or provide particulars or copies of documents other than in an official language of the Party; or (b) furnish any information the disclosure of which would impede law enforcement or otherwise be contrary to the public interest, or would prejudice the legitimate commercial interests of particular enterprises.

Article 913: Committee on Standards–Related Measures

1. The Parties hereby establish a Committee on Standards–Related Measures, comprising representatives of each Party.

2. The Committee's functions shall include: (a) monitoring the implementation and administration of this Chapter, including the progress of the subcommittees and working groups established under paragraph 4, and the operation of the inquiry points established under Article 910; (b) facilitating the process by which the Parties make compatible their standards-related measures; (c) providing a forum for the Parties to consult on issues relating to standards-related measures, including the provision of technical advice and recommendations under Article 914; (d) enhancing cooperation on the development, application and enforcement of standards-related measures; and (e) considering non-governmental, regional and multilateral developments regarding standards-related measures, including under the GATT.

3. The Committee shall: (a) meet on request of any Party and, unless the Parties otherwise agree, at least once each year; and (b) report annually to the Commission on the implementation of this Chapter.

4. The Committee may, as it considers appropriate, establish and determine the scope and mandate of subcommittees or working groups, comprising representatives of each Party. Each subcommittee or working group may: (a) as it considers necessary or desirable, include or consult with (i) representatives of non-governmental bodies, including standardizing bodies, (ii) scientists, and (iii) technical experts; and (b) determine its work program, taking into account relevant international activities.

5. Further to paragraph 4, the Committee shall establish: (a) the following subcommittees (i) Land Transportation Standards Subcommittee, in accordance with Annex 913.5.a–1, (ii) Telecommunications Standards Subcommittee, in accordance with Annex 913.5.a–2, (iii) Automotive Standards Council, in accordance with Annex 913.5.a–3, and (iv) Subcommittee on Labeling of Textile and Apparel Goods, in accordance with Annex 913.5.a–4; and (b) such other subcommittees or working groups as it considers appropriate to address any topic, including (i) identification and nomenclature for goods subject to standards-related measures, (ii) quality and identity standards and technical regulations, (iii) packaging, labeling and presentation of consumer information, including languages, measurement systems, ingredients, sizes, terminology, symbols and related matters, (iv) product approval and post-market surveillance programs, (v) principles for the accreditation and recognition of conformity assessment bodies, procedures and systems, (vi) development and implementation of a uniform chemical hazard classification and communication system, (vii) enforcement programs, including training and inspections by regulatory, analytical and enforcement per-

sonnel, (viii) promotion and implementation of good laboratory practices, (ix) promotion and implementation of good manufacturing practices, (x) criteria for assessment of potential environmental hazards of goods, (xi) methodologies for assessment of risk, (xii) guidelines for testing of chemicals, including industrial and agricultural chemicals, pharmaceuticals and biologicals, (xiii) methods by which consumer protection, including matters relating to consumer redress, can be facilitated, and (xiv) extension of the application of this Chapter to other services.

6.   Each Party shall, on request of another Party, take such reasonable measures as may be available to it to provide for the participation in the activities of the Committee, where and as appropriate, of representatives of state or provincial governments.

7.   A Party requesting technical advice, information or assistance pursuant to Article 911 shall notify the Committee which shall facilitate any such request.

Annex 913.5.a–1

Land Transportation Standards Subcommittee

1.   The Land Transportation Standards Subcommittee, established under Article 913(5)(a)(i), shall comprise representatives of each Party.

2.   The Subcommittee shall implement the following work program for making compatible the Parties' relevant standards-related measures for: (a) bus and truck operations (i) no later than one and one-half years after the date of entry into force of this Agreement, for non-medical standards-related measures respecting drivers, including measures relating to the age of and language used by drivers, (ii) no later than two and one-half years after the date of entry into force of this Agreement, for medical standards-related measures respecting drivers, (iii) no later than three years after the date of entry into force of this Agreement, for standards-related measures respecting vehicles, including measures relating to weights and dimensions, tires, brakes, parts and accessories, securement of cargo, maintenance and repair, inspections, and emissions and environmental pollution levels not covered by the Automotive Standards Council's work program established under Annex 913.5.a–3, (iv) no later than three years after the date of entry into force of this Agreement, for standards-related measures respecting each Party's supervision of motor carriers' safety compliance, and (v) no later than three years after the date of entry into force of this Agreement, for standards-related measures respecting road signs; (b) rail operations (i) no later than one year after the date of entry into force of this Agreement, for standards-related measures respecting operating personnel that are relevant to cross-border operations, and (ii) no later than one year after the date of entry into force of this Agreement, for standards-related measures respecting locomotives and other rail equipment; and (c) transportation of dangerous goods, no later than six years after the date of entry into force of this Agreement, using as their basis the United Nations

Recommendations on the Transport of Dangerous Goods, or such other standards as the Parties may agree.

3. The Subcommittee may address other related standards-related measures as it considers appropriate.

Annex 913.5.a–2

Telecommunications Standards Subcommittee

1. The Telecommunications Standards Subcommittee, established under Article 913(5)(a)(ii), shall comprise representatives of each Party.

2. The Subcommittee shall, within six months of the date of entry into force of this Agreement, develop a work program, including a timetable, for making compatible, to the greatest extent practicable, the standards-related measures of the Parties for authorized equipment as defined in Chapter Thirteen (Telecommunications).

3. The Subcommittee may address other appropriate standards-related matters respecting telecommunications equipment or services and such other matters as it considers appropriate.

4. The Subcommittee shall take into account relevant work carried out by the Parties in other forums, and that of non-governmental standardizing bodies.

Annex 913.5.a–3

Automotive Standards Council

1. The Automotive Standards Council, established under Article 913.5(a)(iii), shall comprise representatives of each Party.

2. The purpose of the Council shall be, to the extent practicable, to facilitate the attainment of compatibility among, and review the implementation of, national standards-related measures of the Parties that apply to automotive goods, and to address other related matters.

3. To facilitate its objectives, the Council may establish subgroups, consultation procedures and other appropriate operational mechanisms. On the agreement of the Parties, the Council may include state and provincial government or private sector representatives in its subgroups.

4. Any recommendation of the Council shall require agreement of the Parties. Where the adoption of a law is not required for a Party, the Council's recommendations shall be implemented by the Party within a reasonable time in accordance with the legal and procedural requirements and international obligations of the Party. Where the adoption of a law is required for a Party, the Party shall use its best efforts to secure the adoption of the law and shall implement any such law within a reasonable time.

5. Recognizing the existing disparity in standards-related measures of the Parties, the Council shall develop a work program for making compatible the national standards-related measures that apply to automotive goods and other related matters based on the following criteria:

(a) the impact on industry integration; (b) the extent of the barriers to trade; (c) the level of trade affected; and (d) the extent of the disparity. In developing its work program, the Council may address other related matters, including emissions from on-road and non-road mobile sources.

6.   Each Party shall take such reasonable measures as may be available to it to promote the objectives of this Annex with respect to standards-related measures that are maintained by state and provincial government authorities and private sector organizations. The Council shall make every effort to assist these entities with such activities, especially the identification of priorities and the establishment of work schedules.

Annex 913.5.a–4

Subcommittee on Labeling of Textile and Apparel Goods

1.   The Subcommittee on Labelling of Textile and Apparel Goods, established under Article 913(5)(a)(iv), shall comprise representatives of each Party.

2.   The Subcommittee shall include, and consult with, technical experts as well as a broadly representative group from the manufacturing and retailing sectors in the territory of each Party.

3.   The Subcommittee shall develop and pursue a work program on the harmonization of labelling requirements to facilitate trade in textile and apparel goods between the Parties through the adoption of uniform labelling provisions. The work program should include the following matters: (a) pictograms and symbols to replace, where possible, required written information, as well as other methods to reduce the need for labels on textile and apparel goods in multiple languages; (b) care instructions for textile and apparel goods; (c) fiber content information for textile and apparel goods; (d) uniform methods acceptable for the attachment of required information to textile and apparel goods; and (e) use in the territory of the other Parties of each Party's national registration numbers for manufacturers or importers of textile and apparel goods.

Article 914: Technical Consultations

1.   Where a Party requests consultations regarding the application of this Chapter to a standards-related measure, and so notifies the Committee, the Committee may facilitate the consultations, if it does not consider the matter itself, by referring the matter for non-binding technical advice or recommendations to a subcommittee or working group, including an ad hoc subcommittee or working group, or to another forum.

2.   The Committee should consider any matter referred to it under paragraph 1 as expeditiously as possible and promptly forward to the Parties any technical advice or recommendations that it develops or

receives concerning the matter. The Parties involved shall provide a written response to the Committee concerning the technical advice or recommendations within such time as the Committee may request.

3. Where the involved Parties have had recourse to consultations facilitated by the Committee under paragraph 1, the consultations shall, on the agreement of the Parties involved, constitute consultations under Article 2006 (Consultations).

4. The Parties confirm that a Party asserting that a standards-related measure of another Party is inconsistent with this Chapter shall have the burden of establishing the inconsistency.

Article 915: Definitions

1. For purposes of this Chapter:

approval procedure means any registration, notification or other mandatory administrative procedure for granting permission for a good or service to be produced, marketed or used for a stated purpose or under stated conditions;

assessment of risk means evaluation of the potential for adverse effects;

conformity assessment procedure means any procedure used, directly or indirectly, to determine that a technical regulation or standard is fulfilled, including sampling, testing, inspection, evaluation, verification, monitoring, auditing, assurance of conformity, accreditation, registration or approval used for such a purpose, but does not mean an approval procedure;

international standard means a standards-related measure, or other guide or recommendation, adopted by an international standardizing body and made available to the public;

international standardizing body means a standardizing body whose membership is open to the relevant bodies of at least all the parties to the GATT Agreement on Technical Barriers to Trade, including the International Organization for Standardization (ISO), the International Electrotechnical Commission (IEC), Codex Alimentarius Commission, the World Health Organization (WHO), the Food and Agriculture Organization (FAO), the International Telecommunication Union (ITU); or any other body that the Parties designate;

land transportation service means a transportation service provided by means of motor carrier or rail;

legitimate objective includes an objective such as: (a) safety, (b) protection of human, animal or plant life or health, the environment or consumers, including matters relating to quality and identifiability of goods or services, and (c) sustainable development, considering, among other things, where appropriate, fundamental climatic or other geographical factors, technological or infrastructural factors, or scientific justification but does not include the protection of domestic production;

make compatible means bring different standards-related measures of the same scope approved by different standardizing bodies to a level such that they are either identical, equivalent or have the effect of permitting goods or services to be used in place of one another or fulfill the same purpose;

services means land transportation services and telecommunications services;

standard means a document, approved by a recognized body, that provides, for common and repeated use, rules, guidelines or characteristics for goods or related processes and production methods, or for services or related operating methods, with which compliance is not mandatory. It may also include or deal exclusively with terminology, symbols, packaging, marking or labeling requirements as they apply to a good, process, or production or operating method;

standardizing body means a body having recognized activities in standardization; standards-related measure means a standard, technical regulation or conformity assessment procedure;

technical regulation means a document which lays down goods' characteristics or their related processes and production methods, or services' characteristics or their related operating methods, including the applicable administrative provisions, with which compliance is mandatory. It may also include or deal exclusively with terminology, symbols, packaging, marking or labeling requirements as they apply to a good, process, or production or operating method; and

telecommunications service means a service provided by means of the transmission and reception of signals by any electromagnetic means, but does not mean the cable, broadcast or other electromagnetic distribution of radio or television programming to the public generally.

2.   Except as they are otherwise defined in this Agreement, other terms in this Chapter shall be interpreted in accordance with their ordinary meaning in context and in the light of the objectives of this Agreement, and where appropriate by reference to the terms presented in the sixth edition of the ISO/IEC Guide 2: 1991, General Terms and Their Definitions Concerning Standardization and Related Activities.

Part Four
GOVERNMENT PROCUREMENT

Chapter Ten

GOVERNMENT PROCUREMENT

Section A—Scope and Coverage
and National Treatment

Article 1001: Scope and Coverage

1. This Chapter applies to measures adopted or maintained by a Party relating to procurement: (a) by a federal government entity set out in Annex 1001.1a–1, a government enterprise set out in Annex 1001.1a–2, or a state or provincial government entity set out in Annex 1001.1a–3 in accordance with Article 1024; (b) of goods in accordance with Annex 1001.1b–1, services in accordance with Annex 1001.1b–2, or construction services in accordance with Annex 1001.1b–3; and (c) where the value of the contract to be awarded is estimated to be equal to or greater than a threshold, calculated and adjusted according to the U.S. inflation rate as set out in Annex 1001.1c, of (i) for federal government entities, US$50,-000 for contracts for goods, services or any combination thereof, and US$6.5 million for contracts for construction services, (ii) for government enterprises, US$250,000 for contracts for goods, services or any combination thereof, and US$8.0 million for contracts for construction services, and (iii) for state and provincial government entities, the applicable threshold, as set out in Annex 1001.1a–3 in accordance with Article 1024.

2. Paragraph 1 is subject to: (a) the transitional provisions set out in Annex 1001.2a; (b) the General Notes set out in Annex 1001.2b; and (c) Annex 1001.2c, for the Parties specified therein.

3. Subject to paragraph 4, where a contract to be awarded by an entity is not covered by this Chapter, this Chapter shall not be construed to cover any good or service component of that contract.

4. No Party may prepare, design or otherwise structure any procurement contract in order to avoid the obligations of this Chapter.

5. Procurement includes procurement by such methods as purchase, lease or rental, with or without an option to buy. Procurement does not include: (a) non-contractual agreements or any form of government assistance, including cooperative agreements, grants, loans, equity

infusions, guarantees, fiscal incentives, and government provision of goods and services to persons or state, provincial and regional governments; and (b) the acquisition of fiscal agency or depository services, liquidation and management services for regulated financial institutions and sale and distribution services for government debt.

Article 1002: Valuation of Contracts

1.   Each Party shall ensure that its entities, in determining whether a contract is covered by this Chapter, apply paragraphs 2 through 7 in calculating the value of that contract.

2.   The value of a contract shall be estimated as at the time of publication of a notice in accordance with Article 1010.

3.   In calculating the value of a contract, an entity shall take into account all forms of remuneration, including premiums, fees, commissions and interest.

4.   Further to Article 1001(4), an entity may not select a valuation method, or divide procurement requirements into separate contracts, to avoid the obligations of this Chapter.

5.   Where an individual requirement for a procurement results in the award of more than one contract, or in contracts being awarded in separate parts, the basis for valuation shall be either: (a) the actual value of similar recurring contracts concluded over the prior fiscal year or 12 months adjusted, where possible, for anticipated changes in quantity and value over the subsequent 12 months; or (b) the estimated value of recurring contracts in the fiscal year or 12 months subsequent to the initial contract.

6.   In the case of a contract for lease or rental, with or without an option to buy, or in the case of a contract that does not specify a total price, the basis for valuation shall be: (a) in the case of a fixed-term contract, where the term is 12 months or less, the total contract value, for its duration or, where the term exceeds 12 months, the total contract value, including the estimated residual value; or (b) in the case of a contract for an indefinite period, the estimated monthly installment multiplied by 48. If the entity is uncertain as to whether a contract is for a fixed or an indefinite term, the entity shall calculate the value of the contract using the method set out in subparagraph (b).

7.   Where tender documentation requires option clauses, the basis for valuation shall be the total value of the maximum permissible procurement, including all possible optional purchases.

Article 1003: National Treatment and Non-discrimination

1.   With respect to measures covered by this Chapter, each Party shall accord to goods of another Party, to the suppliers of such goods and to service suppliers of another Party, treatment no less favorable than

the most favorable treatment that the Party accords to: (a) its own goods and suppliers; and (b) goods and suppliers of another Party.

2.   With respect to measures covered by this Chapter, no Party may: (a) treat a locally established supplier less favorably than another locally established supplier on the basis of degree of foreign affiliation or ownership; or (b) discriminate against a locally established supplier on the basis that the goods or services offered by that supplier for the particular procurement are goods or services of another Party.

3.   Paragraph 1 does not apply to measures respecting customs duties or other charges of any kind imposed on or in connection with importation, the method of levying such duties or charges or other import regulations, including restrictions and formalities.

Article 1004: Rules of Origin

No Party may apply rules of origin to goods imported from another Party for purposes of government procurement covered by this Chapter that are different from or inconsistent with the rules of origin the Party applies in the normal course of trade, which may be the Marking Rules established under Annex 311 if they become the rules of origin applied by that Party in the normal course of its trade.

Article 1005: Denial of Benefits

1.   Subject to prior notification and consultation in accordance with Articles 1803 (Notification and Provision of Information) and 2006 (Consultations), a Party may deny the benefits of this Chapter to a service supplier of another Party where the Party establishes that the service is being provided by an enterprise that is owned or controlled by persons of a non-Party and that has no substantial business activities in the territory of any Party.

2.   A Party may deny to an enterprise of another Party the benefits of this Chapter if nationals of a non-Party own or control the enterprise and: (a) the circumstance set out in Article 1113(1)(a) (Denial of Benefits) is met; or (b) the denying Party adopts or maintains measures with respect to the non-Party that prohibit transactions with the enterprise or that would be violated or circumvented if the benefits of this Chapter were accorded to the enterprise.

Article 1006: Prohibition of Offsets

Each Party shall ensure that its entities do not, in the qualification and selection of suppliers, goods or services, in the evaluation of bids or the award of contracts, consider, seek or impose offsets. For purposes of this Article, offsets means conditions imposed or considered by an entity prior to or in the course of its procurement process that encourage local development or improve its Party's balance of payments accounts, by means of requirements of local content, licensing of technology, investment, counter-trade or similar requirements.

Article 1007: Technical Specifications

1.   Each Party shall ensure that its entities do not prepare, adopt or apply any technical specification with the purpose or the effect of creating unnecessary obstacles to trade.

2.   Each Party shall ensure that any technical specification prescribed by its entities is, where appropriate: (a) specified in terms of performance criteria rather than design or descriptive characteristics; and (b) based on international standards, national technical regulations, recognized national standards, or building codes.

3.   Each Party shall ensure that the technical specifications prescribed by its entities do not require or refer to a particular trademark or name, patent, design or type, specific origin or producer or supplier unless there is no sufficiently precise or intelligible way of otherwise describing the procurement requirements and provided that, in such cases, words such as "or equivalent" are included in the tender documentation.

4.   Each Party shall ensure that its entities do not seek or accept, in a manner that would have the effect of precluding competition, advice that may be used in the preparation or adoption of any technical specification for a specific procurement from a person that may have a commercial interest in that procurement.

Section B—Tendering Procedures

Article 1008: Tendering Procedures

1.   Each Party shall ensure that the tendering procedures of its entities are: (a) applied in a non-discriminatory manner; and (b) consistent with this Article and Articles 1009 through 1016.

2.   In this regard, each Party shall ensure that its entities: (a) do not provide to any supplier information with regard to a specific procurement in a manner that would have the effect of precluding competition; and (b) provide all suppliers equal access to information with respect to a procurement during the period prior to the issuance of any notice or tender documentation.

Article 1009: Qualification of Suppliers

1.   Further to Article 1003, no entity of a Party may, in the process of qualifying suppliers in a tendering procedure, discriminate between suppliers of the other Parties or between domestic suppliers and suppliers of the other Parties.

2.   The qualification procedures followed by an entity shall be consistent with the following: (a) conditions for participation by suppli-

ers in tendering procedures shall be published sufficiently in advance so as to provide the suppliers adequate time to initiate and, to the extent that it is compatible with efficient operation of the procurement process, to complete the qualification procedures; (b) conditions for participation by suppliers in tendering procedures, including financial guarantees, technical qualifications and information necessary for establishing the financial, commercial and technical capacity of suppliers, as well as the verification of whether a supplier meets those conditions, shall be limited to those that are essential to ensure the fulfillment of the contract in question; (c) the financial, commercial and technical capacity of a supplier shall be judged both on the basis of that supplier's global business activity, including its activity in the territory of the Party of the supplier, and its activity, if any, in the territory of the Party of the procuring entity; (d) an entity shall not misuse the process of, including the time required for, qualification in order to exclude suppliers of another Party from a suppliers' list or from being considered for a particular procurement; (e) an entity shall recognize as qualified suppliers those suppliers of another Party that meet the conditions for participation in a particular procurement; (f) an entity shall consider for a particular procurement those suppliers of another Party that request to participate in the procurement and that are not yet qualified, provided there is sufficient time to complete the qualification procedure; (g) an entity that maintains a permanent list of qualified suppliers shall ensure that suppliers may apply for qualification at any time, that all qualified suppliers so requesting are included in the list within a reasonably short period of time and that all qualified suppliers included in the list are notified of the termination of the list or of their removal from it; (h) where, after publication of a notice in accordance with Article 1010, a supplier that is not yet qualified requests to participate in a particular procurement, the entity shall promptly start the qualification procedure; (i) an entity shall advise any supplier that requests to become a qualified supplier of its decision as to whether that supplier has become qualified; and (j) where an entity rejects a supplier's application to qualify or ceases to recognize a supplier as qualified, the entity shall, on request of the supplier, promptly provide pertinent information concerning the entity's reasons for doing so.

3.   Each Party shall: (a) ensure that each of its entities uses a single qualification procedure, except that an entity may use additional qualification procedures where the entity determines the need for a different procedure and is prepared, on request of another Party, to demonstrate that need; and (b) endeavor to minimize differences in the qualification procedures of its entities.

4.   Nothing in paragraphs 2 and 3 shall prevent an entity from excluding a supplier on grounds such as bankruptcy or false declarations.

Article 1010: Invitation to Participate

1. Except as otherwise provided in Article 1016, an entity shall publish an invitation to participate for all procurements in accordance with paragraphs 2, 3 and 5, in the appropriate publication referred to in Annex 1010.1.

2. The invitation to participate shall take the form of a notice of proposed procurement that shall contain the following information: (a) a description of the nature and quantity of the goods or services to be procured, including any options for further procurement and, if possible, (i) an estimate of when such options may be exercised, and (ii) in the case of recurring contracts, an estimate of when the subsequent notices will be issued; (b) a statement as to whether the procedure is open or selective and whether it will involve negotiation; (c) any date for starting or completion of delivery of the goods or services to be procured; (d) the address to which an application to be invited to tender or to qualify for the suppliers' lists must be submitted, the final date for receiving the application and the language or languages in which it may be submitted; (e) the address to which tenders must be submitted, the final date for receiving tenders and the language or languages in which tenders may be submitted; (f) the address of the entity that will award the contract and that will provide any information necessary for obtaining specifications and other documents; (g) a statement of any economic or technical requirements and of any financial guarantees, information and documents required from suppliers; (h) the amount and terms of payment of any sum payable for the tender documentation; and (i) a statement as to whether the entity is inviting offers for purchase, lease or rental, with or without an option to buy.

3. Notwithstanding paragraph 2, an entity listed in Annex 1001.1a–2 or 1001.1a–3 may use as an invitation to participate a notice of planned procurement that shall contain as much of the information referred to in paragraph 2 as is available to the entity, but that shall include, at a minimum, the following information: (a) a description of the subject matter of the procurement; (b) the time limits set for the receipt of tenders or applications to be invited to tender; (c) the address to which requests for documents relating to the procurement should be submitted; (d) a statement that interested suppliers should express their interest in the procurement to the entity; and (e) the identification of a contact point within the entity from which further information may be obtained.

4. An entity that uses a notice of planned procurement as an invitation to participate shall subsequently invite suppliers that have expressed an interest in the procurement to confirm their interest on the basis of information provided by the entity, which shall include at least the information referred to in paragraph 2.

5. Notwithstanding paragraph 2, an entity listed in Annex 1001.1a–2 or 1001.1a–3 may use as an invitation to participate a notice

regarding a qualification system. An entity that uses such a notice shall, subject to the considerations referred to Article 1015(8), provide in a timely manner information that allows all suppliers that have expressed an interest in participating in the procurement to have a meaningful opportunity to assess their interest. The information shall normally include the information required for notices referred to in paragraph 2. Information provided to any interested supplier shall be provided in a non-discriminatory manner to all other interested suppliers.

6.   In the case of selective tendering procedures, an entity that maintains a permanent list of qualified suppliers shall publish annually in the appropriate publication referred to in Annex 1010.1 a notice containing the following information: (a) an enumeration of any such lists maintained, including their headings, in relation to the goods or services or categories of goods or services to be procured through the lists; (b) the conditions to be fulfilled by suppliers in view of their inscription on the lists and the methods according to which each of those conditions will be verified by the entity concerned; and (c) the period of validity of the lists and the formalities for their renewal.

7.   Where, after publication of an invitation to participate, but before the time set for the opening or receipt of tenders as specified in the notices or the tender documentation, an entity finds that it has become necessary to amend or reissue the notice or tender documentation, the entity shall ensure that the amended or reissued notice or tender documentation is given the same circulation as the original. Any significant information given by an entity to a supplier with respect to a particular procurement shall be given simultaneously to all other interested suppliers and sufficiently in advance so as to provide all suppliers concerned adequate time to consider the information and to respond.

8.   An entity shall indicate in the notices referred to in this Article that the procurement is covered by this Chapter.

Article 1011: Selective Tendering Procedures

1.   To ensure optimum effective competition between the suppliers of the Parties under selective tendering procedures, an entity shall, for each procurement, invite tenders from the maximum number of domestic suppliers and suppliers of the other Parties, consistent with the efficient operation of the procurement system.

2.   Subject to paragraph 3, an entity that maintains a permanent list of qualified suppliers may select suppliers to be invited to tender for a particular procurement from among those listed. In the process of making a selection, the entity shall provide for equitable opportunities for suppliers on the list.

3.   Subject to Article 1009(2)(f), an entity shall allow a supplier that requests to participate in a particular procurement to submit a tender and shall consider the tender. The number of additional suppliers

permitted to participate shall be limited only by the efficient operation of the procurement system.

4.   Where an entity does not invite or admit a supplier to tender, the entity shall, on request of the supplier, promptly provide pertinent information concerning its reasons for not doing so.

Article 1012: Time Limits for Tendering and Delivery

1.   An entity shall: (a) in prescribing a time limit, provide adequate time to allow suppliers of another Party to prepare and submit tenders before the closing of the tendering procedures; (b) in determining a time limit, consistent with its own reasonable needs, take into account such factors as the complexity of the procurement, the extent of subcontracting anticipated, and the time normally required for transmitting tenders by mail from foreign as well as domestic points; and (c) take due account of publication delays when setting the final date for receipt of tenders or applications to be invited to tender.

2.   Subject to paragraph 3, an entity shall provide that: (a) in open tendering procedures, the period for the receipt of tenders is no less than 40 days from the date of publication of a notice in accordance with Article 1010; (b) in selective tendering procedures not involving the use of a permanent list of qualified suppliers, the period for submitting an application to be invited to tender is no less than 25 days from the date of publication of a notice in accordance with Article 1010, and the period for receipt of tenders is no less than 40 days from the date of issuance of the invitation to tender; and (c) in selective tendering procedures involving the use of a permanent list of qualified suppliers, the period for receipt of tenders is no less than 40 days from the date of the initial issuance of invitations to tender, but where the date of initial issuance of invitations to tender does not coincide with the date of publication of a notice in accordance with Article 1010, there shall not be less than 40 days between those two dates.

3.   An entity may reduce the periods referred to in paragraph 2 in accordance with the following: (a) where a notice referred to in Article 1010(3) or (5) has been published for a period of no less than 40 days and no more than 12 months, the 40–day limit for receipt of tenders may be reduced to no less than 24 days; (b) in the case of the second or subsequent publications dealing with recurring contracts within the meaning of Article 1010(2)(a), the 40–day limit for receipt of tenders may be reduced to no less than 24 days; (c) where a state of urgency duly substantiated by the entity renders impracticable the periods in question, the periods may be reduced to no less than 10 days from the date of publication of a notice in accordance with Article 1010; or (d) where an entity listed in Annex 1001.1a–2 or 1001.1a–3 is using as an invitation to participate a notice referred to in Article 1010(5), the periods may be fixed by mutual agreement between the entity and all selected suppliers but, in the absence of agreement, the entity may fix periods that shall be

sufficiently long to allow for responsive bidding and in any event shall be no less than 10 days.

4. An entity shall, in establishing a delivery date for goods or services and consistent with its own reasonable needs, take into account such factors as the complexity of the procurement, the extent of subcontracting anticipated and the time realistically required for production, destocking and transport of goods from the points of supply.

Article 1013: Tender Documentation

1. Where an entity provides tender documentation to suppliers, the documentation shall contain all information necessary to permit suppliers to submit responsive tenders, including information required to be published in the notice referred to in Article 1010(2), except for the information required under Article 1010(2)(h). The documentation shall also include: (a) the address of the entity to which tenders should be submitted; (b) the address to which requests for supplementary information should be submitted; (c) the language or languages in which tenders and tendering documents may be submitted; (d) the closing date and time for receipt of tenders and the length of time during which tenders should be open for acceptance; (e) the persons authorized to be present at the opening of tenders and the date, time and place of the opening; (f) a statement of any economic or technical requirements and of any financial guarantees, information and documents required from suppliers; (g) a complete description of the goods or services to be procured and any other requirements, including technical specifications, conformity certification and necessary plans, drawings and instructional materials; (h) the criteria for awarding the contract, including any factors other than price that are to be considered in the evaluation of tenders and the cost elements to be included in evaluating tender prices, such as transportation, insurance and inspection costs, and in the case of goods or services of another Party, customs duties and other import charges, taxes and the currency of payment; (i) the terms of payment; and (j) any other terms or conditions.

2. An entity shall: (a) forward tender documentation on the request of a supplier that is participating in open tendering procedures or has requested to participate in selective tendering procedures, and reply promptly to any reasonable request for explanations relating thereto; and (b) reply promptly to any reasonable request for relevant information made by a supplier participating in the tendering procedure, on condition that such information does not give that supplier an advantage over its competitors in the procedure for the award of the contract.

Article 1014: Negotiation Disciplines

1. An entity may conduct negotiations only: (a) in the context of procurement in which the entity has, in a notice published in accordance with Article 1010, indicated its intent to negotiate; or (b) where it

appears to the entity from the evaluation of the tenders that no one tender is obviously the most advantageous in terms of the specific evaluation criteria set out in the notices or tender documentation.

2. An entity shall use negotiations primarily to identify the strengths and weaknesses in the tenders.

3. An entity shall treat all tenders in confidence. In particular, no entity may provide to any person information intended to assist any supplier to bring its tender up to the level of any other tender.

4. No entity may, in the course of negotiations, discriminate between suppliers. In particular, an entity shall: (a) carry out any elimination of suppliers in accordance with the criteria set out in the notices and tender documentation; (b) provide in writing all modifications to the criteria or technical requirements to all suppliers remaining in the negotiations; (c) permit all remaining suppliers to submit new or amended tenders on the basis of the modified criteria or requirements; and (d) when negotiations are concluded, permit all remaining suppliers to submit final tenders in accordance with a common deadline.

Article 1015: Submission, Receipt and Opening of Tenders and Awarding of Contracts

1. An entity shall use procedures for the submission, receipt and opening of tenders and the awarding of contracts that are consistent with the following: (a) tenders shall normally be submitted in writing directly or by mail; (b) where tenders by telex, telegram, telecopy or other means of electronic transmission are permitted, the tender made thereby must include all the information necessary for the evaluation of the tender, in particular the definitive price proposed by the supplier and a statement that the supplier agrees to all the terms and conditions of the invitation to tender; (c) a tender made by telex, telegram, telecopy or other means of electronic transmission must be confirmed promptly by letter or by the dispatch of a signed copy of the telex, telegram, telecopy or electronic message; (d) the content of the telex, telegram, telecopy or electronic message shall prevail where there is a difference or conflict between that content and the content of any documentation received after the time limit for submission of tenders; (e) tenders presented by telephone shall not be permitted; (f) requests to participate in selective tendering procedures may be submitted by telex, telegram or telecopy and if permitted, may be submitted by other means of electronic transmission; and (g) the opportunities that may be given to suppliers to correct unintentional errors of form between the opening of tenders and the awarding of the contract shall not be administered in a manner that would result in discrimination between suppliers. In this paragraph, "means of electronic transmission" consists of means capable of producing for the recipient at the destination of the transmission a printed copy of the tender.

2. No entity may penalize a supplier whose tender is received in the office designated in the tender documentation after the time speci-

fied for receiving tenders if the delay is due solely to mishandling on the part of the entity. An entity may also consider, in exceptional circumstances, tenders received after the time specified for receiving tenders if the entity's procedures so provide.

3.   All tenders solicited by an entity under open or selective tendering procedures shall be received and opened under procedures and conditions guaranteeing the regularity of the opening of tenders. The entity shall retain the information on the opening of tenders. The information shall remain at the disposal of the competent authorities of the Party for use, if required, under Article 1017, Article 1019 or Chapter Twenty (Institutional Arrangements and Dispute Settlement Procedures).

4.   An entity shall award contracts in accordance with the following: (a) to be considered for award, a tender must, at the time of opening, conform to the essential requirements of the notices or tender documentation and have been submitted by a supplier that complies with the conditions for participation; (b) if the entity has received a tender that is abnormally lower in price than other tenders submitted, the entity may inquire of the supplier to ensure that it can comply with the conditions of participation and is or will be capable of fulfilling the terms of the contract; (c) unless the entity decides in the public interest not to award the contract, the entity shall make the award to the supplier that has been determined to be fully capable of undertaking the contract and whose tender is either the lowest-priced tender or the tender determined to be the most advantageous in terms of the specific evaluation criteria set out in the notices or tender documentation; (d) awards shall be made in accordance with the criteria and essential requirements specified in the tender documentation; and (e) option clauses shall not be used in a manner that circumvents this Chapter.

5.   No entity of a Party may make it a condition of the awarding of a contract that the supplier has previously been awarded one or more contracts by an entity of that Party or that the supplier has prior work experience in the territory of that Party.

6.   An entity shall: (a) on request, promptly inform suppliers participating in tendering procedures of decisions on contract awards and, if so requested, inform them in writing; and (b) on request of a supplier whose tender was not selected for award, provide pertinent information to that supplier concerning the reasons for not selecting its tender, the relevant characteristics and advantages of the tender selected and the name of the winning supplier.

7.   No later than 72 days after the award of a contract, an entity shall publish a notice in the appropriate publication referred to in Annex 1010.1 that shall contain the following information: (a) a description of the nature and quantity of goods or services included in the contract; (b) the name and address of the entity awarding the contract; (c) the date of the award; (d) the name and address of each winning supplier; (e) the value of the contract, or the highest-priced and lowest-priced tenders

considered in the process of awarding the contract; and (f) the tendering procedure used.

8. Notwithstanding paragraphs 1 through 7, an entity may withhold certain information on the award of a contract where disclosure of the information: (a) would impede law enforcement or otherwise be contrary to the public interest; (b) would prejudice the legitimate commercial interest of a particular person; or (c) might prejudice fair competition between suppliers.

Article 1016: Limited Tendering Procedures

1. An entity of a Party may, in the circumstances and subject to the conditions set out in paragraph 2, use limited tendering procedures and thus derogate from Articles 1008 through 1015, provided that such limited tendering procedures are not used with a view to avoiding maximum possible competition or in a manner that would constitute a means of discrimination between suppliers of the other Parties or protection of domestic suppliers.

2. An entity may use limited tendering procedures in the following circumstances and subject to the following conditions, as applicable: (a) in the absence of tenders in response to an open or selective call for tenders, or where the tenders submitted either have resulted from collusion or do not conform to the essential requirements of the tender documentation, or where the tenders submitted come from suppliers that do not comply with the conditions for participation provided for in accordance with this Chapter, on condition that the requirements of the initial procurement are not substantially modified in the contract as awarded; (b) where, for works of art, or for reasons connected with the protection of patents, copyrights or other exclusive rights, or proprietary information or where there is an absence of competition for technical reasons, the goods or services can be supplied only by a particular supplier and no reasonable alternative or substitute exists; (c) in so far as is strictly necessary where, for reasons of extreme urgency brought about by events unforeseeable by the entity, the goods or services could not be obtained in time by means of open or selective tendering procedures; (d) for additional deliveries by the original supplier that are intended either as replacement parts or continuing services for existing supplies, services or installations, or as the extension of existing supplies, services or installations, where a change of supplier would compel the entity to procure equipment or services not meeting requirements of interchangeability with already existing equipment or services, including software to the extent that the initial procurement of the software was covered by this Chapter; (e) where an entity procures a prototype or a first good or service that is developed at its request in the course of and for a particular contract for research, experiment, study or original development. Where such contracts have been fulfilled, subsequent procurement of goods or services shall be subject to Articles 1008 through 1015. Original development of a first good may include limited produc-

tion in order to incorporate the results of field testing and to demonstrate that the good is suitable for production in quantity to acceptable quality standards, but does not include quantity production to establish commercial viability or to recover research and development costs; (f) for goods purchased on a commodity market; (g) for purchases made under exceptionally advantageous conditions that only arise in the very short term, such as unusual disposals by enterprises that are not normally suppliers or disposal of assets of businesses in liquidation or receivership, but not routine purchases from regular suppliers; (h) for a contract to be awarded to the winner of an architectural design contest, on condition that the contest is (i) organized in a manner consistent with the principles of this Chapter, including regarding publication of an invitation to suitably qualified suppliers to participate in the contest, (ii) organized with a view to awarding the design contract to the winner, and (iii) to be judged by an independent jury; and (i) where an entity needs to procure consulting services regarding matters of a confidential nature, the disclosure of which could reasonably be expected to compromise government confidences, cause economic disruption or similarly be contrary to the public interest.

3. An entity shall prepare a report in writing on each contract awarded by it under paragraph 2. Each report shall contain the name of the procuring entity, indicate the value and kind of goods or services procured, the name of the country of origin, and a statement indicating the circumstances and conditions described in paragraph 2 that justified the use of limited tendering. The entity shall retain each report. They shall remain at the disposal of the competent authorities of the Party for use, if required, under Article 1017, Article 1019 or Chapter Twenty (Institutional Arrangements and Dispute Settlement Procedures).

Section C—Bid Challenge

Article 1017: Bid Challenge

1. In order to promote fair, open and impartial procurement procedures, each Party shall adopt and maintain bid challenge procedures for procurement covered by this Chapter in accordance with the following: (a) each Party shall allow suppliers to submit bid challenges concerning any aspect of the procurement process, which for the purposes of this Article begins after an entity has decided on its procurement requirement and continues through the contract award; (b) a Party may encourage a supplier to seek a resolution of any complaint with the entity concerned prior to initiating a bid challenge; (c) each Party shall ensure that its entities accord fair and timely consideration to any complaint regarding procurement covered by this Chapter; (d) whether or not a supplier has attempted to resolve its complaint with the entity, or following an unsuccessful attempt at such a resolution, no Party may prevent the supplier from initiating a bid challenge or seeking any other relief; (e) a Party may require a supplier to notify the entity on initiation

of a bid challenge; (f) a Party may limit the period within which a supplier may initiate a bid challenge, but in no case shall the period be less than 10 working days from the time when the basis of the complaint became known or reasonably should have become known to the supplier; (g) each Party shall establish or designate a reviewing authority with no substantial interest in the outcome of procurements to receive bid challenges and make findings and recommendations concerning them; (h) on receipt of a bid challenge, the reviewing authority shall expeditiously investigate the challenge; (i) a Party may require its reviewing authority to limit its considerations to the challenge itself; (j) in investigating the challenge, the reviewing authority may delay the awarding of the proposed contract pending resolution of the challenge, except in cases of urgency or where the delay would be contrary to the public interest; (k) the reviewing authority shall issue a recommendation to resolve the challenge, which may include directing the entity to re-evaluate offers, terminate or re-compete the contract in question; (*l*) entities normally shall follow the recommendations of the reviewing authority; (m) each Party should authorize its reviewing authority, following the conclusion of a bid challenge procedure, to make additional recommendations in writing to an entity respecting any facet of the entity's procurement process that is identified as problematic during the investigation of the challenge, including recommendations for changes in the procurement procedures of the entity to bring them into conformity with this Chapter; (n) the reviewing authority shall provide its findings and recommendations respecting bid challenges in writing and in a timely manner, and shall make them available to the Parties and interested persons; (*o*) each Party shall specify in writing and shall make generally available all its bid challenge procedures; and (p) each Party shall ensure that each of its entities maintains complete documentation regarding each of its procurements, including a written record of all communications substantially affecting each procurement, for at least three years from the date the contract was awarded, to allow verification that the procurement process was carried out in accordance with this Chapter.

2.   A Party may require that a bid challenge be initiated only after the notice of procurement has been published or, where a notice is not published, after tender documentation has been made available. Where a Party imposes such a requirement, the 10–working day period described in paragraph 1(f) shall begin no earlier than the date that the notice is published or the tender documentation is made available.

Section D—General Provisions

Article 1018: Exceptions

1.   Nothing in this Chapter shall be construed to prevent a Party from taking any action or not disclosing any information which it considers necessary for the protection of its essential security interests relating to the procurement of arms, ammunition or war materials, or to

procurement indispensable for national security or for national defense purposes.

2. Provided that such measures are not applied in a manner that would constitute a means of arbitrary or unjustifiable discrimination between Parties where the same conditions prevail or a disguised restriction on trade between the Parties, nothing in this Chapter shall be construed to prevent any Party from adopting or maintaining measures: (a) necessary to protect public morals, order or safety; (b) necessary to protect human, animal or plant life or health; (c) necessary to protect intellectual property; or (d) relating to goods or services of handicapped persons, of philanthropic institutions or of prison labor.

Article 1019: Provision of Information

1. Further to Article 1802(1) (Publication), each Party shall promptly publish any law, regulation, precedential judicial decision, administrative ruling of general application and any procedure, including standard contract clauses, regarding government procurement covered by this Chapter in the appropriate publications referred to in Annex 1010.1.

2. Each Party shall: (a) on request, explain to another Party its government procurement procedures; (b) ensure that its entities, on request from a supplier, promptly explain their procurement practices and procedures; and (c) designate by January 1, 1994 one or more contact points to (i) facilitate communication between the Parties, and (ii) answer all reasonable inquiries from other Parties to provide relevant information on matters covered by this Chapter.

3. A Party may seek such additional information on the award of the contract as may be necessary to determine whether the procurement was made fairly and impartially, in particular with respect to unsuccessful tenders. To this end, the Party of the procuring entity shall provide information on the characteristics and relative advantages of the winning tender and the contract price. Where release of this information would prejudice competition in future tenders, the information shall not be released by the requesting Party except after consultation with and agreement of the Party that provided the information.

4. On request, each Party shall provide to another Party information available to that Party and its entities concerning covered procurement of its entities and the individual contracts awarded by its entities.

5. No Party may disclose confidential information the disclosure of which would prejudice the legitimate commercial interests of a particular person or might prejudice fair competition between suppliers, without the formal authorization of the person that provided the information to that Party.

6. Nothing in this Chapter shall be construed as requiring any Party to disclose confidential information the disclosure of which would impede law enforcement or otherwise be contrary to the public interest.

7. With a view to ensuring effective monitoring of procurement covered by this Chapter, each Party shall collect statistics and provide to the other Parties an annual report in accordance with the following reporting requirements, unless the Parties otherwise agree: (a) statistics on the estimated value of all contracts awarded, both above and below the applicable threshold values, broken down by entities; (b) statistics on the number and total value of contracts above the applicable threshold values, broken down by entities, by categories of goods and services established in accordance with classification systems developed under this Chapter and by the country of origin of the goods and services procured; (c) statistics on the number and total value of contracts awarded under each use of the procedures referred to in Article 1016, broken down by entities, by categories of goods and services, and by country of origin of the goods and services procured; and (d) statistics on the number and total value of contracts awarded under derogations to this Chapter set out in Annexes 1001.2a and 1001.2b, broken down by entities.

8. Each Party may organize by state or province any portion of a report referred to in paragraph 7 that pertains to entities listed in Annex 1001.1a–3.

Article 1020: Technical Cooperation

1. The Parties shall cooperate, on mutually agreed terms, to increase understanding of their respective government procurement systems, with a view to maximizing access to government procurement opportunities for the suppliers of all Parties.

2. Each Party shall provide to the other Parties and to the suppliers of such Parties, on a cost recovery basis, information concerning training and orientation programs regarding its government procurement system, and access on a non-discriminatory basis to any program it conducts.

3. The training and orientation programs referred to in paragraph 2 include: (a) training of government personnel directly involved in government procurement procedures; (b) training of suppliers interested in pursuing government procurement opportunities; (c) an explanation and description of specific elements of each Party's government procurement system, such as its bid challenge mechanism; and (d) information about government procurement market opportunities.

4. Each Party shall establish by January 1, 1994 at least one contact point to provide information on the training and orientation programs referred to in this Article.

Article 1021: Joint Programs for Small Business

1. The Parties shall establish, within 12 months after the date of entry into force of this Agreement, the Committee on Small Business,

comprising representatives of the Parties. The Committee shall meet as mutually agreed, but not less than once each year, and shall report annually to the Commission on the efforts of the Parties to promote government procurement opportunities for their small businesses.

2.   The Committee shall work to facilitate the following activities of the Parties: (a) identification of available opportunities for the training of small business personnel in government procurement procedures; (b) identification of small businesses interested in becoming trading partners of small businesses in the territory of another Party; (c) development of data bases of small businesses in the territory of each Party for use by entities of another Party wishing to procure from small businesses; (d) consultations regarding the factors that each Party uses in establishing its criteria for eligibility for any small business programs; and (e) activities to address any related matter.

Article 1022: Rectifications or Modifications

1.   A Party may modify its coverage under this Chapter only in exceptional circumstances.

2.   Where a Party modifies its coverage under this Chapter, the Party shall: (a) notify the other Parties and its Section of the Secretariat of the modification; (b) reflect the change in the appropriate Annex; and (c) propose to the other Parties appropriate compensatory adjustments to its coverage in order to maintain a level of coverage comparable to that existing prior to the modification.

3.   Notwithstanding paragraphs 1 and 2, a Party may make rectifications of a purely formal nature and minor amendments to its Schedules to Annexes 1001.1a–1 through 1001.1b–3 and Annexes 1001.2a and 1001.2b, provided that it notifies such rectifications to the other Parties and its Section of the Secretariat, and another Party does not object to such proposed rectification within 30 days. In such cases, compensation need not be proposed.

4.   Notwithstanding any other provision of this Chapter, a Party may undertake reorganizations of its government procurement entities covered by this Chapter, including programs through which the procurement of such entities is decentralized or the corresponding government functions cease to be performed by any government entity, whether or not subject to this Chapter. In such cases, compensation need not be proposed. No Party may undertake such reorganizations or programs to avoid the obligations of this Chapter.

5.   Where a Party considers that: (a) an adjustment proposed under paragraph (2)(c) is not adequate to maintain a comparable level of mutually agreed coverage, or (b) a rectification or a minor amendment under paragraph 3 or a reorganization under paragraph 4 does not meet the applicable requirements of those paragraphs and should require compensation, the Party may have recourse to dispute settlement proce-

dures under Chapter Twenty (Institutional Arrangements and Dispute Settlement Procedures).

Article 1023: Divestiture of Entities

1.   Nothing in this Chapter shall be construed to prevent a Party from divesting an entity covered by this Chapter.

2.   If, on the public offering of shares of an entity listed in Annex 1001.1a-2, or through other methods, the entity is no longer subject to federal government control, the Party may delete the entity from its Schedule to that Annex, and withdraw the entity from the coverage of this Chapter, on notification to the other Parties and its Section of the Secretariat.

3.   Where a Party objects to the withdrawal on the grounds that the entity remains subject to federal government control, that Party may have recourse to dispute settlement procedures under Chapter Twenty.

Article 1024: Further Negotiations

1.   The Parties shall commence further negotiations no later than December 31, 1998, with a view to the further liberalization of their respective government procurement markets.

2.   In such negotiations, the Parties shall review all aspects of their government procurement practices for purposes of: (a) assessing the functioning of their government procurement systems; (b) seeking to expand the coverage of this Chapter, including by adding (i) other government enterprises, and (ii) procurement otherwise subject to legislated or administrative exceptions; and (c) reviewing thresholds.

3.   Prior to such review, the Parties shall endeavor to consult with their state and provincial governments with a view to obtaining commitments, on a voluntary and reciprocal basis, to include within this Chapter procurement by state and provincial government entities and enterprises.

4.   If the negotiations pursuant to Article IX:6(b) of the GATT Agreement on Government Procurement ("the Code") are completed prior to such review, the Parties shall: (a) immediately begin consultations with their state and provincial governments with a view to obtaining commitments, on a voluntary and reciprocal basis, to include within this Chapter procurement by state and provincial government entities and enterprises; and (b) increase the obligations and coverage of this Chapter to a level at least commensurate with that of the Code.

5.   The Parties shall undertake further negotiations, to commence no later than one year after the date of entry into force of this Agreement, on the subject of electronic transmission.

Article 1025: Definitions

For purposes of this Chapter:

construction services contract means a contract for the realization by any means of civil or building works listed in Appendix 1001.1b–3–A;

entity means an entity listed in Annex 1001.1a–1, 1001.1a–2 or 1001.1a–3;

goods of another Party means goods originating in the territory of another Party, determined in accordance with Article 1004;

international standard means "international standard", as defined in Article 915 (Standards–Related Measures—Definitions);

limited tendering procedures means procedures where an entity contacts suppliers individually, only in the circumstances and under the conditions specified in Article 1016;

locally established supplier includes a natural person resident in the territory of the Party, an enterprise organized or established under the Party's law, and a branch or representative office located in the Party's territory;

open tendering procedures means those procedures under which all interested suppliers may submit a tender;

selective tendering procedures means procedures under which, consistent with Article 1011, those suppliers invited to do so by an entity may submit a tender;

services includes construction services contracts, unless otherwise specified;

standard means "standard", as defined in Article 915;

supplier means a person that has provided or could provide goods or services in response to an entity's call for tender;

technical regulation means "technical regulation", as defined in Article 915;

technical specification means a specification which lays down goods characteristics or their related processes and production methods, or services characteristics or their related operating methods, including the applicable administrative provisions. It may also include or deal exclusively with terminology, symbols, packaging, marking or labelling requirements as they apply to a good, process, or production or operating method; and

tendering procedures means open tendering procedures, selective tendering procedures and limited tendering procedures.

Part Five

INVESTMENT, SERVICES AND RELATED MATTERS

Chapter Eleven

INVESTMENT

Section A—Investment

Article 1101: Scope and Coverage

1. This Chapter applies to measures adopted or maintained by a Party relating to: (a) investors of another Party; (b) investments of investors of another Party in the territory of the Party; and (c) with respect to Articles 1106 and 1114, all investments in the territory of the Party.

2. A Party has the right to perform exclusively the economic activities set out in Annex III and to refuse to permit the establishment of investment in such activities.

3. This Chapter does not apply to measures adopted or maintained by a Party to the extent that they are covered by Chapter Fourteen (Financial Services).

4. Nothing in this Chapter shall be construed to prevent a Party from providing a service or performing a function such as law enforcement, correctional services, income security or insurance, social security or insurance, social welfare, public education, public training, health, and child care, in a manner that is not inconsistent with this Chapter.

Article 1102: National Treatment

1. Each Party shall accord to investors of another Party treatment no less favorable than that it accords, in like circumstances, to its own investors with respect to the establishment, acquisition, expansion, management, conduct, operation, and sale or other disposition of investments.

2. Each Party shall accord to investments of investors of another Party treatment no less favorable than that it accords, in like circumstances, to investments of its own investors with respect to the establishment, acquisition, expansion, management, conduct, operation, and sale or other disposition of investments.

3. The treatment accorded by a Party under paragraphs 1 and 2 means, with respect to a state or province, treatment no less favorable than the most favorable treatment accorded, in like circumstances, by that state or province to investors, and to investments of investors, of the Party of which it forms a part.

4. For greater certainty, no Party may: (a) impose on an investor of another Party a requirement that a minimum level of equity in an enterprise in the territory of the Party be held by its nationals, other than nominal qualifying shares for directors or incorporators of corporations; or (b) require an investor of another Party, by reason of its nationality, to sell or otherwise dispose of an investment in the territory of the Party.

Article 1103: Most–Favored–Nation Treatment

1. Each Party shall accord to investors of another Party treatment no less favorable than that it accords, in like circumstances, to investors of any other Party or of a non-Party with respect to the establishment, acquisition, expansion, management, conduct, operation, and sale or other disposition of investments.

2. Each Party shall accord to investments of investors of another Party treatment no less favorable than that it accords, in like circumstances, to investments of investors of any other Party or of a non-Party with respect to the establishment, acquisition, expansion, management, conduct, operation, and sale or other disposition of investments.

Article 1104: Standard of Treatment

Each Party shall accord to investors of another Party and to investments of investors of another Party the better of the treatment required by Articles 1102 and 1103.

Article 1105: Minimum Standard of Treatment

1. Each Party shall accord to investments of investors of another Party treatment in accordance with international law, including fair and equitable treatment and full protection and security.

2. Without prejudice to paragraph 1 and notwithstanding Article 1108(7)(b), each Party shall accord to investors of another Party, and to investments of investors of another Party, non-discriminatory treatment with respect to measures it adopts or maintains relating to losses suffered by investments in its territory owing to armed conflict or civil strife.

3. Paragraph 2 does not apply to existing measures relating to subsidies or grants that would be inconsistent with Article 1102 but for Article 1108(7)(b).

Article 1106: Performance Requirements

1. No Party may impose or enforce any of the following requirements, or enforce any commitment or undertaking, in connection with the establishment, acquisition, expansion, management, conduct or operation of an investment of an investor of a Party or of a non-Party in its territory: (a) to export a given level or percentage of goods or services; (b) to achieve a given level or percentage of domestic content; (c) to purchase, use or accord a preference to goods produced or services provided in its territory, or to purchase goods or services from persons in its territory; (d) to relate in any way the volume or value of imports to the volume or value of exports or to the amount of foreign exchange inflows associated with such investment; (e) to restrict sales of goods or services in its territory that such investment produces or provides by relating such sales in any way to the volume or value of its exports or foreign exchange earnings; (f) to transfer technology, a production process or other proprietary knowledge to a person in its territory, except when the requirement is imposed or the commitment or undertaking is enforced by a court, administrative tribunal or competition authority to remedy an alleged violation of competition laws or to act in a manner not inconsistent with other provisions of this Agreement; or (g) to act as the exclusive supplier of the goods it produces or services it provides to a specific region or world market.

2. A measure that requires an investment to use a technology to meet generally applicable health, safety or environmental requirements shall not be construed to be inconsistent with paragraph 1(f). For greater certainty, Articles 1102 and 1103 apply to the measure.

3. No Party may condition the receipt or continued receipt of an advantage, in connection with an investment in its territory of an investor of a Party or of a non-Party, on compliance with any of the following requirements: (a) to achieve a given level or percentage of domestic content; (b) to purchase, use or accord a preference to goods produced in its territory, or to purchase goods from producers in its territory; (c) to relate in any way the volume or value of imports to the volume or value of exports or to the amount of foreign exchange inflows associated with such investment; or (d) to restrict sales of goods or services in its territory that such investment produces or provides by relating such sales in any way to the volume or value of its exports or foreign exchange earnings.

4. Nothing in paragraph 3 shall be construed to prevent a Party from conditioning the receipt or continued receipt of an advantage, in connection with an investment in its territory of an investor of a Party or of a non-Party, on compliance with a requirement to locate production, provide a service, train or employ workers, construct or expand particular facilities, or carry out research and development, in its territory.

5. Paragraphs 1 and 3 do not apply to any requirement other than the requirements set out in those paragraphs.

6. Provided that such measures are not applied in an arbitrary or unjustifiable manner, or do not constitute a disguised restriction on international trade or investment, nothing in paragraph 1(b) or (c) or 3(a) or (b) shall be construed to prevent any Party from adopting or maintaining measures, including environmental measures: (a) necessary to secure compliance with laws and regulations that are not inconsistent with the provisions of this Agreement; (b) necessary to protect human, animal or plant life or health; or (c) necessary for the conservation of living or non-living exhaustible natural resources.

Article 1107: Senior Management and Boards of Directors

1. No Party may require that an enterprise of that Party that is an investment of an investor of another Party appoint to senior management positions individuals of any particular nationality.

2. A Party may require that a majority of the board of directors, or any committee thereof, of an enterprise of that Party that is an investment of an investor of another Party, be of a particular nationality, or resident in the territory of the Party, provided that the requirement does not materially impair the ability of the investor to exercise control over its investment.

Article 1108: Reservations and Exceptions

1. Articles 1102, 1103, 1106 and 1107 do not apply to: (a) any existing non-conforming measure that is maintained by (i) a Party at the federal level, as set out in its Schedule to Annex I or III, (ii) a state or province, for two years after the date of entry into force of this Agreement, and thereafter as set out by a Party in its Schedule to Annex I in accordance with paragraph 2, or (iii) a local government; (b) the continuation or prompt renewal of any non-conforming measure referred to in subparagraph (a); or (c) an amendment to any non-conforming measure referred to in subparagraph (a) to the extent that the amendment does not decrease the conformity of the measure, as it existed immediately before the amendment, with Articles 1102, 1103, 1106 and 1107.

2. Each Party may set out in its Schedule to Annex I, within two years of the date of entry into force of this Agreement, any existing non-conforming measure maintained by a state or province, not including a local government.

3. Articles 1102, 1103, 1106 and 1107 do not apply to any measure that a Party adopts or maintains with respect to sectors, subsectors or activities, as set out in its Schedule to Annex II.

4. No Party may, under any measure adopted after the date of entry into force of this Agreement and covered by its Schedule to Annex

II, require an investor of another Party, by reason of its nationality, to sell or otherwise dispose of an investment existing at the time the measure becomes effective.

5.   Articles 1102 and 1103 do not apply to any measure that is an exception to, or derogation from, the obligations under Article 1703 (Intellectual Property—National Treatment) as specifically provided for in that Article.

6.   Article 1103 does not apply to treatment accorded by a Party pursuant to agreements, or with respect to sectors, set out in its Schedule to Annex IV.

7.   Articles 1102, 1103 and 1107 do not apply to: (a) procurement by a Party or a state enterprise; or (b) subsidies or grants provided by a Party or a state enterprise, including government-supported loans, guarantees and insurance.

8.   The provisions of: (a) Article 1106(1)(a), (b) and (c), and (3)(a) and (b) do not apply to qualification requirements for goods or services with respect to export promotion and foreign aid programs; (b) Article 1106(1)(b), (c), (f) and (g), and (3)(a) and (b) do not apply to procurement by a Party or a state enterprise; and (c) Article 1106(3)(a) and (b) do not apply to requirements imposed by an importing Party relating to the content of goods necessary to qualify for preferential tariffs or preferential quotas.

Article 1109: Transfers

1.   Each Party shall permit all transfers relating to an investment of an investor of another Party in the territory of the Party to be made freely and without delay. Such transfers include: (a) profits, dividends, interest, capital gains, royalty payments, management fees, technical assistance and other fees, returns in kind and other amounts derived from the investment; (b) proceeds from the sale of all or any part of the investment or from the partial or complete liquidation of the investment; (c) payments made under a contract entered into by the investor, or its investment, including payments made pursuant to a loan agreement; (d) payments made pursuant to Article 1110; and (e) payments arising under Section B.

2.   Each Party shall permit transfers to be made in a freely usable currency at the market rate of exchange prevailing on the date of transfer with respect to spot transactions in the currency to be transferred.

3.   No Party may require its investors to transfer, or penalize its investors that fail to transfer, the income, earnings, profits or other amounts derived from, or attributable to, investments in the territory of another Party.

4.   Notwithstanding paragraphs 1 and 2, a Party may prevent a transfer through the equitable, non-discriminatory and good faith appli-

cation of its laws relating to: (a) bankruptcy, insolvency or the protection of the rights of creditors; (b) issuing, trading or dealing in securities; (c) criminal or penal offenses; (d) reports of transfers of currency or other monetary instruments; or (e) ensuring the satisfaction of judgments in adjudicatory proceedings.

5. Paragraph 3 shall not be construed to prevent a Party from imposing any measure through the equitable, non-discriminatory and good faith application of its laws relating to the matters set out in subparagraphs (a) through (e) of paragraph 4.

6. Notwithstanding paragraph 1, a Party may restrict transfers of returns in kind in circumstances where it could otherwise restrict such transfers under this Agreement, including as set out in paragraph 4.

Article 1110: Expropriation and Compensation

1. No Party may directly or indirectly nationalize or expropriate an investment of an investor of another Party in its territory or take a measure tantamount to nationalization or expropriation of such an investment ("expropriation"), except: (a) for a public purpose; (b) on a non-discriminatory basis; (c) in accordance with due process of law and Article 1105(1); and (d) on payment of compensation in accordance with paragraphs 2 through 6.

2. Compensation shall be equivalent to the fair market value of the expropriated investment immediately before the expropriation took place ("date of expropriation"), and shall not reflect any change in value occurring because the intended expropriation had become known earlier. Valuation criteria shall include going concern value, asset value including declared tax value of tangible property, and other criteria, as appropriate, to determine fair market value.

3. Compensation shall be paid without delay and be fully realizable.

4. If payment is made in a G7 currency, compensation shall include interest at a commercially reasonable rate for that currency from the date of expropriation until the date of actual payment.

5. If a Party elects to pay in a currency other than a G7 currency, the amount paid on the date of payment, if converted into a G7 currency at the market rate of exchange prevailing on that date, shall be no less than if the amount of compensation owed on the date of expropriation had been converted into that G7 currency at the market rate of exchange prevailing on that date, and interest had accrued at a commercially reasonable rate for that G7 currency from the date of expropriation until the date of payment.

6. On payment, compensation shall be freely transferable as provided in Article 1109.

7. This Article does not apply to the issuance of compulsory licenses granted in relation to intellectual property rights, or to the revocation,

limitation or creation of intellectual property rights, to the extent that such issuance, revocation, limitation or creation is consistent with Chapter Seventeen (Intellectual Property).

8. For purposes of this Article and for greater certainty, a nondiscriminatory measure of general application shall not be considered a measure tantamount to an expropriation of a debt security or loan covered by this Chapter solely on the ground that the measure imposes costs on the debtor that cause it to default on the debt.

Article 1111: Special Formalities and Information Requirements

1. Nothing in Article 1102 shall be construed to prevent a Party from adopting or maintaining a measure that prescribes special formalities in connection with the establishment of investments by investors of another Party, such as a requirement that investors be residents of the Party or that investments be legally constituted under the laws or regulations of the Party, provided that such formalities do not materially impair the protections afforded by a Party to investors of another Party and investments of investors of another Party pursuant to this Chapter.

2. Notwithstanding Articles 1102 or 1103, a Party may require an investor of another Party, or its investment in its territory, to provide routine information concerning that investment solely for informational or statistical purposes. The Party shall protect such business information that is confidential from any disclosure that would prejudice the competitive position of the investor or the investment. Nothing in this paragraph shall be construed to prevent a Party from otherwise obtaining or disclosing information in connection with the equitable and good faith application of its law.

Article 1112: Relation to Other Chapters

1. In the event of any inconsistency between this Chapter and another Chapter, the other Chapter shall prevail to the extent of the inconsistency.

2. A requirement by a Party that a service provider of another Party post a bond or other form of financial security as a condition of providing a service into its territory does not of itself make this Chapter applicable to the provision of that cross-border service. This Chapter applies to that Party's treatment of the posted bond or financial security.

Article 1113: Denial of Benefits

1. A Party may deny the benefits of this Chapter to an investor of another Party that is an enterprise of such Party and to investments of such investor if investors of a non-Party own or control the enterprise and the denying Party: (a) does not maintain diplomatic relations with the non-Party; or (b) adopts or maintains measures with respect to the

non-Party that prohibit transactions with the enterprise or that would be violated or circumvented if the benefits of this Chapter were accorded to the enterprise or to its investments.

2.   Subject to prior notification and consultation in accordance with Articles 1803 (Notification and Provision of Information) and 2006 (Consultations), a Party may deny the benefits of this Chapter to an investor of another Party that is an enterprise of such Party and to investments of such investors if investors of a non-Party own or control the enterprise and the enterprise has no substantial business activities in the territory of the Party under whose law it is constituted or organized.

Article 1114: Environmental Measures

1.   Nothing in this Chapter shall be construed to prevent a Party from adopting, maintaining or enforcing any measure otherwise consistent with this Chapter that it considers appropriate to ensure that investment activity in its territory is undertaken in a manner sensitive to environmental concerns.

2.   The Parties recognize that it is inappropriate to encourage investment by relaxing domestic health, safety or environmental measures. Accordingly, a Party should not waive or otherwise derogate from, or offer to waive or otherwise derogate from, such measures as an encouragement for the establishment, acquisition, expansion or retention in its territory of an investment of an investor. If a Party considers that another Party has offered such an encouragement, it may request consultations with the other Party and the two Parties shall consult with a view to avoiding any such encouragement.

Section B—Settlement of Disputes Between a Party and an Investor of Another Party

Article 1115: Purpose

Without prejudice to the rights and obligations of the Parties under Chapter Twenty (Institutional Arrangements and Dispute Settlement Procedures), this Section establishes a mechanism for the settlement of investment disputes that assures both equal treatment among investors of the Parties in accordance with the principle of international reciprocity and due process before an impartial tribunal.

Article 1116: Claim by an Investor of a Party on Its Own Behalf

1.   An investor of a Party may submit to arbitration under this Section a claim that another Party has breached an obligation under: (a) Section A or Article 1503(2) (State Enterprises), or (b) Article 1502(3)(a) (Monopolies and State Enterprises) where the monopoly has acted in a

manner inconsistent with the Party's obligations under Section A, and that the investor has incurred loss or damage by reason of, or arising out of, that breach.

2. An investor may not make a claim if more than three years have elapsed from the date on which the investor first acquired, or should have first acquired, knowledge of the alleged breach and knowledge that the investor has incurred loss or damage.

Article 1117: Claim by an Investor of a Party on Behalf of an Enterprise

1. An investor of a Party, on behalf of an enterprise of another Party that is a juridical person that the investor owns or controls directly or indirectly, may submit to arbitration under this Section a claim that the other Party has breached an obligation under: (a) Section A or Article 1503(2) (State Enterprises), or (b) Article 1502(3)(a) (Monopolies and State Enterprises) where the monopoly has acted in a manner inconsistent with the Party's obligations under Section A, and that the enterprise has incurred loss or damage by reason of, or arising out of, that breach.

2. An investor may not make a claim on behalf of an enterprise described in paragraph 1 if more than three years have elapsed from the date on which the enterprise first acquired, or should have first acquired, knowledge of the alleged breach and knowledge that the enterprise has incurred loss or damage.

3. Where an investor makes a claim under this Article and the investor or a non-controlling investor in the enterprise makes a claim under Article 1116 arising out of the same events that gave rise to the claim under this Article, and two or more of the claims are submitted to arbitration under Article 1120, the claims should be heard together by a Tribunal established under Article 1126, unless the Tribunal finds that the interests of a disputing party would be prejudiced thereby.

4. An investment may not make a claim under this Section.

Article 1118: Settlement of a Claim Through Consultation and Negotiation

The disputing parties should first attempt to settle a claim through consultation or negotiation.

Article 1119: Notice of Intent to Submit a Claim to Arbitration

The disputing investor shall deliver to the disputing Party written notice of its intention to submit a claim to arbitration at least 90 days before the claim is submitted, which notice shall specify: (a) the name and address of the disputing investor and, where a claim is made under

Article 1117, the name and address of the enterprise; (b) the provisions of this Agreement alleged to have been breached and any other relevant provisions; (c) the issues and the factual basis for the claim; and (d) the relief sought and the approximate amount of damages claimed.

Article 1120: Submission of a Claim to Arbitration

1. Except as provided in Annex 1120.1, and provided that six months have elapsed since the events giving rise to a claim, a disputing investor may submit the claim to arbitration under: (a) the ICSID Convention, provided that both the disputing Party and the Party of the investor are parties to the Convention; (b) the Additional Facility Rules of ICSID, provided that either the disputing Party or the Party of the investor, but not both, is a party to the ICSID Convention; or (c) the UNCITRAL Arbitration Rules.

2. The applicable arbitration rules shall govern the arbitration except to the extent modified by this Section.

Annex 1120.1

Submission of a Claim to Arbitration

Mexico

With respect to the submission of a claim to arbitration: (a) an investor of another Party may not allege that Mexico has breached an obligation under: (i) Section A or Article 1503(2) (State Enterprises), or (ii) Article 1502(3)(a) (Monopolies and State Enterprises) where the monopoly has acted in a manner inconsistent with the Party's obligations under Section A, both in an arbitration under this Section and in proceedings before a Mexican court or administrative tribunal; and (b) where an enterprise of Mexico that is a juridical person that an investor of another Party owns or controls directly or indirectly alleges in proceedings before a Mexican court or administrative tribunal that Mexico has breached an obligation under: (i) Section A or Article 1503(2) (State Enterprises), or (ii) Article 1502(3)(a) (Monopolies and State Enterprises) where the monopoly has acted in a manner inconsistent with the Party's obligations under Section A, the investor may not allege the breach in an arbitration under this Section.

Article 1121: Conditions Precedent to Submission of a Claim to Arbitration

1. A disputing investor may submit a claim under Article 1116 to arbitration only if: (a) the investor consents to arbitration in accordance with the procedures set out in this Agreement; and (b) the investor and, where the claim is for loss or damage to an interest in an enterprise of another Party that is a juridical person that the investor owns or controls directly or indirectly, the enterprise, waive their right to initiate or continue before any administrative tribunal or court under the law of

any Party, or other dispute settlement procedures, any proceedings with respect to the measure of the disputing Party that is alleged to be a breach referred to in Article 1116, except for proceedings for injunctive, declaratory or other extraordinary relief, not involving the payment of damages, before an administrative tribunal or court under the law of the disputing Party.

2. A disputing investor may submit a claim under Article 1117 to arbitration only if both the investor and the enterprise: (a) consent to arbitration in accordance with the procedures set out in this Agreement; and (b) waive their right to initiate or continue before any administrative tribunal or court under the law of any Party, or other dispute settlement procedures, any proceedings with respect to the measure of the disputing Party that is alleged to be a breach referred to in Article 1117, except for proceedings for injunctive, declaratory or other extraordinary relief, not involving the payment of damages, before an administrative tribunal or court under the law of the disputing Party.

3. A consent and waiver required by this Article shall be in writing, shall be delivered to the disputing Party and shall be included in the submission of a claim to arbitration.

4. Only where a disputing Party has deprived a disputing investor of control of an enterprise: (a) a waiver from the enterprise under paragraph 1(b) or 2(b) shall not be required; and (b) Annex 1120.1(b) shall not apply.

Article 1122: Consent to Arbitration

1. Each Party consents to the submission of a claim to arbitration in accordance with the procedures set out in this Agreement.

2. The consent given by paragraph 1 and the submission by a disputing investor of a claim to arbitration shall satisfy the requirement of: (a) Chapter II of the ICSID Convention (Jurisdiction of the Centre) and the Additional Facility Rules for written consent of the parties; (b) Article II of the New York Convention for an agreement in writing; and (c) Article I of the Inter–American Convention for an agreement.

Article 1123: Number of Arbitrators and Method of Appointment

Except in respect of a Tribunal established under Article 1126, and unless the disputing parties otherwise agree, the Tribunal shall comprise three arbitrators, one arbitrator appointed by each of the disputing parties and the third, who shall be the presiding arbitrator, appointed by agreement of the disputing parties.

Article 1124: Constitution of a Tribunal When a Party Fails to Appoint an Arbitrator or the Disputing Parties Are Unable to Agree on a Presiding Arbitrator

1. The Secretary–General shall serve as appointing authority for an arbitration under this Section.

2. If a Tribunal, other than a Tribunal established under Article 1126, has not been constituted within 90 days from the date that a claim is submitted to arbitration, the Secretary–General, on the request of either disputing party, shall appoint, in his discretion, the arbitrator or arbitrators not yet appointed, except that the presiding arbitrator shall be appointed in accordance with paragraph 3.

3. The Secretary–General shall appoint the presiding arbitrator from the roster of presiding arbitrators referred to in paragraph 4, provided that the presiding arbitrator shall not be a national of the disputing Party or a national of the Party of the disputing investor. In the event that no such presiding arbitrator is available to serve, the Secretary–General shall appoint, from the ICSID Panel of Arbitrators, a presiding arbitrator who is not a national of any of the Parties.

4. On the date of entry into force of this Agreement, the Parties shall establish, and thereafter maintain, a roster of 45 presiding arbitrators meeting the qualifications of the Convention and rules referred to in Article 1120 and experienced in international law and investment matters. The roster members shall be appointed by consensus and without regard to nationality.

Article 1125: Agreement to Appointment of Arbitrators

For purposes of Article 39 of the ICSID Convention and Article 7 of Schedule C to the ICSID Additional Facility Rules, and without prejudice to an objection to an arbitrator based on Article 1124(3) or on a ground other than nationality: (a) the disputing Party agrees to the appointment of each individual member of a Tribunal established under the ICSID Convention or the ICSID Additional Facility Rules; (b) a disputing investor referred to in Article 1116 may submit a claim to arbitration, or continue a claim, under the ICSID Convention or the ICSID Additional Facility Rules, only on condition that the disputing investor agrees in writing to the appointment of each individual member of the Tribunal; and (c) a disputing investor referred to in Article 1117(1) may submit a claim to arbitration, or continue a claim, under the ICSID Convention or the ICSID Additional Facility Rules, only on condition that the disputing investor and the enterprise agree in writing to the appointment of each individual member of the Tribunal.

Article 1126: Consolidation

1. A Tribunal established under this Article shall be established under the UNCITRAL Arbitration Rules and shall conduct its proceedings in accordance with those Rules, except as modified by this Section.

2. Where a Tribunal established under this Article is satisfied that claims have been submitted to arbitration under Article 1120 that have a question of law or fact in common, the Tribunal may, in the interests of fair and efficient resolution of the claims, and after hearing the disputing parties, by order: (a) assume jurisdiction over, and hear and determine together, all or part of the claims; or (b) assume jurisdiction over, and hear and determine one or more of the claims, the determination of which it believes would assist in the resolution of the others.

3. A disputing party that seeks an order under paragraph 2 shall request the Secretary–General to establish a Tribunal and shall specify in the request: (a) the name of the disputing Party or disputing investors against which the order is sought; (b) the nature of the order sought; and (c) the grounds on which the order is sought.

4. The disputing party shall deliver to the disputing Party or disputing investors against which the order is sought a copy of the request.

5. Within 60 days of receipt of the request, the Secretary–General shall establish a Tribunal comprising three arbitrators. The Secretary–General shall appoint the presiding arbitrator from the roster referred to in Article 1124(4). In the event that no such presiding arbitrator is available to serve, the Secretary–General shall appoint, from the ICSID Panel of Arbitrators, a presiding arbitrator who is not a national of any of the Parties. The Secretary–General shall appoint the two other members from the roster referred to in Article 1124(4), and to the extent not available from that roster, from the ICSID Panel of Arbitrators, and to the extent not available from that Panel, in the discretion of the Secretary–General. One member shall be a national of the disputing Party and one member shall be a national of a Party of the disputing investors.

6. Where a Tribunal has been established under this Article, a disputing investor that has submitted a claim to arbitration under Article 1116 or 1117 and that has not been named in a request made under paragraph 3 may make a written request to the Tribunal that it be included in an order made under paragraph 2, and shall specify in the request: (a) the name and address of the disputing investor; (b) the nature of the order sought; and (c) the grounds on which the order is sought.

7. A disputing investor referred to in paragraph 6 shall deliver a copy of its request to the disputing parties named in a request made under paragraph 3.

8.   A Tribunal established under Article 1120 shall not have jurisdiction to decide a claim, or a part of a claim, over which a Tribunal established under this Article has assumed jurisdiction.

9.   On application of a disputing party, a Tribunal established under this Article, pending its decision under paragraph 2, may order that the proceedings of a Tribunal established under Article 1120 be stayed, unless the latter Tribunal has already adjourned its proceedings.

10.   A disputing Party shall deliver to the Secretariat, within 15 days of receipt by the disputing Party, a copy of: (a) a request for arbitration made under paragraph (1) of Article 36 of the ICSID Convention; (b) a notice of arbitration made under Article 2 of Schedule C of the ICSID Additional Facility Rules; or (c) a notice of arbitration given under the UNCITRAL Arbitration Rules.

11.   A disputing Party shall deliver to the Secretariat a copy of a request made under paragraph 3: (a) within 15 days of receipt of the request, in the case of a request made by a disputing investor; (b) within 15 days of making the request, in the case of a request made by the disputing Party.

12.   A disputing Party shall deliver to the Secretariat a copy of a request made under paragraph 6 within 15 days of receipt of the request.

13.   The Secretariat shall maintain a public register of the documents referred to in paragraphs 10, 11 and 12.

Article 1127: Notice

A disputing Party shall deliver to the other Parties: (a) written notice of a claim that has been submitted to arbitration no later than 30 days after the date that the claim is submitted; and (b) copies of all pleadings filed in the arbitration.

Article 1128: Participation by a Party

On written notice to the disputing parties, a Party may make submissions to a Tribunal on a question of interpretation of this Agreement.

Article 1129: Documents

1.   A Party shall be entitled to receive from the disputing Party, at the cost of the requesting Party a copy of: (a) the evidence that has been tendered to the Tribunal; and (b) the written argument of the disputing parties.

2.   A Party receiving information pursuant to paragraph 1 shall treat the information as if it were a disputing Party.

Article 1130: Place of Arbitration

Unless the disputing parties agree otherwise, a Tribunal shall hold an arbitration in the territory of a Party that is a party to the New York Convention, selected in accordance with: (a) the ICSID Additional Facility Rules if the arbitration is under those Rules or the ICSID Convention; or (b) the UNCITRAL Arbitration Rules if the arbitration is under those Rules.

Article 1131: Governing Law

1.   A Tribunal established under this Section shall decide the issues in dispute in accordance with this Agreement and applicable rules of international law.

2.   An interpretation by the Commission of a provision of this Agreement shall be binding on a Tribunal established under this Section.

Article 1132: Interpretation of Annexes

1.   Where a disputing Party asserts as a defense that the measure alleged to be a breach is within the scope of a reservation or exception set out in Annex I, Annex II, Annex III or Annex IV, on request of the disputing Party, the Tribunal shall request the interpretation of the Commission on the issue. The Commission, within 60 days of delivery of the request, shall submit in writing its interpretation to the Tribunal.

2.   Further to Article 1131(2), a Commission interpretation submitted under paragraph 1 shall be binding on the Tribunal. If the Commission fails to submit an interpretation within 60 days, the Tribunal shall decide the issue.

Article 1133: Expert Reports

Without prejudice to the appointment of other kinds of experts where authorized by the applicable arbitration rules, a Tribunal, at the request of a disputing party or, unless the disputing parties disapprove, on its own initiative, may appoint one or more experts to report to it in writing on any factual issue concerning environmental, health, safety or other scientific matters raised by a disputing party in a proceeding, subject to such terms and conditions as the disputing parties may agree.

Article 1134: Interim Measures of Protection

A Tribunal may order an interim measure of protection to preserve the rights of a disputing party, or to ensure that the Tribunal's jurisdiction is made fully effective, including an order to preserve evidence in the possession or control of a disputing party or to protect the Tribunal's jurisdiction. A Tribunal may not order attachment or enjoin the application of the measure alleged to constitute a breach referred to in Article

1116 or 1117. For purposes of this paragraph, an order includes a recommendation.

Article 1135: Final Award

1. Where a Tribunal makes a final award against a Party, the Tribunal may award, separately or in combination, only: (a) monetary damages and any applicable interest; (b) restitution of property, in which case the award shall provide that the disputing Party may pay monetary damages and any applicable interest in lieu of restitution.

A tribunal may also award costs in accordance with the applicable arbitration rules.

2. Subject to paragraph 1, where a claim is made under Article 1117(1): (a) an award of restitution of property shall provide that restitution be made to the enterprise; (b) an award of monetary damages and any applicable interest shall provide that the sum be paid to the enterprise; and (c) the award shall provide that it is made without prejudice to any right that any person may have in the relief under applicable domestic law.

3. A Tribunal may not order a Party to pay punitive damages.

Article 1136: Finality and Enforcement of an Award

1. An award made by a Tribunal shall have no binding force except between the disputing parties and in respect of the particular case.

2. Subject to paragraph 3 and the applicable review procedure for an interim award, a disputing party shall abide by and comply with an award without delay.

3. A disputing party may not seek enforcement of a final award until: (a) in the case of a final award made under the ICSID Convention (i) 120 days have elapsed from the date the award was rendered and no disputing party has requested revision or annulment of the award, or (ii) revision or annulment proceedings have been completed; and (b) in the case of a final award under the ICSID Additional Facility Rules or the UNCITRAL Arbitration Rules (i) three months have elapsed from the date the award was rendered and no disputing party has commenced a proceeding to revise, set aside or annul the award, or (ii) a court has dismissed or allowed an application to revise, set aside or annul the award and there is no further appeal.

4. Each Party shall provide for the enforcement of an award in its territory.

5. If a disputing Party fails to abide by or comply with a final award, the Commission, on delivery of a request by a Party whose investor was a party to the arbitration, shall establish a panel under Article 2008 (Request for an Arbitral Panel). The requesting Party may seek in such proceedings: (a) a determination that the failure to abide by

or comply with the final award is inconsistent with the obligations of this Agreement; and (b) a recommendation that the Party abide by or comply with the final award.

6.   A disputing investor may seek enforcement of an arbitration award under the ICSID Convention, the New York Convention or the Inter–American Convention regardless of whether proceedings have been taken under paragraph 5.

7.   A claim that is submitted to arbitration under this Section shall be considered to arise out of a commercial relationship or transaction for purposes of Article I of the New York Convention and Article I of the Inter–American Convention.

Article 1137: General

Time When a Claim Is Submitted to Arbitration

1.   A claim is submitted to arbitration under this Section when: (a) the request for arbitration under paragraph (1) of Article 36 of the ICSID Convention has been received by the Secretary–General; (b) the notice of arbitration under Article 2 of Schedule C of the ICSID Additional Facility Rules has been received by the Secretary–General; or (c) the notice of arbitration given under the UNCITRAL Arbitration Rules is received by the disputing Party.

Service of Documents

2.   Delivery of notice and other documents on a Party shall be made to the place named for that Party in Annex 1137.2.

Receipts Under Insurance or Guarantee Contracts

3.   In an arbitration under this Section, a Party shall not assert, as a defense, counterclaim, right of setoff or otherwise, that the disputing investor has received or will receive, pursuant to an insurance or guarantee contract, indemnification or other compensation for all or part of its alleged damages.

Publication of an Award

4.   Annex 1137.4 applies to the Parties specified in that Annex with respect to publication of an award.

Annex 1137.2

Service of Documents on a Party Under Section B

Each Party shall set out in this Annex and publish in its official journal by January 1, 1994, the place for delivery of notice and other documents under this Section.

Annex 1137.4

Publication of an Award

Canada

Where Canada is the disputing Party, either Canada or a disputing investor that is a party to the arbitration may make an award public.

Mexico

Where Mexico is the disputing Party, the applicable arbitration rules apply to the publication of an award.

United States

Where the United States is the disputing Party, either the United States or a disputing investor that is a party to the arbitration may make an award public.

Article 1138: Exclusions

1. Without prejudice to the applicability or non-applicability of the dispute settlement provisions of this Section or of Chapter Twenty (Institutional Arrangements and Dispute Settlement Procedures) to other actions taken by a Party pursuant to Article 2102 (National Security), a decision by a Party to prohibit or restrict the acquisition of an investment in its territory by an investor of another Party, or its investment, pursuant to that Article shall not be subject to such provisions.

2. The dispute settlement provisions of this Section and of Chapter Twenty shall not apply to the matters referred to in Annex 1138.2.

Annex 1138.2

Exclusions From Dispute Settlement

Canada

A decision by Canada following a review under the Investment Canada Act, with respect to whether or not to permit an acquisition that is subject to review, shall not be subject to the dispute settlement provisions of Section B or of Chapter Twenty (Institutional Arrangements and Dispute Settlement Procedures).

Mexico

A decision by the National Commission on Foreign Investment ("Comision Nacional de Inversiones Extranjeras") following a review pursuant to Annex I, page I–M–4, with respect to whether or not to permit an acquisition that is subject to review, shall not be subject to the dispute settlement provisions of Section B or of Chapter Twenty.

Section C—Definitions

Article 1139: Definitions

For purposes of this Chapter:

disputing investor means an investor that makes a claim under Section B;

disputing parties means the disputing investor and the disputing Party;

disputing party means the disputing investor or the disputing Party;

disputing Party means a Party against which a claim is made under Section B;

enterprise means an "enterprise" as defined in Article 201 (Definitions of General Application), and a branch of an enterprise;

enterprise of a Party means an enterprise constituted or organized under the law of a Party, and a branch located in the territory of a Party and carrying out business activities there.

equity or debt securities includes voting and non-voting shares, bonds, convertible debentures, stock options and warrants;

G7 Currency means the currency of Canada, France, Germany, Italy, Japan, the United Kingdom of Great Britain and Northern Ireland or the United States;

ICSID means the International Centre for Settlement of Investment Disputes;

ICSID Convention means the Convention on the Settlement of Investment Disputes between States and Nationals of other States, done at Washington, March 18, 1965;

Inter–American Convention means the Inter–American Convention on International Commercial Arbitration, done at Panama, January 30, 1975;

investment means: (a) an enterprise; (b) an equity security of an enterprise; (c) a debt security of an enterprise (i) where the enterprise is an affiliate of the investor, or (ii) where the original maturity of the debt security is at least three years, but does not include a debt security, regardless of original maturity, of a state enterprise; (d) a loan to an enterprise (i) where the enterprise is an affiliate of the investor, or (ii) where the original maturity of the loan is at least three years, but does not include a loan, regardless of original maturity, to a state enterprise; (e) an interest in an enterprise that entitles the owner to share in income or profits of the enterprise; (f) an interest in an enterprise that entitles the owner to share in the assets of that enterprise on dissolution, other than a debt security or a loan excluded from subparagraph (c) or (d); (g) real estate or other property, tangible or intangible, acquired in the expectation or used for the purpose of economic benefit or other business purposes; and (h) interests arising from the commitment of capital or other resources in the territory of a Party to economic activity in such territory, such as under (i) contracts involving the presence of an investor's property in the territory of the Party, including turnkey or construction contracts, or concessions, or (ii) contracts where remuneration depends substantially on the production, revenues or profits of an enterprise; but investment does not mean, (i) claims to money that arise solely from (i) commercial contracts for the sale of goods or services by a national or enterprise in the territory of a Party to an enterprise in the territory of another Party, or (ii) the extension of credit in connection with a commercial transaction, such as trade financing, other than a loan covered by subparagraph (d); or (j) any other claims to money, that do not involve the kinds of interests set out in subparagraphs (a) through (h);

investment of an investor of a Party means an investment owned or controlled directly or indirectly by an investor of such Party;

investor of a Party means a Party or state enterprise thereof, or a national or an enterprise of such Party, that seeks to make, is making or has made an investment;

investor of a non-Party means an investor other than an investor of a Party, that seeks to make, is making or has made an investment;

New York Convention means the United Nations Convention on the Recognition and Enforcement of Foreign Arbitral Awards, done at New York, June 10, 1958;

Secretary–General means the Secretary–General of ICSID;

transfers means transfers and international payments;

Tribunal means an arbitration tribunal established under Article 1120 or 1126; and

UNCITRAL Arbitration Rules means the arbitration rules of the United Nations Commission on International Trade Law, approved by the United Nations General Assembly on December 15, 1976.

Chapter Twelve

CROSS–BORDER TRADE IN SERVICES

Article 1201: Scope and Coverage

1. This Chapter applies to measures adopted or maintained by a Party relating to cross-border trade in services by service providers of another Party, including measures respecting: (a) the production, distribution, marketing, sale and delivery of a service; (b) the purchase or use of, or payment for, a service; (c) the access to and use of distribution and transportation systems in connection with the provision of a service; (d) the presence in its territory of a service provider of another Party; and (e) the provision of a bond or other form of financial security as a condition for the provision of a service.

2. This Chapter does not apply to: (a) financial services, as defined in Chapter Fourteen (Financial Services); (b) air services, including domestic and international air transportation services, whether scheduled or non-scheduled, and related services in support of air services, other than (i) aircraft repair and maintenance services during which an aircraft is withdrawn from service, and (ii) specialty air services; (c) procurement by a Party or a state enterprise; or (d) subsidies or grants provided by a Party or a state enterprise, including government-supported loans, guarantees and insurance.

3. Nothing in this Chapter shall be construed to: (a) impose any obligation on a Party with respect to a national of another Party seeking access to its employment market, or employed on a permanent basis in its territory, or to confer any right on that national with respect to that access or employment; or (b) prevent a Party from providing a service or performing a function such as law enforcement, correctional services, income security or insurance, social security or insurance, social welfare, public education, public training, health, and child care, in a manner that is not inconsistent with this Chapter.

Article 1202: National Treatment

1.   Each Party shall accord to service providers of another Party treatment no less favorable than that it accords, in like circumstances, to its own service providers.

2.   The treatment accorded by a Party under paragraph 1 means, with respect to a state or province, treatment no less favorable than the most favorable treatment accorded, in like circumstances, by that state or province to service providers of the Party of which it forms a part.

Article 1203: Most–Favored–Nation Treatment

Each Party shall accord to service providers of another Party treatment no less favorable than that it accords, in like circumstances, to service providers of any other Party or of a non-Party.

Article 1204: Standard of Treatment

Each Party shall accord to service providers of any other Party the better of the treatment required by Articles 1202 and 1203.

Article 1205: Local Presence

No Party may require a service provider of another Party to establish or maintain a representative office or any form of enterprise, or to be resident, in its territory as a condition for the cross-border provision of a service.

Article 1206: Reservations

1.   Articles 1202, 1203 and 1205 do not apply to: (a) any existing non-conforming measure that is maintained by (i) a Party at the federal level, as set out in its Schedule to Annex I, (ii) a state or province, for two years after the date of entry into force of this Agreement, and thereafter as set out by a Party in its Schedule to Annex I in accordance with paragraph 2, or (iii) a local government; (b) the continuation or prompt renewal of any non-conforming measure referred to in subparagraph (a); or (c) an amendment to any non-conforming measure referred to in subparagraph (a) to the extent that the amendment does not decrease the conformity of the measure, as it existed immediately before the amendment, with Articles 1202, 1203 and 1205.

2.   Each Party may set out in its Schedule to Annex I, within two years of the date of entry into force of this Agreement, any existing non-conforming measure maintained by a state or province, not including a local government.

3.   Articles 1202, 1203 and 1205 do not apply to any measure that a Party adopts or maintains with respect to sectors, subsectors or activities, as set out in its Schedule to Annex II.

Article 1207: Quantitative Restrictions

1. Each Party shall set out in its Schedule to Annex V any quantitative restriction that it maintains at the federal level.

2. Within one year of the date of entry into force of this Agreement, each Party shall set out in its Schedule to Annex V any quantitative restriction maintained by a state or province, not including a local government.

3. Each Party shall notify the other Parties of any quantitative restriction that it adopts, other than at the local government level, after the date of entry into force of this Agreement and shall set out the restriction in its Schedule to Annex V.

4. The Parties shall periodically, but in any event at least every two years, endeavor to negotiate the liberalization or removal of the quantitative restrictions set out in Annex V pursuant to paragraphs 1 through 3.

Article 1208: Liberalization of Non-discriminatory Measures

Each Party shall set out in its Schedule to Annex VI its commitments to liberalize quantitative restrictions, licensing requirements, performance requirements or other non-discriminatory measures.

Article 1209: Procedures

The Commission shall establish procedures for: (a) a Party to notify and include in its relevant Schedule (i) state or provincial measures in accordance with Article 1206(2), (ii) quantitative restrictions in accordance with Article 1207(2) and (3), (iii) commitments pursuant to Article 1208, and (iv) amendments of measures referred to in Article 1206(1)(c); and (b) consultations on reservations, quantitative restrictions or commitments with a view to further liberalization.

Article 1210: Licensing and Certification

1. With a view to ensuring that any measure adopted or maintained by a Party relating to the licensing or certification of nationals of another Party does not constitute an unnecessary barrier to trade, each Party shall endeavor to ensure that any such measure: (a) is based on objective and transparent criteria, such as competence and the ability to provide a service; (b) is not more burdensome than necessary to ensure the quality of a service; and (c) does not constitute a disguised restriction on the cross-border provision of a service.

2. Where a Party recognizes, unilaterally or by agreement, education, experience, licenses or certifications obtained in the territory of another Party or of a non-Party: (a) nothing in Article 1203 shall be

construed to require the Party to accord such recognition to education, experience, licenses or certifications obtained in the territory of another Party; and (b) the Party shall afford another Party an adequate opportunity to demonstrate that education, experience, licenses or certifications obtained in that other Party's territory should also be recognized or to conclude an agreement or arrangement of comparable effect.

3.   Each Party shall, within two years of the date of entry into force of this Agreement, eliminate any citizenship or permanent residency requirement set out in its Schedule to Annex I that it maintains for the licensing or certification of professional service providers of another Party. Where a Party does not comply with this obligation with respect to a particular sector, any other Party may, in the same sector and for such period as the non-complying Party maintains its requirement, solely have recourse to maintaining an equivalent requirement set out in its Schedule to Annex I or reinstating: (a) any such requirement at the federal level that it eliminated pursuant to this Article; or (b) on notification to the non-complying Party, any such requirement at the state or provincial level existing on the date of entry into force of this Agreement.

4.   The Parties shall consult periodically with a view to determining the feasibility of removing any remaining citizenship or permanent residency requirement for the licensing or certification of each other's service providers.

5.   Annex 1210.5 applies to measures adopted or maintained by a Party relating to the licensing or certification of professional service providers.

Annex 1210.5

Professional Services

Section A—General Provisions

Processing of Applications for Licenses and Certifications

1.   Each Party shall ensure that its competent authorities, within a reasonable time after the submission by a national of another Party of an application for a license or certification: (a) where the application is complete, make a determination on the application and inform the applicant of that determination; or (b) where the application is not complete, inform the applicant without undue delay of the status of the application and the additional information that is required under the Party's law.

Development of Professional Standards

2.   The Parties shall encourage the relevant bodies in their respective territories to develop mutually acceptable standards and criteria for licensing and certification of professional service providers and to provide recommendations on mutual recognition to the Commission.

3. The standards and criteria referred to in paragraph 2 may be developed with regard to the following matters: (a) education—accreditation of schools or academic programs; (b) examinations—qualifying examinations for licensing, including alternative methods of assessment such as oral examinations and interviews; (c) experience—length and nature of experience required for licensing; (d) conduct and ethics—standards of professional conduct and the nature of disciplinary action for non-conformity with those standards; (e) professional development and re-certification—continuing education and ongoing requirements to maintain professional certification; (f) scope of practice—extent of, or limitations on, permissible activities; (g) local knowledge—requirements for knowledge of such matters as local laws, regulations, language, geography or climate; and (h) consumer protection—alternatives to residency requirements, including bonding, professional liability insurance and client restitution funds, to provide for the protection of consumers.

4. On receipt of a recommendation referred to in paragraph 2, the Commission shall review the recommendation within a reasonable time to determine whether it is consistent with this Agreement. Based on the Commission's review, each Party shall encourage its respective competent authorities, where appropriate, to implement the recommendation within a mutually agreed time.

Temporary Licensing

5. Where the Parties agree, each Party shall encourage the relevant bodies in its territory to develop procedures for the temporary licensing of professional service providers of another Party.

Review

6. The Commission shall periodically, and at least once every three years, review the implementation of this Section.

Section B—Foreign Legal Consultants

1. Each Party shall, in implementing its obligations and commitments regarding foreign legal consultants as set out in its relevant Schedules and subject to any reservations therein, ensure that a national of another Party is permitted to practice or advise on the law of any country in which that national is authorized to practice as a lawyer.

Consultations With Professional Bodies

2. Each Party shall consult with its relevant professional bodies to obtain their recommendations on: (a) the form of association or partnership between lawyers authorized to practice in its territory and foreign legal consultants; (b) the development of standards and criteria for the authorization of foreign legal consultants in conformity with Article 1210; and (c) other matters relating to the provision of foreign legal consultancy services.

3. Prior to initiation of consultations under paragraph 7, each Party shall encourage its relevant professional bodies to consult with the relevant professional bodies designated by each of the other Parties regarding the development of joint recommendations on the matters referred to in paragraph 2.

Future Liberalization

4. Each Party shall establish a work program to develop common procedures throughout its territory for the authorization of foreign legal consultants.

5. Each Party shall promptly review any recommendation referred to in paragraphs 2 and 3 to ensure its consistency with this Agreement. If the recommendation is consistent with this Agreement, each Party shall encourage its competent authorities to implement the recommendation within one year.

6. Each Party shall report to the Commission within one year of the date of entry into force of this Agreement, and each year thereafter, on its progress in implementing the work program referred to in paragraph 4.

7. The Parties shall meet within one year of the date of entry into force of this Agreement with a view to: (a) assessing the implementation of paragraphs 2 through 5; (b) amending or removing, where appropriate, reservations on foreign legal consultancy services; and (c) assessing further work that may be appropriate regarding foreign legal consultancy services.

Section C—Temporary Licensing of Engineers

1. The Parties shall meet within one year of the date of entry into force of this Agreement to establish a work program to be undertaken by each Party, in conjunction with its relevant professional bodies, to provide for the temporary licensing in its territory of nationals of another Party who are licensed as engineers in the territory of that other Party.

2. To this end, each Party shall consult with its relevant professional bodies to obtain their recommendations on: (a) the development of procedures for the temporary licensing of such engineers to permit them to practice their engineering specialties in each jurisdiction in its territory; (b) the development of model procedures for adoption by the competent authorities throughout its territory to facilitate the temporary licensing of such engineers; (c) the engineering specialties to which priority should be given in developing temporary licensing procedures; and (d) other matters relating to the temporary licensing of engineers identified by the Party in such consultations.

3. Each Party shall request its relevant professional bodies to make recommendations on the matters referred to in paragraph 2 within two years of the date of entry into force of this Agreement.

4.   Each Party shall encourage its relevant professional bodies to meet at the earliest opportunity with the relevant professional bodies of the other Parties with a view to cooperating in the development of joint recommendations on the matters referred to in paragraph 2 within two years of the date of entry into force of this Agreement. Each Party shall request an annual report from its relevant professional bodies on the progress achieved in developing those recommendations.

5.   The Parties shall promptly review any recommendation referred to in paragraph 3 or 4 to ensure its consistency with this Agreement. If the recommendation is consistent with this Agreement, each Party shall encourage its competent authorities to implement the recommendation within one year.

6.   The Commission shall review the implementation of this Section within two years of the date of entry into force of this Section.

7.   Appendix 1210.5–C applies to the Parties specified therein.

Appendix 1210.5–C

Civil Engineers

The rights and obligations of Section C of Annex 1210.5 apply to Mexico with respect to civil engineers ("ingenieros civiles") and to such other engineering specialties that Mexico may designate.

Article 1211: Denial of Benefits

1.   A Party may deny the benefits of this Chapter to a service provider of another Party where the Party establishes that: (a) the service is being provided by an enterprise owned or controlled by nationals of a non-Party, and (i) the denying Party does not maintain diplomatic relations with the non-Party, or (ii) the denying Party adopts or maintains measures with respect to the non-Party that prohibit transactions with the enterprise or that would be violated or circumvented if the benefits of this Chapter were accorded to the enterprise; or (b) the cross-border provision of a transportation service covered by this Chapter is provided using equipment not registered by any Party.

2.   Subject to prior notification and consultation in accordance with Articles 1803 (Notification and Provision of Information) and 2006 (Consultations), a Party may deny the benefits of this Chapter to a service provider of another Party where the Party establishes that the service is being provided by an enterprise that is owned or controlled by persons of a non-Party and that has no substantial business activities in the territory of any Party.

Article 1212: Sectoral Annex

Annex 1212 applies to specific sectors.

Annex 1212

Land Transportation

Contact Points

1. Further to Article 1801 (Contact Points), each Party shall designate by January 1, 1994 contact points to provide information published by that Party relating to land transportation services regarding operating authority, safety requirements, taxation, data, studies and technology, and to provide assistance in contacting its relevant government agencies.

Review Process

2. The Commission shall, during the fifth year after the date of entry into force of this Agreement and during every second year thereafter until the liberalization for bus and truck transportation set out in the Parties' Schedules to Annex I is complete, receive and consider a report from the Parties that assesses progress respecting liberalization, including: (a) the effectiveness of the liberalization; (b) specific problems for, or unanticipated effects on, each Party's bus and truck transportation industries arising from liberalization; and (c) modifications to the period for liberalization. The Commission shall endeavor to resolve any matter arising from its consideration of a report.

3. The Parties shall consult, no later than seven years after the date of entry into force of this Agreement, to consider further liberalization commitments.

Article 1213: Definitions

1. For purposes of this Chapter, a reference to a federal, state or provincial government includes any non-governmental body in the exercise of any regulatory, administrative or other governmental authority delegated to it by that government.

2. For purposes of this Chapter:

cross-border provision of a service or cross-border trade in services means the provision of a service: (a) from the territory of a Party into the territory of another Party, (b) in the territory of a Party by a person of that Party to a person of another Party, or (c) by a national of a Party in the territory of another Party, but does not include the provision of a service in the territory of a Party by an investment, as defined in Article 1139 (Investment—Definitions), in that territory;

enterprise means an "enterprise" as defined in Article 201 (Definitions of General Application), and a branch of an enterprise;

enterprise of a Party means an enterprise constituted or organized under the law of a Party, and a branch located in the territory of a Party and carrying out business activities there;

professional services means services, the provision of which requires specialized post-secondary education, or equivalent training or experience, and for which the right to practice is granted or restricted by a Party, but does not include services provided by trades-persons or vessel and aircraft crew members;

quantitative restriction means a non-discriminatory measure that imposes limitations on: (a) the number of service providers, whether in the form of a quota, a monopoly or an economic needs test, or by any other quantitative means; or (b) the operations of any service provider, whether in the form of a quota or an economic needs test, or by any other quantitative means;

service provider of a Party means a person of a Party that seeks to provide or provides a service; and

specialty air services means aerial mapping, aerial surveying, aerial photography, forest fire management, fire fighting, aerial advertising, glider towing, parachute jumping, aerial construction, heli-logging, aerial sightseeing, flight training, aerial inspection and surveillance, and aerial spraying services.

Chapter Thirteen

TELECOMMUNICATIONS

Article 1301: Scope and Coverage

1.   This Chapter applies to: (a) measures adopted or maintained by a Party relating to access to and use of public telecommunications transport networks or services by persons of another Party, including access and use by such persons operating private networks; (b) measures adopted or maintained by a Party relating to the provision of enhanced or value-added services by persons of another Party in the territory, or across the borders, of a Party; and (c) standards-related measures relating to attachment of terminal or other equipment to public telecommunications transport networks.

2.   Except to ensure that persons operating broadcast stations and cable systems have continued access to and use of public telecommunications transport networks and services, this Chapter does not apply to any measure adopted or maintained by a Party relating to broadcast or cable distribution of radio or television programming.

3.   Nothing in this Chapter shall be construed to: (a) require a Party to authorize a person of another Party to establish, construct, acquire, lease, operate or provide telecommunications transport networks or telecommunications transport services; (b) require a Party, or require a Party to compel any person, to establish, construct, acquire, lease, operate or provide telecommunications transport networks or telecommunications transport services not offered to the public generally; (c) prevent a Party from prohibiting persons operating private networks from using their networks to provide public telecommunications transport networks or services to third persons; or (d) require a Party to compel any person engaged in the broadcast or cable distribution of radio or television programming to make available its cable or broadcast facilities as a public telecommunications transport network.

Article 1302: Access to and Use of Public Telecommunications Transport Networks and Services

1. Each Party shall ensure that persons of another Party have access to and use of any public telecommunications transport network or service, including private leased circuits, offered in its territory or across its borders for the conduct of their business, on reasonable and nondiscriminatory terms and conditions, including as set out in paragraphs 2 through 8.

2. Subject to paragraphs 6 and 7, each Party shall ensure that such persons are permitted to: (a) purchase or lease, and attach terminal or other equipment that interfaces with the public telecommunications transport network; (b) interconnect private leased or owned circuits with public telecommunications transport networks in the territory, or across the borders, of that Party, including for use in providing dial-up access to and from their customers or users, or with circuits leased or owned by another person on terms and conditions mutually agreed by those persons; (c) perform switching, signalling and processing functions; and (d) use operating protocols of their choice.

3. Each Party shall ensure that: (a) the pricing of public telecommunications transport services reflects economic costs directly related to providing the services; and (b) private leased circuits are available on a flat-rate pricing basis. Nothing in this paragraph shall be construed to prevent cross-subsidization between public telecommunications transport services.

4. Each Party shall ensure that persons of another Party may use public telecommunications transport networks or services for the movement of information in its territory or across its borders, including for intracorporate communications, and for access to information contained in data bases or otherwise stored in machine-readable form in the territory of any Party.

5. Further to Article 2101 (General Exceptions), nothing in this Chapter shall be construed to prevent a Party from adopting or enforcing any measure necessary to: (a) ensure the security and confidentiality of messages; or (b) protect the privacy of subscribers to public telecommunications transport networks or services.

6. Each Party shall ensure that no condition is imposed on access to and use of public telecommunications transport networks or services, other than that necessary to: (a) safeguard the public service responsibilities of providers of public telecommunications transport networks or services, in particular their ability to make their networks or services available to the public generally; or (b) protect the technical integrity of public telecommunications transport networks or services.

7. Provided that conditions for access to and use of public telecommunications transport networks or services satisfy the criteria set out in paragraph 6, such conditions may include: (a) a restriction on resale or

shared use of such services; (b) a requirement to use specified technical interfaces, including interface protocols, for interconnection with such networks or services; (c) a restriction on interconnection of private leased or owned circuits with such networks or services or with circuits leased or owned by another person, where the circuits are used in the provision of public telecommunications transport networks or services; and (d) a licensing, permit, registration or notification procedure which, if adopted or maintained, is transparent and applications filed thereunder are processed expeditiously.

8. For purposes of this Article, "non-discriminatory" means on terms and conditions no less favorable than those accorded to any other customer or user of like public telecommunications transport networks or services in like circumstances.

Article 1303: Conditions for the Provision of Enhanced or Value–Added Services

1. Each Party shall ensure that: (a) any licensing, permit, registration or notification procedure that it adopts or maintains relating to the provision of enhanced or value-added services is transparent and non-discriminatory, and that applications filed thereunder are processed expeditiously; and (b) information required under such procedures is limited to that necessary to demonstrate that the applicant has the financial solvency to begin providing services or to assess conformity of the applicant's terminal or other equipment with the Party's applicable standards or technical regulations.

2. No Party may require a person providing enhanced or value-added services to: (a) provide those services to the public generally; (b) cost-justify its rates; (c) file a tariff; (d) interconnect its networks with any particular customer or network; or (e) conform with any particular standard or technical regulation for interconnection other than for interconnection to a public telecommunications transport network.

3. Notwithstanding paragraph 2(c), a Party may require the filing of a tariff by: (a) such provider to remedy a practice of that provider that the Party has found in a particular case to be anticompetitive under its law; or (b) a monopoly to which Article 1305 applies.

Article 1304: Standards–Related Measures

1. Further to Article 904(4) (Unnecessary Obstacles), each Party shall ensure that its standards-related measures relating to the attachment of terminal or other equipment to the public telecommunications transport networks, including those measures relating to the use of testing and measuring equipment for conformity assessment procedures, are adopted or maintained only to the extent necessary to: (a) prevent technical damage to public telecommunications transport networks; (b) prevent technical interference with, or degradation of, public telecommu-

nications transport services; (c) prevent electromagnetic interference, and ensure compatibility, with other uses of the electromagnetic spectrum; (d) prevent billing equipment malfunction; or (e) ensure users' safety and access to public telecommunications transport networks or services.

2.   A Party may require approval for the attachment to the public telecommunications transport network of terminal or other equipment that is not authorized, provided that the criteria for that approval are consistent with paragraph 1.

3.   Each Party shall ensure that the network termination points for its public telecommunications transport networks are defined on a reasonable and transparent basis.

4.   No Party may require separate authorization for equipment that is connected on the customer's side of authorized equipment that serves as a protective device fulfilling the criteria of paragraph 1.

5.   Further to Article 904(3) (Non–Discriminatory Treatment), each Party shall: (a) ensure that its conformity assessment procedures are transparent and non-discriminatory and that applications filed thereunder are processed expeditiously; (b) permit any technically qualified entity to perform the testing required under the Party's conformity assessment procedures for terminal or other equipment to be attached to the public telecommunications transport network, subject to the Party's right to review the accuracy and completeness of the test results; and (c) ensure that any measure that it adopts or maintains requiring persons to be authorized to act as agents for suppliers of telecommunications equipment before the Party's relevant conformity assessment bodies is non-discriminatory.

6.   No later than one year after the date of entry into force of this Agreement, each Party shall adopt, as part of its conformity assessment procedures, provisions necessary to accept the test results from laboratories or testing facilities in the territory of another Party for tests performed in accordance with the accepting Party's standards-related measures and procedures.

7.   The Telecommunications Standards Subcommittee established under Article 913(5) (Committee on Standards–Related Measures) shall perform the functions set out in Annex 913.5.a–2.

Article 1305: Monopolies

1.   Where a Party maintains or designates a monopoly to provide public telecommunications transport networks or services, and the monopoly, directly or through an affiliate, competes in the provision of enhanced or value-added services or other telecommunications-related services or telecommunications-related goods, the Party shall ensure that the monopoly does not use its monopoly position to engage in anticompetitive conduct in those markets, either directly or through its dealings

with its affiliates, in such a manner as to affect adversely a person of another Party. Such conduct may include cross-subsidization, predatory conduct and the discriminatory provision of access to public telecommunications transport networks or services.

2.   To prevent such anticompetitive conduct, each Party shall adopt or maintain effective measures, such as: (a) accounting requirements; (b) requirements for structural separation; (c) rules to ensure that the monopoly accords its competitors access to and use of its public telecommunications transport networks or services on terms and conditions no less favorable than those it accords to itself or its affiliates; or (d) rules to ensure the timely disclosure of technical changes to public telecommunications transport networks and their interfaces.

Article 1306: Transparency

Further to Article 1802 (Publication), each Party shall make publicly available its measures relating to access to and use of public telecommunications transport networks or services, including measures relating to: (a) tariffs and other terms and conditions of service; (b) specifications of technical interfaces with the networks or services; (c) information on bodies responsible for the preparation and adoption of standards-related measures affecting such access and use; (d) conditions applying to attachment of terminal or other equipment to the networks; and (e) notification, permit, registration or licensing requirements.

Article 1307: Relation to Other Chapters

In the event of any inconsistency between this Chapter and another Chapter, this Chapter shall prevail to the extent of the inconsistency.

Article 1308: Relation to International Organizations and Agreements

The Parties recognize the importance of international standards for global compatibility and interoperability of telecommunication networks or services and undertake to promote those standards through the work of relevant international bodies, including the International Telecommunication Union and the International Organization for Standardization.

Article 1309: Technical Cooperation and Other Consultations

1.   To encourage the development of interoperable telecommunications transport services infrastructure, the Parties shall cooperate in the exchange of technical information, the development of government-to-government training programs and other related activities. In implementing this obligation, the Parties shall give special emphasis to existing exchange programs.

2.   The Parties shall consult with a view to determining the feasibility of further liberalizing trade in all telecommunications services, including public telecommunications transport networks and services.

Article 1310: Definitions

For purposes of this Chapter:

authorized equipment means terminal or other equipment that has been approved for attachment to the public telecommunications transport network in accordance with a Party's conformity assessment procedures;

conformity assessment procedure means "conformity assessment procedure" as defined in Article 915 (Standards–Related Measures—Definitions), and includes the procedures referred to in Annex 1310;

enhanced or value-added services means those telecommunications services employing computer processing applications that: (a) act on the format, content, code, protocol or similar aspects of a customer's transmitted information; (b) provide a customer with additional, different or restructured information; or (c) involve customer interaction with stored information;

flat-rate pricing basis means pricing on the basis of a fixed charge per period of time regardless of the amount of use;

intracorporate communications means telecommunications through which an enterprise communicates: (a) internally or with or among its subsidiaries, branches or affiliates, as defined by each Party, or (b) on a non-commercial basis with other persons that are fundamental to the economic activity of the enterprise and that have a continuing contractual relationship with it, but does not include telecommunications services provided to persons other than those described herein;

network termination point means the final demarcation of the public telecommunications transport network at the customer's premises;

private network means a telecommunications transport network that is used exclusively for intracorporate communications;

protocol means a set of rules and formats that govern the exchange of information between two peer entities for purposes of transferring signaling or data information;

public telecommunications transport network means public telecommunications infrastructure that permits telecommunications between defined network termination points;

public telecommunications transport networks or services means public telecommunications transport networks or public telecommunications transport services;

public telecommunications transport service means any telecommunications transport service required by a Party, explicitly or in effect, to be offered to the public generally, including telegraph, telephone, telex and data transmission, that typically involves the real-time transmission of customer-supplied information between two or more points without any end-to-end change in the form or content of the customer's information;

standards-related measure means a "standards-related measure" as defined in Article 915;

telecommunications means the transmission and reception of signals by any electromagnetic means; and

terminal equipment means any digital or analog device capable of processing, receiving, switching, signaling or transmitting signals by electromagnetic means and that is connected by radio or wire to a public telecommunications transport network at a termination point.

Annex 1310

Conformity Assessment Procedures

For Canada:

Department of Communications, Terminal Attachment Program Certification Procedures (CP–01) Department of Communications Act, R.S.C.1985, c. C–35 Railway Act, R.S.C.1985, c. R–3 Radiocommunication Act, R.S.C.1985, c. R–2, as amended by S.C.1989, c. 17 Telecommunications Act (Bill C–62)

For Mexico:

Secretaria de Comunicaciones y Transportes

Subsecretaria de Comunicaciones y Desarrollo Tecnologico Reglamento de Telecomunicaciones, Capitulo X

For the United States:

Part 15 and Part 68 of the Federal Communications Commission's Rules, Title 47 of the Code of Federal Regulations

Chapter Fourteen

FINANCIAL SERVICES

Article 1401: Scope and Coverage

1. This Chapter applies to measures adopted or maintained by a Party relating to: (a) financial institutions of another Party; (b) investors of another Party, and investments of such investors, in financial institutions in the Party's territory; and (c) cross-border trade in financial services.

2. Articles 1109 through 1111, 1113, 1114 and 1211 are hereby incorporated into and made a part of this Chapter. Articles 1115 through 1138 are hereby incorporated into and made a part of this Chapter solely for breaches by a Party of Articles 1109 through 1111, 1113 and 1114, as incorporated into this Chapter.

3. Nothing in this Chapter shall be construed to prevent a Party, including its public entities, from exclusively conducting or providing in its territory: (a) activities or services forming part of a public retirement plan or statutory system of social security; or (b) activities or services for the account or with the guarantee or using the financial resources of the Party, including its public entities.

4. Annex 1401.4 applies to the Parties specified in that Annex.

Annex 1401.4

Country–Specific Commitments

For Canada and the United States, Article 1702(1) and (2) of the Canada–United States Free Trade Agreement is hereby incorporated into and made a part of this Agreement.

Article 1402: Self–Regulatory Organizations

Where a Party requires a financial institution or a cross-border financial service provider of another Party to be a member of, participate in, or have access to, a self-regulatory organization to provide a financial service in or into the territory of that Party, the Party shall ensure observance of the obligations of this Chapter by such self-regulatory organization.

Article 1403: Establishment of Financial Institutions

1.   The Parties recognize the principle that an investor of another Party should be permitted to establish a financial institution in the territory of a Party in the juridical form chosen by such investor.

2.   The Parties also recognize the principle that an investor of another Party should be permitted to participate widely in a Party's market through the ability of such investor to: (a) provide in that Party's territory a range of financial services through separate financial institutions as may be required by that Party; (b) expand geographically in that Party's territory; and (c) own financial institutions in that Party's territory without being subject to ownership requirements specific to foreign financial institutions.

3.   Subject to Annex 1403.3, at such time as the United States permits commercial banks of another Party located in its territory to expand through subsidiaries or direct branches into substantially all of the United States market, the Parties shall review and assess market access provided by each Party in relation to the principles in paragraphs 1 and 2 with a view to adopting arrangements permitting investors of another Party to choose the juridical form of establishment of commercial banks.

4.   Each Party shall permit an investor of another Party that does not own or control a financial institution in the Party's territory to establish a financial institution in that territory. A Party may: (a) require an investor of another Party to incorporate under the Party's law any financial institution it establishes in the Party's territory; or (b) impose terms and conditions on establishment that are consistent with Article 1405.

5.   For purposes of this Article, "investor of another Party" means an investor of another Party engaged in the business of providing financial services in the territory of that Party.

Annex 1403.3

Review of Market Access

The review of market access referred to in Article 1403(3) shall not include the market access limitations specified in Section B of the Schedule of Mexico to Annex VII.

Article 1404: Cross–Border Trade

1.   No Party may adopt any measure restricting any type of cross-border trade in financial services by cross-border financial service providers of another Party that the Party permits on the date of entry into force of this Agreement, except to the extent set out in Section B of the Party's Schedule to Annex VII.

2.   Each Party shall permit persons located in its territory, and its nationals wherever located, to purchase financial services from cross-

border financial service providers of another Party located in the territory of that other Party or of another Party. This obligation does not require a Party to permit such providers to do business or solicit in its territory. Subject to paragraph 1, each Party may define "doing business" and "solicitation" for purposes of this obligation.

3.   Without prejudice to other means of prudential regulation of cross-border trade in financial services, a Party may require the registration of cross-border financial service providers of another Party and of financial instruments.

4.   The Parties shall consult on future liberalization of cross-border trade in financial services as set out in Annex 1404.4.

Annex 1404.4

Consultations on Liberalization of Cross–Border Trade

No later than January 1, 2000, the Parties shall consult on further liberalization of cross-border trade in financial services. In such consultations the Parties shall, with respect to insurance: (a) consider the possibility of allowing a wider range of insurance services to be provided on a cross-border basis in or into their respective territories; and (b) determine whether the limitations on cross-border insurance services specified in Section A of the Schedule of Mexico to Annex VII shall be maintained, modified or eliminated.

Article 1405: National Treatment

1.   Each Party shall accord to investors of another Party treatment no less favorable than that it accords to its own investors, in like circumstances, with respect to the establishment, acquisition, expansion, management, conduct, operation, and sale or other disposition of financial institutions and investments in financial institutions in its territory.

2.   Each Party shall accord to financial institutions of another Party and to investments of investors of another Party in financial institutions treatment no less favorable than that it accords to its own financial institutions and to investments of its own investors in financial institutions, in like circumstances, with respect to the establishment, acquisition, expansion, management, conduct, operation, and sale or other disposition of financial institutions and investments.

3.   Subject to Article 1404, where a Party permits the cross-border provision of a financial service it shall accord to the cross-border financial service providers of another Party treatment no less favorable than that it accords to its own financial service providers, in like circumstances, with respect to the provision of such service.

4.   The treatment that a Party is required to accord under paragraphs 1, 2 and 3 means, with respect to a measure of any state or province: (a) in the case of an investor of another Party with an investment in a financial institution, an investment of such investor in a

financial institution, or a financial institution of such investor, located in a state or province, treatment no less favorable than the treatment accorded to an investor of the Party in a financial institution, an investment of such investor in a financial institution, or a financial institution of such investor, located in that state or province, in like circumstances; and (b) in any other case, treatment no less favorable than the most favorable treatment accorded to an investor of the Party in a financial institution, its financial institution or its investment in a financial institution, in like circumstances. For greater certainty, in the case of an investor of another Party with investments in financial institutions or financial institutions of such investor, located in more than one state or province, the treatment required under subparagraph (a) means: (c) treatment of the investor that is no less favorable than the most favorable treatment accorded to an investor of the Party with an investment located in such states or provinces, in like circumstances; and (d) with respect to an investment of the investor in a financial institution or a financial institution of such investor, located in a state or province, treatment no less favorable than that accorded to an investment of an investor of the Party, or a financial institution of such investor, located in that state or province, in like circumstances.

5. A Party's treatment of financial institutions and cross-border financial service providers of another Party, whether different or identical to that accorded to its own institutions or providers in like circumstances, is consistent with paragraphs 1 through 3 if the treatment affords equal competitive opportunities.

6. A Party's treatment affords equal competitive opportunities if it does not disadvantage financial institutions and cross-border financial services providers of another Party in their ability to provide financial services as compared with the ability of the Party's own financial institutions and financial services providers to provide such services, in like circumstances.

7. Differences in market share, profitability or size do not in themselves establish a denial of equal competitive opportunities, but such differences may be used as evidence regarding whether a Party's treatment affords equal competitive opportunities.

Article 1406: Most–Favored–Nation Treatment

1. Each Party shall accord to investors of another Party, financial institutions of another Party, investments of investors in financial institutions and cross-border financial service providers of another Party treatment no less favorable than that it accords to the investors, financial institutions, investments of investors in financial institutions and cross-border financial service providers of any other Party or of a non-Party, in like circumstances.

2. A Party may recognize prudential measures of another Party or of a non-Party in the application of measures covered by this Chapter.

Such recognition may be: (a) accorded unilaterally; (b) achieved through harmonization or other means; or (c) based upon an agreement or arrangement with the other Party or non-Party.

3. A Party according recognition of prudential measures under paragraph 2 shall provide adequate opportunity to another Party to demonstrate that circumstances exist in which there are or would be equivalent regulation, oversight, implementation of regulation, and if appropriate, procedures concerning the sharing of information between the Parties.

4. Where a Party accords recognition of prudential measures under paragraph 2(c) and the circumstances set out in paragraph 3 exist, the Party shall provide adequate opportunity to another Party to negotiate accession to the agreement or arrangement, or to negotiate a comparable agreement or arrangement.

Article 1407: New Financial Services and Data Processing

1. Each Party shall permit a financial institution of another Party to provide any new financial service of a type similar to those services that the Party permits its own financial institutions, in like circumstances, to provide under its domestic law. A Party may determine the institutional and juridical form through which the service may be provided and may require authorization for the provision of the service. Where such authorization is required, a decision shall be made within a reasonable time and the authorization may only be refused for prudential reasons.

2. Each Party shall permit a financial institution of another Party to transfer information in electronic or other form, into and out of the Party's territory, for data processing where such processing is required in the ordinary course of business of such institution.

Article 1408: Senior Management and Boards of Directors

1. No Party may require financial institutions of another Party to engage individuals of any particular nationality as senior managerial or other essential personnel.

2. No Party may require that more than a simple majority of the board of directors of a financial institution of another Party be composed of nationals of the Party, persons residing in the territory of the Party, or a combination thereof.

Article 1409: Reservations and Specific Commitments

1. Articles 1403 through 1408 do not apply to: (a) any existing non-conforming measure that is maintained by (i) a Party at the federal level,

as set out in Section A of its Schedule to Annex VII, (ii) a state or province, for the period ending on the date specified in Annex 1409.1 for that state or province, and thereafter as described by the Party in Section A of its Schedule to Annex VII in accordance with Annex 1409.1, or (iii) a local government; (b) the continuation or prompt renewal of any non-conforming measure referred to in subparagraph (a); or (c) an amendment to any non-conforming measure referred to in subparagraph (a) to the extent that the amendment does not decrease the conformity of the measure, as it existed immediately before the amendment, with Articles 1403 through 1408.

2.   Articles 1403 through 1408 do not apply to any non-conforming measure that a Party adopts or maintains in accordance with Section B of its Schedule to Annex VII.

3.   Section C of each Party's Schedule to Annex VII sets out certain specific commitments by that Party.

4.   Where a Party has set out a reservation to Article 1102, 1103, 1202 or 1203 in its Schedule to Annex I, II, III or IV, the reservation shall be deemed to constitute a reservation to Article 1405 or 1406, as the case may be, to the extent that the measure, sector, subsector or activity set out in the reservation is covered by this Chapter.

Annex 1409.1

Provincial and State Reservations

1.   Canada may set out in Section A of its Schedule to Annex VII by the date of entry into force of this Agreement any existing non-conforming measure maintained at the provincial level.

2.   The United States may set out in Section A of its Schedule to Annex VII by the date of entry into force of this Agreement any existing non-conforming measures maintained by California, Florida, Illinois, New York, Ohio and Texas. Existing non-conforming state measures of all other states may be set out by January 1, 1995.

Article 1410: Exceptions

1.   Nothing in this Part shall be construed to prevent a Party from adopting or maintaining reasonable measures for prudential reasons, such as: (a) the protection of investors, depositors, financial market participants, policy-holders, policy-claimants, or persons to whom a fiduciary duty is owed by a financial institution or cross-border financial service provider; (b) the maintenance of the safety, soundness, integrity or financial responsibility of financial institutions or cross-border financial service providers; and (c) ensuring the integrity and stability of a Party's financial system.

2.   Nothing in this Part applies to non-discriminatory measures of general application taken by any public entity in pursuit of monetary and related credit policies or exchange rate policies. This paragraph shall

not affect a Party's obligations under Article 1106 (Performance Requirements) with respect to measures covered by Chapter Eleven (Investment) or Article 1109 (Transfers).

3. Article 1405 shall not apply to the granting by a Party to a financial institution of an exclusive right to provide a financial service referred to in Article 1401(3)(a).

4. Notwithstanding Article 1109(1), (2) and (3), as incorporated into this Chapter, and without limiting the applicability of Article 1109(4), as incorporated into this Chapter, a Party may prevent or limit transfers by a financial institution or cross-border financial services provider to, or for the benefit of, an affiliate of or person related to such institution or provider, through the equitable, non-discriminatory and good faith application of measures relating to maintenance of the safety, soundness, integrity or financial responsibility of financial institutions or cross-border financial service providers. This paragraph does not prejudice any other provision of this Agreement that permits a Party to restrict transfers.

Article 1411: Transparency

1. In lieu of Article 1802(2) (Publication), each Party shall, to the extent practicable, provide in advance to all interested persons any measure of general application that the Party proposes to adopt in order to allow an opportunity for such persons to comment on the measure. Such measure shall be provided: (a) by means of official publication; (b) in other written form; or (c) in such other form as permits an interested person to make informed comments on the proposed measure.

2. Each Party's regulatory authorities shall make available to interested persons their requirements for completing applications relating to the provision of financial services.

3. On the request of an applicant, the regulatory authority shall inform the applicant of the status of its application. If such authority requires additional information from the applicant, it shall notify the applicant without undue delay.

4. A regulatory authority shall make an administrative decision on a completed application of an investor in a financial institution, a financial institution or a cross-border financial service provider of another Party relating to the provision of a financial service within 120 days, and shall promptly notify the applicant of the decision. An application shall not be considered complete until all relevant hearings are held and all necessary information is received. Where it is not practicable for a decision to be made within 120 days, the regulatory authority shall notify the applicant without undue delay and shall endeavor to make the decision within a reasonable time thereafter.

5. Nothing in this Chapter requires a Party to furnish or allow access to: (a) information related to the financial affairs and accounts of individual customers of financial institutions or cross-border financial

service providers; or (b) any confidential information, the disclosure of which would impede law enforcement or otherwise be contrary to the public interest or prejudice legitimate commercial interests of particular enterprises.

6.   Each Party shall maintain or establish one or more inquiry points no later than 180 days after the date of entry into force of this Agreement, to respond in writing as soon as practicable, to all reasonable inquiries from interested persons regarding measures of general application covered by this Chapter.

Article 1412: Financial Services Committee

1.   The Parties hereby establish the Financial Services Committee. The principal representative of each Party shall be an official of the Party's authority responsible for financial services set out in Annex 1412.1.

2.   Subject to Article 2001(2)(d) (Free Trade Commission), the Committee shall: (a) supervise the implementation of this Chapter and its further elaboration; (b) consider issues regarding financial services that are referred to it by a Party; and (c) participate in the dispute settlement procedures in accordance with Article 1415.

3.   The Committee shall meet annually to assess the functioning of this Agreement as it applies to financial services. The Committee shall inform the Commission of the results of each annual meeting.

Annex 1412.1

Authorities Responsible for Financial Services

The authority of each Party responsible for financial services shall be: (a) for Canada, the Department of Finance of Canada; (b) for Mexico, the Secretaria de Hacienda y Credito Publico; and (c) for the United States, the Department of the Treasury for banking and other financial services and the Department of Commerce for insurance services.

Article 1413: Consultations

1.   A Party may request consultations with another Party regarding any matter arising under this Agreement that affects financial services. The other Party shall give sympathetic consideration to the request. The consulting Parties shall report the results of their consultations to the Committee at its annual meeting.

2.   Consultations under this Article shall include officials of the authorities specified in Annex 1412.1.

3.   A Party may request that regulatory authorities of another Party participate in consultations under this Article regarding that other Party's measures of general application which may affect the operations of financial institutions or cross-border financial service providers in the requesting Party's territory.

4.   Nothing in this Article shall be construed to require regulatory authorities participating in consultations under paragraph 3 to disclose information or take any action that would interfere with individual regulatory, supervisory, administrative or enforcement matters.

5.   Where a Party requires information for supervisory purposes concerning a financial institution in another Party's territory or a cross-border financial service provider in another Party's territory, the Party may approach the competent regulatory authority in the other Party's territory to seek the information.

6.   Annex 1413.6 shall apply to further consultations and arrangements.

Annex 1413.6

Further Consultations and Arrangements

Section A—Limited Scope Financial Institutions

Three years after the date of entry into force of this Agreement, the Parties shall consult on the aggregate limit on limited scope financial institutions described in paragraph 8 of Section B of the Schedule of Mexico to Annex VII.

Section B—Payments System Protection

1.   If the sum of the authorized capital of foreign commercial bank affiliates (as such term is defined in the Schedule of Mexico to Annex VII), measured as a percentage of the aggregate capital of all commercial banks in Mexico, reaches 25 percent, Mexico may request consultations with the other Parties on the potential adverse effects arising from the presence of commercial banks of the other Parties in the Mexican market and the possible need for remedial action, including further temporary limitations on market participation. The consultations shall be completed expeditiously.

2.   In considering the potential adverse effects, the Parties shall take into account: (a) the threat that the Mexican payments system may be controlled by non-Mexican persons; (b) the effects foreign commercial banks established in Mexico may have on Mexico's ability to conduct monetary and exchange-rate policy effectively; and (c) the adequacy of this Chapter in protecting the Mexican payments system.

3.   If no consensus is reached on the matters referred to in paragraph 1, any Party may request the establishment of an arbitral panel under Article 1414 or Article 2008 (Request for an Arbitral Panel). The panel proceedings shall be conducted in accordance with the Model Rules of Procedure established under Article 2012 (Rules of Procedure). The Panel shall present its determination within 60 days after the last panelist is selected or such other period as the Parties to the proceeding may agree. Article 2018 (Implementation of Final Report) and 2019 (Non–Implementation—Suspension of Benefits) shall not apply in such proceedings.

Article 1414: Dispute Settlement

1.   Section B of Chapter Twenty (Institutional Arrangements and Dispute Settlement Procedures) applies as modified by this Article to the settlement of disputes arising under this Chapter.

2.   The Parties shall establish by January 1, 1994 and maintain a roster of up to 15 individuals who are willing and able to serve as financial services panelists. Financial services roster members shall be appointed by consensus for terms of three years, and may be reappointed.

3.   Financial services roster members shall: (a) have expertise or experience in financial services law or practice, which may include the regulation of financial institutions; (b) be chosen strictly on the basis of objectivity, reliability and sound judgment; and (c) meet the qualifications set out in Article 2009(2)(b) and (c) (Roster).

4.   Where a Party claims that a dispute arises under this Chapter, Article 2011 (Panel Selection) shall apply, except that: (a) where the disputing Parties so agree, the panel shall be composed entirely of panelists meeting the qualifications in paragraph 3; and (b) in any other case, (i) each disputing Party may select panelists meeting the qualifications set out in paragraph 3 or in Article 2010(1) (Qualifications of Panelists), and (ii) if the Party complained against invokes Article 1410, the chair of the panel shall meet the qualifications set out in paragraph 3.

5.   In any dispute where a panel finds a measure to be inconsistent with the obligations of this Agreement and the measure affects: (a) only the financial services sector, the complaining Party may suspend benefits only in the financial services sector; (b) the financial services sector and any other sector, the complaining Party may suspend benefits in the financial services sector that have an effect equivalent to the effect of the measure in the Party's financial services sector; or (c) only a sector other than the financial services sector, the complaining Party may not suspend benefits in the financial services sector.

Article 1415: Investment Disputes in Financial Services

1.   Where an investor of another Party submits a claim under Article 1116 or 1117 to arbitration under Section B of Chapter Eleven (Investment—Settlement of Disputes between a Party and an Investor of Another Party) against a Party and the disputing Party invokes Article 1410, on request of the disputing Party, the Tribunal shall refer the matter in writing to the Committee for a decision. The Tribunal may not proceed pending receipt of a decision or report under this Article.

2.   In a referral pursuant to paragraph 1, the Committee shall decide the issue of whether and to what extent Article 1410 is a valid defense to the claim of the investor. The Committee shall transmit a

copy of its decision to the Tribunal and to the Commission. The decision shall be binding on the Tribunal.

3.   Where the Committee has not decided the issue within 60 days of the receipt of the referral under paragraph 1, the disputing Party or the Party of the disputing investor may request the establishment of an arbitral panel under Article 2008 (Request for an Arbitral Panel). The panel shall be constituted in accordance with Article 1414. Further to Article 2017 (Final Report), the panel shall transmit its final report to the Committee and to the Tribunal. The report shall be binding on the Tribunal.

4.   Where no request for the establishment of a panel pursuant to paragraph 3 has been made within 10 days of the expiration of the 60–day period referred to in paragraph 3, the Tribunal may proceed to decide the matter.

Article 1416: Definitions

For purposes of this Chapter:

cross-border financial service provider of a Party means a person of a Party that is engaged in the business of providing a financial service within the territory of the Party and that seeks to provide or provides financial services through the cross-border provision of such services;

cross-border provision of a financial service or cross-border trade in financial services means the provision of a financial service: (a) from the territory of a Party into the territory of another Party, (b) in the territory of a Party by a person of that Party to a person of another Party, or (c) by a national of a Party in the territory of another Party, but does not include the provision of a service in the territory of a Party by an investment in that territory;

financial institution means any financial intermediary or other enterprise that is authorized to do business and regulated or supervised as a financial institution under the law of the Party in whose territory it is located;

financial institution of another Party means a financial institution, including a branch, located in the territory of a Party that is controlled by persons of another Party;

financial service means a service of a financial nature, including insurance, and a service incidental or auxiliary to a service of a financial nature;

financial service provider of a Party means a person of a Party that is engaged in the business of providing a financial service within the territory of that Party;

investment means "investment" as defined in Article 1139 (Investment—Definitions), except that, with respect to "loans" and "debt securities" referred to in that Article: (a) a loan to or debt security issued by a financial institution is an investment only where it is treated as regulatory capital by the Party in whose territory the financial institution is located; and (b) a loan granted by or debt security owned by a financial institution, other than a loan to or debt security of a financial institution referred to in subparagraph (a), is not an investment; for greater certainty: (c) a loan to, or debt security issued by, a Party or a state enterprise thereof is not an investment; and (d) a loan granted by or debt security owned by a cross-border financial service provider, other than a loan to or debt security issued by a financial institution, is an investment if such loan or debt security meets the criteria for investments set out in Article 1139;

investor of a Party means a Party or state enterprise thereof, or a person of that Party, that seeks to make, makes, or has made an investment;

new financial service means a financial service not provided in the Party's territory that is provided within the territory of another Party, and includes any new form of delivery of a financial service or the sale of a financial product that is not sold in the Party's territory;

person of a Party means "person of a Party" as defined in Chapter Two (General Definitions) and, for greater certainty, does not include a branch of an enterprise of a non-Party;

public entity means a central bank or monetary authority of a Party, or any financial institution owned or controlled by a Party; and

self-regulatory organization means any non-governmental body, including any securities or futures exchange or market, clearing agency, or other organization or association, that exercises its own or delegated regulatory or supervisory authority over financial service providers or financial institutions.

Chapter Fifteen

COMPETITION POLICY, MONOPOLIES AND STATE ENTERPRISES

Article 1501: Competition Law

1.   Each Party shall adopt or maintain measures to proscribe anti-competitive business conduct and take appropriate action with respect thereto, recognizing that such measures will enhance the fulfillment of the objectives of this Agreement. To this end the Parties shall consult from time to time about the effectiveness of measures undertaken by each Party.

2.   Each Party recognizes the importance of cooperation and coordination among their authorities to further effective competition law enforcement in the free trade area. The Parties shall cooperate on issues of competition law enforcement policy, including mutual legal assistance, notification, consultation and exchange of information relating to the enforcement of competition laws and policies in the free trade area.

3.   No Party may have recourse to dispute settlement under this Agreement for any matter arising under this Article.

Article 1502: Monopolies and State Enterprises

1.   Nothing in this Agreement shall be construed to prevent a Party from designating a monopoly.

2.   Where a Party intends to designate a monopoly and the designation may affect the interests of persons of another Party, the Party shall: (a) wherever possible, provide prior written notification to the other Party of the designation; and (b) endeavor to introduce at the time of the designation such conditions on the operation of the monopoly as will minimize or eliminate any nullification or impairment of benefits in the sense of Annex 2004 (Nullification and Impairment).

3.   Each Party shall ensure, through regulatory control, administrative supervision or the application of other measures, that any privately-

owned monopoly that it designates and any government monopoly that it maintains or designates: (a) acts in a manner that is not inconsistent with the Party's obligations under this Agreement wherever such a monopoly exercises any regulatory, administrative or other governmental authority that the Party has delegated to it in connection with the monopoly good or service, such as the power to grant import or export licenses, approve commercial transactions or impose quotas, fees or other charges; (b) except to comply with any terms of its designation that are not inconsistent with subparagraph (c) or (d), acts solely in accordance with commercial considerations in its purchase or sale of the monopoly good or service in the relevant market, including with regard to price, quality, availability, marketability, transportation and other terms and conditions of purchase or sale; (c) provides non-discriminatory treatment to investments of investors, to goods and to service providers of another Party in its purchase or sale of the monopoly good or service in the relevant market; and (d) does not use its monopoly position to engage, either directly or indirectly, including through its dealings with its parent, its subsidiary or other enterprise with common ownership, in anticompetitive practices in a non-monopolized market in its territory that adversely affect an investment of an investor of another Party, including through the discriminatory provision of the monopoly good or service, cross-subsidization or predatory conduct.

4.   Paragraph 3 does not apply to procurement by governmental agencies of goods or services for governmental purposes and not with a view to commercial resale or with a view to use in the production of goods or the provision of services for commercial sale.

5.   For purposes of this Article "maintain" means designate prior to the date of entry into force of this Agreement and existing on January 1, 1994.

Article 1503: State Enterprises

1.   Nothing in this Agreement shall be construed to prevent a Party from maintaining or establishing a state enterprise.

2.   Each Party shall ensure, through regulatory control, administrative supervision or the application of other measures, that any state enterprise that it maintains or establishes acts in a manner that is not inconsistent with the Party's obligations under Chapters Eleven (Investment) and Fourteen (Financial Services) wherever such enterprise exercises any regulatory, administrative or other governmental authority that the Party has delegated to it, such as the power to expropriate, grant licenses, approve commercial transactions or impose quotas, fees or other charges.

3.   Each Party shall ensure that any state enterprise that it maintains or establishes accords non-discriminatory treatment in the sale of its goods or services to investments in the Party's territory of investors of another Party.

Article 1504: Working Group on Trade and Competition

The Commission shall establish a Working Group on Trade and Competition, comprising representatives of each Party, to report, and to make recommendations on further work as appropriate, to the Commission within five years of the date of entry into force of this Agreement on relevant issues concerning the relationship between competition laws and policies and trade in the free trade area.

Article 1505: Definitions

For purposes of this Chapter:

designate means to establish, designate or authorize, or to expand the scope of a monopoly to cover an additional good or service, after the date of entry into force of this Agreement;

discriminatory provision includes treating: (a) a parent, a subsidiary or other enterprise with common ownership more favorably than an unaffiliated enterprise, or (b) one class of enterprises more favorably than another, in like circumstances;

government monopoly means a monopoly that is owned, or controlled through ownership interests, by the federal government of a Party or by another such monopoly;

in accordance with commercial considerations means consistent with normal business practices of privately-held enterprises in the relevant business or industry;

market means the geographic and commercial market for a good or service;

monopoly means an entity, including a consortium or government agency, that in any relevant market in the territory of a Party is designated as the sole provider or purchaser of a good or service, but does not include an entity that has been granted an exclusive intellectual property right solely by reason of such grant;

non-discriminatory treatment means the better of national treatment and most-favored-nation treatment, as set out in the relevant provisions of this Agreement; and

state enterprise means, except as set out in Annex 1505, an enterprise owned, or controlled through ownership interests, by a Party.

Annex 1505

Country—Specific Definitions of State Enterprises

For purposes of Article 1503(3), "**state enterprise**": (a) with respect to Canada, means a Crown corporation within the meaning of the Financial Administration Act (Canada), a Crown corporation within the meaning of any comparable provincial law or equivalent entity that is incorporated under other applicable provincial law; and (b) with respect to Mexico, does not include, the Compania Nacional de Subsistencias Populares (National Company for Basic Commodities) and its existing affiliates, or any successor enterprise or its affiliates, for purposes of sales of maize, beans and powdered milk.

Chapter Sixteen

TEMPORARY ENTRY FOR
BUSINESS PERSONS

Article 1601: General Principles

Further to Article 102 (Objectives), this Chapter reflects the preferential trading relationship between the Parties, the desirability of facilitating temporary entry on a reciprocal basis and of establishing transparent criteria and procedures for temporary entry, and the need to ensure border security and to protect the domestic labor force and permanent employment in their respective territories.

Article 1602: General Obligations

1.   Each Party shall apply its measures relating to the provisions of this Chapter in accordance with Article 1601 and, in particular, shall apply expeditiously those measures so as to avoid unduly impairing or delaying trade in goods or services or conduct of investment activities under this Agreement.

2.   The Parties shall endeavor to develop and adopt common criteria, definitions and interpretations for the implementation of this Chapter.

Article 1603: Grant of Temporary Entry

1.   Each Party shall grant temporary entry to business persons who are otherwise qualified for entry under applicable measures relating to public health and safety and national security, in accordance with this Chapter, including the provisions of Annex 1603.

2.   A Party may refuse to issue an immigration document authorizing employment to a business person where the temporary entry of that person might affect adversely: (a) the settlement of any labor dispute that is in progress at the place or intended place of employment; or (b) the employment of any person who is involved in such dispute.

3.   When a Party refuses pursuant to paragraph 2 to issue an immigration document authorizing employment, it shall: (a) inform in

writing the business person of the reasons for the refusal; and (b) promptly notify in writing the Party whose business person has been refused entry of the reasons for the refusal.

4.   Each Party shall limit any fees for processing applications for temporary entry of business persons to the approximate cost of services rendered.

Annex 1603

Temporary Entry for Business Persons
Section A—Business Visitors

1.   Each Party shall grant temporary entry to a business person seeking to engage in a business activity set out in Appendix 1603.A.1, without requiring that person to obtain an employment authorization, provided that the business person otherwise complies with existing immigration measures applicable to temporary entry, on presentation of: (a) proof of citizenship of a Party; (b) documentation demonstrating that the business person will be so engaged and describing the purpose of entry; and (c) evidence demonstrating that the proposed business activity is international in scope and that the business person is not seeking to enter the local labor market.

2.   Each Party shall provide that a business person may satisfy the requirements of paragraph 1(c) by demonstrating that: (a) the primary source of remuneration for the proposed business activity is outside the territory of the Party granting temporary entry; and (b) the business person's principal place of business and the actual place of accrual of profits, at least predominantly, remain outside such territory. A Party shall normally accept an oral declaration as to the principal place of business and the actual place of accrual of profits. Where the Party requires further proof, it shall normally consider a letter from the employer attesting to these matters as sufficient proof.

3.   Each Party shall grant temporary entry to a business person seeking to engage in a business activity other than those set out in Appendix 1603.A.1, without requiring that person to obtain an employment authorization, on a basis no less favorable than that provided under the existing provisions of the measures set out in Appendix 1603.A.3, provided that the business person otherwise complies with existing immigration measures applicable to temporary entry.

4.   No Party may: (a) as a condition for temporary entry under paragraph 1 or 3, require prior approval procedures, petitions, labor certification tests or other procedures of similar effect; or (b) impose or maintain any numerical restriction relating to temporary entry under paragraph 1 or 3.

5.   Notwithstanding paragraph 4, a Party may require a business person seeking temporary entry under this Section to obtain a visa or its equivalent prior to entry. Before imposing a visa requirement, the Party shall consult with a Party whose business persons would be affected with

a view to avoiding the imposition of the requirement. With respect to an existing visa requirement, a Party shall consult, on request, with a Party whose business persons are subject to the requirement with a view to its removal.

Section B—Traders and Investors

1.   Each Party shall grant temporary entry and provide confirming documentation to a business person seeking to: (a) carry on substantial trade in goods or services principally between the territory of the Party of which the business person is a citizen and the territory of the Party into which entry is sought, or (b) establish, develop, administer or provide advice or key technical services to the operation of an investment to which the business person or the business person's enterprise has committed, or is in the process of committing, a substantial amount of capital, in a capacity that is supervisory, executive or involves essential skills, provided that the business person otherwise complies with existing immigration measures applicable to temporary entry.

2.   No Party may: (a) as a condition for temporary entry under paragraph 1, require labor certification tests or other procedures of similar effect; or (b) impose or maintain any numerical restriction relating to temporary entry under paragraph 1.

3.   Notwithstanding paragraph 2, a Party may require a business person seeking temporary entry under this Section to obtain a visa or its equivalent prior to entry.

Section C—Intra–Company Transferees

1.   Each Party shall grant temporary entry and provide confirming documentation to a business person employed by an enterprise who seeks to render services to that enterprise or a subsidiary or affiliate thereof, in a capacity that is managerial, executive or involves specialized knowledge, provided that the business person otherwise complies with existing immigration measures applicable to temporary entry. A Party may require the business person to have been employed continuously by the enterprise for one year within the three-year period immediately preceding the date of the application for admission.

2.   No Party may: (a) as a condition for temporary entry under paragraph 1, require labor certification tests or other procedures of similar effect; or (b) impose or maintain any numerical restriction relating to temporary entry under paragraph 1.

3.   Notwithstanding paragraph 2, a Party may require a business person seeking temporary entry under this Section to obtain a visa or its equivalent prior to entry. Before imposing a visa requirement, the Party shall consult with a Party whose business persons would be affected with a view to avoiding the imposition of the requirement. With respect to an existing visa requirement, a Party shall consult, on request, with a Party whose business persons are subject to the requirement with a view to its removal.

Section D—Professionals

1. Each Party shall grant temporary entry and provide confirming documentation to a business person seeking to engage in a business activity at a professional level in a profession set out in Appendix 1603.D.1, if the business person otherwise complies with existing immigration measures applicable to temporary entry, on presentation of: (a) proof of citizenship of a Party; and (b) documentation demonstrating that the business person will be so engaged and describing the purpose of entry.

2. No Party may: (a) as a condition for temporary entry under paragraph 1, require prior approval procedures, petitions, labor certification tests or other procedures of similar effect; or (b) impose or maintain any numerical restriction relating to temporary entry under paragraph 1.

3. Notwithstanding paragraph 2, a Party may require a business person seeking temporary entry under this Section to obtain a visa or its equivalent prior to entry. Before imposing a visa requirement, the Party shall consult with a Party whose business persons would be affected with a view to avoiding the imposition of the requirement. With respect to an existing visa requirement, a Party shall consult, on request, with a Party whose business persons are subject to the requirement with a view to its removal.

4. Notwithstanding paragraphs 1 and 2, a Party may establish an annual numerical limit, which shall be set out in Appendix 1603.D.4, regarding temporary entry of business persons of another Party seeking to engage in business activities at a professional level in a profession set out in Appendix 1603.D.1, if the Parties concerned have not agreed otherwise prior to the date of entry into force of this Agreement for those Parties. In establishing such a limit, the Party shall consult with the other Party concerned.

5. A Party establishing a numerical limit pursuant to paragraph 4, unless the Parties concerned agree otherwise: (a) shall, for each year after the first year after the date of entry into force of this Agreement, consider increasing the numerical limit set out in Appendix 1603.D.4 by an amount to be established in consultation with the other Party concerned, taking into account the demand for temporary entry under this Section; (b) shall not apply its procedures established pursuant to paragraph 1 to the temporary entry of a business person subject to the numerical limit, but may require the business person to comply with its other procedures applicable to the temporary entry of professionals; and (c) may, in consultation with the other Party concerned, grant temporary entry under paragraph 1 to a business person who practices in a profession where accreditation, licensing, and certification requirements are mutually recognized by those Parties.

6. Nothing in paragraph 4 or 5 shall be construed to limit the ability of a business person to seek temporary entry under a Party's

applicable immigration measures relating to the entry of professionals other than those adopted or maintained pursuant to paragraph 1.

7.   Three years after a Party establishes a numerical limit pursuant to paragraph 4, it shall consult with the other Party concerned with a view to determining a date after which the limit shall cease to apply.

Appendix 1603.A.1

Business Visitors

Research and Design

—Technical, scientific and statistical researchers conducting independent research or research for an enterprise located in the territory of another Party.

Growth, Manufacture and Production

—Harvester owner supervising a harvesting crew admitted under applicable law.

—Purchasing and production management personnel conducting commercial transactions for an enterprise located in the territory of another Party.

Marketing

—Market researchers and analysts conducting independent research or analysis or research or analysis for an enterprise located in the territory of another Party.

—Trade fair and promotional personnel attending a trade convention.

Sales

—Sales representatives and agents taking orders or negotiating contracts for goods or services for an enterprise located in the territory of another Party but not delivering goods or providing services.

—Buyers purchasing for an enterprise located in the territory of another Party.

Distribution

—Transportation operators transporting goods or passengers to the territory of a Party from the territory of another Party or loading and transporting goods or passengers from the territory of a Party, with no unloading in that territory, to the territory of another Party.

—With respect to temporary entry into the territory of the United States, Canadian customs brokers performing brokerage duties relating to the export of goods from the territory of the United States to or through the territory of Canada.

—With respect to temporary entry into the territory of Canada, United States customs brokers performing brokerage duties relating to the export of goods from the territory of Canada to or through the territory of the United States.

—Customs brokers providing consulting services regarding the facilitation of the import or export of goods.

After–Sales Service

—Installers, repair and maintenance personnel, and supervisors, possessing specialized knowledge essential to a seller's contractual obligation, performing services or training workers to perform services, pursuant to a warranty or other service contract incidental to the sale of commercial or industrial equipment or machinery, including computer software, purchased from an enterprise located outside the territory of the Party into which temporary entry is sought, during the life of the warranty or service agreement.

General Service

—Professionals engaging in a business activity at a professional level in a profession set out in Appendix 1603.D.1.

—Management and supervisory personnel engaging in a commercial transaction for an enterprise located in the territory of another Party.

—Financial services personnel (insurers, bankers or investment brokers) engaging in commercial transactions for an enterprise located in the territory of another Party.

—Public relations and advertising personnel consulting with business associates, or attending or participating in conventions.

—Tourism personnel (tour and travel agents, tour guides or tour operators) attending or participating in conventions or conducting a tour that has begun in the territory of another Party.

—Tour bus operators entering the territory of a Party: (a) with a group of passengers on a bus tour that has begun in, and will return to, the territory of another Party; (b) to meet a group of passengers on a bus tour that will end, and the predominant portion of which will take place, in the territory of another Party; or (c) with a group of passengers on a bus tour to be unloaded in the territory of the Party into which temporary entry is sought, and returning with no passengers or reloading with the group for transportation to the territory of another Party.

—Translators or interpreters performing services as employees of an enterprise located in the territory of another Party.

Definitions

For purposes of this Appendix:

territory of another Party means the territory of a Party other than the territory of the Party into which temporary entry is sought;

tour bus operator means a natural person, including relief personnel accompanying or following to join, necessary for the operation of a tour bus for the duration of a trip; and

transportation operator means a natural person, other than a tour bus operator, including relief personnel accompanying or following to join, necessary for the operation of a vehicle for the duration of a trip.

Appendix 1603.A.3

Existing Immigration Measures

1. In the case of Canada, subsection 19(1) of the Immigration Regulations, 1978, SOR/78–172, as amended, made under the Immigration Act, R.S.C. 1985, c. I–2, as amended.

2. In the case of the United States, section 101(a)(15)(B) of the Immigration and Nationality Act, 1952, as amended.

3. In the case of Mexico, Chapter III of the General Demography Law ("Ley General de Poblacion"), 1974, as amended.

* * *

Appendix 1603.D.4

United States

1. Beginning on the date of entry into force of this Agreement as between the United States and Mexico, the United States shall annually approve as many as 5,500 initial petitions of business persons of Mexico seeking temporary entry under Section D of Annex 1603 to engage in a business activity at a professional level in a profession set out in Appendix 1603.D.1.

2. For purposes of paragraph 1, the United States shall not take into account: (a) the renewal of a period of temporary entry; (b) the entry of a spouse or children accompanying or following to join the principal business person; (c) an admission under section 101(a)(15)(H)(i)(b) of the Immigration and Nationality Act, 1952, as may be amended, including the worldwide numerical limit established by section 214(g)(1)(A) of that Act; or (d) an admission under any other provision of section 101(a)(15) of that Act relating to the entry of professionals.

3. Paragraphs 4 and 5 of Section D of Annex 1603 shall apply as between the United States and Mexico for no longer than: (a) the period that such paragraphs or similar provisions may apply as between the United States and any other Party other than Canada or any non-Party; or (b) 10 years after the date of entry into force of this Agreement as between such Parties, whichever period is shorter.

Article 1604: Provision of Information

1. Further to Article 1802 (Publication), each Party shall: (a) provide to the other Parties such materials as will enable them to become acquainted with its measures relating to this Chapter; and (b) no later than one year after the date of entry into force of this Agreement, prepare, publish and make available in its own territory, and in the territories of the other Parties, explanatory material in a consolidated document regarding the requirements for temporary entry under this Chapter in such a manner as will enable business persons of the other Parties to become acquainted with them.

2. Subject to Annex 1604.2, each Party shall collect and maintain, and make available to the other Parties in accordance with its domestic law, data respecting the granting of temporary entry under this Chapter to business persons of the other Parties who have been issued immigration documentation, including data specific to each occupation, profession or activity.

Annex 1604.2

Provision of Information

The obligations under Article 1604(2) shall take effect with respect to Mexico one year after the date of entry into force of this Agreement.

Article 1605: Working Group

1. The Parties hereby establish a Temporary Entry Working Group, comprising representatives of each Party, including immigration officials.

2. The Working Group shall meet at least once each year to consider: (a) the implementation and administration of this Chapter; (b) the development of measures to further facilitate temporary entry of business persons on a reciprocal basis; (c) the waiving of labor certification tests or procedures of similar effect for spouses of business persons who have been granted temporary entry for more than one year under Section B, C or D of Annex 1603; and (d) proposed modifications of or additions to this Chapter.

Article 1606: Dispute Settlement

1. A Party may not initiate proceedings under Article 2007 (Commission—Good Offices, Conciliation and Mediation) regarding a refusal to grant temporary entry under this Chapter or a particular case arising under Article 1602(1) unless: (a) the matter involves a pattern of practice; and (b) the business person has exhausted the available administrative remedies regarding the particular matter.

2. The remedies referred to in paragraph (1)(b) shall be deemed to be exhausted if a final determination in the matter has not been issued

by the competent authority within one year of the institution of an administrative proceeding, and the failure to issue a determination is not attributable to delay caused by the business person.

Article 1607: Relation to Other Chapters

Except for this Chapter, Chapters One (Objectives), Two (General Definitions), Twenty (Institutional Arrangements and Dispute Settlement Procedures) and Twenty–Two (Final Provisions) and Articles 1801 (Contact Points), 1802 (Publication), 1803 (Notification and Provision of Information) and 1804 (Administrative Proceedings), no provision of this Agreement shall impose any obligation on a Party regarding its immigration measures.

Article 1608: Definitions

For purposes of this Chapter:

business person means a citizen of a Party who is engaged in trade in goods, the provision of services or the conduct of investment activities;

citizen means "citizen" as defined in Annex 1608 for the Parties specified in that Annex;

existing means "existing" as defined in Annex 1608 for the Parties specified in that Annex; and

temporary entry means entry into the territory of a Party by a business person of another Party without the intent to establish permanent residence.

Annex 1608

Country—Specific Definitions

For purposes of this Chapter:

citizen means, with respect to Mexico, a national or a citizen according to the existing provisions of Articles 30 and 34, respectively, of the Mexican Constitution; and

existing means, as between: (a) Canada and Mexico, and Mexico and the United States, in effect on the date of entry into force of this Agreement; and (b) Canada and the United States, in effect on January 1, 1989.

Part Six
INTELLECTUAL PROPERTY

Chapter Seventeen

INTELLECTUAL PROPERTY

Article 1701: Nature and Scope of Obligations

1.   Each Party shall provide in its territory to the nationals of another Party adequate and effective protection and enforcement of intellectual property rights, while ensuring that measures to enforce intellectual property rights do not themselves become barriers to legitimate trade.

2.   To provide adequate and effective protection and enforcement of intellectual property rights, each Party shall, at a minimum, give effect to this Chapter and to the substantive provisions of: (a) the Geneva Convention for the Protection of Producers of Phonograms Against Unauthorized Duplication of their Phonograms, 1971 (Geneva Convention); (b) the Berne Convention for the Protection of Literary and Artistic Works, 1971 (Berne Convention); (c) the Paris Convention for the Protection of Industrial Property, 1967 (Paris Convention); and (d) the International Convention for the Protection of New Varieties of Plants, 1978 (UPOV Convention), or the International Convention for the Protection of New Varieties of Plants, 1991 (UPOV Convention). If a Party has not acceded to the specified text of any such Conventions on or before the date of entry into force of this Agreement, it shall make every effort to accede.

3.   Annex 1701.3 applies to the Parties specified in that Annex.

Annex 1701.3

Intellectual Property Conventions

1.   Mexico shall: (a) make every effort to comply with the substantive provisions of the 1978 or 1991 UPOV Convention as soon as possible and shall do so no later than two years after the date of signature of this Agreement; and (b) accept from the date of entry into force of this Agreement applications from plant breeders for varieties in all plant genera and species and grant protection, in accordance with such substantive provisions, promptly after complying with subparagraph (a).

2. Notwithstanding Article 1701(2)(b), this Agreement confers no rights and imposes no obligations on the United States with respect to Article 6bis of the Berne Convention, or the rights derived from that Article.

Article 1702: More Extensive Protection

A Party may implement in its domestic law more extensive protection of intellectual property rights than is required under this Agreement, provided that such protection is not inconsistent with this Agreement.

Article 1703: National Treatment

1. Each Party shall accord to nationals of another Party treatment no less favorable than that it accords to its own nationals with regard to the protection and enforcement of all intellectual property rights. In respect of sound recordings, each Party shall provide such treatment to producers and performers of another Party, except that a Party may limit rights of performers of another Party in respect of secondary uses of sound recordings to those rights its nationals are accorded in the territory of such other Party.

2. No Party may, as a condition of according national treatment under this Article, require right holders to comply with any formalities or conditions in order to acquire rights in respect of copyright and related rights.

3. A Party may derogate from paragraph 1 in relation to its judicial and administrative procedures for the protection or enforcement of intellectual property rights, including any procedure requiring a national of another Party to designate for service of process an address in the Party's territory or to appoint an agent in the Party's territory, if the derogation is consistent with the relevant Convention listed in Article 1701(2), provided that such derogation: (a) is necessary to secure compliance with measures that are not inconsistent with this Chapter; and (b) is not applied in a manner that would constitute a disguised restriction on trade.

4. No Party shall have any obligation under this Article with respect to procedures provided in multilateral agreements concluded under the auspices of the World Intellectual Property Organization relating to the acquisition or maintenance of intellectual property rights.

Article 1704: Control of Abusive or Anticompetitive Practices or Conditions

Nothing in this Chapter shall prevent a Party from specifying in its domestic law licensing practices or conditions that may in particular cases constitute an abuse of intellectual property rights having an adverse effect on competition in the relevant market. A Party may adopt or maintain, consistent with the other provisions of this Agreement, appropriate measures to prevent or control such practices or conditions.

Article 1705: Copyright

1. Each Party shall protect the works covered by Article 2 of the Berne Convention, including any other works that embody original expression within the meaning of that Convention. In particular: (a) all types of computer programs are literary works within the meaning of the Berne Convention and each Party shall protect them as such; and (b) compilations of data or other material, whether in machine readable or other form, which by reason of the selection or arrangement of their contents constitute intellectual creations, shall be protected as such. The protection a Party provides under subparagraph (b) shall not extend to the data or material itself, or prejudice any copyright subsisting in that data or material.

2. Each Party shall provide to authors and their successors in interest those rights enumerated in the Berne Convention in respect of works covered by paragraph 1, including the right to authorize or prohibit: (a) the importation into the Party's territory of copies of the work made without the right holder's authorization; (b) the first public distribution of the original and each copy of the work by sale, rental or otherwise; (c) the communication of a work to the public; and (d) the commercial rental of the original or a copy of a computer program. Subparagraph (d) shall not apply where the copy of the computer program is not itself an essential object of the rental. Each Party shall provide that putting the original or a copy of a computer program on the market with the right holder's consent shall not exhaust the rental right.

3. Each Party shall provide that for copyright and related rights: (a) any person acquiring or holding economic rights may freely and separately transfer such rights by contract for purposes of their exploitation and enjoyment by the transferee; and (b) any person acquiring or holding such economic rights by virtue of a contract, including contracts of employment underlying the creation of works and sound recordings, shall be able to exercise those rights in its own name and enjoy fully the benefits derived from those rights.

4. Each Party shall provide that, where the term of protection of a work, other than a photographic work or a work of applied art, is to be calculated on a basis other than the life of a natural person, the term shall be not less than 50 years from the end of the calendar year of the first authorized publication of the work or, failing such authorized publication within 50 years from the making of the work, 50 years from the end of the calendar year of making.

5. Each Party shall confine limitations or exceptions to the rights provided for in this Article to certain special cases that do not conflict with a normal exploitation of the work and do not unreasonably prejudice the legitimate interests of the right holder.

6. No Party may grant translation and reproduction licenses permitted under the Appendix to the Berne Convention where legitimate needs in that Party's territory for copies or translations of the work could be met by the right holder's voluntary actions but for obstacles created by the Party's measures.

7. Annex 1705.7 applies to the Parties specified in that Annex.

Annex 1705.7

Copyright

The United States shall provide protection to motion pictures produced in another Party's territory that have been declared to be in the public domain pursuant to 17 U.S.C. section 405. This obligation shall apply to the extent that it is consistent with the Constitution of the United States, and is subject to budgetary considerations.

Article 1706: Sound Recordings

1. Each Party shall provide to the producer of a sound recording the right to authorize or prohibit: (a) the direct or indirect reproduction of the sound recording; (b) the importation into the Party's territory of copies of the sound recording made without the producer's authorization; (c) the first public distribution of the original and each copy of the sound recording by sale, rental or otherwise; and (d) the commercial rental of the original or a copy of the sound recording, except where expressly otherwise provided in a contract between the producer of the sound recording and the authors of the works fixed therein. Each Party shall provide that putting the original or a copy of a sound recording on the market with the right holder's consent shall not exhaust the rental right.

2. Each Party shall provide a term of protection for sound recordings of at least 50 years from the end of the calendar year in which the fixation was made.

3. Each Party shall confine limitations or exceptions to the rights provided for in this Article to certain special cases that do not conflict with a normal exploitation of the sound recording and do not unreasonably prejudice the legitimate interests of the right holder.

Article 1707: Protection of Encrypted Program–Carrying Satellite Signals

Within one year from the date of entry into force of this Agreement, each Party shall make it: (a) a criminal offense to manufacture, import, sell, lease or otherwise make available a device or system that is primarily of assistance in decoding an encrypted program-carrying satellite signal without the authorization of the lawful distributor of such signal; and (b) a civil offense to receive, in connection with commercial activities, or further distribute, an encrypted program-carrying satellite signal that has been decoded without the authorization of the lawful distributor of the signal or to engage in any activity prohibited under subparagraph (a). Each Party shall provide that any civil offense established under subparagraph (b) shall be actionable by any person that holds an interest in the content of such signal.

Article 1708: Trademarks

1. For purposes of this Agreement, a trademark consists of any sign, or any combination of signs, capable of distinguishing the goods or services of one person from those of another, including personal names, designs, letters, numerals, colors, figurative elements, or the shape of goods or of their packaging. Trademarks shall include service marks and collective marks, and may include certification marks. A Party may require, as a condition for registration, that a sign be visually perceptible.

2. Each Party shall provide to the owner of a registered trademark the right to prevent all persons not having the owner's consent from using in commerce identical or similar signs for goods or services that are identical or similar to those goods or services in respect of which the owner's trademark is registered, where such use would result in a likelihood of confusion. In the case of the use of an identical sign for identical goods or services, a likelihood of confusion shall be presumed. The rights described above shall not prejudice any prior rights, nor shall they affect the possibility of a Party making rights available on the basis of use.

3. A Party may make registrability depend on use. However, actual use of a trademark shall not be a condition for filing an application for registration. No Party may refuse an application solely on the ground that intended use has not taken place before the expiry of a period of three years from the date of application for registration.

4. Each Party shall provide a system for the registration of trademarks, which shall include: (a) examination of applications; (b) notice to be given to an applicant of the reasons for the refusal to register a trademark; (c) a reasonable opportunity for the applicant to respond to the notice; (d) publication of each trademark either before or promptly after it is registered; and (e) a reasonable opportunity for interested persons to petition to cancel the registration of a trademark. A Party may provide for a reasonable opportunity for interested persons to oppose the registration of a trademark.

5. The nature of the goods or services to which a trademark is to be applied shall in no case form an obstacle to the registration of the trademark.

6. Article 6bis of the Paris Convention shall apply, with such modifications as may be necessary, to services. In determining whether a trademark is well-known, account shall be taken of the knowledge of the trademark in the relevant sector of the public, including knowledge in

the Party's territory obtained as a result of the promotion of the trademark. No Party may require that the reputation of the trademark extend beyond the sector of the public that normally deals with the relevant goods or services.

7.   Each Party shall provide that the initial registration of a trademark be for a term of at least 10 years and that the registration be indefinitely renewable for terms of not less than 10 years when conditions for renewal have been met.

8.   Each Party shall require the use of a trademark to maintain a registration. The registration may be canceled for the reason of non-use only after an uninterrupted period of at least two years of non-use, unless valid reasons based on the existence of obstacles to such use are shown by the trademark owner. Each Party shall recognize, as valid reasons for non-use, circumstances arising independently of the will of the trademark owner that constitute an obstacle to the use of the trademark, such as import restrictions on, or other government requirements for, goods or services identified by the trademark.

9.   Each Party shall recognize use of a trademark by a person other than the trademark owner, where such use is subject to the owner's control, as use of the trademark for purposes of maintaining the registration.

10.   No Party may encumber the use of a trademark in commerce by special requirements, such as a use that reduces the trademark's function as an indication of source or a use with another trademark.

11.   A Party may determine conditions on the licensing and assignment of trademarks, it being understood that the compulsory licensing of trademarks shall not be permitted and that the owner of a registered trademark shall have the right to assign its trademark with or without the transfer of the business to which the trademark belongs.

12.   A Party may provide limited exceptions to the rights conferred by a trademark, such as fair use of descriptive terms, provided that such exceptions take into account the legitimate interests of the trademark owner and of other persons.

13.   Each Party shall prohibit the registration as a trademark of words, at least in English, French or Spanish, that generically designate goods or services or types of goods or services to which the trademark applies.

14.   Each Party shall refuse to register trademarks that consist of or comprise immoral, deceptive or scandalous matter, or matter that may disparage or falsely suggest a connection with persons, living or dead, institutions, beliefs or any Party's national symbols, or bring them into contempt or disrepute.

Article 1709: Patents

1.   Subject to paragraphs 2 and 3, each Party shall make patents available for any inventions, whether products or processes, in all fields of technology, provided that such inventions are new, result from an inventive step and are capable of industrial application. For purposes of this Article, a Party may deem the terms "inventive step" and "capable of industrial application" to be synonymous with the terms "non-obvious" and "useful", respectively.

2.   A Party may exclude from patentability inventions if preventing in its territory the commercial exploitation of the inventions is necessary to protect ordre public or morality, including to protect human, animal or plant life or health or to avoid serious prejudice to nature or the environment, provided that the exclusion is not based solely on the ground that the Party prohibits commercial exploitation in its territory of the subject matter of the patent.

3.   A Party may also exclude from patentability: (a) diagnostic, therapeutic and surgical methods for the treatment of humans or animals; (b) plants and animals other than microorganisms; and (c) essentially biological processes for the production of plants or animals, other than non-biological and microbiological processes for such production. Notwithstanding subparagraph (b), each Party shall provide for the protection of plant varieties through patents, an effective scheme of sui generis protection, or both.

4.   If a Party has not made available product patent protection for pharmaceutical or agricultural chemicals commensurate with paragraph 1: (a) as of January 1, 1992, for subject matter that relates to naturally occurring substances prepared or produced by, or significantly derived from, microbiological processes and intended for food or medicine, and (b) as of July 1, 1991, for any other subject matter, that Party shall provide to the inventor of any such product or its assignee the means to obtain product patent protection for such product for the unexpired term of the patent for such product granted in another Party, as long as the product has not been marketed in the Party providing protection under this paragraph and the person seeking such protection makes a timely request.

5.   Each Party shall provide that: (a) where the subject matter of a patent is a product, the patent shall confer on the patent owner the right to prevent other persons from making, using or selling the subject matter of the patent, without the patent owner's consent; and (b) where the subject matter of a patent is a process, the patent shall confer on the patent owner the right to prevent other persons from using that process and from using, selling, or importing at least the product obtained directly by that process, without the patent owner's consent.

6.   A Party may provide limited exceptions to the exclusive rights conferred by a patent, provided that such exceptions do not unreason-

ably conflict with a normal exploitation of the patent and do not unreasonably prejudice the legitimate interests of the patent owner, taking into account the legitimate interests of other persons.

7. Subject to paragraphs 2 and 3, patents shall be available and patent rights enjoyable without discrimination as to the field of technology, the territory of the Party where the invention was made and whether products are imported or locally produced.

8. A Party may revoke a patent only when: (a) grounds exist that would have justified a refusal to grant the patent; or (b) the grant of a compulsory license has not remedied the lack of exploitation of the patent.

9. Each Party shall permit patent owners to assign and transfer by succession their patents, and to conclude licensing contracts.

10. Where the law of a Party allows for use of the subject matter of a patent, other than that use allowed under paragraph 6, without the authorization of the right holder, including use by the government or other persons authorized by the government, the Party shall respect the following provisions: (a) authorization of such use shall be considered on its individual merits; (b) such use may only be permitted if, prior to such use, the proposed user has made efforts to obtain authorization from the right holder on reasonable commercial terms and conditions and such efforts have not been successful within a reasonable period of time. The requirement to make such efforts may be waived by a Party in the case of a national emergency or other circumstances of extreme urgency or in cases of public non-commercial use. In situations of national emergency or other circumstances of extreme urgency, the right holder shall, nevertheless, be notified as soon as reasonably practicable. In the case of public non-commercial use, where the government or contractor, without making a patent search, knows or has demonstrable grounds to know that a valid patent is or will be used by or for the government, the right holder shall be informed promptly; (c) the scope and duration of such use shall be limited to the purpose for which it was authorized; (d) such use shall be non-exclusive; (e) such use shall be non-assignable, except with that part of the enterprise or goodwill that enjoys such use; (f) any such use shall be authorized predominantly for the supply of the Party's domestic market; (g) authorization for such use shall be liable, subject to adequate protection of the legitimate interests of the persons so authorized, to be terminated if and when the circumstances that led to it cease to exist and are unlikely to recur. The competent authority shall have the authority to review, on motivated request, the continued existence of these circumstances; (h) the right holder shall be paid adequate remuneration in the circumstances of each case, taking into account the economic value of the authorization; (i) the legal validity of any decision relating to the authorization shall be subject to judicial or other independent review by a distinct higher authority; (j) any decision relating to the remuneration provided in respect of such use shall be subject to judicial or other independent review by a distinct higher authority; (k) the Party

shall not be obliged to apply the conditions set out in subparagraphs (b) and (f) where such use is permitted to remedy a practice determined after judicial or administrative process to be anticompetitive. The need to correct anticompetitive practices may be taken into account in determining the amount of remuneration in such cases. Competent authorities shall have the authority to refuse termination of authorization if and when the conditions that led to such authorization are likely to recur; (*l*) the Party shall not authorize the use of the subject matter of a patent to permit the exploitation of another patent except as a remedy for an adjudicated violation of domestic laws regarding anticompetitive practices.

11.   Where the subject matter of a patent is a process for obtaining a product, each Party shall, in any infringement proceeding, place on the defendant the burden of establishing that the allegedly infringing product was made by a process other than the patented process in one of the following situations: (a) the product obtained by the patented process is new; or (b) a substantial likelihood exists that the allegedly infringing product was made by the process and the patent owner has been unable through reasonable efforts to determine the process actually used. In the gathering and evaluation of evidence, the legitimate interests of the defendant in protecting its trade secrets shall be taken into account.

12.   Each Party shall provide a term of protection for patents of at least 20 years from the date of filing or 17 years from the date of grant. A Party may extend the term of patent protection, in appropriate cases, to compensate for delays caused by regulatory approval processes.

Article 1710: Layout Designs of Semiconductor Integrated Circuits

1.   Each Party shall protect layout designs (topographies) of integrated circuits ("layout designs") in accordance with Articles 2 through 7, 12 and 16(3), other than Article 6(3), of the Treaty on Intellectual Property in Respect of Integrated Circuits as opened for signature on May 26, 1989.

2.   Subject to paragraph 3, each Party shall make it unlawful for any person without the right holder's authorization to import, sell or otherwise distribute for commercial purposes any of the following: (a) a protected layout design; (b) an integrated circuit in which a protected layout design is incorporated; or (c) an article incorporating such an integrated circuit, only insofar as it continues to contain an unlawfully reproduced layout design.

3.   No Party may make unlawful any of the acts referred to in paragraph 2 performed in respect of an integrated circuit that incorporates an unlawfully reproduced layout design, or any article that incorporates such an integrated circuit, where the person performing those acts or ordering those acts to be done did not know and had no reasonable ground to know, when it acquired the integrated circuit or article

incorporating such an integrated circuit, that it incorporated an unlawfully reproduced layout design.

4. Each Party shall provide that, after the person referred to in paragraph 3 has received sufficient notice that the layout design was unlawfully reproduced, such person may perform any of the acts with respect to the stock on hand or ordered before such notice, but shall be liable to pay the right holder for doing so an amount equivalent to a reasonable royalty such as would be payable under a freely negotiated license in respect of such a layout design.

5. No Party may permit the compulsory licensing of layout designs of integrated circuits.

6. Any Party that requires registration as a condition for protection of a layout design shall provide that the term of protection shall not end before the expiration of a period of 10 years counted from the date of: (a) filing of the application for registration; or (b) the first commercial exploitation of the layout design, wherever in the world it occurs.

7. Where a Party does not require registration as a condition for protection of a layout design, the Party shall provide a term of protection of not less than 10 years from the date of the first commercial exploitation of the layout design, wherever in the world it occurs.

8. Notwithstanding paragraphs 6 and 7, a Party may provide that the protection shall lapse 15 years after the creation of the layout design.

9. Annex 1710.9 applies to the Parties specified in that Annex.

Annex 1710.9

Layout Designs

Mexico shall make every effort to implement the requirements of Article 1710 as soon as possible, and shall do so no later than four years after the date of entry into force of this Agreement.

Article 1711: Trade Secrets

1. Each Party shall provide the legal means for any person to prevent trade secrets from being disclosed to, acquired by, or used by others without the consent of the person lawfully in control of the information in a manner contrary to honest commercial practices, in so far as: (a) the information is secret in the sense that it is not, as a body or in the precise configuration and assembly of its components, generally known among or readily accessible to persons that normally deal with the kind of information in question; (b) the information has actual or potential commercial value because it is secret; and (c) the person lawfully in control of the information has taken reasonable steps under the circumstances to keep it secret.

2. A Party may require that to qualify for protection a trade secret must be evidenced in documents, electronic or magnetic means, optical discs, microfilms, films or other similar instruments.

3.   No Party may limit the duration of protection for trade secrets, so long as the conditions in paragraph 1 exist.

4.   No Party may discourage or impede the voluntary licensing of trade secrets by imposing excessive or discriminatory conditions on such licenses or conditions that dilute the value of the trade secrets.

5.   If a Party requires, as a condition for approving the marketing of pharmaceutical or agricultural chemical products that utilize new chemical entities, the submission of undisclosed test or other data necessary to determine whether the use of such products is safe and effective, the Party shall protect against disclosure of the data of persons making such submissions, where the origination of such data involves considerable effort, except where the disclosure is necessary to protect the public or unless steps are taken to ensure that the data is protected against unfair commercial use.

6.   Each Party shall provide that for data subject to paragraph 5 that are submitted to the Party after the date of entry into force of this Agreement, no person other than the person that submitted them may, without the latter's permission, rely on such data in support of an application for product approval during a reasonable period of time after their submission. For this purpose, a reasonable period shall normally mean not less than five years from the date on which the Party granted approval to the person that produced the data for approval to market its product, taking account of the nature of the data and the person's efforts and expenditures in producing them. Subject to this provision, there shall be no limitation on any Party to implement abbreviated approval procedures for such products on the basis of bioequivalence and bioavailability studies.

7.   Where a Party relies on a marketing approval granted by another Party, the reasonable period of exclusive use of the data submitted in connection with obtaining the approval relied on shall begin with the date of the first marketing approval relied on.

Article 1712: Geographical Indications

1.   Each Party shall provide, in respect of geographical indications, the legal means for interested persons to prevent: (a) the use of any means in the designation or presentation of a good that indicates or suggests that the good in question originates in a territory, region or locality other than the true place of origin, in a manner that misleads the public as to the geographical origin of the good; (b) any use that constitutes an act of unfair competition within the meaning of Article 10bis of the Paris Convention.

2.   Each Party shall, on its own initiative if its domestic law so permits or at the request of an interested person, refuse to register, or invalidate the registration of, a trademark containing or consisting of a geographical indication with respect to goods that do not originate in the indicated territory, region or locality, if use of the indication in the

trademark for such goods is of such a nature as to mislead the public as to the geographical origin of the good.

3. Each Party shall also apply paragraphs 1 and 2 to a geographical indication that, although correctly indicating the territory, region or locality in which the goods originate, falsely represents to the public that the goods originate in another territory, region or locality.

4. Nothing in this Article shall be construed to require a Party to prevent continued and similar use of a particular geographical indication of another Party in connection with goods or services by any of its nationals or domiciliaries who have used that geographical indication in a continuous manner with regard to the same or related goods or services in that Party's territory, either: (a) for at least 10 years, or (b) in good faith, before the date of signature of this Agreement.

5. Where a trademark has been applied for or registered in good faith, or where rights to a trademark have been acquired through use in good faith, either: (a) before the date of application of these provisions in that Party, or (b) before the geographical indication is protected in its Party of origin, no Party may adopt any measure to implement this Article that prejudices eligibility for, or the validity of, the registration of a trademark, or the right to use a trademark, on the basis that such a trademark is identical with, or similar to, a geographical indication.

6. No Party shall be required to apply this Article to a geographical indication if it is identical to the customary term in common language in that Party's territory for the goods or services to which the indication applies.

7. A Party may provide that any request made under this Article in connection with the use or registration of a trademark must be presented within five years after the adverse use of the protected indication has become generally known in that Party or after the date of registration of the trademark in that Party, provided that the trademark has been published by that date, if such date is earlier than the date on which the adverse use became generally known in that Party, provided that the geographical indication is not used or registered in bad faith.

8. No Party shall adopt any measure implementing this Article that would prejudice any person's right to use, in the course of trade, its name or the name of its predecessor in business, except where such name forms all or part of a valid trademark in existence before the geographical indication became protected and with which there is a likelihood of confusion, or such name is used in such a manner as to mislead the public.

9. Nothing in this Chapter shall be construed to require a Party to protect a geographical indication that is not protected, or has fallen into disuse, in the Party of origin.

Article 1713: Industrial Designs

1. Each Party shall provide for the protection of independently created industrial designs that are new or original. A Party may provide that: (a) designs are not new or original if they do not significantly differ from known designs or combinations of known design features; and (b) such protection shall not extend to designs dictated essentially by technical or functional considerations.

2. Each Party shall ensure that the requirements for securing protection for textile designs, in particular in regard to any cost, examination or publication, do not unreasonably impair a person's opportunity to seek and obtain such protection. A Party may comply with this obligation through industrial design law or copyright law.

3. Each Party shall provide the owner of a protected industrial design the right to prevent other persons not having the owner's consent from making or selling articles bearing or embodying a design that is a copy, or substantially a copy, of the protected design, when such acts are undertaken for commercial purposes.

4. A Party may provide limited exceptions to the protection of industrial designs, provided that such exceptions do not unreasonably conflict with the normal exploitation of protected industrial designs and do not unreasonably prejudice the legitimate interests of the owner of the protected design, taking into account the legitimate interests of other persons.

5. Each Party shall provide a term of protection for industrial designs of at least 10 years.

Article 1714: Enforcement of Intellectual Property Rights: General Provisions

1. Each Party shall ensure that enforcement procedures, as specified in this Article and Articles 1715 through 1718, are available under its domestic law so as to permit effective action to be taken against any act of infringement of intellectual property rights covered by this Chapter, including expeditious remedies to prevent infringements and remedies to deter further infringements. Such enforcement procedures shall be applied so as to avoid the creation of barriers to legitimate trade and to provide for safeguards against abuse of the procedures.

2. Each Party shall ensure that its procedures for the enforcement of intellectual property rights are fair and equitable, are not unnecessarily complicated or costly, and do not entail unreasonable time-limits or unwarranted delays.

3. Each Party shall provide that decisions on the merits of a case in judicial and administrative enforcement proceedings shall: (a) preferably be in writing and preferably state the reasons on which the decisions are based; (b) be made available at least to the parties in a proceeding

without undue delay; and (c) be based only on evidence in respect of which such parties were offered the opportunity to be heard.

4. Each Party shall ensure that parties in a proceeding have an opportunity to have final administrative decisions reviewed by a judicial authority of that Party and, subject to jurisdictional provisions in its domestic laws concerning the importance of a case, to have reviewed at least the legal aspects of initial judicial decisions on the merits of a case. Notwithstanding the above, no Party shall be required to provide for judicial review of acquittals in criminal cases.

5. Nothing in this Article or Articles 1715 through 1718 shall be construed to require a Party to establish a judicial system for the enforcement of intellectual property rights distinct from that Party's system for the enforcement of laws in general.

6. For the purposes of Articles 1715 through 1718, the term "right holder" includes federations and associations having legal standing to assert such rights.

Article 1715: Specific Procedural and Remedial Aspects of Civil and Administrative Procedures

1. Each Party shall make available to right holders civil judicial procedures for the enforcement of any intellectual property right provided in this Chapter. Each Party shall provide that: (a) defendants have the right to written notice that is timely and contains sufficient detail, including the basis of the claims; (b) parties in a proceeding are allowed to be represented by independent legal counsel; (c) the procedures do not include imposition of overly burdensome requirements concerning mandatory personal appearances; (d) all parties in a proceeding are duly entitled to substantiate their claims and to present relevant evidence; and (e) the procedures include a means to identify and protect confidential information.

2. Each Party shall provide that its judicial authorities shall have the authority: (a) where a party in a proceeding has presented reasonably available evidence sufficient to support its claims and has specified evidence relevant to the substantiation of its claims that is within the control of the opposing party, to order the opposing party to produce such evidence, subject in appropriate cases to conditions that ensure the protection of confidential information; (b) where a party in a proceeding voluntarily and without good reason refuses access to, or otherwise does not provide relevant evidence under that party's control within a reasonable period, or significantly impedes a proceeding relating to an enforcement action, to make preliminary and final determinations, affirmative or negative, on the basis of the evidence presented, including the complaint or the allegation presented by the party adversely affected by the denial of access to evidence, subject to providing the parties an opportunity to be heard on the allegations or evidence; (c) to order a party in a proceeding to desist from an infringement, including to

prevent the entry into the channels of commerce in their jurisdiction of imported goods that involve the infringement of an intellectual property right, which order shall be enforceable at least immediately after customs clearance of such goods; (d) to order the infringer of an intellectual property right to pay the right holder damages adequate to compensate for the injury the right holder has suffered because of the infringement where the infringer knew or had reasonable grounds to know that it was engaged in an infringing activity; (e) to order an infringer of an intellectual property right to pay the right holder's expenses, which may include appropriate attorney's fees; and (f) to order a party in a proceeding at whose request measures were taken and who has abused enforcement procedures to provide adequate compensation to any party wrongfully enjoined or restrained in the proceeding for the injury suffered because of such abuse and to pay that party's expenses, which may include appropriate attorney's fees.

3.   With respect to the authority referred to in subparagraph 2(c), no Party shall be obliged to provide such authority in respect of protected subject matter that is acquired or ordered by a person before that person knew or had reasonable grounds to know that dealing in that subject matter would entail the infringement of an intellectual property right.

4.   With respect to the authority referred to in subparagraph 2(d), a Party may, at least with respect to copyrighted works and sound recordings, authorize the judicial authorities to order recovery of profits or payment of pre-established damages, or both, even where the infringer did not know or had no reasonable grounds to know that it was engaged in an infringing activity.

5.   Each Party shall provide that, in order to create an effective deterrent to infringement, its judicial authorities shall have the authority to order that: (a) goods that they have found to be infringing be, without compensation of any sort, disposed of outside the channels of commerce in such a manner as to avoid any injury caused to the right holder or, unless this would be contrary to existing constitutional requirements, destroyed; and (b) materials and implements the predominant use of which has been in the creation of the infringing goods be, without compensation of any sort, disposed of outside the channels of commerce in such a manner as to minimize the risks of further infringements. In considering whether to issue such an order, judicial authorities shall take into account the need for proportionality between the seriousness of the infringement and the remedies ordered as well as the interests of other persons. In regard to counterfeit goods, the simple removal of the trademark unlawfully affixed shall not be sufficient, other than in exceptional cases, to permit release of the goods into the channels of commerce.

6.   In respect of the administration of any law pertaining to the protection or enforcement of intellectual property rights, each Party shall only exempt both public authorities and officials from liability to

appropriate remedial measures where actions are taken or intended in good faith in the course of the administration of such laws.

7. Notwithstanding the other provisions of Articles 1714 through 1718, where a Party is sued with respect to an infringement of an intellectual property right as a result of its use of that right or use on its behalf, that Party may limit the remedies available against it to the payment to the right holder of adequate remuneration in the circumstances of each case, taking into account the economic value of the use.

8. Each Party shall provide that, where a civil remedy can be ordered as a result of administrative procedures on the merits of a case, such procedures shall conform to principles equivalent in substance to those set out in this Article.

Article 1716: Provisional Measures

1. Each Party shall provide that its judicial authorities shall have the authority to order prompt and effective provisional measures: (a) to prevent an infringement of any intellectual property right, and in particular to prevent the entry into the channels of commerce in their jurisdiction of allegedly infringing goods, including measures to prevent the entry of imported goods at least immediately after customs clearance; and (b) to preserve relevant evidence in regard to the alleged infringement.

2. Each Party shall provide that its judicial authorities shall have the authority to require any applicant for provisional measures to provide to the judicial authorities any evidence reasonably available to that applicant that the judicial authorities consider necessary to enable them to determine with a sufficient degree of certainty whether: (a) the applicant is the right holder; (b) the applicant's right is being infringed or such infringement is imminent; and (c) any delay in the issuance of such measures is likely to cause irreparable harm to the right holder, or there is a demonstrable risk of evidence being destroyed. Each Party shall provide that its judicial authorities shall have the authority to require the applicant to provide a security or equivalent assurance sufficient to protect the interests of the defendant and to prevent abuse.

3. Each Party shall provide that its judicial authorities shall have the authority to require an applicant for provisional measures to provide other information necessary for the identification of the relevant goods by the authority that will execute the provisional measures.

4. Each Party shall provide that its judicial authorities shall have the authority to order provisional measures on an ex parte basis, in particular where any delay is likely to cause irreparable harm to the right holder, or where there is a demonstrable risk of evidence being destroyed.

5. Each Party shall provide that where provisional measures are adopted by that Party's judicial authorities on an ex parte basis: (a) a

person affected shall be given notice of those measures without delay but in any event no later than immediately after the execution of the measures; (b) a defendant shall, on request, have those measures reviewed by that Party's judicial authorities for the purpose of deciding, within a reasonable period after notice of those measures is given, whether the measures shall be modified, revoked or confirmed, and shall be given an opportunity to be heard in the review proceedings.

6.   Without prejudice to paragraph 5, each Party shall provide that, on the request of the defendant, the Party's judicial authorities shall revoke or otherwise cease to apply the provisional measures taken on the basis of paragraphs 1 and 4 if proceedings leading to a decision on the merits are not initiated: (a) within a reasonable period as determined by the judicial authority ordering the measures where the Party's domestic law so permits; or (b) in the absence of such a determination, within a period of no more than 20 working days or 31 calendar days, whichever is longer.

7.   Each Party shall provide that, where the provisional measures are revoked or where they lapse due to any act or omission by the applicant, or where the judicial authorities subsequently find that there has been no infringement or threat of infringement of an intellectual property right, the judicial authorities shall have the authority to order the applicant, on request of the defendant, to provide the defendant appropriate compensation for any injury caused by these measures.

8.   Each Party shall provide that, where a provisional measure can be ordered as a result of administrative procedures, such procedures shall conform to principles equivalent in substance to those set out in this Article.

Article 1717: Criminal Procedures and Penalties

1.   Each Party shall provide criminal procedures and penalties to be applied at least in cases of willful trademark counterfeiting or copyright piracy on a commercial scale. Each Party shall provide that penalties available include imprisonment or monetary fines, or both, sufficient to provide a deterrent, consistent with the level of penalties applied for crimes of a corresponding gravity.

2.   Each Party shall provide that, in appropriate cases, its judicial authorities may order the seizure, forfeiture and destruction of infringing goods and of any materials and implements the predominant use of which has been in the commission of the offense.

3.   A Party may provide criminal procedures and penalties to be applied in cases of infringement of intellectual property rights, other than those in paragraph 1, where they are committed wilfully and on a commercial scale.

Article 1718: Enforcement of Intellectual Property Rights at the Border

1.   Each Party shall, in conformity with this Article, adopt procedures to enable a right holder, who has valid grounds for suspecting that the importation of counterfeit trademark goods or pirated copyright goods may take place, to lodge an application in writing with its competent authorities, whether administrative or judicial, for the suspension by the customs administration of the release of such goods into free circulation. No Party shall be obligated to apply such procedures to goods in transit. A Party may permit such an application to be made in respect of goods that involve other infringements of intellectual property rights, provided that the requirements of this Article are met. A Party may also provide for corresponding procedures concerning the suspension by the customs administration of the release of infringing goods destined for exportation from its territory.

2.   Each Party shall require any applicant who initiates procedures under paragraph 1 to provide adequate evidence: (a) to satisfy that Party's competent authorities that, under the domestic laws of the country of importation, there is prima facie an infringement of its intellectual property right; and (b) to supply a sufficiently detailed description of the goods to make them readily recognizable by the customs administration. The competent authorities shall inform the applicant within a reasonable period whether they have accepted the application and, if so, the period for which the customs administration will take action.

3.   Each Party shall provide that its competent authorities shall have the authority to require an applicant under paragraph 1 to provide a security or equivalent assurance sufficient to protect the defendant and the competent authorities and to prevent abuse. Such security or equivalent assurance shall not unreasonably deter recourse to these procedures.

4.   Each Party shall provide that, where pursuant to an application under procedures adopted pursuant to this Article, its customs administration suspends the release of goods involving industrial designs, patents, integrated circuits or trade secrets into free circulation on the basis of a decision other than by a judicial or other independent authority, and the period provided for in paragraphs 6 through 8 has expired without the granting of provisional relief by the duly empowered authority, and provided that all other conditions for importation have been complied with, the owner, importer or consignee of such goods shall be entitled to their release on the posting of a security in an amount sufficient to protect the right holder against any infringement. Payment of such security shall not prejudice any other remedy available to the right holder, it being understood that the security shall be released if the right holder fails to pursue its right of action within a reasonable period of time.

5. Each Party shall provide that its customs administration shall promptly notify the importer and the applicant when the customs administration suspends the release of goods pursuant to paragraph 1.

6. Each Party shall provide that its customs administration shall release goods from suspension if, within a period not exceeding 10 working days after the applicant under paragraph 1 has been served notice of the suspension, the customs administration has not been informed that: (a) a party other than the defendant has initiated proceedings leading to a decision on the merits of the case, or (b) a competent authority has taken provisional measures prolonging the suspension, provided that all other conditions for importation or exportation have been met. Each Party shall provide that, in appropriate cases, the customs administration may extend the suspension by another 10 working days.

7. Each Party shall provide that if proceedings leading to a decision on the merits of the case have been initiated, a review, including a right to be heard, shall take place on request of the defendant with a view to deciding, within a reasonable period, whether these measures shall be modified, revoked or confirmed.

8. Notwithstanding paragraphs 6 and 7, where the suspension of the release of goods is carried out or continued in accordance with a provisional judicial measure, Article 1716(6) shall apply.

9. Each Party shall provide that its competent authorities shall have the authority to order the applicant under paragraph 1 to pay the importer, the consignee and the owner of the goods appropriate compensation for any injury caused to them through the wrongful detention of goods or through the detention of goods released pursuant to paragraph 6.

10. Without prejudice to the protection of confidential information, each Party shall provide that its competent authorities shall have the authority to give the right holder sufficient opportunity to have any goods detained by the customs administration inspected in order to substantiate the right holder's claims. Each Party shall also provide that its competent authorities have the authority to give the importer an equivalent opportunity to have any such goods inspected. Where the competent authorities have made a positive determination on the merits of a case, a Party may provide the competent authorities the authority to inform the right holder of the names and addresses of the consignor, the importer and the consignee, and of the quantity of the goods in question.

11. Where a Party requires its competent authorities to act on their own initiative and to suspend the release of goods in respect of which they have acquired prima facie evidence that an intellectual property right is being infringed: (a) the competent authorities may at any time seek from the right holder any information that may assist them to exercise these powers; (b) the importer and the right holder shall be promptly notified of the suspension by the Party's competent authorities, and where the importer lodges an appeal against the suspen-

sion with competent authorities, the suspension shall be subject to the conditions, with such modifications as may be necessary, set out in paragraphs 6 through 8; and (c) the Party shall only exempt both public authorities and officials from liability to appropriate remedial measures where actions are taken or intended in good faith.

12. Without prejudice to other rights of action open to the right holder and subject to the defendant's right to seek judicial review, each Party shall provide that its competent authorities shall have the authority to order the destruction or disposal of infringing goods in accordance with the principles set out in Article 1715(5). In regard to counterfeit goods, the authorities shall not allow the re-exportation of the infringing goods in an unaltered state or subject them to a different customs procedure, other than in exceptional circumstances.

13. A Party may exclude from the application of paragraphs 1 through 12 small quantities of goods of a non-commercial nature contained in travellers' personal luggage or sent in small consignments that are not repetitive.

14. Annex 1718.14 applies to the Parties specified in that Annex.

Annex 1718.14

Enforcement of Intellectual Property Rights

Mexico shall make every effort to comply with the requirements of Article 1718 as soon as possible and shall do so no later than three years after the date of signature of this Agreement.

Article 1719: Cooperation and Technical Assistance

1. The Parties shall provide each other on mutually agreed terms with technical assistance and shall promote cooperation between their competent authorities. Such cooperation shall include the training of personnel.

2. The Parties shall cooperate with a view to eliminating trade in goods that infringe intellectual property rights. For this purpose, each Party shall establish and notify the other Parties by January 1, 1994 of contact points in its federal government and shall exchange information concerning trade in infringing goods.

Article 1720: Protection of Existing Subject Matter

1. Except as required under Article 1705(7), this Agreement does not give rise to obligations in respect of acts that occurred before the date of application of the relevant provisions of this Agreement for the Party in question.

2. Except as otherwise provided for in this Agreement, each Party shall apply this Agreement to all subject matter existing on the date of application of the relevant provisions of this Agreement for the Party in

question and that is protected in a Party on such date, or that meets or subsequently meets the criteria for protection under the terms of this Chapter. In respect of this paragraph and paragraphs 3 and 4, a Party's obligations with respect to existing works shall be solely determined under Article 18 of the Berne Convention and with respect to the rights of producers of sound recordings in existing sound recordings shall be determined solely under Article 18 of that Convention, as made applicable under this Agreement.

3.   Except as required under Article 1705(7), and notwithstanding the first sentence of paragraph 2, no Party may be required to restore protection to subject matter that, on the date of application of the relevant provisions of this Agreement for the Party in question, has fallen into the public domain in its territory.

4.   In respect of any acts relating to specific objects embodying protected subject matter that become infringing under the terms of laws in conformity with this Agreement, and that were begun or in respect of which a significant investment was made, before the date of entry into force of this Agreement for that Party, any Party may provide for a limitation of the remedies available to the right holder as to the continued performance of such acts after the date of application of this Agreement for that Party. In such cases, the Party shall, however, at least provide for payment of equitable remuneration.

5. No Party shall be obliged to apply Article 1705(2)(d) or 1706(1)(d) with respect to originals or copies purchased prior to the date of application of the relevant provisions of this Agreement for that Party.

6. No Party shall be required to apply Article 1709(10), or the requirement in Article 1709(7) that patent rights shall be enjoyable without discrimination as to the field of technology, to use without the authorization of the right holder where authorization for such use was granted by the government before the text of the Draft Final Act Embodying the Results of the Uruguay Round of Multilateral Trade Negotiations became known.

7.   In the case of intellectual property rights for which protection is conditional on registration, applications for protection that are pending on the date of application of the relevant provisions of this Agreement for the Party in question shall be permitted to be amended to claim any enhanced protection provided under this Agreement. Such amendments shall not include new matter.

Article 1721: Definitions

1.   For purposes of this Chapter:

confidential information includes trade secrets, privileged information and other materials exempted from disclosure under the Party's domestic law.

2.   For purposes of this Agreement:

encrypted program-carrying satellite signal means a program-carrying satellite signal that is transmitted in a form whereby the aural or visual characteristics, or both, are modified or altered for the purpose of preventing the unauthorized reception, by persons without the authorized equipment that is designed to eliminate the effects of such modification or alteration, of a program carried in that signal;

geographical indication means any indication that identifies a good as originating in the territory of a Party, or a region or locality in that territory, where a particular quality, reputation or other characteristic of the good is essentially attributable to its geographical origin;

in a manner contrary to honest commercial practices means at least practices such as breach of contract, breach of confidence and inducement to breach, and includes the acquisition of undisclosed information by other persons who knew, or were grossly negligent in failing to know, that such practices were involved in the acquisition;

intellectual property rights refers to copyright and related rights, trademark rights, patent rights, rights in layout designs of semiconductor integrated circuits, trade secret rights, plant breeders' rights, rights in geographical indications and industrial design rights;

nationals of another Party means, in respect of the relevant intellectual property right, persons who would meet the criteria for eligibility for protection provided for in the Paris Convention (1967), the Berne Convention (1971), the Geneva Convention (1971), the International Convention for the Protection of Performers, Producers of Phonograms and Broadcasting Organizations (1961), the UPOV Convention (1978), the UPOV Convention (1991) or the Treaty on Intellectual Property in Respect of Integrated Circuits, as if each Party were a party to those Conventions, and with respect to intellectual property rights that are not the subject of these Conventions, "nationals of another Party" shall be understood to be at least individuals who are citizens or permanent residents of that Party and also includes any other natural person referred to in Annex 201.1 (Country–Specific Definitions);

public includes, with respect to rights of communication and performance of works provided for under Articles 11, 11bis(1) and 14(1)(ii) of the Berne Convention, with respect to dramatic, dramatico-musical, musical and cinematographic works, at least, any aggregation of individuals intended to be the object of, and capable of perceiving, communications or performances of works, regardless of whether they can do so at the same or different times or in the same or different places, provided that such an aggregation is larger than a family and its immediate circle of acquaintances or is not a group comprising a limited number of individuals having similarly close ties that has not been formed for the principal purpose of receiving such performances and communications of works; and

secondary uses of sound recordings means the use directly for broadcasting or for any other public communication of a sound recording.

Part Seven
ADMINISTRATIVE AND INSTITUTIONAL PROVISIONS

Chapter Eighteen

PUBLICATION, NOTIFICATION AND ADMINISTRATION OF LAWS

Article 1801: Contact Points

Each Party shall designate a contact point to facilitate communications between the Parties on any matter covered by this Agreement. On the request of another Party, the contact point shall identify the office or official responsible for the matter and assist, as necessary, in facilitating communication with the requesting Party.

Article 1802: Publication

1. Each Party shall ensure that its laws, regulations, procedures and administrative rulings of general application respecting any matter covered by this Agreement are promptly published or otherwise made available in such a manner as to enable interested persons and Parties to become acquainted with them.

2. To the extent possible, each Party shall: (a) publish in advance any such measure that it proposes to adopt; and (b) provide interested persons and Parties a reasonable opportunity to comment on such proposed measures.

Article 1803: Notification and Provision of Information

1. To the maximum extent possible, each Party shall notify any other Party with an interest in the matter of any proposed or actual measure that the Party considers might materially affect the operation of this Agreement or otherwise substantially affect that other Party's interests under this Agreement.

2. On request of another Party, a Party shall promptly provide information and respond to questions pertaining to any actual or proposed measure, whether or not that other Party has been previously notified of that measure.

3.   Any notification or information provided under this Article shall be without prejudice as to whether the measure is consistent with this Agreement.

Article 1804: Administrative Proceedings

With a view to administering in a consistent, impartial and reasonable manner all measures of general application affecting matters covered by this Agreement, each Party shall ensure that in its administrative proceedings applying measures referred to in Article 1802 to particular persons, goods or services of another Party in specific cases that: (a) wherever possible, persons of another Party that are directly affected by a proceeding are provided reasonable notice, in accordance with domestic procedures, when a proceeding is initiated, including a description of the nature of the proceeding, a statement of the legal authority under which the proceeding is initiated and a general description of any issues in controversy; (b) such persons are afforded a reasonable opportunity to present facts and arguments in support of their positions prior to any final administrative action, when time, the nature of the proceeding and the public interest permit; and (c) its procedures are in accordance with domestic law.

Article 1805: Review and Appeal

1.   Each Party shall establish or maintain judicial, quasi-judicial or administrative tribunals or procedures for the purpose of the prompt review and, where warranted, correction of final administrative actions regarding matters covered by this Agreement. Such tribunals shall be impartial and independent of the office or authority entrusted with administrative enforcement and shall not have any substantial interest in the outcome of the matter.

2.   Each Party shall ensure that, in any such tribunals or procedures, the parties to the proceeding are provided with the right to: (a) a reasonable opportunity to support or defend their respective positions; and (b) a decision based on the evidence and submissions of record or, where required by domestic law, the record compiled by the administrative authority.

3.   Each Party shall ensure, subject to appeal or further review as provided in its domestic law, that such decisions shall be implemented by, and shall govern the practice of, the offices or authorities with respect to the administrative action at issue.

Article 1806: Definitions

For purposes of this Chapter:

administrative ruling of general application means an administrative ruling or interpretation that applies to all persons and fact situations that fall generally within its ambit and that establishes a norm of conduct but does not include: (a) a determination or ruling made in an administrative or quasi-judicial proceeding that applies to a particular person, good or service of another Party in a specific case; or (b) a ruling that adjudicates with respect to a particular act or practice.

Chapter Nineteen

REVIEW AND DISPUTE SETTLE-MENT IN ANTIDUMPING AND COUNTERVAILING DUTY MAT-TERS

Article 1901: General Provisions

1. Article 1904 applies only with respect to goods that the competent investigating authority of the importing Party, applying the importing Party's antidumping or countervailing duty law to the facts of a specific case, determines are goods of another Party.

2. For purposes of Articles 1903 and 1904, panels shall be established in accordance with Annex 1901.2.

3. Except for Article 2203 (Entry into Force), no provision of any other Chapter of this Agreement shall be construed as imposing obligations on a Party with respect to the Party's antidumping law or countervailing duty law.

Annex 1901.2

Establishment of Binational Panels

1. On the date of entry into force of this Agreement, the Parties shall establish and thereafter maintain a roster of individuals to serve as panelists in disputes under this Chapter. The roster shall include judges or former judges to the fullest extent practicable. The Parties shall consult in developing the roster, which shall include at least 75 candidates. Each Party shall select at least 25 candidates, and all candidates shall be citizens of Canada, Mexico or the United States. Candidates shall be of good character, high standing and repute, and shall be chosen strictly on the basis of objectivity, reliability, sound judgment and general familiarity with international trade law. Candidates shall not be affiliated with a Party, and in no event shall a candidate take instructions from a Party. The Parties shall maintain the roster, and may amend it, when necessary, after consultations.

2. A majority of the panelists on each panel shall be lawyers in good standing. Within 30 days of a request for a panel, each involved Party shall appoint two panelists, in consultation with the other involved Party. The involved Parties normally shall appoint panelists from the roster. If a panelist is not selected from the roster, the panelist shall be chosen in accordance with and be subject to the criteria of paragraph 1. Each involved Party shall have the right to exercise four peremptory challenges, to be exercised simultaneously and in confidence, disqualifying from appointment to the panel up to four candidates proposed by the other involved Party. Peremptory challenges and the selection of alternative panelists shall occur within 45 days of the request for the panel. If an involved Party fails to appoint its members to a panel within 30 days or if a panelist is struck and no alternative panelist is selected within 45 days, such panelist shall be selected by lot on the 31st or 46th day, as the case may be, from that Party's candidates on the roster.

3. Within 55 days of the request for a panel, the involved Parties shall agree on the selection of a fifth panelist. If the involved Parties are unable to agree, they shall decide by lot which of them shall select, by the 61st day, the fifth panelist from the roster, excluding candidates eliminated by peremptory challenges.

4. On appointment of the fifth panelist, the panelists shall promptly appoint a chair from among the lawyers on the panel by majority vote of the panelists. If there is no majority vote, the chair shall be appointed by lot from among the lawyers on the panel.

5. Decisions of the panel shall be by majority vote and based on the votes of all members of the panel. The panel shall issue a written decision with reasons, together with any dissenting or concurring opinions of panelists.

6. Panelists shall be subject to the code of conduct established pursuant to Article 1909. If an involved Party believes that a panelist is in violation of the code of conduct, the involved Parties shall consult and if they agree, the panelist shall be removed and a new panelist shall be selected in accordance with the procedures of this Annex.

7. When a panel is convened pursuant to Article 1904 each panelist shall be required to sign: (a) an application for a protective order for information supplied by the United States or its persons covering business proprietary and other privileged information; (b) an undertaking for information supplied by Canada or its persons covering confidential, personal, business proprietary and other privileged information; or (c) an undertaking for information supplied by Mexico or its persons covering confidential, business proprietary and other privileged information.

8. On a panelist's acceptance of the obligations and terms of an application for a protective order or disclosure undertaking, the importing Party shall grant access to the information covered by such order or disclosure undertaking. Each Party shall establish appropriate sanctions for violations of protective orders or disclosure undertakings issued by or given to any Party. Each Party shall enforce such sanctions with respect

to any person within its jurisdiction. Failure by a panelist to sign an application for a protective order or disclosure undertaking shall result in disqualification of the panelist.

9.   If a panelist becomes unable to fulfill panel duties or is disqualified, proceedings of the panel shall be suspended pending the selection of a substitute panelist in accordance with the procedures of this Annex.

10.   Subject to the code of conduct established pursuant to Article 1909, and provided that it does not interfere with the performance of the duties of such panelist, a panelist may engage in other business during the term of the panel.

11.   While acting as a panelist, a panelist may not appear as counsel before another panel.

12.   With the exception of violations of protective orders or disclosure undertakings, signed pursuant to paragraph 7, panelists shall be immune from suit and legal process relating to acts performed by them in their official capacity.

Article 1902: Retention of Domestic Antidumping Law and Countervailing Duty Law

1.   Each Party reserves the right to apply its antidumping law and countervailing duty law to goods imported from the territory of any other Party. Antidumping law and countervailing duty law include, as appropriate for each Party, relevant statutes, legislative history, regulations, administrative practice and judicial precedents.

2.   Each Party reserves the right to change or modify its antidumping law or countervailing duty law, provided that in the case of an amendment to a Party's antidumping or countervailing duty statute: (a) such amendment shall apply to goods from another Party only if the amending statute specifies that it applies to goods from that Party or from the Parties to this Agreement; (b) the amending Party notifies in writing the Parties to which the amendment applies of the amending statute as far in advance as possible of the date of enactment of such statute; (c) following notification, the amending Party, on request of any Party to which the amendment applies, consults with that Party prior to the enactment of the amending statute; and (d) such amendment, as applicable to that other Party, is not inconsistent with (i) the General Agreement on Tariffs and Trade (GATT), the Agreement on Implementation of Article VI of the General Agreement on Tariffs and Trade (the Antidumping Code) or the Agreement on the Interpretation and Application of Articles VI, XVI and XXIII of the General Agreement on Tariffs and Trade (the Subsidies Code), or any successor agreement to which all the original signatories to this Agreement are party, or (ii) the object and purpose of this Agreement and this Chapter, which is to establish fair and predictable conditions for the progressive liberalization of trade between the Parties to this Agreement while maintaining effective and fair disciplines on unfair trade practices, such object and purpose to be

ascertained from the provisions of this Agreement, its preamble and objectives, and the practices of the Parties.

Article 1903: Review of Statutory Amendments

1. A Party to which an amendment of another Party's antidumping or countervailing duty statute applies may request in writing that such amendment be referred to a binational panel for a declaratory opinion as to whether: (a) the amendment does not conform to Article 1902(2)(d)(i) or (ii); or (b) such amendment has the function and effect of overturning a prior decision of a panel made pursuant to Article 1904 and does not conform to Article 1902(2)(d)(i) or (ii). Such declaratory opinion shall have force or effect only as provided in this Article.

2. The panel shall conduct its review in accordance with the procedures of Annex 1903.2.

3. In the event that the panel recommends modifications to the amending statute to remedy a non-conformity that it has identified in its opinion: (a) the two Parties shall immediately begin consultations and shall seek to achieve a mutually satisfactory solution to the matter within 90 days of the issuance of the panel's final declaratory opinion. Such solution may include seeking corrective legislation with respect to the statute of the amending Party; (b) if corrective legislation is not enacted within nine months from the end of the 90–day consultation period referred to in subparagraph (a) and no other mutually satisfactory solution has been reached, the Party that requested the panel may (i) take comparable legislative or equivalent executive action, or (ii) terminate this Agreement with regard to the amending Party on 60–day written notice to that Party.

Annex 1903.2

Panel Procedures Under Article 1903

1. The panel shall establish its own rules of procedure unless the Parties otherwise agree prior to the establishment of that panel. The procedures shall ensure a right to at least one hearing before the panel, as well as the opportunity to provide written submissions and rebuttal arguments. The proceedings of the panel shall be confidential, unless the two Parties otherwise agree. The panel shall base its decisions solely on the arguments and submissions of the two Parties.

2. Unless the Parties to the dispute otherwise agree, the panel shall, within 90 days after its chair is appointed, present to the two Parties an initial written declaratory opinion containing findings of fact and its determination pursuant to Article 1903.

3. If the findings of the panel are affirmative, the panel may include in its report its recommendations as to the means by which the amending statute could be brought into conformity with Article 1902(2)(d). In determining what, if any, recommendations are appropriate, the panel shall consider the extent to which the amending statute

affects interests under this Agreement. Individual panelists may provide separate opinions on matters not unanimously agreed. The initial opinion of the panel shall become the final declaratory opinion, unless a Party to the dispute requests a reconsideration of the initial opinion pursuant to paragraph 4.

4. Within 14 days of the issuance of the initial declaratory opinion, a Party to the dispute disagreeing in whole or in part with the opinion may present a written statement of its objections and the reasons for those objections to the panel. In such event, the panel shall request the views of both Parties and shall reconsider its initial opinion. The panel shall conduct any further examination that it deems appropriate, and shall issue a final written opinion, together with dissenting or concurring views of individual panelists, within 30 days of the request for reconsideration.

5. Unless the Parties to the dispute otherwise agree, the final declaratory opinion of the panel shall be made public, along with any separate opinions of individual panelists and any written views that either Party may wish to be published.

6. Unless the Parties to the dispute otherwise agree, meetings and hearings of the panel shall take place at the office of the amending Party's Section of the Secretariat.

Article 1904: Review of Final Antidumping and Countervailing Duty Determinations

1. As provided in this Article, each Party shall replace judicial review of final antidumping and countervailing duty determinations with binational panel review.

2. An involved Party may request that a panel review, based on the administrative record, a final antidumping or countervailing duty determination of a competent investigating authority of an importing Party to determine whether such determination was in accordance with the antidumping or countervailing duty law of the importing Party. For this purpose, the antidumping or countervailing duty law consists of the relevant statutes, legislative history, regulations, administrative practice and judicial precedents to the extent that a court of the importing Party would rely on such materials in reviewing a final determination of the competent investigating authority. Solely for purposes of the panel review provided for in this Article, the antidumping and countervailing duty statutes of the Parties, as those statutes may be amended from time to time, are incorporated into and made a part of this Agreement.

3. The panel shall apply the standard of review set out in Annex 1911 and the general legal principles that a court of the importing Party otherwise would apply to a review of a determination of the competent investigating authority.

4. A request for a panel shall be made in writing to the other involved Party within 30 days following the date of publication of the

final determination in question in the official journal of the importing Party. In the case of final determinations that are not published in the official journal of the importing Party, the importing Party shall immediately notify the other involved Party of such final determination where it involves goods from the other involved Party, and the other involved Party may request a panel within 30 days of receipt of such notice. Where the competent investigating authority of the importing Party has imposed provisional measures in an investigation, the other involved Party may provide notice of its intention to request a panel under this Article, and the Parties shall begin to establish a panel at that time. Failure to request a panel within the time specified in this paragraph shall preclude review by a panel.

5. An involved Party on its own initiative may request review of a final determination by a panel and shall, on request of a person who would otherwise be entitled under the law of the importing Party to commence domestic procedures for judicial review of that final determination, request such review.

6. The panel shall conduct its review in accordance with the procedures established by the Parties pursuant to paragraph 14. Where both involved Parties request a panel to review a final determination, a single panel shall review that determination.

7. The competent investigating authority that issued the final determination in question shall have the right to appear and be represented by counsel before the panel. Each Party shall provide that other persons who, pursuant to the law of the importing Party, otherwise would have had the right to appear and be represented in a domestic judicial review proceeding concerning the determination of the competent investigating authority, shall have the right to appear and be represented by counsel before the panel.

8. The panel may uphold a final determination, or remand it for action not inconsistent with the panel's decision. Where the panel remands a final determination, the panel shall establish as brief a time as is reasonable for compliance with the remand, taking into account the complexity of the factual and legal issues involved and the nature of the panel's decision. In no event shall the time permitted for compliance with a remand exceed an amount of time equal to the maximum amount of time (counted from the date of the filing of a petition, complaint or application) permitted by statute for the competent investigating authority in question to make a final determination in an investigation. If review of the action taken by the competent investigating authority on remand is needed, such review shall be before the same panel, which shall normally issue a final decision within 90 days of the date on which such remand action is submitted to it.

9. The decision of a panel under this Article shall be binding on the involved Parties with respect to the particular matter between the Parties that is before the panel.

10. This Agreement shall not affect: (a) the judicial review procedures of any Party, or (b) cases appealed under those procedures, with respect to determinations other than final determinations.

11. A final determination shall not be reviewed under any judicial review procedures of the importing Party if an involved Party requests a panel with respect to that determination within the time limits set out in this Article. No Party may provide in its domestic legislation for an appeal from a panel decision to its domestic courts.

12. This Article shall not apply where: (a) neither involved Party seeks panel review of a final determination; (b) a revised final determination is issued as a direct result of judicial review of the original final determination by a court of the importing Party in cases where neither involved Party sought panel review of that original final determination; or (c) a final determination is issued as a direct result of judicial review that was commenced in a court of the importing Party before the date of entry into force of this Agreement.

13. Where, within a reasonable time after the panel decision is issued, an involved Party alleges that: (a) (i) a member of the panel was guilty of gross misconduct, bias, or a serious conflict of interest, or otherwise materially violated the rules of conduct, (ii) the panel seriously departed from a fundamental rule of procedure, or (iii) the panel manifestly exceeded its powers, authority or jurisdiction set out in this Article, for example by failing to apply the appropriate standard of review, and (b) any of the actions set out in subparagraph (a) has materially affected the panel's decision and threatens the integrity of the binational panel review process, that Party may avail itself of the extraordinary challenge procedure set out in Annex 1904.13.

14. To implement this Article, the Parties shall adopt rules of procedure by January 1, 1994. Such rules shall be based, where appropriate, on judicial rules of appellate procedure, and shall include rules concerning: the content and service of requests for panels; a requirement that the competent investigating authority transmit to the panel the administrative record of the proceeding; the protection of business proprietary, government classified, and other privileged information (including sanctions against persons participating before panels for improper release of such information); participation by private persons; limitations on panel review to errors alleged by the Parties or private persons; filing and service; computation and extensions of time; the form and content of briefs and other papers; pre-and post-hearing conferences; motions; oral argument; requests for rehearing; and voluntary terminations of panel reviews. The rules shall be designed to result in final decisions within 315 days of the date on which a request for a panel is made, and shall allow: (a) 30 days for the filing of the complaint; (b) 30 days for designation or certification of the administrative record and its filing with the panel; (c) 60 days for the complainant to file its brief; (d) 60 days for the respondent to file its brief; (e) 15 days for the filing of

reply briefs; (f) 15 to 30 days for the panel to convene and hear oral argument; and (g) 90 days for the panel to issue its written decision.

15. In order to achieve the objectives of this Article, the Parties shall amend their antidumping and countervailing duty statutes and regulations with respect to antidumping or countervailing duty proceedings involving goods of the other Parties, and other statutes and regulations to the extent that they apply to the operation of the antidumping and countervailing duty laws. In particular, without limiting the generality of the foregoing, each Party shall: (a) amend its statutes or regulations to ensure that existing procedures concerning the refund, with interest, of antidumping or countervailing duties operate to give effect to a final panel decision that a refund is due; (b) amend its statutes or regulations to ensure that its courts shall give full force and effect, with respect to any person within its jurisdiction, to all sanctions imposed pursuant to the laws of the other Parties to enforce provisions of any protective order or undertaking that such other Party has promulgated or accepted in order to permit access for purposes of panel review or of the extraordinary challenge procedure to confidential, personal, business proprietary or other privileged information; (c) amend its statutes or regulations to ensure that (i) domestic procedures for judicial review of a final determination may not be commenced until the time for requesting a panel under paragraph 4 has expired, and (ii) as a prerequisite to commencing domestic judicial review procedures to review a final determination, a Party or other person intending to commence such procedures shall provide notice of such intent to the Parties concerned and to other persons entitled to commence such review procedures of the same final determination no later than 10 days prior to the latest date on which a panel may be requested; and (d) make the further amendments set out in its Schedule to Annex 1904.15.

Annex 1904.13

Extraordinary Challenge Procedure

1. The involved Parties shall establish an extraordinary challenge committee, comprising three members, within 15 days of a request pursuant to Article 1904(13). The members shall be selected from a 15–person roster comprised of judges or former judges of a federal judicial court of the United States or a judicial court of superior jurisdiction of Canada, or a federal judicial court of Mexico. Each Party shall name five persons to this roster. Each involved Party shall select one member from this roster and the involved Parties shall decide by lot which of them shall select the third member from the roster.

2. The Parties shall establish by the date of entry into force of the Agreement rules of procedure for committees. The rules shall provide for a decision of a committee within 90 days of its establishment.

3. Committee decisions shall be binding on the Parties with respect to the particular matter between the Parties that was before the panel. After examination of the legal and factual analysis underlying the

findings and conclusions of the panel's decision in order to determine whether one of the grounds set out in Article 1904(13) has been established, and on finding that one of those grounds has been established, the committee shall vacate the original panel decision or remand it to the original panel for action not inconsistent with the committee's decision; if the grounds are not established, it shall deny the challenge and, therefore, the original panel decision shall stand affirmed. If the original decision is vacated, a new panel shall be established pursuant to Annex 1901.2.

Annex 1904.15

Amendments to Domestic Laws

Schedule of Canada

1. Canada shall amend sections 56 and 58 of the Special Import Measures Act, as amended, to allow the United States with respect to goods of the United States or Mexico with respect to goods of Mexico or a United States or a Mexican manufacturer, producer, or exporter, without regard to payment of duties, to make a written request for a redetermination; and section 59 to require the Deputy Minister to make a ruling on a request for a redetermination within one year of a request to a designated officer or other customs officer.

2. Canada shall amend section 18.3(1) of the Federal Court Act, as amended, to render that section inapplicable to the United States and to Mexico; and shall provide in its statutes or regulations that persons (including producers of goods subject to an investigation) have standing to ask Canada to request a panel review where such persons would be entitled to commence domestic procedures for judicial review if the final determination were reviewable by the Federal Court pursuant to section 18.1(4).

3. Canada shall amend the Special Import Measures Act, as amended, and any other relevant provisions of law, to provide that the following actions of the Deputy Minister shall be deemed for the purposes of this Article to be final determinations subject to judicial review: (a) a determination by the Deputy Minister pursuant to section 41; (b) a re-determination by the Deputy Minister pursuant to section 59; and (c) a review by the Deputy Minister of an undertaking pursuant to section 53(1).

4. Canada shall amend Part II of the Special Import Measures Act, as amended, to provide for binational panel review respecting goods of Mexico and the United States.

5. Canada shall amend Part II of the Special Import Measures Act, as amended, to provide for definitions related to this Chapter, as may be required.

6. Canada shall amend Part II of the Special Import Measures Act, as amended, to permit the governments of Mexico and the United States

to request binational panel review of final determinations respecting goods of Mexico and the United States.

7.   Canada shall amend Part II of the Special Import Measures Act, as amended, to provide for the establishment of binational panels requested to review final determinations in respect of goods of Mexico and the United States.

8.   Canada shall amend Part II of the Special Import Measures Act, as amended, to provide that binational panel review of a final determination shall be conducted in accordance with this Chapter.

9.   Canada shall amend Part II of the Special Import Measures Act, as amended, to provide that an extraordinary challenge proceeding shall be requested and conducted in accordance with Article 1904 and Annex 1904.13.

10.   Canada shall amend Part II of the Special Import Measures Act, as amended, to provide for a code of conduct, immunity for anything done or omitted to be done during the course of panel proceedings, the signing of and compliance with disclosure undertakings respecting confidential information, and remuneration for members of panels and committees established pursuant to this Chapter.

11.   Canada shall make such amendments as are necessary to establish a Canadian Secretariat for this Agreement and generally to facilitate the operation of this Chapter and the work of the binational panels, extraordinary challenge committees and special committees convened under this Chapter.

Schedule of Mexico

Mexico shall amend its antidumping and countervailing duty statutes and regulations, and other statutes and regulations to the extent that they apply to the operation of the antidumping and countervailing duty laws, to provide the following:

(a) elimination of the possibility of imposing duties within the five-day period after the acceptance of a petition;

(b) substitution of the term Initial Resolution ("Resolucion de Inicio") for the term Provisional Resolution ("Resolucion Provisional") and the term Provisional Resolution ("Resolucion Provisional") for the term Resolution Reviewing the Provisional Resolution ("Resolucion que revisa a la Resolucion Provisional");

(c) full participation in the administrative process for interested parties, as well as the right to administrative appeal and judicial review of final determinations of investigations, reviews, product coverage or other final decisions affecting them;

(d) elimination of the possibility of imposing provisional duties before the issuance of a preliminary determination;

(e) the right to immediate access to review of final determinations by binational panels for interested parties, without the need to exhaust first the administrative appeal;

(f) explicit and adequate timetables for determinations of the competent investigating authority and for the submission of questionnaires, evidence and comments by interested parties, as well as an opportunity for them to present facts and arguments in support of their positions prior to any final determination, to the extent time permits, including an opportunity to be adequately informed in a timely manner of and to comment on all aspects of preliminary determinations of dumping or subsidization;

(g) written notice to interested parties of any of the actions or resolutions rendered by the competent investigating authority, including initiation of an administrative review as well as its conclusion;

(h) disclosure meetings with interested parties by the competent investigating authority conducting its investigations and reviews, within seven calendar days after the date of publication in the Federal Official Journal ("Diario Oficial de la Federacion") of preliminary and final determinations, to explain the margins of dumping and the amount of subsidies calculations and to provide the interested parties with copies of sample calculations and, if used, computer programs;

(i) timely access by eligible counsel of interested parties during the course of the proceeding (including disclosure meetings) and on appeal, either before a national tribunal or a panel, to all information contained in the administrative record of the proceeding, including confidential information, excepting proprietary information of such a high degree of sensitivity that its release would lead to substantial and irreversible harm to the owner as well as government classified information, subject to an undertaking for confidentiality that strictly forbids use of the information for personal benefit and its disclosure to persons who are not authorized to receive such information; and for sanctions that are specific to violations of undertakings in proceedings before national tribunals or panels;

(j) timely access by interested parties during the course of the proceeding, to all non-confidential information contained in the administrative record and access to such information by interested parties or their representatives in any proceeding after 90 days following the issuance of the final determination;

(k) a mechanism requiring that any person submitting documents to the competent investigating authority shall simultaneously serve on interested persons, including foreign interests, any submissions after the complaint;

(*l*) preparation of summaries of ex parte meetings held between the competent investigating authority and any interested party and the inclusion in the administrative record of such summaries, which shall be made available to parties to the proceeding; if such summaries contain business proprietary information, the documents must be disclosed to a party's representative under an undertaking to ensure confidentiality;

(m) maintenance by the competent investigating authority of an administrative record as defined in this Chapter and a requirement that the final determination be based solely on the administrative record;

(n) informing interested parties in writing of all data and information the administering authority requires them to submit for the investigation, review, product coverage proceeding, or other antidumping or countervailing duty proceeding;

(o) the right to an annual individual review on request by the interested parties through which they can obtain their own dumping margin or countervailing duty rate, or can change the margin or rate they received in the investigation or a previous review, reserving to the competent investigating authority the ability to initiate a review, at any time, on its own motion and requiring that the competent investigating authority issue a notice of initiation within a reasonable period of time after the request;

(p) application of determinations issued as a result of judicial, administrative, or panel review, to the extent they are relevant to interested parties in addition to the plaintiff, so that all interested parties will benefit;

(q) issuance of binding decisions by the competent investigating authority if an interested party seeks clarification outside the context of an antidumping or countervailing duty investigation or review with respect to whether a particular product is covered by an antidumping or countervailing duty order;

(r) a detailed statement of reasons and the legal basis for final determinations in a manner sufficient to permit interested parties to make an informed decision as to whether to seek judicial or panel review, including an explanation of methodological or policy issues raised in the calculation of dumping or subsidization;

(s) written notice to interested parties and publication in the Federal Official Journal ("Diario Oficial de la Federacion") of initiation of investigations setting forth the nature of the proceeding, the legal authority under which the proceeding is initiated, and a description of the product at issue;

(t) documentation in writing of all advisory bodies' decisions or recommendations, including the basis for the decisions, and release of such written decisions to parties to the proceeding; all decisions or recommendations of any advisory body shall be placed in the administrative record and made available to parties to the proceeding; and

(u) a standard of review to be applied by binational panels as set out in subparagraph (c) of the definition of "standard of review" in Annex 1911.

Schedule of the United States

1. The United States shall amend section 301 of the Customs Courts Act of 1980, as amended, and any other relevant provisions of law, to eliminate the authority to issue declaratory judgments in any civil action involving an antidumping or countervailing duty proceeding regarding a class or kind of Canadian or Mexican merchandise.

2. The United States shall amend section 405(a) of the United States–Canada Free–Trade Agreement Implementation Act of 1988, to provide that the interagency group established under section 242 of the Trade Expansion Act of 1962 shall prepare a list of individuals qualified to serve as members of binational panels, extraordinary challenge committees and special committees convened under this Chapter.

3. The United States shall amend section 405(b) of the United States–Canada Free–Trade Agreement Implementation Act of 1988, to provide that panelists selected to serve on panels or committees convened pursuant to this Chapter, and individuals designated to assist such appointed individuals, shall not be considered employees of the United States.

4. The United States shall amend section 405(c) of the United States–Canada Free–Trade Agreement Implementation Act of 1988, to provide that panelists selected to serve on panels or committees convened pursuant to this Chapter, and individuals designated to assist the individuals serving on such panels or committees, shall be immune from suit and legal process relating to acts performed by such individuals in their official capacity and within the scope of their functions as such panelists or committee members, except with respect to the violation of protective orders described in section 777f(d)(3) of the Tariff Act of 1930, as amended.

5. The United States shall amend section 405(d) of the United States–Canada Free–Trade Agreement Implementation Act of 1988, to establish a United States Secretariat to facilitate the operation of this Chapter and the work of the binational panels, extraordinary challenge committees and special committees convened under this Chapter.

6. The United States shall amend section 407 of the United States–Canada Free–Trade Agreement Implementation Act of 1988, to provide that an extraordinary challenge committee convened pursuant to Article 1904 and Annex 1904.13 shall have authority to obtain information in the event of an allegation that a member of a binational panel was guilty of gross misconduct, bias, or a serious conflict of interest, or otherwise materially violated the rules of conduct, and for the committee to summon the attendance of witnesses, order the taking of depositions and obtain the assistance of any district or territorial court of the United States in aid of the committee's investigation.

7. The United States shall amend section 408 of the United States–Canada Free–Trade Agreement Implementation Act of 1988, to provide that, in the case of a final determination of a competent investigating

authority of Mexico, as well as Canada, the filing with the United States Secretary of a request for binational panel review by a person described in Article 1904(5) shall be deemed, on receipt of the request by the Secretary, to be a request for binational panel review within the meaning of Article 1904(4).

8.   The United States shall amend section 516A of the Tariff Act of 1930, as amended, to provide that judicial review of antidumping or countervailing duty cases regarding Mexican, as well as Canadian, merchandise shall not be commenced in the Court of International Trade if binational panel review is requested.

9.   The United States shall amend section 516A(a) of the Tariff Act of 1930, as amended, to provide that the time limits for commencing an action in the Court of International Trade with regard to antidumping or countervailing duty proceedings involving Mexican or Canadian merchandise shall not begin to run until the 31st day after the date of publication in the Federal Register of notice of the final determination or the antidumping duty order.

10.   The United States shall amend section 516A(g) of the Tariff Act of 1930, as amended, to provide, in accordance with the terms of this Chapter, for binational panel review of antidumping and countervailing duty cases involving Mexican or Canadian merchandise. Such amendment shall provide that if binational panel review is requested such review will be exclusive.

11.   The United States shall amend section 516A(g) of the Tariff Act of 1930, as amended, to provide that the competent investigating authority shall, within the period specified by any panel formed to review a final determination regarding Mexican or Canadian merchandise, take action not inconsistent with the decision of the panel or committee.

12.   The United States shall amend section 777 of the Tariff Act of 1930, as amended, to provide for the disclosure to authorized persons under protective order of proprietary information in the administrative record, if binational panel review of a final determination regarding Mexican or Canadian merchandise is requested.

13.   The United States shall amend section 777 of the Tariff Act of 1930, as amended, to provide for the imposition of sanctions on any person who the competent investigating authority finds to have violated a protective order issued by the competent investigating authority of the United States or disclosure undertakings entered into with an authorized agency of Mexico or with a competent investigating authority of Canada to protect proprietary material during binational panel review.

Article 1905: Safeguarding the Panel Review System

1.   Where a Party alleges that the application of another Party's domestic law: (a) has prevented the establishment of a panel requested by the complaining Party; (b) has prevented a panel requested by the

complaining Party from rendering a final decision; (c) has prevented the implementation of the decision of a panel requested by the complaining Party or denied it binding force and effect with respect to the particular matter that was before the panel; or (d) has resulted in a failure to provide opportunity for review of a final determination by a panel or court of competent jurisdiction that is independent of the competent investigating authorities, that examines the basis for the competent investigating authority's determination and whether the competent investigating authority properly applied domestic antidumping and countervailing duty law in reaching the challenged determination, and that employs the relevant standard of review identified in Article 1911, the Party may request in writing consultations with the other Party regarding the allegations. The consultations shall begin within 15 days of the date of the request.

2. If the matter has not been resolved within 45 days of the request for consultations, or such other period as the consulting Parties may agree, the complaining Party may request the establishment of a special committee.

3. Unless otherwise agreed by the disputing Parties, the special committee shall be established within 15 days of a request and perform its functions in a manner consistent with this Chapter.

4. The roster for special committees shall be that established under Annex 1904.13.

5. The special committee shall comprise three members selected in accordance with the procedures set out in Annex 1904.13.

6. The Parties shall establish rules of procedure in accordance with the principles set out in Annex 1905.6.

7. Where the special committee makes an affirmative finding with respect to one of the grounds specified in paragraph 1, the complaining Party and the Party complained against shall begin consultations within 10 days thereafter and shall seek to achieve a mutually satisfactory solution within 60 days of the issuance of the committee's report.

8. If, within the 60–day period, the Parties are unable to reach a mutually satisfactory solution to the matter, or the Party complained against has not demonstrated to the satisfaction of the special committee that it has corrected the problem or problems with respect to which the committee has made an affirmative finding, the complaining Party may suspend: (a) the operation of Article 1904 with respect to the Party complained against; or (b) the application to the Party complained against of such benefits under this Agreement as may be appropriate under the circumstances. If the complaining Party decides to take action under this paragraph, it shall do so within 30 days after the end of the 60–day consultation period.

9. In the event that a complaining Party suspends the operation of Article 1904 with respect to the Party complained against, the latter Party may reciprocally suspend the operation of Article 1904 within 30

days after the suspension of the operation of Article 1904 by the complaining Party. If either Party decides to suspend the operation of Article 1904, it shall provide written notice of such suspension to the other Party.

10. On the request of the Party complained against, the special committee shall reconvene to determine whether: (a) the suspension of benefits by the complaining Party pursuant to paragraph 8(b) is manifestly excessive; or (b) the Party complained against has corrected the problem or problems with respect to which the committee has made an affirmative finding. The special committee shall, within 45 days of the request, present a report to both Parties containing its determination. Where the special committee determines that the Party complained against has corrected the problem or problems, any suspension effected by the complaining Party or the Party complained against, or both, pursuant to paragraph 8 or 9 shall be terminated.

11. If the special committee makes an affirmative finding with respect to one of the grounds specified in paragraph 1, then effective as of the day following the date of issuance of the special committee's report: (a) binational panel or extraordinary challenge committee review under Article 1904 shall be stayed (i) in the case of review of any final determination of the complaining Party requested by the Party complained against, if such review was requested after the date on which consultations were requested pursuant to paragraph 1, and in no case more than 150 days prior to an affirmative finding by the special committee, or (ii) in the case of review of any final determination of the Party complained against requested by the complaining Party, on the request of the complaining Party; and (b) the time set out in Article 1904(4) or Annex 1904.13 for requesting panel or committee review shall not run unless and until resumed in accordance with paragraph 12.

12. If either Party suspends the operation of Article 1904 pursuant to paragraph 8(a), the panel or committee review stayed under paragraph 11(a) shall be terminated and the challenge to the final determination shall be irrevocably referred to the appropriate domestic court for decision, as provided below: (a) in the case of review of any final determination of the complaining Party requested by the Party complained against, on the request of either Party, or of a party to the panel review under Article 1904; or (b) in the case of review of any final determination of the Party complained against requested by the complaining Party, on the request of the complaining Party, or of a person of the complaining Party that is a party to the panel review under Article 1904. If either Party suspends the operation of Article 1904 pursuant to paragraph 8(a), any running of time suspended under paragraph 11(b) shall resume.

If the suspension of the operation of Article 1904 does not become effective, panel or committee review stayed under paragraph 11(a), and any running of time suspended under paragraph 11(b), shall resume.

13. If the complaining Party suspends the application to the Party complained against of such benefits under the Agreement as may be appropriate under the circumstances pursuant to paragraph 8(b), panel or committee review stayed under paragraph 11(a), and any running of time suspended under paragraph 11(b), shall resume.

14. Each Party shall provide in its domestic law that, in the event of an affirmative finding by the special committee, the time for requesting judicial review of a final antidumping or countervailing duty determination shall not run unless and until the Parties concerned have negotiated a mutually satisfactory solution under paragraph 7, or have suspended the operation of Article 1904 or the application of other benefits under paragraph 8.

Annex 1905.6

Special Committee Procedures

The Parties shall establish rules of procedure by the date of entry into force of this Agreement in accordance with the following principles: (a) the procedures shall assure a right to at least one hearing before the special committee as well as the opportunity to provide initial and rebuttal written submissions; (b) the procedures shall assure that the special committee shall prepare an initial report typically within 60 days of the appointment of the last member, and shall afford the Parties 14 days to comment on that report prior to issuing a final report 30 days after presentation of the initial report; (c) the special committee's hearings, deliberations and initial report, and all written submissions to, and communications with, the special committee shall be confidential; (d) unless the Parties to the dispute otherwise agree, the decision of the special committee shall be published 10 days after it is transmitted to the disputing Parties, along with any separate opinions of individual members and any written views that either Party may wish to be published; and (e) unless the Parties to the dispute otherwise agree, meetings and hearings of the special committee shall take place at the office of the Section of the Secretariat of the Party complained against.

Article 1906: Prospective Application

This Chapter shall apply only prospectively to: (a) final determinations of a competent investigating authority made after the date of entry into force of this Agreement; and (b) with respect to declaratory opinions under Article 1903, amendments to antidumping or countervailing duty statutes enacted after the date of entry into force of this Agreement.

Article 1907: Consultations

1. The Parties shall consult annually, or on the request of any Party, to consider any problems that may arise with respect to the implementation or operation of this Chapter and recommend solutions, where appropriate. The Parties shall each designate one or more offi-

cials, including officials of the competent investigating authorities, to be responsible for ensuring that consultations occur, when required, so that the provisions of this Chapter are carried out expeditiously.

2. The Parties further agree to consult on: (a) the potential to develop more effective rules and disciplines concerning the use of government subsidies; and (b) the potential for reliance on a substitute system of rules for dealing with unfair transborder pricing practices and government subsidization.

3. The competent investigating authorities of the Parties shall consult annually, or on the request of any Party, and may submit reports to the Commission, where appropriate. In the context of these consultations, the Parties agree that it is desirable in the administration of antidumping and countervailing duty laws to: (a) publish notice of initiation of investigations in the importing Party's official journal, setting forth the nature of the proceeding, the legal authority under which the proceeding is initiated, and a description of the goods at issue; (b) provide notice of the times for submissions of information and for decisions that the competent investigating authorities are expressly required by statute or regulations to make; (c) provide explicit written notice and instructions as to the information required from interested parties and reasonable time to respond to requests for information; (d) accord reasonable access to information, noting that in this context (i) "reasonable access" means access during the course of the investigation, to the extent practicable, so as to permit an opportunity to present facts and arguments as set out in subparagraph (e); when it is not practicable to provide access to information during the investigation in such time as to permit an opportunity to present facts and arguments, reasonable access shall mean in time to permit the adversely affected party to make an informed decision as to whether to seek judicial or panel review, and (ii) "access to information" means access to representatives determined by the competent investigating authority to be qualified to have access to information received by that competent investigating authority, including access to confidential (business proprietary) information, but does not include information of such high degree of sensitivity that its release would lead to substantial and irreversible harm to the owner or which is required to be kept confidential in accordance with domestic law of a Party; any privileges arising under the domestic law of the importing Party relating to communications between the competent investigating authorities and a lawyer in the employ of, or providing advice to, those authorities may be maintained; (e) provide an opportunity for interested parties to present facts and arguments, to the extent time permits, including an opportunity to comment on the preliminary determination of dumping or of subsidization; (f) protect confidential (business proprietary) information received by the competent investigating authority to ensure that there is no disclosure except to representatives determined by the competent investigating authority to be qualified; (g) prepare administrative records, including recommendations of official advisory bodies that may be required to be kept, and any record of ex parte

meetings that may be required to be kept; (h) provide disclosure of relevant information, including an explanation of the calculation or the methodology used to determine the margin of dumping or the amount of the subsidy, on which any preliminary or final determination of dumping or of subsidization is based, within a reasonable time after a request by interested parties; (i) provide a statement of reasons concerning the final determination of dumping or subsidization; and (j) provide a statement of reasons for final determinations concerning material injury to a domestic industry, threat of material injury to a domestic industry or material retardation of the establishment of such an industry. Inclusion of an item in subparagraphs (a) through (j) is not intended to serve as guidance to a binational panel reviewing a final antidumping or countervailing duty determination pursuant to Article 1904 in determining whether such determination was in accordance with the antidumping or countervailing duty law of the importing Party.

Article 1908: Special Secretariat Provisions

1. Each Party shall establish a division within its section of the Secretariat established pursuant to Article 2002 to facilitate the operation of this Chapter, including the work of panels or committees that may be convened pursuant to this Chapter.

2. The Secretaries of the Secretariat shall act jointly to provide administrative assistance to all panels or committees established pursuant to this Chapter. The Secretary for the Section of the Party in which a panel or committee proceeding is held shall prepare a record thereof and shall preserve an authentic copy of the same in that Party's Section office. Such Secretary shall, on request, provide to the Secretary for the Section of any other Party a copy of such portion of the record as is requested, except that only public portions of the record shall be provided to the Secretary for the Section of any Party that is not an involved Party.

3. Each Secretary shall receive and file all requests, briefs and other papers properly presented to a panel or committee in any proceeding before it that is instituted pursuant to this Chapter and shall number in numerical order all requests for a panel or committee. The number given to a request shall be the file number for briefs and other papers relating to such request.

4. The Secretary for the Section of the Party in which a panel or committee proceeding is held shall forward to the Secretary for the Section of the other involved Party copies of all official letters, documents or other papers received or filed with that Party's Section office pertaining to any proceeding before a panel or committee, except for the administrative record, which shall be handled in accordance with paragraph 2. The Secretary for the Section of an involved Party shall provide on request to the Secretary for the Section of a Party that is not an involved Party in the proceeding a copy of such public documents as are requested.

Article 1909: Code of Conduct

The Parties shall, by the date of entry into force of this Agreement, exchange letters establishing a code of conduct for panelists and members of committees established pursuant to Articles 1903, 1904 and 1905.

Article 1910: Miscellaneous

On request of another Party, the competent investigating authority of a Party shall provide to the other Party copies of all public information submitted to it for purposes of an antidumping or countervailing duty investigation with respect to goods of that other Party.

Article 1911: Definitions

For purposes of this Chapter:

administrative record means, unless otherwise agreed by the Parties and the other persons appearing before a panel: (a) all documentary or other information presented to or obtained by the competent investigating authority in the course of the administrative proceeding, including any governmental memoranda pertaining to the case, and including any record of ex parte meetings as may be required to be kept; (b) a copy of the final determination of the competent investigating authority, including reasons for the determination; (c) all transcripts or records of conferences or hearings before the competent investigating authority; and (d) all notices published in the official journal of the importing Party in connection with the administrative proceeding;

antidumping statute as referred to in Articles 1902 and 1903 means "antidumping statute" of a Party as defined in Annex 1911;

competent investigating authority means "competent investigating authority" of a Party as defined in Annex 1911;

countervailing duty statute as referred to in Articles 1902 and 1903 means "countervailing duty statute" of a Party as defined in Annex 1911;

domestic law for purposes of Article 1905(1) means a Party's constitution, statutes, regulations and judicial decisions to the extent they are relevant to the antidumping and countervailing duty laws;

final determination means "final determination" of a Party as defined in Annex 1911;

foreign interests includes exporters or producers of the Party whose goods are the subject of the proceeding or, in the case of a countervailing duty proceeding, the government of the Party whose goods are the subject of the proceeding;

general legal principles includes principles such as standing, due process, rules of statutory construction, mootness and exhaustion of administrative remedies;

goods of a Party means domestic products as these are understood in the General Agreement on Tariffs and Trade;

importing Party means the Party that issued the final determination;

interested parties includes foreign interests;

involved Party means: (a) the importing Party; or (b) a Party whose goods are the subject of the final determination;

remand means a referral back for a determination not inconsistent with the panel or committee decision; and

standard of review means the "standard of review" for each Party as defined in Annex 1911.

Annex 1911

Country–Specific Definitions

For purposes of this Chapter:

antidumping statute means:

(a) in the case of Canada, the relevant provisions of the Special Import Measures Act, as amended, and any successor statutes;

(b) in the case of the United States, the relevant provisions of Title VII of the Tariff Act of 1930, as amended, and any successor statutes;

(c) in the case of Mexico, the relevant provisions of the Foreign Trade Act Implementing Article 131 of the Constitution of the United Mexican States ("Ley Reglamentaria del Articulo 131 de la Constitucion Politica de los Estados Unidos Mexicanos en Materia de Comercio Exterior"), as amended, and any successor statutes; and

(d) the provisions of any other statute that provides for judicial review of final determinations under subparagraph (a), (b) or (c), or indicates the standard of review to be applied to such determinations;

competent investigating authority means:

(a) in the case of Canada, (i) the Canadian International Trade Tribunal, or its successor, or (ii) the Deputy Minister of National Revenue for Customs and Excise as defined in the Special Import Measures Act, as amended, or the Deputy Minister's successor;

(b) in the case of the United States, (i) the International Trade Administration of the U.S. Department of Commerce, or its successor, or (ii) the U.S. International Trade Commission, or its successor; and

(c) in the case of Mexico, the designated authority within the Secretariat of Trade and Industrial Development ("Secretaria de Comercio y Fomento Industrial"), or its successor;

countervailing duty statute means:

(a) in the case of Canada, the relevant provisions of the Special Import Measures Act, as amended, and any successor statutes;

(b) in the case of the United States, section 303 and the relevant provisions of Title VII of the Tariff Act of 1930, as amended, and any successor statutes;

(c) in the case of Mexico, the relevant provisions of the Foreign Trade Act Implementing Article 131 of the Constitution of the United Mexican States ("Ley Reglamentaria del Articulo 131 de la Constitucion Politica de los Estados Unidos Mexicanos en Materia de Comercio Exterior"), as amended, and any successor statutes; and

(d) the provisions of any other statute that provides for judicial review of final determinations under subparagraph (a), (b) or (c), or indicates the standard of review to be applied to such determinations;

final determination means:

(a) in the case of Canada, (i) an order or finding of the Canadian International Trade Tribunal under subsection 43(1) of the Special Import Measures Act, (ii) an order by the Canadian International Trade Tribunal under subsection 76(4) of the Special Import Measures Act, as amended, continuing an order or finding made under subsection 43(1) of the Act with or without amendment, (iii) a determination by the Deputy Minister of National Revenue for Customs and Excise pursuant to section 41 of the Special Import Measures Act, as amended, (iv) a re-determination by the Deputy Minister pursuant to section 59 of the Special Import Measures Act, as amended, (v) a decision by the Canadian International Trade Tribunal pursuant to subsection 76(3) of the Special Import Measures Act, as amended, not to initiate a review, (vi) a reconsideration by the Canadian International Trade Tribunal pursuant to subsection 91(3) of the Special Import Measures Act, as amended, and (vii) a review by the Deputy Minister of an undertaking pursuant to subsection 53(1) of the Special Import Measures Act, as amended,

(b) in the case of the United States, (i) a final affirmative determination by the International Trade Administration of the U.S. Department of Commerce or by the U.S. International Trade Commission under section 705 or 735 of the Tariff Act of 1930, as amended, including any negative part of such a determination, (ii) a final negative determination by the International Trade Administration of the U.S. Department of Commerce or by the U.S. International Trade Commission under section 705 or 735 of the Tariff Act of 1930, as amended, including any affirmative part of such a determination, (iii) a final determination, other than a determination in (iv), under section 751 of the Tariff Act of 1930, as amended, (iv) a determination by the U.S. International Trade Commission under section 751(b) of the Tariff Act of 1930, as amended, not to review a determination based on changed circumstances, and (v) a final determination by the International Trade Administration of the U.S. Department of Commerce as to whether a particular type of merchandise is within the class or kind of merchandise described in an existing finding of dumping or antidumping or countervailing duty order; and

(c) in the case of Mexico, (i) a final resolution regarding antidumping or countervailing duties investigations by the Secretariat of Trade and Industrial Development ("Secretaria de Comercio y Fomento Industrial"), pursuant to Article 13 of the Foreign Trade Act Implementing Article 131 of the Constitution of the United Mexican States ("Ley Reglamentaria del Articulo 131 de la Constitucion Politica de los Estados Unidos Mexicanos en Materia de Comercio Exterior"), as amended, (ii) a final resolution regarding an annual administrative review of antidumping or countervailing duties by the Secretariat of Trade and Industrial Development ("Secretaria de Comercio y Fomento Industrial"), as described in paragraph (*o*) of its Schedule to Annex 1904.15, and (iii) a final resolution by the Secretariat of Trade and Industrial Development ("Secretaria de Comercio y Fomento Industrial") as to whether a particular type of merchandise is within the class or kind of merchandise described in an existing antidumping or countervailing duty resolution; and

standard of review means the following standards, as may be amended from time to time by the relevant Party:

(a) in the case of Canada, the grounds set out in subsection 18.1(4) of the Federal Court Act, as amended, with respect to all final determinations;

(b) in the case of the United States, (i) the standard set out in section 516A(b)(1)(B) of the Tariff Act of 1930, as amended, with the exception of a determination referred to in (ii), and (ii) the standard set out in section 516A(b)(1)(A) of the Tariff Act of 1930, as amended, with respect to a determination by the U.S. International Trade Commission not to initiate a review pursuant to section 751(b) of the Tariff Act of 1930, as amended; and

(c) in the case of Mexico, the standard set out in Article 238 of the Federal Fiscal Code ("Codigo Fiscal de la Federacion"), or any successor statutes, based solely on the administrative record.

Chapter Twenty

INSTITUTIONAL ARRANGEMENTS AND DISPUTE SETTLEMENT PROCEDURES

Section A—Institutions

Article 2001: The Free Trade Commission

1.   The Parties hereby establish the Free Trade Commission, comprising cabinet-level representatives of the Parties or their designees.

2.   The Commission shall: (a) supervise the implementation of this Agreement; (b) oversee its further elaboration; (c) resolve disputes that may arise regarding its interpretation or application; (d) supervise the work of all committees and working groups established under this Agreement, referred to in Annex 2001.2; and (e) consider any other matter that may affect the operation of this Agreement.

3.   The Commission may: (a) establish, and delegate responsibilities to, ad hoc or standing committees, working groups or expert groups; (b) seek the advice of non-governmental persons or groups; and (c) take such other action in the exercise of its functions as the Parties may agree.

4.   The Commission shall establish its rules and procedures. All decisions of the Commission shall be taken by consensus, except as the Commission may otherwise agree.

5.   The Commission shall convene at least once a year in regular session. Regular sessions of the Commission shall be chaired successively by each Party.

Annex 2001.2

Committees and Working Groups

A.   Committees:

1.   Committee on Trade in Goods (Article 316)

2.   Committee on Trade in Worn Clothing (Annex 300–B, Section 9.1)

3.   Committee on Agricultural Trade (Article 706)—Advisory Committee on Private Commercial Disputes Regarding Agricultural Goods (Article 707)

4.   Committee on Sanitary and Phytosanitary Measures (Article 722)

5.   Committee on Standards–Related Measures (Article 913)—Land Transportation Standards Subcommittee (Article 913(5))—Telecommunications Standards Subcommittee (Article 913(5))—Automotive Standards Council (Article 913(5))—Subcommittee on Labelling of Textile and Apparel Goods (Article 913(5))

6.   Committee on Small Business (Article 1021)

7.   Financial Services Committee (Article 1412)

8.   Advisory Committee on Private Commercial Disputes (Article 2022(4))

B.   Working Groups:

1.   Working Group on Rules of Origin (Article 513)—Customs Subgroup (Article 513(6))

2.   Working Group on Agricultural Subsidies (Article 705(6))

3.   Bilateral Working Group (Mexico—United States) (Annex 703.2(A)(25))

4.   Bilateral Working Group (Canada—Mexico) (Annex 703.2(B)(13))

5.   Working Group on Trade and Competition (Article 1504)

6.   Temporary Entry Working Group (Article 1605)

C.   Other Committees and Working Groups Established under this Agreement

Article 2002: The Secretariat

1.   The Commission shall establish and oversee a Secretariat comprising national Sections.

2.   Each Party shall: (a) establish a permanent office of its Section; (b) be responsible for (i) the operation and costs of its Section, and (ii) the remuneration and payment of expenses of panelists and members of committees and scientific review boards established under this Agreement, as set out in Annex 2002.2; (c) designate an individual to serve as Secretary for its Section, who shall be responsible for its administration and management; and (d) notify the Commission of the location of its Section's office.

3.   The Secretariat shall: (a) provide assistance to the Commission; (b) provide administrative assistance to (i) panels and committees estab-

lished under Chapter Nineteen (Review and Dispute Settlement in Antidumping and Countervailing Duty Matters), in accordance with the procedures established pursuant to Article 1908, and (ii) panels established under this Chapter, in accordance with procedures established pursuant to Article 2012; and (c) as the Commission may direct (i) support the work of other committees and groups established under this Agreement, and (ii) otherwise facilitate the operation of this Agreement.

Annex 2002.2

Remuneration and Payment of Expenses

1. The Commission shall establish the amounts of remuneration and expenses that will be paid to the panelists, committee members and members of scientific review boards.

2. The remuneration of panelists or committee members and their assistants, members of scientific review boards, their travel and lodging expenses, and all general expenses of panels, committees or scientific review boards shall be borne equally by: (a) in the case of panels or committees established under Chapter Nineteen (Review and Dispute Settlement in Antidumping and Countervailing Duty Matters), the involved Parties, as they are defined in Article 1911; or (b) in the case of panels and scientific review boards established under this Chapter, the disputing Parties.

3. Each panelist or committee member shall keep a record and render a final account of the person's time and expenses, and the panel, committee or scientific review board shall keep a record and render a final account of all general expenses.

Section B—Dispute Settlement

Article 2003: Cooperation

The Parties shall at all times endeavor to agree on the interpretation and application of this Agreement, and shall make every attempt through cooperation and consultations to arrive at a mutually satisfactory resolution of any matter that might affect its operation.

Article 2004: Recourse to Dispute Settlement Procedures

Except for the matters covered in Chapter Nineteen (Review and Dispute Settlement in Antidumping and Countervailing Duty Matters) and as otherwise provided in this Agreement, the dispute settlement provisions of this Chapter shall apply with respect to the avoidance or settlement of all disputes between the Parties regarding the interpretation or application of this Agreement or wherever a Party considers that an actual or proposed measure of another Party is or would be inconsistent with the obligations of this Agreement or cause nullification or impairment in the sense of Annex 2004.

Annex 2004

Nullification and Impairment

1.   If any Party considers that any benefit it could reasonably have expected to accrue to it under any provision of: (a) Part Two (Trade in Goods), except for those provisions of Annex 300–A (Automotive Sector) or Chapter Six (Energy) relating to investment, (b) Part Three (Technical Barriers to Trade), (c) Chapter Twelve (Cross–Border Trade in Services), or (d) Part Six (Intellectual Property), is being nullified or impaired as a result of the application of any measure that is not inconsistent with this Agreement, the Party may have recourse to dispute settlement under this Chapter.

2.   A Party may not invoke: (a) paragraph 1(a) or (b), to the extent that the benefit arises from any cross-border trade in services provision of Part Two or Three, or (b) paragraph 1(c) or (d), with respect to any measure subject to an exception under Article 2101 (General Exceptions).

Article 2005: GATT Dispute Settlement

1.   Subject to paragraphs 2, 3 and 4, disputes regarding any matter arising under both this Agreement and the General Agreement on Tariffs and Trade, any agreement negotiated thereunder, or any successor agreement (GATT), may be settled in either forum at the discretion of the complaining Party.

2.   Before a Party initiates a dispute settlement proceeding in the GATT against another Party on grounds that are substantially equivalent to those available to that Party under this Agreement, that Party shall notify any third Party of its intention. If a third Party wishes to have recourse to dispute settlement procedures under this Agreement regarding the matter, it shall inform promptly the notifying Party and those Parties shall consult with a view to agreement on a single forum. If those Parties cannot agree, the dispute normally shall be settled under this Agreement.

3.   In any dispute referred to in paragraph 1 where the responding Party claims that its action is subject to Article 104 (Relation to Environmental and Conservation Agreements) and requests in writing that the matter be considered under this Agreement, the complaining Party may, in respect of that matter, thereafter have recourse to dispute settlement procedures solely under this Agreement.

4.   In any dispute referred to in paragraph 1 that arises under Section B of Chapter Seven (Sanitary and Phytosanitary Measures) or Chapter Nine (Standards–Related Measures): (a) concerning a measure adopted or maintained by a Party to protect its human, animal or plant life or health, or to protect its environment, and (b) that raises factual issues concerning the environment, health, safety or conservation, including directly related scientific matters, where the responding Party requests in writing that the matter be considered under this Agreement,

the complaining Party may, in respect of that matter, thereafter have recourse to dispute settlement procedures solely under this Agreement.

5. The responding Party shall deliver a copy of a request made pursuant to paragraph 3 or 4 to the other Parties and to its Section of the Secretariat. Where the complaining Party has initiated dispute settlement proceedings regarding any matter subject to paragraph 3 or 4, the responding Party shall deliver its request no later than 15 days thereafter. On receipt of such request, the complaining Party shall promptly withdraw from participation in those proceedings and may initiate dispute settlement procedures under Article 2007.

6. Once dispute settlement procedures have been initiated under Article 2007 or dispute settlement proceedings have been initiated under the GATT, the forum selected shall be used to the exclusion of the other, unless a Party makes a request pursuant to paragraph 3 or 4.

7. For purposes of this Article, dispute settlement proceedings under the GATT are deemed to be initiated by a Party's request for a panel, such as under Article XXIII:2 of the General Agreement on Tariffs and Trade 1947, or for a committee investigation, such as under Article 20.1 of the Customs Valuation Code.

Consultations

Article 2006: Consultations

1. Any Party may request in writing consultations with any other Party regarding any actual or proposed measure or any other matter that it considers might affect the operation of this Agreement.

2. The requesting Party shall deliver the request to the other Parties and to its Section of the Secretariat.

3. Unless the Commission otherwise provides in its rules and procedures established under Article 2001(4), a third Party that considers it has a substantial interest in the matter shall be entitled to participate in the consultations on delivery of written notice to the other Parties and to its Section of the Secretariat.

4. Consultations on matters regarding perishable agricultural goods shall commence within 15 days of the date of delivery of the request.

5. The consulting Parties shall make every attempt to arrive at a mutually satisfactory resolution of any matter through consultations under this Article or other consultative provisions of this Agreement. To this end, the consulting Parties shall: (a) provide sufficient information to enable a full examination of how the actual or proposed measure or other matter might affect the operation of this Agreement; (b) treat any confidential or proprietary information exchanged in the course of consultations on the same basis as the Party providing the information; and

(c) seek to avoid any resolution that adversely affects the interests under this Agreement of any other Party.

Initiation of Procedures

Article 2007: Commission—Good Offices, Conciliation and Mediation

1.   If the consulting Parties fail to resolve a matter pursuant to Article 2006 within: (a) 30 days of delivery of a request for consultations, (b) 45 days of delivery of such request if any other Party has subsequently requested or has participated in consultations regarding the same matter, (c) 15 days of delivery of a request for consultations in matters regarding perishable agricultural goods, or (d) such other period as they may agree, any such Party may request in writing a meeting of the Commission.

2.   A Party may also request in writing a meeting of the Commission where: (a) it has initiated dispute settlement proceedings under the GATT regarding any matter subject to Article 2005(3) or (4), and has received a request pursuant to Article 2005(5) for recourse to dispute settlement procedures under this Chapter; or (b) consultations have been held pursuant to Article 513 (Working Group on Rules of Origin), Article 723 (Sanitary and Phytosanitary Measures—Technical Consultations) and Article 914 (Standards–Related Measures—Technical Consultations).

3.   The requesting Party shall state in the request the measure or other matter complained of and indicate the provisions of this Agreement that it considers relevant, and shall deliver the request to the other Parties and to its Section of the Secretariat.

4.   Unless it decides otherwise, the Commission shall convene within 10 days of delivery of the request and shall endeavor to resolve the dispute promptly.

5.   The Commission may: (a) call on such technical advisers or create such working groups or expert groups as it deems necessary, (b) have recourse to good offices, conciliation, mediation or such other dispute resolution procedures, or (c) make recommendations, as may assist the consulting Parties to reach a mutually satisfactory resolution of the dispute.

6.   Unless it decides otherwise, the Commission shall consolidate two or more proceedings before it pursuant to this Article regarding the same measure. The Commission may consolidate two or more proceedings regarding other matters before it pursuant to this Article that it determines are appropriate to be considered jointly.

Panel Proceedings

Article 2008: Request for an Arbitral Panel

1. If the Commission has convened pursuant to Article 2007(4), and the matter has not been resolved within: (a) 30 days thereafter, (b) 30 days after the Commission has convened in respect of the matter most recently referred to it, where proceedings have been consolidated pursuant to Article 2007(6), or (c) such other period as the consulting Parties may agree, any consulting Party may request in writing the establishment of an arbitral panel. The requesting Party shall deliver the request to the other Parties and to its Section of the Secretariat.

2. On delivery of the request, the Commission shall establish an arbitral panel.

3. A third Party that considers it has a substantial interest in the matter shall be entitled to join as a complaining Party on delivery of written notice of its intention to participate to the disputing Parties and its Section of the Secretariat. The notice shall be delivered at the earliest possible time, and in any event no later than seven days after the date of delivery of a request by a Party for the establishment of a panel.

4. If a third Party does not join as a complaining Party in accordance with paragraph 3, it normally shall refrain thereafter from initiating or continuing: (a) a dispute settlement procedure under this Agreement, or (b) a dispute settlement proceeding in the GATT on grounds that are substantially equivalent to those available to that Party under this Agreement, regarding the same matter in the absence of a significant change in economic or commercial circumstances.

5. Unless otherwise agreed by the disputing Parties, the panel shall be established and perform its functions in a manner consistent with the provisions of this Chapter.

Article 2009: Roster

1. The Parties shall establish by January 1, 1994 and maintain a roster of up to 30 individuals who are willing and able to serve as panelists. The roster members shall be appointed by consensus for terms of three years, and may be reappointed.

2. Roster members shall: (a) have expertise or experience in law, international trade, other matters covered by this Agreement or the resolution of disputes arising under international trade agreements, and shall be chosen strictly on the basis of objectivity, reliability and sound judgment; (b) be independent of, and not be affiliated with or take instructions from, any Party; and (c) comply with a code of conduct to be established by the Commission.

Article 2010: Qualifications of Panelists

1. All panelists shall meet the qualifications set out in Article 2009(2).

2. Individuals may not serve as panelists for a dispute in which they have participated pursuant to Article 2007(5).

Article 2011: Panel Selection

1. Where there are two disputing Parties, the following procedures shall apply: (a) The panel shall comprise five members. (b) The disputing Parties shall endeavor to agree on the chair of the panel within 15 days of the delivery of the request for the establishment of the panel. If the disputing Parties are unable to agree on the chair within this period, the disputing Party chosen by lot shall select within five days as chair an individual who is not a citizen of that Party. (c) Within 15 days of selection of the chair, each disputing Party shall select two panelists who are citizens of the other disputing Party. (d) If a disputing Party fails to select its panelists within such period, such panelists shall be selected by lot from among the roster members who are citizens of the other disputing Party.

2. Where there are more than two disputing Parties, the following procedures shall apply: (a) The panel shall comprise five members. (b) The disputing Parties shall endeavor to agree on the chair of the panel within 15 days of the delivery of the request for the establishment of the panel. If the disputing Parties are unable to agree on the chair within this period, the Party or Parties on the side of the dispute chosen by lot shall select within 10 days a chair who is not a citizen of such Party or Parties. (c) Within 15 days of selection of the chair, the Party complained against shall select two panelists, one of whom is a citizen of a complaining Party, and the other of whom is a citizen of another complaining Party. The complaining Parties shall select two panelists who are citizens of the Party complained against. (d) If any disputing Party fails to select a panelist within such period, such panelist shall be selected by lot in accordance with the citizenship criteria of subparagraph (c).

3. Panelists shall normally be selected from the roster. Any disputing Party may exercise a peremptory challenge against any individual not on the roster who is proposed as a panelist by a disputing Party within 15 days after the individual has been proposed.

4. If a disputing Party believes that a panelist is in violation of the code of conduct, the disputing Parties shall consult and if they agree, the panelist shall be removed and a new panelist shall be selected in accordance with this Article.

Article 2012: Rules of Procedure

1.   The Commission shall establish by January 1, 1994, Model Rules of Procedure, in accordance with the following principles: (a) the procedures shall assure a right to at least one hearing before the panel as well as the opportunity to provide initial and rebuttal written submissions; and (b) the panel's hearings, deliberations and initial report, and all written submissions to and communications with the panel shall be confidential.

2.   Unless the disputing Parties otherwise agree, the panel shall conduct its proceedings in accordance with the Model Rules of Procedure.

3.   Unless the disputing Parties otherwise agree within 20 days from the date of the delivery of the request for the establishment of the panel, the terms of reference shall be: "To examine, in the light of the relevant provisions of the Agreement, the matter referred to the Commission (as set out in the request for a Commission meeting) and to make findings, determinations and recommendations as provided in Article 2016(2)."

4.   If a complaining Party wishes to argue that a matter has nullified or impaired benefits, the terms of reference shall so indicate.

5.   If a disputing Party wishes the panel to make findings as to the degree of adverse trade effects on any Party of any measure found not to conform with the obligations of the Agreement or to have caused nullification or impairment in the sense of Annex 2004, the terms of reference shall so indicate.

Article 2013: Third Party Participation

A Party that is not a disputing Party, on delivery of a written notice to the disputing Parties and to its Section of the Secretariat, shall be entitled to attend all hearings, to make written and oral submissions to the panel and to receive written submissions of the disputing Parties.

Article 2014: Role of Experts

On request of a disputing Party, or on its own initiative, the panel may seek information and technical advice from any person or body that it deems appropriate, provided that the disputing Parties so agree and subject to such terms and conditions as such Parties may agree.

Article 2015: Scientific Review Boards

1.   On request of a disputing Party or, unless the disputing Parties disapprove, on its own initiative, the panel may request a written report of a scientific review board on any factual issue concerning environmental, health, safety or other scientific matters raised by a disputing Party in a proceeding, subject to such terms and conditions as such Parties may agree.

2. The board shall be selected by the panel from among highly qualified, independent experts in the scientific matters, after consultations with the disputing Parties and the scientific bodies set out in the Model Rules of Procedure established pursuant to Article 2012(1).

3. The participating Parties shall be provided: (a) advance notice of, and an opportunity to provide comments to the panel on, the proposed factual issues to be referred to the board; and (b) a copy of the board's report and an opportunity to provide comments on the report to the panel.

4. The panel shall take the board's report and any comments by the Parties on the report into account in the preparation of its report.

Article 2016: Initial Report

1. Unless the disputing Parties otherwise agree, the panel shall base its report on the submissions and arguments of the Parties and on any information before it pursuant to Article 2014 or 2015.

2. Unless the disputing Parties otherwise agree, the panel shall, within 90 days after the last panelist is selected or such other period as the Model Rules of Procedure established pursuant to Article 2012(1) may provide, present to the disputing Parties an initial report containing: (a) findings of fact, including any findings pursuant to a request under Article 2012(5); (b) its determination as to whether the measure at issue is or would be inconsistent with the obligations of this Agreement or cause nullification or impairment in the sense of Annex 2004, or any other determination requested in the terms of reference; and (c) its recommendations, if any, for resolution of the dispute.

3. Panelists may furnish separate opinions on matters not unanimously agreed.

4. A disputing Party may submit written comments to the panel on its initial report within 14 days of presentation of the report.

5. In such an event, and after considering such written comments, the panel, on its own initiative or on the request of any disputing Party, may: (a) request the views of any participating Party; (b) reconsider its report; and (c) make any further examination that it considers appropriate.

Article 2017: Final Report

1. The panel shall present to the disputing Parties a final report, including any separate opinions on matters not unanimously agreed, within 30 days of presentation of the initial report, unless the disputing Parties otherwise agree.

2. No panel may, either in its initial report or its final report, disclose which panelists are associated with majority or minority opinions.

3. The disputing Parties shall transmit to the Commission the final report of the panel, including any report of a scientific review board established under Article 2015, as well as any written views that a disputing Party desires to be appended, on a confidential basis within a reasonable period of time after it is presented to them.

4. Unless the Commission decides otherwise, the final report of the panel shall be published 15 days after it is transmitted to the Commission.

Implementation of Panel Reports

Article 2018: Implementation of Final Report

1. On receipt of the final report of a panel, the disputing Parties shall agree on the resolution of the dispute, which normally shall conform with the determinations and recommendations of the panel, and shall notify their Sections of the Secretariat of any agreed resolution of any dispute.

2. Wherever possible, the resolution shall be non-implementation or removal of a measure not conforming with this Agreement or causing nullification or impairment in the sense of Annex 2004 or, failing such a resolution, compensation.

Article 2019: Non–implementation—Suspension of Benefits

1. If in its final report a panel has determined that a measure is inconsistent with the obligations of this Agreement or causes nullification or impairment in the sense of Annex 2004 and the Party complained against has not reached agreement with any complaining Party on a mutually satisfactory resolution pursuant to Article 2018(1) within 30 days of receiving the final report, such complaining Party may suspend the application to the Party complained against of benefits of equivalent effect until such time as they have reached agreement on a resolution of the dispute.

2. In considering what benefits to suspend pursuant to paragraph 1: (a) a complaining Party should first seek to suspend benefits in the same sector or sectors as that affected by the measure or other matter that the panel has found to be inconsistent with the obligations of this Agreement or to have caused nullification or impairment in the sense of Annex 2004; and (b) a complaining Party that considers it is not practicable or effective to suspend benefits in the same sector or sectors may suspend benefits in other sectors.

3. On the written request of any disputing Party delivered to the other Parties and its Section of the Secretariat, the Commission shall establish a panel to determine whether the level of benefits suspended by a Party pursuant to paragraph 1 is manifestly excessive.

4. The panel proceedings shall be conducted in accordance with the Model Rules of Procedure. The panel shall present its determination within 60 days after the last panelist is selected or such other period as the disputing Parties may agree.

Section C—Domestic Proceedings and Private Commercial Dispute Settlement

Article 2020: Referrals of Matters from Judicial or Administrative Proceedings

1. If an issue of interpretation or application of this Agreement arises in any domestic judicial or administrative proceeding of a Party that any Party considers would merit its intervention, or if a court or administrative body solicits the views of a Party, that Party shall notify the other Parties and its Section of the Secretariat. The Commission shall endeavor to agree on an appropriate response as expeditiously as possible.

2. The Party in whose territory the court or administrative body is located shall submit any agreed interpretation of the Commission to the court or administrative body in accordance with the rules of that forum.

3. If the Commission is unable to agree, any Party may submit its own views to the court or administrative body in accordance with the rules of that forum.

Article 2021: Private Rights

No Party may provide for a right of action under its domestic law against any other Party on the ground that a measure of another Party is inconsistent with this Agreement.

Article 2022: Alternative Dispute Resolution

1. Each Party shall, to the maximum extent possible, encourage and facilitate the use of arbitration and other means of alternative dispute resolution for the settlement of international commercial disputes between private parties in the free trade area.

2. To this end, each Party shall provide appropriate procedures to ensure observance of agreements to arbitrate and for the recognition and enforcement of arbitral awards in such disputes.

3. A Party shall be deemed to be in compliance with paragraph 2 if it is a party to and is in compliance with the 1958 United Nations Convention on the Recognition and Enforcement of Foreign Arbitral Awards or the 1975 Inter–American Convention on International Commercial Arbitration.

4. The Commission shall establish an Advisory Committee on Private Commercial Disputes comprising persons with expertise or experience in the resolution of private international commercial disputes.

The Committee shall report and provide recommendations to the Commission on general issues referred to it by the Commission respecting the availability, use and effectiveness of arbitration and other procedures for the resolution of such disputes in the free trade area.

Part Eight
OTHER PROVISIONS

Chapter Twenty–One

EXCEPTIONS

Article 2101: General Exceptions

1. For purposes of: (a) Part Two (Trade in Goods), except to the extent that a provision of that Part applies to services or investment, and (b) Part Three (Technical Barriers to Trade), except to the extent that a provision of that Part applies to services, GATT Article XX and its interpretative notes, or any equivalent provision of a successor agreement to which all Parties are party, are incorporated into and made part of this Agreement. The Parties understand that the measures referred to in GATT Article XX(b) include environmental measures necessary to protect human, animal or plant life or health, and that GATT Article XX(g) applies to measures relating to the conservation of living and non-living exhaustible natural resources.

2. Provided that such measures are not applied in a manner that would constitute a means of arbitrary or unjustifiable discrimination between countries where the same conditions prevail or a disguised restriction on trade between the Parties, nothing in: (a) Part Two (Trade in Goods), to the extent that a provision of that Part applies to services, (b) Part Three (Technical Barriers to Trade), to the extent that a provision of that Part applies to services, (c) Chapter Twelve (Cross–Border Trade in Services), and (d) Chapter Thirteen (Telecommunications), shall be construed to prevent the adoption or enforcement by any Party of measures necessary to secure compliance with laws or regulations that are not inconsistent with the provisions of this Agreement, including those relating to health and safety and consumer protection.

Article 2102: National Security

1. Subject to Articles 607 (Energy—National Security Measures) and 1018 (Government Procurement—Exceptions), nothing in this Agreement shall be construed: (a) to require any Party to furnish or allow access to any information the disclosure of which it determines to be contrary to its essential security interests; (b) to prevent any Party from taking any actions that it considers necessary for the protection of

its essential security interests (i) relating to the traffic in arms, ammunition and implements of war and to such traffic and transactions in other goods, materials, services and technology undertaken directly or indirectly for the purpose of supplying a military or other security establishment, (ii) taken in time of war or other emergency in international relations, or (iii) relating to the implementation of national policies or international agreements respecting the non-proliferation of nuclear weapons or other nuclear explosive devices; or (c) to prevent any Party from taking action in pursuance of its obligations under the United Nations Charter for the maintenance of international peace and security.

Article 2103: Taxation

1. Except as set out in this Article, nothing in this Agreement shall apply to taxation measures.

2. Nothing in this Agreement shall affect the rights and obligations of any Party under any tax convention. In the event of any inconsistency between this Agreement and any such convention, that convention shall prevail to the extent of the inconsistency.

3. Notwithstanding paragraph 2: (a) Article 301 (Market Access—National Treatment) and such other provisions of this Agreement as are necessary to give effect to that Article shall apply to taxation measures to the same extent as does Article III of the GATT; and (b) Article 314 (Market Access—Export Taxes) and Article 604 (Energy—Export Taxes) shall apply to taxation measures.

4. Subject to paragraph 2: (a) Article 1202 (Cross–Border Trade in Services—National Treatment) and Article 1405 (Financial Services—National Treatment) shall apply to taxation measures on income, capital gains or the taxable capital of corporations, and to those taxes listed in paragraph 1 of Annex 2103.4, that relate to the purchase or consumption of particular services, and (b) Articles 1102 and 1103 (Investment—National Treatment and Most–Favored Nation Treatment), Articles 1202 and 1203 (Cross–Border Trade in Services—National Treatment and Most–Favored–Nation Treatment) and Articles 1405 and 1406 (Financial Services—National Treatment and Most–Favored–Nation Treatment) shall apply to all taxation measures, other than those on income, capital gains or on the taxable capital of corporations, taxes on estates, inheritances, gifts and generation-skipping transfers and those taxes listed in paragraph 1 of Annex 2103.4, except that nothing in those Articles shall apply (c) any most-favored-nation obligation with respect to an advantage accorded by a Party pursuant to a tax convention, (d) to a non-conforming provision of any existing taxation measure, (e) to the continuation or prompt renewal of a non-conforming provision of any existing taxation measure, (f) to an amendment to a non-conforming provision of any existing taxation measure to the extent that the amendment does not decrease its conformity, at the time of the amendment, with any of those Articles, (g) to any new taxation measure aimed at ensuring the equitable and effective imposition or collection of taxes and that does not

arbitrarily discriminate between persons, goods or services of the Parties or arbitrarily nullify or impair benefits accorded under those Articles, in the sense of Annex 2004, or (h) to the measures listed in paragraph 2 of Annex 2103.4.

5. Subject to paragraph 2 and without prejudice to the rights and obligations of the Parties under paragraph 3, Article 1106(3), (4) and (5) (Performance Requirements) shall apply to taxation measures.

6. Article 1110 (Expropriation and Compensation) shall apply to taxation measures except that no investor may invoke that Article as the basis for a claim under Article 1116 (Claim by an Investor of a Party on its Own Behalf) or 1117 (Claim by an Investor of a Party on Behalf of an Enterprise), where it has been determined pursuant to this paragraph that the measure is not an expropriation. The investor shall refer the issue of whether the measure is not an expropriation for a determination to the appropriate competent authorities set out in Annex 2103.6 at the time that it gives notice under Article 1119 (Notice of Intent to Submit a Claim to Arbitration). If the competent authorities do not agree to consider the issue or, having agreed to consider it, fail to agree that the measure is not an expropriation within a period of six months of such referral, the investor may submit its claim to arbitration under Article 1120 (Submission of a Claim to Arbitration).

Annex 2103.4

Specific Taxation Measures

1. For purposes of Article 2103(4)(a) and (b), the listed tax is the asset tax under the Asset Tax Law ("Ley del Impuesto al Activo") of Mexico.

2. For purposes of Article 2103(4)(h), the listed tax is any excise tax on insurance premiums adopted by Mexico to the extent that such tax would, if levied by Canada or the United States, be covered by Article 2103(4)(d), (e) or (f).

Annex 2103.6

Competent Authorities

For purposes of this Chapter:

competent authority means (a) in the case of Canada, the Assistant Deputy Minister for Tax Policy, Department of Finance; (b) in the case of Mexico, the Deputy Minister of Revenue of the Ministry of Finance and Public Credit ("Secretaria de Hacienda y Credito Publico"); and (c) in the case of the United States, the Assistant Secretary of the Treasury (Tax Policy), Department of the Treasury.

Article 2104: Balance of Payments

1. Nothing in this Agreement shall be construed to prevent a Party from adopting or maintaining measures that restrict transfers where the

Party experiences serious balance of payments difficulties, or the threat thereof, and such restrictions are consistent with paragraphs 2 through 4 and are: (a) consistent with paragraph 5 to the extent they are imposed on transfers other than cross-border trade in financial services; or (b) consistent with paragraphs 6 and 7 to the extent they are imposed on cross-border trade in financial services.

General Rules

2. As soon as practicable after a Party imposes a measure under this Article, the Party shall: (a) submit any current account exchange restrictions to the IMF for review under Article VIII of the Articles of Agreement of the IMF; (b) enter into good faith consultations with the IMF on economic adjustment measures to address the fundamental underlying economic problems causing the difficulties; and (c) adopt or maintain economic policies consistent with such consultations.

3. A measure adopted or maintained under this Article shall: (a) avoid unnecessary damage to the commercial, economic or financial interests of another Party; (b) not be more burdensome than necessary to deal with the balance of payments difficulties or threat thereof; (c) be temporary and be phased out progressively as the balance of payments situation improves; (d) be consistent with paragraph 2(c) and with the Articles of Agreement of the IMF; and (e) be applied on a national treatment or most-favored-nation treatment basis, whichever is better.

4. A Party may adopt or maintain a measure under this Article that gives priority to services that are essential to its economic program, provided that a Party may not impose a measure for the purpose of protecting a specific industry or sector unless the measure is consistent with paragraph 2(c) and with Article VIII(3) of the Articles of Agreement of the IMF.

Restrictions on Transfers Other Than Cross–Border Trade in Financial Services

5. Restrictions imposed on transfers, other than on cross-border trade in financial services: (a) where imposed on payments for current international transactions, shall be consistent with Article VIII(3) of the Articles of Agreement of the IMF; (b) where imposed on international capital transactions, shall be consistent with Article VI of the Articles of Agreement of the IMF and be imposed only in conjunction with measures imposed on current international transactions under paragraph 2(a); (c) where imposed on transfers covered by Article 1109 (Investment—Transfers) and transfers related to trade in goods, may not substantially impede transfers from being made in a freely usable currency at a market rate of exchange; and (d) may not take the form of tariff surcharges, quotas, licenses or similar measures.

Restrictions on Cross–Border Trade in Financial Services

6. A Party imposing a restriction on cross-border trade in financial services: (a) may not impose more than one measure on any transfer,

unless consistent with paragraph 2(c) and with Article VIII(3) of the Articles of Agreement of the IMF; and (b) shall promptly notify and consult with the other Parties to assess the balance of payments situation of the Party and the measures it has adopted, taking into account among other elements (i) the nature and extent of the balance of payments difficulties of the Party, (ii) the external economic and trading environment of the Party, and (iii) alternative corrective measures that may be available.

7. In consultations under paragraph 6(b), the Parties shall: (a) consider if measures adopted under this Article comply with paragraph 3, in particular paragraph 3(c); and (b) accept all findings of statistical and other facts presented by the IMF relating to foreign exchange, monetary reserves and balance of payments, and shall base their conclusions on the assessment by the IMF of the balance of payments situation of the Party adopting the measures.

Article 2105: Disclosure of Information

Nothing in this Agreement shall be construed to require a Party to furnish or allow access to information the disclosure of which would impede law enforcement or would be contrary to the Party's law protecting personal privacy or the financial affairs and accounts of individual customers of financial institutions.

Article 2106: Cultural Industries

Annex 2106 applies to the Parties specified in that Annex with respect to cultural industries.

Annex 2106
Cultural Industries

Notwithstanding any other provision of this Agreement, as between Canada and the United States, any measure adopted or maintained with respect to cultural industries, except as specifically provided in Article 302 (Market Access—Tariff Elimination), and any measure of equivalent commercial effect taken in response, shall be governed under this Agreement exclusively in accordance with the provisions of the Canada–United States Free Trade Agreement. The rights and obligations between Canada and any other Party with respect to such measures shall be identical to those applying between Canada and the United States.

Article 2107: Definitions

For purposes of this Chapter:

cultural industries means persons engaged in any of the following activities: (a) the publication, distribution, or sale of books, magazines, periodicals or newspapers in print or machine readable form but not including the sole activity of printing or typesetting any of the foregoing; (b) the production, distribution, sale or exhibition of film or video recordings; (c) the production, distribution, sale or exhibition of audio or video music recordings; (d) the publication, distribution or sale of music in print or machine readable form; or (e) radiocommunications in which the transmissions are intended for direct reception by the general public, and all radio, television and cable broadcasting undertakings and all satellite programming and broadcast network services;

international capital transactions means "international capital transactions" as defined under the Articles of Agreement of the IMF;

IMF means the International Monetary Fund;

payments for current international transactions means "payments for current international transactions" as defined under the Articles of Agreement of the IMF;

tax convention means a convention for the avoidance of double taxation or other international taxation agreement or arrangement;

taxes and taxation measures do not include: (a) a "customs duty" as defined in Article 318 (Market Access—Definitions); or (b) the measures listed in exceptions (b), (c), (d) and (e) of that definition; and

transfers means international transactions and related international transfers and payments.

Chapter Twenty–Two

FINAL PROVISIONS

Article 2201: Annexes

The Annexes to this Agreement constitute an integral part of this Agreement.

Article 2202: Amendments

1. The Parties may agree on any modification of or addition to this Agreement.

2. When so agreed, and approved in accordance with the applicable legal procedures of each Party, a modification or addition shall constitute an integral part of this Agreement.

Article 2203: Entry into Force

This Agreement shall enter into force on January 1, 1994, on an exchange of written notifications certifying the completion of necessary legal procedures.

Article 2204: Accession

1. Any country or group of countries may accede to this Agreement subject to such terms and conditions as may be agreed between such country or countries and the Commission and following approval in accordance with the applicable legal procedures of each country.

2. This Agreement shall not apply as between any Party and any acceding country or group of countries if, at the time of accession, either does not consent to such application.

Article 2205: Withdrawal

A Party may withdraw from this Agreement six months after it provides written notice of withdrawal to the other Parties. If a Party withdraws, the Agreement shall remain in force for the remaining Parties.

Article 2206: Authentic Texts

The English, French and Spanish texts of this Agreement are equally authentic.

General Annexes (Selected Provisions)

IN WITNESS WHEREOF, the undersigned, being duly authorized by their respective Governments, have signed this Agreement.

DONE in triplicate at

Ottawa, on the 11th day and the 17th day of December 1992,

Mexico, D.F., on the 14th day and the 17th day of December 1992,

Washington, D.C., on the 8th day and the 17th day of December 1992.

FOR THE GOVERNMENT OF CANADA

FOR THE GOVERNMENT OF THE UNITED MEXICAN STATES

FOR THE GOVERNMENT OF THE UNITED STATES OF AMERICA

Notes

1. Article 201 (Definitions of General Application): A good of a Party may include materials of other countries.

2. Article 301 (Market Access—National Treatment): "goods of the Party" as used in paragraph 2 includes goods produced in the state or province of that Party.

3. Article 302(1) (Tariff Elimination): this paragraph is not intended to prevent any Party from modifying its non-NAFTA tariffs on originating goods for which no NAFTA tariff preference is claimed.

4. Article 302(1): this paragraph does not prohibit a Party from raising a tariff back to an agreed level in accordance with the NAFTA's phase-out schedule following a unilateral reduction.

5. Article 302(1) and (2): paragraphs 1 and 2 are not intended to prevent a Party from maintaining or increasing a customs duty as may be authorized by any dispute settlement provision of the GATT or any agreement negotiated under the GATT.

6. Article 303 (Restriction on Drawback and Duty Deferral): in applying the definition of "used" in Article 415 to this Article, the definition of "consumed" in Article 318 shall not apply.

7. Article 305(2)(d) (Temporary Admission of Goods): where another form of monetary security is used, it shall not be more burdensome than the bonding requirement referred to in this subparagraph. Where a Party uses a non-monetary form of security, it shall not be more burdensome than existing forms of security used by that Party.

8. Article 307(1) (Goods Re-entered After Repair or Alteration): this paragraph does not cover goods imported in bond, into foreign-trade zones or

in similar status, that are exported for repairs and are not re-imported in bond, into foreign-trade zones or in similar status.

9.   Article 307(1): for purposes of this paragraph, alteration includes laundering used textile and apparel goods and sterilizing previously sterilized textile and apparel goods.

10.   Article 318 (Market Access—Definitions): 10–digit items set out in the Tariff Schedule of Canada are included for statistical purposes only.

11.   Article 318: with respect to the definition of "repair or alteration", an operation or process that is part of the production or assembly of an unfinished good into a finished good is not a repair or alteration of the unfinished good; a component of a good is a good that may be subject to repair or alteration.

12.   Annex 300–A (Trade and Investment in the Automotive Sector), Appendix 300–A.1—Canada: paragraphs 1 and 2 shall not be construed to modify the rights and obligations set out in Chapter Ten of the Canada–United States Free Trade Agreement, except that the NAFTA rules of origin shall replace the Canada–United States Free Trade Agreement rules of origin for purposes of Article 1005(1).

13.   Annex 300–A, Appendix 300–A.2—Mexico: citations to the Auto Decree and the Auto Decree Implementing Regulations included in parentheses are provided for purposes of reference only.

14.   Annex 300–B (Textile and Apparel Goods), Section 1 (Scope and Coverage): the general provisions of Chapter Two (Definitions), Chapter Three (Market Access), Chapter Four (Rules of Origin) and Chapter Eight (Emergency Action) are subject to the specific rules for textiles and apparel goods set out in the Annex.

15.   Annex 300–B, Section 2 (Tariff Elimination): with respect to paragraph 1, "as otherwise provided in this Agreement" refers to such provisions as Section 4, Article 802 (Global Actions) and Chapter 22 (General Exceptions).

16.   Annex 300–B, Sections 4 (Bilateral Emergency Actions (Tariff Actions)) and 5 (Bilateral Emergency Actions (Quantitative Restrictions)): for purposes of Sections 4 and 5: (a) "increased quantities" is intended to be interpreted more broadly than the standard provided in Article 801(1), which considers imports "in absolute terms" only. For purposes of these Sections, "increased quantities" is intended to be interpreted in the same manner as this standard is interpreted in the draft Agreement on Textiles and Clothing, contained in the Draft Final Act Embodying the Results of the Uruguay Round of Multilateral Trade Negotiations (GATT document MTN. TNC/W/FA) issued by the Director–General of the GATT on December 20, 1991 ("Draft Uruguay Round Agreement on Textiles and Clothing"); and (b) "serious damage" is intended as a less stringent standard than "serious injury" under Article 801(1). The "serious damage" standard is drawn from the Draft Uruguay Round Agreement on Textiles and Clothing. The factors to be considered in determining whether the standard has been met are set out in Section 4.2 and are also drawn from that Draft. "Serious damage" is to be interpreted in the light of its meaning in Annex A of the Multifiber Arrangement or any successor agreement.

17. Annex 300–B, Section 5: in paragraph 5(c), the term "equitable treatment" is intended to have the same meaning as it has in customary practice under the Multifiber Arrangement.

18. Annex 300–B, Section 7, paragraph 1(c) (Review and Revision of Rules of Origin): for subheading 6212.10, the rule and paragraph 1 shall not be applied if the Parties agree, prior to entry into force of this Agreement, on measures to ease the administrative burden and reduce costs associated with the application of the rule for headings 62.06 through 62.11 to the apparel in subheading 6212.10.

19. Annex 300–B, Section 7, paragraph (2)(d)(ii): with respect to provisions (a) through (i) of the rule for subheadings 6205.20 through 6205.30, prior to the entry into force of this Agreement the Parties will extend cooperation as necessary in an effort to encourage production in the free trade area of shirting fabrics specifically identified in the rule.

20. Annex 300–B, Appendix 3.1, paragraph 17 (Administration of Import and Export Prohibitions, Restrictions and Consultation Levels): for purposes of applying paragraph 17, the determination of the component that determines the tariff classification of the good shall be based on GRI 3(b) of the Harmonized System, and if the component cannot be determined on the basis of GRI 3(b), then the determination will be based on GRI 3(c) or, if GRI 3(c) is inapplicable, GRI 4. When the component that determines the tariff classification is a blend of two or more yarns or fibers, all yarns and, where applicable, fibers, in that component are to be considered.

21. Annex 300–B, Schedule 3.1.3. (Conversion Factors): the conversion factors in this Schedule are those used for imports into the United States. Canada and Mexico may by mutual agreement develop their own conversion factors for trade between them.

22. Article 401 (Originating Goods): the phrase "specifically describes" is intended solely to prevent Article 401(d) from being used to qualify a part of another part, where the heading or subheading covers the final good, the part made from the other part and the other part.

23. Article 402 (Regional Value Content): (a) Article 402(4) applies to intermediate materials, and VNM in paragraphs 2 and 3 does not include (i) the value of any non-originating materials used by another producer to produce an originating material that is subsequently acquired and used in the production of the good by the producer of the good, and (ii) the value of non-originating materials used by the producer to produce an originating self-produced material that is designated by the producer as an intermediate material pursuant to Article 402(10); (b) with respect to paragraph 4, where an originating intermediate material is subsequently used by the producer with non-originating materials (whether or not produced by the producer) to produce the good, the value of such non-originating materials shall be included in the VNM of the good; (c) with respect to paragraph 8, sales promotion, marketing and after-sales service costs, royalties, shipping and packing costs, and non-allowable interest costs included in the value of materials used in the production of the good are not subtracted out of the net cost in the calculation under Article 402(3); (d) with respect to paragraph 10, an intermediate material used by another producer in the production of a material that is subsequently acquired and used by the producer of the good

shall not be taken into account in applying the proviso set out in that paragraph, except where two or more producers accumulate their production under Article 404; (e) with respect to paragraph 10, if a producer designates a self-produced material as an originating intermediate material and the Customs Administration of the importing Party subsequently determines that the intermediate material is not originating, the producer may rescind the designation and recalculate the value content of the good accordingly; in such a case, the producer shall retain its rights of appeal or review with regard to the determination of the origin of the intermediate material; and (f) under paragraph 4, with respect to any self-produced material that is not designated as an intermediate material, only the value of non-originating materials used to produce the self-produced material shall be included in VNM of the good.

24. Article 403 (Automotive Goods): (a) for purposes of paragraph 1, "first person in the territory of a Party" means the first person who uses the imported good in production or resells the imported good; and (b) for purposes of paragraph 2, (i) a producer may not designate as an intermediate material any assembly, including a component identified in Annex 403.2, containing one or more of the materials listed in Annex 403.2, and (ii) a producer of a material listed in Annex 403.2 may designate a self-produced material used in the production of that material as an intermediate material, in accordance with the provisions of Article 402(10).

25. Article 405(6) (De Minimis): for purposes of applying paragraph 6, the determination of the component that determines the tariff classification of the good shall be based on GRI 3(b) of the Harmonized System. If the component cannot be determined on the basis of GRI 3(b), then the determination will be based on GRI 3(c) or, if GRI 3(c) is inapplicable, GRI 4. When the component that determines the tariff classification is a blend of two or more yarns or fibers, all yarns and, where applicable, fibers, in that component are to be taken into account.

26. Article 413 (Interpretation and Application): the rules of origin under Chapter Four are based on the 1992 Harmonized System, amended by the new tariff items created for rules of origin purposes.

27. Article 415 (Rules of Origin—Definitions): the phrase "except for the application of Article 403(1) or 403(2)(a)" in the definition of "transaction value" is intended solely to ensure that the determination of transaction value in the context of Article 403(1) or (2)(a) shall not be limited to the transaction of the producer of the good.

28. Article 514 (Customs Procedures—Definitions): the Uniform Regulations will clarify that "determination of origin" includes a denial of preferential tariff treatment under Article 506(4), and that such denial is subject to review and appeal.

29. Article 603, paragraphs 1 through 5 (Energy—Import and Export Restrictions): these paragraphs shall be interpreted consistently with Article 309 (Import and Export Restrictions).

30. Article 703 (Agriculture—Market Access): the most-favored-nation rate as of July 1, 1991 is the over-quota tariff rate specified in Annex 302.2.

31. Annex 703.2, Section A (Mexico and the United States): this quota replaces Mexico's current access under the "first tier" of the U.S. tariff rate quota as described in Additional Note 3(b)(i) of Chapter 17 of the Harmonized Tariff Schedule of the United States prior to the date of entry into force of this Agreement.

32. Annex 703.2, Section A (Mexico and the United States): the United States operates a re-export program under Additional U.S. Note 3 to Chapter 17 of the U.S. Harmonized Tariff Schedule and under 7 C.F.R. Part 1530 (subparts A and B).

33. Annex 703.2, Section B (Canada and Mexico): the incorporation in paragraph 6 is not intended to override the exceptions to Articles 301 and 309 set out in Canada's and Mexico's respective Schedules to Annex 301.3.

34. Article 906(4) and (6) (Compatibility and Equivalence): these paragraphs are not intended to restrict the right of the importing Party to revise its measures.

35. Article 908(2) (Conformity Assessment): this paragraph does not treat the issue of membership in the Parties' respective conformity assessment bodies.

36. Article 915 (Standards–Related Measures—Definitions): the definition of "standard" shall be interpreted to mean—(a) characteristics for a good or a service, (b) characteristics, rules or guidelines for (i) processes or production methods relating to such good, or (ii) operating methods relating to such service, and (c) provisions specifying terminology, symbols, packaging, marking or labelling for (i) a good or its related process or production method, or (ii) a service or its related operating method, for common and repeated use, including explanatory and other related provisions, set out in a document approved by a standardizing body, with which compliance is not mandatory.

37. Article 915: the definition of "technical regulation" shall be interpreted to mean—(a) characteristics or their related processes and production methods for a good, (b) characteristics for a service or its related operating methods, or (c) provisions specifying terminology, symbols, packaging, marking, or labelling for (i) a good or its related process or production method, or (ii) a service or its related operating method, set out in a document, including applicable administrative, explanatory and other related provisions, with which compliance is mandatory.

38. Annex 1001.2c (Country Specific Thresholds): Canada and the United States will consult regarding this Annex before the entry into force of this Agreement.

39. Article 1101 (Investment—Scope and Coverage): this Chapter covers investments existing on the date of entry into force of this Agreement as well as investments made or acquired thereafter.

40. Article 1101(2) and Annex 602.3: to the extent that a Party allows an investment to be made in an activity set out in Annex III or Annex 602.3, the investment shall be entitled to the protection of Chapter Eleven (Investment).

41.   Article 1106 (Performance Requirements): Article 1106 does not preclude enforcement of any commitment, undertaking or requirement between private parties.

42.   Article 1305 (Monopolies): for purposes of this Article, "monopoly" means an entity, including a consortium or government agency, that in any relevant market in the territory of a Party is maintained or designated as the sole provider of public telecommunications transport networks or services.

43.   Article 1501 (Competition Law): no investor may have recourse to investor-state arbitration under the Investment Chapter for any matter arising under this Article.

44.   Article 1502 (Monopolies and State Enterprises): nothing in this Article shall be construed to prevent a monopoly from charging different prices in different geographic markets, where such differences are based on normal commercial considerations, such as taking account of supply and demand conditions in those markets.

45.   Article 1502(3): a "delegation" includes a legislative grant, and a government order, directive or other act transferring to the monopoly, or authorizing the exercise by the monopoly of, governmental authority.

46.   Article 1502(3)(b): differences in pricing between classes of customers, between affiliated and non-affiliated firms, and cross-subsidization are not in themselves inconsistent with this provision; rather, they are subject to this subparagraph when they are used as instruments of anticompetitive behavior by the monopoly firm.

47.   Article 2005(2) (GATT Dispute Settlement): this obligation is not intended to be subject to dispute settlement under this Chapter.

General Annexes

Annex I: Reservations for Existing Measures and Liberalization Commitments

> **Schedule of Canada**
>
> **Schedule of Mexico**
>
> **Schedule of the United States**

Annex II: Reservations for Future Measures

Annex III: Activities Reserved to the State

Annex IV: Exceptions from Most-Favored-Nation Treatment

Annex V: Quantitative Restrictions

Annex VI: Miscellaneous Commitments

Annex VII: Reservations, Specific Commitments and Other Items

ANNEX I

Reservations for Existing Measures and Liberalization Commitments

1.   The Schedule of a Party sets out, pursuant to Articles 1108(1) (Investment), 1206(1) (Cross-Border Trade in Services) and 1409(4) (Financial Services), the reservations taken by that Party with respect to existing measures that do not conform with obligations imposed by:

(a) Article 1102, 1202 or 1405 (National Treatment),

(b) Article 1103, 1203 or 1406 (Most-Favored-Nation Treatment),

(c) Article 1205 (Local Presence),

(d) Article 1106 (Performance Requirements), or

(e) Article 1107 (Senior Management and Boards of Directors), and, in certain cases, sets out commitments for immediate or future liberalization.

2.   Each reservation sets out the following elements:

(a) **Sector** refers to the general sector in which the reservation is taken;

(b) **Sub-Sector** refers to the specific sector in which the reservation is taken;

(c) **Industry Classification** refers, where applicable, to the activity covered by the reservation according to domestic industry classification codes;

(d) **Type of Reservation** specifies the obligation referred to in paragraph 1 for which a reservation is taken;

(e) **Level of Government** indicates the level of government maintaining the measure for which a reservation is taken;

(f) **Measures** identifies the laws, regulations or other measures, as qualified, where indicated, by the **Description** element, for which the reservation is taken. A measure cited in the **Measures** element

(i) means the measure as amended, continued or renewed as of the date of entry into force of this Agreement, and

(ii) includes any subordinate measure adopted or maintained under the authority of and consistent with the measure;

(g) **Description** sets out commitments, if any, for liberalization on the date of entry into force of this Agreement, and the remaining non-conforming aspects of the existing measures for which the reservation is taken; and

(h) **Phase-Out** sets out commitments, if any, for liberalization after the date of entry into force of this Agreement.

3.   In the interpretation of a reservation, all elements of the reservation shall be considered. A reservation shall be interpreted in the light of the relevant provisions of the Chapters against which the reservation is taken. To the extent that:

(a) the **Phase-Out** element provides for the phasing out of nonconforming aspects of measures, the **Phase-Out** element shall prevail over all other elements;

(b) the **Measures** element is qualified by a liberalization commitment from the **Description** element, the **Measures** element as so qualified shall prevail over all other elements; and

(c) the **Measures** element is not so qualified, the **Measures** element shall prevail over all other elements, unless any discrepancy between the **Measures** element and the other elements considered in their totality is so substantial and material that it would be unreasonable to conclude that the **Measures** element should prevail, in which case the other elements shall prevail to the extent of that discrepancy.

4.   Where a Party maintains a measure that requires that a service provider be a citizen, permanent resident or resident of its territory as a condition to the provision of a service in its territory, a reservation for that measure taken with respect to Article 1202, 1203 or 1205 or Article 1404, 1405 or 1406 shall operate as a reservation with respect to Article 1102, 1103 or 1106 to the extent of that measure.

5.   For purposes of this Annex:

CMAP means Clasificación Mexicana de Actividades y Productos (CMAP) numbers as set out in Instituto Nacional de Estadística, Geografía e Informática, *Clasificación Mexicana de Actividades y Productos*, 1988;

concession means an authorization provided by the State to a person to exploit a natural resource or provide a service, for which Mexican nationals and Mexican enterprises are granted priority over foreigners;

CPC means Central Product Classification (CPC) numbers as set out in Statistical Office of the United Nations, Statistical Papers, Series M, No. 77, *Provisional Central Product Classification*, 1991;

foreigners' exclusion clause means the express provision in an enterprise's by-laws stating that the enterprise shall not allow foreigners, directly or indirectly, to become partners or shareholders of the enterprise;

international cargo means goods that have an origin or destination outside the territory of a Party;

Mexican enterprise means an enterprise constituted under the law of Mexico; and

SIC means:

(a) with respect to Canada, Standard Industrial Classification (SIC) numbers as set out in Statistics Canada, *Standard Industri l Classification*, fourth edition, 1980; and

(b) with respect to the United States, Standard Industrial Classification (SIC) numbers as set out in the United States Office of Management and Budget, *Standard Industrial Classification Manual*, 1987.

Sector: All Sectors (I-C-2 to I-C-6)

Sub-Sector:

Industry Classification:

Type of Reservation: National Treatment (Article 1102)
Performance Requirements (Article 1106)
Senior Management (Article 1107)

Level of Government: Federal

Measures: *Investment Canada Act*, R.S.C. 1985, c. 28 (1st Supp.)

Investment Canada Regulations, SOR/85-611

As qualified by paragraphs 8 through 12 of the **Description** element

Description: Investment

1. Under the *Investment Canada Act*, the following acquisitions of Canadian businesses by "non-Canadians" are subject to review by Investment Canada:

(a) all direct acquisitions of Canadian businesses with assets of C$5 million or more;

(b) all indirect acquisitions of Canadian businesses with assets of C$50 million or more; and

(c) indirect acquisitions of Canadian businesses with assets between C$5 million and C$50 million that represent more than 50 percent of the value of the assets of all the entities the control of which is being acquired, directly or indirectly, in the transaction in question.

2.   A "non-Canadian" is an individual, government or agency thereof or an entity that is not "Canadian" . "Canadian" means a Canadian citizen or permanent resident, government in Canada or agency thereof or Canadian-controlled entity as provided for in the *Investment Canada Act*.

3.   In addition, specific acquisitions or new businesses in designated types of business activities relating to Canada's cultural heritage or national identity, which are normally notifiable, may be reviewed if the Governor in Council authorizes a review in the public interest.

4.   An investment subject to review under the *Investment Canada Act* may not be implemented unless the Minister responsible for the *Investment Canada Act* advises the applicant that the investment is likely to be of net benefit to Canada. Such a determination is made in accordance with six factors described in the Act, summarized as follows:

(a)   the effect of the investment on the level and nature of economic activity in Canada, including the effect on employment, on the utilization of parts, components and services produced in Canada, and on exports from Canada;

(b)   the degree and significance of participation by Canadians in the investment;

(c)   the effect of the investment on productivity, industrial efficiency, technological development and product innovation in Canada;

(d)   the effect of the investment on competition within any industry or industries in Canada;

(e)   the compatibility of the investment with national industrial, economic and cultural policies, taking into consideration industrial, economic and cultural policy objectives enunciated by the government or legislature of any province likely to be significantly affected by the investment; and

(f)   the contribution of the investment to Canada's ability to compete in world markets.

5.   In making a net benefit determination, the Minister, through Investment Canada, may review plans under which the applicant demonstrates the net benefit to Canada of the proposed acquisition. An applicant may also submit undertakings to the Minister in connection with any proposed acquisition which is the subject of review. In the event of noncompliance with an undertaking by an applicant, the Minister may seek a court order directing compliance or any other remedy authorized under the Act.

6.   Non-Canadians who establish or acquire Canadian businesses, other than those described above, must notify Investment Canada.

7.   Investment Canada will review an "acquisition of control", as defined in the *Investment Canada Act*, of a Canadian business by an investor of Mexico or of the United States if the value of the gross assets of the Canadian business is not less than the applicable threshold.

8.   The review threshold applicable to investors of Mexico or of the United States, calculated as set out in the **Phase-Out** element, is higher than those described in paragraph 1. However, this higher review threshold does not apply in the following sectors: uranium production and ownership of uranium producing properties; oil and gas; financial services; transportation services; and cultural businesses.

9.   Notwithstanding the definition of "investor of a Party" in Article 1138, only investors who are nationals, or entities controlled by nationals as provided

for in the *Investment Canada Act*, of Mexico or of the United States may benefit from the higher review threshold.

10. An indirect "acquisition of control" of a Canadian business by an investor of Mexico or of the United States is not reviewable.

11. Notwithstanding Article 1106(1), Canada may impose requirements, or enforce any commitment or undertaking, in connection with the establishment, acquisition, expansion, conduct or operation of an investment of an investor of another Party or of a non-Party for the transfer of technology, production process or other proprietary knowledge to a national or enterprise, affiliated to the transferor, in Canada, in connection with the review of an acquisition of an investment under the *Investment Canada Act*.

12. Except for requirements, commitments or undertakings relating to technology transfer as set out in paragraph 11, Article 1106(1) shall apply to requirements, commitments or undertakings imposed or enforced under the *Investment Canada Act*. Article 1106(1) shall not be construed to apply to any requirement, commitment or undertaking imposed or enforced in connection with a review under the *Investment Canada Act*, to locate production, carry out research and development, employ or train workers, or to construct or expand particular facilities, in Canada.

Phase-Out:

For investors of Mexico or of the United States, the applicable threshold for the review of a direct acquisition of control of a Canadian business will be:

(a)   for the 12-month period beginning on the date of entry into force of this Agreement, the monetary amount as determined in accordance with Annex 1607.3 of the *Canada - United States Free Trade Agreement*; and

(b) beginning one year after the date of entry into force of this Agreement, the monetary amount for the preceding year multiplied by an annual adjustment representing the increase in nominal Gross Domestic Product, as set out below.

The calculation of the annual adjustment will be determined in January of each year after 1994 using the most recently available data published by Statistics Canada and using the following formula:

Annual Adjustment =

$$\frac{\text{Current nominal GDP at market prices}}{\text{Previous year nominal GDP at market prices}}$$

"Current nominal GDP at market prices" means the arithmetic mean of the nominal Gross Domestic Product at market prices for the most recent four consecutive quarters (seasonally adjusted at annual rates).

"Previous year nominal GDP at market prices" means the arithmetic mean of the nominal Gross Domestic Product at market prices for the four consecutive quarters (seasonally adjusted at annual rates) for the comparable period in the year preceding the year used in calculating the "current nominal GDP at market prices".

The amounts determined in this manner will be rounded to the nearest million dollars.

Sector: All Sectors (I-C-7 to I-C-8)

Sub-Sector:

Industry Classification:

Type of Reservation: National Treatment (Article 1102)
                                   Senior Management (Article 1107)

Level of Government: Federal

Provincial

Measures: As set out in the **Description** element

Description: Investment

Canada or any province, when selling or disposing of its equity interests in, or the assets of, an existing state enterprise or an existing governmental entity, may prohibit or impose limitations on the ownership of such interests or assets, and on the ability of owners of such interests or assets to control any resulting enterprise, by investors of another Party or of a non-Party or their investments. With respect to such a sale or other disposition, Canada or any province may adopt or maintain any measure relating to the nationality of senior management or members of the board of directors.

For purposes of this reservation:

(a)   any measure maintained or adopted after the date of entry into force of this Agreement that, at the time of sale or other disposition, prohibits or imposes limitations on the ownership of equity interests or assets or imposes nationality requirements described in this reservation shall be deemed to be an existing measure; and

(b)   "state enterprise" means an enterprise owned or controlled through ownership interests by Canada or a province and includes an enterprise established after the date of entry into force of this Agreement solely for the purposes of selling or disposing of equity interests in, or the assets of, an existing state enterprise or governmental entity.

Phase-Out: None

Sector: All Sectors (I-C-9)

Sub-Sector:

Industry Classification:

Type of Reservation:	National Treatment (Article 1102)
Level of Government:	Federal
Measures:	*Canada Business Corporations Act*, R.S.C. 1985, c. C-44
	Canada Corporations Act, R.S.C. 1970, c. C-32
	Canada Business Corporations Act Regulations, SOR/79-316
Description:	Investment

"Constraints" may be placed on the issue, transfer and ownership of shares in federally incorporated corporations. The object is to permit corporations to meet Canadian ownership requirements, under certain laws set out in the *Canada Business Corporations Act Regulations*, in sectors where ownership is required as a condition to operate or to receive licenses, permits, grants, payments or other benefits. In order to maintain certain "Canadian" ownership levels, a corporation is permitted to sell shareholders' shares without the consent of those shareholders, and to purchase its own shares on the open market. "Canadian" is defined in the *Canada Business Corporations Act Regulations*.

Phase-Out:	None
Sector:	All Sectors (I-C-10 to I-C-11)
Sub-Sector:	
Industry Classification:	
Type of Reservation:	Senior Management (Article 1107)
Level of Government:	Federal
Measures:	*Canada Business Corporations Act*, R.S.C. 1985, c. C-44
	Canada Business Corporations Act Regulations, SOR/79-316

Canada Corporations Act, R.S.C. 1970, c. C-32

Special Acts of Parliament incorporating specific companies

Description: <u>Investment</u>

The *Canada Business Corporations Act* requires that a simple majority of the board of directors, or of a committee thereof, of a federally-incorporated corporation be resident Canadians. For purposes of the Act, "resident Canadian" means an individual who is a Canadian citizen ordinarily resident in Canada, a citizen who is a member of a class set out in the *Canada Business Corporations Act Regulations,* or a permanent resident as defined in the *Immigration Act* other than one who has been ordinarily resident in Canada for more than one year after he became eligible to apply for Canadian citizenship.

In the case of a holding corporation, not more than one-third of the directors need be resident Canadians if the earnings in Canada of the holding corporation and its subsidiaries are less than five percent of the gross earnings of the holding corporation and its subsidiaries.

Under the *Canada Corporations Act,* a simple majority of the elected directors of a Special Act corporation must be resident in Canada and citizens of a Commonwealth country. This requirement applies to every joint stock company incorporated subsequent to June 22, 1869 by any Special Act of Parliament.

Phase-Out: None

Sector: Business Service Industries (I-C-22)

Sub-Sector: Patent Agents and Agencies

Industry Classification: SIC 999   Other Services, Not Elsewhere Classified (limited to patent agency)

Type of Reservation: National Treatment (Article 1202)
Local Presence (Article 1205)

Level of Government: Federal

Measures: *Patent Act*, R.S.C. 1985, c. P-4

Patent Rules, C.R.C. 1978, c. 1250

Patent Cooperation Treaty Regulations, SOR/89-453

Description: <u>Cross-Border Services</u>

To represent persons in the presentation and prosecution of applications for patents or in other business before the Patent Office, a patent agent must be resident in Canada and registered by the Patent Office.

A registered patent agent who is not resident in Canada must appoint a registered patent agent who is resident in Canada as an associate to prosecute an application for a patent.

An enterprise may be added to the patent register provided that it has at least one member who is also on the register.

Phase-Out: Citizenship and permanent residency requirements are subject to removal within two years of the date of entry into force of this Agreement in accordance with Article 1210(3).

Sector: Transportation (I-C-38)

Sub-Sector: Land Transportation

Industry Classification:

SIC 456	Truck Transport Industries
SIC 4572	Interurban and Rural Transit Systems Industry
SIC 4573	School Bus Operations Industry
SIC 4574	Charter and Sightseeing Bus Services Industry

Type of Reservation: National Treatment (Article 1202)
Local Presence (Article 1205)

Measures: *Motor Vehicle Transport Act,* 1987, R.S.C.
                             1985, c. 29 (3rd Supp.), Parts I and II

                             National Transportation Act, 1987, R.S.C.
                             1985, c. 28 (3rd Supp.), Part IV

                             Customs Tariff, R.S.C. 1985, c. 41 (3rd
                             Supp.)

Description: Cross-Border Services

                             Only persons of Canada, using Canadian-
                             registered and either Canadian-built or
                             duty-paid trucks or buses, may provide
                             truck or bus services between points in
                             the territory of Canada.

Phase-Out: None

Annex I
Schedule of Mexico

Sector: All Sectors (I-M-1 to I-M-2)

Sub-Sector:

Industry Classification:

Type of Reservation: National Treatment (Article 1102)

Level of Government: Federal

Measures: *Constitución Política de los Estados Uni-
                             dos Mexicanos,* Artículo 27

                             Ley de Nacionalidad y Naturalización,
                             Capítulos IV, VI

                             *Ley Orgánica de la Fracción I del Artículo
                             27 de la Constitución*

                             *Ley para Promover la Inversión Mexicana
                             y Regular la Inversión Extranjera,* Capí-
                             tulos I, IV, V

                             *Reglamento de la Ley para Promover la
                             Inversión Mexicana y Regular la Inver-
                             sión Extranjera,* Título I; Título II, Capí-
                             tulos I, II; Título III, Capítulo III; Título
                             VI; Título VIII, Capítulo IV

Description: Investment

Foreign nationals or foreign enterprises, or Mexican enterprises without a foreigners' exclusion clause, may not acquire property rights ("dominio directo") over land and water in a 100-kilometer strip along the country's borders or in a 50-kilometer strip inland from its coasts (the Restricted Zone). Lease of land for more than 10 years is deemed to be an acquisition.

Foreign nationals, foreign enterprises or Mexican enterprises may acquire "Certificados de Participación Inmobiliaria" (CPI's). CPI's grant the beneficiaries the right to use and enjoy property and to receive the profits that it may obtain from the profitable use of property.

CPI's are issued by a Mexican credit institution that has been granted authorization to acquire through trust the title to real estate intended for industrial and tourism activities in the Restricted Zone for a period not to exceed 30 years. The trust is renewable if:

(a)   the beneficiaries of the trust that is to be extinguished or terminated will be the beneficiaries of the new trust;

(b)   the new trust is to be executed under the same terms and conditions as the trust that is to be extinguished or terminated, in respect of the purposes of the trust, the use of the property and its characteristics;

(c)   the respective permits are requested within a period of 360 to 181 days preceding the termination or extinction of the trust; and

(d)   the provisions of the *Ley para Promover la Inversión Mexicana y Regular la Inversión Extranjera* are observed.

Phase-Out: None

Sector:	All Sectors (I-M-3)
Sub-Sector:	
Industry Classification:	
Type of Reservation:	National Treatment (Article 1102)
Level of Government:	Federal
Measures:	*Ley para Promover la Inversión Mexicana y Regular la Inversión Extranjera*, Capítulos I, II, III, V, VI

Reglamento de la Ley para Promover la Inversión Mexicana y Regular la Inversión Extranjera, Título I; Título II, Capítulos I, III, IV; Título IV; Título V; Título VIII, Capítulos I-V; Título IX, Capítulos I, II, III

As qualified by the **Description** element

Description: Investment

The Comisión Nacional de Inversiones Extranjeras, in order to evaluate applications submitted for its consideration (acquisitions or establishment of investments in restricted activities as set out in this Schedule), shall take into account the following criteria:

(a)   its effects on employment and training;

(b)   its technological contribution; or

(c)   in general, its contribution to increase Mexican industrial productivity and competitiveness.

The Comisión Nacional de Inversiones Extranjeras may impose performance requirements that are not prohibited by Article 1106.

Phase-Out:	None
Sector:	All Sectors (I-M-4 to I-M-6)
Sub-Sector:	
Industry Classification:	

Type of Reservation: National Treatment (Article 1102)

Level of Government: Federal

Measures: *Ley Para Promover la Inversión Mexicana y Regular la Inversión Extranjera*, Capítulos I, II, III, V, VI

Reglamento de la Ley Para Promover la Inversión Mexicana y Regular la Inversión Extranjera, Título I; Título II, Capítulo I; Título IV; Título V; Título VIII, Capítulos I-V; Título IX, Capítulos I, II, III

As qualified by the **Description** element

Description: Investment

The Comisión Nacional de Inversiones Extranjeras will only review direct or indirect acquisitions by an investor of another Party of more than 49 percent of the ownership interest in a Mexican enterprise in an unrestricted sector, that is directly or indirectly owned or controlled by Mexican nationals, if the value of the gross assets of the Mexican enterprise is not less than the applicable threshold.

Phase-Out: For investors and investments of investors of Canada or the United States, the applicable threshold for the review of an acquisition of a Mexican enterprise will be:

(a)   US$25 million, for the three year period beginning on the date of entry into force of this Agreement;

(b)   US$50 million, for the three year period beginning three years after the date of entry into force of this Agreement;

(c)   US$75 million, for the three year period beginning six years after the date of entry into force of this Agreement; and

(d)   US$150 million, beginning nine years after the date of entry into force of this Agreement.

Beginning one year after the date of entry into force of this Agreement, each of these thresholds will be adjusted annually for cumulative inflation from the date of entry into force of this Agreement, based on the implicit price deflator for U.S. Gross Domestic Product (GDP) or any successor index published by the Council of Economic Advisors in "Economics Indicators" .

The value of a threshold adjusted for cumulative inflation up to January of each year following 1994 shall be equal to the original value of the threshold multiplied by the following ratio:

(a)   the implicit GDP price deflators or any successor index published by the Council of Economic Advisors in "Economic Indicators", current as of January of that year; to

(b)   the implicit GDP price deflator or any successor index published by the Council of Economic Advisors in "Economic Indicators", current as of the date of entry into force of this Agreement,

provided that the implicit GDP price deflators under paragraphs (a) and (b) have the same base year.

The resulting adjusted threshold will be rounded to the nearest million dollars.

Beginning ten years after the date of entry into force of this Agreement, the threshold will be adjusted annually by the rate of growth of the nominal Mexican GDP, as published by the Instituto Nacional de Estadística, Geografía e Informática. Whenever the U.S. dollar amount calculated for the threshold is, at the prevailing market exchange rates, equal to or higher than the amount calculated pursuant to Schedule of Canada, Annex I, page I-C-2, the calculation of the applicable threshold will be made according to the rules established therein. In no case will the threshold, as converted into U.S. dollars, exceed that of Canada.

Sector: Manufacture of Goods (I-M-34 to I-M-35)

Sub-Sector: Maquiladora Industry

Industry Classification:

Type of Reservation: Performance Requirements (Article 1106)

Level of Government: Federal

Measures: *Ley Aduanera*, Título IV, Capítulos I, III; 1Título V, Capítulo II; Título VI

Decreto para el Fomento y Operación de la Industria Maquiladora de Exportación ("Maquiladora Decree")

As qualified by the **Description** element

Description: Investment

Persons authorized by the Secretaría de Comercio y Fomento Industrial to operate under the Maquiladora Decree may not sell to the domestic market more than 55 percent of the total value of its annual exports in the previous year.

Phase-Out: Sales of a maquiladora to the domestic market may not exceed:

(a)   one year after the date of entry into force of this Agreement, 60 percent of the total value of its annual exports in the previous year;

(b)   two years after the date of entry into force of this Agreement, 65 percent of the total value of its annual exports in the previous year;

(c)   three year after the date of entry into force of this Agreement, 70 percent of the total value of its annual exports in the previous year;

(d)   four years after the date of entry into force of this Agreement, 75 percent of the total value of its annual exports in the previous year;

(e)   five years after the date of entry into force of this Agreement, 80 percent of the total value of its annual exports in the previous year; and

(f)   six years after the date of entry into force of this Agreement, 85 percent of the total value of its annual exports in the previous year.

Seven years after the date of entry into force of this Agreement, sales of a maquiladora to the domestic market will not be subject to any percentage requirement.

Sector: Printing, Editing and Associated Industries (I-M-42)

Sub-Sector: Newspaper Publishing

Industry Classification: CMAP 342001   Newspaper Publishing

Type of Reservation: National Treatment (Article 1102)

Level of Government: Federal

Measures: *Ley para Promover la Inversión Mexicana y Regular la Inversión Extranjera*, Capítulos I, II, III, V, VI

Reglamento de la Ley para Promover la Inversión Mexicana y Regular la Inversión Extranjera, Título I; Título II, Capítulo I; Título IV; Título V; Título VIII, Capítulos I, II, III, V; Título IX, Capítulo I

As qualified by the **Description** element

Description: Investment

Investors of another Party or their investments may own, directly or indirectly, 100 percent of the ownership interest in an enterprise established or to be established in the territory of Mexico engaged in the simultaneous printing and distribution in the territory of Mexico of a daily newspaper that is published outside of the territory of Mexico.

Investors of another Party or their investments may only own, directly or indirectly, up to 49 percent of the ownership interest in an enterprise established or to be established in the territory of Mexico engaged in the printing or publication of daily newspapers written primarily for a Mexican audience and distributed in the territory of Mexico.

For purposes of this reservation, daily newspapers are those published at least five days a week.

Phase-Out: None

Sector: Professional, Technical and Specialized Services (I-M-45)

Sub-Sector: Professional Services

Industry Classification: CMAP 9510   Professional, Technical and Specialized Services (limited to professional services)

Type of Reservation: National Treatment (Article 1202)
Local Presence (Article 1205)

Level of Government: Federal and State

Measures: *Ley Reglamentaria del Artículo 5o. Constitucional, relativo al Ejercicio de las Profesiones en el Distrito Federal*, Capítulo III, Sección Tercera, Capítulos IV, V

Ley General de Población, Título III, Capítulo III

Reglamento de la Ley Reglamentaria del Artículo 5o. Constitucional, relativo al Ejercicio de las Profesiones en el Distrito Federal, Capítulo III

Description: Cross-Border Services

Only Mexican nationals may be licensed in professions that require a professional license ("cédula profesional").

An "inmigrado" or an "inmigrante" may seek a judicial order to obtain such a license.

Phase-Out:

Citizenship and permanent residency requirements are subject to removal within two years of the date of entry into force of this Agreement in accordance with Article 1210(3). On removal of these requirements, a foreign professional will be required to have an address in Mexico.

With respect to legal services, see Schedule of Mexico, Annex I, page I-M-46, Schedule of Mexico Annex II, page II-M-10, and Schedule of Mexico, Annex VI, page VI-M-2.

Sector:

Professional, Technical and Specialized Services (I-M-46 to I-M-47)

Sub-Sector:

Professional Services

Industry Classification:

CMAP 951002   Legal Services (including foreign legal consultancy)

Type of Reservation:

National Treatment (Articles 1102, 1202)
Most-Favored-Nation Treatment (Articles 1103, 1203)
Local Presence (Article 1205)

Level of Government:

Federal

Measures:

Ley Reglamentaria del Artículo 5o. Constitucional, relativo al Ejercicio de las Profesiones en el Distrito Federal, Capítulo I, Capítulo III, Sección III

Ley para Promover la Inversión Mexicana y Regular la Inversión Extranjera, Capítulos I, II, III, V, VI

Reglamento de la Ley Reglamentaria del Artículo 5o. Constitucional, relativo al Ejercicio de las Profesiones en el Distrito Federal, Capítulos I, II, V

Reglamento de la Ley para Promover la Inversión Mexicana y Regular la Inversión Extranjera, Título I; Título II, Capítulo I; Título IV; Título V; Título VIII, Capítulos I, II, III, V; Título IX, Capítulo I

As qualified by the **Description** element

Description: Cross Border Services and Investment

Except as provided for in this reservation, only lawyers licensed in Mexico may have an ownership interest in a law firm established in the territory of Mexico.

Lawyers licensed in a Canadian province that permits partnerships between those lawyers and lawyers licensed in Mexico will be permitted to form partnerships with lawyers licensed in Mexico.

The number of lawyers licensed in Canada serving as partners, and their ownership interest in the partnership, may not exceed the number of lawyers licensed in Mexico serving as partners, and their ownership interest in the partnership. A lawyer licensed in Canada may not practice or advise on Mexican law.

A law firm established by a partnership of lawyers licensed in Canada and lawyers licensed in Mexico may hire lawyers licensed in Mexico as employees.

Lawyers licensed in Canada will be subject to Schedule of Mexico, Annex VI, page VI-M-2.

Lawyers licensed in the United States will be subject to Schedule of Mexico, Annex II, page II-M-10 and Schedule of Mexico, Annex VI, page VI-M-2.

Phase-Out: None

Sector: Professional, Technical and Specialized Services (I-M-48)

Sub-Sector: Professional Services

Industry Classification: CMAP 951003 Accounting and Auditing Services (limited to accounting services)

Type of Reservation: National Treatment (Article 1202)
Local Presence (Article 1205)

Level of Government: Federal

Measures: *Código Fiscal de la Federación*, Título III

                            Reglamento del Código Fiscal de la Federación, Capítulo II

Description: <u>Cross-Border Services</u>

                            Only Mexican nationals who are licensed as accountants in Mexico are authorized to perform audits for tax purposes on behalf of:

                            (a) state enterprises;

                            (b) enterprises that are authorized to receive tax-deductible donations;

                            (c) enterprises with income, capital stock, number of employees and operations above levels specified annually by the Secretaría de Hacienda y Crédito Público; or

                            (d) enterprises undergoing a merger or divestiture.

Phase-Out: Citizenship and permanent residency requirements are subject to removal within two years of the date of entry into force of this Agreement in accordance with Article 1210(3). On removal of these requirements, a foreign professional will be required to have an address in Mexico.

Sector: Professional, Technical and Specialized Services (I-M-49)

Sub-Sector: Specialized Services (Commercial Public Notaries)

Industry Classification:

Type of Reservation: National Treatment (Articles 1102, 1202)
                            Local Presence (Article 1205)

Level of Government: Federal

Measures: *Código de Comercio*, Libro I, Título III

Ley para Promover la Inversión Mexicana y Regular la Inversión Extranjera, Capítulos I, II, III, V, VI

Reglamento de la Ley para Promover la Inversión Mexicana y Regular la Inversión Extranjera, Título I; Título II, Capítulo I; Título IV; Título V; Título VIII, Capítulos I, II, III, V; Título II, Capítulo I

Description: Cross-Border Services

1. Only a Mexican national by birth may be licensed to be a commercial public notary ("corredor público").

2. A commercial public notary may not have a business affiliation with any person for the provision of commercial public notary services.

Phase-Out: 1. Citizenship and permanent residency requirements are subject to removal within two years of the date of entry into force of this Agreement in accordance with Article 1210(3). On removal of these requirements, a foreign professional will be required to have an address in Mexico.

2. None

Sector: Professional, Technical and Specialized Services (I-M-50)

Sub-Sector: Specialized Services

Industry Classification: CMAP 951001   Public Notary

Type of Reservation: National Treatment (Articles 1102, 1202)
Local Presence (Article 1205)

Level of Government: Federal and State

Measures: *Ley para Promover la Inversión Mexicana y Regular la Inversión Extranjera*, Capítulos I, II, III, V, VI

Leyes del Notariado para los Estados de: Aguascalientes, Baja California, Baja California Sur, Campeche, Coahuila, Colima, Chiapas, Chihuahua, Distrito Federal, Durango, Guanajuato, Guerrero, Hidalgo, Jalisco, México, Michoacán, Morelos,

Nayarit, Nuevo León, Oaxaca, Puebla, Querétaro, Quintana Roo, San Luis Potosí, Sonora, Tabasco, Tamaulipas, Tlaxcala, Veracruz, Yucatán and Zacatecas.

Reglamento de la Ley para Promover la Inversión Mexicana y Regular la Inversión Extranjera, Título I; Título II, Capítulo I; Título IV; Título V; Título VIII, Capítulos I, II, III, V; Título IX, Capítulo I

Description: Cross-Border Services and Investment

Only Mexican nationals by birth may be granted a fiat ("patente") to be public notaries ("notarios públicos").

A public notary may not have a business affiliation with any person for the provision of public notary services.

Phase-Out: None

Sector: Transportation (I-M-56 to I-M-57)

Sub-Sector: Air Transportation

Industry Classification: CMAP 713001 Transportation Services on Mexican-Registered Aircraft
CMAP 713002 Air Taxi Transportation Services

Type of Reservation: National Treatment (Article 1102)
Senior Management (Article 1107)

Level of Government: Federal

Measures: *Ley de Vías Generales de Comunicación*, Libro IV, Capítulo I, X, XI

Ley para Promover la Inversión Mexicana y Regular la Inversión Extranjera, Capítulos I, II, III, V, VI

Reglamento de la Ley para Promover la Inversión Mexicana y Regular la Inversión Extranjera, Título I; Título II, Capítulo I; Título IV; Título V; Título VIII, Capítulos I, II, III, V; Título IX, Capítulo I

As qualified by the **Description** element

Description:

Investment

Investors of another Party or their investments may only own, directly or indirectly, up to 25 percent of the voting interest in an enterprise established or to be established in the territory of Mexico that provides commercial air services on Mexican-registered aircraft. The chairman and at least two-thirds of the board of directors and two-thirds of managing officers of such an enterprise must be Mexican nationals.

Only Mexican nationals and Mexican enterprises with 75 percent of the voting interest owned or controlled by Mexican nationals and with the chairman and at least two-thirds of the managing officers of such an enterprise Mexican nationals, may register aircraft in Mexico.

Only Mexican-registered aircraft may provide the following commercial air transport services:

(a) "domestic services" (air services between points, or from and to the same point, in the territory of Mexico, or between a point in the territory of Mexico and a point not in the territory of another country);

(b) "scheduled international services" (scheduled air services between a point in the territory of Mexico and a point in the territory of another country) where those services have been reserved to Mexican carriers under existing or future bilateral agreements; and

(c) "non-scheduled international services" (non-scheduled air services between a point in the territory of Mexico and a point in the territory of another country) where those services have been reserved to Mexican carriers under existing or future bilateral agreements.

Phase-Out:

None

Sector: Transportation (I-M-58 to I-M-59)

Sub-Sector: Specialty Air Services

Industry Classification:

Type of Reservation: National Treatment (Articles 1102, 1202)
Local Presence (Article 1205)
Senior Management (Article 1107)

Level of Government: Federal

Measures: *Ley de Vías Generales de Comunicación*, Libro I, Capítulos I, II, III; Libro IV, Capítulo XII

As qualified by paragraphs 2, 3 and 4 of the **Description** element

Description: Cross-Border Services

1. A permit issued by the Secretaría de Comunicaciones y Transportes (SCT) is required to provide all specialty air services in the territory of Mexico.

2. A person of Canada or the United States may obtain such a permit to provide flight training, forest fire-management, fire-fighting, glider towing, and parachute jumping services in Mexico, subject to compliance with Mexican safety requirements.

3. Such a permit may not be issued to a person of Canada or the United States to provide aerial advertising, aerial sightseeing, aerial construction, heli-logging, inspection and surveillance, mapping, photography, surveying and aerial spraying services.

Investment

4. Investors of another Party or their investments may only own, directly or indirectly, up to 25 percent of the voting interests in an enterprise established or to be established in the territory of Mexico that provides specialty air services in Mexican-registered aircraft. The chairman and at least two-thirds of the board of directors and two-thirds of managing

officers of such an enterprise must be Mexican nationals. Only Mexican nationals and Mexican enterprises with 75 percent of the voting interest owned or controlled by Mexican nationals and with the chairman and at least two-thirds of the managing officers of such an enterprise Mexican nationals, may register aircraft in Mexico.

Phase-Out:

Cross-Border Services

A person of Canada or the United States will be allowed to obtain a permit by SCT to provide, subject to compliance with Mexican safety requirements, the following specialty air services:

(a) three years after the date of entry into force of this Agreement, aerial advertising, aerial sightseeing services, aerial construction and heli-logging; and

(b) six years after the date of entry into force of this Agreement, inspection and surveillance, mapping, photography, surveying and aerial spraying services.

Investment

None

Sector:

Transportation (I-M-63 to I-M-64)

Sub-Sector:

Land Transportation

Industry Classification:

CMAP 973101   Bus and Truck Station Administration and Ancillary Services (main bus and truck terminals and bus and truck stations)

Type of Reservation:

National Treatment (Articles 1102, 1202)
Local Presence (Article 1205)

Level of Government:

Federal

Measures:

Ley de Vías Generales de Comunicación, Libro I, Capítulo I, II, III; Libro II, Título

II, Capítulos I, II; Título III, Capítulo Unico

Reglamento para el Aprovechamiento del Derecho de Vía de las Carreteras Federales y Zonas Aledañas, Capítulos II, IV

Reglamento del Servicio Público de Autotransporte Federal de Pasajeros, Capítulo III, IV

As qualified by paragraph 1 of the **Description** element

Description: Cross-Border Services

1. A permit issued by the Secretaría de Comunicaciones y Transportes is required to establish, or operate, a bus or truck station or terminal. Only Mexican nationals and Mexican enterprises with a foreigners' exclusion clause may obtain such a permit.

Investment

2. Investors of another Party or their investments may not own, directly or indirectly, ownership interest in an enterprise established or to be established in the territory of Mexico engaged in the establishment or operation of bus or truck stations or terminals.

Phase-Out: Cross-Border Services

Three years after the date of signature of this Agreement, such a permit may be obtained by Mexican nationals and Mexican enterprises.

Investment

With respect to an enterprise established or to be established in the territory of Mexico engaged in the establishment or operation of bus or truck station or terminals, investors of another Party or their investments may, directly or indirectly:

(a)   only own three years after the date of signature of this Agreement, up to 49 percent of the ownership interest in the enterprise;

(b)   only own seven years after the date of entry into force of this Agreement, up to 51 percent of the ownership interest in the enterprise; and

(c)   own ten years after the date of entry into force of this Agreement, 100 percent of the ownership interest in the enterprise.

Sector: Transportation (I-M-67 to I-M-68)

Sub-Sector: Land Transportation

Industry Classification:
- CMAP 711312   Urban and Suburban Passenger Transportation Service by Bus
- CMAP 711315   Collective Automobile Transportation Service
- CMAP 711316   Established Route Automobile Transportation Service
- CMAP 711317   Automobile Transportation Services from a Specific Station
- CMAP 711318   School and Tourist Transportation Services (limited to school transportation services)

Type of Reservation: National Treatment (Article 1102, 1202)

Level of Government: Federal

Measures:

Ley para Promover la Inversión Mexicana y Regular la Inversión Extranjera, Capítulos I, II, III, V, VI

Ley de Vías Generales de Comunicación, Libro I, Capítulos I, II, III; Libro II, Título II, Capítulo II

Ley de Nacionalidad y Naturalización, Capítulo IV

Reglamento de la Ley para Promover la Inversión Mexicana y Regular la Inversión Extranjera, Título I; Título II, Capítulo I; Título IV; Título V; Título VIII,

Capítulos I, II, III, V; Título IX, Capítulo I

Reglamento del Servicio Público de Auto-transporte Federal de Pasajeros, Capítulo II

Description: Cross-Border Services and Investment

Only Mexican nationals and Mexican enterprises with a foreigners' exclusion clause may provide local bus services, school bus services and taxi and other collective transportation services.

Phase-Out: None

Sector: Transportation (I-M-69 to I-M-72)

Sub-Sector: Land Transportation

Industry Classification:

CMAP 711201	Road Transport Services for Construction Materials
CMAP 711202	Road Transport Moving Services
CMAP 711203	Other Services of Specialized Cargo Transportation
CMAP 711204	General Trucking Services
CMAP 711311	Inter-City Busing Services
CMAP 711318	School and Tourist Transportation Services (limited to tourist transportation services)

Type of Reservation: National Treatment (Articles 1102, 1202)
Local Presence (Article 1205)

Level of Government: Federal

Measures: *Memorandum de Entendimiento entre los Estados Unidos Mexicanos y los Estados Unidos de Norteamérica para la promoción de Servicios de Transporte Turístico de Ruta Fija*, 3 de diciembre de 1990

Ley de Vías Generales de Comunicación, Libro I, Capítulos I, II, III; Libro II, Título II, Capítulo II; Título III, Capítulo Unico

Ley para Promover la Inversión Mexicana y Regular la Inversión Extranjera, Capítulos I, II, III, V, VI

Reglamento de la Ley para Promover la Inversión Mexicana y Regular la Inversión Extranjera, Título I; Título II, Capítulo I; Título IV; Título V; Título VIII, Capítulos I, II, III, V; Título IX, Capítulo I

As qualified by paragraphs 1 and 3 of the **Description** element

Description:

Cross-Border Services

1. A permit issued by the Secretaría de Comunicaciones y Transportes is required to provide inter-city bus services, tourist transportation services or truck services for the transportation of goods or passengers to or from the territory of Mexico.

2. Only Mexican nationals and Mexican enterprises with a foreigners' exclusion clause may provide such services.

3. Notwithstanding paragraph 2, a person of Canada or the United States will be permitted to provide international charter or tour bus services into the territory of Mexico.

4. Only Mexican nationals and Mexican enterprises with a foreigners' exclusion clause, using Mexican-registered equipment and drivers who are Mexican nationals, may provide bus or truck services for the transportation of goods or passengers between points in the territory of Mexico.

Investment

5. Investors of another Party or their investments may not own directly or indirectly, an ownership interest in an enterprise established or to be established in the territory of Mexico engaged in bus or truck transportation services as set out in the **Industry Classification** element.

Phase-Out:

Cross-Border Services

A person of Canada or of the United States will be permitted to provide:

(a)   three years after the date of signature of this Agreement, cross-border truck services to or from the territory of border states (Baja California, Chihuahua, Coahuila, Nuevo León, Sonora and Tamaulipas), and such a person will be permitted to enter and depart Mexico through different ports of entry in such states;

(b)   three years after the date of entry into force of this Agreement, cross-border scheduled bus services to or from the territory of Mexico; and

(c)   six years after the date of entry into force of this Agreement, cross-border truck services to or from the territory of Mexico.

Three years after the date of signature of this Agreement, only Mexican nationals and Mexican enterprises, using Mexican-registered equipment and drivers who are Mexican nationals, may provide bus or truck services for the transportation of international cargo or passengers between points in the territory of Mexico. For domestic cargo, paragraph 4 of the **Description** element will continue to apply.

Investment

With respect to an enterprise established or to be established in the territory of Mexico providing inter-city bus services, tourist transportation services, or truck services for the transportation of international cargo between points in the territory of Mexico, investors of another Party or their investments may, directly or indirectly:

(a)   only own, three years after the date of signature of this Agreement, up to 49 percent of ownership interest in such an enterprise;

(b) only own, seven years after the date of entry into force of this Agreement, up to 51 percent of the ownership interest in such an enterprise; and

(c) own, ten years after the date of entry into force of this Agreement, 100 percent of the ownership interest in such an enterprise.

Investors of another Party or their investments may not own, directly or indirectly, an ownership interest in an enterprise providing truck services for the carriage of domestic cargo.

Sector: Professional Services (I-U-9 to I-U-10)

Sub-Sector: Patent Attorneys and Patent Agents and other Practice before the Patent and Trademark Office

Industry Classification: SIC 7389 Business Services, Not Elsewhere Classified
SIC 8111 Legal Services

Type of Reservation: National Treatment (Article 1202)
Most-Favored-Nation Treatment (Article 1203)
Local Presence (Article 1205)

Level of Government: Federal

Measures: 35 U.S.C. Chapter 3 (practice before the U.S. Patent and Trademark Office)

37 C.F.R. Part 10 (representation of others before the U.S. Patent and Trademark Office)

Description: Cross-Border Services

As a condition to be registered to practice for others before the U.S. Patent and Trademark Office (USPTO):

(a) a patent attorney must be a U.S. citizen or an alien lawfully residing in the United States (37 C.F.R. § 10.6(a));

(b)   a patent agent must be a U.S. citizen, an alien lawfully residing in the United States or a non-resident who is registered to practice in a country that permits patent agents registered to practice before the USPTO to practice in that country (37 C.F.R. § 10.6(c)); and

(c)   a practitioner in trademark and non-patent cases must be an attorney licensed in the United States, a "grandfathered" agent, an attorney licensed to practice in a country that accords equivalent treatment to attorneys licensed in the United States, or an agent registered to practice in such a country (37 C.F.R. § 10.14(a)-(c)).

Phase-Out: Citizenship and permanent residency requirements are subject to removal within two years of the date of entry into force of this Agreement in accordance with Article 1210(3).

Sector: Transportation (I-U-18 to I-U-20)

Sub-Sector: Land Transportation

Industry Classification:

SIC 4213	Trucking, Except Local
SIC 4215	Courier Services, Except by Air
SIC 4131	Intercity and Rural Bus Transportation
SIC 4142	Bus Charter Service, Except Local
SIC 4151	School Buses (limited to interstate transportation not related to school activity)

Type of Reservation: National Treatment (Articles 1102, 1202)
Most-Favored-Nation Treatment (Articles 1103, 1203)
Local Presence (Article 1205)

Level of Government: Federal

Measures: 49 U.S.C. § 10922(*l*) (1) and (2)

49 U.S.C. § 10530 (3)

49 U.S.C. §§ 10329, 10330 and 11705

19 U.S.C. § 1202

49 C.F.R. § 1044

Memorandum of Understanding Between the United States of America and the United Mexican States on Facilitation of Charter/Tour Bus Service, December 3, 1990

As qualified by paragraph 2 of the **Description** element

Description:

Cross-Border Services

1.   Operating authority from the Interstate Commerce Commission (ICC) is required to provide interstate or cross-border bus or truck services in the territory of the United States. A moratorium remains in place on new grants of operating authority for persons of Mexico.

2.   The moratorium does not apply to the provision of cross-border charter or tour bus services.

3.   Under the moratorium, persons of Mexico without operating authority may operate only within ICC Border Commercial Zones, for which ICC operating authority is not required. Persons of Mexico providing truck services, including for hire, private, and exempt services, without operating authority are required to obtain a certificate of registration from the ICC to enter the United States and operate in the ICC Border Commercial Zones. Persons of Mexico providing bus services are not required to obtain an ICC certificate of registration to provide these services within the ICC Border Commercial Zones.

4.   A person providing bus or truck services between points in the United States is required to use U.S.-registered and either U.S.-built or duty-paid equipment.

Investment

5. The moratorium has the effect of being an investment restriction because enterprises of the United States providing bus or truck services that are owned or controlled by persons of Mexico may not obtain ICC operating authority.

Phase-Out:

Cross-Border Services

A person of Mexico will be permitted to obtain operating authority to provide:

(a) three years after the date of signature of this Agreement, cross-border truck services to or from border states (California, Arizona, New Mexico and Texas), and such persons will be permitted to enter and depart the territory of United States through different ports of entry;

(b) three years after the date of entry into force of this Agreement, cross-border scheduled bus services; and

(c) six years after the date of entry into force of this Agreement, cross-border truck services.

Investment

A person of Mexico will be permitted to establish an enterprise in the United States to provide:

(a) three years after the date of signature of this Agreement, truck services for the distribution of international cargo between points in the United States; and

(b) seven years after the date of entry into force of this Agreement, bus services between points in the United States.

The moratorium will remain in place on grants of authority for the provision of truck services by persons of Mexico between points in the United States for the transportation of goods other than international cargo.

ANNEX II

Reservations for Future Measures

1.   The Schedule of a Party sets out, pursuant to Articles 1108(3) (Investment) and 1206(3) (Cross-Border Trade in Services), the reservations taken by that Party with respect to specific sectors, sub-sectors or activities for which it may maintain existing, or adopt new or more restrictive, measures that do not conform with obligations imposed by:

(a) Article 1102 or 1202 (National Treatment);

(b) Article 1103 or 1203 (Most-Favored-Nation Treatment);

(c) Article 1205 (Local Presence);

(d) Article 1106 (Performance Requirements); or

(e) Article 1107 (Senior Management and Boards of Directors).

2.   Each reservation sets out the following elements:

(a) **Sector** refers to the general sector in which the reservation is taken;

(b) **Sub-Sector** refers to the specific sector in which the reservation is taken;

(c) **Industry Classification** refers, where applicable, to the activity covered by the reservation according to domestic industry classification codes;

(d) **Type of Reservation** specifies the obligation referred to in paragraph 1 for which a reservation is taken;

(e) **Description** sets out the scope of the sector, sub-sector or activities covered by the reservation; and

(f) **Existing Measures** identifies, for transparency purposes, existing measures that apply to the sector, sub-sector or activities covered by the reservation.

3.   In the interpretation of a reservation, all elements of the reservation shall be considered. The **Description** element shall prevail over all other elements.

4.   For purposes of this Annex:

CMAP means Clasificación Mexicana de Actividades y Productos (CMAP) numbers as set out in Instituto Nacional de Estadística, Geografía e Informática, *Clasificación Mexicana de Actividades y Productos*, 1988;

CPC means Central Product Classification (CPC) numbers as set out in Statistical Office of the United Nations, Statistical Papers, Series M, No. 77, *Provisional Central Product Classification*, 1991; and

SIC means:

(a) with respect to Canada, Standard Industrial Classification (SIC) numbers as set out in Statistics Canada, *Standard Industrial Classification*, fourth edition, 1980; and

(b) with respect to the United States, Standard Industrial Classification (SIC) numbers as set out in the United States Office of Management and Budget, *Standard Industrial Classification Manual*, 1987.

Sector: **All Sectors** (II-C-2)

Sub-Sector:

Industry Classification:

Type of Reservation: National Treatment (Article 1102)

Description: Investment

Canada and each province reserve the right to adopt or maintain any measure relating to residency requirements for the ownership by investors of another Party, or their investments, of oceanfront land.

Existing Measures:

Annex II
Schedule of Mexico

Sector: All Sectors (II-M-1)

Sub-Sector:

Industry Classification:

Type of Reservation: National Treatment (Article 1102, 1202)

Description: Cross-Border and Investment

Mexico reserves the right to adopt or maintain any measure restricting the acquisition, sale or other disposition of bonds, treasury bills or any other kind of debt security issued by the federal, state or local governments, except with respect to ownership by "a financial institution of another Party", as defined in Chapter Fourteen (Financial Services).

Existing Measures:

Sector: Professional, Technical and Specialized Services (II-M-10)

Sub-Sector: Professional Services

Industry Classification: CMAP 951002   Legal Services (including foreign legal consultancy)

Type of Reservation: National Treatment (Article 1102, 1202)
                                   Most-Favored-Nation Treatment (Article 1103, 1203)
                                   Local Presence (Article 1205)
                                   Senior Management (Article 1107)

Description: Cross-Border Services and Investment

                                   Subject to Schedule of Mexico, Annex VI, page VI-M-2, Mexico reserves the right to adopt or maintain any measure relating to the provision of legal services and foreign legal consultancy services by persons of the United States.

Existing Measures: *Ley Reglamentaria del Artículo 5o. Constitucional, relativo al ejercicio de las profesiones en el Distrito Federal*

                                   Ley para Promover la Inversión Mexicana y Regular la Inversión Extranjera

Annex II
Schedule of United States

Sector: All Sectors (II-U-1)

Sub-Sector:

Industry Classification:

Type of Reservation: National Treatment (Article 1102)
                                   Most-Favored-Nation Treatment (Article 1103)

Description: Investment

                                   The United States and each state reserve the right to adopt or maintain any measure relating to residency requirements for the ownership by investors of Canada, or their investments, of oceanfront land.

Existing Measures:

Sector:	Professional Services (II-U-7)
Sub-Sector:	Legal Services
Industry Classification:	SIC 8111　　　Legal Services
Type of Reservation:	National Treatment (Articles 1102, 1202) Most-Favored-Nation Treatment (Articles 1103, 1203) Local Presence (Article 1205) Senior Management (Article 1107)
Description:	Cross-Border Services and Investment Subject to Schedule of the United States, Annex VI, page VI-U-3, the United States reserves the right to adopt or maintain any measure relating to the provision of legal services, including foreign legal consultancy services, by persons of Mexico.

Existing Measures:

Sector:	Publishing (II-U-8)
Sub-Sector:	Newspaper Publishing
Industry Classification:	SIC 2711　　　Newspapers: Publishing, or Publishing and Printing
Type of Reservation:	National Treatment (Article 1102) Most-Favored-Nation Treatment (Article 1103)
Description:	Investment Subject to Article 2106, the United States reserves the right to adopt or maintain any measure that accords equivalent treatment to persons of any country that limits ownership by persons of the United States in an enterprise engaged in the publication of daily newspapers primarily written for audiences and distributed in that country. For purposes of this reservation, daily newspapers are newspapers published at least five days each week.

Existing Measures:

ANNEX III
Activities Reserved to the State
Schedule of Mexico
Section A – Activities Reserved to the Mexican State (III-M1 to III-M-4)

Mexico reserves the right to perform exclusively, and to refuse to permit the establishment of investments in, the following activities:

    1.   Petroleum, Other Hydrocarbons and Basic Petrochemicals

       (a) Description of activities

          (i) exploration and exploitation of crude oil and natural gas; refining or processing of crude oil and natural gas; and production of artificial gas, basic petrochemicals and their feedstocks and pipelines; and

          (ii) foreign trade; transportation, storage and distribution up to and including first hand sales of the following goods: crude oil; natural and artificial gas; goods covered by Chapter Six (Energy and Basic Petrochemicals) obtained from the refining or processing of crude oil and natural gas; and basic petrochemicals.

       (b) Measures:

Annex III
Schedule of Mexico

A.   Activities Reserved to the Mexican State

Mexico reserves the right to perform exclusively, and to refuse to permit the establishment of investments in, the following activities:

    1.   Petroleum, Other Hydrocarbons and Basic Petrochemicals

       (a) Description of activities

          (i) exploration and exploitation of crude oil and natural gas; refining or processing of crude oil and natural gas; and production of artificial gas, basic petrochemicals and their feedstocks and pipelines; and

          (ii) foreign trade; transportation, storage and distribution up to and including first hand sales of the following goods: crude oil; natural and artificial gas; goods covered by Chapter Six (Energy and Basic Petrochemicals) obtained from the refining or processing of crude oil and natural gas; and basic petrochemicals.

       (b) Measures:

       Constitución Política de los Estados Unidos Mexicanos, Artículos 25, 27 y 28

Ley Reglamentaria del Artículo 27 Constitucional en el Ramo del Petróleo

Ley Orgánica de Petróleos Mexicanos y Organismos Subsidiarios

2. Electricity

(a) Description of activities: the supply of electricity as a public service in Mexico, including, the generation, transmission, transformation, distribution and sale of electricity.

(b) Measures:

Constitución Política de los Estados Unidos Mexicanos, Artículos 25, 27, 28

Ley del Servicio Público de Energía Eléctrica

3. Nuclear Power and Treatment of Radioactive Minerals

(a) Description of activities: exploration, exploitation and processing of radioactive minerals, the nuclear fuel cycle, the generation of nuclear energy, the transportation and storage of nuclear wastes, the use and reprocessing of nuclear fuels and the regulation of their applications for other purposes and the production of heavy water.

(b) Measures:

Constitución Política de los Estados Unidos Mexicanos, Artículos 25, 27, 28

Ley Reglamentaria del Artículo 27 Constitucional en Materia de Energía Nuclear

4. Satellite Communications

(a) Description of activities: the establishment, operation and ownership of satellite systems and earth stations with international links.

(b) Measures:

Constitución Política de los Estados Unidos Mexicanos, Artículos 25, 28

Ley de Vías Generales de Comunicación

5. Telegraph Services

Measures:

Constitución Política de los Estados Unidos Mexicanos, Artículos 25, 28

Ley de Vías Generales de Comunicación

6. Radiotelegraph Services

Measures:

Constitución Política de los Estados Unidos Mexicanos, Artículos 25, 28

Ley de Vías Generales de Comunicación

7. Postal Services

(a) Description of activities: operation, administration and organization of first class mail.

(b) Measures:

Constitución Política de los Estados Unidos Mexicanos, Artículos 25, 28

Ley del Servicio Postal Mexicano

8. Railroads

(a) Description of activities: operation, administration and control of traffic within the Mexican railway system; supervision and management of railway right-of-way; operation, construction and maintenance of basic railway infrastructure.

(b) Measures:

Constitución Política de los Estados Unidos Mexicanos, Artículos 25, 28

Ley Orgánica de Ferrocarriles Nacionales de México

9. Issuance of Bills (currency) and Minting of Coinage

Measures:

Constitución Política de los Estados Unidos Mexicanos, Artículos 25, 28

Ley Orgánica del Banco de México

Ley Orgánica de la Casa de Moneda de México

10. Control, Inspection and Surveillance of Maritime and Inland Ports

Measures:

Ley de Navegación y Comercio Marítimos, Artículos 43, 47

Ley de Vías Generales de Comunicación, Artículo 272

11. Control, Inspection and Surveillance of Airports and Heliports

Measures:

Ley de Vías Generales de Comunicación, Artículo 327

The legal citations are provided for transparency purposes. A measure cited in the Measures category includes any subordinate measure adopted or maintained under the authority of and consistent with the measures.

B. Deregulation of Activities Reserved to the State (III-M-4)

1. The activities set out in Section A are reserved to the Mexican State, and private equity investment is prohibited under Mexican Law. Where Mexico allows private investment to participate in such activities through service contracts, concessions, lending arrangements or any

other type of contractual arrangement, such participation shall not be construed to affect the State's reservation of those activities.

2. If Mexican law is amended to allow private equity investment in an activity set out in Section A, Mexico may impose restrictions on foreign investment participation notwithstanding Article 1102, and describe them in Annex I. Mexico may also impose derogations from Article 1102 on foreign equity investment participation when selling an asset or ownership interest in an enterprise engaged in activities set out in Section A, and describe them in Annex I.

C. Activities Formerly Reserved to the Mexican State (III-M-5)

Where an activity was reserved to the Mexican State on January 1, 1992 and is not reserved to the Mexican State on entry into force of this Agreement, Mexico may restrict the initial sale of a state-owned asset or an ownership interest in a state enterprise that performs that activity to enterprises with majority ownership by Mexican nationals, as defined by the Mexican Constitution. For a period not to exceed three years from the initial sale, Mexico may restrict the transfer of such asset or ownership interest to other enterprises with majority ownership by Mexican nationals, as defined by the Mexican Constitution. On expiration of the three year period, the obligations of national treatment set out in Article 1102 (National Treatment) apply. This provision is subject to Article 1108 (Reservations and Exceptions).

ANNEX IV
Exceptions to Most-Favored-Nation Treatment
Schedule of Canada

Canada takes an exception to Article 1103 for treatment accorded under all bilateral or multilateral international agreements in force or signed prior to the date of entry into force of this Agreement.

For international agreements in force or signed after the date of entry into force of this Agreement, Canada takes an exception to Article 1103 for treatment accorded under those agreements involving:

(a) aviation;

(b) fisheries;

(c) maritime matters, including salvage; or

(d) telecommunications transport networks and telecommunications transport services (this exception does not apply to measures covered by Chapter Thirteen (Telecommunications)).

With respect to state measures not yet set out in Annex I pursuant to Article 1108(2), Canada takes an exception to Article 1103 for international agreements signed within two years of the date of entry into force of this Agreement.

For greater certainty, Article 1103 does not apply to any current or future foreign aid program to promote economic development, such as those governed by the Energy Economic Cooperation Program with Central America and the Caribbean (Pacto de San José) and the OECD Agreement on Export Credits.

Schedule of Mexico

Mexico takes an exception to Article 1103 for treatment accorded under all bilateral or multilateral international agreements in force or signed prior to the date of entry into force of this Agreement.

For international agreements in force or signed after the date of entry into force of this Agreement, Mexico takes an exception to Article 1103 for treatment accorded under those agreements involving:

(a) aviation;

(b) fisheries;

(c) maritime matters, including salvage; or

(d) telecommunications transport networks and telecommunications transport services (this exception does not apply to measures covered by Chapter Thirteen (Telecommunications) or to the production, sale or licensing of radio or television programming).

With respect to state measures not yet set out in Annex I pursuant Article 1108(2), Mexico takes an exception to Article 1103 for international agreements signed within two years of the date of entry into force of this Agreement.

For greater certainty, Article 1103 does not apply to any current or future foreign aid program to promote economic development, such as those governed by the Energy Economic Cooperation Program with Central America and the Caribbean (Pacto de San José) and the OECD Agreement on Export Credits.

Schedule of the United States

The United States takes an exception to Article 1103 for treatment accorded under all bilateral or multilateral international agreements in force or signed prior to the date of entry into force of this Agreement.

For international agreements in force or signed after the date of entry into force of this Agreement, the United States takes an exception to Article 1103 for treatment accorded under those agreements involving:

(a) aviation;

(b) fisheries;

(c) maritime matters, including salvage; or

(d) telecommunications transport networks and telecommunications transport services (this exception does not apply to measures covered by Chapter Thirteen (Telecommunications) or the production, sale or licensing of radio or television programming).

With respect to state measures not yet set out in Annex I pursuant to Article 1108(2), the United States takes an exception to Article 1103 for international agreements signed within two years of the date of entry into force of this Agreement.

For greater certainty, Article 1103 does not apply to any current or future foreign aid program to promote economic development, such as those governed by the Energy Economic Cooperation Program with Central America and the Caribbean (Pacto de San José) and the OECD Agreement on Export Credits.

ANNEX V
Quantitative Restrictions and Other Items

1. The Schedule of a Party sets out the non-discriminatory quantitative restrictions maintained by that Party pursuant to Article 1207.

2. Each entry sets out the following elements:

(a) **Sector** refers to the general sector in which the quantitative restriction is maintained;

(b) **Sub-Sector** refers to the specific sector in which the quantitative restriction is maintained;

(c) **Industry Classification** refers, where applicable, to the activity covered by the quantitative restriction according to domestic industry classification codes;

(d) **Level of Government** indicates the level of government maintaining the quantitative restriction;

(e) **Measures** identifies the measures under which the quantitative restriction is maintained; and

(f) **Description** sets out the scope of the sector, sub-sector or activities covered by the quantitative restriction.

3. For purposes of this Annex:

CMAP means Clasificación Mexicana de Actividades y Productos (CMAP) numbers as set out in Instituto Nacional de Estadística, Geografía e Informática, *Clasificación Mexicana de Actividades y Productos*, 1988;

CPC means Central Product Classification (CPC) numbers as set out in Statistical Office of the United Nations, Statistical Papers, Series M, No. 77, *Provisional Central Product Classification*, 1991; and

SIC means:

(a) with respect to Canada, Standard Industrial Classification (SIC) numbers as set out in Statistics Canada, *Standard Industrial Classification*, fourth edition, 1980; and

(b) with respect to the United States, Standard Industrial Classification (SIC) numbers as set out in the United States

Office of Management and Budget, *Standard Industrial Classification Manual*, 1987.

Schedule of Canada

Sector:	Transportation
Sub-Sector:	Land Transportation
Industry Classification:	SIC 457 — Public Passenger Transit Systems
Level of Government:	Federal (administration delegated to provinces)
Measures:	*National Transportation Act, 1987*, R.S.C. 1985, c. 28 (3rd Supp.)
Description:	Provincial transport boards have been delegated the authority to permit persons to provide extra-provincial (inter-provincial and cross-border) bus services in their respective provinces and territories on the same basis as local bus services. All provinces, except New Brunswick, Prince Edward Island and Yukon Territory, permit the provision of local and extra-provincial bus services on the basis of a public convenience and necessity test.

ANNEX VI
Miscellaneous Commitments

1.   The Schedule of a Party sets out the commitments to liberalize non-discriminatory measures undertaken by that Party pursuant to Article 1208.

2.   Each commitment sets out the following elements:

(a) **Sector** refers to the general sector in which the commitment to liberalize is undertaken;

(b) **Sub-Sector** refers to the specific sector in which the commitment to liberalize is undertaken;

(c) **Industry Classification** refers, where applicable, to the activity covered by the non-discriminatory measure to be liberalized according to domestic industry classification codes;

(d) **Level of Government** indicates the level of government maintaining the non-discriminatory measure to be liberalized;

(e) **Measures** identifies the non-discriminatory measures to be liberalized; and

(f) **Description** sets out the commitment undertaken by the Party to liberalize a non-discriminatory measure.

3. In the interpretation of a commitment, all elements of the commitment shall be considered. The **Description** element shall prevail over all other elements.

4. For purposes of this Annex:

CMAP means Clasificación Mexicana de Actividades y Productos (CMAP) numbers as set out in Instituto Nacional de Estadística, Geografía e Informática, *Clasificación Mexicana de Actividades y Productos*, 1988;

CPC means Central Product Classification (CPC) numbers as set out in Statistical Office of the United Nations, Statistical Papers, Series M, No. 77, *Provisional Central Product Classification*, 1991; and

SIC means:

> (a) with respect to Canada, Standard Industrial Classification (SIC) numbers as set out in Statistics Canada, *Standard Industrial Classification*, fourth edition, 1980; and

> (b) with respect to the United States, Standard Industrial Classification (SIC) numbers as set out in the United States Office of Management and Budget, *Standard Industrial Classification Manual*, 1987.

Sector:	Professional Services
Sub-Sector:	Lawyers
Industry Classification:	SIC 7761 —Offices of Lawyers and Notaries
Level of Government:	Provincial
Measures:	British Columbia: *Legal Profession Act*, S.B.C. 1987, c. 25 Ontario: *Law Society Act*, R.S.O. 1990, c. L-8 Saskatchewan: *Legal Profession Act*, S.Sask. 1990, c. L-10.1
Description:	Lawyers authorized to practice in Mexico or the United States and law firms headquartered in Mexico or the United States will be permitted to provide foreign legal consultancy services, and to establish for that purpose, in British Columbia, Ontario and Saskatchewan, and in any other province that so permits by the date of entry into force of this Agreement.

Schedule of Canada

Sector:	Professional, Technical and Specialized Services (V1-M-2)
Sub-Sector:	Professional Services
Industry Classification:	CMAP 951002 Legal Services (limited to foreign legal consultancy)
Level of Government:	Federal and State
Measures:	
Description:	1. Mexico will ensure that:

(a)   a lawyer authorized to practice in a province of Canada or a state of the United States who seeks to practice as a foreign legal consultant in Mexico will be granted a license to do so if lawyers licensed in Mexico are accorded equivalent treatment in such province or state; and

(b)   a law firm headquartered in a province of Canada or a state of the United States that seeks to establish in Mexico to provide legal services through licensed foreign legal consultants will be authorized to do so if law firms headquartered in Mexico are accorded equivalent treatment in such province or state.

2.   Mexico will, pursuant to paragraph 1(a), deny benefits to foreign lawyers employed by or associated with foreign legal consultancy firms established in Mexico, pursuant to paragraph 1(b), if such lawyers are not authorized to practice in a province of Canada or a state of the United States that authorizes lawyers licensed in Mexico to practice as foreign legal consultants in its territory.

3.   Subject to paragraphs 1 and 2, Mexico will adopt measures regarding the practice of foreign legal consultants in the territory of Mexico, including matters related to association with and hiring of lawyers licensed in Mexico.

Sector:	Transportation (V1-M-3)
Sub-Sector:	Land Transportation
Industry Classification:	CMAP 711201 Road Transport Services for Construction Materials CMAP 711202 Road Transport Moving Services CMAP 711203 Other Services of Specialized Cargo Transportation CMAP 711204 General Trucking Services CMAP 711311 Inter-City Busing Services CMAP 711318 School and Tourist Transportation Services (limited to tourist transportation services)

Measures:

Description: An enterprise authorized in Mexico to provide bus or truck transportation services may use equipment of its own, leased vehicles with an option to purchase (financial leasing), leased vehicles (operational leasing), or short-term rental vehicles.

Federal measures will be established in relation to leasing and rental operations.

Schedule of the United States

Sector:	Professional Services
Sub-Sector:	Legal Services
Industry Classification:	SIC 8111 — Legal Services
Level of Government:	State
Measures:	Alaska Bar R. 44.1
	California R. Ct. 988
	Connecticut Pract, Book § 24A
	D.C. Ct. App. R. 46(c)(4) (Washington, D.C.)
	Rules Regulating the Florida Bar, Chapter 16, as adopted in *Amendment to Rules Regulating the* Florida Bar, 605 So. 2d 252 (1992)

Rules and Regulations of the State Bar of Georgia, Part II, Rule 2–101, Part D

Hawaii Sup. Ct. R. 14

Illinois Rev. Stat. Ch. 110A, par. 712 (Sup. Ct. R. 712)

Michigan Bd. of Law Examiners R. 5(E)

New Jersey Sup. Ct. R. 1:21–9

New York Admn. Code tit. 22, Section 521

Ohio Sup. Ct. R. for the Government of the Bar XI

Rules Regulating Admission to Practice Law in Oregon, Chapter 10

Texas R. Governing Admission to the Bar of Texas XVI

Wash. R. of Ct. 14

Description: Lawyers authorized to practice in Canada or Mexico and law firms headquartered in Canada or Mexico will be permitted to provide foreign legal consultancy services, and to establish for that purpose, in Alaska, California, Connecticut, District of Columbia, Florida, Georgia, Hawaii, Illinois, Michigan, New Jersey, New York, Ohio, Oregon, Texas and Washington, or in any other state that so permits by the date of entry into force of this Agreement.

ANNEX VII
Reservations, Specific Commitments and Other Items

1. Section A of the Schedule of a Party sets out the reservations taken by that Party, pursuant to Article 1409(1) (Financial Services), with respect to existing measures that do not conform with obligations imposed by:

(a) Article 1403 (Establishment of Financial Institutions);

(b) Article 1404 (Cross-Border Trade);

(c) Article 1405 (National Treatment);

(d) Article 1406 (Most-Favored-Nation Treatment);

(e) Article 1407 (New Financial Services and Data Processing); or

(f) Article 1408 (Senior Management and Boards of Directors).

2.   Each reservation in Section A sets out the following elements:

(a) **Sector** refers to the general sector in which the reservation is taken;

(b) **Sub-Sector** refers to the specific sector in which the reservation is taken;

(c) **Industry Classification** refers, where applicable, to the activity covered by the reservation according to domestic industry classification codes;

(d) **Type of Reservation** specifies the obligation referred to in paragraph 1 for which the reservation is taken;

(e) **Level of Government** indicates the level of government maintaining the measure for which the reservation is taken;

(f) **Measures** identifies the laws, regulations or other measures, as qualified by the **Description** element, for which the reservation is taken. A measure cited in the **Measures** element

(i) means the measure as amended, continued or renewed as of the date of entry into force of this Agreement, and

(ii) includes any subordinate measure adopted or maintained under the authority of and consistent with the measure;

(g) **Description** sets out references, if any, for liberalization on the date of entry into force of this Agreement pursuant to other sections of a Party's Schedule to this Annex, and the remaining non-conforming aspects of the existing measures for which the reservation is taken; and

(h) **Phase-Out** sets out commitments, if any, for liberalization after the date of entry into force of this Agreement.

3.   In the interpretation of a reservation, all elements of the reservation shall be considered. A reservation shall be interpreted in the light of the relevant provisions of the Chapter against which the reservation is taken. To the extent that:

(a) the **Phase-Out** element provides for the phasing out of the non-conforming aspects of measures, the **Phase-Out** element shall prevail over all other elements;

(b) the **Measures** element is qualified by a specific reference in the **Description** element, the **Measures** element as so qualified shall prevail over all other elements; and

(c) the **Measures** element is not so qualified, the **Measures** element shall prevail over all other elements, unless any discrepancy between the **Measures** element and the other elements considered in their totality is so substantial and material that it would be unreasonable to conclude that the **Measures** element should prevail, in which case the other elements shall prevail to the extent of that discrepancy.

4.   Section B of the Schedule of a Party sets out reservations taken by the Party, pursuant to Article 1409(2), for measures the Party may adopt or maintain that do not conform with obligations imposed by Article 1403, 1404, 1405, 1406, 1407 or 1408.

5.   Section C of the Schedule of a Party sets out the commitments to liberalize measures undertaken by that Party pursuant to Article 1409(3).

6.   For purposes of this Annex:

CMAP means Clasificación Mexicana de Actividades y Productos (CMAP) numbers as set out in Instituto Nacional de Estadística, Geografía e Informática, *Clasificación Mexicana de Actividades y Productos*, 1988;

CPC means Central Product Classification (CPC) numbers as set out in Statistical Office of the United Nations, Statistical Papers, Series M, No. 77, *Provisional Central Product Classification*, 1991; and

SIC means:

(a) with respect to Canada, Standard Industrial Classification (SIC) number as set out in Statistics Canada, *Standard Industrial Classification*, fourth edition, 1980; and

(b) with respect to the United States, Standards Industrial Classification (SIC) numbers as set out in the United States Office of Management and Budget, *Standard Industrial Classification Manual*, 1987.

Schedule of Canada
Section A

Sector: Financial Services (VII-C-1 to V11-C-4)

Sub-Sector: Insurance

Industrial Classification:

Type of Reservation: Cross-Border Trade (Article 1404)

Level of Government: Federal

Measures: *Insurance Companies Act*, S.C. 1991, c. 47
                                    Reinsurance (Canadian Companies) Regulations, SOR/92-298
                                    Reinsurance (Foreign Companies) Regulations, SOR/92-596

Description: The purchase of reinsurance services by a Canadian insurer, other than a life insurer or a reinsurer, from a non-resident reinsurer is limited to no more than 25 percent of the risks undertaken by the insurer purchasing the reinsurance.

Phase-Out: None

Section B

1. Canada reserves the right to derogate from Article 1405(1) for the securities sector. With respect to this Article, Canada reserves the right to adopt or maintain measures affecting cross-border trade in securities services that are more restrictive than existing such measures.

2. For purposes of restrictions that limit foreign ownership of Canadian-controlled financial institutions, and for purposes of restrictions on total domestic assets of foreign bank subsidiaries in Canada, Canada reserves the right to adopt or maintain measures that require an enterprise of another Party be controlled by one or more residents of the other Party in order to be entitled to the benefits of this Chapter. For these purposes:

(a) an enterprise controlled by one or more residents of another Party means controlled, directly or indirectly, by such residents;

(b) an enterprise that is a body corporate is controlled by one or more persons if

(i) securities of the enterprise to which are attached more than 50 percent of the votes that may be cast to elect directors of the enterprise are beneficially owned by the person or persons and the votes attached to those shares are sufficient, if exercised, to elect a majority of the directors of the enterprise, and

(ii) the person or persons has or have, directly or indirectly, control in fact of the enterprise;

(c) an enterprise that is an unincorporated entity is controlled by one or more persons if

(i) more than 50 percent of ownership interests, however designated, into which the enterprise is divided is beneficially owned by the person or persons and the person or persons is or are able to direct the business and affairs of the enterprise, and

(ii) the person or persons has or have, directly or indirectly, control in fact of the enterprise;

(d) a limited partnership is controlled by the general partner;

(e) ordinarily resident in a country generally means sojourning in that country for a period of, or periods the aggregate of which is, 183 days or more during the relevant year; and

(f) a person ordinarily resident in another Party means

(i) in the case of an enterprise, an enterprise legally constituted or organized under the laws of that Party and controlled,
directly or indirectly, by one or more individuals of that Party
described in clause (ii), and

(ii) in the case of an individual, an individual who is
ordinarily resident in the territory of that Party.

Section C

1. For purposes of restrictions that limit foreign ownership of
Canadian-controlled financial institutions and for purposes of limitations
on total domestic assets of foreign bank subsidiaries in Canada, Canada
shall give to Mexico the same treatment that Canada gives under the
Bank Act, the *Insurance Companies Act (Canada)*, the *Trust and Loan
Companies Act (Canada)*, and the *Investment Companies Act*, to United
States residents and to institutions controlled by United States resi-
dents.

2. Canada shall exempt foreign bank subsidiaries in Canada controlled by Mexican residents from the requirement to obtain approval of
the Minister of Finance prior to opening branches within Canada in the
same manner as it exempts foreign bank subsidiaries in Canada controlled by United States residents.

Annex VII

Section A

Schedule of Mexico

Sector:	Financial Services (VII-M-1)
Sub-Sector:	Holding Companies (Sociedades Controla-doras) Commercial Banks (Instituciones de Cré-dito)
Industry Classification:	Holding Companies (Not applicable) CMAP 811030 Commercial Banks
Type of Reservation:	Establishment of Financial Institutions (Article 1403) National Treatment (Article 1405)
Level of Government:	Federal
Measures:	*Ley para Regular las Agrupaciones Financieras*, Artículo 18 *Ley de Instituciones de Crédito*, Artículos 11, 15
Description:	Aggregate foreign investments in holding companies and in commercial banks are

limited to 30 percent of common stock capital ("capital ordinario"). These percentage limits do not apply to investments in foreign financial affiliates as such term is defined in, and subject to terms and conditions under, Sections B and C of the Schedule of Mexico to Annex VII.

Phase-Out: None

Sector: Financial Services (VII-M-2)

Sub-Sector: Securities Firms (Casas de Bolsa)
Securities Specialists (Especialistas Bursátiles)

Industry Classification: CMAP 812001 Securities Firms
Securities Specialists (Not Applicable)

Type of Reservation: Establishment of Financial Institutions (Article 1403)
National Treatment (Article 1405)

Level of Government: Federal

Measures: *Ley del Mercado de Valores*, Artículo 17-II

Description: Aggregate foreign investments in securities firms and securities specialists are limited to 30 percent of capital ("capital social") and individual foreign investments are limited to 10 percent of capital, while individual investments by Mexicans may, with approval from the Secretaría de Hacienda y Crédito Público, rise to 15 percent of capital. These percentage limits do not apply to investments in foreign financial affiliates as such term is defined in, and subject to terms and conditions under, Sections B and C of the Schedule of Mexico to Annex VII.

Phase-Out: None

Sector: Financial Services (VII-M-3)

Sub-Sector: General Deposit Warehouses (Almacenes Generales de Depósito)
Financial Leasing Companies (Arrendadoras Financieras)
Financial Factoring Companies (Empresas de Factoraje Financiero)

Bonding Companies (Instituciones de Fianzas)

Industry Classification: CMAP 811042 General Deposit Warehouses
CMAP 811043 Financial Leasing Companies
Financial Factoring Companies (Not Applicable)
CMAP 813001 Bonding Companies

Type of Reservation: Establishment of Financial Intitutions (Article 1403)
National Treatment (Article 1405)

Level of Government: Federal

Measures: *Ley General de Organizaciones y Actividades Auxiliares del Crédito*, Artículo 8-III-1

Ley Federal de Instituciones de Fianzas, Artículo 15-XIII

Description: Aggregate foreign investments in general deposit warehouses, financial leasing companies, financial factoring companies and bonding companies must be less than 50 percent of paid-in capital ("capital pagado"). These percentage limits do not apply to investments in foreign financial affiliates as such term is defined in, and subject to terms and conditions under, Section B of the Schedule of Mexico to Annex VII.

Phase-Out: None

Sector: Financial Services (VII-M-4)

Sub-Sector: Credit Unions (Uniones de Crédito)
Financial Agents (Comisionistas Financieros)
Foreign Exchange Firms (Casas de Cambio)

Industry Classification: CMAP 811041 Credit Unions
Financial Agents (Not Applicable)
CMAP 811044 Foreign Exchange Firms

Type of Reservation: Establishment of Financial Institutions (Article 1403)
National Treatment (Article 1405)

Level of Government: Federal

Measures: *Ley General de Organizaciones y Activi-dades Auxiliares del Crédito*, Artículos 8-III-1, 82-III

Ley de Instituciones de Crédito, Artículo 92

Reglas de la Secretaría de Hacienda y Crédito Público

Description: Foreign investments in credit unions, financial agents and foreign exchange firms are not allowed. This limitation does not apply to investments in foreign financial affiliates as such term is defined in, and subject to terms and conditions under, Section B of the Schedule of Mexico to Annex VII.

Phase-Out: None

Sector: Financial Services (VII-M-5)

Sub-Sector: Development Banks (Bancos de Desarrollo)

Industry Classification: CMAP 811021   Development Banks

Type of Reservation: Establishment of Financial Institutions (Article 1403)
National Treatment (Article 1405)

Level of Government: Federal

Measures: *Ley de Instituciones de Crédito*, Artículo 33

Description: Foreign investments in development banks are not allowed.

Phase-Out: None

Sector: Financial Services (VII-M-6)

Sub-Sector: Insurance Companies (Instituciones de Seguros)

Industry Classification: CMAP 813002   Insurance Companies

Type of Reservation: Establishment of Financial Institutions
(Article 1403)
National Treatment (Article 1405)

Level of Government: Federal

Measures: *Ley General de Instituciones y Sociedades
Mutualistas de Seguros*, Artículo 29-I

Description: Aggregate foreign investments in insurance companies must be less than 50 per-
cent of paid-in capital ("capital pagado").
This percentage limit does not apply to
investments in foreign financial affiliates
as such term is defined in Sections B and
C of the Schedule of Mexico to Annex VII,
or in insurance companies, in both cases
subject to terms and conditions under
Sections B and C of the Schedule of Mexico to Annex VII.

Phase-Out: None

Sector: Financial Services (VII-M-7 to VII-M-8)

Sub-Sector: Holding Companies (Sociedades Controla-
doras)
Securities Firms (Casas de Bolsa)
Securities Specialists (Especialistas Bur-
sátiles)
General Deposit Warehouses (Almacenes
Generales de Depósito)
Financial Leasing Companies (Arrendado-
ras Financieras)
Financial Factoring Companies (Empre-
sas de Factoraje Financiero)
Savings and Loan Companies (Sociedades
de Ahorro y Préstamo)
Managing Companies of Investment Com-
panies (Sociedades Operadoras de Socie-
dades de Inversión)
Investment Companies (Sociedades de In-
versión)
Bonding Companies (Instituciones de Fi-
anzas)
Insurance Companies (Instituciones de
Seguros)

Industry Classification: Holding Companies (Not Applicable)
CMAP 812001 Securities Firms
Securities Specialists (Not Applicable)
CMAP 811042 General Deposit Ware-
   houses

CMAP 811043 Financial Leasing Companies

Financial Factoring Companies (Not Applicable)

Saving and Loans Companies (Not Applicable)

CMAP 812003 Managing Companies of Investment Companies

CMAP 812002 Investment Companies

CMAP 813001 Bonding Companies

CMAP 813002 Insurance Companies

Type of Reservation: Establishment of Financial Institutions (Article 1403)
National Treatment (Article 1405)

Level of Government: Federal

Measures: *Ley para Regular las Agrupaciones Financieras*, Artículo 18

Ley del Mercado de Valores, Artículo 17-II

Ley General de Organizaciones y Actividades Auxiliares del Crédito, Artículos 8-III-1, 38-G

Ley de Sociedades de Inversión, Artículos 9-III, 29-VI

Ley Federal de Instituciones de Fianzas, Artículo 15-XIII

Ley General de Instituciones y Sociedades Mutualistas de Seguros, Artículo 29-I

Description: Foreign governments and foreign state enterprises may not invest, directly or indirectly, in holding companies, securities firms, securities specialists, general deposit warehouses, financial leasing companies, financial factoring companies, savings and loan companies, managing companies of investment companies, investment companies, bonding companies or insurance companies.

Phase-Out: None

Sector: Financial Services (VII-M-9)

Sub-Sector: Commercial Banks (Instituciones de Crédito)

Industry Classification: CMAP 811030   Commercial Banks

Type of Reservation: Establishment of Financial Institutions (Article 1403)
National Treatment (Article 1405)

Level of Government: Federal

Measures: *Ley de Instituciones de Crédito*, Artículo 15

Description: Foreign entities that exercise governmental functions may not invest, directly or indirectly, in commercial banks.

Phase-Out: None

Sector: Financial Services (VII-M-10 to VII-M-11)

Sub-Sector: Insurance

Industry Classification: CMAP 813002   Insurance

Type of Reservation: Cross-Border Trade (Article 1404)
National Treatment (Article 1405)

Level of Government: Federal

Measures: *Ley General de Instituciones y Sociedades Mutualistas de Seguros*, Artículo 3

Description: Mexico reserves its existing prohibitions and restrictions on cross-border trade in insurance services, which do not now include restrictions on the right of individuals to purchase, by physical mobility, life and health insurance. Mexico is not reserving its present restrictions with respect to the ability of residents of Mexico to purchase from cross-border insurance providers of another Party the following types of insurance:

(a)   tourist insurance (including travel accident and motor vehicle insurance for non-resident tourists, but not insurance of risks of liability to third parties) for individuals, purchased without solicitation via physical mobility of such individuals;

(b)   (1) cargo insurance to and from each Party, purchased without solicitation, for goods in international transit from point of origin to final destination, and

          (2) insurance purchased without solicitation for a vehicle during the period of its use in transportation of cargo (other than insurance of risks of liabilities to third parties), provided such vehicle is licensed and registered outside Mexico (including vehicles in maritime shipping, commercial aviation, space launching and freight (including satellites)); and

(c)   intermediary services incidental to (a) and (b) purchased without solicitation.

For greater clarity, this reservation does not apply to reinsurance.

Phase-Out: None

Sector: Financial Services (VII-M-12)

Sub-Sector: Banking

Industry Classification: CMAP 811021   Development Banks
CMAP 811030   Commercial Banks

Type of Reservation: Establishment of Financial Institutions (Article 1403)
Cross-Border Trade (Article 1404)
National Treatment (Article 1405)

Level of Government: Federal

Measures: *Ley Orgánica de Nacional Financiera*, Artículo 7

Ley Orgánica del Banco Nacional del Ejército, la Fuerza Aérea y la Armada

Description: The following activities are reserved solely to Mexican development banks:

(1)   acting as custodians of securities and cash funds deposited by or in the administrative or judiciary au-

thorities, and acting as custodian of goods that have been seized according to Mexican measures;

(2)   managing the savings funds, retirement plans and any other funds or property of the personnel of the Secretaría de la Defensa Nacional, Secretaría de Marina and the Mexican armed forces, and performing other financial activities pertaining to the financial resources of such personnel.

Phase-Out: None

Section B

ESTABLISHMENT AND OPERATION OF FINANCIAL INSTITUTIONS (VII-M-13 to VII-M-18)

Type of Reservation: Establishment of Financial Institutions (Article 1403)
National Treatment (Article 1405)

1.   The provisions of paragraphs 2 through 10 of this Section of the Schedule of Mexico shall apply during the transition period, except as otherwise specifically provided in paragraphs 9 and 10 of this Section of the Schedule of Mexico.

2.   For the types of financial institutions listed in the chart in this paragraph, the maximum capital to be authorized by Mexico for a foreign financial affiliate, measured as a percentage of the aggregate capital of all financial institutions of the same type in Mexico, shall not exceed the percentage set forth in the chart in this paragraph:

Type of Financial Institution	Maximum Individual Capital to be Authorized (Percentage of the Aggregate Capital of all Institutions of the same type)
Commercial Banks	1.5%
Securities Firms	4.0%
Insurance Companies	
Casualty	1.5%
Life and Health	1.5%

In the case of an acquisition by an investor of another Party of a financial institution established in Mexico, the sum of the authorized capital of the acquired institution and the authorized capital of any foreign financial affiliate already controlled by the acquiror may not, at the time of acquisition or at any time thereafter during the transition period, exceed the applicable limit set forth in the chart in this paragraph.

This paragraph will not apply to new or existing Mexican insurance companies invested in by insurance investors of another Party (or their affiliates) pursuant to paragraph 7 of this Section or paragraph 4 of Section C of the Schedule of Mexico.

3.   For purposes of the proper administration of the capital limits in this Section, the following provisions shall apply:

(a) Each foreign financial affiliate shall have an authorized capital determined by Mexico, and the paid-in capital of such an institution shall not be less than that authorized at the time of approval of its establishment. After the time of establishment, Mexico may permit authorized capital to exceed paid-in capital. Authorized capital shall not be reduced by any measure of Mexico (other than prudential measures) below paid-in capital. The maximum size of the operations of each foreign financial affiliate shall be determined, on a national treatment basis, as a function of the lesser of its capital or its authorized capital.

(b) Mexico reserves the right to impose limitations on transfers of assets or liabilities by foreign financial affiliates that have the effect of evading the capital limits set forth in the Schedule of Mexico. This subparagraph does not apply to *bona fide* transfers of funds to make overnight deposits or *bona fide* transfers of banking liabilities.

4.   No foreign financial affiliate may issue subordinated debentures, other than to the investor of another Party that owns and controls the affiliate.

5.   The aggregate of the authorized capital of all foreign financial affiliates of the same type, measured as a percentage of the aggregate capital of all financial institutions of such type in Mexico, shall not exceed the percentage set forth in the chart in this paragraph for that type of institution, except for insurance companies as set out in paragraph 6 of this Section. Beginning one year after the entry into force of this Agreement, these initial limits shall increase annually in equal increments so as to reach the final limits specified in the chart in this paragraph at the beginning of the last year of the transition period:

Type of Financial Institution	Percentage of Total Capital	
	Initial Limit	Final Limit
Commercial banks	8%	15%
Securities firms	10%	20%
Factoring companies	10%	20%
Leasing companies	10%	20%

Any capital in existence as of the date of signature of this Agreement of a foreign bank branch established in Mexico prior to such date shall be excluded from each of the aggregate capital limits referred to in the Schedule of Mexico.

6.   The aggregate of the authorized capital of all foreign insurance affiliates, measured as a percentage of the aggregate capital of all insurance companies in Mexico, shall not exceed the percentage set forth in the chart in this paragraph for the respective one-year periods beginning on each of the following dates:

Date	Percentage of Total Capital
January 1, 1994	6%
January 1, 1995	8%
January 1, 1996	9%
January 1, 1997	10%
January 1, 1998	11%
January 1, 1999	12%

If the entry into force of this Agreement occurs on a date prior to January 1, 1994, that date shall become the initial date for purposes of this chart, and each succeeding anniversary of the entry into force of this Agreement shall become the next succeeding date in this chart, with the percentages listed in this chart applying to each of the respective periods as so adjusted. If the entry into force of this Agreement occurs on a date after January 1, 1994, the dates and corresponding limits in this chart shall not be changed.

The individual and aggregate capital limits described in paragraphs 2 and 6 of this Section shall be measured separately (through separate accounting) for life and non-life insurance operations, but both types of insurance operations may be conducted either by a single or separate foreign financial affiliates.

7.   An insurance investor of another Party may elect an alternative procedure for investment in Mexico through phasing-in an equity interest in a new or existing Mexican insurance company, and thereby exempt such Mexican company from the capital limits in paragraphs 2 and 6 of this Section. In order to qualify, the percentage of the Mexican insurance company's common voting stock that is owned by Mexican persons must not be less than the levels set forth in the chart in this paragraph for the respective one-year periods beginning on each of the following dates:

Date	Mexican Interest
January 1, 1994	70%
January 1, 1995	65%
January 1, 1996	60%
January 1, 1997	55%
January 1, 1998	49%
January 1, 1999	25%

If the entry into force of this Agreement occurs on a date prior to January 1, 1994, that date shall become the initial date for purposes of this chart, and each succeeding anniversary of the entry into force of this Agreement shall become the next succeeding date in this chart, with the percentages listed in this chart applying to each of the respective periods as so adjusted. If the entry into force of this Agreement occurs on a date after January 1, 1994, the dates and corresponding limits in this chart shall nonetheless not be changed.

On and after January 1, 2000 (or, if the entry into force of this Agreement occurs on a date prior to January 1, 1994, on and after the sixth anniversary of such date), the percentage requirement of Mexican ownership set forth in this paragraph shall no longer apply.

This paragraph is further modified by paragraph 4 of Section C of the Schedule of Mexico to the extent set forth therein.

8. The aggregate assets of foreign financial affiliates that are limited scope financial institutions within the meaning of paragraph 2 of Section C of the Schedule of Mexico shall not exceed 3% of the sum of (1) the aggregate assets of all commercial banks in Mexico plus (2) the aggregate assets of all types of limited scope financial institutions in Mexico. Lending by affiliates of automobile manufacturing companies with respect to the manufacturers' vehicles shall not be subject to or taken into account in determining compliance with this 3% limit.

9. The limits in paragraphs 2, 5, 6 and 8 of this Section shall be removed at the end of the transition period. If the sum of the authorized capital of foreign financial affiliates, measured as a percentage of the aggregate capital of all financial institutions of such type in Mexico, reaches the percentage set forth in the chart in this paragraph for such type of institutions, then Mexico shall have the right, once during the four years following the end of the transition period, to freeze such aggregate capital percentage at its then-existing level:

| Commercial banks | 25% |
| Securities firms | 30% |

If applied, such a restriction will have a duration not to exceed a period of 3 years.

10. Mexico may deny a license to establish a foreign financial affiliate during the transition period (and, in the case of paragraph 9 of this Section, during the additional periods described in that paragraph) if after such issuance the sum of the authorized capital of all foreign financial affiliates of the same type would exceed the applicable percentage limit for that type of institution in paragraph 5, 6, 8 or 9 of this Section.

11. The provisions of the following paragraphs 12 through 17 of this Section shall apply immediately upon the entry into force of this Agreement and at all times thereafter, except as otherwise specifically

provided in such paragraphs. Any amendment or modification to a measure adopted or maintained pursuant to paragraphs 12 through 15 of this Section shall not decrease the conformity of the measure, as it existed immediately before such amendment or modification, with Articles 1403 through 1408 of this Agreement.

12. Mexico may require that a foreign financial affiliate (other than a foreign insurance affiliate) be wholly-owned by an investor of another Party (except for directors' nominal qualifying shares). Mexico may also restrict any foreign financial affiliate from establishing agencies, branches, or other direct or indirect subsidiaries in the territory of any other country.

13. Following the transition period, acquisition of a commercial bank established in Mexico, or of the assets or liabilities thereof, by an investor of another Party will only be authorized by Mexico, subject to reasonable prudential considerations on a case by case basis, if the sum of the capital of the acquired commercial bank and the capital of any foreign commercial bank affiliate already controlled by the acquiror would not exceed 4% of the aggregate capital of all commercial banks in Mexico.

14. Mexico may adopt measures that (i) limit eligibility to establish a foreign financial affiliate in Mexico to an investor of another Party that is, directly or through any of its affiliates, engaged in the same general type of financial services in the territory of the other Party; and (ii) limit such investor (together with its affiliates) to no more than one institution of the same type in Mexico. In determining what types of operations an investor of another Party is engaged in for purposes of the preceding sentence, all types of insurance shall be considered to be only one type of financial service; but both life and non-life insurance operations may be conducted either by a single or separate foreign financial affiliates.

GOVERNMENTAL INSURANCE PROGRAMS (VII-M-18)

Type of Reservation: Establishment of Financial Institutions (Articles 1403)
Cross-Border Trade (Article 1404)
National Treatment (Article 1405)

15. The activities and operations of the existing Mexican governmental insurance programs conducted by Aseguradora Mexicana, S.A. or Aseguradora Hidalgo, S.A. (including insurance for government employees, agencies, instrumentalities and public entities) are excluded from Articles 1403, 1404 and 1405 for so long as such firm is controlled by the government of Mexico and for a commercially reasonable time after such governmental control ceases.

CROSS-BORDER TRADE (VII-M-18)

Type of Reservation: Cross-Border Trade (Article 1404)

16. In order to avoid impairment of the conduct of Mexico's monetary and exchange rate policies, cross-border financial service providers

of another Party shall not be permitted to provide financial services into the territory of Mexico or to residents of Mexico, and residents of Mexico may not purchase financial services from cross-border financial service providers of another Party, if such transactions are denominated in Mexican pesos.

EXISTING OPERATIONS OF FOREIGN COMMERCIAL BANKS (VII-M-18 & VII-M-19)

Type of Reservation: Establishment of Financial Institutions (Article 1403)
National Treatment (Article 1405)
Most-Favored-Nation Treatment (Article 1406)
New Financial Services and Data Processing (Article 1407)
Senior Management and Boards of Directors (Article 1408)

17. The benefits of this Agreement shall not be extended to a foreign bank branch existing in Mexico on the date of entry into force of this Agreement. The existing legal regime will continue to apply to such a branch for so long as it operates in that form. Such a branch shall be permitted to convert to a subsidiary pursuant to the terms of this Schedule, and upon conversion shall be covered by this Agreement. In the event of conversion the existing capital of such branch on the date of signature of this Agreement shall not be counted against such foreign commercial bank affiliate's individual capital limit, or the aggregate capital limits for commercial banks.

Section C
SPECIFIC COMMITMENTS (VII-2-tO VII-M-21)

1. Mexico shall retain discretion to approve, on a case-by-case basis, any affiliation of a commercial bank or securities firm with a commercial or industrial corporation that is established in Mexico, if Mexico determines that such affiliation is harmless and, in the case of banking, either (a) not substantial, or (b) the financial-related activities of the commercial or industrial corporation account for at least 90 percent of its annual income worldwide, and the non-financial activities of such commercial or industrial corporation are of a type that Mexico determines to be acceptable. Affiliation with a non-resident commercial or industrial corporation that is not established in Mexico will not be a reason for denial of an application to establish or acquire a commercial bank or securities firm in Mexico.

2. Non-bank investors of another Party shall be permitted to establish one or more limited scope financial institutions in Mexico to provide separately consumer lending, commercial lending, mortgage lending or credit card services on terms no less favorable than those applied to like domestic firms under Mexican measures. Mexico may permit lending services closely related to the principal authorized busi-

ness of a limited scope financial institution to be carried out by that institution. Such institutions shall be provided the opportunity to raise funds in the securities market for business operations subject to normal terms and conditions. Mexico may restrict such limited scope financial institutions from taking deposits.

3. Within two years of the entry into force of this Agreement, Mexico shall conduct a study of the desirability of and, if desirable, the possible methods of establishing limited scope securities firms which would have more limited powers than current securities firms. Such limited scope securities firms would be subject to differing capital requirements, depending on the type and extent of business conducted, that would permit lower minimum capital requirements than those currently applicable to Mexican securities firms. The basis of the study will be prudential considerations and opportunities for investment in the securities sector. As part of the second annual meeting of the Committee required under Article 1412, Mexico shall report to the other Parties on the outcome of the study, including any plans for the establishment of new categories of securities firms.

4. Notwithstanding paragraph 7 of Section B of the Schedule of Mexico, an insurance investor of another Party that together with its affiliates had as of July 1, 1992 an active investment or ownership interest of 10% or more in a Mexican insurance company that was specifically approved by Mexico, may: (1) exercise any contract right or option in existence as of July 1, 1992 with respect to ownership interests in such Mexican insurance company; and (2) effective the earlier of January 1, 1996 or two years following the date of entry into force of this Agreement, acquire a controlling interest of up to 100% in such Mexican insurance company. Before the effective date described in clause (2) of the preceding sentence, an insurance investor of another Party (together with its affiliates) described in that sentence may exercise any existing contract right or option described in clause (1) of that sentence, and choose to expand its interest in such Mexican insurance company to the extent consistent with paragraph 7 of Section B of the Schedule of Mexico, or maintain its existing interest. Mexico shall maintain discretion to permit acceleration of the schedule for equity participation in a Mexican insurance company by an insurance investor of another Party described in the first sentence of this paragraph.

5. An investor of another Party that in accordance with Section B is authorized to and establishes or acquires a commercial bank or securities firm, respectively, in Mexico may also establish a financial holding company in Mexico, and thereby establish or acquire other types of financial institutions in Mexico, under the terms of Mexican measures.

6. Mexico shall administer its licensing and approval procedures during the transition period in a manner that does not deny the benefits of the liberalization of existing measures described in the Schedule of Mexico to enterprises of another Party ultimately controlled by nationals of that Party.

DEFINITIONS (VII-M-22)

For purposes of Sections B and C of the Schedule of Mexico:

capital means the following, as defined in Mexican measures, applied on a national treatment basis:

Type of Financial Institution	Concept of "Capital"
commercial banks	capital neto
securities firms	capital global
insurance companies	
casualty	requerimiento bruto de solvencia (allocation to casualty insurance)
life and health	requerimiento bruto de solvencia (allocation to life and health insurance)
factoring companies	capital contable
leasing companies	capital contable;

investor of another Party means an investor of another Party as defined in Article 1403(5);

foreign commercial bank affiliate means a foreign financial affiliate that is a commercial bank;

foreign financial affiliate means a financial institution established in Mexico and owned and controlled by an investor of another Party;

foreign insurance affiliate means a foreign financial affiliate that is an insurance company;

insurance investor of another Party means an investor of another Party that is an insurance company; and

transition period means the period beginning with the entry into force of this Agreement and ending on the earlier of i) January 1, 2000, or ii) six years from the entry into force of this Agreement.

Annex VII

Section A

Schedule of the United States

Sector: Financial Services (VII-U-1)

Sub-Sector: Banking

Industry Classification: SIC 6021 National Commercial Banks

Type of Reservation: Senior Management and Boards of Directors (Article 1408)

Level of Government: Federal

Measures:	*The National Bank Act*, 12 U.S.C. § 72
Description:	All directors of a national bank must be citizens of the United States. Because the chief executive officer of a national bank must be a director, the chief executive officer of a national bank must be a citizen of the United States. An exception exists for a national bank affiliated with or owned by a foreign bank. Such a bank need only have citizens constitute a simple majority of the board and thus need not employ citizens as its chief executive officer.
	Two-thirds of the directors of a national bank must (i) have resided for one year prior to their election, and (ii) continue to reside, in the state in which the bank is located or within 100 miles of the bank.
Phase-Out:	None
Sector:	Financial Services (VII-U-2 to VII-U-3)
Sub-Sector:	Banking
Industry Classification:	SIC 6021 National Commercial Banks SIC 6022 State Commercial Banks SIC 6029 Other Commercial Banks SIC 6081 Branches and Agencies of Foreign Banks SIC 6712 Bank Holding Companies Foreign Banks (Not Applicable)
Type of Reservation:	National Treatment (Article 1405)
Level of Government:	Federal
Measures:	*Bank Holding Company Act of 1956*, 12 U.S.C. § 1842(d) *International Banking Act of 1978*, 12 U.S.C. § 3103(a)(5)
Description:	Federal authorities may not approve the establishment of, or acquisition of an interest in, a bank subsidiary within a state ("the target state") by a foreign bank that has a full-service branch in the United States, unless the measures of the target state expressly permit such an establishment or acquisition by domestic

bank holding companies with their principal place of banking operations (as that term is described under the *Bank Holding Company Act*) in the foreign bank's "home state" (as that term is defined in the *International Banking Act*).

Federal authorities also may not approve the establishment of, or acquisition of an interest in, a bank subsidiary within a state ("the target state") by a bank holding company, including a foreign bank, that has principal place of banking operations in another state, as defined under the *Bank Holding Company Act*, unless the measures of the target state expressly permit the establishment and acquisition by bank holding companies from the state of the company's or bank's principal place of banking operations.

Due to these Federal measures and certain state measures, foreign banks with direct deposit-taking branches or bank subsidiaries in the United States are not permitted to establish or acquire interests in banks located in some states on the same basis as domestic bank holding companies from the state of the foreign bank's principal of banking operations or the foreign bank's home state. The following types of measures, inter alia, fall into this category:

(a) foreign banks are expressly excluded from the authority to own banks under certain regional holding company laws;

(b) foreign banks are implicitly excluded from the definition of an eligible owner under certain state laws that require a majority of a banking company's deposits to be in the United States, in a particular region of the United States, or in a particular state;

(c) foreign banks that do not already own a banking subsidiary in the United States are interpreted as not qualifying as an eligible "bank holding company" entitled to own a bank; and

(d)   where a foreign bank's principal place of business is in a state which is different from its home state and the measures of the target state accord better treatment to bank holding companies from one of these states, the foreign bank will be subject to the more restrictive rule.

Phase-Out: None

Sector: Financial Services (VII-U-4)

Sub-Sector: Banking

Industry Classification: SIC 6082 Foreign Trade and International Banking Institutions

Type of Reservation: National Treatment (Article 1405)

Level of Government: Federal

Measures: *Federal Reserve Act*, 12 U.S.C. § 619

Description: Edge corporations (specialized international banking companies chartered under Federal law) may be owned by domestically-owned banks and bank holding companies, and by domestic non-bank companies willing to restrict their business activities to those closely related to banking. Foreign ownership of Edge corporations is limited to foreign banks and U.S. subsidiaries of foreign banks. Other foreign persons may neither directly nor indirectly own Edge corporations.

Phase-Out: None

Sector: Financial Services (VII-U-6)

Sub-Sector: Banking

Industry Classification: SIC 6081 Branches of Foreign Banks

Type of Reservation: National Treatment (Article 1405)

Level of Government: Federal

Measures: *International Banking Act of 1978*, 12
                          U.S.C. §3104(c)

Description: In order to accept or maintain domestic
                          retail deposit accounts having balances of
                          less than $100,000, a foreign bank must
                          establish an insured banking subsidiary.
                          This prohibition does not apply to a for-
                          eign bank branch that was engaged in
                          insured deposit-taking activities on De-
                          cember 19, 1991.

Phase-Out: None

Sector: Financial Services (VII-U-7)

Sub-Sector: Banking

Industry Classification: SIC 6081 Branches and Agencies of For-
                          eign Banks

Type of Reservation: National Treatment (Article 1405)

Level of Government: Federal

Measures: *Federal Reserve Act*, 12 U.S.C. §§ 221,
                          302, 321

Description: Foreign banks with branches and agen-
                          cies in the United States may not be
                          members of the Federal Reserve System,
                          and may thus not vote for directors of a
                          Federal Reserve Bank.

Phase-Out: None

Sector: Financial Services (VII-U-8)

Sub-Sector: Banking and Securities

Industry Classification: SIC 6021 National Commercial Banks
                          SIC 6022 State Commercial Banks
                          SIC 6029 Other Commercial Banks
                          SIC 6081 Branches and Agencies of For-
                          eign Banks
                          SIC 6211 Security Brokers, Dealers and
                          Flotation Companies

Type of Reservation: National Treatment (Article 1405)
                          Most-Favored-Nation Treatment (Article
                          1406)

Level of Government: Federal

Measures: The *Primary Dealers Act of 1988*, 22 U.S.C. §§ 5341-5342

Description: The *Primary Dealers Act of 1988* prohibits a foreign firm from being designated as a primary dealer in U.S. government debt obligations unless the home country of the foreign firm accords to U.S. firms the same competitive opportunities as are accorded to domestic firms in the underwriting and distribution of government debt instruments in the firm's home country.

Phase-Out: None

Sector: Financial Services (VII-U-8)

Sub-Sector: Banking and Securities

Industry Classification: SIC 6289 Services Allied with the Exchange of Securities or Commodities

Type of Reservation: Cross-Border Trade (Article 1404)
National Treatment (Article 1405)
Most-Favored-Nation Treatment (Article 1406)
Senior Management and Boards of Directors (Article 1408)

Level of Government: Federal

Measures: *Trust Indenture Act of 1939*, 15 U.S.C. § 77jjj(a)(1)

Description: Under the *Trust Indenture Act of 1939*, a foreign firm located outside the United States may be prohibited from acting as the sole trustee under an indenture for debt securities sold in the United States if U.S. institutional trustees cannot act as sole trustees for securities sold in the foreign firm's home country.

Phase-Out: None

Sector: Financial Services (VII-U-9)

Sub-Sector: Banking and Securities

Industry Classification: SIC 6211 Security Brokers, Dealers and Flotation Companies

Type of Reservation: Most-Favored-Nation Treatment (Article 1406)

Level of Government: Federal

Measures: *Securities Exchange Act of 1934*, 15 U.S.C. § 78o(c)

17 C.F.R. § 240.15c3-3

Description: A broker-dealer that maintains its principal place of business in Canada may maintain its required reserves at a bank in Canada subject to supervision by an authority of Canada. A broker-dealer that maintains its principal place of business in any other foreign country must maintain reserves in the United States.

Phase-Out: None

Sector: Financial Services (VII-U-10)

Sub-Sector: Commodity Futures and Options

Industry Classification: SIC 6221 Commodity Contracts Broker and Dealers
SIC 6231 Commodity Exchanges
SIC 6282 Investment Advice
SIC 6289 Services Allied with the Exchange of Commodities

Type of Reservation: Cross-Border Trade (Article 1404)
New Financial Services and Data Processing (Article 1407)

Level of Government: Federal

Measures: *Commodity Exchange Act*, 7 U.S.C. §§ 2, 13-1

Description: Federal law prohibits the offer or sale of futures contracts on onions, options contracts on onions and options on futures contracts on onions in the United States and services related thereto.

Phase-Out: None

Sector: Financial Services (VII-U-11)

Sub-Sector: Insurance

Industry Classification:	SIC 6351 Surety Insurance
Type of Reservation:	Cross-Border Trade (Article 1405) National Treatment (Article 1405)
Level of Government:	Federal
Measures:	31 U.S.C. § 9304
Description:	Branches of foreign insurance companies are not permitted to provide surety bonds for U.S. Government contracts.
Phase-Out:	None
Sector:	Financial Services (VII-U-12)
Sub-Sector:	Banking and Securities
Industry Classification:	SIC 6081 Branches and Agencies of Foreign Banks SIC 6282 Investment Advice
Type of Reservation:	National Treatment (Article 1405)
Level of Government:	Federal
Measures:	*Investment Advisers Act of 1940*, 15 U.S.C. §§ 80b-2, 80b-3
Description:	Foreign banks are required to register as investment advisers under the *Investment Advisers Act of 1940* to engage in securities advisory services in the United States, while domestic banks are exempt from registration.
Phase-Out:	None

Annex VII

Section B

Schedule of the United States (VII-V-13)

The United States reserves the right to derogate from Articles 1404(1) and 1406 for the securities sector with respect to Canada. With respect to these Articles, the United States may adopt or maintain measures affecting cross-border trade in securities services that are more restrictive than measures existing on the date of entry into force of this Agreement.

Annex VII

Section C

Schedule of the United States (VII-V-14)

The United States commits to permit an eligible *grupo financiero* that, in formation of the *grupo* in Mexico before the entry into force of this Agreement, lawfully acquires an eligible Mexican bank and a Mexican securities firm which owns or controls a securities company in the United States, to continue to engage through the U.S. securities company in the activities in which that securities company was engaged on the date of acquisition by the *grupo* for a time period of five years from the date of that acquisition. The U.S. securities company: (i) shall not be permitted to expand through acquisition in the United States during such period; and (ii) shall be subject to measures consistent with national treatment that restrict transactions between the company and its affiliates. For purposes of this paragraph: an "eligible *grupo financiero*" is a Mexican financial group that has not previously benefitted from this commitment; and an "eligible Mexican bank" means any Mexican *institución de crédito* that owned or controlled a subsidiary bank, or operated a branch or agency, in the United States on January 1, 1992.

DOCUMENT 2

UNDERSTANDING BETWEEN THE PARTIES TO THE NORTH AMERICAN FREE TRADE AGREEMENT CONCERNING CHAPTER EIGHT—EMERGENCY ACTION

Article 1: Objectives

The objectives of this Understanding are to establish additional procedures to facilitate the effective use of Chapter Eight of the North American Free Trade Agreement (NAFTA).

Article 2: Working Group on Emergency Action

1. The Parties hereby establish a Working Group on Emergency Action comprising one representative of each Party to the NAFTA. The Working Group shall be deemed to be a working group established under Article 2001(2)(d) of the NAFTA.

2. The Working Group shall report to the Free Trade Commission established under the NAFTA, and shall be subject to the supervision of the Commission.

3. The NAFTA Secretariat shall provide technical support to the Working Group.

4. The Working Group shall meet at least annually, unless the Parties otherwise agree, and on request of any Party.

5. The Working Group may call on the assistance of such experts and advisers as it deems appropriate.

6. All decisions of the Working Group shall be taken by consensus, except as otherwise agreed or provided for in this Understanding.

Article 3: Functions of the Working Group

1. The Working Group shall consider any issue related to recourse to Chapter Eight of the NAFTA and may make recommendations to the Commission.

2. The Working Group shall consider any recourse to Article XIX of the General Agreement on Tariffs and Trade by any Party to the NAFTA, and, at the request of any Party, may serve as a forum for consultations before or during any such use of Article XIX.

3. The Parties may consult in the Working Group on the request of a Party where a Party considers that: (a) in accordance with Article 801

or 802, goods originating in the territory of another Party are being imported in such increased quantities as to constitute a substantial cause of, or contribute importantly to, serious injury, or threat thereof, to its domestic industry, as evidenced by the factors set out in Annex 803.3(9) of the NAFTA, including trade, productivity, and employment; or (b) another Party is contemplating having recourse to Chapter Eight.

Any consultations under this paragraph shall be without prejudice as to whether any subsequent emergency action proceeding is consistent with the NAFTA.

4.   The Parties may agree that consultations under paragraph 3 shall constitute consultations under Article 801(2) or 802(5) of the NAFTA.

5.   Subject to the rights and obligations of the Parties under the NAFTA, the Working Group shall serve as a forum for examining, at the request of any Party and with the agreement of two-thirds of the Parties, trade, productivity, employment and other economic factors with respect to any good, provided that such discussions shall not serve as a justification for restricting or prohibiting trade in any manner inconsistent with Chapter Eight.

6.   The Working Group may make recommendations to the Commission for any improvements to Chapter Eight of the NAFTA that the Working Group deems appropriate, consistent with the objectives of the NAFTA and of this Understanding.

Article 4: Definitions

Unless otherwise specified, all terms of this Understanding shall have the meaning assigned to them in the NAFTA.

B. THE SIDE AGREEMENTS— ENVIRONMENT AND LABOR

DOCUMENT 3

NORTH AMERICAN AGREEMENT ON ENVIRONMENTAL COOPERATION

PREAMBLE

The Government of the United States of America, the Government of Canada and the Government of the United Mexican States:

CONVINCED of the importance of the conservation, protection and enhancement of the environment in their territories and the essential role of cooperation in these areas in achieving sustainable development for the well-being of present and future generations;

REAFFIRMING the sovereign right of States to exploit their own resources pursuant to their own environmental and development policies and their responsibility to ensure that activities within their jurisdiction or control do not cause damage to the environment of other States or of areas beyond the limits of national jurisdiction;

RECOGNIZING the interrelationship of their environments;

ACKNOWLEDGING the growing economic and social links between them, including the North American Free Trade Agreement (NAFTA);

RECONFIRMING the importance of the environmental goals and objectives of the NAFTA, including enhanced levels of environmental protection;

EMPHASIZING the importance of public participation in conserving, protecting and enhancing the environment;

NOTING the existence of differences in their respective natural endowments, climatic and geographical conditions, and economic, technological and infrastructural capabilities;

REAFFIRMING the Stockholm Declaration on the Human Environment of 1972 and the Rio Declaration on Environment and Development of 1992;

RECALLING their tradition of environmental cooperation and expressing their desire to support and build on international environmental agreements and existing policies and laws, in order to promote cooperation between them; and

CONVINCED of the benefits to be derived from a framework, including a Commission, to facilitate effective cooperation on the conservation, protection and enhancement of the environment in their territories;

HAVE AGREED AS FOLLOWS:

PART ONE

OBJECTIVES

Article 1: Objectives

The objectives of this Agreement are to: (a) foster the protection and improvement of the environment in the territories of the Parties for the well-being of present and future generations; (b) promote sustainable development based on cooperation and mutually supportive environmental and economic policies; (c) increase cooperation between the Parties to better conserve, protect, and enhance the environment, including wild flora and fauna; (d) support the environmental goals and objectives of the NAFTA; (e) avoid creating trade distortions or new trade barriers; (f) strengthen cooperation on the development and improvement of environmental laws, regulations, procedures, policies and practices; (g) enhance compliance with, and enforcement of, environmental laws and regulations; (h) promote transparency and public participation in the development of environmental laws, regulations and policies; (i) promote economically efficient and effective environmental measures; and (j) promote pollution prevention policies and practices.

PART TWO

OBLIGATIONS

Article 2: General Commitments

1. Each Party shall, with respect to its territory: (a) periodically prepare and make publicly available reports on the state of the environment; (b) develop and review environmental emergency preparedness measures; (c) promote education in environmental matters, including environmental law; (d) further scientific research and technology development in respect of environmental matters; (e) assess, as appropriate, environmental impacts; and (f) promote the use of economic instruments for the efficient achievement of environmental goals.

2. Each Party shall consider implementing in its law any recommendation developed by the Council under Article 10(5)(b).

3. Each Party shall consider prohibiting the export to the territories of the other Parties of a pesticide or toxic substance whose use is prohibited within the Party's territory. When a Party adopts a measure prohibiting or severely restricting the use of a pesticide or toxic sub-

stance in its territory, it shall notify the other Parties of the measure, either directly or through an appropriate international organization.

Article 3: Levels of Protection

Recognizing the right of each Party to establish its own levels of domestic environmental protection and environmental development policies and priorities, and to adopt or modify accordingly its environmental laws and regulations, each Party shall ensure that its laws and regulations provide for high levels of environmental protection and shall strive to continue to improve those laws and regulations.

Article 4: Publication

1. Each Party shall ensure that its laws, regulations, procedures and administrative rulings of general application respecting any matter covered by this Agreement are promptly published or otherwise made available in such a manner as to enable interested persons and Parties to become acquainted with them.

2. To the extent possible, each Party shall: (a) publish in advance any such measure that it proposes to adopt; and (b) provide interested persons and Parties a reasonable opportunity to comment on such proposed measures.

Article 5: Government Enforcement Action

1. With the aim of achieving high levels of environmental protection and compliance with its environmental laws and regulations, each Party shall effectively enforce its environmental laws and regulations through appropriate governmental action, subject to Article 37, such as: (a) appointing and training inspectors; (b) monitoring compliance and investigating suspected violations, including through on-site inspections; (c) seeking assurances of voluntary compliance and compliance agreements; (d) publicly releasing non-compliance information; (e) issuing bulletins or other periodic statements on enforcement procedures; (f) promoting environmental audits; (g) requiring record keeping and reporting; (h) providing or encouraging mediation and arbitration services; (i) using licenses, permits or authorizations; (j) initiating, in a timely manner, judicial, quasi-judicial or administrative proceedings to seek appropriate sanctions or remedies for violations of its environmental laws and regulations; (k) providing for search, seizure or detention; or (*l*) issuing administrative orders, including orders of a preventative, curative or emergency nature.

2. Each Party shall ensure that judicial, quasi-judicial or administrative enforcement proceedings are available under its law to sanction or remedy violations of its environmental laws and regulations.

3. Sanctions and remedies provided for a violation of a Party's environmental laws and regulations shall, as appropriate: (a) take into

consideration the nature and gravity of the violation, any economic benefit derived from the violation by the violator, the economic condition of the violator, and other relevant factors; and (b) include compliance agreements, fines, imprisonment, injunctions, the closure of facilities, and the cost of containing or cleaning up pollution.

Article 6: Private Access to Remedies

1.   Each Party shall ensure that interested persons may request the Party's competent authorities to investigate alleged violations of its environmental laws and regulations and shall give such requests due consideration in accordance with law.

2.   Each Party shall ensure that persons with a legally recognized interest under its law in a particular matter have appropriate access to administrative, quasi-judicial or judicial proceedings for the enforcement of the Party's environmental laws and regulations.

3.   Private access to remedies shall include rights, in accordance with the Party's law, such as: (a) to sue another person under that Party's jurisdiction for damages; (b) to seek sanctions or remedies such as monetary penalties, emergency closures or orders to mitigate the consequences of violations of its environmental laws and regulations; (c) to request the competent authorities to take appropriate action to enforce that Party's environmental laws and regulations in order to protect the environment or to avoid environmental harm; or (d) to seek injunctions where a person suffers, or may suffer, loss, damage or injury as a result of conduct by another person under that Party's jurisdiction contrary to that Party's environmental laws and regulations or from tortious conduct.

Article 7: Procedural Guarantees

1.   Each Party shall ensure that its administrative, quasi-judicial and judicial proceedings referred to in Articles 5(2) and 6(2) are fair, open and equitable, and to this end shall provide that such proceedings: (a) comply with due process of law; (b) are open to the public, except where the administration of justice otherwise requires; (c) entitle the parties to the proceedings to support or defend their respective positions and to present information or evidence; and (d) are not unnecessarily complicated and do not entail unreasonable charges or time limits or unwarranted delays.

2.   Each Party shall provide that final decisions on the merits of the case in such proceedings are: (a) in writing and preferably state the reasons on which the decisions are based; (b) made available without undue delay to the parties to the proceedings and, consistent with its law, to the public; and (c) based on information or evidence in respect of which the parties were offered the opportunity to be heard.

3.   Each Party shall provide, as appropriate, that parties to such proceedings have the right, in accordance with its law, to seek review

and, where warranted, correction of final decisions issued in such proceedings.

4.   Each Party shall ensure that tribunals that conduct or review such proceedings are impartial and independent and do not have any substantial interest in the outcome of the matter.

PART THREE

COMMISSION FOR ENVIRONMENTAL COOPERATION

Article 8: The Commission

1.   The Parties hereby establish the Commission for Environmental Cooperation.

2.   The Commission shall comprise a Council, a Secretariat and a Joint Public Advisory Committee.

Section A: The Council

Article 9: Council Structure and Procedures

1.   The Council shall comprise cabinet-level or equivalent representatives of the Parties, or their designees.

2.   The Council shall establish its rules and procedures.

3.   The Council shall convene: (a) at least once a year in regular session; and (b) in special session at the request of any Party. Regular sessions shall be chaired successively by each Party.

4.   The Council shall hold public meetings in the course of all regular sessions. Other meetings held in the course of regular or special sessions shall be public where the Council so decides.

5.   The Council may: (a) establish, and assign responsibilities to, ad hoc or standing committees, working groups or expert groups; (b) seek the advice of non-governmental organizations or persons, including independent experts; and (c) take such other action in the exercise of its functions as the Parties may agree.

6.   All decisions and recommendations of the Council shall be taken by consensus, except as the Council may otherwise decide or as otherwise provided in this Agreement.

7.   All decisions and recommendations of the Council shall be made public, except as the Council may otherwise decide or as otherwise provided in this Agreement.

Article 10: Council Functions

1.   The Council shall be the governing body of the Commission and shall: (a) serve as a forum for the discussion of environmental matters within the scope of this Agreement; (b) oversee the implementation and

develop recommendations on the further elaboration of this Agreement and, to this end, the Council shall, within four years after the date of entry into force of this Agreement, review its operation and effectiveness in the light of experience; (c) oversee the Secretariat; (d) address questions and differences that may arise between the Parties regarding the interpretation or application of this Agreement; (e) approve the annual program and budget of the Commission; and (f) promote and facilitate cooperation between the Parties with respect to environmental matters.

2. The Council may consider, and develop recommendations regarding: (a) comparability of techniques and methodologies for data gathering and analysis, data management and electronic data communications on matters covered by this Agreement; (b) pollution prevention techniques and strategies; (c) approaches and common indicators for reporting on the state of the environment; (d) the use of economic instruments for the pursuit of domestic and internationally agreed environmental objectives; (e) scientific research and technology development in respect of environmental matters; (f) promotion of public awareness regarding the environment; (g) transboundary and border environmental issues, such as the long-range transport of air and marine pollutants; (h) exotic species that may be harmful; (i) the conservation and protection of wild flora and fauna and their habitat, and specially protected natural areas; (j) the protection of endangered and threatened species; (k) environmental emergency preparedness and response activities; (*l*) environmental matters as they relate to economic development; (m) the environmental implications of goods throughout their life cycles; (n) human resource training and development in the environmental field; (*o*) the exchange of environmental scientists and officials; (p) approaches to environmental compliance and enforcement; (q) ecologically sensitive national accounts; (r) eco-labelling; and (s) other matters as it may decide.

3. The Council shall strengthen cooperation on the development and continuing improvement of environmental laws and regulations, including by: (a) promoting the exchange of information on criteria and methodologies used in establishing domestic environmental standards; and (b) without reducing levels of environmental protection, establishing a process for developing recommendations on greater compatibility of environmental technical regulations, standards and conformity assessment procedures in a manner consistent with the NAFTA.

4. The Council shall encourage: (a) effective enforcement by each Party of its environmental laws and regulations; (b) compliance with those laws and regulations; and (c) technical cooperation between the Parties.

5. The Council shall promote and, as appropriate, develop recommendations regarding: (a) public access to information concerning the environment that is held by public authorities of each Party, including information on hazardous materials and activities in its communities,

and opportunity to participate in decision-making processes related to such public access; and (b) appropriate limits for specific pollutants, taking into account differences in ecosystems.

6. The Council shall cooperate with the NAFTA Free Trade Commission to achieve the environmental goals and objectives of the NAFTA by: (a) acting as a point of inquiry and receipt for comments from nongovernmental organizations and persons concerning those goals and objectives; (b) providing assistance in consultations under Article 1114 of the NAFTA where a Party considers that another Party is waiving or derogating from, or offering to waive or otherwise derogate from, an environmental measure as an encouragement to establish, acquire, expand or retain an investment of an investor, with a view to avoiding any such encouragement; (c) contributing to the prevention or resolution of environment-related trade disputes by: (i) seeking to avoid disputes between the Parties, (ii) making recommendations to the Free Trade Commission with respect to the avoidance of such disputes, and (iii) identifying experts able to provide information or technical advice to NAFTA committees, working groups and other NAFTA bodies; (d) considering on an ongoing basis the environmental effects of the NAFTA; and (e) otherwise assisting the Free Trade Commission in environment-related matters.

7. Recognizing the significant bilateral nature of many transboundary environmental issues, the Council shall, with a view to agreement between the Parties pursuant to this Article within three years on obligations, consider and develop recommendations with respect to: (a) assessing the environmental impact of proposed projects subject to decisions by a competent government authority and likely to cause significant adverse transboundary effects, including a full evaluation of comments provided by other Parties and persons of other Parties; (b) notification, provision of relevant information and consultation between Parties with respect to such projects; and (c) mitigation of the potential adverse effects of such projects.

8. The Council shall encourage the establishment by each Party of appropriate administrative procedures pursuant to its environmental laws to permit another Party to seek the reduction, elimination or mitigation of transboundary pollution on a reciprocal basis.

9. The Council shall consider and, as appropriate, develop recommendations on the provision by a Party, on a reciprocal basis, of access to and rights and remedies before its courts and administrative agencies for persons in another Party's territory who have suffered or are likely to suffer damage or injury caused by pollution originating in its territory as if the damage or injury were suffered in its territory.

Section B: The Secretariat

Article 11: Secretariat Structure and Procedures

1. The Secretariat shall be headed by an Executive Director, who shall be chosen by the Council for a three-year term, which may be

renewed by the Council for one additional three-year term. The position of Executive Director shall rotate consecutively between nationals of each Party. The Council may remove the Executive Director solely for cause.

2. The Executive Director shall appoint and supervise the staff of the Secretariat, regulate their powers and duties and fix their remuneration in accordance with general standards to be established by the Council. The general standards shall provide that: (a) staff shall be appointed and retained, and their conditions of employment shall be determined, strictly on the basis of efficiency, competence and integrity; (b) in appointing staff, the Executive Director shall take into account lists of candidates prepared by the Parties and by the Joint Public Advisory Committee; (c) due regard shall be paid to the importance of recruiting an equitable proportion of the professional staff from among the nationals of each Party; and (d) the Executive Director shall inform the Council of all appointments.

3. The Council may decide, by a two-thirds vote, to reject any appointment that does not meet the general standards. Any such decision shall be made and held in confidence.

4. In the performance of their duties, the Executive Director and the staff shall not seek or receive instructions from any government or any other authority external to the Council. Each Party shall respect the international character of the responsibilities of the Executive Director and the staff and shall not seek to influence them in the discharge of their responsibilities.

5. The Secretariat shall provide technical, administrative and operational support to the Council and to committees and groups established by the Council, and such other support as the Council may direct.

6. The Executive Director shall submit for the approval of the Council the annual program and budget of the Commission, including provision for proposed cooperative activities and for the Secretariat to respond to contingencies.

7. The Secretariat shall, as appropriate, provide the Parties and the public information on where they may receive technical advice and expertise with respect to environmental matters.

8. The Secretariat shall safeguard: (a) from disclosure information it receives that could identify a non-governmental organization or person making a submission if the person or organization so requests or the Secretariat otherwise considers it appropriate; and (b) from public disclosure any information it receives from any non-governmental organization or person where the information is designated by that non-governmental organization or person as confidential or proprietary.

Article 12: Annual Report of the Commission

1. The Secretariat shall prepare an annual report of the Commission in accordance with instructions from the Council. The Secretariat shall submit a draft of the report for review by the Council. The final report shall be released publicly.

2. The report shall cover: (a) activities and expenses of the Commission during the previous year; (b) the approved program and budget of the Commission for the subsequent year; (c) the actions taken by each Party in connection with its obligations under this Agreement, including data on the Party's environmental enforcement activities; (d) relevant views and information submitted by non-governmental organizations and persons, including summary data regarding submissions, and any other relevant information the Council deems appropriate; (e) recommendations made on any matter within the scope of this Agreement; and (f) any other matter that the Council instructs the Secretariat to include.

3. The report shall periodically address the state of the environment in the territories of the Parties.

Article 13: Secretariat Reports

1. The Secretariat may prepare a report for the Council on any matter within the scope of the annual program. Should the Secretariat wish to prepare a report on any other environmental matter related to the cooperative functions of this Agreement, it shall notify the Council and may proceed unless, within 30 days of such notification, the Council objects by a two-thirds vote to the preparation of the report. Such other environmental matters shall not include issues related to whether a Party has failed to enforce its environmental laws and regulations. Where the Secretariat does not have specific expertise in the matter under review, it shall obtain the assistance of one or more independent experts of recognized experience in the matter to assist in the preparation of the report.

2. In preparing such a report, the Secretariat may draw upon any relevant technical, scientific or other information, including information: (a) that is publicly available; (b) submitted by interested non-governmental organizations and persons; (c) submitted by the Joint Public Advisory Committee; (d) furnished by a Party; (e) gathered through public consultations, such as conferences, seminars and symposia; or (f) developed by the Secretariat, or by independent experts engaged pursuant to paragraph 1.

3. The Secretariat shall submit its report to the Council, which shall make it publicly available, normally within 60 days following its submission, unless the Council otherwise decides.

Article 14: Submissions on Enforcement Matters

1. The Secretariat may consider a submission from any non-governmental organization or person asserting that a Party is failing to effectively enforce its environmental law, if the Secretariat finds that the submission: (a) is in writing in a language designated by that Party in a notification to the Secretariat; (b) clearly identifies the person or organization making the submission; (c) provides sufficient information to allow the Secretariat to review the submission, including any documentary evidence on which the submission may be based; (d) appears to be aimed at promoting enforcement rather than at harassing industry; (e) indicates that the matter has been communicated in writing to the relevant authorities of the Party and indicates the Party's response, if any; and (f) is filed by a person or organization residing or established in the territory of a Party.

2. Where the Secretariat determines that a submission meets the criteria set out in paragraph 1, the Secretariat shall determine whether the submission merits requesting a response from the Party. In deciding whether to request a response, the Secretariat shall be guided by whether: (a) the submission alleges harm to the person or organization making the submission; (b) the submission, alone or in combination with other submissions, raises matters whose further study in this process would advance the goals of this Agreement; (c) private remedies available under the Party's law have been pursued; and (d) the submission is drawn exclusively from mass media reports. Where the Secretariat makes such a request, it shall forward to the Party a copy of the submission and any supporting information provided with the submission.

3. The Party shall advise the Secretariat within 30 days or, in exceptional circumstances and on notification to the Secretariat, within 60 days of delivery of the request: (a) whether the matter is the subject of a pending judicial or administrative proceeding, in which case the Secretariat shall proceed no further; and (b) of any other information that the Party wishes to submit, such as (i) whether the matter was previously the subject of a judicial or administrative proceeding, and (ii) whether private remedies in connection with the matter are available to the person or organization making the submission and whether they have been pursued.

Article 15: Factual Record

1. If the Secretariat considers that the submission, in the light of any response provided by the Party, warrants developing a factual record, the Secretariat shall so inform the Council and provide its reasons.

2. The Secretariat shall prepare a factual record if the Council, by a two-thirds vote, instructs it to do so.

3. The preparation of a factual record by the Secretariat pursuant to this Article shall be without prejudice to any further steps that may be taken with respect to any submission.

4. In preparing a factual record, the Secretariat shall consider any information furnished by a Party and may consider any relevant technical, scientific or other information: (a) that is publicly available; (b) submitted by interested non-governmental organizations or persons; (c) submitted by the Joint Public Advisory Committee; or (d) developed by the Secretariat or by independent experts.

5. The Secretariat shall submit a draft factual record to the Council. Any Party may provide comments on the accuracy of the draft within 45 days thereafter.

6. The Secretariat shall incorporate, as appropriate, any such comments in the final factual record and submit it to the Council.

7. The Council may, by a two-thirds vote, make the final factual record publicly available, normally within 60 days following its submission.

Section C: Advisory Committees

Article 16: Joint Public Advisory Committee

1. The Joint Public Advisory Committee shall comprise 15 members, unless the Council otherwise decides. Each Party or, if the Party so decides, its National Advisory Committee convened under Article 17, shall appoint an equal number of members.

2. The Council shall establish the rules of procedure for the Joint Public Advisory Committee, which shall choose its own chair.

3. The Joint Public Advisory Committee shall convene at least once a year at the time of the regular session of the Council and at such other times as the Council, or the Committee's chair with the consent of a majority of its members, may decide.

4. The Joint Public Advisory Committee may provide advice to the Council on any matter within the scope of this Agreement, including on any documents provided to it under paragraph 6, and on the implementation and further elaboration of this Agreement, and may perform such other functions as the Council may direct.

5. The Joint Public Advisory Committee may provide relevant technical, scientific or other information to the Secretariat, including for purposes of developing a factual record under Article 15. The Secretariat shall forward to the Council copies of any such information.

6. The Secretariat shall provide to the Joint Public Advisory Committee at the time they are submitted to the Council copies of the proposed annual program and budget of the Commission, the draft annual report, and any report the Secretariat prepares pursuant to Article 13.

7. The Council may, by a two-thirds vote, make a factual record available to the Joint Public Advisory Committee.

Article 17: National Advisory Committees

Each Party may convene a national advisory committee, comprising members of its public, including representatives of non-governmental organizations and persons, to advise it on the implementation and further elaboration of this Agreement.

Article 18: Governmental Committees

Each Party may convene a governmental committee, which may comprise or include representatives of federal and state or provincial governments, to advise it on the implementation and further elaboration of this Agreement.

Section D: Official Languages

Article 19: Official Languages

The official languages of the Commission shall be English, French and Spanish. All annual reports under Article 12, reports submitted to the Council under Article 13, factual records submitted to the Council under Article 15(6) and panel reports under Part Five shall be available in each official language at the time they are made public. The Council shall establish rules and procedures regarding interpretation and translation.

PART FOUR

COOPERATION AND PROVISION OF INFORMATION

Article 20: Cooperation

1. The Parties shall at all times endeavor to agree on the interpretation and application of this Agreement, and shall make every attempt through cooperation and consultations to resolve any matter that might affect its operation.

2. To the maximum extent possible, each Party shall notify any other Party with an interest in the matter of any proposed or actual environmental measure that the Party considers might materially affect the operation of this Agreement or otherwise substantially affect that other Party's interests under this Agreement.

3. On request of any other Party, a Party shall promptly provide information and respond to questions pertaining to any such actual or proposed environmental measure, whether or not that other Party has been previously notified of that measure.

4. Any Party may notify any other Party of, and provide to that Party, any credible information regarding possible violations of its environmental law, specific and sufficient to allow the other Party to inquire into the matter. The notified Party shall take appropriate steps in accordance with its law to so inquire and to respond to the other Party.

Article 21: Provision of Information

1. On request of the Council or the Secretariat, each Party shall, in accordance with its law, provide such information as the Council or the Secretariat may require, including: (a) promptly making available any information in its possession required for the preparation of a report or factual record, including compliance and enforcement data; and (b) taking all reasonable steps to make available any other such information requested.

2. If a Party considers that a request for information from the Secretariat is excessive or otherwise unduly burdensome, it may so notify the Council. The Secretariat shall revise the scope of its request to comply with any limitations established by the Council by a two-thirds vote.

3. If a Party does not make available information requested by the Secretariat, as may be limited pursuant to paragraph 2, it shall promptly advise the Secretariat of its reasons in writing.

PART FIVE

CONSULTATION AND RESOLUTION OF DISPUTES

Article 22: Consultations

1. Any Party may request in writing consultations with any other Party regarding whether there has been a persistent pattern of failure by that other Party to effectively enforce its environmental law.

2. The requesting Party shall deliver the request to the other Parties and to the Secretariat.

3. Unless the Council otherwise provides in its rules and procedures established under Article 9(2), a third Party that considers it has a substantial interest in the matter shall be entitled to participate in the consultations on delivery of written notice to the other Parties and to the Secretariat.

4. The consulting Parties shall make every attempt to arrive at a mutually satisfactory resolution of the matter through consultations under this Article.

Article 23: Initiation of Procedures

1. If the consulting Parties fail to resolve the matter pursuant to Article 22 within 60 days of delivery of a request for consultations, or

such other period as the consulting Parties may agree, any such Party may request in writing a special session of the Council.

2. The requesting Party shall state in the request the matter complained of and shall deliver the request to the other Parties and to the Secretariat.

3. Unless it decides otherwise, the Council shall convene within 20 days of delivery of the request and shall endeavor to resolve the dispute promptly.

4. The Council may: (a) call on such technical advisers or create such working groups or expert groups as it deems necessary, (b) have recourse to good offices, conciliation, mediation or such other dispute resolution procedures, or (c) make recommendations, as may assist the consulting Parties to reach a mutually satisfactory resolution of the dispute. Any such recommendations shall be made public if the Council, by a two-thirds vote, so decides.

5. Where the Council decides that a matter is more properly covered by another agreement or arrangement to which the consulting Parties are party, it shall refer the matter to those Parties for appropriate action in accordance with such other agreement or arrangement.

Article 24: Request for an Arbitral Panel

1. If the matter has not been resolved within 60 days after the Council has convened pursuant to Article 23, the Council shall, on the written request of any consulting Party and by a two-thirds vote, convene an arbitral panel to consider the matter where the alleged persistent pattern of failure by the Party complained against to effectively enforce its environmental law relates to a situation involving workplaces, firms, companies or sectors that produce goods or provide services: (a) traded between the territories of the Parties; or (b) that compete, in the territory of the Party complained against, with goods or services produced or provided by persons of another Party.

2. A third Party that considers it has a substantial interest in the matter shall be entitled to join as a complaining Party on delivery of written notice of its intention to participate to the disputing Parties and the Secretariat. The notice shall be delivered at the earliest possible time, and in any event no later than seven days after the date of the vote of the Council to convene a panel.

3. Unless otherwise agreed by the disputing Parties, the panel shall be established and perform its functions in a manner consistent with the provisions of this Part.

Article 25: Roster

1. The Council shall establish and maintain a roster of up to 45 individuals who are willing and able to serve as panelists. The roster members shall be appointed by consensus for terms of three years, and may be reappointed.

2.   Roster members shall: (a) have expertise or experience in environmental law or its enforcement, or in the resolution of disputes arising under international agreements, or other relevant scientific, technical or professional expertise or experience; (b) be chosen strictly on the basis of objectivity, reliability and sound judgment; (c) be independent of, and not be affiliated with or take instructions from, any Party, the Secretariat or the Joint Public Advisory Committee; and (d) comply with a code of conduct to be established by the Council.

Article 26: Qualifications of Panelists

1.   All panelists shall meet the qualifications set out in Article 25(2).

2.   Individuals may not serve as panelists for a dispute in which: (a) they have participated pursuant to Article 23(4); or (b) they have, or a person or organization with which they are affiliated has, an interest, as set out in the code of conduct established under Article 25(2)(d).

Article 27: Panel Selection

1.   Where there are two disputing Parties, the following procedures shall apply: (a) The panel shall comprise five members. (b) The disputing Parties shall endeavor to agree on the chair of the panel within 15 days after the Council votes to convene the panel. If the disputing Parties are unable to agree on the chair within this period, the disputing Party chosen by lot shall select within five days a chair who is not a citizen of that Party. (c) Within 15 days of selection of the chair, each disputing Party shall select two panelists who are citizens of the other disputing Party. (d) If a disputing Party fails to select its panelists within such period, such panelists shall be selected by lot from among the roster members who are citizens of the other disputing Party.

2.   Where there are more than two disputing Parties, the following procedures shall apply: (a) The panel shall comprise five members. (b) The disputing Parties shall endeavor to agree on the chair of the panel within 15 days after the Council votes to convene the panel. If the disputing Parties are unable to agree on the chair within this period, the Party or Parties on the side of the dispute chosen by lot shall select within 10 days a chair who is not a citizen of such Party or Parties. (c) Within 30 days of selection of the chair, the Party complained against shall select two panelists, one of whom is a citizen of a complaining Party, and the other of whom is a citizen of another complaining Party. The complaining Parties shall select two panelists who are citizens of the Party complained against. (d) If any disputing Party fails to select a panelist within such period, such panelist shall be selected by lot in accordance with the citizenship criteria of subparagraph (c).

3.   Panelists shall normally be selected from the roster. Any disputing Party may exercise a peremptory challenge against any individual

not on the roster who is proposed as a panelist by a disputing Party within 30 days after the individual has been proposed.

4. If a disputing Party believes that a panelist is in violation of the code of conduct, the disputing Parties shall consult and, if they agree, the panelist shall be removed and a new panelist shall be selected in accordance with this Article.

Article 28: Rules of Procedure

1. The Council shall establish Model Rules of Procedure. The procedures shall provide: (a) a right to at least one hearing before the panel; (b) the opportunity to make initial and rebuttal written submissions; and (c) that no panel may disclose which panelists are associated with majority or minority opinions.

2. Unless the disputing Parties otherwise agree, panels convened under this Part shall be established and conduct their proceedings in accordance with the Model Rules of Procedure.

3. Unless the disputing Parties otherwise agree within 20 days after the Council votes to convene the panel, the terms of reference shall be: "To examine, in light of the relevant provisions of the Agreement, including those contained in Part Five, whether there has been a persistent pattern of failure by the Party complained against to effectively enforce its environmental law, and to make findings, determinations and recommendations in accordance with Article 31(2)."

Article 29: Third Party Participation

A Party that is not a disputing Party, on delivery of a written notice to the disputing Parties and to the Secretariat, shall be entitled to attend all hearings, to make written and oral submissions to the panel and to receive written submissions of the disputing Parties.

Article 30: Role of Experts

On request of a disputing Party, or on its own initiative, the panel may seek information and technical advice from any person or body that it deems appropriate, provided that the disputing Parties so agree and subject to such terms and conditions as such Parties may agree.

Article 31: Initial Report

1. Unless the disputing Parties otherwise agree, the panel shall base its report on the submissions and arguments of the Parties and on any information before it pursuant to Article 30.

2. Unless the disputing Parties otherwise agree, the panel shall, within 180 days after the last panelist is selected, present to the disputing Parties an initial report containing: (a) findings of fact; (b) its

determination as to whether there has been a persistent pattern of failure by the Party complained against to effectively enforce its environmental law, or any other determination requested in the terms of reference; and (c) in the event the panel makes an affirmative determination under subparagraph (b), its recommendations, if any, for the resolution of the dispute, which normally shall be that the Party complained against adopt and implement an action plan sufficient to remedy the pattern of non-enforcement.

3.   Panelists may furnish separate opinions on matters not unanimously agreed.

4.   A disputing Party may submit written comments to the panel on its initial report within 30 days of presentation of the report.

5.   In such an event, and after considering such written comments, the panel, on its own initiative or on the request of any disputing Party, may: (a) request the views of any participating Party; (b) reconsider its report; and (c) make any further examination that it considers appropriate.

Article 32: Final Report

1.   The panel shall present to the disputing Parties a final report, including any separate opinions on matters not unanimously agreed, within 60 days of presentation of the initial report, unless the disputing Parties otherwise agree.

2.   The disputing Parties shall transmit to the Council the final report of the panel, as well as any written views that a disputing Party desires to be appended, on a confidential basis within 15 days after it is presented to them.

3.   The final report of the panel shall be published five days after it is transmitted to the Council.

Article 33: Implementation of Final Report

If, in its final report, a panel determines that there has been a persistent pattern of failure by the Party complained against to effectively enforce its environmental law, the disputing Parties may agree on a mutually satisfactory action plan, which normally shall conform with the determinations and recommendations of the panel. The disputing Parties shall promptly notify the Secretariat and the Council of any agreed resolution of the dispute.

Article 34: Review of Implementation

1.   If, in its final report, a panel determines that there has been a persistent pattern of failure by the Party complained against to effectively enforce its environmental law, and: (a) the disputing Parties have not agreed on an action plan under Article 33 within 60 days of the date of

the final report, or (b) the disputing Parties cannot agree on whether the Party complained against is fully implementing (i) an action plan agreed under Article 33, (ii) an action plan deemed to have been established by a panel under paragraph 2, or (iii) an action plan approved or established by a panel under paragraph 4, any disputing Party may request that the panel be reconvened. The requesting Party shall deliver the request in writing to the other Parties and to the Secretariat. The Council shall reconvene the panel on delivery of the request to the Secretariat.

2. No Party may make a request under paragraph 1(a) earlier than 60 days, or later than 120 days, after the date of the final report. If the disputing Parties have not agreed to an action plan and if no request was made under paragraph 1(a), the last action plan, if any, submitted by the Party complained against to the complaining Party or Parties within 60 days of the date of the final report, or such other period as the disputing Parties may agree, shall be deemed to have been established by the panel 120 days after the date of the final report.

3. A request under paragraph 1(b) may be made no earlier than 180 days after an action plan has been: (a) agreed under Article 33; (b) deemed to have been established by a panel under paragraph 2; or (c) approved or established by a panel under paragraph 4; and only during the term of any such action plan.

4. Where a panel has been reconvened under paragraph 1(a), it: (a) shall determine whether any action plan proposed by the Party complained against is sufficient to remedy the pattern of non-enforcement and (i) if so, shall approve the plan, or (ii) if not, shall establish such a plan consistent with the law of the Party complained against, and (b) may, where warranted, impose a monetary enforcement assessment in accordance with Annex 34, within 90 days after the panel has been reconvened or such other period as the disputing Parties may agree.

5. Where a panel has been reconvened under paragraph 1(b), it shall determine either that: (a) the Party complained against is fully implementing the action plan, in which case the panel may not impose a monetary enforcement assessment, or (b) the Party complained against is not fully implementing the action plan, in which case the panel shall impose a monetary enforcement assessment in accordance with Annex 34, within 60 days after it has been reconvened or such other period as the disputing Parties may agree.

6. A panel reconvened under this Article shall provide that the Party complained against shall fully implement any action plan referred to in paragraph 4(a)(ii) or 5(b), and pay any monetary enforcement assessment imposed under paragraph 4(b) or 5(b), and any such provision shall be final.

Annex 34

Monetary Enforcement Assessments

1. For the first year after the date of entry into force of this Agreement, any monetary enforcement assessment shall be no greater

than 20 million dollars (U.S.) or its equivalent in the currency of the Party complained against. Thereafter, any monetary enforcement assessment shall be no greater than .007 percent of total trade in goods between the Parties during the most recent year for which data are available.

2. In determining the amount of the assessment, the panel shall take into account: (a) the pervasiveness and duration of the Party's persistent pattern of failure to effectively enforce its environmental law; (b) the level of enforcement that could reasonably be expected of a Party given its resource constraints; (c) the reasons, if any, provided by the Party for not fully implementing an action plan; (d) efforts made by the Party to begin remedying the pattern of non-enforcement after the final report of the panel; and (e) any other relevant factors.

3. All monetary enforcement assessments shall be paid in the currency of the Party complained against into a fund established in the name of the Commission by the Council and shall be expended at the direction of the Council to improve or enhance the environment or environmental law enforcement in the Party complained against, consistent with its law.

Article 35: Further Proceeding

A complaining Party may, at any time beginning 180 days after a panel determination under Article 34(5)(b), request in writing that a panel be reconvened to determine whether the Party complained against is fully implementing the action plan. On delivery of the request to the other Parties and the Secretariat, the Council shall reconvene the panel. The panel shall make the determination within 60 days after it has been reconvened or such other period as the disputing Parties may agree.

Article 36: Suspension of Benefits

1. Subject to Annex 36A, where a Party fails to pay a monetary enforcement assessment within 180 days after it is imposed by a panel: (a) under Article 34(4)(b), or (b) under Article 34(5)(b), except where benefits may be suspended under paragraph 2(a), any complaining Party or Parties may suspend, in accordance with Annex 36B, the application to the Party complained against of NAFTA benefits in an amount no greater than that sufficient to collect the monetary enforcement assessment.

2. Subject to Annex 36A, where a panel has made a determination under Article 34(5)(b) and the panel: (a) has previously imposed a monetary enforcement assessment under Article 34(4)(b) or established an action plan under Article 34(4)(a)(ii); or (b) has subsequently determined under Article 35 that a Party is not fully implementing an action plan; the complaining Party or Parties may, in accordance with Annex 36B, suspend annually the application to the Party complained against of

NAFTA benefits in an amount no greater than the monetary enforcement assessment imposed by the panel under Article 34(5)(b).

3. Where more than one complaining Party suspends benefits under paragraph 1 or 2, the combined suspension shall be no greater than the amount of the monetary enforcement assessment.

4. Where a Party has suspended benefits under paragraph 1 or 2, the Council shall, on the delivery of a written request by the Party complained against to the other Parties and the Secretariat, reconvene the panel to determine whether the monetary enforcement assessment has been paid or collected, or whether the Party complained against is fully implementing the action plan, as the case may be. The panel shall submit its report within 45 days after it has been reconvened. If the panel determines that the assessment has been paid or collected, or that the Party complained against is fully implementing the action plan, the suspension of benefits under paragraph 1 or 2, as the case may be, shall be terminated.

5. On the written request of the Party complained against, delivered to the other Parties and the Secretariat, the Council shall reconvene the panel to determine whether the suspension of benefits by the complaining Party or Parties pursuant to paragraph 1 or 2 is manifestly excessive. Within 45 days of the request, the panel shall present a report to the disputing Parties containing its determination.

Annex 36A

Canadian Domestic Enforcement and Collection

1. For the purposes of this Annex, "panel determination" means: (a) a determination by a panel under Article 34(4)(b) or 5(b) that provides that Canada shall pay a monetary enforcement assessment; and (b) a determination by a panel under Article 34(5)(b) that provides that Canada shall fully implement an action plan where the panel: (i) has previously established an action plan under Article 34(4)(a)(ii) or imposed a monetary enforcement assessment under Article 34(4)(b); or (ii) has subsequently determined under Article 35 that Canada is not fully implementing an action plan.

2. Canada shall adopt and maintain procedures that provide that: (a) subject to subparagraph (b), the Commission, at the request of a complaining Party, may in its own name file in a court of competent jurisdiction a certified copy of a panel determination; (b) the Commission may file in court a panel determination that is a panel determination described in paragraph 1(a) only if Canada has failed to comply with the determination within 180 days of when the determination was made; (c) when filed, the panel determination, for purposes of enforcement, shall become an order of the court; (d) the Commission may take proceedings for enforcement of a panel determination that is made an order of the court, in that court, against the person against whom the panel determination is addressed in accordance with paragraph 6 of Annex 41; (e) proceedings to enforce a panel determination that has been made an

order of the court shall be conducted by way of summary proceedings; (f) in proceedings to enforce a panel determination that is a panel determination described in paragraph 1(b) and that has been made an order of the court, the court shall promptly refer any question of fact or any question of interpretation of the panel determination to the panel that made the panel determination, and the decision of the panel shall be binding on the court; (g) a panel determination that has been made an order of the court shall not be subject to domestic review or appeal; and (h) an order made by the court in proceedings to enforce a panel determination that has been made an order of the court shall not be subject to review or appeal.

3.   Where Canada is the Party complained against, the procedures adopted and maintained by Canada under this Annex shall apply and the procedures set out in Article 36 shall not apply.

4.   Any change by Canada to the procedures adopted and maintained by Canada under this Annex that have the effect of undermining the provisions of this Annex shall be considered a breach of this Agreement.

Annex 36B

Suspension of Benefits

1.   Where a complaining Party suspends NAFTA tariff benefits in accordance with this Agreement, the Party may increase the rates of duty on originating goods of the Party complained against to levels not to exceed the lesser of: (a) the rate that was applicable to those goods immediately prior to the date of entry into force of the NAFTA, and (b) the Most–Favored–Nation rate applicable to those goods on the date the Party suspends such benefits, and such increase may be applied only for such time as is necessary to collect, through such increase, the monetary enforcement assessment.

2.   In considering what tariff or other benefits to suspend pursuant to Article 36(1) or (2): (a) a complaining Party shall first seek to suspend benefits in the same sector or sectors as that in respect of which there has been a persistent pattern of failure by the Party complained against to effectively enforce its environmental law; and (b) a complaining Party that considers it is not practicable or effective to suspend benefits in the same sector or sectors may suspend benefits in other sectors.

PART SIX

GENERAL PROVISIONS

Article 37: Enforcement Principle

Nothing in this Agreement shall be construed to empower a Party's authorities to undertake environmental law enforcement activities in the territory of another Party.

Article 38: Private Rights

No Party may provide for a right of action under its law against any other Party on the ground that another Party has acted in a manner inconsistent with this Agreement.

Article 39: Protection of Information

1.   Nothing in this Agreement shall be construed to require a Party to make available or allow access to information: (a) the disclosure of which would impede its environmental law enforcement; or (b) that is protected from disclosure by its law governing business or proprietary information, personal privacy or the confidentiality of governmental decision making.

2.   If a Party provides confidential or proprietary information to another Party, the Council, the Secretariat or the Joint Public Advisory Committee, the recipient shall treat the information on the same basis as the Party providing the information.

3.   Confidential or proprietary information provided by a Party to a panel under this Agreement shall be treated in accordance with the rules of procedure established under Article 28.

Article 40: Relation to Other Environmental Agreements

Nothing in this Agreement shall be construed to affect the existing rights and obligations of the Parties under other international environmental agreements, including conservation agreements, to which such Parties are party.

Article 41: Extent of Obligations

Annex 41 applies to the Parties specified in that Annex.

Annex 41

Extent of Obligations

1.   On the date of signature of this Agreement, or of the exchange of written notifications under Article 47, Canada shall set out in a declaration a list of any provinces for which Canada is to be bound in respect of matters within their jurisdiction. The declaration shall be effective on delivery to the other Parties, and shall carry no implication as to the internal distribution of powers within Canada. Canada shall notify the other Parties six months in advance of any modification to its declaration.

2.   When considering whether to instruct the Secretariat to prepare a factual record pursuant to Article 15, the Council shall take into account whether the submission was made by a non-governmental

organization or enterprise incorporated or otherwise organized under the laws of a province included in the declaration made under paragraph 1.

3.   Canada may not request consultations under Article 22 or a Council meeting under Article 23 or request the establishment of a panel or join as a complaining Party under Article 24 against another Party at the instance, or primarily for the benefit, of any government of a province not included in the declaration made under paragraph 1.

4.   Canada may not request a Council meeting under Article 23, or request the establishment of a panel or join as a complaining Party under Article 24 concerning whether there has been a persistent pattern of failure by another Party to effectively enforce its environmental law, unless Canada states in writing that the matter would be under federal jurisdiction if it were to arise within the territory of Canada, or: (a) Canada states in writing that the matter would be under provincial jurisdiction if it were to arise within the territory of Canada; and (b) the provinces included in the declaration account for at least 55 percent of Canada's Gross Domestic Product (GDP) for the most recent year in which data are available, and (c) where the matter concerns a specific industry or sector, at least 55 percent of total Canadian production in that industry or sector is accounted for by the provinces included in the declaration for the most recent year in which data are available.

5.   No other Party may request a Council meeting under Article 23 or request the establishment of a panel or join as a complaining Party under Article 24 concerning whether there has been a persistent failure to effectively enforce an environmental law of a province unless that province is included in the declaration made under paragraph 1 and the requirements of subparagraphs 4(b) and (c) have been met.

6.   Canada shall, no later than the date on which an arbitral panel is convened pursuant to Article 24 respecting a matter within the scope of paragraph 5 of this Annex, notify in writing the complaining Parties and the Secretariat of whether any monetary enforcement assessment or action plan imposed by a panel under Article 34(4) or 34(5) against Canada shall be addressed to Her Majesty in right of Canada or Her Majesty in right of the province concerned.

7.   Canada shall use its best efforts to make this Agreement applicable to as many of its provinces as possible.

8.   Two years after the date of entry into force of this Agreement, the Council shall review the operation of this Annex and, in particular, shall consider whether the Parties should amend the thresholds established in paragraph 4.

Article 42: National Security

Nothing in this Agreement shall be construed: (a) to require any Party to make available or provide access to information the disclosure of which it determines to be contrary to its essential security interests; or (b) to prevent any Party from taking any actions that it considers necessary for the protection of its essential security interests relating to (i) arms, ammunition and implements of war, or (ii) the implementation of national policies or international agreements respecting the non-proliferation of nuclear weapons or other nuclear explosive devices.

Article 43: Funding of the Commission

Each Party shall contribute an equal share of the annual budget of the Commission, subject to the availability of appropriated funds in accordance with the Party's legal procedures. No Party shall be obligated to pay more than any other Party in respect of an annual budget.

Article 44: Privileges and Immunities

The Executive Director and staff of the Secretariat shall enjoy in the territory of each Party such privileges and immunities as are necessary for the exercise of their functions.

Article 45: Definitions

1.   For purposes of this Agreement:

A Party has not failed to "effectively enforce its environmental law" or to comply with Article 5(1) in a particular case where the action or inaction in question by agencies or officials of that Party: (a) reflects a reasonable exercise of their discretion in respect of investigatory, prose-cutorial, regulatory or compliance matters; or (b) results from bona fide decisions to allocate resources to enforcement in respect of other environmental matters determined to have higher priorities;

"non-governmental organization" means any scientific, professional, business, non-profit, or public interest organization or association which is neither affiliated with, nor under the direction of, a government;

"persistent pattern" means a sustained or recurring course of action or inaction beginning after the date of entry into force of this Agreement;

"province" means a province of Canada, and includes the Yukon Territory and the Northwest Territories and their successors; and

"territory" means for a Party the territory of that Party as set out in Annex 45.

2.   For purposes of Article 14(1) and Part Five: (a) "environmental law" means any statute or regulation of a Party, or provision thereof, the primary purpose of which is the protection of the environment, or the prevention of a danger to human life or health, through (i) the prevention, abatement or control of the release, discharge, or emission of pollutants or environmental contaminants, (ii) the control of environmentally hazardous or toxic chemicals, substances, materials and wastes, and the dissemination of information related thereto, or (iii) the protection of wild flora or fauna, including endangered species, their habitat,

and specially protected natural areas in the Party's territory, but does not include any statute or regulation, or provision thereof, directly related to worker safety or health. (b) For greater certainty, the term "environmental law" does not include any statute or regulation, or provision thereof, the primary purpose of which is managing the commercial harvest or exploitation, or subsistence or aboriginal harvesting, of natural resources. (c) The primary purpose of a particular statutory or regulatory provision for purposes of subparagraphs (a) and (b) shall be determined by reference to its primary purpose, rather than to the primary purpose of the statute or regulation of which it is part.

3. For purposes of Article 14(3), "judicial or administrative proceeding" means: (a) a domestic judicial, quasi-judicial or administrative action pursued by the Party in a timely fashion and in accordance with its law. Such actions comprise: mediation; arbitration; the process of issuing a license, permit, or authorization; seeking an assurance of voluntary compliance or a compliance agreement; seeking sanctions or remedies in an administrative or judicial forum; and the process of issuing an administrative order; and (b) an international dispute resolution proceeding to which the Party is party.

Annex 45

Country–Specific Definitions

For purposes of this Agreement:

"territory" means: (a) with respect to Canada, the territory to which its customs laws apply, including any areas beyond the territorial seas of Canada within which, in accordance with international law and its domestic law, Canada may exercise rights with respect to the seabed and subsoil and their natural resources; (b) with respect to Mexico, (i) the states of the Federation and the Federal District, (ii) the islands, including the reefs and keys, in adjacent seas, (iii) the islands of Guadalupe and Revillagigedo situated in the Pacific Ocean, (iv) the continental shelf and the submarine shelf of such islands, keys and reefs, (v) the waters of the territorial seas, in accordance with international law, and its interior maritime waters, (vi) the space located above the national territory, in accordance with international law, and (vii) any areas beyond the territorial seas of Mexico within which, in accordance with international law, including the United Nations Convention on the Law of the Sea, and its domestic law, Mexico may exercise rights with respect to the seabed and subsoil and their natural resources; and (c) with respect to the United States, (i) the customs territory of the United States, which includes the 50 states, the District of Columbia and Puerto Rico, (ii) the foreign trade zones located in the United States and Puerto Rico, and (iii) any areas beyond the territorial seas of the United States within which, in accordance with international law and its domestic law, the United States may exercise rights with respect to the seabed and subsoil and their natural resources.

PART SEVEN

FINAL PROVISIONS

Article 46: Annexes

The Annexes to this Agreement constitute an integral part of the Agreement.

Article 47: Entry into Force

This Agreement shall enter into force on January 1, 1994, immediately after entry into force of the NAFTA, on an exchange of written notifications certifying the completion of necessary legal procedures.

Article 48: Amendments

1. The Parties may agree on any modification of or addition to this Agreement.

2. When so agreed, and approved in accordance with the applicable legal procedures of each Party, a modification or addition shall constitute an integral part of this Agreement.

Article 49: Accession

Any country or group of countries may accede to this Agreement subject to such terms and conditions as may be agreed between such country or countries and the Council and following approval in accordance with the applicable legal procedures of each country.

Article 50: Withdrawal

A Party may withdraw from this Agreement six months after it provides written notice of withdrawal to the other Parties. If a Party withdraws, the Agreement shall remain in force for the remaining Parties.

Article 51: Authentic Texts

The English, French, and Spanish texts of this Agreement are equally authentic.

IN WITNESS WHEREOF, the undersigned, being duly authorized by the respective Governments, have signed this Agreement.

DOCUMENT 4

GUIDELINES FOR SUBMISSIONS ON ENFORCEMENT MATTERS UNDER ARTICLES 14 AND 15 OF THE NORTH AMERICAN AGREEMENT ON ENVIRONMENTAL COOPERATION (www.cec.org (June 28, 1999))

1. *What is a submission on enforcement matters?*

1.1 A "submission on enforcement matters" ("submission") is a documented assertion that a Party to the North American Agreement on Environmental Cooperation ("Agreement") is failing to effectively enforce its environmental law. The relevant Articles of the Agreement are annexed to these guidelines.

2. *Who can make submissions on enforcement matters?*

2.1 Any nongovernmental organization or person established or residing in the territory of a Party to the Agreement may make a submission on enforcement matters for consideration by the Secretariat of the Commission for Environmental Cooperation ("Secretariat"). The term "nongovernmental organization" is defined in Article 45(1) of the Agreement.

2.2 The submission must clearly identify the person(s) or organization(s) making the submission ("Submitter").

3. *How are they to be submitted?*

3.1 A written copy of the submission must be received by the Secretariat at the following address:

Commission for Environmental Cooperation
393, rue St–Jacques Ouest, Bureau 200
Montréal (Québec)
Canada H2Y 1N9

3.2 Submissions may be made in English, French or Spanish, which are the languages currently designated by the Parties for submissions.

3.3 Submissions should not exceed 15 pages of typed, letter-sized paper, excluding supporting information. Submissions will not be accepted by fax or any other electronic means. Where possible, a copy of the submission on computer diskette should also be provided.

3.4 Submissions must include the complete mailing address of the Submitter.

3.5 The Secretariat will promptly acknowledge the receipt of any correspondence or written document(s) relating to the initiation of the submission process.

3.6 Any correspondence or written document(s) will be considered a submission by the Secretariat if it contains the supporting information necessary to enable the Secretariat, at the proper time, to assess the submission based on the criteria listed in Article 14(1) of the Agreement.

3.7 Formal notifications by the Secretariat to a Submitter will be made in writing and sent by any reliable means of notification which provides a record of the notification having been sent and received.

3.8 The Secretariat will inform the Council of the initiation and progress of all submissions.

3.9 The Secretariat will inform the Submitter of the progress of its submission, as provided for in these guidelines.

3.10 The Secretariat may at any time notify the Submitter of any minor errors of form in the submission in order for the Submitter to rectify them.

3.11 The Secretariat will make its best efforts to take all actions necessary to process a submission in a timely manner.

4. What should be included in a submission?

4.1 The Secretariat may only consider a submission on enforcement matters if that submission meets the criteria set forth in Article 14(1) of the Agreement, as specified in these guidelines.

INITIAL CONSIDERATION OF A SUBMISSION BY THE SECRETARIAT

5. What criteria must a submission address?

5.1 The submission must assert that a Party is failing to effectively enforce its environmental law and should focus on any acts or omissions of the Party asserted to demonstrate such failure. For purposes of determining if a submission meets the criteria of Article 14(1) of the Agreement, the term "environmental law" is defined in Article 45(2) of the Agreement.

5.2 The Submitter must identify the applicable statute or regulation, or provision thereof, as defined in Article 45(2) of the Agreement. In the case of the General Ecological Equilibrium and Environmental Protection Law of Mexico, the Submitter must identify the applicable chapter or provision of the Law.

5.3 Submissions must contain a succinct account of the facts on which such an assertion is based and must provide sufficient information to allow the Secretariat to review the submission, including any documentary evidence on which the submission may be based.

5.4 A submission must appear to be aimed at promoting enforcement rather than at harassing industry. In making that determination, the Secretariat will consider such factors as whether or not:

(a) the submission is focused on the acts or omissions of a Party rather than on compliance by a particular company or business; especially if the Submitter is a competitor that may stand to benefit economically from the submission;

(b) the submission appears frivolous.

5.5 The submission must indicate that the matter has been communicated in writing to the relevant authorities of the Party in question and indicate the Party's response, if any. The Submitter must include, with the submission, copies of any relevant correspondence with the relevant authorities. The relevant authorities are the agencies of the government responsible under the law of the Party for the enforcement of the environmental law in question.

5.6 The Submission should address the factors for consideration identified in Article 14(2) to assist the Secretariat in its review under this provision. Thus, the Submission should address:

(a) The issue of harm (Article 14(2)(a));

(b) Whether further study of the matters raised would advance the goals of the Agreement (Article 14(2)(b));

(c) The actions, including private remedies, available under the Party's law that have been pursued(Article 14(2)(c));

(d) The extent to which the Submission is drawn exclusively from mass media reports (Article 14(2)(d)).[1]

6. *What if the submission does not meet these criteria?*

6.1 Where the Secretariat determines that a submission does not meet the criteria set out in Article 14(1) of the Agreement or any other requirement set out in these guidelines, with the exception of minor errors of form contemplated in section 3.10 of these guidelines, the Secretariat will promptly notify the Submitter of the reason(s) why it has determined not to consider the submission.

6.2 After receipt of such notification from the Secretariat, the Submitter will have 30 days to provide the Secretariat with a submission that conforms to the criteria of Article 14(1) of the Agreement and to the requirements set out in these guidelines.

6.3 If the Secretariat again determines that the Submitter has not met the criteria of Article 14(1) of the Agreement or the requirements set out in these guidelines, the Secretariat will promptly

---

1. *Editor's Note*: Provision 5.6 was added to the Guidelines by the Council in June 1999.

inform the Submitter of its reason(s), and inform the Submitter that the process is terminated with respect to that submission.

DETERMINING WHETHER A SUBMISSION ON ENFORCEMENT MATTERS WARRANTS PREPARATION OF A FACTUAL RECORD

7. *When is a response from the Party to the submission merited?*

7.1 Where the Secretariat determines that the submission meets the criteria set out in Article 14(1) of the Agreement, the Secretariat will determine whether the submission merits requesting a response from the Party concerned. The Secretariat will accordingly notify the Council and the Submitter.[2]

7.2 The notification to the Council and the Submitter of the Secretariat's determination concerning whether or not a submission meets the criteria in Article 14(1) will include, as appropriate, an explanation of how the submission meets or fails to meet each of those criteria. The notification to the Council and the Submitter of the Secretariat's determination concerning whether or not the submission merits requesting a response from the Party concerned will include an explanation of the factors that guided the Secretariat in making the determination, including each consideration set forth in Article 14(2) of the Agreement, if applicable. These notifications will be available on the registry referred to in section 15 of these guidelines and in the public file referred to in section 16 of these guidelines at the same time they are provided to the Council and the Submitter.[3]

7.3 As set forth in Article 14(2) of the Agreement, the Secretariat will, in making that determination, be guided by whether:

(a) the submission alleges harm to the person or organization making the submission;

(b) the submission, alone or in combination with other submissions, raises matters whose further study in this process would advance the goals of the Agreement;

(c) private remedies available under the Party's law have been pursued; and

(d) the submission is drawn exclusively from mass media reports.

7.4 In considering whether the submission alleges harm to the person or organization making the submission, the Secretariat will consider such factors as whether:

(a) the alleged harm is due to the asserted failure to effectively enforce environmental law; and

2. *Editor's Note*: The final sentence of provision 7.1 was added to the Guidelines by the Council in June 1999.

3. *Editor's Note*: This version of provision 7.2 was added to the Guidelines by the Council in June 1999.

(b) the alleged harm relates to the protection of the environment or the prevention of danger to human life or health (but not directly related to worker safety or health), as stated in Article 45(2) of the Agreement.

7.5 In considering whether private remedies available under the Party's law have been pursued, the Secretariat will be guided by whether:

(a) requesting a response to the submission is appropriate if the preparation of a factual record on the submission could duplicate or interfere with private remedies that are being pursued or have been pursued by the Submitter; and

(b) reasonable actions have been taken to pursue such remedies prior to initiating a submission, bearing in mind that barriers to the pursuit of such remedies may exist in some cases.[4]

7.6 In considering whether a response from the Party concerned should be requested when the submission is drawn exclusively from mass media reports, the Secretariat will determine if other sources of information relevant to the assertion in the submission were reasonably available to the Submitter.

8.   What if it is determined that no response from the Party is merited?

8.1 The Secretariat may consider new or supplemental information from the Submitter within 30 days following receipt by the Submitter of notification that the Secretariat has determined that no response from the Party is necessary. If no new or supplemental information is received by the Secretariat within this time period, or if the Secretariat determines that no response from the Party is merited in light of the new or supplemental information provided by the Submitter, the process will be terminated with respect to that submission, and the Secretariat will so notify the Submitter.

9.   How is a response from the Party requested?

9.1 Where the Secretariat determines that a submission merits a response from the Party concerned, the Secretariat will forward to the Party a copy of the submission and any supporting information provided by the Submitter. The Secretariat will translate the submission and supporting information into the official language(s) of the Party from which a response is requested, unless that Party directs otherwise.

9.2 The Party will advise the Secretariat within 30 days, or in exceptional circumstances and on notification to the Secretariat within 60 days, of delivery of the request for a response:

---

4. *Editor's Note*: Provision 7.5 was added to the Guidelines by the Council in June   1999.

(a) whether the matter is the subject of a pending judicial or administrative proceeding, and

(b) of any other information that the Party wishes to submit such as

i) whether the matter was previously the subject of a judicial or administrative proceeding, and

ii) whether private remedies in connection with the matter are available to the Submitter, and whether such remedies have been pursued.

9.3 The Party may include in its response whether environmental policies have been defined or actions have been taken in connection with the matter in question.

9.4 If the Party informs the Secretariat that the matter raised in the submission is the subject of a pending judicial or administrative proceeding, as defined in Article 45(3) of the Agreement, the Secretariat will proceed no further with the submission, and will notify the Submitter and the Council of its reason(s) and that the submission process is terminated.

9.5 Upon receipt of a response from the Party or following the expiration of the response period, the Secretariat may begin its consideration of whether it will inform the Council that the submission warrants developing a factual record.

9.6 If the Secretariat considers that the submission, in light of any response provided by the Party, does not warrant development of a factual record, the Secretariat will notify the Submitter and the Council of its reason(s) in accordance with section 7.2 of these guidelines, and that the submission process is terminated with respect to that submission.

10. *How is a decision on whether or not to prepare a factual record taken?*

10.1 If the Secretariat considers that the submission, in light of any response provided by the Party or after the response period has expired, warrants developing a factual record, the Secretariat will so inform the Council. When the Secretariat informs the Council that it considers that a factual record is warranted, the Secretariat will provide sufficient explanation of its reasoning to allow the Council to make an informed decision. In addition, it will provide a copy of the submission, the supporting information provided with the submission, and any other relevant information, when these items have not been provided to the Council. The Council may request further explanation of the Secretariat's reasons, which the Council will receive prior to taking its decision under Article 15(2) of the Agreement concerning whether or not a factual record will be prepared.[5]

5. *Editor's Note*: The second and fourth   sentences of provision 10.1 were added to

10.2 Thirty days after the Council has been informed by the Secretariat that the Secretariat considers that the submission warrants developing a factual record, notice that the Council has been so informed will be placed by the Secretariat in the registry referred to in section 15 of these guidelines and in the public file referred to in section 16 of these guidelines. The explanation of the Secretariat's reasoning as to why it has informed the Council that it considers that a factual record is warranted will be placed on the registry and in the public file by the Secretariat as soon as practicable after the Council has reached its decision under Article 15(2) of the Agreement.[6]

10.3 The Secretariat may consolidate two or more submissions that relate to the same facts and the same asserted failure to effectively enforce an environmental law. In other situations where two or more submissions relate essentially to the same facts and enforcement matter and the Secretariat considers that it would be more efficient or cost-effective to consolidate them, it may so propose to the Council.

10.4 The Secretariat will prepare a factual record if the Council, by a two-thirds vote, instructs it to do so. If the Council votes to instruct the Secretariat not to prepare a factual record, the Secretariat will so inform the Submitter and will inform the Submitter that the submission process is terminated. Unless the Council decides otherwise, any such decision will be noted in the registry and in the public file described in these guidelines.

11. *How is a factual record prepared?*

11.1 In preparing draft and final factual records, the Secretariat will consider any information furnished by a Party, including information developed by experts and furnished by a Party. The Secretariat may consider any relevant technical, scientific or other information:

(a) that is publicly available;

(b) submitted by interested nongovernmental organizations or persons;

(c) submitted by the Joint Public Advisory Committee (JPAC); or

(d) developed by the Secretariat or by independent experts.

11.2 If the JPAC provides relevant technical, scientific or other information to the Secretariat relating to the development of a factual record, the Secretariat will forward copies of the information to the Council.

the Guidelines by the Council in June 1999.

6. *Editor's Note*: This version of provision 10.2 was added to the Guidelines by the Council in June 1999.

11.3 All contributors to the factual record process are encouraged to submit only relevant information, reducing wherever possible the volume of material submitted.

11.4 The Secretariat will submit the draft factual record to the Council. Any Party may provide comments on the accuracy of the draft within 45 days. The Secretariat will then prepare the final factual record for the Council, incorporating any such comments as appropriate.

12. What is included in a factual record?

12.1 Draft and final factual records prepared by the Secretariat will contain:

(a) a summary of the submission that initiated the process;

(b) a summary of the response, if any, provided by the concerned Party;

(c) a summary of any other relevant factual information; and

(d) the facts presented by the Secretariat with respect to the matters raised in the submission.

12.2 The final factual record will incorporate, as appropriate, the comments of any Party. If a Party so desires, its comments on the draft factual record will be posted on the registry referred to in section 15 of these guidelines.[7]

13. Will the final factual record be made public?

13.1 After receiving the final factual record, the Council may decide, by a two-thirds vote, to make it public. If it so decides, the final factual record will be made public as soon as it is available in the three official languages of the Commission and a copy will be provided to the Submitter. This should normally be within 60 days of the submission of the final factual record to the Council.

13.2 If the Council decides not to make a factual record available to the public, the Secretariat will inform the Submitter that the factual record will not be made public.

13.3 Independent of any Council decision with respect to the public availability of a factual record, the Council may, by a two-thirds vote, make a factual record available to the JPAC for their information in accordance with Article 16(7) of the Agreement and the JPAC Rules of Procedure.

14. Can a submission under consideration be withdrawn?

14.1 If a Submitter informs the Secretariat in writing before the response from the Party is received by the Secretariat that it no

---

7. *Editor's Note*: The final sentence of provision 12.2 was added to the Guidelines   by the Council in June 1999.

longer wishes to have the submission process continue with respect to its submission, the Secretariat will proceed no further with the submission and so inform the Council. If two or more submitters have made a joint submission, all of the Submitters must inform the Secretariat in writing that they no longer wish to have the submission process continue, before the submission may be withdrawn.

14.2 If the Submitter informs the Secretariat in writing that it wishes to withdraw its submission after the response from the Party is received by the Secretariat, the Secretariat will proceed no further unless the Party concerned informs it that consideration of the Submission should continue. The Secretariat shall inform the Council of any such notice of withdrawal and of whether or not the Party concerned wants consideration of the submission to continue.[8]

14.3 If the Submitter withdraws its submission after the Secretariat is instructed by the Council to prepare a factual record, the Secretariat will so inform the Council. The withdrawal of the submission will be without prejudice to any further steps that may be taken with respect to the factual record, as stated in Article 15(3) of the Agreement.[9]

15. *How will information on the status of submissions and factual records be made publicly available?*

15.1 The Secretariat will establish a registry to provide summary information so that any interested nongovernmental organization or person, as well as the JPAC, may follow the status of any given submission during the submission process envisaged under Articles 14 and 15 of the Agreement. The registry will be accessible to the public. The Secretariat will provide periodically a copy of the registry to the Council. Subject to the confidentiality provisions of the Agreement and of these guidelines, the registry will include the following information unless decided otherwise by the Council:

(a) a list of all the submissions including:

i) the name of the Submitter and the name of the Party addressed in each submission;

ii) a summary of the matter addressed in the submission that initiated the process, including a brief description of the asserted failure(s) to effectively enforce environmental law;

iii) the name and citation of the environmental law(s) in question;

(b) a summary of the response provided by the Party, if any;

(c) a summary of the following notifications, as applicable:

---

8. *Editor's Note:* Provision 14.2 was added to the Guidelines by the Council in June 1999.

9. *Editor's Note:* Provision 14.3 was added to the Guidelines by the Council in June 1999.

i) a given submission does not meet the criteria set forth in Article 14(1) of the Agreement;

ii) a response is requested from the Party concerned;

iii) the Secretariat has determined that no response from the Party concerned is merited;

iv) as specified in section 10.2 of these guidelines, the Secretariat considers that, in its view, a preparation of a factual record is warranted;

v) the Council has instructed the Secretariat not to prepare a factual record;

vi) the final factual record has been provided to the Council;

vii) the Council has decided not to make the factual record available to the public;

(d) as specified in section 10.2 of these guidelines, the explanation of the Secretariat's reasoning as to why it has informed the Council that it considers that a factual record is warranted; [10]

(e) the Council's decision on the preparation of a factual record; and

(f) the Council's decision regarding whether the factual record will be made publicly available.

15.2   Any summary will contain information sufficient to enable interested nongovernmental organizations or persons or the JPAC to provide relevant information to the Secretariat for the development of a factual record.

16.   *Does the public have access to documents relating to individual submissions?*

16.1   The Secretariat will maintain a file on each submission at its headquarters in a manner suitable for public access, inspection and photocopying. A reasonable cost may be requested for photocopying. Photocopies may also be obtained by mail at a reasonable cost to the public. Subject to confidentiality provisions of the Agreement and of these guidelines, the file will contain:

a) the submission and supporting information, including any documentary evidence on which the submission may be based;

b) any response by a Party, developed under Article 14(2) of the Agreement;

c) any notifications placed on the registry by the Secretariat in accordance with section 15.1(c) of these guidelines; and

d) the final factual record, where the Council has decided to make it publicly available pursuant to Article 15(7) of the Agree-

---

10.   *Editor's Note*: Provision 15.1(d) was added to the Guidelines by the Council in   June 1999.

ment and, any other information considered by the Secretariat under Article 15(4) of the Agreement.

16.2   These documents will be placed in the public file in a timely manner.

16.3   As specified in section 10.2 of these guidelines, the explanation of the Secretariat's reasoning as to why it has informed the Council that it considers that a factual record is warranted.[11]

16.4   When a submission received by the Secretariat names an individual or entity, the Party concerned may notify that individual or entity of the existence of that submission.

17.   *How will privacy and confidentiality be safeguarded?*

17.1   In accordance with Article 11(8)(a) of the Agreement, the Secretariat will safeguard from disclosure any information it receives that could identify a Submitter if the Submitter so requests, or the Secretariat otherwise considers it appropriate. In accordance with Article 11(8)(b) of the Agreement, the Secretariat will safeguard from disclosure to the public any information received from a nongovernmental organization or person where the information is designated by that nongovernmental organization or person as confidential or proprietary. The Parties will have access to this confidential or proprietary information, except information that could identify the Submitter pursuant to Article 11(8)(a) of the Agreement.

17.2   The Secretariat will safeguard from disclosure any information provided by the Council or a Party and designated as confidential.

17.3   Given the fact that confidential or proprietary information provided by a Party, a nongovernmental organization or a person may substantially contribute to the opinion of the Secretariat that a factual record is, or is not, warranted, contributors are encouraged to furnish a summary of such information or a general explanation of why the information is considered confidential or proprietary.

17.4   If a Party provides information relating to a submission on enforcement matters to the Secretariat, the Council, the JPAC or another Party, that is confidential or proprietary, the recipient will treat the information on the same basis as the Party providing the information.

18.   *What is the relationship between these guidelines and the*
Agreement?

18.1   These guidelines are not intended to modify the Agreement. If there is a conflict between any provision of these guidelines and any provision of the Agreement, the provision of the Agreement will prevail to the extent of the inconsistency.

---

11.   *Editor's Note*: This version of provision 16.3 was added to the Guidelines by the Council in June 1999.

DOCUMENT 5

NORTH AMERICAN AGREEMENT
ON LABOR COOPERATION

PREAMBLE

The Government of the United States of America, the Government of Canada and the Government of the United Mexican States:

RECALLING their resolve in the North American Free Trade Agreement (NAFTA) to:—create an expanded and secure market for the goods and services produced in their territories,—enhance the competitiveness of their firms in global markets,—create new employment opportunities and improve working conditions and living standards in their respective territories, and—protect, enhance and enforce basic workers' rights;

AFFIRMING their continuing respect for each Party's constitution and law;

DESIRING to build on their respective international commitments and to strengthen their cooperation on labor matters;

RECOGNIZING that their mutual prosperity depends on the promotion of competition based on innovation and rising levels of productivity and quality;

SEEKING to complement the economic opportunities created by the NAFTA with the human resource development, labor-management cooperation and continuous learning that characterize high-productivity economies;

ACKNOWLEDGING that protecting basic workers' rights will encourage firms to adopt high-productivity competitive strategies;

RESOLVED to promote, in accordance with their respective laws, high-skill, high-productivity economic development in North America by:—investing in continuous human resource development, including for entry into the workforce and during periods of unemployment;—promoting employment security and career opportunities for all workers through referral and other employment services;—strengthening labor-management cooperation to promote greater dialogue between worker organizations and employers and to foster creativity and productivity in the workplace;—promoting higher living standards as productivity increases;—encouraging consultation and dialogue between labor, business and government both in each country and in North America;—fostering investment with due regard for the importance of labor laws and principles;—encouraging employers and employees in each country to comply with labor laws and to work together in maintaining a progressive, fair, safe and healthy working environment;

BUILDING on existing institutions and mechanisms in Canada, Mexico and the United States to achieve the preceding economic and social goals; and

CONVINCED of the benefits to be gained from further cooperation between them on labor matters;

HAVE AGREED as follows:

PART ONE

OBJECTIVES

Article 1: Objectives

The objectives of this Agreement are to: (a) improve working conditions and living standards in each Party's territory; (b) promote, to the maximum extent possible, the labor principles set out in Annex 1; (c) encourage cooperation to promote innovation and rising levels of productivity and quality; (d) encourage publication and exchange of information, data development and coordination, and joint studies to enhance mutually beneficial understanding of the laws and institutions governing labor in each Party's territory; (e) pursue cooperative labor-related activities on the basis of mutual benefit; (f) promote compliance with, and effective enforcement by each Party of, its labor law; and (g) foster transparency in the administration of labor law.

Annex 1

Labor Principles

The following are guiding principles that the Parties are committed to promote, subject to each Party's domestic law, but do not establish common minimum standards for their domestic law. They indicate broad areas of concern where the Parties have developed, each in its own way, laws, regulations, procedures and practices that protect the rights and interests of their respective workforces.

1. Freedom of association and protection of the right to organize

The right of workers exercised freely and without impediment to establish and join organizations of their own choosing to further and defend their interests.

2. The right to bargain collectively

The protection of the right of organized workers to freely engage in collective bargaining on matters concerning the terms and conditions of employment.

3. The right to strike

The protection of the right of workers to strike in order to defend their collective interests.

4. Prohibition of forced labor

The prohibition and suppression of all forms of forced or compulsory labor, except for types of compulsory work generally considered acceptable by the Parties, such as compulsory military service, certain civic obligations, prison labor not for private purposes and work exacted in cases of emergency.

5. Labor protections for children and young persons

The establishment of restrictions on the employment of children and young persons that may vary taking into consideration relevant factors likely to jeopardize the full physical, mental and moral development of young persons, including schooling and safety requirements.

6. Minimum employment standards

The establishment of minimum employment standards, such as minimum wages and overtime pay, for wage earners, including those not covered by collective agreements.

7. Elimination of employment discrimination

Elimination of employment discrimination on such grounds as race, religion, age, sex or other grounds, subject to certain reasonable exceptions, such as, where applicable, bona fide occupational requirements or qualifications and established practices or rules governing retirement ages, and special measures of protection or assistance for particular groups designed to take into account the effects of discrimination.

8. Equal pay for women and men

Equal wages for women and men by applying the principle of equal pay for equal work in the same establishment.

9. Prevention of occupational injuries and illnesses

Prescribing and implementing standards to minimize the causes of occupational injuries and illnesses.

10. Compensation in cases of occupational injuries and illnesses

The establishment of a system providing benefits and compensation to workers or their dependents in cases of occupational injuries, accidents or fatalities arising out of, linked with or occurring in the course of employment.

11. Protection of migrant workers

Providing migrant workers in a Party's territory with the same legal protection as the Party's nationals in respect of working conditions.

PART TWO

OBLIGATIONS

Article 2: Levels of Protection

Affirming full respect for each Party's constitution, and recognizing the right of each Party to establish its own domestic labor standards, and to adopt or modify accordingly its labor laws and regulations, each Party shall ensure that its labor laws and regulations provide for high labor standards, consistent with high quality and productivity workplaces, and shall continue to strive to improve those standards in that light.

Article 3: Government Enforcement Action

1. Each Party shall promote compliance with and effectively enforce its labor law through appropriate government action, subject to Article 42, such as: (a) appointing and training inspectors; (b) monitoring compliance and investigating suspected violations, including through on-site inspections; (c) seeking assurances of voluntary compliance; (d) requiring record keeping and reporting; (e) encouraging the establishment of worker-management committees to address labor regulation of the workplace; (f) providing or encouraging mediation, conciliation and arbitration services; or (g) initiating, in a timely manner, proceedings to seek appropriate sanctions or remedies for violations of its labor law.

2. Each Party shall ensure that its competent authorities give due consideration in accordance with its law to any request by an employer, employee or their representatives, or other interested person, for an investigation of an alleged violation of the Party's labor law.

Article 4: Private Action

1. Each Party shall ensure that persons with a legally recognized interest under its law in a particular matter have appropriate access to administrative, quasi-judicial, judicial or labor tribunals for the enforcement of the Party's labor law.

2. Each Party's law shall ensure that such persons may have recourse to, as appropriate, procedures by which rights arising under: (a) its labor law, including in respect of occupational safety and health, employment standards, industrial relations and migrant workers, and (b) collective agreements, can be enforced.

Article 5: Procedural Guarantees

1. Each Party shall ensure that its administrative, quasi-judicial, judicial and labor tribunal proceedings for the enforcement of its labor law are fair, equitable and transparent and, to this end, each Party shall provide that: (a) such proceedings comply with due process of law; (b) any hearings in such proceedings are open to the public, except where the administration of justice otherwise requires; (c) the parties to such proceedings are entitled to support or defend their respective positions and to present information or evidence; and (d) such proceedings are not unnecessarily complicated and do not entail unreasonable charges or time limits or unwarranted delays.

2. Each Party shall provide that final decisions on the merits of the case in such proceedings are: (a) in writing and preferably state the

reasons on which the decisions are based; (b) made available without undue delay to the parties to the proceedings and, consistent with its law, to the public; and (c) based on information or evidence in respect of which the parties were offered the opportunity to be heard.

3. Each Party shall provide, as appropriate, that parties to such proceedings have the right, in accordance with its law, to seek review and, where warranted, correction of final decisions issued in such proceedings.

4. Each Party shall ensure that tribunals that conduct or review such proceedings are impartial and independent and do not have any substantial interest in the outcome of the matter.

5. Each Party shall provide that the parties to administrative, quasi-judicial, judicial or labor tribunal proceedings may seek remedies to ensure the enforcement of their labor rights. Such remedies may include, as appropriate, orders, compliance agreements, fines, penalties, imprisonment, injunctions or emergency workplace closures.

6. Each Party may, as appropriate, adopt or maintain labor defense offices to represent or advise workers or their organizations.

7. Nothing in this Article shall be construed to require a Party to establish, or to prevent a Party from establishing, a judicial system for the enforcement of its labor law distinct from its system for the enforcement of laws in general.

8. For greater certainty, decisions by each Party's administrative, quasi-judicial, judicial or labor tribunals, or pending decisions, as well as related proceedings shall not be subject to revision or reopened under the provisions of this Agreement.

Article 6: Publication

1. Each Party shall ensure that its laws, regulations, procedures and administrative rulings of general application respecting any matter covered by this Agreement are promptly published or otherwise made available in such a manner as to enable interested persons and Parties to become acquainted with them.

2. When so established by its law, each Party shall: (a) publish in advance any such measure that it proposes to adopt; and (b) provide interested persons a reasonable opportunity to comment on such proposed measures.

Article 7: Public Information and Awareness

Each Party shall promote public awareness of its labor law, including by: (a) ensuring that public information is available related to its labor law and enforcement and compliance procedures; and (b) promoting public education regarding its labor law.

PART THREE

COMMISSION FOR LABOR COOPERATION

Article 8: The Commission

1.   The Parties hereby establish the Commission for Labor Cooperation.

2.   The Commission shall comprise a ministerial Council and a Secretariat. The Commission shall be assisted by the National Administrative Office of each Party.

Section A: The Council

Article 9: Council Structure and Procedures

1.   The Council shall comprise labor ministers of the Parties or their designees.

2.   The Council shall establish its rules and procedures.

3.   The Council shall convene: (a) at least once a year in regular session, and (b) in special session at the request of any Party. Regular sessions shall be chaired successively by each Party.

4.   The Council may hold public sessions to report on appropriate matters.

5.   The Council may: (a) establish, and assign responsibilities to, committees, working groups or expert groups; and (b) seek the advice of independent experts.

6.   All decisions and recommendations of the Council shall be taken by consensus, except as the Council may otherwise decide or as otherwise provided in this Agreement.

Article 10: Council Functions

1.   The Council shall be the governing body of the Commission and shall: (a) oversee the implementation and develop recommendations on the further elaboration of this Agreement and, to this end, the Council shall, within four years after the date of entry into force of this Agreement, review its operation and effectiveness in the light of experience; (b) direct the work and activities of the Secretariat and of any committees or working groups convened by the Council; (c) establish priorities for cooperative action and, as appropriate, develop technical assistance programs on the matters set out in Article 11; (d) approve the annual plan of activities and budget of the Commission; (e) approve for publication, subject to such terms or conditions as it may impose, reports and studies prepared by the Secretariat, independent experts or working groups; (f) facilitate Party-to-Party consultations, including through the exchange of information; (g) address questions and differences that may

arise between the Parties regarding the interpretation or application of this Agreement; and (h) promote the collection and publication of comparable data on enforcement, labor standards and labor market indicators.

2.   The Council may consider any other matter within the scope of this Agreement and take such other action in the exercise of its functions as the Parties may agree.

Article 11: Cooperative Activities

1.   The Council shall promote cooperative activities between the Parties, as appropriate, regarding: (a) occupational safety and health; (b) child labor; (c) migrant workers of the Parties; (d) human resource development; (e) labor statistics; (f) work benefits; (g) social programs for workers and their families; (h) programs, methodologies and experiences regarding productivity improvement; (i) labor-management relations and collective bargaining procedures; (j) employment standards and their implementation; (k) compensation for work-related injury or illness; (*l*) legislation relating to the formation and operation of unions, collective bargaining and the resolution of labor disputes, and its implementation; (m) the equality of women and men in the workplace; (n) forms of cooperation among workers, management and government; (o) the provision of technical assistance, at the request of a Party, for the development of its labor standards; and (p) such other matters as the Parties may agree.

2.   In carrying out the activities referred to in paragraph 1, the Parties may, commensurate with the availability of resources in each Party, cooperate through: (a) seminars, training sessions, working groups and conferences; (b) joint research projects, including sectoral studies; (c) technical assistance; and (d) such other means as the Parties may agree.

3.   The Parties shall carry out the cooperative activities referred to in paragraph 1 with due regard for the economic, social, cultural and legislative differences between them.

Section B: The Secretariat

Article 12: Secretariat Structure and Procedures

1.   The Secretariat shall be headed by an Executive Director, who shall be chosen by the Council for a three-year term, which may be renewed by the Council for one additional three-year term. The position of Executive Director shall rotate consecutively between nationals of each Party. The Council may remove the Executive Director solely for cause.

2.   The Executive Director shall appoint and supervise the staff of the Secretariat, regulate their powers and duties and fix their remunera-

tion in accordance with general standards to be established by the Council. The general standards shall provide that: (a) staff shall be appointed and retained, and their conditions of employment shall be determined, strictly on the basis of efficiency, competence and integrity; (b) in appointing staff, the Executive Director shall take into account lists of candidates prepared by the Parties; (c) due regard shall be paid to the importance of recruiting an equitable proportion of the professional staff from among the nationals of each Party; and (d) the Executive Director shall inform the Council of all appointments.

3.   The number of staff positions shall initially be set at 15 and may be changed thereafter by the Council.

4.   The Council may decide, by a two-thirds vote, to reject any appointment that does not meet the general standards. Any such decision shall be made and held in confidence.

5.   In the performance of their duties, the Executive Director and the staff shall not seek or receive instructions from any government or any other authority external to the Council. Each Party shall respect the international character of the responsibilities of the Executive Director and the staff and shall not seek to influence them in the discharge of their responsibilities.

6.   The Secretariat shall safeguard: (a) from disclosure information it receives that could identify an organization or person if the person or organization so requests or the Secretariat otherwise considers it appropriate; and (b) from public disclosure any information it receives from any organization or person where the information is designated by that organization or person as confidential or proprietary.

7.   The Secretariat shall act under the direction of the Council in accordance with Article 10(1)(b).

Article 13: Secretariat Functions

1.   The Secretariat shall assist the Council in exercising its functions and shall provide such other support as the Council may direct.

2.   The Executive Director shall submit for the approval of the Council the annual plan of activities and budget for the Commission, including provision for contingencies and proposed cooperative activities.

3.   The Secretariat shall report to the Council annually on its activities and expenditures.

4.   The Secretariat shall periodically publish a list of matters resolved under Part Four or referred to Evaluation Committees of Experts.

Article 14: Secretariat Reports and Studies

1.   The Secretariat shall periodically prepare background reports setting out publicly available information supplied by each Party on: (a) labor law and administrative procedures; (b) trends and administrative

strategies related to the implementation and enforcement of labor law; (c) labor market conditions such as employment rates, average wages and labor productivity; and (d) human resource development issues such as training and adjustment programs.

2.   The Secretariat shall prepare a study on any matter as the Council may request. The Secretariat shall prepare any such study in accordance with terms of reference established by the Council, and may (a) consider any relevant information; (b) where it does not have specific expertise in the matter, engage one or more independent experts of recognized experience; and (c) include proposals on the matter.

3.   The Secretariat shall submit a draft of any report or study that it prepares pursuant to paragraph 1 or 2 to the Council. If the Council considers that a report or study is materially inaccurate or otherwise deficient, the Council may remand it to the Secretariat for reconsideration or other disposition.

4.   Secretariat reports and studies shall be made public 45 days after their approval by the Council, unless the Council otherwise decides.

Section C: National Administrative Offices

Article 15: National Administrative Office Structure

1.   Each Party shall establish a National Administrative Office (NAO) at the federal government level and notify the Secretariat and the other Parties of its location.

2.   Each Party shall designate a Secretary for its NAO, who shall be responsible for its administration and management.

3.   Each Party shall be responsible for the operation and costs of its NAO.

Article 16: NAO Functions

1.   Each NAO shall serve as a point of contact with: (a) governmental agencies of that Party; (b) NAOs of the other Parties; and (c) the Secretariat.

2.   Each NAO shall promptly provide publicly available information requested by: (a) the Secretariat for reports under Article 14(1); (b) the Secretariat for studies under Article 14(2); (c) a NAO of another Party; and (d) an ECE.

3.   Each NAO shall provide for the submission and receipt, and periodically publish a list, of public communications on labor law matters arising in the territory of another Party. Each NAO shall review such matters, as appropriate, in accordance with domestic procedures.

Section D: National Committees

Article 17: National Advisory Committee

Each Party may convene a national advisory committee, comprising members of its public, including representatives of its labor and business organizations and other persons, to advise it on the implementation and further elaboration of this Agreement.

Article 18: Governmental Committee

Each Party may convene a governmental committee, which may comprise or include representatives of federal and state or provincial governments, to advise it on the implementation and further elaboration of this Agreement.

Section E: Official Languages

Article 19: Official Languages

The official languages of the Commission shall be English, French and Spanish. The Council shall establish rules and procedures regarding interpretation and translation.

PART FOUR
COOPERATIVE CONSULTATIONS AND EVALUATIONS

Article 20: Cooperation

The Parties shall at all times endeavor to agree on the interpretation and application of this Agreement, and shall make every attempt through cooperation and consultations to resolve any matter that might affect its operation.

Section A: Cooperative Consultations

Article 21: Consultations Between NAOs

1. A NAO may request consultations, to be conducted in accordance with the procedures set out in paragraph 2, with another NAO in relation to the other Party's labor law, its administration, or labor market conditions in its territory. The requesting NAO shall notify the NAOs of the other Parties and the Secretariat of its request.

2. In such consultations, the requested NAO shall promptly provide such publicly available data or information, including: (a) descriptions of its laws, regulations, procedures, policies or practices, (b) proposed changes to such procedures, policies or practices, and (c) such clarifications and explanations related to such matters, as may assist the consulting NAOs to better understand and respond to the issues raised.

3. Any other NAO shall be entitled to participate in the consultations on notice to the other NAOs and the Secretariat.

Article 22: Ministerial Consultations

1. Any Party may request in writing consultations with another Party at the ministerial level regarding any matter within the scope of this Agreement. The requesting Party shall provide specific and sufficient information to allow the requested Party to respond.

2. The requesting Party shall promptly notify the other Parties of the request. A third Party that considers it has a substantial interest in the matter shall be entitled to participate in the consultations on notice to the other Parties.

3. The consulting Parties shall make every attempt to resolve the matter through consultations under this Article, including through the exchange of sufficient publicly available information to enable a full examination of the matter.

Section B: Evaluations

Article 23: Evaluation Committee of Experts

1. If a matter has not been resolved after ministerial consultations pursuant to Article 22, any consulting Party may request in writing the establishment of an Evaluation Committee of Experts (ECE). The requesting Party shall deliver the request to the other Parties and to the Secretariat. Subject to paragraphs 3 and 4, the Council shall establish an ECE on delivery of the request.

2. The ECE shall analyze, in the light of the objectives of this Agreement and in a non-adversarial manner, patterns of practice by each Party in the enforcement of its occupational safety and health or other technical labor standards as they apply to the particular matter considered by the Parties under Article 22.

3. No ECE may be convened if a Party obtains a ruling under Annex 23 that the matter: (a) is not trade-related; or (b) is not covered by mutually recognized labor laws.

4. No ECE may be convened regarding any matter that was previously the subject of an ECE report in the absence of such new information as would warrant a further report.

Annex 23

Interpretive Ruling

1. Where a Party has requested the Council to convene an ECE, the Council shall, on the written request of any other Party, select an independent expert to make a ruling concerning whether the matter is: (a) trade-related; or (b) covered by mutually recognized labor laws.

2. The Council shall establish rules of procedure for the selection of the expert and for submissions by the Parties. Unless the Council decides otherwise, the expert shall present a ruling within 15 days after the expert is selected.

Article 24: Rules of Procedure

1. The Council shall establish rules of procedure for ECEs, which shall apply unless the Council otherwise decides. The rules of procedure shall provide that: (a) an ECE shall normally comprise three members; (b) the chair shall be selected by the Council from a roster of experts developed in consultation with the ILO pursuant to Article 45 and, where possible, other members shall be selected from a roster developed by the Parties; (c) ECE members shall (i) have expertise or experience in labor matters or other appropriate disciplines, (ii) be chosen strictly on the basis of objectivity, reliability and sound judgment, (iii) be independent of, and not be affiliated with or take instructions from, any Party or the Secretariat, and (iv) comply with a code of conduct to be established by the Council; (d) an ECE may invite written submissions from the Parties and the public; (e) an ECE may consider, in preparing its report, any information provided by (i) the Secretariat, (ii) the NAO of each Party, (iii) organizations, institutions and persons with relevant expertise, and (iv) the public; and (f) each Party shall have a reasonable opportunity to review and comment on information that the ECE receives and to make written submissions to the ECE.

2. The Secretariat and the NAOs shall provide appropriate administrative assistance to an ECE, in accordance with the rules of procedure established by the Council under paragraph 1.

Article 25: Draft Evaluation Reports

1. Within 120 days after it is established, or such other period as the Council may decide, the ECE shall present a draft report for consideration by the Council, which shall contain: (a) a comparative assessment of the matter under consideration; (b) its conclusions; and (c) where appropriate, practical recommendations that may assist the Parties in respect of the matter.

2. Each Party may submit written views to the ECE on its draft report. The ECE shall take such views into account in preparing its final report.

Article 26: Final Evaluation Reports

1. The ECE shall present a final report to the Council within 60 days after presentation of the draft report, unless the Council otherwise decides.

2. The final report shall be published within 30 days after its presentation to the Council, unless the Council otherwise decides.

3. The Parties shall provide to each other and the Secretariat written responses to the recommendations contained in the ECE report within 90 days of its publication.

4. The final report and such written responses shall be tabled for consideration at the next regular session of the Council. The Council may keep the matter under review.

PART FIVE

RESOLUTION OF DISPUTES

Article 27: Consultations

1. Following presentation to the Council under Article 26(1) of an ECE final report that addresses the enforcement of a Party's occupational safety and health, child labor or minimum wage technical labor standards, any Party may request in writing consultations with any other Party regarding whether there has been a persistent pattern of failure by that other Party to effectively enforce such standards in respect of the general subject matter addressed in the report.

2. The requesting Party shall deliver the request to the other Parties and to the Secretariat.

3. Unless the Council otherwise provides in its rules and procedures established under Article 9(2), a third Party that considers it has a substantial interest in the matter shall be entitled to participate in the consultations on delivery of written notice to the other Parties and to the Secretariat.

4. The consulting Parties shall make every attempt to arrive at a mutually satisfactory resolution of the matter through consultations under this Article.

Article 28: Initiation of Procedures

1. If the consulting Parties fail to resolve the matter pursuant to Article 27 within 60 days of delivery of a request for consultations, or such other period as the consulting Parties may agree, any such Party may request in writing a special session of the Council.

2. The requesting Party shall state in the request the matter complained of and shall deliver the request to the other Parties and to the Secretariat.

3. Unless it decides otherwise, the Council shall convene within 20 days of delivery of the request and shall endeavor to resolve the dispute promptly.

4. The Council may: (a) call on such technical advisers or create such working groups or expert groups as it deems necessary, (b) have recourse to good offices, conciliation, mediation or such other dispute resolution procedures, or (c) make recommendations, as may assist the

consulting Parties to reach a mutually satisfactory resolution of the dispute. Any such recommendations shall be made public if the Council, by a two-thirds vote, so decides.

5.   Where the Council decides that a matter is more properly covered by another agreement or arrangement to which the consulting Parties are party, it shall refer the matter to those Parties for appropriate action in accordance with such other agreement or arrangement.

Article 29: Request for an Arbitral Panel

1.   If the matter has not been resolved within 60 days after the Council has convened pursuant to Article 28, the Council shall, on the written request of any consulting Party and by a two-thirds vote, convene an arbitral panel to consider the matter where the alleged persistent pattern of failure by the Party complained against to effectively enforce its occupational safety and health, child labor or minimum wage technical labor standards is: (a) trade-related; and (b) covered by mutually recognized labor laws.

2.   A third Party that considers it has a substantial interest in the matter shall be entitled to join as a complaining Party on delivery of written notice of its intention to participate to the disputing Parties and the Secretariat. The notice shall be delivered at the earliest possible time, and in any event no later than seven days after the date of the vote of the Council to convene a panel.

3.   Unless otherwise agreed by the disputing Parties, the panel shall be established and perform its functions in a manner consistent with the provisions of this Part.

Article 30: Roster

1.   The Council shall establish and maintain a roster of up to 45 individuals who are willing and able to serve as panelists. The roster members shall be appointed by consensus for terms of three years, and may be reappointed.

2.   Roster members shall: (a) have expertise or experience in labor law or its enforcement, or in the resolution of disputes arising under international agreements, or other relevant scientific, technical or professional expertise or experience; (b) be chosen strictly on the basis of objectivity, reliability and sound judgment; (c) be independent of, and not be affiliated with or take instructions from, any Party or the Secretariat; and (d) comply with a code of conduct to be established by the Council.

Article 31: Qualifications of Panelists

1.   All panelists shall meet the qualifications set out in Article 30.

2.   Individuals may not serve as panelists for a dispute where: (a) they have participated pursuant to Article 28(4) or participated as

members of an ECE that addressed the matter; or (b) they have, or a person or organization with which they are affiliated has, an interest in the matter, as set out in the code of conduct established under Article 30(2)(d).

Article 32: Panel Selection

1.   Where there are two disputing Parties, the following procedures shall apply: (a) The panel shall comprise five members. (b) The disputing Parties shall endeavor to agree on the chair of the panel within 15 days after the Council votes to convene the panel. If the disputing Parties are unable to agree on the chair within this period, the disputing Party chosen by lot shall select within five days a chair who is not a citizen of that Party. (c) Within 15 days of selection of the chair, each disputing Party shall select two panelists who are citizens of the other disputing Party. (d) If a disputing Party fails to select its panelists within such period, such panelists shall be selected by lot from among the roster members who are citizens of the other disputing Party.

2.   Where there are more than two disputing Parties, the following procedures shall apply: (a) The panel shall comprise five members. (b) The disputing Parties shall endeavor to agree on the chair of the panel within 15 days after the Council votes to convene the panel. If the disputing Parties are unable to agree on the chair within this period, the Party or Parties on the side of the dispute chosen by lot shall select within 10 days a chair who is not a citizen of such Party or Parties. (c) Within 30 days of selection of the chair, the Party complained against shall select two panelists, one of whom is a citizen of a complaining Party, and the other of whom is a citizen of another complaining Party. The complaining Parties shall select two panelists who are citizens of the Party complained against. (d) If any disputing Party fails to select a panelist within such period, such panelist shall be selected by lot in accordance with the citizenship criteria of subparagraph (c).

3.   Panelists shall normally be selected from the roster. Any disputing Party may exercise a peremptory challenge against any individual not on the roster who is proposed as a panelist by a disputing Party within 30 days after the individual has been proposed.

4.   If a disputing Party believes that a panelist is in violation of the code of conduct, the disputing Parties shall consult and, if they agree, the panelist shall be removed and a new panelist shall be selected in accordance with this Article.

Article 33: Rules of Procedure

1.   The Council shall establish Model Rules of Procedure. The procedures shall provide: (a) a right to at least one hearing before the panel; (b) the opportunity to make initial and rebuttal written submissions; and (c) that no panel may disclose which panelists are associated with majority or minority opinions.

2. Unless the disputing Parties otherwise agree, panels convened under this Part shall be established and conduct their proceedings in accordance with the Model Rules of Procedure.

3. Unless the disputing Parties otherwise agree within 20 days after the Council votes to convene the panel, the terms of reference shall be: "To examine, in light of the relevant provisions of the Agreement, including those contained in Part Five, whether there has been a persistent pattern of failure by the Party complained against to effectively enforce its occupational safety and health, child labor or minimum wage technical labor standards, and to make findings, determinations and recommendations in accordance with Article 36(2)."

Article 34: Third Party Participation

A Party that is not a disputing Party, on delivery of a written notice to the disputing Parties and the Secretariat, shall be entitled to attend all hearings, to make written and oral submissions to the panel and to receive written submissions of the disputing Parties.

Article 35: Role of Experts

On request of a disputing Party, or on its own initiative, the panel may seek information and technical advice from any person or body that it deems appropriate, provided that the disputing Parties so agree and subject to such terms and conditions as such Parties may agree.

Article 36: Initial Report

1. Unless the disputing Parties otherwise agree, the panel shall base its report on the submissions and arguments of the disputing Parties and on any information before it pursuant to Article 35.

2. Unless the disputing Parties otherwise agree, the panel shall, within 180 days after the last panelist is selected, present to the disputing Parties an initial report containing: (a) findings of fact; (b) its determination as to whether there has been a persistent pattern of failure by the Party complained against to effectively enforce its occupational safety and health, child labor or minimum wage technical labor standards in a matter that is trade-related and covered by mutually recognized labor laws, or any other determination requested in the terms of reference; and (c) in the event the panel makes an affirmative determination under subparagraph (b), its recommendations, if any, for the resolution of the dispute, which normally shall be that the Party complained against adopt and implement an action plan sufficient to remedy the pattern of non-enforcement.

3. Panelists may furnish separate opinions on matters not unanimously agreed.

4. A disputing Party may submit written comments to the panel on its initial report within 30 days of presentation of the report.

5. In such an event, and after considering such written comments, the panel, on its own initiative or on the request of any disputing Party, may: (a) request the views of any participating Party; (b) reconsider its report; and (c) make any further examination that it considers appropriate.

Article 37: Final Report

1. The panel shall present to the disputing Parties a final report, including any separate opinions on matters not unanimously agreed, within 60 days of presentation of the initial report, unless the disputing Parties otherwise agree.

2. The disputing Parties shall transmit to the Council the final report of the panel, as well as any written views that a disputing Party desires to be appended, on a confidential basis within 15 days after it is presented to them.

3. The final report of the panel shall be published five days after it is transmitted to the Council.

Article 38: Implementation of Final Report

If, in its final report, a panel determines that there has been a persistent pattern of failure by the Party complained against to effectively enforce its occupational safety and health, child labor or minimum wage technical labor standards, the disputing Parties may agree on a mutually satisfactory action plan, which normally shall conform with the determinations and recommendations of the panel. The disputing Parties shall promptly notify the Secretariat and the Council of any agreed resolution of the dispute.

Article 39: Review of Implementation

1. If, in its final report, a panel determines that there has been a persistent pattern of failure by the Party complained against to effectively enforce its occupational safety and health, child labor or minimum wage technical labor standards, and: (a) the disputing Parties have not agreed on an action plan under Article 38 within 60 days of the date of the final report, or (b) the disputing Parties cannot agree on whether the Party complained against is fully implementing (i) an action plan agreed under Article 38, (ii) an action plan deemed to have been established by a panel under paragraph 2, or (iii) an action plan approved or established by a panel under paragraph 4, any disputing Party may request that the panel be reconvened. The requesting Party shall deliver the request in writing to the other Parties and to the Secretariat. The Council shall reconvene the panel on delivery of the request to the Secretariat.

2. No Party may make a request under paragraph 1(a) earlier than 60 days, or later than 120 days, after the date of the final report. If the

disputing Parties have not agreed to an action plan and if no request was made under paragraph 1(a), the last action plan, if any, submitted by the Party complained against to the complaining Party or Parties within 60 days of the date of the final report, or such other period as the disputing Parties may agree, shall be deemed to have been established by the panel 120 days after the date of the final report.

3. A request under paragraph 1(b) may be made no earlier than 180 days after an action plan has been: (a) agreed under Article 38, (b) deemed to have been established by a panel under paragraph 2, or (c) approved or established by a panel under paragraph 4, and only during the term of any such action plan.

4. Where a panel has been reconvened under paragraph 1(a), it: (a) shall determine whether any action plan proposed by the Party complained against is sufficient to remedy the pattern of non-enforcement and (i) if so, shall approve the plan, or (ii) if not, shall establish such a plan consistent with the law of the Party complained against, and (b) may, where warranted, impose a monetary enforcement assessment in accordance with Annex 39, within 90 days after the panel has been reconvened or such other period as the disputing Parties may agree.

5. Where a panel has been reconvened under paragraph 1(b), it shall determine either that: (a) the Party complained against is fully implementing the action plan, in which case the panel may not impose a monetary enforcement assessment, or (b) the Party complained against is not fully implementing the action plan, in which case the panel shall impose a monetary enforcement assessment in accordance with Annex 39, within 60 days after it has been reconvened or such other period as the disputing Parties may agree.

6. A panel reconvened under this Article shall provide that the Party complained against shall fully implement any action plan referred to in paragraph 4(a)(ii) or 5(b), and pay any monetary enforcement assessment imposed under paragraph 4(b) or 5(b), and any such provision shall be final.

Annex 39

Monetary Enforcement Assessments

1. For the first year after the date of entry into force of this Agreement, any monetary enforcement assessment shall be no greater than 20 million dollars (U.S.) or its equivalent in the currency of the Party complained against. Thereafter, any monetary enforcement assessment shall be no greater than .007 percent of total trade in goods between the Parties during the most recent year for which data are available.

2. In determining the amount of the assessment, the panel shall take into account: (a) the pervasiveness and duration of the Party's persistent pattern of failure to effectively enforce its occupational safety and health, child labor or minimum wage technical labor standards; (b)

the level of enforcement that could reasonably be expected of a Party given its resource constraints; (c) the reasons, if any, provided by the Party for not fully implementing an action plan; (d) efforts made by the Party to begin remedying the pattern of non-enforcement after the final report of the panel; and (e) any other relevant factors.

3. All monetary enforcement assessments shall be paid in the currency of the Party complained against into a fund established in the name of the Commission by the Council and shall be expended at the direction of the Council to improve or enhance the labor law enforcement in the Party complained against, consistent with its law.

Article 40: Further Proceeding

A complaining Party may, at any time beginning 180 days after a panel determination under Article 39(5)(b), request in writing that a panel be reconvened to determine whether the Party complained against is fully implementing the action plan. On delivery of the request to the other Parties and the Secretariat, the Council shall reconvene the panel. The panel shall make the determination within 60 days after it has been reconvened or such other period as the disputing Parties may agree.

Article 41: Suspension of Benefits

1. Subject to Annex 41A, where a Party fails to pay a monetary enforcement assessment within 180 days after it is imposed by a panel: (a) under Article 39(4)(b), or (b) under Article 39(5)(b), except where benefits may be suspended under paragraph 2(a), any complaining Party or Parties may suspend, in accordance with Annex 41B, the application to the Party complained against of NAFTA benefits in an amount no greater than that sufficient to collect the monetary enforcement assessment.

2. Subject to Annex 41A, where a panel has made a determination under Article 39(5)(b) and the panel: (a) has previously imposed a monetary enforcement assessment under Article 39(4)(b) or established an action plan under Article 39(4)(a)(ii), or (b) has subsequently determined under Article 40 that a Party is not fully implementing an action plan, the complaining Party or Parties may, in accordance with Annex 41B, suspend annually the application to the Party complained against of NAFTA benefits in an amount no greater than the monetary enforcement assessment imposed by the panel under Article 39(5)(b).

3. Where more than one complaining Party suspends benefits under paragraph 1 or 2, the combined suspension shall be no greater than the amount of the monetary enforcement assessment.

4. Where a Party has suspended benefits under paragraph 1 or 2, the Council shall, on the delivery of a written request by the Party complained against to the other Parties and the Secretariat, reconvene the panel to determine whether the monetary enforcement assessment

has been paid or collected, or whether the Party complained against is fully implementing the action plan, as the case may be. The panel shall submit its report within 45 days after it has been reconvened. If the panel determines that the assessment has been paid or collected, or that the Party complained against is fully implementing the action plan, the suspension of benefits under paragraph 1 or 2, as the case may be, shall be terminated.

5. On the written request of the Party complained against, delivered to the other Parties and the Secretariat, the Council shall reconvene the panel to determine whether the suspension of benefits by the complaining Party or Parties pursuant to paragraph 1 or 2 is manifestly excessive. Within 45 days of the request, the panel shall present a report to the disputing Parties containing its determination.

Annex 41A

Canadian Domestic Enforcement and Collection

1. For the purposes of this Annex, "panel determination" means: (a) a determination by a panel under Article 39(4)(b) or 5(b) that provides that Canada shall pay a monetary enforcement assessment; and (b) a determination by a panel under Article 39(5)(b) that provides that Canada shall fully implement an action plan where the panel: (i) has previously established an action plan under Article 39(4)(a)(ii) or imposed a monetary enforcement assessment under Article 39(4)(b); or (ii) has subsequently determined under Article 40 that Canada is not fully implementing an action plan.

2. Canada shall adopt and maintain procedures that provide that: (a) subject to subparagraph (b), the Commission, at the request of a complaining Party, may in its own name file in a court of competent jurisdiction a certified copy of a panel determination; (b) the Commission may file in court a panel determination that is a panel determination described in paragraph 1(a) only if Canada has failed to comply with the determination within 180 days of when the determination was made; (c) when filed, the panel determination, for purposes of enforcement, shall become an order of the court; (d) the Commission may take proceedings for enforcement of a panel determination that is made an order of the court, in that court, against the person against whom the panel determination is addressed in accordance with paragraph 6 of Annex 46; (e) proceedings to enforce a panel determination that has been made an order of the court shall be conducted by way of summary proceedings; (f) in proceedings to enforce a panel determination that is a panel determination described in paragraph 1(b) and that has been made an order of the court, the court shall promptly refer any question of fact or any question of interpretation of the panel determination to the panel that made the panel determination, and the decision of the panel shall be binding on the court; (g) a panel determination that has been made an order of the court shall not be subject to domestic review or appeal; and (h) an order made by the court in proceedings to enforce a panel

determination that has been made an order of the court shall not be subject to review or appeal.

3.   Where Canada is the Party complained against, the procedures adopted and maintained by Canada under this Annex shall apply and the procedures set out in Article 41 shall not apply.

4.   Any change by Canada to the procedures adopted and maintained by Canada under this Annex that have the effect of undermining the provisions of this Annex shall be considered a breach of this Agreement.

Annex 41B

Suspension of Benefits

1.   Where a complaining Party suspends NAFTA tariff benefits in accordance with this Agreement, the Party may increase the rates of duty on originating goods of the Party complained against to levels not to exceed the lesser of: (a) the rate that was applicable to those goods immediately prior to the date of entry into force of the NAFTA, and (b) the Most–Favored–Nation rate applicable to those goods on the date the Party suspends such benefits, and such increase may be applied only for such time as is necessary to collect, through such increase, the monetary enforcement assessment.

2.   In considering what tariff or other benefits to suspend pursuant to Article 41(1) or (2): (a) a complaining Party shall first seek to suspend benefits in the same sector or sectors as that in respect of which there has been a persistent pattern of failure by the Party complained against to effectively enforce its occupational safety and health, child labor or minimum wage technical labor standards; and (b) a complaining Party that considers it is not practicable or effective to suspend benefits in the same sector or sectors may suspend benefits in other sectors.

PART SIX

GENERAL PROVISIONS

Article 42: Enforcement Principle

Nothing in this Agreement shall be construed to empower a Party's authorities to undertake labor law enforcement activities in the territory of another Party.

Article 43: Private Rights

No Party may provide for a right of action under its domestic law against any other Party on the ground that another Party has acted in a manner inconsistent with this Agreement.

Article 44: Protection of Information

1. If a Party provides confidential or proprietary information to another Party, including its NAO, the Council or the Secretariat, the recipient shall treat the information on the same basis as the Party providing the information.

2. Confidential or proprietary information provided by a Party to an ECE or a panel under this Agreement shall be treated in accordance with the rules of procedure established under Articles 24 and 33.

Article 45: Cooperation with the ILO

The Parties shall seek to establish cooperative arrangements with the ILO to enable the Council and Parties to draw on the expertise and experience of the ILO for purposes of implementing Article 24(1).

Article 46: Extent of Obligations

Annex 46 applies to the Parties specified in that Annex.

Annex 46

Extent of Obligations

1. On the date of signature of this Agreement, or of the exchange of written notifications under Article 51, Canada shall set out in a declaration a list of any provinces for which Canada is to be bound in respect of matters within their jurisdiction. The declaration shall be effective on delivery to the other Parties, and shall carry no implication as to the internal distribution of powers within Canada. Canada shall notify the other Parties six months in advance of any modification to its declaration.

2. Unless a communication relates to a matter that would be under federal jurisdiction if it were to arise within the territory of Canada, the Canadian NAO shall identify the province of residence or establishment of the author of any communication regarding the labor law of another Party that it forwards to the NAO of another Party. That NAO may choose not to respond if that province is not included in the declaration made under paragraph 1.

3. Canada may not request consultations under Article 22, the establishment of an Evaluation Committee of Experts under Article 23, consultations under Article 27, the initiation of procedures under Article 28 or the establishment of a panel or join as a complaining Party under Article 29 at the instance, or primarily for the benefit, of any government of a province not included in the declaration made under paragraph 1.

4. Canada may not request consultations under Article 22, the establishment of an Evaluation Committee of Experts under Article 23,

consultations under Article 27, the initiation of procedures under Article 28 or the establishment of a panel or join as a complaining Party under Article 29, unless Canada states in writing that the matter would be under federal jurisdiction if it were to arise within the territory of Canada, or: (a) Canada states in writing that the matter would be under provincial jurisdiction if it were to arise within the territory of Canada; and (b) the federal government and the provinces included in the declaration account for at least 35 percent of Canada's labor force for the most recent year in which data are available, and (c) where the matter concerns a specific industry or sector, at least 55 percent of the workers concerned are employed in provinces included in Canada's declaration under paragraph 1.

5. No other Party may request consultations under Article 22, the establishment of an Evaluation Committee of Experts under Article 23, consultations under Article 27, the initiation of procedures under Article 28 or the establishment of a panel or join as a complaining Party under Article 29, concerning a matter related to a labor law of a province unless that province is included in the declaration made under paragraph 1 and the requirements of subparagraphs 4(b) and (c) have been met.

6. Canada shall, no later than the date on which an arbitral panel is convened pursuant to Article 29 respecting a matter within the scope of paragraph 5 of this Annex, notify in writing the complaining Parties and the Secretariat of whether any monetary enforcement assessment or action plan imposed by a panel under Article 39(4) or (5) against Canada shall be addressed to Her Majesty in right of Canada or Her Majesty in right of the province concerned.

7. Canada shall use its best efforts to make the Agreement applicable to as many of its provinces as possible.

8. Two years after the date of entry into force of this Agreement, the Council shall review the operation of this Annex and, in particular, shall consider whether the Parties should amend the thresholds established in paragraph 4.

Article 47: Funding of the Commission

Each Party shall contribute an equal share of the annual budget of the Commission, subject to the availability of appropriated funds in accordance with the Party's legal procedures. No Party shall be obligated to pay more than any other Party in respect of an annual budget.

Article 48: Privileges and Immunities

The Executive Director and staff of the Secretariat shall enjoy in the territory of each of the Parties such privileges and immunities as are necessary for the exercise of their functions.

Article 49: Definitions

1.   For purposes of this Agreement:

A Party has not failed to "effectively enforce its occupational safety and health, child labor or minimum wage technical labor standards" or comply with Article 3(1) in a particular case where the action or inaction by agencies or officials of that Party: (a) reflects a reasonable exercise of the agency's or the official's discretion with respect to investigatory, prosecutorial, regulatory or compliance matters; or (b) results from bona fide decisions to allocate resources to enforcement in respect of other labor matters determined to have higher priorities;

"labor law" means laws and regulations, or provisions thereof, that are directly related to: (a) freedom of association and protection of the right to organize; (b) the right to bargain collectively; (c) the right to strike; (d) prohibition of forced labor; (e) labor protections for children and young persons; (f) minimum employment standards, such as minimum wages and overtime pay, covering wage earners, including those not covered by collective agreements; (g) elimination of employment discrimination on the basis of grounds such as race, religion, age, sex, or other grounds as determined by each Party's domestic laws; (h) equal pay for men and women; (i) prevention of occupational injuries and illnesses; (j) compensation in cases of occupational injuries and illnesses; (k) protection of migrant workers;

"mutually recognized labor laws" means laws of both a requesting Party and the Party whose laws were the subject of ministerial consultations under Article 22 that address the same general subject matter in a manner that provides enforceable rights, protections or standards;

"pattern of practice" means a course of action or inaction beginning after the date of entry into force of the Agreement, and does not include a single instance or case;

"persistent pattern" means a sustained or recurring pattern of practice;

"province" means a province of Canada, and includes the Yukon Territory and the Northwest Territories and their successors;

"publicly available information" means information to which the public has a legal right under the statutory laws of the Party;

"technical labor standards" means laws and regulations, or specific provisions thereof, that are directly related to subparagraphs (d) through (k) of the definition of labor law. For greater certainty and consistent with the provisions of this Agreement, the setting of all standards and levels in respect of minimum wages and labor protections for children and young persons by each Party shall not be subject to obligations under this Agreement. Each Party's obligations under this Agreement pertain to enforcing the level of the general minimum wage and child labor age limits established by that Party;

"territory" means for a Party the territory of that Party as set out in Annex 49; and

"trade-related" means related to a situation involving workplaces, firms, companies or sectors that produce goods or provide services: (a) traded between the territories of the Parties; or (b) that compete, in the territory of the Party whose labor law was the subject of ministerial consultations under Article 22, with goods or services produced or provided by persons of another Party.

Annex 49

Country–Specific Definitions

For purposes of this Agreement:

"territory" means: (a) with respect to Canada, the territory to which its customs laws apply, including any areas beyond the territorial seas of Canada within which, in accordance with international law and its domestic law, Canada may exercise rights with respect to the seabed and subsoil and their natural resources; (b) with respect to Mexico, (i) the states of the Federation and the Federal District, (ii) the islands, including the reefs and keys, in adjacent seas, (iii) the islands of Guadalupe and Revillagigedo situated in the Pacific Ocean, (iv) the continental shelf and the submarine shelf of such islands, keys and reefs, (v) the waters of the territorial seas, in accordance with international law, and its interior maritime waters, (vi) the space located above the national territory, in accordance with international law, and (vii) any areas beyond the territorial seas of Mexico within which, in accordance with international law, including the United Nations Convention on the Law of the Sea, and its domestic law, Mexico may exercise rights with respect to the seabed and subsoil and their natural resources; and (c) with respect to the United States, (i) the customs territory of the United States, which includes the 50 states, the District of Columbia and Puerto Rico, (ii) the foreign trade zones located in the United States and Puerto Rico, and (iii) any areas beyond the territorial seas of the United States within which, in accordance with international law and its domestic law, the United States may exercise rights with respect to the seabed and subsoil and their natural resources.

PART SEVEN

FINAL PROVISIONS

Article 50: Annexes

The Annexes to this Agreement constitute an integral part of the Agreement.

Article 51: Entry into Force

This Agreement shall enter into force on January 1, 1994, immediately after entry into force of the NAFTA, on an exchange of written notifications certifying the completion of necessary legal procedures.

Article 52: Amendments

1. The Parties may agree on any modification of or addition to this Agreement.

2. When so agreed, and approved in accordance with the applicable legal procedures of each Party, a modification or addition shall constitute an integral part of this Agreement.

Article 53: Accession

Any country or group of countries may accede to this Agreement subject to such terms and conditions as may be agreed between such country or countries and the Council and following approval in accordance with the applicable legal procedures of each country.

Article 54: Withdrawal

A Party may withdraw from this Agreement six months after it provides written notice of withdrawal to the other Parties. If a Party withdraws, the Agreement shall remain in force for the remaining Parties.

Article 55: Authentic Texts

The English, French and Spanish texts of this Agreement are equally authentic.

IN WITNESS WHEREOF, the undersigned, being duly authorized by the respective Governments, have signed this Agreement.

C. NAFTA DISPUTE RESOLUTION CODE OF CONDUCT AND RULES OF PROCEDURE

DOCUMENT 6

CODE OF CONDUCT FOR DISPUTE SETTLEMENT PROCEDURES UNDER CHAPTERS 19 AND 20 OF THE NORTH AMERICAN FREE TRADE AGREEMENT

Preamble

Whereas the Parties place prime importance on the integrity and impartiality of proceedings conducted pursuant to Chapters 19 and 20 of the North American Free Trade Agreement between the Government of Canada, the Government of the United Mexican States and the Government of the United States of America, this Code of Conduct is hereby established to ensure that these principles are respected.

Interpretation

A. In this Code of Conduct,

"Agreement" means the North American Free Trade Agreement;

"assistant" means a person who, under the terms of appointment of a member, conducts research or provides support for the member;

"candidate" means

a) an individual whose name appears on a roster or list established under Article 1414, Annex 1901.2 or 1904.13 or Article 2009,

b) an individual who is under consideration for appointment as a member of a panel pursuant to Annex 1901.2 or Article 1903, 1904 or 2011, or

c) an individual who is under consideration for appointment as a member of a committee pursuant to Annex 1904.13 or Article 1905;

"member" means

a) a member of a panel constituted pursuant to Annex 1901.2 or Article 1414, 1903, 1904, 2008 or 2011,

b) a member of an extraordinary challenge committee constituted pursuant to Annex 1904.13, or

420

c) a member of a special committee constituted pursuant to Article 1905;

"participant" has the meaning assigned in the Rules of Procedure for Article 1904 Binational Panel Reviews;

"Party" means a Party to the Agreement;

"proceeding" , unless otherwise specified, means

a) a panel review under Article 1903 or 1904,

b) an extraordinary challenge proceeding under Annex 1904.13,

c) a special committee proceeding under Article 1905,

d) a panel proceeding under Chapter 20, or

e) a proceeding in a dispute arising under Chapter 11 or 14 to which Chapter 20 applies;

"Secretariat" means the Secretariat established pursuant to Article 2002; and

"staff" , in respect of a member, means persons under the direction and control of the member, other than assistants.

B. Any reference made in this Code of Conduct to an Article, Annex or Chapter is a reference to the appropriate Article, Annex or Chapter of the Agreement.

I. Responsibilities to the Process

Every candidate, member and former member shall avoid impropriety and the appearance of impropriety and shall observe high standards of conduct so that the integrity and impartiality of the dispute settlement process is preserved.

II. Disclosure Obligations

Introductory Note:

The governing principle of this Code of Conduct is that a candidate or member must disclose the existence of any interest, relationship or matter that is likely to affect the candidate's or member's independence or impartiality or that might reasonably create an appearance of impropriety or an apprehension of bias. An appearance of impropriety or an apprehension of bias is created where a reasonable person, with knowledge of all the relevant circumstances that a reasonable inquiry would disclose, would conclude that a candidate's or member's ability to carry out the duties with integrity, impartiality and competence is impaired.

These disclosure obligations, however, should not be interpreted so that the burden of detailed disclosure makes it impractical for persons in the legal or business community to serve as members, thereby depriving the Parties and participants of the services of those who might be best qualified to serve as members. Thus, candidates and members should not be called upon to disclose interests, relationships or matters whose bearing on their role in the proceeding would be trivial.

Throughout the proceeding, candidates and members have a continuing obligation to disclose interests, relationships and matters that may bear on the integrity or impartiality of the dispute settlement process.

This Code of Conduct does not determine whether or under what circumstances the Parties will disqualify a candidate or member from being appointed to, or serving as a member of, a panel or committee on the basis of disclosures made.

A.   A candidate shall disclose any interest, relationship or matter that is likely to affect the candidate's independence or impartiality or that might reasonably create an appearance of impropriety or an apprehension of bias in the proceeding. To this end, a candidate shall make all reasonable efforts to become aware of any such interests, relationships and matters.

The candidate shall disclose such interests, relationships and matters by completing an Initial Disclosure Statement provided by the Secretariat and sending it to the Secretariat.

Without limiting the generality of the foregoing, candidates shall disclose the following interests, relationships and matters:

1) any financial interest of the candidate

(a) in the proceeding or in its outcome, and

(b) in an administrative proceeding, a domestic court proceeding or another panel or committee proceeding that involves issues that may be decided in the proceeding for which the candidate is under consideration;

2) any financial interest of the candidate's employer, partner, business associate or family member

(a) in the proceeding or in its outcome, and

(b) in an administrative proceeding, a domestic court proceeding or another panel or committee proceeding that involves issues that may be decided in the proceeding for which the candidate is under consideration;

3) any past or existing financial, business, professional, family or social relationship with any interested parties in the proceeding, or their counsel, or any such relationship involving a candidate's employer, partner, business associate or family member; and

4) public advocacy or legal or other representation concerning an issue in dispute in the proceeding or involving the same goods.

B.   A member in an Article 1904 proceeding shall, after receiving the complaint, disclose any interests, advocacy or representation referred to in paragraph A (1)(b) or (2)(b) or subsection (4) by completing a Supplementary Disclosure Statement provided by the Secretariat and sending it to the Secretariat for consideration by the appropriate Parties.

C.   Once appointed, a member shall continue to make all reasonable efforts to become aware of any interests, relationships or matters referred to in section A and shall disclose them. The obligation to disclose is a continuing duty which requires a member to disclose any such interests, relationships and matters that may arise during any stage of the proceeding.

The member shall disclose such interests, relationships and matters by communicating them in writing to the Secretariat for consideration by the appropriate Parties.

III.   The Performance of Duties By Candidates and Members

A.   A candidate who accepts an appointment as a member shall be available to perform, and shall perform, a member's duties thoroughly and expeditiously throughout the course of the proceeding.

B.   A member shall ensure that the Secretariat can, at all reasonable times, contact the member in order to conduct panel or committee business.

C.   A member shall carry out all duties fairly and diligently.

D.   A member shall comply with the provisions of Chapter 19 or 20 and the applicable rules.

E.   A member shall not deny other members the opportunity to participate in all aspects of the proceeding.

F.   A member shall consider only those issues raised in the proceeding and necessary to a decision and shall not delegate the duty to decide to any other person, except as provided in the applicable rules.

G.   A member shall take all reasonable steps to ensure that the member's assistant and staff comply with Parts I, II and VI of this Code of Conduct.

H.   A member shall not engage in ex parte contacts concerning the proceeding.

I.   A candidate or member shall not communicate matters concerning actual or potential violations of this Code of Conduct unless the communication is to the Secretariat or is necessary to ascertain whether that candidate or member has violated or may violate the Code.

IV.   Independence and Impartiality of Members

A.   A member shall be independent and impartial. A member shall act in a fair manner and shall avoid creating an appearance of impropriety or an apprehension of bias.

B.   A member shall not be influenced by self-interest, outside pressure, political considerations, public clamour, loyalty to a Party or fear of criticism.

C.   A member shall not, directly or indirectly, incur any obligation or accept any benefit that would in any way interfere, or appear to interfere, with the proper performance of the member's duties.

D. A member shall not use the member's position on the panel or committee to advance any personal or private interests. A member shall avoid actions that may create the impression that others are in a special position to influence the member. A member shall make every effort to prevent or discourage others from representing themselves as being in such a position.

E. A member shall not allow past or existing financial, business, professional, family or social relationships or responsibilities to influence the member's conduct or judgment.

F. A member shall avoid entering into any relationship, or acquiring any financial interest, that is likely to affect the member's impartiality or that might reasonably create an appearance of impropriety or an apprehension of bias.

V. Duties in Certain Situations

A. For a period of one year after the completion of an Article 1904 proceeding, a former member shall not personally advise or represent any participant in the proceeding with regard to antidumping or countervailing duty matters.

B. In the case of an Article 1904 proceeding, a member or a former member shall not represent a participant in an administrative proceeding, a domestic court proceeding or another Article 1904 proceeding involving the same goods.

C. A former member shall avoid actions that may create the appearance that the member was biased in carrying out the member's duties or would benefit from the decision of the panel or committee.

VI. Maintenance of Confidentiality

A. A member or former member shall not at any time disclose or use any non-public information concerning the proceeding or acquired during the proceeding except for the purposes of the proceeding and shall not, in any case, disclose or use any such information to gain personal advantage or advantage for others or to affect adversely the interest of another.

B. A member shall not disclose a declaratory opinion under Article 1903 or a panel or extraordinary challenge committee order or decision under Article 1904 prior to its issuance by the panel or committee.

C. A member shall not disclose a special committee report or decision under Article 1905 prior to its public release by the Secretariat. A member or former member shall not at any time disclose which members are associated with majority or minority opinions in an Article 1905 proceeding.

D. A member shall not disclose a panel report issued under Chapter 20 prior to its publication by the Commission. A member or former member shall not at any time disclose which members are associated with majority or minority opinions in a proceeding under Chapter 20.

E.　A member or former member shall not at any time disclose the deliberations of a panel or committee, or any member's view, except as required by law.

VII.　Responsibilities of Assistants and Staff

Parts I (Responsibilities to the Process), II (Disclosure Obligations) and VI (Maintenance of Confidentiality) of this Code of Conduct apply also to assistants and staff.

Dated: February 10, 1994.
Timothy J. Hauser,
Deputy Under Secretary for
International Trade.

DOCUMENT 7

RULES OF PROCEDURE FOR ARTICLE 1904 BINATIONAL PANEL REVIEWS

Preamble

The Parties,

Having regard to Chapter Nineteen of the North American Free Trade Agreement between Canada, the United Mexican States and the United States of America;

Acting pursuant to Article 1904.14 of the Agreement;

Adopt the following Rules of Procedure, which shall come into force on the same day as the Agreement enters into force and from that day shall govern all panel reviews conducted pursuant to Article 1904 of the Agreement.

Short Title

1. These rules may be cited as the *NAFTA Article 1904 Panel Rules*.

Statement of General Intent

2. These rules are intended to give effect to the provisions of Chapter Nineteen of the Agreement with respect to panel reviews

426

conducted pursuant to Article 1904 of the Agreement and are designed to result in decisions of panels within 315 days after the commencement of the panel review. The purpose of these rules is to secure the just, speedy and inexpensive review of final determinations in accordance with the objectives and provisions of Article 1904. Where a procedural question arises that is not covered by these rules, a panel may adopt the procedure to be followed in the particular case before it by analogy to these rules or may refer for guidance to rules of procedure of a court that would otherwise have had jurisdiction in the importing country. In the event of any inconsistency between the provisions of these rules and the Agreement, the Agreement shall prevail.

Definitions and Interpretation

3.   In these rules,

"**Agreement**" means the North American Free Trade Agreement; (*Accord*) (*Tratado*)

"**Code of Conduct**" means the code of conduct established by the Parties pursuant to Article 1909 of the Agreement; (*Code de conduite*) (*Código de Conducta*)

"**complainant**" means a Party or interested person who files a Complaint pursuant to rule 39; (*plaignant*) (*demandante*)

"**counsel**" means

(a) with respect to a panel review of a final determination made in Canada, a person entitled to appear as counsel before the Federal Court of Canada,

(b) with respect to a panel review of a final determination made in Mexico, a person entitled to appear as counsel before the Tribunal Fiscal de la Federación, and B,r

(c) with respect to a panel review of a final determination made in the United States, a person entitled to appear as counsel before a federal court in the United States; (*avocat*) (*representante*)

"**counsel of record**" means a counsel referred to in subrule1(1); (*avocat au dossier*) (*representante legal acreditado*)

"**Deputy Minister**" means the Deputy Minister of National Revenue for Customs and Excise, or the successor thereto, and includes any person authorized to perform a power, duty or function of the Deputy Minister under the Special Import Measures Act, as amended; (*sous-ministre*) (Deputy Minister)

"**final determination**" means, in the case of Canada, a definitive decision within the meaning of subsection 77.01(1) of the Special Import Measures Act, as amended; (*décision définitive*) (*resolución definitiva*)

"**first Request for Panel Review**" means

(a) where only one Request for Panel Review is filed for review of a final determination, that Request, and

(b) where more than one Request for Panel Review is filed for review of the same final determination, the Request that is filed first; (*premiṛe demande de révision par un groupe spécial*) (*primera solicitud de revisión del panel*)

"**government information**" means

(a) with respect to a panel review of a final determination made in Canada, information

(i) the disclosure of which would be injurious to international relations or national defence or security,

(ii) that constitutes a confidence of the Queen's Privy Council for Canada, or

(iii) contained in government-to-government correspondence that is transmitted in confidence,

(b) with respect to a panel review of a final determination made in Mexico, information the disclosure of which is prohibited under the laws and regulations of Mexico, including

(i) data, statistics and documents referring to national security and strategic activities for scientific and technological development, and

(ii) information contained in government-to-government correspondence that is transmitted in confidence, and

(c) with respect to a panel review of a final determination made in the United States, information classified in accordance with Executive Order No. 12065 or its successor; (*renseignements gouvernementaux*) (*información gubernamental*)

"**interested person**" means a person who, pursuant to the laws of the country in which a final determination was made, would be entitled to appear and be represented in a judicial review of the final determination; (*personne intéressée*) (*persona interesada*)

"**investigating authority**" means the competent investigating authority that issued the final determination subject to review and includes, in respect of the issuance, amendment, modification or revocation of a Proprietary Information Access Order, any person authorized by the investigating authority; (*autorité chargée de l'enquête*) (*autoridad investigadora*)

"**involved Secretariat**" means the section of the Secretariat located in the country of an involved Party; (*Secrétariat en cause*) (*Secretariado implicado*)

"**legal holiday**" means

(a) with respect to the Canadian Section of the Secretariat, every Saturday and Sunday, New Year's Day (January 1), Good Friday, Easter Monday, Victoria Day, Canada Day (July 1), Labour Day (first Monday in September), Thanksgiving Day (second Monday in October), Remembrance Day (November 11), Christmas Day

(December 25), Boxing Day (December 26), any other day fixed as a statutory holiday by the Government of Canada or by the province in which the Section is located and any day on which the offices of the Canadian Section of the Secretariat are officially closed in whole or in part,

(b) with respect to the Mexican Section of the Secretariat, every Saturday and Sunday, New Year's Day (January 1), Constitution Day (February 5), Benito Juárez's Birthday (March 21), Labor Day (May 1), Battle of Puebla (May), Independence Day (September 16), Congressional Opening Day (November 1), Revolution Day (November 20), Transmission of the Federal Executive Branch (every six years on December 1), Christmas Day (December 25), any day designated as a statutory holiday by the Federal Laws or, in the case of Ordinary Elections, by the Local Electoral Laws and any day on which the offices of the Mexican Section of the Secretariat are officially closed in whole or in part, and

(c) with respect to the United States Section of the Secretariat, every Saturday and Sunday, New Year's Day (January 1), Martin Luther King's Birthday (third Monday in January), Presidents' Day (third Monday in February), Memorial Day (last Monday in May), Independence Day (July 4), Labor Day (first Monday in September), Columbus Day (second Monday in October), Veterans' Day (November 11), Thanksgiving Day (fourth Thursday in November), Christmas Day (December 25), any day designated as a holiday by the President or the Congress of the United States and any day on which the offices of the Government of the United States located in the District of Columbia or the offices of the United States Section of the Secretariat are officially closed in whole or in part; (*jour férié*) (*días inhábiles*)

"**Mexico**" means the United Mexican States; (*Mexique*) (*Mexico*)

"**official publication**" means

(a) in the case of the Government of Canada, the *Canada Gazette*;

(b) in the case of the Government of Mexico, the *Diario Oficial de la Federación*, and

(c) in the case of the Government of United States, the *Federal Register*; (*journal officiel*) (*publicación oficial*)

"**panel**" means a binational panel established pursuant to Annex 1901.2 to Chapter Nineteen of the Agreement for the purpose of reviewing a final determination; (*groupe spécial*) (*panel*)

"**participant**" means any of the following persons who files a Complaint pursuant to rule 39 or a Notice of Appearance pursuant to rule 40:

(a) a Party,

(b) an investigating authority, and

(c) an interested person; (*participant*) (*participante*)

"**Party**" means the Government of Canada, the Government of Mexico or the Government of the United States; (*Partie*) (*Parte*)

"**person**" means

(a) an individual,

(b) a Party,

(c) an investigating authority,

(d) a government of a province, state or other political subdivision of the country of a Party,

(e) a department, agency or body of a Party or of a government referred to in paragraph (d), or

(f) a partnership, corporation or association; (personne) (persona)

"**pleading**" means a Request for Panel Review, a Complaint, a Notice of Appearance, a Change of Service Address, a Notice of Motion, a Notice of Change of Counsel of Record, a brief or any other written submission filed by a participant; (*acte de procédure*) (*promoción*)

"**privileged information**" means

(a) with respect to a panel review of a final determination made in Canada, information of the investigating authority that is subject to solicitor-client privilege under the laws of Canada, or that constitutes part of the deliberative process with respect to the final determination, and with respect to which the privilege has not been waived,

(b) with respect to a panel review of a final determination made in Mexico,

(i) information of the investigating authority that is subject to attorney-client privilege under the laws of Mexico, or

(ii) internal communications between officials of the Secretaría de Comercio y Fomento Industrial in charge of antidumping and countervailing duty investigations or communications between those officials and other government officials, where those communications constitute part of the deliberative process with respect to the final determination, and

(c) with respect to a panel review of a final determination made in the United States, information of the investigating authority that is subject to the attorney-client, attorney work product or government deliberative process privilege under the laws of the United States with respect to which the privilege has not been waived; (*renseignements protégés*) (*información privilegiada*)

"**proof of service**" means

(a) with respect to a panel review of a final determination made in Canada or Mexico,

(i) an affidavit of service stating by whom the document was served, the date on which it was served, where it was served and the manner of service, or

(ii) an acknowledgement of service by counsel for a participant stating by whom the document was served, the date on which it was served and the manner of service and, where the acknowledgement is signed by a person other than the counsel, the name of that person followed by a statement that the person is signing as agent for the counsel, and

(b) with respect to a panel review of a final determination made in the United States, a certificate of service in the form of a statement of the date and manner of service and of the name of the person served, signed by the person who made service; *(preuve de signification)* *(comprobante de envío)*

"proprietary information" means

(a) with respect to a panel review of a final determination made in Canada, information referred to in subsection 84(3) of the *Special Import Measures Act*, as amended, or subsection 45(3) of the *Canadian International Trade Tribunal Act*, as amended, with respect to which the person who designated or submitted the information has not withdrawn the person's claim as to the confidentiality of the information,

(b) with respect to a panel review of a final determination made in Mexico, *información confidencial*, as defined under article 80 of the *Ley de Comercio Exterior* and its regulations, and

(c) with respect to a panel review of a final determination made in the United States, business proprietary information under section 777(f) of the *Tariff Act of 1930*, as amended, and any regulations made under that Act; *(renseignements de nature exclusive)* *(información confidencial)*

"Proprietary Information Access Application" means

(a) with respect to a panel review of a final determination made in Canada, a disclosure undertaking in the prescribed form, which form

(i) in respect of a final determination by the Deputy Minister, is available from the Deputy Minister, and

(ii) in respect of a final determination by the Tribunal, is available from the Tribunal,

(b) with respect to a panel review of a final determination made in Mexico, a disclosure undertaking in the prescribed form, which form is available from the Secretaría de Comercio y Fomento Industrial, and

(c) with respect to a panel review of a final determination made in the United States, a Protective Order Application

(i) in respect of a final determination by the International Trade Administration of the United States Department of Commerce, in a form prescribed by, and available from, the International Trade Administration of the United States Department of Commerce, and

(ii) in respect of a final determination by the United States International Trade Commission, in a form prescribed by, and available from, the United States International Trade Commission; (*demande relative à la communication de renseignements*) (*compromiso de confidencialidad*)

"**Proprietary Information Access Order**" means

(a) in the case of Canada, a Disclosure Order issued by the Deputy Minister or the Tribunal pursuant to a Proprietary Information Access Application,

(b) in the case of Mexico, a Disclosure Order issued by the Secretaría de Comercio y Fomento Industrial pursuant to a Proprietary Information Access Application, and

(c) in the case of the United States, a Protective Order issued by the International Trade Administration of the United States Department of Commerce or the United States International Trade Commission pursuant to a Proprietary Information Access Application; (*ordonnance relative à la communication de renseignements*) (*autorización de acceso a la información confidencial*)

"**responsible Secretariat**" means the section of the Secretariat located in the country in which the final determination under review was made; (*Secrétariat responsable*) (*Secretariado responsable*)

"**responsible Secretary**" means the Secretary of the responsible Secretariat; (*secrétaire responsable*) (*Secretario responsable*)

"**Secretariat**" means the Secretariat established pursuant to Article 2002 of the Agreement; (*Secrétariat*) (*Secretariado*)

"**Secretary**" means the Secretary of the United States Section of the Secretariat, the Secretary of the Mexican Section of the Secretariat or the Secretary of the Canadian Section of the Secretariat and includes any person authorized to act on behalf of that Secretary; (*secrétaire*) (*Secretario*)

"**service address**" means

(a) with respect to a Party, the address filed with the Secretariat as the service address of the Party, including any facsimile number submitted with that address,

(b) with respect to a participant other than a Party, the address of the counsel of record for the person, including any facsimile number submitted with that address or, where the person is not represented by counsel, the address set out by the participant in a Request for Panel Review, Complaint or Notice of Appearance as the address at which the participant may be served, including any facsimile number submitted with that address, or

(c) where a Change of Service Address has been filed by a Party or participant, the address set out as the new service address in that form, including any facsimile number submitted with that address; (*adresse aux fins de signification*) (*domicilio para oír y recibir notificaciones*)

"**service list**" means, with respect to a panel review,

(a) where the final determination was made in Canada, a list comprising the other involved Party and

(i) in the case of a final determination made by the Deputy Minister, persons named on the list maintained by the Deputy Minister who participated in the proceedings before the Deputy Minister and who were exporters or importers of goods of the country of the other involved Party or complainants referred to in section 34 of the Special Import Measures Act, as amended, and

(ii) in the case of a final determination made by the Tribunal, persons named on the list maintained by the Tribunal of parties in the proceedings before the Tribunal who were exporters or importers of goods of the country of the other involved Party, complainants referred to in section 31 of the Special Import Measures Act, as amended, or other domestic parties whose interest in the findings of the Tribunal is with respect to goods of the country of the other involved Party, and

(b) where the final determination was made in Mexico or the United States, the list, maintained by the investigating authority of persons who have been served in the proceedings leading to the final determination; (*liste de signification*) (*lista de correo*)

"**Tribunal**" means the Canadian International Trade Tribunal or its successor and includes any person authorized to act on its behalf; (*Tribunal*) (*Tribunal*)

"**United States**" means the United States of America. (*États-Unis*)

4.   The definitions set forth in Article 1911 of the Agreement and Annex 1911 to Chapter Nineteen of the Agreement are hereby incorporated into these rules.

5.   Where these rules require that notice be given, it shall be given in writing.

PART I
GENERAL
Duration and Scope of Panel Review

6.   A panel review commences on the day on which a first Request for Panel Review is filed with the Secretariat and terminates on the day on which a Notice of Completion of Panel Review is effective.

7.   A panel review shall be limited to

(a) the allegations of error of fact or law, including challenges to the jurisdiction of the investigating authority, that are set out in the Complaints filed in the panel review; and

(b) procedural and substantive defenses raised in the panel review.

Responsibilities of the Secretary

8.   The normal business hours of the Secretariat, during which the offices of the Secretariat shall be open to the public, shall be from 9:00 a.m. to 5:00 p.m. on each weekday other than

(a) in the case of the United States Section of the Secretariat, legal holidays of that Section;

(b) in the case of the Canadian Section of the Secretariat, legal holidays of that Section; and

(c) in the case of the Mexican Section of the Secretariat, legal holidays of that Section.

9.   The responsible Secretary shall provide administrative support for each panel review and shall make the arrangements necessary for the oral proceedings and meetings of each panel, including, if required, interpreters to provide simultaneous translation.

10.   (1) Each Secretary shall maintain a file for each panel review. Subject to subrules (3) and (4), the file shall be comprised of either the original or a copy of all documents filed, whether or not filed in accordance with these rules, in the panel review.

(2) The file number assigned to a first Request for Panel Review shall be the Secretariat file number for all documents filed or issued in that panel review. All documents filed shall be stamped by the Secretariat to show the date and time of receipt.

(3) Where, after notification of the selection of a panel pursuant to rule 42, a document is filed that is not provided for in these rules or that is not in accordance with the rules, the responsible Secretary may refer the unauthorized filing to the chairperson of the Panel for instructions, provided such authority has been delegated by the Panel to its chairperson pursuant to rule 17.

(4) On a referral referred to in subrule (3), the chairperson may instruct the responsible Secretary to

(a) retain the document in the file, without prejudice to a motion to strike such document; or

(b) return the document to the person who filed the document, without prejudice to a motion for leave to file the document.

11.   The responsible Secretary shall forward to the other involved Secretary a copy of all documents filed in the office of the responsible

Secretary in a panel review and of all orders and decisions issued by the panel.

12.   Where under these rules a responsible Secretary is required to publish a notice or other document in the official publications of the involved Parties, the responsible Secretary and the other involved Secretary shall cause the notice or other document to be published in the official publication of the country in which that section of the Secretariat is located.

13.   (1) Each Secretary and every member of the staff of the Secretariat shall, before taking up duties, file a Proprietary Information Access Application with each of the Deputy Minister, the Tribunal, the Secretaría de Comercio y Fomento Industrial, the International Trade Administration of the United States Department of Commerce and the United States International Trade Commission.

(2) Where a Secretary or a member of the staff of the Secretariat files a Proprietary Information Access Application in accordance with subrule (1), the appropriate investigating authority shall issue to the Secretary or to the member a Proprietary Information Access Order.

14.   (1) The responsible Secretary shall file with the investigating authority one original, and any additional copies required by the investigating authority, of every Proprietary Information Access Application and any amendments or modifications thereto, filed by a panelist, assistant to a panelist, court reporter, interpreter or translator pursuant to rule 47.

(2) The responsible Secretary shall ensure that every panelist, assistant to a panelist, court reporter, interpreter and translator, before taking up duties in a panel review, files with the responsible Secretariat a copy of a Proprietary Information Access Order.

15.   Where a document containing proprietary information or privileged information is filed with the responsible Secretariat, each involved Secretary shall ensure that

(a) the document is stored, maintained, handled and distributed in accordance with the terms of any applicable Proprietary Information Access Order;

(b) the inner wrapper of the document is clearly marked to indicate that it contains proprietary information or privileged information; and

(c) access to the document is limited to officials of, and counsel for, the investigating authority whose final determination is under review and

(i) in the case of proprietary information, the person who submitted the proprietary information to the investigating authority or counsel for that person and any persons who have been granted access to the information under a Proprietary Information Access Order with respect to the document, and

(ii) in the case of privileged information filed in a panel review of a final determination made in the United States, persons with respect to whom the panel has ordered disclosure of the privileged information under rule 52, if the persons have filed with the responsible Secretariat a Proprietary Information Access Order with respect to the document.

16. (1) Each Secretary shall permit access by any person to the information in the file in a panel review that is not proprietary information or privileged information and shall provide copies of that information on request and payment of an appropriate fee.

(2) Each Secretary shall, in accordance with subrule 15(c) and the terms of the applicable Proprietary Information Access Order or order of the panel,

(a) permit access to proprietary information or privileged information in the file of a panel review; and

(b) on payment of an appropriate fee, provide a copy of the information referred to in subrule (a).

(3) No document filed in a panel review shall be removed from the offices of the Secretariat except in the ordinary course of the business of the Secretariat or pursuant to the direction of a panel.

Internal Functioning of Panels

17. (1) A panel may adopt its own internal procedures, not inconsistent with these rules, for routine administrative matters.

(2) A panel may delegate to its chairperson

(a) the authority to accept or reject filings in accordance with subrule 10(4); and

(b) the authority to grant motions consented to by all participants, other than a motion filed pursuant to rule 20 or 52, a motion for remand of a final determination or a motion that is inconsistent with an order or decision previously made by the panel.

(3) A decision of the chairperson referred to in subrule (2) shall be issued as an order of the panel.

(4) Subject to subrule 26(b), meetings of a panel may be conducted by means of a telephone conference call.

18. Only panelists may take part in the deliberations of a panel, which shall take place in private and remain secret. Staff of the involved Secretariats and assistants to panelists may be present by permission of the panel.

Computation of Time

19.   (1) In computing any time period fixed in these rules or by an order or decision of a panel, the day from which the time period begins to run shall be excluded and, subject to subrule (2), the last day of the time period shall be included.

(2) Where the last day of a time period computed in accordance with subrule (1) falls on a legal holiday of the responsible Secretariat, that day and any other legal holidays of the responsible Secretariat immediately following that day shall be excluded from the computation.

20.   (1) A panel may extend any time period fixed in these rules if

(a) adherence to the time period would result in unfairness or prejudice to a participant or the breach of a general legal principle of the country in which the final determination was made;

(b) the time period is extended only to the extent necessary to avoid the unfairness, prejudice or breach;

(c) the decision to extend the time period is concurred in by four of the five panelists; and

(d) in fixing the extension, the panel takes into account the intent of the rules to secure just, speedy and inexpensive reviews of final determinations.

(2) A participant may request an extension of time by filing a Notice of Motion no later than the tenth day prior to the last day of the time period. Any response to the Notice of Motion shall be filed no later than seven days after the Notice of Motion is filed.

(3) A participant who fails to request an extension of time pursuant to subrule (2) may file a notice of motion for leave to file out of time, which shall include reasons why additional time is required and why the participant has failed to comply with the provisions of subrule (2).

(4) The panel will normally rule on such a motion before the last day of the time period which is the subject of the motion.

Counsel of Record

21.   (1) A counsel who signs a document filed pursuant to these rules on behalf of a participant shall be the counsel of record for the participant from the date of filing until a change is effected in accordance with subrule (2).

(2) A participant may change its counsel of record by filing with the responsible Secretariat a Notice of Change of Counsel of Record signed by the new counsel, together with proof of service on the former counsel and other participants.

Filing, Service and Communications

22.   (1) Subject to subrule 46(1), rule 47 and subrules 52(3) and 73(2)(a), no document is filed with the Secretariat until one original and eight copies of the document are received by the responsible Secretariat during its normal business hours and within the time period fixed for filing.

(2) The responsible Secretariat shall accept, date and time stamp and place in the appropriate file every document submitted to the responsible Secretariat.

(3) Receipt, date and time stamping or placement in the file of a document by the responsible Secretariat does not constitute a waiver of any time period fixed for filing or an acknowledgement that the document has been filed in accordance with these rules.

23.   The responsible Secretary shall be responsible for the service of

(a) Notices of Intent to Commence Judicial Review and Complaints on each Party;

(b) Requests for Panel Review on the Parties, the investigating authority and the persons listed on the service list; and

(c) Notices of Appearance, Proprietary Information Access Orders granted to panelists, assistants to panelists, court reporters, interpreter or translators and any amendments or modifications thereto or notices of revocation thereof, decisions and orders of a panel, Notices of Final Panel Action and Notices of Completion of Panel Review on the participants.

24.   (1) Subject to subrules (4) and (5), all documents filed by a participant, other than the administrative record, any supplementary remand record and any document required by rule 23 to be served by the responsible Secretary, shall be served by the participant on the counsel of record of each of the other participants, or where a participant is not represented by counsel, on the participant.

(2) A proof of service shall appear on, or be affixed to, all documents referred to in subrule (1).

(3) Where a document is served by expedited delivery courier or expedited mail service, the date of service set out in the affidavit of service or certificate of service shall be the day on which the document is consigned to the expedited delivery courier or expedited mail service.

(4) A document containing proprietary information or privileged information shall be filed and served under seal in accordance with rule 44, and shall be served only on

(a) the investigating authority; and

(b) participants who have been granted access to the proprietary information or privileged information under a Proprietary Information Access Order or an order of the panel.

(5) A complainant shall serve a Complaint on the investigating authority and on all persons listed on the service list.

25.   Subject to subrule 26(a), a document may be served by

(a) delivering a copy of the document to the service address of the participant;

(b) sending a copy of the document to the service address of the participant by facsimile transmission or by expedited delivery courier or expedited mail service, such as express mail in the United States or Priority Post in Canada; or

(c) personal service on the participant.

26.   Where proprietary information or privileged information is disclosed in a panel review to a person pursuant to a Proprietary Information Access Order, the person shall not

(a) file, serve or otherwise communicate the proprietary information or privileged information by facsimile transmission; or

(b) communicate the proprietary information or privileged information by telephone.

27.   Service on an investigating authority does not constitute service on a Party and service on a Party does not constitute service on an investigating authority.

Pleadings and Simultaneous Translation
of Panel Reviews in Canada

28.   Rules 29 to 31 apply with respect to a panel review of a final determination made in Canada.

29.   Either English or French may be used by any person or panelist in any document or oral proceeding.

30.   (1) Subject to subrule (2), any order or decision including the reasons therefor, issued by a panel shall be made available simultaneously in both English and French where

(a) in the opinion of the panel, the order or decision is in respect of a question of law of general public interest or importance; or

(b) the proceedings leading to the issuance of the order or decision were conducted in whole or in part in both English and French.

(2) Where

(a) an order or decision issued by a panel is not required by subrule (1) to be made available simultaneously in English and French, or

(b) an order or decision is required by subrule (1)(a) to be made available simultaneously in both English and French but the panel is of the opinion that to make the order or decision available simultaneously in both English and French would occasion a delay prejudicial to the public interest or result in injustice or hardship to any participant,

the order or decision, including the reasons therefor, shall be issued in the first instance in either English or French and thereafter at the earliest possible time in the other language, each version to be effective from the time the first version is effective.

(3) Nothing in subrule (1) or (2) shall be construed as prohibiting the oral delivery in either English or French of any order or decision or any reasons therefor.

(4) No order or decision is invalid by reason only that it was not made or issued in both English and French.

31.   (1) Any oral proceeding conducted in both English and French shall be translated simultaneously.

(2) Where a participant requests simultaneous translation of oral proceedings in a panel review, the request shall be made as early as possible in the panel review and preferably at the time of filing a Complaint or Notice of Appearance.

(3) Where the chairperson of a panel is of the opinion that there is a public interest in the panel review, the chairperson may direct the responsible Secretary to arrange for simultaneous translation of any of the oral proceedings in the panel review.

Costs

32.   Each participant shall bear the costs of, and those incidental to, its own participation in a panel review.

PART II
COMMENCEMENT OF PANEL REVIEW
Notice of Intent to Commence Judicial Review

33.   (1) Where an interested person intends to commence judicial review of a final determination, the interested person shall

(a) where the final determination was made in Canada, publish a notice to that effect in the *Canada Gazette* and serve a Notice of Intent to Commence Judicial Review on both involved Secretaries and on all persons listed on the service list; and

(b) where the final determination was made in Mexico or the United States, within 20 days after the date referred to in subrule (3)(b) or (c), serve a Notice of Intent to Commence Judicial Review on

(i) both involved Secretaries,

(ii) the investigating authority, and

(iii) all persons listed on the service list.

(2) Where the final determination referred to in subrule (1) was made in Canada, the Secretary of the Canadian Section of the

Secretariat shall serve a copy of the Notice of Intent to Commence Judicial Review on the investigating authority.

(3) Every Notice of Intent to Commence Judicial Review referred to in subrule (1) shall include the following information (model form provided in the Schedule):

(a) the information set out in subrules 55(1)(c) to (f);

(b) the title of the final determination for which judicial review is sought, the investigating authority that issued the final determination, the file number assigned by the investigating authority and, if the final determination was published in an official publication, the appropriate citation, including the date of publication; and

(c) the date on which the notice of the final determination was received by the other Party if the final determination was not published in an official publication.

Request for Panel Review

34. (1) A Request for Panel Review shall be made in accordance with the requirements of

(a) section 77.011 or 96.21 of the *Special Import Measures Act*, as amended, and any regulations made thereunder;

(b) section 516A of the *Tariff Act of 1930*, as amended, and any regulations made thereunder;

(c) section 404 of the *United States North American Free Trade Agreement Implementation Act* and any regulations made thereunder; or

(d) articles 97 and 98 of the *Ley de Comercio Exterior* and its regulations.

(2) A Request for Panel Review shall contain the following information (model form provided in the Schedule):

(a) the information set out in subrule 55(1);

(b) the title of the final determination for which panel review is requested, the investigating authority that issued the final determination, the file number assigned by the investigating authority and, if the final determination was published in an official publication, the appropriate citation;

(c) the date on which the notice of the final determination was received by the other Party if the final determination was not published in an official publication;

(d) where a Notice of Intent to Commence Judicial Review has been served and the sole reason that the Request for Panel Review is made is to require review of the final determination by a panel, a statement to that effect; and

(e) the service list, as defined in rule 3.

35. (1) On receipt of a first Request for Panel Review, the responsible Secretary shall

(a) forthwith forward a copy of the Request to the other involved Secretary;

(b) forthwith inform the other involved Secretary of the Secretariat file number; and

(c) serve a copy of the first Request for Panel Review on the persons listed on the service list together with a statement setting out the date on which the Request was filed and stating that

(i) a Party or interested person may challenge the final determination in whole or in part by filing a Complaint in accordance with rule 39 within 30 days after the filing of the first Request for Panel Review,

(ii) a Party, an investigating authority or other interested person who does not file a Complaint but who intends to participate in the panel review shall file a Notice of Appearance in accordance with rule 40 within 45 days after the filing of the first Request for Panel Review, and

(iii) the panel review will be limited to the allegations of error of fact or law, including challenges to the jurisdiction of the investigating authority, that are set out in the Complaints filed in the panel review and to the procedural and substantive defenses raised in the panel review.

(2) On the filing of a first Request for Panel Review, the responsible Secretary shall forthwith publish a notice of that Request in the official publications of the involved Parties, stating that a Request for Panel Review has been received and specifying the date on which the Request was filed, the final determination for which panel review is requested and the information set out in subrule (1)(c).

Joint Panel Reviews

36. (1) Subject to rule 37, where

(a) a panel is established to review a final determination made under paragraph 41(1)(a) of the *Special Import Measures Act*, as amended, with respect to particular goods of the United States or Mexico and a Request for Panel Review of a final determination made under subsection 43(1) of that Act with respect to those goods is filed, or

(b) a panel is established to review a final determination made under section 705(a) or 735(a) of the *Tariff Act of 1930*, as amended, with respect to particular goods of Canada or Mexico and a Request for Panel Review of a final determination made under section 705(b) or 735(b) of that Act with respect to those goods is filed,

within 10 days after that Request is filed, a participant in the former panel review, the investigating authority in the latter panel review or an interested person listed in the service list of the latter panel review may file a motion in the former panel review requesting that both final determinations be reviewed jointly by one panel.

(2) Any participant in the former panel review, the investigating authority in the latter panel review or an interested person listed in the service list of the latter panel review who certifies an intention to become a participant in the latter panel review may, within 10 days after a motion is filed under subrule (1), file an objection to the motion, in which case the motion shall be deemed to be denied and separate panel reviews shall be held.

37.   (1) Where a panel is established to review a final determination made under paragraph 41(1)(a) of the *Special Import Measures Act*, as amended, that applies with respect to particular goods of the United States or Mexico and a Request for Panel Review of a negative final determination made under subsection 43(1) of that Act with respect to those goods is filed, the final determinations shall be reviewed jointly by one panel.

(2) Where a panel is established to review a final determination made under section 705(a) or 735(a) of the *Tariff Act of 1930*, as amended, that applies with respect to particular goods of Canada or Mexico and a Request for Panel Review of a negative final determination made under section 705(b) or 735(b) of that Act with respect to those goods is filed, the final determinations shall be reviewed jointly by one panel.

38.   (1) Subject to subrules (2) and (3), where final determinations are reviewed jointly pursuant to rule 36 or 37, the time periods fixed under these rules for the review of the final determination made under subsection 43(1) of the *Special Import Measures Act*, as amended, or section 705(b) or 735(b) of the *Tariff Act of 1930*, as amended, shall apply to the joint review, commencing with the date fixed for filing briefs pursuant to rule 57.

(2) Unless otherwise ordered by a panel as a result of a motion under subrule (3), where final determinations are reviewed jointly pursuant to rule 37, the panel shall issue its decision with respect to the final determination made under subsection 43(1) of the *Special Import Measures Act*, as amended, or section 705(b) or 735(b) of the *Tariff Act of 1930*, as amended, and where the panel remands the final determination to the investigating authority and the Determination on Remand is affirmative, the panel shall thereafter issue its decision with respect to the final determination made under paragraph 41(1)(a) of the *Special Import Measures Act*, as amended, or section 705(a) or 735(a) of the *Tariff Act of 1930*, as amended.

(3) Where the final determinations are reviewed jointly pursuant to rule 36 or 37, any participant may, unilaterally or with the consent of the other participants, request by motion that time periods, other than the time periods referred to in subrule (1), be fixed for the filing of pleadings, oral proceedings, decisions and other matters.

(4) A Notice of Motion pursuant to subrule (3) shall be filed no later than 10 days after the date fixed for filing Notices of Appearance in the review of the final determination made under subsection 43(1) of the *Special Import Measures Act*, as amended, or section 705(b) or 735(b) of the *Tariff Act of 1930*, as amended.

(5) Unless otherwise ordered by a panel, where the panel has not issued a ruling on a motion filed pursuant to subrule (3) within 30 days after the filing of the Notice of Motion, the motion shall be deemed denied.

Complaint

39.   (1) Subject to subrule (3), any interested person who intends to make allegations of errors of fact or law, including challenges to the jurisdiction of the investigating authority, with respect to a final determination, shall file with the responsible Secretariat, within 30 days after the filing of a first Request for Panel Review of the final determination, a Complaint, together with proof of service on the investigating authority and on all persons listed on the service list.

(2) Every Complaint referred to in subrule (1) shall contain the following information (model form provided in the Schedule):

(a) the information set out in subrule 55(1);

(b) the precise nature of the Complaint, including the applicable standard of review and the allegations of errors of fact or law, including challenges to the jurisdiction of the investigating authority;

(c) a statement describing the interested person's entitlement to file a Complaint under this rule; and

(d) where the final determination was made in Canada, a statement as to whether the complainant

(i) intends to use English or French in pleadings and oral proceedings before the panel, and

(ii) requests simultaneous translation of any oral proceedings.

(3) Only an interested person who would otherwise be entitled to commence proceedings for judicial review of the final determination may file a Complaint.

(4) Subject to subrule (5), an amended Complaint shall be filed no later than 5 days before the expiration of the time period for filing a Notice of Appearance pursuant to rule 40.

(5) An amended Complaint may, with leave of the panel, be filed after the time limit set out in subrule (4) but no later than 20 days

before the expiration of the time period for filing briefs pursuant to subrule 57(1).

(6) Leave to file an amended Complaint may be requested of the panel by the filing of a Notice of Motion for leave to file an amended Complaint accompanied by the proposed amended Complaint.

(7) Where the panel does not grant a motion referred to in subrule (6) within the time period for filing briefs pursuant to subrule 57(1), the motion shall be deemed to be denied.

Notice of Appearance

40.   (1) Within 45 days after the filing of a first Request for Panel Review of a final determination, the investigating authority and any other interested person who proposes to participate in the panel review and who has not filed a Complaint in the panel review shall file with the responsible Secretariat a Notice of Appearance containing the following information (model form provided in the Schedule):

(a) the information set out in subrule 55(1);

(b) a statement as to the basis for the person's claim of entitlement to file a Notice of Appearance under this rule;

(c) in the case of a Notice of Appearance filed by the investigating authority, any admissions with respect to the allegations set out in the Complaints;

(d) a statement as to whether appearance is made

(i) in support of some or all of the allegations set out in a Complaint under subrule 39(2)(b),

(ii) in opposition to some or all of the allegations set out in a Complaint under subrule 39(2)(b), or

(iii) in support of some of the allegations set out in a Complaint under subrule 39(2)(b) and in opposition to some of the allegations set out in a Complaint under subrule 39(2)(b); and

(e) where the final determination was made in Canada, a statement as to whether the person filing the Notice of Appearance

(i) intends to use English or French in pleadings and oral proceedings before the panel, and

(ii) requests simultaneous translation of any oral proceedings.

(2) Any complainant who intends to appear in opposition to allegations set out in a Complaint under subrule 39(2)(b) shall file a Notice of Appearance containing the statements referred to in subrules (1)(b) and (1)(d)(ii) or (iii).

Record for Review

41.   (1) The investigating authority whose final determination is under review shall, within 15 days after the expiration of the time period

fixed for filing a Notice of Appearance, file with the responsible Secretariat

> (a) nine copies of the final determination, including reasons for the final determination;

> (b) two copies of an Index comprised of a descriptive list of all items contained in the administrative record, together with proof of service of the Index on all participants; and

> (c) subject to subrules (3), (4) and (5), two copies of the administrative record.

(2) An Index referred to in subrule (1) shall, where applicable, identify those items that contain proprietary information, privileged information or government information by a statement to that effect.

(3) Where a document containing proprietary information is filed, it shall be filed under seal in accordance with rule4.

(4) No privileged information shall be filed with the responsible Secretariat unless the investigating authority waives the privilege and voluntarily files the information or the information is filed pursuant to an order of a panel.

(5) No government information shall be filed with the responsible Secretariat unless the investigating authority, after having reviewed the government information and, where applicable, after having pursued appropriate review procedures, determines that the information may be disclosed.

PART III
PANELS
Announcement of Panel

42.   On the completion of the selection of a panel, the responsible Secretary shall notify the participants and the other involved Secretary of the names of the panelists.

Violation of Code of Conduct

43.   Where a participant believes that a panelist or an assistant to a panelist is in violation of the Code of Conduct, the participant shall forthwith notify the responsible Secretary in writing of the alleged violation. The responsible Secretary shall promptly notify the other involved Secretary and the involved Parties of the allegations.

PART IV
PROPRIETARY INFORMATION AND PRIVILEGED INFORMATION
Filing or Service under Seal

44.   (1) Where, under these rules, a document containing proprietary information or privileged information is required to be filed under

seal with the Secretariat or is required to be served under seal, the document shall be filed or served in accordance with this rule and, where the document is a pleading, in accordance with rule 56.

(2) A document filed or served under seal shall be

(a) bound separately from all other documents;

(b) clearly marked

(i) with respect to a panel review of a final determination made in Canada,

(A) in the case of a document containing proprietary information, "Proprietary", "Confidential", "De nature exclusive" or "Confidentiel", and

(B) in the case of a document containing privileged information, "Privileged" or 'Protégé",

(ii) with respect to a panel review of a final determination made in Mexico,

(A) in the case of a document containing proprietary information, "Confidencial", and

(B) in the case of a document containing privileged information, "Privilegiada", and

(iii) with respect to a panel review of a final determination made in the United States,

(A) in the case of a document containing proprietary information, "Proprietary", and

(B) in the case of a document containing privileged information, "Privileged" ; and

(c) contained in an opaque inner wrapper and an opaque outer wrapper.

(3) An inner wrapper referred to in subrule (2)(c) shall indicate

(a) that proprietary information or privileged information is enclosed, as the case may be; and

(b) the Secretariat file number of the panel review.

45.   Filing or service of proprietary information or privileged information with the Secretariat does not constitute a waiver of the designation of the information as proprietary information or privileged information.

Proprietary Information Access Orders

46.   (1) A counsel of record, or a professional retained by, or under the control or direction of, a counsel of record, who wishes disclosure of proprietary information in a panel review shall file a Proprietary Information Access Application with respect to the proprietary information as follows:

(a) with the responsible Secretariat, four copies; and

(b) with the investigating authority, one original and any additional copies that the investigating authority requires.

(2) A Proprietary Information Access Application referred to in subrule (1) shall be served

(a) where the Proprietary Information Access Application is filed before the expiration of the time period fixed for filing a Notice of Appearance in the panel review, on the persons listed in the service list; and

(b) in any other case, on all participants other than the investigating authority, in accordance with subrule 24(1).

47. (1) Every panelist, assistant to a panelist, court reporter, interpreter and translator shall, before taking up duties in a panel review, provide to the responsible Secretary a Proprietary Information Access Application.

(2) A panelist, assistant to a panelist, court reporter, interpreter or translator who amends or modifies a Proprietary Information Access Application shall provide the responsible Secretariat with a copy of the amendment or modification.

(3) Where the investigating authority receives, pursuant to subrule 14(1), a Proprietary Information Access Application or an amendment or modification thereto, the investigating authority shall issue a Proprietary Information Access Order, amendment or modification accordingly.

48. The investigating authority shall, within 30 days after a Proprietary Information Access Application is filed in accordance with subrule 46(1), serve on the person who filed the Proprietary Information Access Application

(a) a Proprietary Information Access Order; or

(b) a notification in writing setting out the reasons why a Proprietary Information Access Order is not issued.

49. (1) Where

(a) an investigating authority refuses to issue a Proprietary Information Access Order to a counsel of record or to a professional retained by, or under the control or direction of, a counsel of record, or

(b) an investigating authority issues a Proprietary Information Access Order with terms unacceptable to the counsel of record,

the counsel of record may file with the responsible Secretariat a Notice of Motion requesting that the panel review the decision of the investigating authority.

(2) Where, after consideration of any response made by the investigating authority referred to in subrule (1), the panel decides that a Proprietary Information Access Order should be issued or

that the terms of a Proprietary Information Access Order should be modified or amended, the panel shall so notify counsel for the investigating authority.

(3) Where the final determination was made in the United States and the investigating authority fails to comply with the notification referred to in subrule (2), the panel may issue such orders as are just in the circumstances, including an order refusing to permit the investigating authority to make certain arguments in support of its case or striking certain arguments from its pleadings.

50.   (1) Where a Proprietary Information Access Order is issued to a person in a panel review, the person shall file with the responsible Secretariat a copy of the Proprietary Information Access Order.

(2) Where a Proprietary Information Access Order is revoked, amended or modified by the investigating authority, the investigating authority shall provide to the responsible Secretariat and to all participants a copy of the Notice of Revocation, amendment or modification.

51.   Where a Proprietary Information Access Order is issued to a person, the person is entitled

(a) to access to the document; and

(b) where the person is a counsel of record, to a copy of the document containing the proprietary information, on payment of an appropriate fee, and to service of pleadings containing the proprietary information.

Privileged Information

52.   (1) A Notice of Motion for disclosure of a document in the administrative record identified as containing privileged information shall set out

(a) the reasons why disclosure of the document is necessary to the case of the participant filing the Notice of Motion; and

(b) a statement of any point of law or legal authority relied on, together with a concise argument in support of disclosure.

(2) Within 10 days after a Notice of Motion referred to in subrule (1) is filed, the investigating authority shall, if it intends to respond, file the following in response:

(a) an affidavit of an official of the investigating authority stating that, since the filing of the Notice of Motion, the official has examined the document and has determined that disclosure of the document would constitute disclosure of privileged information; and

(b) a statement of any point of law or legal authority relied on, together with a concise argument in support of non-disclosure.

(3) After having reviewed the Notice of Motion referred to in subrule (1) and any response filed under subrule (2), the panel may order

(a) that the document shall not be disclosed; or

(b) that the investigating authority file two copies of the document under seal with the responsible Secretariat.

(4) Where the panel has issued an order pursuant to subrule (3)(b), the panel shall select two panelists, one of whom shall be a lawyer who is a citizen of the country of one involved Party and the other of whom shall be a lawyer who is a citizen of the country of the other involved Party.

(5) The two panelists selected under subrule (4) shall

(a) examine the document in camera; and

(b) communicate their decision, if any, to the panel.

(6) The decision referred to in subrule (5)(b) shall be issued as an order of the panel.

(7) Where the two panelists selected under subrule (4) fail to come to a decision, the panel shall

(a) examine the document in camera; and

(b) issue an order with respect to the disclosure of the document.

(8) Where an order referred to in subrule (6) or (7) is to the effect that the document shall not be disclosed, the responsible Secretary shall return all copies of the document to the investigating authority by service under seal.

53.   In a panel review of a final determination made in the United States, where, pursuant to rule 52, disclosure of a document is granted,

(a) the panel shall limit disclosure to

(i) persons who must have access in order to permit effective representation in the panel review,

(ii) persons, such as the Secretariat staff, court reporters, interpreters and translators, who must have access for administrative purposes in order to permit effective functioning of the panel, and

(iii) members of an Extraordinary Challenge Committee and their assistants who may need access pursuant to the NAFTA Extraordinary Challenge Committee Rules;

(b) the panel shall issue an order identifying by name and by title or position the persons who are entitled to access and shall allow for future access by new counsel of record and by members of an Extraordinary Challenge Committee and, as necessary, their assistants; and

(c) the investigating authority shall issue a Propriety Information Access Order with respect to that document in accordance with the order of the panel.

Violations of Proprietary Information Access Applications or Orders

54. Where a person alleges that the terms of a Proprietary Information Access Application or of a Proprietary Information Access Order have been violated, the panel shall refer the allegations to the investigating authority for investigation and, where applicable, the imposition of sanctions in accordance with section 77.034 of the *Special Import Measures Act*, as amended, section 777(f) of the *Tariff Act of 1930*, as amended, or article 93 of the *Ley de Comercio Exterior*.

PART V

WRITTEN PROCEEDINGS

Form and Content of Pleadings

55. (1) Every pleading filed in a panel review shall contain the following information:

(a) the title of, and any Secretariat file number assigned for, the panel review;

(b) a brief descriptive title of the pleading;

(c) the name of the Party, investigating authority or interested person filing the document;

(d) the name of counsel of record for the Party, investigating authority or interested person;

(e) the service address, as defined in rule 3; and

(f) the telephone number of the counsel of record referred to in subrule (d) or, where an interested person is not represented by counsel, the telephone number of the interested person.

(2) Every pleading filed in a panel review shall be on paper 8 1/2 11 inches (216 millimetres by 279 millimetres) in size. The text of the pleading shall be printed, typewritten or reproduced legibly on one side only with a margin of approximately 1 1/2 inches (40 millimetres) on the left-hand side with double spacing between each line of text, except for quotations of more than 50 words, which shall be indented and single-spaced. Footnotes, titles, schedules, tables, graphs and columns of figures shall be presented in a readable form. Briefs and appendices shall be securely bound along the left-hand margin.

(3) Every pleading filed on behalf of a participant in a panel review shall be signed by counsel for the participant or, where the participant is not represented by counsel, by the participant.

56.   (1) Where a participant files a pleading that contains proprietary information, the participant shall file two sets of the pleading in the following manner:

    (a) one set containing the proprietary information shall be filed under seal and

        (i) with respect to a panel review of a final determination made in Canada, shall be labelled "Proprietary", "Confidential", "Confidentiel" or "De nature exclusive", with the top of each page that contains proprietary information marked with the word "Proprietary", "Confidential", "Confidentiel" or "De nature exclusive" and with the proprietary information enclosed in brackets,

        (ii) with respect to a panel review of a final determination made in Mexico, shall be labelled "Confidencial", with the top of each page that contains proprietary information marked with the word "Confidencial" and with the proprietary information enclosed in brackets, and

        (iii) with respect to a panel review of a final determination made in the United States, shall be labelled "Proprietary", with the top of each page that contains proprietary information marked with the word "Proprietary" and with the proprietary information enclosed in brackets; and

    (b) no later than one day following the day on which the set of pleadings referred to in subrule (a) is filed, another set not containing proprietary information shall be filed and

        (i) with respect to a panel review of a final determination made in Canada, shall be labelled "Non-Proprietary", "Non-Confidential", "Non confidentiel" or "De nature non exclusive",

        (ii) with respect to a panel review of a final determination made in Mexico, shall be labelled "Noconfidencial", and

        (iii) with respect to a panel review of a final determination made in the United States, shall be labelled "Non-Proprietary",

with each page from which proprietary information has been deleted marked to indicate the location from which the proprietary information was deleted.

(2) Where a participant files a pleading that contains privileged information, the participant shall file two sets of the pleading in the following manner:

    (a) one set containing the privileged information shall be filed under seal and

        (i) with respect to a panel review of a final determination made in Canada, shall be labelled "Privileged" or

"Protégé", with the top of each page that contains privileged information marked with the word "Privileged" or "Protégé" and with the privileged information enclosed in brackets,

(ii) with respect to a panel review of a final determination made in Mexico, shall be labelled "Privilegiada", with the top of each page that contains privileged information marked with the word "Privilegiada", and with the privileged information enclosed in brackets, and

(iii) with respect to a panel review of a final determination made in the United States, shall be labelled "Privileged", with the top of each page that contains privileged information marked with the word "Privileged" and with the privileged information enclosed in brackets; and

(b) no later than one day following the day on which the set of pleadings referred to in subrule (a) is filed, another set not containing privileged information shall be filed and

(i) with respect to a panel review of a final determination made in Canada, shall be labelled "NonPrivileged" or "Non protégé",

(ii) with respect to a panel review of a final determination made in Mexico, shall be labelled "No-privilegiada", and

(iii) with respect to a panel review of a final determination made in the United States, shall be labelled "Non-Privileged",

with each page from which privileged information has been deleted marked to indicate the location from which the privileged information was deleted.

Filing of Briefs

57.   (1) Subject to subrule 38(1), every participant who has filed a Complaint under rule 39 or a Notice of Appearance with a statement under subrule 40(1)(d)(i) or (iii) shall file a brief, setting forth grounds and arguments supporting allegations of the Complaint no later than 60 days after the expiration of the time period fixed, under subrule 41(1), for filing the administrative record.

(2) Every participant who has filed a Notice of Appearance with a statement under subrule 40(1)(d)(ii) or (iii) shall file a brief setting forth grounds and arguments opposing allegations of a Complaint no later than 60 days after the expiration of the time period for filing of briefs referred to in subrule (1).

(3) Every participant who has filed a brief pursuant to subrule (1) may file a brief replying to the grounds and arguments set forth in the briefs filed pursuant to subrule (2) no later than 15 days after

the expiration of the time period for filing of briefs referred to in subrule (2). Reply briefs shall be limited to rebuttal of matters raised in the briefs filed pursuant to subrule (2).

(4) An appendix containing authorities cited in all briefs filed under any of subrules (1) to (3) shall be filed with the responsible Secretariat within 10 days after the last day on which a brief under subrule (3) may be filed.

(5) Any number of participants may join in a single brief and any participant may adopt by reference any part of the brief of another participant.

(6) A participant may file a brief without appearing to present oral argument.

(7) Where a panel review of a final determination made by an investigating authority of United States with respect to certain goods involves issues that may relate to the final determination of the other investigating authority with respect to those goods, the latter investigating authority may file an amicus curiae brief in the panel review in accordance with subrule (2).

Failure to File Briefs

58.   (1) In respect of a panel review of a final determination made in the United States or Canada, where a participant fails to file a brief within the time period fixed and no motion pursuant to rule 20 is pending, on a motion of another participant, the panel may order that the participant who fails to file a brief is not entitled

(a) to present oral argument;

(b) to service of any further pleadings, orders or decisions in the panel review; or

(c) to further notice of the proceedings in the panel review.

(2) Where

(a) no brief is filed by any complainant or by any participant in support of any of the complainants within the time periods established pursuant to these rules, and

(b) no motion pursuant to rule 20 is pending,

the panel may, on its own motion or pursuant to the motion of a participant, issue an order to show cause why the panel review should not be dismissed.

(3) If, pursuant to an order under subrule (2), good cause is not shown, the panel shall issue an order dismissing the panel review.

(4) Where no brief is filed by an investigating authority, or by an interested person in support of the investigating authority, within the time period fixed in subrule 57(2), a panel may issue a decision referred to in rule 72.

Content of Briefs and Appendices

59. (1) Every brief filed pursuant to subrule 57(1) or (2) shall contain information, in the following order, divided into five parts:

Part I:

> (a) A table of contents; and

> (b) A table of authorities cited:

The table of authorities shall contain references to all treaties, statutes and regulations cited, any cases primarily relied on in the briefs, set out alphabetically, and all other documents referred to except documents from the administrative record. The table of authorities shall refer to the page(s) of the brief where each authority is cited and mark, with an asterisk in the margin, those authorities primarily relied on.

Part II: A statement of the case:

> (a) in the brief of a complainant or of a participant filing a brief pursuant to subrule 57(1), this Part shall contain a concise statement of the relevant facts;

> (b) in the brief of an investigating authority or of a participant filing a brief pursuant to subrule 57(2), this Part shall contain a concise statement of the position of the investigating authority or the participant with respect to the statement of facts set out in the briefs referred to in paragraph (a), including a concise statement of other facts relevant to its case; and

> (c) in all briefs, references to evidence in the administrative record shall be made by page and, where practicable, by line.

Part III: A statement of the issues:

> (a) in the brief of a complainant or of a participant filing a brief pursuant to subrule 57(1), this Part shall contain a concise statement of the issues; and

> (b) in the brief of an investigating authority or of a participant filing a brief pursuant to subrule 57(2), this Part shall contain a concise statement of the position of the investigating authority or the participant with respect to each issue relevant to its case.

Part IV: Argument:

This Part shall consist of the argument setting out concisely the points of law relating to the issues, with applicable citations to authorities and the administrative record.

Part V: Relief:

This part shall consist of a concise statement precisely identifying the relief requested.

(2) Paragraphs in Parts I to V of a brief may be numbered consecutively.

(3) A reply brief filed pursuant to rule 57(3) shall include a table of contents and a table of authorities, indicating those principally relied upon in the argument.

Appendix to the Briefs

60.   (1) Authorities referred to in the briefs shall be included in an appendix, which shall be organized as follows: a table of contents, copies of all treaty and statutory references, references to regulations, cases primarily relied on in the briefs, set out alphabetically, and all other documents referred to in the briefs except documents from the administrative record.

(2) The appendix required under subrule 57(4) shall be compiled by a participant who filed a brief under subrule 57(1) and who was so designated by all the participants who filed a brief. Each participant who filed a brief under subrule 57(2) shall provide the designated participant with a copy of each authority on which it primarily relied in its brief that was not primarily relied on in any other brief filed under subrule 57(1). Each participant who filed a brief under subrule 57(3) shall provide the designated participant with a copy of each authority on which it primarily relied in its brief that was not primarily relied on in briefs filed pursuant to subrule 57(1) or (2).

(3) The costs for compiling the appendix shall be borne equally by all participants who file briefs.

Motions

61.   (1) A motion shall be made by Notice of Motion in writing (model form provided in the Schedule) unless the circumstances make it unnecessary or impracticable.

(2) Every Notice of Motion, and any affidavit in support thereof, shall be accompanied by a proposed order of the panel (model form provided in the Schedule) and shall be filed with the responsible Secretariat, together with proof of service on all participants.

(3) Every Notice of Motion shall contain the following information:

(a) the title of the panel review, the Secretariat file number for that panel review and a brief descriptive title indicating the purpose of the motion;

(b) a statement of the precise relief requested;

(c) a statement of the grounds to be argued, including a reference to any rule, point of law or legal authority to be relied on, together with a concise argument in support of the motion; and

(d) where necessary, references to evidence in the administrative record identified by page and, where practicable, by line.

(4) The pendency of any motion in a panel review shall not alter any time period fixed in these rules or by an order or decision of the panel.

(5) A Notice of Motion to which all participants consent shall be entitled a Consent Motion.

62.   Subject to subrules 20(2) and 76(5), unless the panel otherwise orders, a participant may file a response to a Notice of Motion within 10 days after the Notice of Motion is filed.

63.   (1) A panel may dispose of a motion based upon the pleadings filed pertaining to the motion.

(2) The panel may hear oral argument or, subject to subrule 26(b), direct that a motion be heard by means of a telephone conference call with the participants.

(3) A panel may deny a motion before responses to the Notice of Motion have been filed.

64.   Where a panel chooses to hear oral argument or, pursuant to subrule 63(2), directs that a motion be heard by means of a telephone conference call with the participants, the responsible Secretary shall, at the direction of the chairperson, fix a date, time and place for the hearing of the motion and shall notify all participants of the same.

PART VI
ORAL PROCEEDINGS
Location

65.   Oral proceedings in a panel review shall take place at the office of the responsible Secretariat or at such other location as the responsible Secretary may arrange.

Pre-hearing Conference

66.   (1) A panel may hold a pre-hearing conference, in which case the responsible Secretary shall give notice of the conference to all participants.

(2) A participant may request that the panel hold a pre-hearing conference by filing with the responsible Secretariat a written request setting out the matters that the participant proposes to raise at the conference.

(3) The purpose of a pre-hearing conference shall be to facilitate the expeditious advancement of the panel review by addressing such matters as

(a) the clarification and simplification of the issues;

(b) the procedure to be followed at the hearing of oral argument; and

(c) any outstanding motions.

(4) Subject to subrule 26(b), a pre-hearing conference may be conducted by means of a telephone conference call.

(5) Following a pre-hearing conference, the panel shall promptly issue an order setting out its rulings with respect to the matters considered at the conference.

Oral Argument

67. (1) A panel shall commence the hearing of oral argument no later than 30 days after the expiration of the time period fixed under subrule 57(3) for filing reply briefs. At the direction of the panel, the responsible Secretary shall notify all participants of the date, time and place for the oral argument.

(2) Oral argument shall be subject to the time constraints set by the panel and shall, unless the panel otherwise orders, be presented in the following order:

(a) the complainants and any participant who filed a brief in support of the allegations set out in a Complaint or partly in support of the allegations set out in a Complaint and partly in opposition to the allegations set out in a Complaint;

(b) the investigating authority and any participant who filed a brief in opposition to the allegations set out in a Complaint, other than a participant referred to in subrule (a); and

(c) argument in reply, at the discretion of the panel.

(3) If a participant fails to appear at oral argument, the panel may hear argument on behalf of the participants who are present. If no participant appears, the panel may decide the case on the basis of briefs.

(4) Oral argument on behalf of a participant on a motion or at a hearing shall be conducted by the counsel of record for that participant or, where the participant is an individual appearing pro se, by the participant.

(5) Oral argument shall be limited to the issues in dispute.

Subsequent Authorities

68. (1) A participant who has filed a brief may bring to the attention of the panel,

(a) at any time before the conclusion of oral argument, an authority that is relevant to the panel review;

(b) at any time after the conclusion of oral argument and before the panel has issued its decision,

(i) an authority that was reported subsequent to the conclusion of oral argument, or

(ii) with the leave of the panel, an authority that is relevant to the panel review and that came to the attention of counsel of record after the conclusion of oral argument,

by filing with the responsible Secretariat a written request, setting out the citation of the decision or judgment, the page reference of the brief of the participant to which the decision or judgment relates and a concise statement, of no more than one page in length, of the relevance of the decision or judgment.

(2) A request referred to in subrule (1) shall be filed as soon as possible after the issuance of the decision or judgment by the court.

(3) Where a request referred to in subrule (1) is filed with the responsible Secretariat, any other participant may, within five days after the date on which the request was filed, file a concise statement, of no more than one page in length, in response.

Oral Proceedings in Camera

69.   During that part of oral proceedings in which proprietary information or privileged information is presented, a panel shall not permit any person other than the following persons to be present:

(a) the person presenting the proprietary information or privileged information;

(b) a person who has been granted access to the proprietary information or privileged information under a Proprietary Information Access Order or an order of the panel;

(c) in the case of privileged information, a person as to whom the confidentiality of the privileged information has been waived; and

(d) officials of, and counsel for, the investigating authority.

PART VII
DECISIONS AND COMPLETIONS OF PANEL REVIEWS
Orders, Decisions and Terminations

70.   The responsible Secretary shall cause notice of every decision of a panel issued pursuant to rule 72 to be published in the official publications of the involved Parties.

71.   (1) Where a Notice of Motion requesting dismissal of a panel review is filed by a participant, the panel may issue an order dismissing the panel review.

(2) Where a Notice of Motion requesting termination of a panel review is filed by a participant and is consented to by all the participants, and an affidavit to that effect is filed, or where all participants file Notices of Motion requesting termination, the panel review is terminated and, if a panel has been appointed, the panelists are discharged.

72. A panel shall issue a written decision with reasons, together with any dissenting or concurring opinions of the panelists, in accordance with Article 1904.8 of the Agreement. The decision will normally be released by noon on the date of issuance.

Panel Review of Action on Remand

73. (1) An investigating authority shall give notice of the action taken pursuant to a remand of the panel by filing with the responsible Secretariat a Determination on Remand within the time specified by the panel.

(2) If, on remand, the investigating authority has supplemented the administrative record,

(a) the investigating authority shall file with the responsible Secretariat an Index listing each item in the supplementary remand record, and a copy of each non-privileged item listed in that Index, within five days after the date on which the investigating authority filed the Determination on Remand with the panel;

(b) any participant who intends to challenge the Determination on Remand shall file a written submission with respect to the Determination on Remand within 20 days after the date on which the investigating authority filed the Index and supplementary remand record; and

(c) any response to the written submissions referred to in subrule (b) shall be filed by the investigating authority, and by any participant supporting the investigating authority, within 20 days after the last day on which written submissions in opposition to the Determination on Remand may be filed.

(3) If, on remand, the investigating authority has not supplemented the record,

(a) any participant who intends to challenge the Determination on Remand shall file a written submission within 20 days after the date on which the investigating authority filed the Determination on Remand with the panel; and

(b) any response to the written submissions referred to in subrule (a) shall be filed by the investigating authority, and by any participant filing in support of the investigating authority, within 20 days after the last day on which such written submissions may be filed.

(4) In the case of a panel review of a final determination made in Mexico, where a participant who fails to file a brief under rule 57 files a written submission pursuant to subrule (2) or (3), the submission shall be disregarded by the panel.

(5) If no written submissions are filed under subrule (2)(b) or (3)(a) within the time periods established by these rules, and if no motion pursuant to rule 20 is pending, the panel shall, within 10

days after the later of the due date for such written submissions and the date of the denial of a motion pursuant to rule 20, issue an order affirming the investigating authority's Determination on Remand.

(6) Where a Determination on Remand is challenged, the panel shall issue a written decision pursuant to rule 72, either affirming the Determination on Remand or remanding it to the investigating authority, no later than 90 days after the Determination on Remand is filed.

74.   In setting the date by which a Determination on Remand shall be due from the investigating authority, the panel shall take into account, among other factors,

   (a) the date that any Determination on Remand with respect to the same goods is due from the other investigating authority; and

   (b) the effect the Determination on Remand from the other investigating authority might have on the deliberations of the investigating authority with respect to the making of a final Determination on Remand.

Re-examination of Orders and Decisions

75.   A clerical error in an order or decision of a panel, or an error in an order or decision of a panel arising from any accidental oversight, inaccuracy or omission, may be corrected by the panel at any time during the panel review.

76.   (1) A participant may, within 10 days after a panel issues its decision, file a Notice of Motion requesting that the panel re-examine its decision for the purpose of correcting an accidental oversight, inaccuracy or omission, which shall set

   (a) the oversight, inaccuracy or omission with respect to which the request is made;

   (b) the relief requested; and

   (c) if ascertainable, a statement as to whether other participants consent to the motion.

(2) The grounds for a motion referred to in subrule (1) shall be limited to one or both of the following grounds:

   (a) that the decision does not accord with the reasons therefor; or

   (b) that some matter has been accidentally overlooked, stated inaccurately or omitted by the panel.

(3) No Notice of Motion referred to in subrule (1) shall set out any argument already made in the panel review.

(4) There shall be no oral argument in support of a motion referred to in subrule (1).

(5) Except as the panel may otherwise order under subrule (6)(b), no participant shall file a response to a Notice of Motion filed pursuant to subrule (1).

(6) Within seven days after the filing of a Notice of Motion under subrule (1), the panel shall

(a) issue a decision ruling on the motion; or

(b) issue an order identifying further action to be taken concerning the motion.

(7) A decision or order under subrule (6) may be made with the concurrence of any three panelists.

PART VIII
COMPLETION OF PANEL REVIEW

77. (1) Subject to subrule (2), when a panel issues:

(a) an order dismissing a panel review under subrule 58(3) or 71(1),

(b) a decision under rule 72 or subrule 73(6) that is the final action in the panel review, or

(c) an order under subrule 73(5),

the panel shall direct the responsible Secretary to issue a Notice of Final Panel Action (model form provided in the Schedule) on the eleventh day thereafter.

(2) Where a motion is filed pursuant to subrule 76(1) regarding a decision referred to in subrule (1)(b), the responsible Secretary shall issue the Notice of Final Panel Action on the day on which the panel

(a) issues a ruling finally disposing of the motion; or

(b) directs the responsible Secretary to issue the Notice of Final Panel Action, the issuance of which shall constitute a denial of the motion.

78. If no Request for an Extraordinary Challenge Committee is filed, the responsible Secretary shall publish a Notice of Completion of Panel Review in the official publications of the involved Parties, effective

(a) on the day on which a panel is terminated pursuant to subrule 71(2); or

(b) in any other case, on the 31st day following the date on which the responsible Secretary issues a Notice of Final Panel Action.

79. Where a Request for an Extraordinary Challenge Committee has been filed, the responsible Secretary shall publish a Notice of Completion of Panel Review in the official publications of the involved Parties, effective on the day after the day referred to in rule 64 or subrule 65(a) of the NAFTA Extraordinary Challenge Committee Rules.

80.   Panelists are discharged from their duties on the day on which a Notice of Completion of Panel Review is effective, or on the day on which an Extraordinary Challenge Committee vacates a panel review pursuant to subrule 65(b) of the NAFTA Extraordinary Challenge Committee Rules.

Stays and Suspensions

81.   Where a panelist becomes unable to fulfil panel duties, is disqualified or dies, panel proceedings and the running of time periods shall be suspended, pending the appointment of a substitute panelist in accordance with the procedures set out in Annex 1901.2 to Chapter Nineteen of the Agreement.

82.   Where a panelist is disqualified, dies or otherwise becomes unable to fulfil panel duties, after the oral argument, the chairperson may order that the matter be reheard, on such terms as are appropriate, after selection of a substitute panelist.

83.   (1) A Party may make a request, pursuant to Article 905.11(a)(ii) of the Agreement, that an ongoing panel review be stayed by filing the request with the responsible Secretariat.

(2) A Party who files a request under subrule (1) shall forthwith give written notice of the request to the other involved Party and to the other involved Secretariat.

(3) On receipt of a request under subrule (1), the responsible Secretary shall

(a) immediately give written notice of the stay of the panel review to all participants in the panel review; and

(b) publish a notice of the stay of the panel review in the official publications of the involved Parties.

84.   On receipt of a report containing an affirmative finding with respect to a ground specified in Article 1905.1 of the Agreement, the responsible Secretary for panel reviews referred to in Article 1905.11(a)(i) of the Agreement shall

(a) immediately give notice in writing to all participants in those reviews; and

(b) publish a notice of the affirmative finding in the official publications of the involved Parties.

85.   (1) A Party who intends to suspend the operation of Article 1904 of the Agreement pursuant to Article 1905.8 or 1905.9 of the Agreement shall endeavour to give written notice of that intention to the other involved Party and to the involved Secretaries at least five days prior to the suspension.

(2) On receipt of a notice under subrule (1), the involved Secretaries shall publish a notice of the suspension in the official publications of the involved Parties.

ARTICLE 1904 BINATIONAL PANEL REVIEW
pursuant to the
NORTH AMERICAN FREE TRADE AGREEMENT

IN THE MATTER OF:)
)
_____   )
)
_____   )
)
(Title of Final Determination)   )
_____   )

NOTICE OF INTENT TO COMMENCE JUDICIAL REVIEW

Pursuant to Article 1904 of the North American Free-Trade Agreement, notice is hereby served that

_____

(interested person filing notice)

intends to commence judicial review in the

_____

(name of the court)

of the final determination referenced below. The following information is provided pursuant to Rule 33 of the *NAFTA Article 1904 Panel Rules*:

1. _____
   (The name of the interested person filing this notice)

2. _____
   (The name of counsel for the interested person, if any)

3. _____

   _____

   (The service address, as defined by Rule 3 of the *NAFTA Article 1904 Panel Rules*, including facsimile number, if any)

4. _____
   (The telephone number of counsel for the interested person or the telephone number of the interested person, if not represented by counsel)

5. _____
   (The title of the final determination for which notice of intent to commence judicial review is served)

6. _____
   (The investigating authority that issued the final determination)

7. _____
   (The file number of the investigating authority)

8. a) _____
       (The citation and date of publication of the final determination in the Federal Register, Canada Gazette or Diario Oficial de la Federación); or

b) _____

(If the final determination was not published, the date notice of the final determination was received by the other Party)

Date   Signature of Counsel
(or interested person, if not represented by counsel)

ARTICLE 1904 BINATIONAL PANEL REVIEW
pursuant to the
NORTH AMERICAN FREE TRADE AGREEMENT

IN THE MATTER OF:)
)
_____)
)
_____)   Secretariat File No.
(Title of Final Determination)   )
_____)   _____

REQUEST FOR PANEL REVIEW

Pursuant to Article 1904 of the North American Free-Trade Agreement, panel review is hereby requested of the final determination referenced below. The following information is provided pursuant to Rule 34 of the *NAFTA Article 1904 Panel Rules*:

1. _____

(The name of the Party or the interested person filing this request for panel review)

2. _____

(The name of counsel for the Party or the interested person, if any)

3. _____

(The service address, as defined by Rule 3 of the *NAFTA Article 1904 Panel Rules*, including facsimile number, if any)

4. _____

(The telephone number of counsel for the Party or the interested person or the telephone number of the interested person, if not represented by counsel)

5. _____

(The title of the final determination for which panel review is requested)

6. _____

(The investigating authority that issued the final determination)

7. _____

(The file number of the investigating authority)

8. a) _____

(The citation and date of publication of the final determination in the Federal Register, Canada Gazette or Diario Oficial de la Federación); or

b) _____

(If the final determination was not published, the date notice of the final determination was received by the other Party)

9. Yes ___   No ___   Non-Applicable ___
(Where a Notice of Intent to Commence Judicial Review has been served, is the sole reason for requesting review of the final determination to require review by a panel?)

10. The Service List, as defined by Rule 3 of the *NAFTA Article 1904 Panel Rules*, is attached.

_____   _____
Date   Signature of Counsel
                                 (or interested person, if not repre-
                                 sented by counsel)

ARTICLE 1904 BINATIONAL PANEL REVIEW
pursuant to the
NORTH AMERICAN FREE TRADE AGREEMENT

_____

IN THE MATTER OF:)
)
_____   )
)
_____   )   Secretariat File No.
(Title of Final Determination)   )
_____   )   _____

COMPLAINT

1. _____

(The name of the interested person filing the complaint)

2. _____

(The name of counsel for the interested person, if any)

3. _____
   _____
   _____

(The service address, as defined by Rule 3 of the *NAFTA Article 1904 Panel Rules*, including facsimile number, if any)

4. _____

(The telephone number of counsel for the interested person or telephone number of the interested person, if not represented by counsel)

5. Statement of the Precise Nature of the Complaint (See Rule 39 of the *NAFTA Article 1904 Panel Rules*)

   A. The Applicable Standard of Review

   B. Allegations of Errors of Fact or Law

   C. Challenges to the Jurisdiction of the Investigating Authority

6. Statement of the Interested Person's Entitlement to File a Complaint under Rule 39 of the *NAFTA Article 1904 Panel Rules*

7. For Panel Reviews of Determinations Made in Canada:

   a) Complainant intends to use the specified language in pleadings and oral proceedings (Specify one)

      _____ English _____ French

   b) Complainant requests simultaneous translation of oral proceedings (Specify one)

      _____ English _____ French

_____

Date

_____

Signature of Counsel
(or interested person, if not represented by counsel)

ARTICLE 1904 BINATIONAL PANEL REVIEW
pursuant to the
NORTH AMERICAN FREE TRADE AGREEMENT

IN THE MATTER OF:)

_____)

_____) Secretariat File No.
(Title of Final Determination))

_____) _____

NOTICE OF APPEARANCE

1. _____

(The name of the investigating authority or the interested person filing this notice of appearance)

2. _____

(The name of counsel for the investigating authority or the interested person, if any)

3. _____

(The service address, as defined by Rule 3 of the *NAFTA Article 1904 Panel Rules*, including facsimile number, if any)

4. _____

(The telephone number of counsel for the investigating authority or the interested person or the telephone number of the interested person, if not represented by counsel)

5. This Notice of Appearance is made:

  ___ in support of some or all of the allegations set out in a Complaint;

  ___ in opposition to some or all of the allegations set out in a Complaint; or

  ___ in support of some of the allegations set out in a Complaint and in opposition to some of the allegations set out in a Complaint.

6. Statement as to the basis for the interested person's entitlement to file a Notice of Appearance under rule 40 of the *NAFTA Article 1904 Panel Rules*

7. For Notices of Appearance Filed by the Investigating Authority

  Statement by the Investigating Authority regarding any admissions with respect to the allegations set out in the Complaints

8. For Panel Reviews of Determinations Made in Canada:

  a) I intend to use the specified language in pleadings and oral proceedings (Specify one)

  _____ English _____ French

  b) I request simultaneous translation of oral proceedings (Specify one)

  _____ Yes _____ No

_____   _____

Date   Signature of Counsel
                               (or interested person, if not repre-
                               sented by counsel)

ARTICLE 1904 BINATIONAL PANEL REVIEW
pursuant to the
NORTH AMERICAN FREE TRADE AGREEMENT

_____

IN THE MATTER OF:)
)
_____   )
)
_____   ) Secretariat File No.
) _____
(Title of Final Determination))
_____   )

NOTICE OF MOTION

(descriptive title indicating the purpose of the motion)

1. _____

(The name of the investigating authority or the interested person filing this notice of motion)

2. _____

(The name of counsel for the investigating authority or the interested person, if any)

3. _____

_____

(The service address, as defined by Rule 3 of the *NAFTA Article 1904 Panel Rules*, including facsimile number, if any)

4. _____

(The telephone number of the counsel for the investigating authority or the interested person or the telephone number of the interested person, if not represented by counsel)

5. Statement of the precise relief requested

6. Statement of the grounds to be argued, including references to any rule, point of law, or legal authority to be relied on

7. Arguments in support of the motion, including references to evidence in the administrative record by page and, where practicable, by line

8. Draft order attached (see Rule 61 and Form (6) of the *NAFTA Article 1904 Panel Rules*)

_____   _____

Date   Signature of Counsel
                                         (or interested person, if not represented by counsel)

DOCUMENT 8

RULES OF PROCEDURE FOR ARTICLE 1904 EXTRAORDINARY CHALLENGE COMMITTEES

Preamble

The Parties,

Having regard to Chapter Nineteen of the North American Free Trade Agreement between Canada, the United Mexican States and the United States of America;

Acting pursuant to paragraph 2 of Annex 1904.13 to Chapter Nineteen of the Agreement;

Adopted the Rules of Procedure, which shall come into force on the same day as the Agreement enters into force and from that day shall govern all extraordinary challenge committee proceedings conducted pursuant to Article 1904 of the Agreement.

Short Title

1. These rules may be cited as the *NAFTA Extraordinary Challenge Committee Rules.*

Statement of General Intent

2. These rules are intended to give effect to the provisions of Chapter Nineteen of the Agreement with respect to extraordinary challenges conducted pursuant to Article 1904 of the Agreement and are

470

designed to result in decisions within 90 days after the establishment of the committee. Where a procedural question arises that is not covered by these rules, a committee may adopt an appropriate procedure that is not inconsistent with the Agreement. In the event of any inconsistency between the provisions of these Rules and the Agreement, the Agreement shall prevail.

Interpretation

3.   In these rules,

"**Agreement**" means the North American Free Trade Agreement; (*Accord*) (*Tratado*)

"**Code of Conduct**" means the code of conduct established by the Parties pursuant to Article 1909 of the Agreement; (*Code de conduite*) (*Código de Conducta*)

"**committee**" means an extraordinary challenge committee established pursuant to Annex 1904.13 to Chapter Nineteen of the Agreement; (*comité*) (*comite*)

"**counsel**" means

(a) with respect to an extraordinary challenge of a panel review of a final determination made in Canada, a person entitled to appear as counsel before the Federal Court of Canada,

(b) with respect to an extraordinary challenge of a panel review of a final determination made in Mexico, a person entitled to appear as counsel before the Tribunal Fiscal de la Federación, and

(c) with respect to an extraordinary challenge of a panel review of a final determination made in the United States, a person entitled to appear as counsel before a federal court in the United States; (avocat) (representante)

"**counsel of record**" means a counsel referred to in subrule 12(1); (*avocat au dossier*) (*representante legal acreditado*)

"**Deputy Minister**" means the Deputy Minister of National Revenue for Customs and Excise, or the successor thereto, and includes any person authorized to perform a power, duty or function of the Deputy Minister under the Special Import Measures Act, as amended; (*sous-ministre*) (*Deputy Minister*)

"**final determination**" means, in the case of Canada, a definitive decision within the meaning of subsection 77.01(1) of the Special Import Measures Act, as amended; (*décision définitive*) (*resolución definitiva*)

"**investigating authority**" means the competent investigating authority that issued the final determination that was the subject of the panel review to which an extraordinary challenge relates and includes, in respect of the issuance, amendment, modification or revocation of a Proprietary Information Access Order, any person authorized by the investigating authority; (*autorité chargée de l'enquête*) (*autoridad investigadora*) "**involved Secretariat**" means the section of the Secretariat located in the country of an involved Party; (*Secrétariat en cause*) (*Secretariado implicado*)

"**legal holiday**" means

(a) with respect to the Canadian Section of the Secretariat, every Saturday and Sunday, New Year's Day (January 1), Good Friday, Easter Monday, Victoria Day, Canada Day (July 1), Labour Day (first Monday in September), Thanksgiving Day (second Monday in October), Remembrance Day (November 11), Christmas Day (December 25), Boxing Day (December 26), any other day fixed as a statutory holiday by the Government of Canada or by the province in which the Section is located and any day on which the offices of the Canadian Section of the Secretariat are officially closed in whole or in part,

(b) with respect to the Mexican Section of the Secretariat, every Saturday and Sunday, New Year's Day (January 1), Constitution Day (February 5), Benito Jufirez's Birthday (March 21), Labor Day (May 1), Battle of Puebla (May 5), Independence Day (September 16), Congressional Opening Day (November 1), Revolution Day (November 20), Transmission of the Federal Executive Branch (every six years on December 1), Christmas Day (December 25), any day designated as a statutory holiday by the Federal Laws or, in the case of Ordinary Elections, by the Local Electoral Laws and any day on which the offices of the Mexican Section of the Secretariat are officially closed in whole or in part, and

(c) with respect to the United States Section of the Secretariat, every Saturday and Sunday, New Year's Day (January 1), Martin Luther King's Birthday (third Monday in January), Presidents' Day (third Monday in February), Memorial Day (last Monday in May), Independence Day (July 4), Labor Day (first Monday in September), Columbus Day (second Monday in October), Veterans' Day (November 11), Thanksgiving Day (fourth Thursday in November), Christmas Day (December 25), any other day designated as a holiday by the President or the Congress of the United States and any day on which the offices of the Government of the United States located in the District of Columbia or the offices of the United States Section of the Secretariat are officially closed in whole or in part; (jour férié) (días inhfíbiles)

"**Mexico**" means the United Mexican States; (*Mexique*)

"**official publication**" means

(a) in the case of the Government of Canada, the Canada Gazette,

(b) in the case of the Government of Mexico, the Diario Oficial de la Federación, and

(c) in the case of the Government of the United States, the Federal Register; (journal officiel) (publicación oficial) "**panel**" means a binational panel established pursuant to Annex 1901.2 to Chapter Nineteen of the Agreement, the decision of which is the subject of an extraordinary challenge; (*groupe spécial*) (*panel*)

"**participant**" means a Party who files a Request for an Extraordinary Challenge Committee or any of the following persons who files a Notice of Appearance pursuant to these rules:

(a) the other involved Party,

(b) a person who participated in the panel review that is the subject of the extraordinary challenge, and

(c) a panelist against whom an allegation referred to in Article 1904.13(a)(i) of the Agreement is made; (*participant*) (*participante*)

"**Party**" means the Government of Canada, the Government of Mexico or the Government of the United States; (*Partie*) (*Parte*)

"**person**" means

(a) an individual,

(b) a Party,

(c) an investigating authority,

(d) a government of a province, state or other political subdivision of the country of a Party,

(e) a department, agency or body of a Party or of a government referred to in paragraph (d), or

(f) a partnership, corporation or association; (personne) (persona)

"**personal information**" means, with respect to an extraordinary challenge proceeding in which an allegation is made that a member of the panel was guilty of gross misconduct, bias or a serious conflict of interest or otherwise materially violated the rules of conduct, the information referred to in subrule 39(2) and rule 41; (*renseignements personnels*) (*información personal*)

"**pleading**" means a Request for an Extraordinary Challenge Committee, a Notice of Appearance, a Change of Service Address, a Notice of Change of Counsel of Record, a Notice of Motion, a brief or any other written submission filed by a participant; (*acte de procédure*) (*promoción*)

"**privileged information**" means

(a) with respect to an extraordinary challenge of a panel review of a final determination made in Canada, information of the investigating authority that is subject to solicitor-client privilege under the laws of Canada, or that constitutes part of the deliberative process with respect to the final determination, with respect to which the privilege has not been waived,

(b) with respect to an extraordinary challenge of a panel review of a final determination made in Mexico,

(i) information of the investigating authority that is subject to attorney-client privilege under the laws of Mexico, or

(ii) internal communications between officials of the Secretaría de Comercio y Fomento Industrial in charge of antidumping and countervailing duty investigations or communications between those officials and other government officials, where those communications constitute part of the deliberative process with respect to the final determination, and

(c) with respect to an extraordinary challenge of a panel review of a final determination made in the United States, information of the investigating authority that is subject to the attorney-client, attorney work product or government deliberative process privilege under the laws of the United States and with respect to which the privilege has not been waived; (*renseignements protégés*) (*información privilegiada*)

"**proof of service**" means

(a) with respect to an extraordinary challenge of a panel review of a final determination made in Canada or Mexico,

(i) an affidavit of service stating the name of the person who served the document, the date on which it was served, where it was served and the manner of service, or

(ii) a written acknowledgement of service by counsel for a participant stating the name of the person who served the document, the date on which it was served and the manner of service and, where the acknowledgement is signed by a person other than the counsel, the name of that person followed by a statement that the person is signing as agent for the counsel, and

(b) with respect to an extraordinary challenge of a panel review of a final determination made in the United States, a certificate of service in the form of a statement of the date and manner of service and of the name of the person served, signed by the person who made service; (*preuve de signification*) (*comprobante de envio*)

"**proprietary information**" means

(a) with respect to an extraordinary challenge of a panel review of a final determination made in Canada, information referred to in subsection 84(3) of the Special Import Measures Act, as amended, or subsection 45(3) of the Canadian International Trade Tribunal Act, as amended, and with respect to which the person who designated or submitted the information has not withdrawn the person's claim as to the confidentiality of the information,

(b) with respect to an extraordinary challenge of a panel review of a final determination made in Mexico, información confidencial, as defined under article 80 of the Ley de Comercio Exterior and its regulations, and

(c) with respect to an extraordinary challenge of a panel review of a final determination made in the United States, business proprietary information under section 777(f) of the Tariff Act of 1930, as amended, and any regulations made under that Act; (renseignements de nature exclusive) (información confidencial)

"Proprietary Information Access Application" means

(a) with respect to an extraordinary challenge of a panel review of a final determination made in Canada, a disclosure undertaking in the prescribed form, which form

(i) in respect of a final determination by the Deputy Minister, is available from the Deputy Minister, and

(ii) in respect of a final determination by the Tribunal, is available from the Tribunal,

(b) with respect to an extraordinary challenge of a panel review of a final determination made in Mexico, a disclosure undertaking in the prescribed form, which form is available the from Secretaría de Comercio y Fomento Industrial, and

(c) with respect to an extraordinary challenge of a panel review of a final determination made in the United States, a Protective Order Application

(i) in respect of a final determination by the International Trade Administration of the United States Department of Commerce, in a form prescribed by, and available from, the International Trade Administration of the United States Department of Commerce, and

(ii) in respect of a final determination by the United States International Trade Commission, in a form prescribed by, and available from, the United States International Trade Commission; (demande relative à la communication de renseignements) (compromiso de confidencialidad)

"Proprietary Information Access Order" means

(a) in the case of Canada, a Disclosure Order issued by the Deputy Minister or the Tribunal pursuant to a Proprietary Information Access Application,

(b) in the case of Mexico, a Disclosure Order issued by the Secretaría de Comercio y Fomento Industrial pursuant to a Proprietary Information Access Application, and

(c) in the case of the United States, a Protective Order issued by the International Trade Administration of the United States Department of Commerce or the United States International Trade Commission pursuant to a Proprietary Information Access Application; (ordonnance relative à la communication de renseignements) (autorización de acceso a la información confidencial)

"**responsible Secretariat**" means, with respect to an extraordinary challenge of a panel review, the section of the Secretariat located in the country in which the final determination reviewed by the panel was made; (*Secrétariat responsable*) (*Secretariado responsable*)

"**responsible Secretary**" means the Secretary of the responsible Secretariat; (*secrétaire responsable*) (*Secretario responsable*)

"**Secretariat**" means the Secretariat established pursuant to Article 2002 of the Agreement; (*Secrétariat*) (*Secretariado*)

"**Secretary**" means the Secretary of the United States Section of the Secretariat, the Secretary of the Mexican Section of the Secretariat or the Secretary of the Canadian Section of the Secretariat and includes any person authorized to act on behalf of that Secretary; (*secrétaire*) (*Secretario*)

"**service address**" means

(a) with respect to a Party or panelist, the address filed with the Secretariat as the service address of the Party or panelist, including any facsimile number submitted with that address,

(b) with respect to a participant other than a Party or panelist, the service address of the participant in the panel review, or

(c) where a Change of Service Address has been filed by a Party, panelist or participant, the address set out as the new service address of the participant in that form, including any facsimile number submitted with that address; (*adresse aux fins de signification*) (*domicilio para oír y recibir notificaciones*)

"**Tribunal**" means the Canadian International Trade Tribunal or its successor and includes any person authorized to act on its behalf. (*Tribunal*) (*Tribunal*)

"**United States**" means the United States of America. (États-Unis) (*Estados Unidos*)

4.   The definitions set forth in Article 1911 of the Agreement and Annex 1911 to Chapter 19 of the Agreement are hereby incorporated into these rules.

PART I
GENERAL

5.   An extraordinary challenge proceeding commences on the day on which a Request for an Extraordinary Challenge Committee is filed with the Secretariat and terminates on the day on which a Notice of Completion of Extraordinary Challenge is effective.

6.   The general legal principles of the country in which a final determination was made apply in an extraordinary challenge of the decision of a panel with respect to the final determination.

7.   A committee may review any part of the record of the panel review relevant to the extraordinary challenge.

Internal Functioning of Committees

8.   (1) For routine administrative matters governing its own internal functioning, a committee may adopt procedures not inconsistent with these rules or the Agreement.

(2) Subject to subrule 34(b), meetings of a committee may be conducted by means of a telephone conference call.

9.   Only committee members may take part in the *deliberations* of a committee, which shall take place in *private* and remain *secret*. Staff of the involved Secretariats and assistants to committee members may be present by permission of the committee.

Computation of Time

10.   (1) In computing any time period fixed in these rules or by an order or decision of a committee, the day from which the time period begins to run shall be excluded and, subject to subrules (2) and (3), the last day of the time period shall be included.

(2) Where the last day of a time period computed in accordance with subrule (1) falls on a legal holiday of the responsible Secretariat, that day and any other legal holidays of the responsible Secretariat immediately following that day shall be excluded from the computation.

(3) In computing any time period of five days or less fixed in these rules or by an order or decision of a committee, any legal holiday that falls within the time period shall be excluded from the computation.

11.   A committee may extend any time period fixed in these rules if

(a) the extension is made in the interests of fairness and justice; and

(b) in fixing the extension, the committee takes into account the intent of the rules to secure just, speedy and inexpensive final resolutions of challenges to decisions of panels.

Counsel of Record

12.   (1) Subject to subrule (2), the counsel of record for a participant in an extraordinary challenge proceeding shall be

(a) the counsel for the participant in the panel review; or

(b) in the case of a Party who was not a participant in the panel review or of a panelist, the counsel who signs any document filed on behalf of the Party or panelist in the extraordinary challenge proceeding.

(2) A participant may change its counsel of record by filing with the responsible Secretariat a Notice of Change of Counsel of Record signed by the new counsel, together with proof of service on the former counsel and other participants.

Costs

13.   Each participant shall bear the costs of, and incidental to, its own participation in an extraordinary challenge proceeding.

Proprietary Information and Privileged Information

14.   (1) Where proprietary information has been filed in a panel review that is the subject of an extraordinary challenge proceeding, every member of a committee, assistant to a committee member, court reporter, interpreter and translator shall provide the responsible Secretariat with a Proprietary Information Access Application.

(2) Upon receipt of a Proprietary Information Access Application, the responsible Secretary shall file with the appropriate investigating authority the Proprietary Information Access Application and any additional copies of those documents required by the investigating authority.

(3) The investigating authority shall issue the Proprietary Information Access Order and provide the responsible Secretariat with the original and any additional copies of those documents required by the responsible Secretariat.

(4) Upon receipt of a Proprietary Information Access Order, the responsible Secretary shall transmit the original Proprietary Information Access Order to the appropriate member of a committee, assistant to a committee member, court reporter, interpreter or translator.

15.   (1) A member of a committee, assistant to a committee member, court reporter, interpreter or translator who amends or modifies a Proprietary Information Access Application shall provide a copy of the amendment or modification to the responsible Secretariat.

(2) Upon receipt of an amendment or modification to a Proprietary Information Access Application, the responsible Secretary shall file with the appropriate investigating authority that document and any additional copies of that document required by the investigating authority.

(3) Upon receipt of an amendment or modification to a Proprietary Information Access Application, the investigating authority shall, as appropriate, amend, modify or revoke the Proprietary Information Access Order and provide the responsible Secretariat with the original of the amendment, modification or notice of revocation and any additional copies of the document required by the responsible Secretariat.

(4) Upon receipt of an amendment or modification to a Proprietary Information Access Order or a notice of revocation, the responsible Secretary shall transmit the amendment, modification or notice of revocation to the appropriate member of a committee, assistant to a committee member, court reporter, interpreter or translator.

16. The responsible Secretary shall serve Proprietary Information Access Orders granted to members of a committee, assistants to committee members, court reporters, interpreters or translators, and any amendments or modifications thereto or notices of revocation thereof, on all participants other than the investigating authority.

17. (1) A counsel of record, or a professional retained by, or under the control or direction of, a counsel of record, who has not been issued a Proprietary Information Access Order in the panel review or in these proceedings and who wishes disclosure of proprietary information in the file of an extraordinary challenge proceeding, shall file a Proprietary Information Access Application, as follows:

(a) with the responsible Secretariat, four copies; and

(b) with the investigating authority, one original and any additional copies that the investigating authority requires.

(2) A Proprietary Information Access Application referred to in subrule (1) shall be served on all participants.

(3) The investigating authority shall, within 10 days after a Proprietary Information Access Application is filed with it in accordance with subrule (1), serve on the person who filed the Proprietary Information Access Application

(a) a Proprietary Information Access Order; or

(b) a notification in writing setting out the reasons why a Proprietary Information Access Order is not issued.

18. (1) Where

(a) an investigating authority refuses to issue a Proprietary Information Access Order to a counsel of record or to a professional retained by, or under the control or direction of, a counsel of record, or

(b) an investigating authority issues a Proprietary Information Access Order with terms unacceptable to a counsel of record,

the counsel of record may file with the responsible Secretariat a Notice of Motion requesting that the committee review the decision of the investigating authority.

(2) Where, after consideration of any response made by the investigating authority referred to in subrule (1), the committee decides that a Proprietary Information Access Order should be issued or that the terms of a Proprietary Information Access Order should be amended or modified, the committee shall so notify counsel for the investigating authority.

(3) Where the final determination was made in the United States and the investigating authority fails to comply with the notification referred to in subrule (2), the committee may issue such orders as are just in the circumstances, including an order refusing

to permit the investigating authority to make certain arguments in support of its case or striking certain arguments from its pleadings.

19.   (1) Where a Proprietary Information Access Order is issued to a person in an extraordinary challenge proceeding, the person shall file with the responsible Secretariat a copy of the Proprietary Information Access Order.

(2) Where a Proprietary Information Access Order is revoked, amended or modified by an investigating authority, the investigating authority shall provide to the responsible Secretariat and to all participants a copy of the Notice of Revocation, amendment or modification.

20.   In an extraordinary challenge proceeding that commences with a Request for an Extraordinary Challenge Committee pursuant to Article 1904.13(a)(i) of the Agreement, personal information shall be kept confidential

(a) where a Notice of Motion is filed pursuant to subrule 41(1)(c),

(i) until the committee makes an order referred to in subrule 45(1)(a), or

(ii) where the committee makes an order referred to in subrule 45(1)(b), indefinitely, unless otherwise ordered by the committee; and

(b) in any other case, until the day after the expiration of the time period fixed, pursuant to rule 41, for filing a Notice of Motion referred to in subrule 41(1)(c).

21.   Where a person alleges that the terms of a Proprietary Information Access Application or Proprietary Information Access Order have been violated, the committee shall refer the allegations to the investigating authority for investigation and, where applicable, the imposition of sanctions in accordance with section 77.034 of the Special Import Measures Act, as amended, section 777(f) of the Tariff Act of 1930, as amended, or article 93 of the Ley de Comercio Exterior.

Violation of Code of Conduct

22.   Where a participant believes that a committee member or an assistant to a committee member is in violation of the Code of Conduct, the participant shall forthwith notify the responsible Secretary in writing of the alleged violation. The responsible Secretary shall promptly notify the other involved Secretary and the involved Parties of the allegations.

Pleadings and Simultaneous Translation of Extraordinary Challenge Proceedings in Canada

23.   Rules 24 to 26 apply with respect to an extraordinary challenge of a panel review of a final determination made in Canada.

24.   Either English or French may be used by any person, panelist or member of a committee in any document or oral proceeding.

25.   (1) Subject to subrule (2), any order or decision including the reasons therefor, issued by a committee shall be made available simultaneously in both English and French where

(a) in the opinion of the committee, the order or decision is in respect of a question of law of general public interest or importance; or

(b) the proceedings leading to the issuance of the order or decision were conducted in whole or in part in both English and French.

(2) Where

(a) an order or decision issued by a committee is not required by subrule (1) to be made available simultaneously in English and French, or

(b) an order or decision is required by subrule (1)(a) to be made available simultaneously in both English and French but the committee is of the opinion that to make the order or decision available simultaneously in both English and French would occasion a delay prejudicial to the public interest or result in injustice or hardship to any participant, the order or decision, including the reasons therefor, shall be issued in the first instance in either English or French and thereafter at the earliest possible time in the other language, each version to be effective from the time the first version is effective.

(3) Nothing in subrule (1) or (2) shall be construed as prohibiting the oral delivery in either English or French of any order or decision or any reasons therefor.

(4) No order or decision is invalid by reason only that it was not made or issued in both English and French.

26.   (1) Any oral proceeding conducted in both English and French shall be translated simultaneously.

(2) Where a participant requests simultaneous translation of an extraordinary challenge proceeding, the request shall be made as early as possible in the proceedings.

(3) Where a committee is of the opinion that there is a public interest in the extraordinary challenge proceedings, the committee may direct the responsible Secretary to arrange for simultaneous translation of the oral proceedings, if any.

PART II
WRITTEN PROCEEDINGS

27.   Where these rules require that notice be given, it shall be given in writing.

Filing, Service and Communications

28.   (1) No document is filed with the Secretariat until one original and five copies of the document are received by the responsible Secretariat during its normal business hours and within the time period fixed for filing.

(2) The responsible Secretariat shall accept, date and time stamp and place in the appropriate file every document submitted to the responsible Secretariat.

(3) Receipt, date and time stamping or placement in the file of a document by the responsible Secretariat does not constitute a waiver of any time period fixed for filing or an acknowledgement that the document has been filed in accordance with these rules.

29.   (1) All documents filed by a participant, other than documents required by rule 58 to be served by the responsible Secretary and documents referred to in subrule 38(2), rule 39, subrule 40(2)(a) and rule 41 shall be served by the participant on the counsel of record of each of the other participants or, where another participant is not represented by counsel, on the other participant.

(2) Subject to subrule 34(a), a document may be served by

(a) delivering a copy of the document to the service address of the participant;

(b) sending a copy of the document to the service address of the participant by facsimile transmission or by expedited delivery courier or expedited mail service, such as express mail in the United States or Priority Post in Canada; or

(c) personal service on the participant.

(3) A proof of service shall appear on, or be affixed to, all documents referred to in subrule (1).

(4) Where a document is served by expedited delivery courier or expedited mail service, the date of service set out in the affidavit of service or certificate of service shall be the day on which the document is consigned to the expedited delivery courier or expedited mail service.

30.   (1) Where, under these rules, a document containing proprietary information, privileged information or personal information is required to be filed under seal with the Secretariat or is required to be served under seal, the document shall be filed or served in accordance with this rule and, where applicable, in accordance with rule 32.

(2) A document filed or served under seal shall be

(a) bound separately from all other documents;

(b) clearly marked

(i) with respect to an extraordinary challenge of a panel review of a final determination made in Canada,

(A) in the case of a document containing proprietary information, "Proprietary", "Confidential", "De nature exclusive" or "Confidentiel", and

(B) in the case of a document containing privileged information, "Privileged" or "Protégé", and

(C) in the case of a document containing personal information, "Personal Information" or "Renseignements personnels",

(ii) with respect to an extraordinary challenge of a panel review of a final determination made in Mexico,

(A) in the case of a document containing proprietary information, "Confidencial",

(B) in the case of a document containing privileged information, "Privilegiada", and

(C) in the case of a document containing personal information, "Información Personal", and

(iii) with respect to an extraordinary challenge of a panel review of a final determination made in the United States,

(A) in the case of a document containing proprietary information, "Proprietary", and

(B) in the case of a document containing privileged information, "Privileged", and

(C) in the case of a document containing personal information, "Personal Information" ; and

(c) contained in an opaque inner wrapper and an opaque outer wrapper.

(3) An inner wrapper referred to in subrule (2)(c) shall indicate

(a) that proprietary information, privileged information or personal information is enclosed, as the case may be; and

(b) the Secretariat file number of the extraordinary challenge proceeding.

31.   Filing or service of proprietary information, privileged information or personal information with the Secretariat does not constitute a waiver of the designation of the information as proprietary information, privileged information or personal information.

32.   (1) Where a participant files a pleading that contains proprietary information, the participant shall file two sets of the pleading in the following manner:

(a) one set containing the proprietary information shall be filed under seal and

(i) with respect to an extraordinary challenge of a panel review of a final determination made in Canada, shall be labelled "Proprietary", "Confidential", "Confidentiel" or "De nature exclusive", with the top of each page that contains proprietary information marked with the word "Proprietary", "Confidential", "Confidentiel" or "De nature exclusive" and with the proprietary information enclosed in brackets,

(ii) with respect to an extraordinary challenge of a panel review of a final determination made in Mexico, shall be labelled "Confidencial", with the top of each page that contains proprietary information marked with the word "confidencial" and with the proprietary information enclosed in brackets, and

(iii) with respect to an extraordinary challenge of a panel review of a final determination made in the United States, shall be labelled "Proprietary", with the top of each page that contains proprietary information marked with the word "Proprietary" and with the proprietary information enclosed in brackets; and

(b) no later than one day following the day on which the set of pleadings referred to in subrule (a) is filed, another set not containing proprietary information shall be filed and

(i) with respect to an extraordinary challenge of a panel review of a final determination made in Canada, shall be labelled "Non-Proprietary", "Non-Confidential", "Non confidentiel" or "De nature non exclusive",

(ii) with respect to an extraordinary challenge of a panel review of a final determination made in Mexico, shall be labelled "No-confidencial", and

(iii) with respect to an extraordinary challenge of a panel review of a final determination made in the United States, shall be labelled "Non-Proprietary",

with each page from which proprietary information has been deleted marked to indicate the location from which the proprietary information was deleted.

(2) Where a participant files a pleading that contains privileged information, the participant shall file two sets of the pleading in the following manner:

(a) one set containing the privileged information shall be filed under seal and

(i) with respect to an extraordinary challenge of a panel review of a final determination made in Canada, shall be labelled "Privileged" or "Protégé", with the top of each page that contains privileged information marked with the word "Privileged" or "Protégé" and with the privileged information enclosed in brackets,

(ii) with respect to an extraordinary challenge of a panel review of a final determination made in Mexico, shall be labelled "Privilegiada", with the top of each page that contains privileged information marked with the word "Privilegiada" and with the privileged information enclosed in brackets, and

(iii) with respect to an extraordinary challenge of a panel review of a final determination made in the United States, shall be labelled "Privileged", with the top of each page that contains privileged information marked with the word "Privileged" and with the privileged information enclosed in brackets; and

(b) no later than one day following the day on which the set of pleadings referred to in subrule (a) is filed, another set not containing privileged information shall be filed and

(i) with respect to an extraordinary challenge of a panel review of a final determination made in Canada, shall be labelled "Non-Privileged" or "Non protégé",

(ii) with respect to an extraordinary challenge of a panel review of a final determination made in Mexico, shall be labelled "No-privilegiada", and

(iii) with respect to an extraordinary challenge of a panel review of a final determination made in the United States, shall be labelled "Non-Privileged",

with each page from which privileged information has been deleted marked to indicate the location from which the privileged information was deleted.

(3) Where a participant files a pleading that contains personal information, the pleading shall be filed under seal and

(a) with respect to an extraordinary challenge of a panel review of a final determination made in Canada, shall be labelled "Personal Information" or "Renseignements personnels", with the top of each page that contains personal information marked with the words "Personal Information" or "Renseignements personnels" and with the personal information enclosed in brackets;

(b) with respect to an extraordinary challenge of a panel review of a final determination made in Mexico, shall be labelled "Información Personal", with the top of each page that contains personal information marked with the words "Información personal" and with the personal information enclosed in brackets; and

(c) with respect to an extraordinary challenge of a panel review of a final determination made in the United States, shall be labelled "Personal Information", with the top of each page that contains personal information marked with the words "Personal Information" and with the personal information enclosed in brackets.

33.   (1) Subject to subrule (2), a document containing proprietary or privileged information shall be filed under seal in accordance with rule 30 and shall be served only on the investigating authority and on those participants who have been granted access to the information under a Proprietary Information Access Order.

(2) Where all proprietary information contained in a document was submitted to the investigating authority by one participant, the document shall be served on that participant even if that participant has not been granted access to proprietary information under a Proprietary Information Access Order.

(3) A document containing personal information shall be filed under seal in accordance with rule 30 and shall be served only on persons or participants who have been granted access to the information under an order of the committee.

34.   Where proprietary information, privileged information or personal information is disclosed to a person in an extraordinary challenge proceeding, the person shall not

(a) file, serve or otherwise communicate the information by facsimile transmission; or

(b) communicate the information by telephone.

35.   Service on an investigating authority does not constitute service on a Party and service on a Party does not constitute service on an investigating authority.

Form and Content of Pleadings

36.   (1) Every pleading filed in an extraordinary challenge proceeding shall contain the following information:

(a) the title of, and any Secretariat file number assigned for, the extraordinary challenge proceeding;

(b) a brief descriptive title of the pleading;

(c) the name of the participant filing the pleading;

(d) the name of counsel of record for the participant;

(e) the service address, as defined in rule 3; and

(f) the telephone number of the counsel of record of the participant or, where the participant is not represented by counsel, the telephone number of the participant.

(2) Every pleading filed in an extraordinary challenge proceeding shall be on paper 8 1/2 X 11 inches (216 millimetres by 279 millimetres) in size. The text of the pleading shall be printed, typewritten or reproduced legibly on one side only with a margin of approximately 1 1/2 inches (40 millimetres) on the left-hand side

with double spacing between each line of text, except for quotations of more than 50 words, which shall be indented and single-spaced. Footnotes, titles, schedules, tables, graphs and columns of figures shall be presented in a readable form. Briefs and appendices shall be securely bound along the left-hand margin.

(3) Every pleading filed on behalf of a participant in an extraordinary challenge proceeding shall be signed by counsel for the participant or, where the participant is not represented by counsel, by the participant.

Requests for an Extraordinary Challenge Committee

37.   (1) Where a Party, in its discretion, files with the responsible Secretary a Request for an Extraordinary Challenge Committee referred to in Article 1904.13(a)(ii) or (iii) of the Agreement, the Party shall file the Request (*model form available from the Secretariat*) within 30 days after the issuance, pursuant to rule 77 of the NAFTA Article 1904 Panel Rules, of the Notice of Final Panel Action in the panel review that is the subject of the Request.

(2) Where a Party, in its discretion, files with the responsible Secretary a Request for an Extraordinary Challenge Committee referred to in Article 1904.13(a)(i) of the Agreement, the Party shall file the Request (model form available from the Secretariat)

(a) within 30 days after the issuance, pursuant to rule 77 of the NAFTA Article 1904 Panel Rules, of the Notice of Final Panel Action in the panel review that is the subject of the Request; or

(b) subject to subrule (3), where the Party gained knowledge of the action of the panelist giving rise to the allegation more than 30 days after the panel issued a Notice of Final Panel Action, no more than 30 days after gaining knowledge of the action of the panelist.

(3) No Request for an Extraordinary Challenge Committee referred to in subrule (2) may be filed if two years or more have elapsed since the effective date of the Notice of Completion of Panel Review.

(4) Notwithstanding subrules (1) to (3), the running of the time periods referred to in this section

(a) shall be suspended in the circumstances set out in Article 1905.11 of the Agreement; and

(b) where suspended under subrule (a), shall be resumed in the circumstances set out in Articles 1905.12 and 1905.13 of the Agreement.

38.   (1) Subject to subrule (2), every Request for an Extraordinary Challenge Committee shall be in writing and shall

(a) include a concise statement of the allegations relied on, together with a concise statement of how the actions alleged have materially affected the panel's decision and the way in which the integrity of the panel review process is threatened;

(b) contain the name of the Party in the panel review, name of counsel, service address and telephone number; and

(c) where the panel decision was made in Canada, state whether the Party filing the Request for an Extraordinary Challenge Committee

(i) intends to use English or French in pleadings and oral proceedings before the committee, and

(ii) requests simultaneous translation of any oral proceedings.

(2) Where a Request for an Extraordinary Challenge Committee contains an allegation referred to in Article 1904.13(a)(i) of the Agreement, the identity of the panelist against whom such an allegation is made shall be revealed only in a confidential annex filed together with the Request and shall be disclosed only in accordance with rule 60.

39. (1) Every Request for an Extraordinary Challenge Committee (model form available from the Secretariat) shall be accompanied by

(a) those items of the record of the panel review relevant to the allegations contained in the Request; and

(b) an Index of the items referred to in subrule (a).

(2) Where a Request contains an allegation referred to in Article 1904.13(a)(i) of the Agreement, the Request shall be accompanied by, in addition to the requirements of subrule (1),

(a) any other material relevant to the allegations contained in the Request; and

(b) if the Request is filed more than 30 days after the panel issued a Notice of Final Panel Action pursuant to rule 77 of the NAFTA Article 1904 Panel Rules, an affidavit certifying that the Party gained knowledge of the action of the panelist giving rise to the allegation no more than 30 days preceding the filing of the Request.

Notices of Appearance

40. (1) Within 10 days after the Request for an Extraordinary Challenge Committee is filed, a Party or participant in the panel review who proposes to participate in the extraordinary challenge proceeding shall file with the responsible Secretariat a Notice of Appearance (model form available from the Secretariat) containing the following information:

(a) the name of the Party or participant, name of counsel, service address and telephone number;

(b) a statement as to whether appearance is made

(i) in support of the Request, or

(ii) in opposition to the Request; and

(c) where the extraordinary challenge is in respect of a panel review of a final determination made in Canada, a statement as to whether the person filing the Notice of Appearance

(i) intends to use English or French in pleadings and oral proceedings before the committee, and

(ii) requests simultaneous translation of any oral proceedings.

(2) Where a Party or participant referred to in subrule (1) proposes to rely on a document in the record of the panel review that is not specified in the Index filed with the Request for an Extraordinary Challenge Committee, the Party or participant shall file, with the Notice of Appearance,

(a) the document; and

(b) a statement identifying the document and requesting its inclusion in the extraordinary challenge record.

(3) On receipt of a document referred to in subrule (2), the responsible Secretary shall include the document in the extraordinary challenge record.

41.   (1) Within 10 days after a Request for an Extraordinary Challenge Committee referred to in Article 1904.13(a)(i) of the Agreement is filed, a panelist against whom an allegation contained in the Request is made and who proposes to participate in the extraordinary challenge proceeding

(a) shall file a Notice of Appearance;

(b) may file, under seal, documents to be included in the extraordinary challenge record relevant to the panelist's defense against the allegation; and

(c) may file an ex parte motion requesting that the extraordinary challenge proceeding be conducted in camera.

(2) Where a committee issues an order pursuant to subrule 45(1)(a), a panelist who filed documents described in subrule (1)(b) may, within five days after issuance of the order, withdraw any of those documents.

(3) Where a panelist withdraws documents pursuant to subrule (2), the committee shall not consider those documents.

Filing and Content of Briefs and Appendices

42.   (1) The Party who has filed the Request for an Extraordinary Challenge Committee and every participant who has filed a Notice of Appearance under subrule 40(1)(b)(i) shall file a brief, setting forth grounds and arguments in support of the Request, no later than 21 days after the Request for an Extraordinary Challenge Committee is filed.

(2) Every participant who has filed a Notice of Appearance under subrule 40(1)(b)(ii) shall file a brief, setting forth grounds and arguments in opposition to the Request for an Extraordinary Challenge Committee, no later than 21 days after the expiration of the time period for filing of briefs referred to in subrule (1).

(3) The Party who has filed the Request for an Extraordinary Challenge Committee and every participant who has filed a Notice of Appearance under subrule 40(1)(b)(i) may file a brief, replying to the grounds and arguments set forth in the briefs filed pursuant to subrule (2), no later than 10 days after the expiration of the time period for filing of briefs referred to in subrule (2). Reply briefs shall be limited to rebuttal of matters raised in the briefs filed pursuant to subrule (2).

(4) Every brief filed under this rule shall be in the form required by rule 43.

(5) Appendices shall be filed with the briefs.

43.   (1) Briefs shall contain information, in the following order, divided into five parts:

Part I:

   (a) A table of contents; and

   (b) A table of authorities cited:

The table of authorities shall contain references to all treaties, statutes and regulations cited, any cases primarily relied on in the briefs, set out alphabetically, and all other documents referred to except documents from the administrative record. The table of authorities shall refer to the page(s) of the brief where each authority is cited and mark, with an asterisk in the margin, those authorities primarily relied on.

Part II: A statement of the case:

This part shall contain a concise statement of the relevant facts with references to the panel record by page and, where applicable, by line.

Part III: A statement of the issues:

   (a) In the brief of the Party who files the Request for an Extraordinary Challenge Committee, this part shall contain a concise statement of the issues.

(b) In the brief of any other participant, this part shall contain a concise statement of the position of the participant with respect to the issues.

Part IV: Argument:

This part shall consist of the argument, setting out concisely the points of law relating to the issues, with applicable citations to authorities and the panel record.

Part V: Relief:

This part shall consist of a concise statement precisely identifying the relief requested.

(2) Paragraphs in Parts I to V of a brief may be numbered consecutively.

(3) Authorities referred to in the briefs shall be included in an appendix, which shall be organized as follows: a table of contents, copies of all treaty and statutory references, references to regulations, cases primarily relied on in the briefs, set out alphabetically, all documents relied on from the panel record and all other materials relied on.

Motions

44.   (1) Motions, other than motions referred to in subrule 41(1)(c), may be considered at the discretion of the committee.

(2) A committee may dispose of a motion based upon the pleadings filed on the motion.

(3) A committee may hear oral argument in person or, subject to subrule 34(b), direct that a motion be heard by means of a telephone conference call with the participants.

PART III

CONDUCT OF ORAL PROCEEDINGS

45.   (1) The order of a committee on a motion referred to in subrule 41(1)(c) shall set out

(a) that the proceedings shall not be held in camera; or

(b) that the proceedings shall be held in camera and

(i) that all the participants shall keep confidential all information received with respect to the extraordinary challenge proceeding and shall use the information solely for the purposes of the proceeding, and

(ii) which documents containing personal information the responsible Secretary shall serve under seal and on whom the documents shall be served.

(2) The responsible Secretary shall not serve any documents containing personal information until the time period for withdrawal of any documents pursuant to subrule 41(2) has expired.

46. A committee may decide the procedures to be followed in the extraordinary challenge proceeding and may, for that purpose, hold a pre-hearing conference to determine such matters as the presentation of evidence and of oral argument.

47. The decision as to whether oral argument will be heard shall be in the discretion of the committee.

Oral Proceedings in Camera

48. During that part of oral proceedings in which proprietary information or privileged information is presented, a committee shall not permit any person other than the following persons to be present:

(a) the person presenting the proprietary information or privileged information;

(b) a person who has been granted access to the proprietary information or privileged information under a Proprietary Information Access Order or an order of the panel or committee;

(c) in the case of privileged information, a person as to whom the confidentiality of the privileged information has been waived; and

(d) officials of, and counsel for, the investigating authority.

PART IV

RESPONSIBILITIES OF THE SECRETARY

49. The normal business hours of the Secretariat, during which the offices of the Secretariat shall be open to the public, shall be from 9:00 a.m. to 5:00 p.m. on each weekday other than

(a) in the case of the Canadian Section of the Secretariat, legal holidays of that Section;

(b) in the case of the Mexican Section of the Secretariat, legal holidays of that Section; and

(c) in the case of the United States Section of the Secretariat, legal holidays of that Section.

50. On the completion of the selection of the members of a committee, the responsible Secretary shall notify the participants and the other involved Secretary of the names of the members of the committee.

51. The responsible Secretary shall provide administrative support for each extraordinary challenge proceeding and shall make the arrangements necessary for meetings and any oral proceedings, including, if required, interpreters to provide simultaneous translation.

52. Each involved Secretary shall maintain a file for each extraordinary challenge, comprised of either the original or a copy of all documents filed, whether or not filed in accordance with these rules.

53.   The responsible Secretary shall forward to the other involved Secretary a copy of all documents filed with the responsible Secretary and of all orders and decisions issued by a committee.

54.   Where under these rules a notice or other document is required to be published, the responsible Secretary and the other involved Secretary shall each cause the document to be published in the official publication of the country in which that section of the Secretariat is located.

55.   (1) Where a document containing proprietary information or privileged information is filed with the involved Secretariats, each involved Secretary shall ensure that

> (a) the document is stored, maintained, handled, and distributed in accordance with the terms of an applicable Proprietary Information Access Order;

> (b) the inner wrapper of the document is clearly marked to indicate that it contains proprietary information or privileged information; and

> (c) access to the document is limited to

>> (i) in the case of proprietary information, officials of, and counsel for, the investigating authority, the person who submitted the proprietary information to the investigating authority and counsel of record for that person, and any persons who have been granted access to the information under a Proprietary Information Access Order, and

>> (ii) in the case of privileged information relied upon in an extraordinary challenge of a decision of a panel with respect to a final determination made in the United States, committee members and their assistants and persons with respect to whom the panel ordered disclosure of the privileged information under rule 52 of the NAFTA Article 1904 Panel Rules, if those persons have filed with the responsible Secretariat a Proprietary Information Access Order with respect to the document.

(2) Where a document containing personal information is filed with the involved Secretariats, each involved Secretary shall ensure that

> (a) the document is stored, maintained, handled, and distributed in accordance with the terms of any applicable Proprietary Information Access Order;

> (b) the inner wrapper of the document is clearly marked to indicate that it contains personal information; and

> (c) access to the document is limited to persons granted access to the information pursuant to subrule 45(1)(b).

56.   No document filed in an extraordinary challenge proceeding shall be removed from the offices of the Secretariat except in the

ordinary course of the business of the Secretariat or pursuant to the direction of a committee.

57.   (1) Each involved Secretary shall permit access by any person to information in the file of an extraordinary challenge proceeding that is not proprietary information, privileged information or personal information.

(2) Each involved Secretary shall, in accordance with the terms of any applicable Proprietary Information Access Order or order of a panel or committee, permit access to proprietary information, privileged information or personal information in the file of an extraordinary challenge proceeding.

(3) Each involved Secretary shall, on request and on payment of the prescribed fee, provide copies of information in the file of an extraordinary challenge proceeding to any person who has been given access to that information.

58.   (1) Where a Request for an Extraordinary Challenge Committee pursuant to Article 1904.13(a)(ii) or (iii) of the Agreement is filed with the responsible Secretariat, the responsible Secretary shall, upon receipt thereof,

(a) forward a copy of the Request and Index to the other involved Secretary; and

(b) serve a copy of the Request and Index on the other involved Party and on the participants in the panel review, together with a statement setting out the date on which the Request was filed and stating that all briefs of

(i) the Party who has filed the Request and of every participant who files a Notice of Appearance in support of the Request shall be filed no later than 21 days after the date of filing of the Request,

(ii) every participant who files a Notice of Appearance in opposition to the Request shall be filed no later than 21 days after the expiration of the time period, referred to in subrule (i), for filing of briefs, and

(iii) the Party who has filed the Request and of every participant who files a brief under subrule (i) in reply to the grounds and arguments set forth in the briefs filed pursuant to subrule (ii) shall be filed no later than 10 days after the expiration of the time period, referred to in subrule (ii), for filing of briefs.

(2) Where a Request for an Extraordinary Challenge Committee pursuant to Article 1904.13(a)(i) of the Agreement is filed, the responsible Secretary shall, upon receipt thereof,

(a) forward a copy of the Request, Index and annex to the other involved Secretary; and

(b) serve a copy of the Request, Index and annex on the other involved Party, on the panelist against whom the allegation contained in the Request is made and on the participants in the panel review, together with a statement setting out the date on which the Request was filed and stating that all briefs of

(i) the Party who has filed the Request and of every participant who files a Notice of Appearance in support of the Request shall be filed no later than 21 days after the date of filing of the Request,

(ii) every participant who files a Notice of Appearance in opposition to the Request shall be filed no later than 21 days after the expiration of the time period, referred to in subrule (i), for filing of briefs, and

(iii) the Party who has filed the Request and of every participant who files a brief under subrule (i) in reply to the grounds and arguments set forth in the briefs filed pursuant to subrule (ii) shall be filed no later than 10 days after the expiration of the time period, referred to in subrule (ii), for filing of briefs.

(3) The responsible Secretary shall serve orders and decisions of a committee and Notices of Completion of Extraordinary Challenge on the participants.

(4) Where the decision of a committee referred to in subrule (3) relates to a panel review of a final determination made in Canada, the decision shall be served by registered mail.

59.   The responsible Secretary shall cause notice of a final decision of a committee issued pursuant to rule 63, and any order that the committee directs the Secretary to publish, to be published in the official publications of the involved Parties.

60.   Where the time period fixed, pursuant to rule 41, for filing an ex parte motion referred to in subrule 41(1)(c) has expired, the responsible Secretary shall serve on all participants

(a) where no motion is filed pursuant to that subrule, the documents referred to in rules 39 and 41;

(b) where the committee issues an order referred to in subrule 45(1)(a), the documents referred to in rules 39 and 41 in accordance with any order of the committee; and

(c) where the committee issues an order referred to in subrule 45(1)(b), the documents referred to in rules 39 and 41, in accordance with subrule 45(1)(b)(ii) and any order made by the committee.

PART V

ORDERS AND DECISIONS

61.   All orders and decisions of a committee shall be made by a majority of the votes of all members of the committee.

62. (1) Where a Notice of Motion requesting dismissal of an extraordinary challenge proceeding is filed by a participant, the committee may issue an order dismissing the proceeding.

(2) Where the motion referred to in subrule (1) is consented to by all the participants and an affidavit to that effect is filed, or where all participants file Notices of Motion requesting dismissal, the extraordinary challenge proceeding is terminated.

63. (1) A final decision of a committee shall

(a) affirm the decision of the panel;

(b) vacate the decision of the panel; or

(c) remand the decision of the panel to the panel for action not inconsistent with the final decision of the committee.

(2) Every final decision of a committee shall be issued in writing with reasons, together with any dissenting or concurring opinions of the members of the committee.

(3) Subrule (2) shall not be construed as prohibiting the oral delivery of the decision of a committee.

PART VI

COMPLETION OF EXTRAORDINARY CHALLENGES

64. Where all participants consent to the termination of the proceeding pursuant to rule 62, the responsible Secretary shall cause to be published in the official publications of the involved Parties a Notice of Completion of Extraordinary Challenge, effective on the day after the day on which the requirements of rule 62 have been met.

65. Where a committee issues its final decision, the responsible Secretary shall cause to be published in the official publications of the involved Parties a Notice of Completion of Extraordinary Challenge, effective on the day after the day on which

(a) the committee affirms the decision of the panel;

(b) the committee vacates the decision of the panel; or

(c) where the committee remands the decision of the panel, the day the responsible Secretary gives notice to the committee that the panel has given notice that it has taken action not inconsistent with the committee's decision.

66. The members of the committee are discharged from their duties on the day on which a Notice of Completion of Extraordinary Challenge is effective.

67. (1) A Party may make a request, pursuant to Article 1905.11(a)(ii) of the Agreement, that an ongoing extraordinary challenge proceeding be stayed by filing the request with the responsible Secretariat.

(2) A Party who files a request under subrule (1) shall forthwith give written notice of the request to the other involved Party and to the other involved Secretariat.

(3) On receipt of a request under subrule (1), the responsible Secretary shall

(a) immediately give written notice of the stay of the extraordinary challenge proceedings to all participants in the extraordinary challenge proceedings; and

(b) publish a notice of the stay of the extraordinary challenge proceedings in the official publications of the involved Parties.

68. On receipt of a report containing an affirmative finding with respect to a ground specified in Article 1905.1 of the Agreement, the responsible Secretary for extraordinary challenge proceedings referred to in Article 1905.11(a)(i) of the Agreement shall

(a) immediately give notice in writing to all participants in those proceedings; and

(b) publish a notice of the affirmative finding in the official publications of the involved Parties.

69. (1) A Party who intends to suspend the operation of Article 1904 of the Agreement pursuant to Article 1905.8 or 1905.9 of the Agreement shall endeavour to give written notice of that intention to the other involved Party and to the involved Secretaries at least five days prior to the suspension.

(2) On receipt of a notice under subrule (1), the involved Secretaries shall publish a notice of the suspension in the official publications of the involved Parties.

DOCUMENT 9

NAFTA RULES OF PROCEDURE FOR CHAPTER 20 PANELS

(The following were not published in the Federal Register. They are public records and were obtained from the NAFTA Secretariat.)

Model Rules of Procedure for Chapter Twenty of the North American Free Trade Agreement

Application

1. These rules are established under Article 2012(1) and shall apply to dispute settlement proceedings under Chapter Twenty unless the disputing Parties otherwise agree.

Definitions

2. In these rules:

adviser means a person retained by a Party to advise or assist the Party in connection with the panel proceeding;

Agreement means the North American Free Trade Agreement;

complaining Party means any Party that requests the establishment of an arbitral panel under Article 2008(1) or any Party that joins a panel proceeding under Article 2008(3);

disputing Parties means the complaining Party or Parties, and the Party complained against;

legal holiday, with respect to a Party's section of the Secretariat, means every Saturday and Sunday and any other day designated by that Party as a holiday for the purposes of these rules and notified by that Party to its section of the Secretariat and by that section to the other sections of the Secretariat and the other Parties;

panel means a panel established under Article 2008(2);

participating Parties means the disputing Parties and a third Party;

Party means a Party to the Agreement;

representative of a participating Party means an employee of a government department or agency or of any other government entity of a participating Party;

responsible section of the Secretariat means the section of the Secretariat of the Party complained against;

Secretariat means the Secretariat established under Article 2002(1); and

third Party means a Party, other than a disputing Party, that delivers a written notice in accordance with Article 2013.

3.   Any reference made in these rules to an Article, Annex or Chapter is a reference to the appropriate Article, Annex or Chapter of the Agreement.

Terms of Reference

4.   The disputing Parties shall promptly deliver any agreed terms of reference to the responsible section of the Secretariat which, in turn, shall provide for their delivery to any third Party, to the other sections of the Secretariat, and to the panel on selection of the last panelist, by the most expeditious means practicable.

5.   If the disputing Parties have not agreed on terms of reference after 20 days of the request for the establishment of the panel, the complaining Party may so notify the responsible section of the Secretariat. On receipt of such notification, that section shall deliver the terms of reference set out in Article 2012(3) to the participating Parties, to the other sections of the Secretariat, and to the panel on selection of the last panelist, by the most expeditious means practicable.

Written Submissions and Other Documents

6.   A participating Party shall deliver the original and nine copies of each of its written submissions to its section of the Secretariat and shall make a copy of each of its written submissions available to the Embassy of each other participating Party at the time it delivers the written submission to its section.

7.   A complaining Party shall deliver the original and nine copies of its initial written submission to its section of the Secretariat no later than 10 days after the date on which the last panelist is selected. The Party complained against shall deliver the original and nine copies of its written counter-submission to its section of the Secretariat no later than 20 days after the date of delivery of the initial written submission. A third Party shall deliver the original and nine copies of its initial written submission to its section of the Secretariat no later than the date on which the counter-submission is due.

8.   A section of the Secretariat that receives a written submission shall forward it by the most expeditious means practicable to the responsible section of the Secretariat which, in turn, shall provide for delivery of that submission by the most expeditious means practicable to the other sections of the Secretariat, the other participating Parties and the panel.

9.   In the case of any request, notice or other document related to the panel proceeding that is not covered by rule 6, 7 or 8, the participating Party shall deliver the original and nine copies of the document to its section of the Secretariat and, on the same day, it shall deliver a copy to the other participating Parties by facsimile or other means of electronic transmission.

10.   Minor errors of a clerical nature in any request, notice, written submission or other document related to the panel proceeding may be corrected by delivery of a new document clearly indicating the changes.

11.   A participating Party that delivers any request, notice, written submission or other document to its section of the Secretariat shall, to the extent practicable, deliver a copy of the document in electronic form to that section.

12.   Any delivery to a section of the Secretariat under these rules shall be made during the normal business hours of that section.

13.   If the last day for delivery of a document to a section of the Secretariat falls on a legal holiday observed by that section or on any other day on which the offices of that section are closed by order of the government or by *force majeure*, the document may be delivered to that section on the next business day.

Operation of Panels

14.   The chair of the panel shall preside at all of its meetings. A panel may delegate to the chair authority to make administrative and procedural decisions.

15.   Except as otherwise provided in these rules, the panel may conduct its business by any means, including by telephone, facsimile transmission or computer links.

16.   Only panelists may take part in the deliberations of the panel but the panel may permit assistants, Secretariat personnel, interpreters or translators to be present during such deliberations.

17.   Where a procedural question arises that is not covered by these rules, a panel may adopt an appropriate procedure that is not inconsistent with the Agreement.

18.   If a panelist dies, withdraws or is removed, a replacement shall be selected as expeditiously as possible in accordance with the selection procedure followed to select the panelist.

19.   Any time period applicable to the panel proceeding shall be suspended for a period beginning on the date the panelist dies, withdraws or is removed and ending on the date the replacement is selected.

20.   A panel may, in consultation with the disputing Parties, modify any time period applicable in the panel proceeding and make such other procedural or administrative adjustments as may be required in the proceeding, such as where a panelist is replaced or where the Parties are required to reply in writing to the questions of a panel.

Hearings

21.   The chair shall fix the date and time of the hearing in consultation with the participating Parties, the other members of the panel and the responsible section of the Secretariat. The responsible section of the

Secretariat shall notify in writing the participating Parties of the date, time and location of the hearing.

22.   The hearing shall be held in the capital of the Party complained against.

23.   The panel may convene additional hearings if the disputing Parties so agree.

24.   All panelists shall be present at hearings.

25.   The following persons may attend a hearing:

(a) representatives of a participating Party;

(b) advisers to a participating Party provided that they do not address the panel and provided further that neither they nor their employers, partners, business associates or family members have a financial or personal interest in the proceeding;

(c) Secretariat personnel, interpreters, translators and court reporters; and

(d) panelists' assistants.

26.   No later than five days before the date of a hearing, each participating Party shall deliver to the other participating Parties and the responsible section of the Secretariat a list of the names of those persons who will make oral arguments or presentations at the hearing on behalf of that Party and of other representatives or advisers who will be attending the hearing.

27.   The hearing shall be conducted by the panel in the following manner, ensuring that the complaining Party or Parties and the Party complained against are afforded equal time:

Argument—

(i) Argument of the complaining Party or Parties.

(ii) Argument of the Party complained against.

(iii) Presentation of a third Party.

Rebuttal Argument—

(iv) Reply of the complaining Party or Parties.

(v) Counter-reply of the Party complained against.

28.   The panel may direct questions to any participating Party at any time during a hearing.

29.   The responsible section of the Secretariat shall arrange for a transcript of each hearing to be prepared and shall, as soon as possible after it is prepared, deliver a copy of the transcript to the participating Parties, the other sections of the Secretariat and the panel.

Supplementary Written Submissions

30.   The panel may at any time during a proceeding address questions in writing to one or more of the participating Parties. The panel

shall deliver the written questions to the Party or Parties to whom the questions are addressed through the responsible section of the Secretariat which, in turn, shall provide for the delivery of copies of the questions by the most expeditious means practicable to the other sections of the Secretariat and any other participating Party.

31. A participating Party to whom the panel addresses written questions shall deliver a copy of any written reply to its section of the Secretariat which, in turn, shall forward it by the most expeditious means practicable to the responsible section of the Secretariat. The responsible section of the Secretariat shall provide for the delivery of copies of the reply by the most expeditious means practicable to the other sections of the Secretariat and any other participating Party. Each other participating Party shall be given the opportunity to provide written comments on the reply within five days after the date of delivery.

32. Within 10 days after the date of the hearing, each participating Party may deliver to its section of the Secretariat a supplementary written submission responding to any matter that arose during the hearing.

Burden of Proof Regarding Inconsistent Measures and Exceptions

33. A Party asserting that a measure of another Party is inconsistent with the provisions of the Agreement shall have the burden of establishing such inconsistency.

34. A Party asserting that a measure is subject to an exception under the Agreement shall have the burden of establishing that the exception applies.

Availability of Information

35. The Parties shall maintain the confidentiality of the panel's hearings, deliberations and initial report, and all written submissions to and communications with the panel, in accordance with such procedures as may be agreed from time to time between representatives of the Parties.

Ex Parte Contacts

36. The panel shall not meet or contact one participating Party in the absence of the other participating Parties.

37. No panelist may discuss any aspect of the subject matter of the proceeding with a participating Party or Parties in the absence of the other panelists.

Scientific Review Boards

38. No panel may decide to request a written report of a scientific review board any later than 15 days after the date of the hearing, whether on its own initiative or at the request of a disputing Party.

39.   Within five days after the date on which the panel decides to request a written report of a scientific review board, the panel shall request that the scientific bodies designated by each Party from time to time and set out in Appendix I provide, within 15 days after the date of the delivery of the request, a list of the names of possible members of the scientific review board, in such numbers as the panel requests and having expertise in the scientific matters that the panel identifies.

40.   The panel shall deliver the request for the list of names of possible members of the scientific review board to the responsible section of the Secretariat which, in turn, shall provide for the delivery of copies of the request by the most expeditious means practicable to the other sections of the Secretariat and the participating Parties.

41.   Within 25 days after its decision to request a written report of a scientific review board and after consulting the disputing Parties, the panel shall select up to three members to constitute the scientific review board. The panel shall make its selection from the lists provided by the scientific bodies wherever possible.

42.   The panel shall not select as a member of a scientific review board an individual who has, or whose employers, partners, business associates or family members have, a financial or personal interest in the proceeding.

43.   A participating Party may, before the date on which the last member of the scientific review board is selected, submit written comments to the panel on the factual issues to be referred to the board.

44.   Within five days after the date on which the last member of the scientific review board is selected, the panel shall finalize the factual issues to be referred to the board, and may consult with members of the board in this regard.

45.   The panel shall deliver a copy of its referral to the responsible section of the Secretariat which, in turn, shall provide for the delivery of copies of the referral by the most expeditious means practicable to the other sections of the Secretariat, the participating Parties and the board.

46.   A scientific review board shall deliver its report to the responsible section of the Secretariat within 30 days after the date on which the factual issues are referred to the board.

47.   The responsible section of the Secretariat shall deliver the board's report to the participating Parties and their respective sections of the Secretariat. Any participating Party may provide comments on the report to its section of the Secretariat within 14 days after the date of delivery of the report. The appropriate section of the Secretariat shall promptly deliver any such comments to the responsible section of the Secretariat which, in turn, shall no later than the next business day deliver such comments to the other participating Parties and their respective sections of the Secretariat, and shall deliver the report and all such comments to the panel.

48.   Where a request is made for a written report of a scientific review board, any time period applicable to the panel proceeding shall be suspended for a period beginning on the date of delivery of the request and ending on the date the report is delivered to the panel.

Translation and Interpretation

49.   A participating Party shall, within a reasonable period of time before it delivers its initial written submission in a panel proceeding, advise its section of the Secretariat in writing of the language in which its written submissions will be made and in which it wishes to receive the written submissions of the other participating Parties. A section of the Secretariat that is so advised shall promptly notify the responsible section of the Secretariat which, in turn, shall promptly notify the other sections of the Secretariat, the other participating Parties and the panel.

50.   A participating Party shall, within a reasonable period of time before the date of a hearing, advise its section of the Secretariat in writing of the language in which it will make oral arguments or presentations at the hearing and in which it wishes to hear oral arguments and presentations. A section of the Secretariat that is so advised shall promptly notify the responsible section of the Secretariat which, in turn, shall promptly notify the other sections of the Secretariat, the other participating Parties and the panel.

51.   In lieu of the procedure set out in rule 49 or 50, a Party may advise its section of the Secretariat of:

(a) the language in which it will make, and in which it wishes to receive, written submissions in all panel proceedings; or

(b) the language in which it will make, and in which it wishes to hear, oral arguments and presentations at hearings in all panel proceedings.

A section of the Secretariat that is so advised shall promptly notify the other sections of the Secretariat and the other Parties.

52.   Where in accordance with the advice provided by each Party under rules 49 through 51, written submissions or oral arguments and presentations in a panel proceeding will be made in more than one language, or if a panelist requests, the responsible section of the Secretariat shall arrange for the translation of the written submissions and the panel reports or for the interpretation of arguments at any hearing, as the case may be.

53.   Where the responsible section of the Secretariat is required to arrange for the translation of a written submission or report in one or more languages, it shall not provide for the delivery of that written submission as required by rule 8 or for the delivery of that report until all translated versions of that written submission or report have been prepared.

54. Any time period applicable to a panel proceeding shall be suspended for the period necessary to complete the translation of any written submissions.

55. The costs incurred to prepare a translation of a written submission shall be borne by the Party making the submission. The costs incurred to prepare a translation of a final report shall be borne equally by each section of the Secretariat. The costs of all other translation and interpretation requirements in a panel proceeding shall be borne equally by the participating Parties in that proceeding.

56. Any Party may provide comments on a translated version of a document that is prepared in accordance with these rules.

Computation of Time

57. Where anything under the Agreement or these rules is to be done, or the panel requires anything to be done, within a number of days after, before or of a specified date or event, the specified date or the date on which the specified event occurs shall not be included in calculating that number of days.

58. Where, by reason of the operation of rule 13, a participating Party

(a) receives a document on a date other than the date on which the same document is received by any other participating Party, or

(b) receives a document from a second participating Party on a date that is either before or after the date on which it receives the corresponding document from a third participating Party,

any period of time the calculation of which is dependent on such receipt shall be calculated from the date of receipt of the last such document.

Suspension of Benefits Panels

59. These rules shall apply to a panel established under Article 2019(3) except that:

(a) the Party that requests the establishment of the panel shall deliver its initial written submission to its section of the Secretariat within 10 days after the date on which the last panelist is selected;

(b) the responding Party shall deliver its written counter-submission to its section of the Secretariat within 15 days after the date of delivery of the initial written submission;

(c) the panel shall fix the time limit for delivering any further written submissions, including rebuttal written submissions, so as to provide each disputing Party with the opportunity to make an equal number of written submissions subject to the time limits for panel proceedings set out in the Agreement and these Rules; and

(d) unless the disputing Parties disagree, the panel may decide not to convene a hearing.

Panels Regarding Investment Disputes in Financial Services

60. These rules shall apply to a panel convened under Article 1415(3) except that the terms of reference shall be as set out in Article 1415(2).

Responsible Section of the Secretariat

61. The responsible section of the Secretariat shall:

(a) provide administrative assistance to the panel and any scientific review board;

(b) compensate, and provide administrative assistance to, experts, panelists and their assistants, members of scientific review boards, interpreters, translators, court reporters or other individuals that it retains in a panel proceeding;

(c) make available to the panelists, on confirmation of their appointment, copies of the Agreement and other documents relevant to the proceedings, such as the Uniform Regulations and these Rules; and

(d) retain indefinitely a copy of the complete record of the panel proceeding.

Maintenance of Rosters

62. The Parties shall inform each section of the Secretariat of the composition of the roster established under Article 1414(3) and the roster established under Article 2009(1). The Parties shall promptly inform each section of the Secretariat of any changes made to the roster.

Appendix I
Scientific Bodies

Canada

The Royal Society of Canada

Mexico

El Colegio Nacional

United States

The National Research Council of the National Academy of Sciences

The National Academy of Engineering

The Institute of Medicine

THE UNITED STATES TRADE REPRESENTATIVE
Executive Office of the President
Washington, D.C. 20506

July 13, 1995

The Honorable Roy MacLaren
Minister for International Trade
Ottawa K1A OG2
Canada

Dear Minister MacLaren:

I have the honor to refer to discussions between the delegations of the United States of America, Canada and the United Mexican States regarding Model Rules of Procedure for disputes under Chapter Twenty of the North American Free Trade Agreement ("NAFTA").

I have the further honor to propose that the attached rules constitute the Model Rules of Procedure established under Article 2012 of the NAFTA.

I have the further honor to propose that this letter and the text appended, and your letter of confirmation in reply, constitute a decision of the Free Trade Commission, to take effect this day.

Sincerely,

Michael Kantor

Attachment

THE UNITED STATES TRADE REPRESENTATIVE
Executive Office of the President
Washington, D.C. 20506

July 13, 1995

The Honorable Herminio Blanco Mendoza
Secretary of Commerce and Industrial Development
Alfonso Reyes 30, Piso 10
Col. Hipodromo de la Condesa
06179 Mexico City
Mexico

Dear Secretary Blanco:

I have the honor to refer to discussions between the delegations of the United States of America, Canada and the United Mexican States regarding Model Rules of Procedure for disputes under Chapter Twenty of the North American Free Trade Agreement ("NAFTA").

I have the further honor to propose that the attached rules constitute the Model Rules of Procedure established under Article 2012 of the NAFTA.

I have the further honor to propose that this letter and the text appended, and your letter of confirmation in reply, constitute a decision of the Free Trade Commission, to take effect this day.

Sincerely,

Michael Kantor

Attachment

Executive Office of the President
Office of the United States Trade Representative
Washington, D.C. 20506

July 13, 1995

Jonathan T. Fried, Esq.
General Counsel
Trade Law Division
Department of Foreign Affairs and International Trade
Ottawa K1A OG2

Dear Jon:

Pursuant to Rule 35 of the NAFTA Chapter Twenty Model Rules of Procedure, I have the honor to confirm the following understanding reached between representatives of the United States of America, Canada, and the United Mexican States regarding the availability of information in the context of NAFTA Chapter Twenty dispute settlement procedures.

The NAFTA Parties will maintain the confidentiality of the panel's hearings, deliberations and initial report, and all written submissions to and communications with the panel, in accordance with the following procedures:

(1) A Party or, subject to its direction, the Party's section of the Secretariat, may make available to the public at any time the Party's written submissions and those of the other participating Parties. Before such documents are made available to the public they shall be redacted to remove any information designated for confidential treatment by a participating Party pursuant to paragraph (4).

(2) A Party or, subject to its direction, the Party's section of the Secretariat, may make the hearing transcript available to the public 15 days after the final report of the panel is published pursuant to Article 2017(5). Before the transcript is made available to the public it shall be redacted to remove any information designated for confidential treatment by a participating Party pursuant to paragraph (4).

(3) Where information has been removed from a document pursuant to paragraph (1) or (2), the document shall indicate clearly each place where such information has been removed.

(4) To the extent it considers strictly necessary to protect personal privacy or to address essential confidentiality concerns, a participating Party may designate specific informa-

tion included in its written submissions, or that it has present in the panel hearing, for confidential treatment.

(5) A participating Party may disclose to other persons such information in connection with the panel proceedings as it considers necessary for the preparation of its case, but it shall ensure that those persons maintain the confidentiality of any such information.

(6) A participating Party shall treat as confidential the initial report and information submitted by another Party to the panel that the Party has designated as confidential pursuant to paragraph (4).

(7) The responsible section of the Secretariat shall take such reasonable steps as are necessary to ensure that experts, scientific review board members, interpreters, translators, court reporters and other individuals retained by the Secretariat maintain the confidentiality of the panel proceedings.

(8) Except as provided under paragraphs (1) and (2), Secretariat personnel shall maintain the confidentiality of the panel proceedings.

I have the honor to propose that this letter, and your letter of confirmation in reply, constitute an understanding between our two Governments, to take effect on this day.

Sincerely,

Jennifer A. Hillman

General Counsel

DOCUMENT 10

NAFTA RULES OF PROCEDURE FOR ARTICLE 1905 SPECIAL COMMITTEES

59 Federal Register 8714 (February 23, 1994)

AGENCY: North American Free Trade Agreement, NAFTA Secretariat, United States Section, International Trade Administration, Department of Commerce.

ACTION: Rules of Procedure for NAFTA Article 1905 Special Committees.

SUMMARY: Canada, Mexico, and the United States have negotiated the rules of procedure for Article 1905 Special Committees. These rules apply to special committee proceedings conducted pursuant to Article 1905 of the Agreement, unless the involved Parties otherwise agree.

EFFECTIVE DATE: January 1, 1994, the date of the entry into force of the North American Free Trade Agreement ("Agreement"). These Rules of Procedure shall apply to all special committee proceedings commenced on or after the effective date.

FOR FURTHER INFORMATION CONTACT: Lisa B. Koteen, Senior Attorney, Stacy J. Ettinger, Attorney-Advisor, or Terrence J. McCartin, Attorney-Advisor, Office of the Chief Counsel for Import Administration, room B-099, U.S. Department of Commerce, 14th and Constitution Avenue, NW., Washington, DC 20230; telephone: (202) 482–0836, (202) 482–4618, or (202) 482–5031, respectively. For procedural matters involving cases under panel review, contact James R. Holbein, United States Secretary, NAFTA Secretariat, room 2061, U.S. Department of Commerce, 14th and Constitution Avenue, NW., Washington, DC 20230; telephone: (202) 482–5438; fax: (202) 482–0148.

SUPPLEMENTARY INFORMATION:

Background

Chapter Nineteen of the North American Free Trade Agreement ("Agreement") establishes a mechanism for replacing judicial review of final antidumping and countervailing duty determinations involving imports from Canada, Mexico, or the United States with review by independent binational panels. If requested, these panels will expeditiously review final determinations to determine whether they are consistent with the antidumping or countervailing duty law of the importing country. In instances in which one of the Parties to the Agreement alleges, pursuant to Article 1905.1 of the Agreement, that the application of another Party's domestic law (a) has prevented the establishment of a panel; (b) has prevented a panel from rendering a final decision; (c) has prevented the implementation of a panel's decision or denied it binding force and effect; or (d) has resulted in a failure to provide opportunity for proper review of a final determination by a panel or a court of competent jurisdiction, that Party may request the establishment of a special committee. Title IV of the North American Free Trade Agreement Implementation Act of 1993, Public Law No. 103–182, 107 Stat. 2057, amends United States law to implement Chapter Nineteen of the Agreement. The Article 1905 Special Committee Rules are intended to give effect to the special committee provisions of Chapter Nineteen of the Agreement by setting forth the procedures for commencing, conducting, and completing special committee proceedings. These rules are the result of negotiations among Canada, Mexico, and the United States in compliance with the terms of the Agreement.

North American Free Trade Agreement Rules of Procedure for Article 1905 Special Committees

Contents

The Parties,

Having regard to Chapter Nineteen of the North American Free Trade Agreement between Canada, the United Mexican States and the United States of America;

Acting pursuant to Article 1905.6 of the Agreement;

Adopt the following Rules of Procedure, which shall come into force on the same day as the Agreement enters into force and from that day shall govern all special committee proceedings conducted pursuant to Article 1905 of the Agreement.

Short Title

1.   These rules may be cited as the Article 1905 Special Committee Rules.

Statement of General Intent

2.   These rules shall apply to special committee proceedings conducted pursuant to Article 1905 of the Agreement, unless the involved Parties otherwise agree. Where a procedural question arises that is not covered by these rules, a special committee may adopt an appropriate procedure that is not inconsistent with the Agreement. In the event of any inconsistency between the provisions of these rules and the Agreement, the Agreement shall prevail.

Interpretation

3.   In these rules,

"Agreement"   means the North American Free Trade Agreement;

"Complaining Party"   means a Party who requests, pursuant to Article 1905.2 of the Agreement, that a special committee be established;

"involved Secretariat"   means the responsible Secretariat or the section of the Secretariat located in the country of the other involved Party;

"legal holiday"   means

a) with respect to the Canadian Section of the Secretariat, every Saturday and Sunday, New Year's Day (January 1), Good Friday, Easter Monday, Victoria Day, Canada Day (July 1), Labour Day (first Monday in September), Thanksgiving Day (second Monday in October), Remembrance Day (November 11), Christmas Day (December 25), Boxing Day (December 26), any other day fixed as a statutory holiday by the Government of Canada or by the province in which the section is located and any day on which the offices of the Canadian Section of the Secretariat are officially closed in whole or in part,

b) with respect to the Mexican Section of the Secretariat, every Saturday and Sunday, New Year's Day (January 1), Constitution Day (February 5), Benito Juarez's Birthday (March 21), Labor Day (May 1), Battle of Puebla (May 5), Independence Day (September 16), Congressional Opening Day (November 1), Revolution Day

(November 20), Transmission of the Federal Executive Branch (every six years on December 1), Christmas Day (December 25), any day designated as a statutory holiday by the Federal Laws or, in the case of Ordinary Elections, by the Local Electoral Laws and any day on which the offices of the Mexican Section of the Secretariat are officially closed in whole or in part, and

c) with respect to the United States Section of the Secretariat, every Saturday and Sunday, New Year's Day (January 1), Martin Luther King's Birthday (third Monday in January), Presidents' Day (third Monday in February), Memorial Day (last Monday in May), Independence Day (July 4), Labor Day (first Monday in September), Columbus Day (second Monday in October), Veterans' Day (November 11), Thanksgiving Day (fourth Thursday in November), Christmas Day (December 25), any day designated as a holiday by the President or the Congress of the United States and any day on which the offices of the Government of the United States located in the District of Columbia or the offices of the United States Section of the Secretariat are officially closed in whole or in part;

"Mexico" means the United Mexican States;

"official publication" means

a) in the case of the Government of Canada, the Canada Gazette,

b) in the case of the Government of Mexico, the Diario Oficial de la Federacion, and

c) in the case of the Government of the United States, the Federal Register;

"Party" means the Government of Canada, the Government of Mexico or the Government of the United States;

"Responding Party" means the Party against whom an allegation is made under Article 1905.1 of the Agreement;

"responsible Secretariat" means the section of the Secretariat of the Responding Party;

"responsible Secretary" means the Secretary of the responsible Secretariat;

"Secretariat" means the Secretariat established pursuant to Article 2002 of the Agreement;

"Secretary" means the Secretary of the United States Section of the Secretariat, the Secretary of the Mexican Section of the Secretariat or the Secretary of the Canadian Section of the Secretariat and includes any person authorized to act on behalf of that Secretary;

"special committee" means a special committee established pursuant to Article 1905 of the Agreement;

"United States" means the United States of America.

Operation of the Special Committee

4. 1) Subject to subrule (2), unless the involved Parties otherwise agree, special committee meetings shall take place at the offices of the responsible Secretariat or at such alternative location as the committee members may agree.

   2) A special committee may conduct meetings or exchange information by any means, including by means of a telephone conference call or facsimile or computer transmission.

5. The members of a special committee shall select from among themselves a chairperson, who shall preside over all meetings and hearings of the special committee.

6. The chairperson of the special committee shall fix the date and time of its meetings in consultation with other special committee members and the responsible Secretary.

7. All reports, findings, determinations and decisions of a special committee shall be made or issued by a majority vote of all members of the special committee.

8. A special committee proceeding commences on the day on which a request for a special committee is filed with the responsible Secretariat and terminates on the day on which a notice of completion of the special committee proceeding is issued pursuant to rule 36.

9. 1) A special committee may adopt internal procedures of its own, not inconsistent with these rules, for routine administrative matters.

   2) A special committee may delegate to its chairperson the authority to make decisions regarding internal procedures or routine administrative matters.

10. The terms of reference of a special committee shall be limited to

   a) making a finding as to whether any allegations set out in Article 1905.1 of the Agreement made by the Complaining Party regarding the application of the Responding Party's domestic law are substantiated;

   b) determining whether a suspension of benefits by the Complaining Party pursuant to Article 1905.8(b) of the Agreement is manifestly excessive; and

   c) determining whether the Responding Party has corrected a problem with respect to which the special committee has made an affirmative finding.

Service of Documents

11. A document to be filed by an involved Party with the responsible Secretariat shall

a) be served on the other involved Party by express courier, overnight mail or by any other means agreed upon by the involved Parties; and

b) when filed, be accompanied by a proof of service certifying that the document has been served on the other involved Party, indicating the manner, date and time of service.

Written Submissions

12. All written submissions and responses filed with a responsible Secretariat shall be accompanied by four copies thereof.

13. 1) A request for the establishment of a special committee under Article 1905.2 of the Agreement shall be made by filing the request with the responsible Secretariat.

2) On the filing of a request under subrule (1), the responsible Secretary and the other involved Secretary shall cause a notice of the filing of the request to be published in the official publications of the countries in which their sections of the Secretariat are located.

14. The written initial submission of a Complaining Party shall be filed with the responsible Secretariat no later than 10 days after the date on which the last member of the special committee is appointed.

15. A written response by the Responding Party shall be filed with the responsible Secretariat no later than 20 days after the filing of the initial submission of the Complaining Party.

16. A special committee may allow each involved Party the opportunity to make an equal number of further written submissions, within such time as may be fixed by the special committee, having regard to the time limits fixed by Annex 1905.6 to Chapter Nineteen of the Agreement.

17. The responsible Secretary shall forward to the other involved Secretary a copy of all documents filed with the responsible Secretariat and of all reports, findings, determinations and decisions issued by the special committee.

Hearings

18. 1) At least one hearing shall be held before the special committee presents its initial report.

2) The date and time of hearings shall be fixed by the special committee in consultation with the involved Parties and the responsible Secretary.

3) A verbatim transcript shall be taken of all hearings.

19. Unless the involved Parties otherwise agree, special committee hearings shall take place at the offices of the responsible Secretariat.

20. 1) All special committee members must be present during hearings.

2) No later than five days before the date of a hearing, each involved Party shall deliver to the responsible Secretariat and to the other involved Party a list of the names of the persons who will present oral arguments at the hearing on behalf of that Party and of other representatives or advisers of the Party who will be attending the hearing.

21.   Oral proceedings shall be conducted in the following order, ensuring that each involved Party is given equal time:

    a) the argument of the Complaining Party;

    b) the argument of the Responding Party;

    c) a reply of the Complaining Party; and

    d) a counter-reply of the Responding Party.

22.   At the request of an involved Party or at the initiative of the special committee, with the agreement of both involved Parties and subject to such terms and conditions as both involved Parties may agree upon, the special committee may call upon any person to provide information concerning the matter in dispute.

Language of Proceedings

23.   Written and oral proceedings may be in either English, French or Spanish, or in any combination thereof.

24.   Unless the involved Parties otherwise agree, the reports, findings, determinations and decisions of a special committee shall be issued in an official language of the Responding Party and, if necessary, shall be promptly translated into an official language of the other involved Party.

Special Committee Deliberations

25.   1) The deliberations of a special committee shall take place in private and remain confidential.

    2) Only special committee members may take part in the deliberations of a special committee.

    3) Staff of the involved Secretariats, assistants to the special committee members and any necessary support staff may be present during deliberations of a special committee by permission of the special committee.

Reports

26.   In accordance with paragraph (b) of Annex 1905.6 to Chapter Nineteen of the Agreement, a special committee shall prepare and present to the involved Parties an initial report, wherever practicable, within 60 days after the appointment of the last member of the special committee.

27.   The involved Parties may comment in writing or, at the request of the special committee, orally, on an initial report of a special committee within 14 days after the initial report is presented.

28.   An initial report of a special committee shall be kept confidential.

29.   1) A special committee shall issue a final report, together with any separate opinions rendered by individual committee members, within 30 days after the presentation of its initial report.

2) Any separate opinions rendered by individual special committee members shall be anonymous.

3) On the issuance of a final report under subrule (1), the responsible Secretary shall immediately forward copies of the report to the involved Parties.

4) Unless the involved Parties otherwise agree,

(a) within 10 days after the final report is forwarded to the involved Parties, the involved Secretaries shall cause a notice that a final report has been issued by a special committee to be published in the official publications of the involved Parties, indicating that copies of the report and of any separate opinions by individual members or written views of either involved Party are available to the public at the offices of the responsible Secretariat; and

(b) the responsible Secretariat shall make available to the public copies of the final report of a special committee, together with any separate opinions by individual members and any written views that either involved Party may wish to be published.

Reconvening of Special Committee

30.   Where a special committee has made an affirmative finding with respect to grounds specified in Article 1905.1 of the Agreement, a Responding Party may request that the special committee be reconvened by filing a request with the responsible Secretariat

a) where the Responding Party is requesting that the special committee determine whether the Responding Party has corrected a problem with respect to which the special committee has made an affirmative finding, at any time after the affirmative finding was made; or

b) where the Responding Party is requesting that the special committee determine whether a suspension of benefits by the Complaining Party under Article 1905.8 of the Agreement is manifestly excessive, at any time after the suspension was made.

31.   1) Where a request referred to in subrule 30(a) is filed before the fortieth day of the 60-day consultation period referred to in Article 1905.8 of the Agreement, the special committee shall endeavour to present a report containing its determination to the involved Parties before the sixtieth day of that period, and may for that purpose make such orders as to filing of written submissions and responses and the

holding of a hearing as the special committee considers necessary under the circumstances.

2) Rules 32 to 34 apply with respect to requests referred to in subrule 30(a) that are filed on or after the fortieth day of the 60-day consultation period referred to in Article 1905.8 and to requests referred to in subrule 30(b).

32.   1) At the time of filing a request pursuant to rule 30, the Responding Party shall file a written submission in support of the request.

2) A Complaining Party shall file a written response to a submission referred to in subrule (1) within 20 days after that submission is filed.

33.   1) At the time of filing a request pursuant to rule 30 or a written response pursuant to subrule 32(2), an involved Party may request an opportunity to present oral argument in support of its request or response.

2) Where an involved Party requests an opportunity to present oral argument pursuant to subrule (1), the special committee may hold a hearing, at which both involved Parties shall be granted an equal opportunity to present oral argument.

34.   The special committee shall, within 45 days of the filing of a request pursuant to rule 30, present to the involved Parties a written report containing its determination pursuant to Article 1905.10 of the Agreement.

35.   Subrules 29 (2) to (4) apply, with such modifications as are necessary, to reports referred to in subrule 31(1) and rule 34.

Completion of Special Committee Proceedings

36.   1) On completion of a special committee proceeding, as determined by the special committee in consultation with the involved Parties, the special committee shall request the responsible Secretary to issue a notice of completion of the proceeding.

2) A notice referred to in subrule (1) is effective the day after it is issued.

3) The responsible Secretary shall cause a notice issued under subrule (1) to be published in the official publications of the involved Parties.

37.   The members of a special committee are discharged from their duties on the day on which a notice of completion of the special committee proceeding is effective.

Confidentiality

38.   All written submissions to, and communications with, a special committee and all documents filed with the involved Secretariats shall be kept confidential.

39.   1) All hearings of a special committee, and all transcripts thereof, shall be kept confidential.

2) It is the responsibility of each involved Party to ensure that the persons attending oral proceedings of a special committee on its behalf maintain the confidentiality of the proceedings.

Ex Parte Contacts

40.   1) No special committee or member of a special committee shall meet or contact one involved Party in the absence of the other involved Party.

2) No special committee member shall discuss a matter before the special committee with the involved Parties in the absence of other special committee members.

Extension and Computation of Time

41.   A time period fixed by these rules may be extended with the consent of both involved Parties or by a decision of a special committee.

42.   1) In computing any time period fixed in or under these rules, the day or date from which the time period begins to run shall be excluded and, subject to subrule (2), the last day of the time period shall be included.

2) Where the last day of a time period computed in accordance with subrule (1) falls on a legal holiday of the responsible Secretariat, that day and any other legal holidays of the responsible Secretariat immediately following that day shall be excluded from the computation.

3) In computing any time period of five days or less fixed in these rules or by a decision of a special committee, any legal holiday that falls within the time period shall be excluded from the computation.

Responsibilities of the Responsible Secretary

43.   The responsible Secretary shall provide administrative support for each special committee proceeding and shall make the arrangements necessary for the hearings and meetings of the special committee, including the provision of court reporters and, if required, interpreters to provide simultaneous translation.

44.   The responsible Secretary shall maintain a file for each special committee proceeding, comprised of the original or a copy of all documents filed, whether or not filed in accordance with these rules, in the special committee proceeding.

Death or Incapacity

45.   Where a special committee member is disqualified, dies or otherwise becomes unable to fulfil special committee duties,

a) special committee proceedings and computations of time shall be suspended, pending the appointment of a substitute member; and

b) where the disability, disqualification or death occurs after oral argument has begun, the chairperson may order that the matter be reheard, on such terms as are appropriate, after selection of a substitute member.

Dated: February 10, 1994.

Timothy J. Hauser, Deputy Under Secretary for International Trade.

[FR Doc. 94–3931 Filed 2–22–94; 8:45 am]

D. MEXICAN LAW

DOCUMENT 11

FOREIGN INVESTMENT LAW OF THE UNITED MEXICAN STATES

Published in the Official Gazette (Diario Oficial) of the Federation on December 27, 1993 and in force as of December 28, 1993

———

TITLE FIRST
GENERAL PROVISIONS
Chapter I
Purpose of Law

ARTICLE 1

This Law is of public order and general observance throughout the Republic. Its purpose is determination of the rules for channeling foreign investment into Mexico and to insure that it contributes to national development.

ARTICLE 2

For purposes of this Law, the following definitions shall apply:

I. The Commission: The National Foreign Investments Commission;

II. Foreign Investment:

a. Participation of foreign investors in any proportion in the capital of Mexican corporations;

b. That done by Mexican corporations with majority foreign investment; and

c. The participation by foreign investors in the activities and acts included in this Law.

III. Foreign investor: The individual or corporate person with nationality other than Mexican and foreign entities without legal status.

IV. Registry: The National Foreign Investments Registry.

V. The Secretariat: The Secretariat of Commerce and Industrial Development.

VI. Restricted Zone: The strip of Mexican territory one hundred kilometers in depth from the borders and fifty kilometers in depth from the coast lines to which Article 27, paragraph I of the Political Constitution of the United Mexican States refers; and

VII. Exclusion of Foreigners Clause: The express agreement, or pact that forms an integral part of corporate by-laws by which it is provided that the companies at hand shall not admit directly or indirectly, foreign investors nor corporations with an admission of foreigners clause.

ARTICLE 3

For purposes of this Law, investment made by foreigners in Mexico who hold resident alien status shall be considered the same as Mexican investment, except that made in the activities provided for in Titles First and Second hereof.

ARTICLE 4

Foreign investment may participate in any proportion in the capital of Mexican companies, acquire fixed assets, enter new fields of economic activity or manufacture new product lines, open and operate establishments, and expand or relocate existing establishments, except as otherwise provided herein.

The rules for participation of foreign investment in the activities of the financial sector provided for in this Law shall be applied without prejudice to those established by the specific laws for those activities.

Chapter II
Reserved Activities

ARTICLE 5

The functions determined by the laws in the following strategic areas are reserved exclusively to the State:

I.   Petroleum and other hydrocarbons;

II.   Basic petrochemicals;

III.   Electricity;

IV.   Generation of nuclear energy;

V.   Radioactive minerals;

VI.   Satellite communication;

VII.   Telegraph;

VIII.   Radiotelegraph;

IX.   Mail;

X.   Railroads;

XI.   Issue of currency; and

XII.   Minting of coins.

XIII. Control, supervision and oversight of ports, airports, and heliports; and

XIV. Such others as are expressly stated in the applicable legal provisions.

ARTICLE 6

The following economic activities and corporations hereinafter mentioned, are reserved exclusively to Mexicans or to Mexican companies with an Exclusion of Foreigners Clause:

I. National surface transportation of passengers, tourism, and freight, excluding messenger and package delivery service;

II. Retail trade in gasoline and liquid petroleum gas;

III. Radio broadcasting service and other radio and television services different from cable television;

IV. Credit unions;

V. Development banking institutions, pursuant to the provisions of the law on the subject; and

VI. Supply of professional and technical services expressly set forth in the applicable legal provisions.

Foreign investment may not participate in the aforesaid activities and corporations in this article directly or through trusts, agreements, corporate or shareholder pacts, pyramid schemes, or any other mechanism which grants any control or equity participation whatsoever, except as provided by Title Fifth hereof.

Chapter III
Activities and Acquisitions Subject to Specific Regulation

ARTICLE 7

In the economic activities and corporations mentioned hereafter, foreign investment may participate in the following percentages:

I. Up to 10% in:

Cooperative companies for production;

II. Up to 25% in:

    a. Domestic air transportation

    b. Air taxi transportation; and

    c. Specialized air transportation;

III. Up to 30% in:

    a. Holding companies for financial groups;

    b. Commercial (multiple) banking credit institutions;

    c. Securities brokerage firms; and

    d. Securities market specialists;

IV. Up to 49% in:

    a. Insurance institutions;

    b. Bonding institutions;

    c. Currency exchange houses;

    d. General deposit warehouses;

    e. Financial leasing companies;

    f. Financial factoring companies;

    g. Financial companies with purpose limited to those provided for in Article 103, paragraph IV, of the Law of Credit Institutions;

    h. Companies to which Article 12 Bis of the Securities Market Law refers;

    i. Shares representing the fixed capital in investment companies and operating companies of investment corporations;

    j. Manufacture and commercialization of explosives, firearms, cartridges, munitions and fireworks, excluding acquisition and use of explosives for industrial and extraction activities or the preparation of explosive mixtures for use in said activities;

    k. Printing and publication of newspapers for circulation solely throughout Mexico;

    l. Series T shares in companies that own agricultural, ranching, and forestry lands;

    m. Cable television;

    n. Basic telephone services;

    o. Fresh water, coastal, and exclusive economic zone fishing, excluding aquaculture;

    p. Integral port administration;

    q. Piloting port services for vessels to carry out operations of inland navigation operations in the terms of the subject law;

    r. Shipping companies engaged in commercial exploitation of ships for inland and coastal navigation, excluding tourism cruisers and exploitation of marine dredging and implements for port construction, conservation and operation;

    s. Services connected to the railway sector that consist of passenger service, maintenance and rehabilitation of roads, rights of way, repair shops for tractive and hauling equipment, organization and commercialization of unit trains, operation of domestic terminals for freight and railroad telecommunications; and

    t. Supply of fuel and lubricants for ships, airplanes, and railway equipment;

The limitations for foreign investment participation set forth in this article may not be exceeded directly, nor through trusts, agreements, corporate or shareholder pacts, pyramid schemes or any other mechanism which grants control or equity participation greater than that established, except pursuant to Title Fifth of this Law.

ARTICLE 8

Favorable resolution by the Commission is required for foreign investment participation in a percentage greater than 49% in the economic activities and companies referred to hereafter:

I. Port services for ships to effect their inland navigation operations, such as towing, mooring and lighterage;

II. Shipping companies engaged in exploitation of ships solely for high seas traffic;

III. Management of air terminals;

IV. Private education services at the pre-school, primary, secondary, upper middle, upper, and combined levels;

V. Legal services;

VI. Credit information companies;

VII. Securities classification institutions; and

VIII. Insurance agents; and

IX. Cellular telephone.

X. Construction of pipeline for the transportation of petroleum and products derived therefrom; and

XI. Drilling of petroleum and gas wells.

ARTICLE 9

Favorable resolution from the Commission is required for foreign investment to acquire assets or shares in Mexican companies, regardless of the activity they engage in only whose total asset value at the time of acquisition exceeds the amount established annually by said Commission, and provided said acquisition implies that the direct or indirect participation of foreign investment in the capital of the companies in question exceeds 49% thereof.

TITLE SECOND

ACQUISITION OF REAL ESTATE AND TRUSTS

Chapter I

Acquisition of Real Estate

ARTICLE 10

Pursuant to Article 27, paragraph I of the Political Constitution of the United Mexican States, Mexican companies with an Exclusion of

Foreigners Clause or which have executed the agreement to which said provision refers, may acquire ownership of real estate in Mexico.

For companies whose by-laws include the agreement provided for in Constitutional Article 27, paragraph (I), the following shall apply:

I.   They may acquire ownership to real estate located in the Restricted Zone used for realization of non-residential activities, and must record said acquisition with the Secretariat of Foreign Relations; and

II.   They may acquire rights to real property in the Restricted Zone that are used for residential purposes pursuant to the following chapter.

Chapter II
Real Estate Trusts in the Restricted Zone

ARTICLE 11

A permit is required from the Secretariat of Foreign Relations for credit institutions to acquire as trustees, the rights to real estate located in the Restricted Zone when the purpose of the trust is to permit the use and benefit from said property without creating real rights thereto, and the beneficiaries are:

I.   Mexican companies without an Exclusion of Foreigners Clause in the case provided for in Article 10, paragraph (II) of this Law; and

II.   Foreign individuals or corporations.

ARTICLE 12

Use and benefit from real estate located in the Restricted Zone shall mean the rights to use or enjoyment thereof, including, as applicable, receipt of the fruits, products, or generally, any yield resulting from the operation and exploitation for gain done through third parties, or through the trust institution.

ARTICLE 13

The duration of the trusts to which this article refers to shall be a maximum of 50 years, which may be renewed on request by the interested party.

The Secretariat of Foreign Relations reserves the authority to verify at any time compliance with the conditions under which the permits and registrations to which this Title refers to are granted.

ARTICLE 14

The Secretariat of Foreign Relations shall decide on the permits to which this Chapter refers, considering the economic and social benefit that realization of these operations implies for the Nation.

Any application for permit which meets the requirements set forth must be granted by the Secretariat of Foreign Relations within thirty business days following the date of its filing. Recording with the registry to which Article 10, paragraph (I) refers must be decided within a maximum period of fifteen business days following filing of the application. Otherwise, the corresponding permit or registration shall be deemed granted.

TITLE THIRD
COMPANIES
Creation and Modification of Companies

ARTICLE 15

A permit from the Secretariat of Foreign Relations is required for the creation of companies. The Exclusion of Foreigners Clause or the agreement provided for in Constitutional Article 27, paragraph (I) must be included in the by-laws of companies that are created.

ARTICLE 16

A permit from the Secretariat of Foreign Relations for companies created to change their corporate name or to replace the Exclusion of Foreigners Clause with a clause for admission of foreigners.

TITLE FOURTH
INVESTMENT BY FOREIGN CORPORATIONS

ARTICLE 17

Without prejudice to that established in international treaties and conventions to which Mexico is a party, in order for foreign corporations to habitually undertake commercial actions in the Mexican Republic they must obtain authorization from The Secretariat for their consequent registration in the Public Registry of Commerce, pursuant to Articles 250 and 251 of the General Law of Commercial Companies.

Any application to obtain the authorization to which the preceding paragraph refers to which meets the corresponding requirements must be approved by The Secretariat within the 15 business days following the date of its filing.

TITLE FIFTH
NEUTRAL INVESTMENT
Chapter I
Neutral Investment Concept

ARTICLE 18

Neutral investment is that investment made in Mexican companies, or trusts authorized pursuant to this Title and shall not be computed to determine the percentage of foreign investment in the capital of Mexican companies.

Chapter II

Neutral Investment Represented by Instruments Issued by Fiduciary Institutions

ARTICLE 19

The Secretariat may authorize fiduciary institutions to issue neutral investment instruments that shall solely grant, with respect to companies, pecuniary rights to their holders, and, as applicable, limited corporate rights, but without granting their holders voting rights in Shareholders Meetings.

Chapter III

Neutral Investment Represented by Special Stock Series

ARTICLE 20

Investment in shares without voting rights or with limited corporate rights shall be deemed neutral, provided the authorization from The Secretariat, and when applicable, from the National Securities Commission, is previously obtained.

Chapter IV

Neutral Investment in Holding Companies of Financial Groups, Commercial Banks and Brokerage Houses

ARTICLE 21

Upon prior opinion of the Secretariat of Finance and Public Credit and from the National Securities Commission, The Secretariat may decide on neutral investment through the acquisition of Certificates of Ordinary Participation issued by fiduciary institutions authorized therefor, whose assets are constituted by shares representing Series B of the capital stock of holding companies of financial groups, commercial banks, or shares representing Series A of the capital stock of brokerage houses.

Chapter V

Neutral Investment by International Financial Development Corporations

ARTICLE 22

The Commission may decide on neutral investment that international financial development corporations intend to make in the capital of companies pursuant to the terms and conditions established in the Regulations to this Law for such purpose.

TITLE SIXTH

NATIONAL FOREIGN INVESTMENT COMMISSION

Chapter I

Structure of the Commission

ARTICLE 23

The Commission shall be composed of the Secretariats of Interior, of Foreign Relations, of Finance and Public Credit, of Social Development, of Energy, Mines and Quasi-State Industry, of Commerce and Industrial Development, of Communications and Transportation, of Labor and Social Welfare, and of Tourism, who may appoint an Under-Secretary as alternate. Further, those authorities who may have jurisdiction over the issues to be addressed may be invited to participate in Commission meetings.

ARTICLE 24

The Secretary of Commerce and Industrial Development shall preside over the Commission and for its operation it shall have an Executive Secretary and a Committee of Representatives.

ARTICLE 25

The Committee of Representatives shall be composed of the public servants appointed by each of the State Secretariats who sit on the Commission and shall have the authority delegated to it by said Commission.

Chapter II

Authority of the Commission

ARTICLE 26

The Commission shall have the following authority:

I. Declare the policy guidelines for foreign investment and to design mechanisms to promote investment in Mexico;

II. Resolve, through The Secretariat, on the merit, and as applicable, on the terms and conditions for participation of foreign investment in activities or acquisitions subject to specific regulation pursuant to Articles 8 and 9 of this Law;

III. Be the mandatory advisory body on foreign investment to the Federal Public Administration agencies and organizations;

IV. Establish criteria for the application of the legal and regulatory provisions on foreign investment, through issuance of general resolutions; and

V. Such others as correspond to it pursuant hereto.

ARTICLE 27

The Executive Secretary of the Commission shall have the following authority:

    I.   To represent the Commission;

    II.   To give notice of the Resolutions of the Commission, through The Secretariat;

    III.   To undertake the studies entrusted to him by the Commission; and

    IV.   To deliver to the Congress, an annual statistical report on the foreign investment activity in the country, that covers the economic sectors and the regions where same is effected; and

    V.   Such others as pertain to him pursuant to this Law.

Chapter III
Operation of the Commission

ARTICLE 28

The Commission must decide on applications submitted for its consideration within a period not to exceed 45 business days counted from the date the relevant application is filed pursuant to the Regulations to this Law.

If the Commission does not enter a resolution within the aforesaid period, the application shall be deemed approved as filed. Upon request of interested party, The Secretariat must issue the corresponding authorization.

ARTICLE 29

To evaluate the applications submitted to its consideration, the Commission shall observe the following criteria:

    I.   The impact on jobs and training for employees;

    II.   The technological contribution;

    III.   Compliance of environmental requirements contained in the environmental statutes applicable; and

    IV.   Generally, the contribution toward increasing competitiveness in the Mexican production plant.

The Commission, in deciding whether an application is appropriate, may only impose requirements that do not distort international trade.

ARTICLE 30

The Commission may prevent acquisitions by foreign investment for reasons of national security.

TITLE SEVENTH
NATIONAL FOREIGN INVESTMENTS REGISTRY

ARTICLE 31

The Registry shall not have a public character and shall be divided in the sections established by its Regulations, which shall determine its organization and the information that must be provided to said Registry.

ARTICLE 32

The following must register with the Registry:

I.   Mexican companies in which foreign investors participate;

II.   Foreign individuals or corporations who habitually undertake commercial activity in Mexico, and branches of foreign investors established in Mexico; and

III.   Trusts on shares or corporate equity interests, on real estate, and on neutral investment by which rights are derived for the foreign investment.

The obligation to register falls upon the individuals and corporations to which Paragraphs I and II refer, and in the case of Paragraph III, the obligation shall correspond upon the fiduciary institution. The registration must be done within 40 business days counted from the date of the creation of the corporation or the equity participation by foreign investors; of formalization or protocolling of the documents relating to the foreign company; or of the creation of the relevant trust or granting of beneficial rights to foreign investors.

ARTICLE 33

The Registry shall issue the certificates of registration when the following information is included on the application:

I.   In the circumstances provided in Paragraphs I and II:

a.   Name, corporate or business name, domicile, date of creation, if applicable, and principal economic activity to be carried out;

b.   Name and domicile of the legal representative;

c.   Name and domicile of the persons authorized to hear and receive notices;

d.   Name, corporate or business name, nationality and immigration classification, if applicable, domicile of the foreign investors abroad or in Mexico, and their percentage of equity participation;

e.   Amount of capital stock subscribed and paid for, or subscribed and payable; and

f.   Estimated date for start of operations and approximate amount of total investment with the schedule therefor.

II. In the circumstances of Paragraph III:

    a. Name of the fiduciary institution;

    b. Name, corporate or business name, domicile and nationality of the foreign investment, or of the foreign investors grantors;

    c. Name, corporate or business name, domicile and nationality of the foreign investment or of the foreign investors designated beneficiaries;

    d. Date of creation, purposes, and duration of trust; and

    e. Description, value, use, and as applicable, location of the trust estate.

Once the certificate of registration or its renewals are issued, the Registry reserves the authority to request clarifications on the information filed.

Any change in the information filed in the terms of this article must be notified to the Registry pursuant to its Regulations.

ARTICLE 34

In the creation, modification, transformation, merger, separation, dissolution and liquidation of commercial companies, civil companies and associations, and generally, in any legal act or fact where the persons obligated to register with the Registry pursuant to Article 32 hereof, themselves participate or participate through representative, Public Notaries shall require said persons or their representatives to evidence their registration with said Register or, if said registration is being processed, that they evidence same with the relevant application. If it is not so evidenced, the Notary Public may authorize the Public Instrument at hand and shall report such failure to the Registry within the ten business days following the date that the Instrument is authorized.

ARTICLE 35

Those subject to register with the Registry must annually renew their certificate of registration, for which it shall be sufficient to file an economic and financial questionnaire pursuant to the relevant Regulations.

ARTICLE 36

The federal, state and local authorities must provide The Secretariat with the reports and certifications necessary for it to fulfill its functions pursuant to this Law and its regulatory provisions.

TITLE EIGHTH
SANCTIONS

ARTICLE 37

When acts done in contravention to the provisions of this Law are at hand, The Secretariat may revoke the authorizations granted.

Actions, agreements or corporate or shareholder pacts ruled null by The Secretariat due to being contrary to the provisions of this Law shall have no legal effect between the parties and shall be non enforceable against third parties.

ARTICLE 38

The violations to the provisions hereof and its regulatory provisions shall be penalized in accordance with the following:

I.   In the event that foreign investment effects activities, acquisitions or any other act that for its realization requires favorable resolution from the Commission, without previously obtaining said resolution, a fine of one thousand to five thousand salaries* shall be imposed;

II.   In the event that foreign corporations habitually undertake commercial acts in Mexico without previously obtaining the authorization from The Secretariat, a fine of five hundred to a thousand salaries shall be imposed;

III.   In the event that acts are taken in contravention to the provisions of this Law or its regulatory provisions on neutral investment, a fine of one hundred to three hundred salaries* shall be imposed;

IV.   In the event of failure, extemporaneous compliance, filing of incomplete or incorrect information with respect to the registration, reporting or notice obligations to the Registry by those obligated, a fine of thirty to one hundred salaries* shall be imposed;

V.   In the event of simulation of acts with the purpose of permitting enjoyment or disposition of real estate in the Restricted Zone by foreign individuals or corporations, or by Mexican companies without an Exclusion of Foreigners Clause, in contravention of the provisions of Titles Second and Third hereof, the violator shall be penalized with a fine of up to the amount of the operation; and

VI.   In the event of the other violations of this Law or its regulatory provisions, a fine of one hundred to one thousand salaries* shall be imposed.

For determination and imposition of penalties, the interested party must previously be heard and in the case of monetary sanctions, the nature and seriousness of the violation, the economic condition of the offender, the time between the date on which the obligations should have been performed and the date of its performance or remedy, and the total value of the operation must be taken into consideration.

The Secretariat is responsible for imposition of the sanctions except with respect to the offence to which Paragraph V of this article, and the

---

* For purposes of this article, salary means the daily general minimum wage in effect in the Federal District at the time the violation is determined.

others related to Titles Second and Third referred to, which shall be applied by the Secretariat of Foreign Relations.

The imposition of the sanctions to which this Title refers to shall be without prejudice of the civil or criminal liability which may apply.

ARTICLE 39

Notaries Public shall describe, insert and include in the official file or appendix of the instruments in which they intervene, the official communications of the authorizations that must be issued pursuant to this Law. When they authorize documents in which they do not refer to said authorizations, they shall be subject to the sanctions determined by the applicable laws for Notarial functions and the Federal Law for Public Brokerage.

TRANSITIONAL ARTICLES

FIRST

This law shall become effective the day following its publication in the Official Gazette of the Federation.

SECOND

The following are abrogated:

I. The Law to Promote Mexican Investment and to Regulate Foreign Investment, published in the Official Gazette of the Federation, on March 9, 1973;

II. The Organic Law of Constitutional Article 27, Paragraph (I), published in the Official Gazette of the Federation, on January 21, 1926;

III. The Decree Establishing the Temporary Need to Obtain a Permit for Acquisition of Property by Foreigners and for the Creation or Modification of Mexican Companies that Have or May Have Foreign Investors, published in the Official Gazette of the Federation, on July 7, 1944.

THIRD

The following are derogated:

I. Articles 46 and 47 of the Federal Firearms and Explosives Law published in the Official Gazette of the Federation, on January 11, 1972; and

II. All legal, regulatory, and general administrative provisions contrary to this Law.

FOURTH

Until the Regulations to this Law are issued, the Regulations to the Law to Promote Mexican Investment and to Regulate Foreign Investment, published in the Official Gazette of the Federation, on May 16,

1989 shall continue in force on all terms where its terms are not contrary hereto.

FIFTH

Foreign investors and companies with foreign investment who on the date of publication of this Law have programs, requirements, or commitments assumed with the Commission, its Executive Secretary, or the General Bureau of Foreign Investment within The Secretariat, may submit for the consideration of the Direction General cited, the exception of its fulfillment and for which said administrative office must respond accordingly, with no more than 45 days counted as of the filing of the respective application. Those foreign investors that do not request the possibility of the exception referred to, must comply with the commitments agreed upon previously with the commission, parties or public entities stated.

SIXTH

Activities for international land transportation of passengers, tourism and freight between points within the territory of Mexico and administration services of bus stations for passengers and auxiliary services are reserved exclusively to Mexicans or Mexican companies with an Exclusion of Foreigners Clause.

However, foreign investment may participate in the above activities pursuant to the following provisions:

I. Beginning on December 18, 1995, in up to 49% of the capital of Mexican companies;

II. Beginning on January 1, 2001, in up to 51% of the capital of Mexican companies; and

III. Beginning January 1, 2004, up to 100% of the capital of Mexican companies, without need of obtaining favorable resolution from the Commission.

SEVENTH

In activities for manufacture and assembly of automotive industry parts, equipment and accessories, foreign investment may participate up to 49% of the capital of Mexican companies, without prejudice of the terms of the Decree for the Fostering and Modernization of the Automotive Industry. As of January 1, 1999 foreign investment may participate up to 100% of the capital of Mexican companies without need of obtaining a favorable resolution from the Commission.

EIGHTH

With respect to video and packet switching services, foreign investment may participate up to 49% of the capital of Mexican companies. After July 1, 1995, foreign investment may participate up to 100% in the companies engaged in the aforesaid services without need of obtaining a favorable resolution from the Commission.

NINTH

A favorable resolution from the Commission is required for foreign investment to participate in a percentage greater that 49% of the capital of corporations who carry out activities of building, construction and installation of works. After January 1, 1999, foreign investment may participate in up to 100% of the capital of Mexican companies engaged therein, without need of obtaining a favorable resolution from the Commission.

TENTH

For purposes of the provisions of Article 9, and until the Commission establishes the amount of total value of the assets to which said article refers to, the amount set is of eighty-five million new pesos.

ELEVENTH

The terms of Chapter II, of Title Second of this Law, shall be applied to the foreign investors and Mexican corporations with clause accepting foreign investors that have real estate located in a restricted zone in trust for their benefit, upon this Law becoming effective, in everything that benefits them.

This Law was published in the Official Gazette of the Mexican Federation on December 27, 1993 and became effective on December 28, 1993.

E. UNITED STATES LAWS

DOCUMENT 12

NORTH AMERICAN FREE TRADE AGREEMENT IMPLEMENTATION ACT (1993)

(Selected Provisions)

PUBLIC LAW 103–182 of December 8, 1993, 107 Stat. 2060

An Act to implement the North American Free Trade Agreement.

Be it enacted by the Senate and House of Representatives of the United States of America in Congress assembled,

SECTION 1. SHORT TITLE AND TABLE OF CONTENTS.

19 U.S.C. § 3301 NOTE

(a) Short Title.—This Act may be cited as the "North American Free Trade Agreement Implementation Act" .

(b) Table of Contents.

19 U.S.C. § 3301

Sec. 2. Definitions

For purposes of this Act:

(1) Agreement.—The term "Agreement" means the North American Free Trade Agreement approved by the Congress under section 101(a).

(2) HTS.—The term "HTS" means the Harmonized Tariff Schedule of the United States.

(3) Mexico.—Any reference to Mexico shall be considered to be a reference to the United Mexican States.

(4) NAFTA Country.—Except as provided in section 202, the term "NAFTA country" means—

    (A) Canada for such time as the Agreement is in force with respect to, and the United States applies the Agreement to, Canada; and

(B) Mexico for such time as the Agreement is in force with respect to, and the United States applies the Agreement to, Mexico.

(5) International Trade Commission.—The term "International Trade Commission" means the United States International Trade Commission.

(6) Trade Representative.—The term "Trade Representative" means the United States Trade Representative.

TITLE I—APPROVAL OF, AND GENERAL PROVISIONS RELATING TO, THE NORTH AMERICAN FREE TRADE AGREEMENT

19 U.S.C. § 3311

Sec. 101.   Approval and Entry into Force of the North American Free Trade Agreement

(a) Approval of agreement and statement of administrative action.—Pursuant to section 1103 of the Omnibus Trade and Competitiveness Act of 1988 (19 U.S.C. § 2903) and section 151 of the Trade Act of 1974 (19 U.S.C. § 2191), the Congress approves—

(1) the North American Free Trade Agreement entered into on December 17, 1992, with the Governments of Canada and Mexico and submitted to the Congress on November 4, 1993; * * *

19 U.S.C. § 3312

Sec. 102.   Relationship of the Agreement to United States and State law

(a) Relationship of Agreement to United States Law.—

(1) United States law to Prevail in Conflict.—No provision of the Agreement, nor the application of any such provision to any person or circumstance, which is inconsistent with any law of the United States shall have effect.

(2) Construction.—Nothing in this Act shall be construed—

(A) to amend or modify any law of the United States, including any law regarding—

(i) the protection of human, animal, or plant life or health,

(ii) the protection of the environment, or

(iii) motor carrier or worker safety; or

(B) to limit any authority conferred under any law of the United States, including section 301 of the Trade Act of 1974;

unless specifically provided for in this Act.

(b) Relationship of Agreement to State Law.—

(1) Federal-State Consultation.—

(A) In General.—Upon the enactment of this Act, the President shall, through the intergovernmental policy advisory committees on trade established under section 306(c)(2)(A) of the Trade and Tariff Act of 1984, consult with the States for the purpose of achieving conformity of State laws and practices with the Agreement.

(B) Federal-State Consultation Process.—The Trade Representative shall establish within the Office of the United States Trade Representative a Federal-State consultation process for addressing issues relating to the Agreement that directly relate to, or will potentially have a direct impact on, the States. The Federal-State consultation process shall include procedures under which—

(i) the Trade Representative will assist the States in identifying those State laws that may not conform with the Agreement but may be maintained under the Agreement by reason of being in effect before the Agreement entered into force;

(ii) the States will be informed on a continuing basis of matters under the Agreement that directly relate to, or will potentially have a direct impact on, the States;

(iii) the States will be provided opportunity to submit, on a continuing basis, to the Trade Representative information and advice with respect to matters referred to in clause (ii);

(iv) the Trade Representative will take into account the information and advice received from the States under clause (iii) when formulating United States positions regarding matters referred to in clause (ii); and

(v) the States will be involved (including involvement through the inclusion of appropriate representatives of the States) to the greatest extent practicable at each stage of the development of United States positions regarding matters referred to in clause (ii) that will be addressed by committees, subcommittees, or working groups established under the Agreement or through dispute settlement processes provided for under the Agreement.

The Federal Advisory Committee Act (5 U.S.C.App.) shall not apply to the Federal-State consultation process established by this paragraph.

(2) Legal Challenge.—No State law, or the application thereof, may be declared invalid as to any person or circumstance on the ground that the provision or application is inconsistent with the Agreement, except in an action brought by the United States for the purpose of declaring such law or application invalid.

(3) Definition of State law.—For purposes of this subsection, the term "State law" includes—

(A) any law of a political subdivision of a State; and

(B) any State law regulating or taxing the business of insurance.

(c) Effect of Agreement with Respect to Private Remedies.—
No person other than the United States—

(1) shall have any cause of action or defense under—

(A) the Agreement or by virtue of Congressional approval thereof, or

(B) the North American Agreement on Environmental Cooperation or the North American Agreement on Labor Cooperation; or

(2) may challenge, in any action brought under any provision of law, any action or inaction by any department, agency, or other instrumentality of the United States, any State, or any political subdivision of a State on the ground that such action or inaction is inconsistent with the Agreement, the North American Agreement on Environmental Cooperation, or the North American Agreement on Labor Cooperation.

19 U.S.C. § 3315

Sec. 105.   United States Section of the NAFTA Secretariat

(a) Establishment of the United States Section.—The President is authorized to establish within any department or agency of the United States Government a United States Section of the Secretariat established under chapter 20 of the Agreement. The United States Section, subject to the oversight of the interagency group established under section 402, shall carry out its functions within the Secretariat to facilitate the operation of the Agreement, including the operation of chapters 19 and 20 of the Agreement and the work of the panels, extraordinary challenge committees, special committees, and scientific review boards convened under those chapters. The United States Section may not be considered to be an agency for purposes of section 552 of title 5, United States Code.

(b) Authorization of Appropriations.—There are authorized to be appropriated for each fiscal year after fiscal year 1993 to the department or agency within which the United States Section is established the lesser of—

(1) such sums as may be necessary; or

(2) $2,000,000;

for the establishment and operations of the United States Section and for the payment of the United States share of the expenses of binational panels and extraordinary challenge committees convened under chapter 19, and of the expenses incurred in dispute settlement proceedings under chapter 20, of the Agreement.

(c) Reimbursement of Certain Expenses.—If, in accordance with Annex 2002.2 of the Agreement, the Canadian Section or the Mexican Section of the Secretariat provides funds to the United States Section during any fiscal year, as reimbursement for expenses by the Canadian Section or the Mexican Section in connection with settlement proceedings under chapter 19 or 20 of the Agreement, the United States Section may retain and use such funds to carry out the functions described in subsection (a).

19 U.S.C. § 3316

Sec. 106.   Appointments to chapter 20 panel proceedings

(a) Consultation

The Trade Representative shall consult with the Committee on Ways and Means of the House of Representatives and the Committee on Finance of the Senate regarding the selection and appointment of candidates for the rosters described in article 2009 of the Agreement.

(b) Selection of individuals with environmental expertise

The United States shall, to the maximum extent practicable, encourage the selection of individuals who have expertise and experience in environmental issues for service in panel proceedings under chapter 20 of the Agreement to hear any challenge to a United States or State environmental law.

19 U.S.C. § 2112 NOTE

Sec. 107.   Termination or suspension of United States-Canada Free Trade Agreement

Section 501(c) of the United States-Canada Free Trade Implementation Act of 1988 (19 U.S.C. § 2112 note) is amended to read as follows:

"(c) **TERMINATION OR SUSPENSION OF AGREEMENT.—**

"(1) *TERMINATION OF AGREEMENT.*—On the date the Agreement ceases to be in force, the provisions of this Act (other than this paragraph and section 410(b)), and the amendments made by this Act, shall cease to have effect.

"(2) *EFFECT OF AGREEMENT SUSPENSION.*—An agreement by the United States and Canada to suspend the operation of the Agreement shall not be deemed to cause the Agreement to cease to be in force within the meaning of paragraph (1).

"(3) *SUSPENSION RESULTING FROM NAFTA.*—On the date the United States and Canada agree to suspend the operation of the Agreement by reason of the entry into force between them of the North American Free Trade Agreement, the following provisions of this Act are suspended and shall remain suspended until such time as the suspension of the Agreement may be terminated:

"(A) Sections 204(a) and (b) and 205(a).

"(B) Sections 302 and 304(f).

"(C) Sections 404, 409, and 410(b)." .

19 U.S.C. § 3317

Sec. 108.   Congressional Intent Regarding Future Accessions

(a) **In General.**—Section 101(a) may not be construed as conferring Congressional approval of the entry into force of the Agreement for the United States with respect to countries other than Canada and Mexico.

* * *

19 U.S.C. § 2112 NOTE

Sec. 109.   Effective Dates; Effect of Termination of NAFTA Status

* * *

(b) Termination of NAFTA Status.—During any period in which a country ceases to be a NAFTA country, sections 101 through 106 shall cease to have effect with respect to such country.

TITLE II—CUSTOMS PROVISIONS
19 U.S.C. § 3331

Sec. 201.   Tariff Modifications

(a) Tariff Modifications Provided for in the Agreement.—

(1) Proclamation Authority.—The President may proclaim—

(A) such modifications or continuation of any duty,

(B) such continuation of duty-free or excise treatment, or

(C) such additional duties,

as the President determines to be necessary or appropriate to carry out or apply articles 302, 305, 307, 308, and 703 and Annexes 302.2, 307.1, 308.1, 308.2, 300-B, 703.2, and 703.3 of the Agreement.

(2) Effect on Mexican GSP Status.—Notwithstanding section 502(a)(2) of the Trade Act of 1974 (19 U.S.C. § 2462(a)(2)), the President shall terminate the designation of Mexico as a beneficiary developing country for purposes of title V of the Trade Act of 1974 on the date of entry into force of the Agreement between the United States and Mexico.

(b) Other Tariff Modifications.—

* * *

(c) Conversion to Ad Valorem Rates For Certain Textiles.—

* * *

19 U.S.C. § 3332

Sec. 202.   Rules of Origin

(a) Originating Goods.—

(1) In General.—For purposes of implementing the tariff treatment and quantitative restrictions provided for under the Agreement, except as otherwise provided in this section, a good originates in the territory of a NAFTA country if—

(A) the good is wholly obtained or produced entirely in the territory of one or more of the NAFTA countries;

(B)(i) each nonoriginating material used in the production of the good—

(I) undergoes an applicable change in tariff classification set out in Annex 401 of the Agreement as a result of production occurring entirely in the territory of one or more of the NAFTA countries; or

(II) where no change in tariff classification is required, the good otherwise satisfies the applicable requirements of such Annex; and

(ii) the good satisfies all other applicable requirements of this section;

(C) the good is produced entirely in the territory of one or more of the NAFTA countries exclusively from originating materials; or

(D) except for a good provided for in chapters 61 through 63 of the HTS, the good is produced entirely in the territory of one or more of the NAFTA countries, but one or more of the nonoriginating materials, that are provided for as parts under the HTS and are used in the production of the good, does not undergo a change in tariff classification because—

(i) the good was imported into the territory of a NAFTA country in an unassembled or a disassembled form but was classified as an assembled good pursuant to General Rule of Interpretation 2(a) of the HTS; or

(ii)(I) the heading for the good provides for and specifically describes both the good itself and its parts and is not further subdivided into subheadings; or

(II) the subheading for the good provides for and specifically describes both the good itself and its parts.

(2) Special Rules.—

(A) Foreign-Trade Zones.—Subparagraph (B) of paragraph (1) shall not apply to a good produced in a foreign-trade zone or subzone (established pursuant to the Act of June 18, 1934, commonly known as the Foreign Trade Zones Act) that is entered for consumption in the customs territory of the United States.

(B) Regional Value-Content Requirement.—For purposes of subparagraph (D) of paragraph (1), a good shall be treated as originating in a NAFTA country if the regional value-content of the good, determined in accordance with subsection (b), is not less than 60 percent where the transaction value method is used, or not less than 50 percent where the net cost method is used, and the good satisfies all other applicable requirements of this section.

(b) Regional Value-Content.—

(1) In General.—Except as provided in paragraph (5), the regional value-content of a good shall be calculated, at the choice of the exporter or producer of the good, on the basis of—

(A) the transaction value method described in paragraph (2); or

(B) the net cost method described in paragraph (3).

(2) Transaction Value Method.—

(A) In General.—An exporter or producer may calculate the regional value-content of a good on the basis of the following transaction value method:

$$RVC = \frac{TV - VNM}{TV} - 100$$

(B) Definitions.—For purposes of subparagraph (A):

(i) The term "RVC" means the regional value-content, expressed as a percentage.

(ii) The term "TV" means the transaction value of the good adjusted to a F.O.B. basis.

(iii) The term "VNM" means the value of nonoriginating materials used by the producer in the production of the good.

(3) Net Cost Method.—

(A) In General.—An exporter or producer may calculate the regional value-content of a good on the basis of the following net cost method:

$$RVC = \frac{NC - VNM}{NC} \times 100$$

(B) Definitions.—For purposes of subparagraph (A):

(i) The term "RVC" means the regional value-content, expressed as a percentage.

(ii) The term "NC" means the net cost of the good.

(iii) The term "VNM" means the value of nonoriginating materials used by the producer in the production of the good.

(4) Value of Nonoriginating Materials Used in Originating Materials.—Except as provided in subsection (c)(1), and for a motor vehicle identified in subsection (c)(2) or a component identified in Annex 403.2 of the Agreement, the value of nonoriginating materials used by the producer in the production of a good shall not, for purposes of calculating the regional value-content of the good under paragraph (2) or (3), include the value of nonoriginating materials used to produce originating materials that are subsequently used in the production of the good.

(5) Net Cost Method Must be Used in Certain Cases.—An exporter or producer shall calculate the regional value-content of a good solely on the basis of the net cost method described in paragraph (3), if—

(A) there is no transaction value for the good;

(B) the transaction value of the good is unacceptable under Article 1 of the Customs Valuation Code;

(C) the good is sold by the producer to a related person and the volume, by units of quantity, of sales of identical or similar goods to related persons during the six-month period immediately preceding the month in which the good is sold exceeds 85 percent of the producer's total sales of such goods during that period;

(D) the good is—

(i) a motor vehicle provided for in heading 8701 or 8702, subheadings 8703.21 through 8703.90, or heading 8704, 8705, or 8706;

(ii) identified in Annex 403.1 or 403.2 of the Agreement and is for use in a motor vehicle provided for in heading 8701 or 8702, subheadings 8703.21 through 8703.90, or heading 8704, 8705, or 8706;

(iii) provided for in subheadings 6401.10 through 6406.10; or

(iv) a word processing machine provided for in subheading 8469.10.00;

(E) the exporter or producer chooses to accumulate the regional value-content of the good in accordance with subsection (d); or

(F) the good is designated as an intermediate material under paragraph (10) and is subject to a regional value-content requirement.

(6) Net Cost Method Allowed for Adjustments.—If an exporter or producer of a good calculates the regional value-content of the good on the basis of the transaction value method and a NAFTA country subsequently notifies the exporter or producer, during the course of a verification conducted in accordance with chapter 5 of the Agreement, that the transaction value of the good or the value of any material used in the production of the good must be adjusted or is unacceptable under Article 1 of the Customs Valuation Code, the exporter or producer may calculate the regional value-content of the good on the basis of the net cost method.

(7) Review of Adjustment.—Nothing in paragraph (6) shall be construed to prevent any review or appeal available in accordance with article 510 of the Agreement with respect to an adjustment to or a rejection of—

(A) the transaction value of a good; or

(B) the value of any material used in the production of a good.

(8) Calculating Net Cost.—The producer may, consistent with regulations implementing this section, calculate the net cost of a good under paragraph (3), by—

(A) calculating the total cost incurred with respect to all goods produced by that producer, subtracting any sales promotion, marketing and after-sales service costs, royalties, shipping and packing costs, and nonallowable interest costs that are included in the total cost of all such goods, and reasonably allocating the resulting net cost of those goods to the good;

(B) calculating the total cost incurred with respect to all goods produced by that producer, reasonably allocating the total cost to the good, and subtracting any sales promotion, marketing and after-sales service costs, royalties, shipping and packing costs, and nonallowable interest costs that are included in the portion of the total cost allocated to the good; or

(C) reasonably allocating each cost that is part of the total cost incurred with respect to the good so that the aggregate of these costs does not include any sales promotion, marketing and after-sales service costs, royalties, shipping and packing costs, or nonallowable interest costs.

(9) Value of Material Used in Production.—Except as provided in paragraph (11), the value of a material used in the production of a good—

(A) shall—

(i) be the transaction value of the material determined in accordance with Article 1 of the Customs Valuation Code; or

(ii) in the event that there is no transaction value or the transaction value of the material is unacceptable under Article 1 of the Customs Valuation Code, be determined in accordance with Articles 2 through 7 of the Customs Valuation Code; and

(B) if not included under clause (i) or (ii) of subparagraph (A), shall include—

(i) freight, insurance, packing, and all other costs incurred in transporting the material to the location of the producer;

(ii) duties, taxes, and customs brokerage fees paid on the material in the territory of one or more of the NAFTA countries; and

(iii) the cost of waste and spoilage resulting from the use of the material in the production of the good, less the value of renewable scrap or by-product.

(10) Intermediate Material.—Except for goods described in subsection (c)(1), any self-produced material, other than a component identified in Annex 403.2 of the Agreement, that is used in the production of a good may be designated by the producer of the good as an intermediate material for the purpose of calculating the regional value-content of the good under paragraph (2) or (3); provided that if the intermediate material is subject to a regional value-content requirement, no other self-produced material that is subject to a regional value-content require-

ment, and is used in the production of the intermediate material may be designated by the producer as an intermediate material.

(11) Value of Intermediate Material.—The value of an intermediate material shall be—

(A) the total cost incurred with respect to all goods produced by the producer of the good that can be reasonably allocated to the intermediate material; or

(B) the aggregate of each cost that is part of the total cost incurred with respect to the intermediate material that can be reasonably allocated to that intermediate material.

(12) Indirect Material.—The value of an indirect material shall be based on the Generally Accepted Accounting Principles applicable in the territory of the NAFTA country in which the good is produced.

(c) Automotive Goods.—

* * *

(d) Accumulation.—

(1) Determination of Originating Good.—For purposes of determining whether a good is an originating good, the production of the good in the territory of one or more of the NAFTA countries by one or more producers shall, at the choice of the exporter or producer of the good, be considered to have been performed in the territory of any of the NAFTA countries by that exporter or producer, if—

(A) all nonoriginating materials used in the production of the good undergo an applicable tariff classification change set out in Annex 401 of the Agreement;

(B) the good satisfies any applicable regional value-content requirement; and

(C) the good satisfies all other applicable requirements of this section.

The requirements of subparagraphs (A) and (B) must be satisfied entirely in the territory of one or more of the NAFTA countries.

(2) Treatment as Single Producer.—For purposes of subsection (b)(10), the production of a producer that chooses to accumulate its production with that of other producers under paragraph (1) shall be treated as the production of a single producer.

(e) De Minimis Amounts of Nonoriginating Materials.—

(1) In General.—Except as provided in paragraphs (3), (4), (5), and (6), a good shall be considered to be an originating good if—

(A) the value of all nonoriginating materials used in the production of the good that do not undergo an applicable change in tariff classification (set out in Annex 401 of the Agreement) is not more than 7 percent of the transaction value of the good, adjusted to an F.O.B. basis, or

(B) where the transaction value of the good is unacceptable under Article 1 of the Customs Valuation Code, the value of all such nonoriginating materials is not more than 7 percent of the total cost of the good,

provided that the good satisfies all other applicable requirements of this section and, if the good is subject to a regional value-content requirement, the value of such nonoriginating materials is taken into account in calculating the regional value-content of the good.

(2) Goods Not Subject to Regional Value-Content Requirement. A good that is otherwise subject to a regional value-content requirement shall not be required to satisfy such requirement if—

(A)(i) the value of all nonoriginating materials used in the production of the good is not more than 7 percent of the transaction value of the good, adjusted to an F.O.B. basis; or

(ii) where the transaction value of the good is unacceptable under Article 1 of the Customs Valuation Code, the value of all nonoriginating materials is not more than 7 percent of the total cost of the good; and

(B) the good satisfies all other applicable requirements of this section.

(3) Dairy Products, Etc. * * *

* * *

(4) Certain Fruit Juices. * * *

* * *

(f) Fungible Goods and Materials.* * *

* * *

(g) Accessories, Spare Parts, or Tools.

* * *

(h) Indirect Materials. * * *

(i) Packaging Materials and Containers for Retail Sale. * * *

(j) Packing Materials and Containers for Shipment.—* * *

(k) Transshipment.—A good shall not be considered to be an originating good by reason of having undergone production that satisfies the requirements of subsection (a) if, subsequent to that production, the good undergoes further production or any other operation outside the territories of the NAFTA countries, other than unloading, reloading, or any other operation necessary to preserve it in good condition or to transport the good to the territory of a NAFTA country.

* * *

(m) Interpretation and Application.—For purposes of this section:

(1) The basis for any tariff classification is the HTS.

(2) Except as otherwise expressly provided, whenever in this section there is a reference to a heading or subheading such reference shall be a reference to a heading or subheading of the HTS.

(3) In applying subsection (a)(4), the determination of whether a heading or subheading under the HTS provides for and specifically describes both a good and its parts shall be made on the basis of the nomenclature of the heading or subheading, the rules of interpretation, or notes of the HTS.

(4) In applying the Customs Valuation Code—

(A) the principles of the Customs Valuation Code shall apply to domestic transactions, with such modifications as may be required by the circumstances, as would apply to international transactions;

(B) the provisions of this section shall take precedence over the Customs Valuation Code to the extent of any difference; and

(C) the definitions in subsection (*o*) shall take precedence over the definitions in the Customs Valuation Code to the extent of any difference.

(5) All costs referred to in this section shall be recorded and maintained in accordance with the Generally Accepted Accounting Principles applicable in the territory of the NAFTA country in which the good is produced.

* * *

(*o*) Special Rule for Certain Agricultural Products. * * *

(p) Definitions. * * *

TITLE III—APPLICATION OF AGREEMENT TO SECTORS AND SERVICES

Subtitle A—Safeguards

PART 1—RELIEF FROM IMPORTS BENEFITING FROM THE AGREEMENT

19 U.S.C. § 3351

Sec. 301. Definitions

As used in this part:

(1) *Canadian Article.*—The term "Canadian article" means an article that—

(A) is an originating good under chapter 4 of the Agreement; and

(B) qualifies under the Agreement to be marked as a good of Canada.

(2) *Mexican Article.*—The term "Mexican article" means an article that—

(A) is an originating good under chapter 4 of the Agreement; and

(B) qualifies under the Agreement to be marked as a good of Mexico.

19 U.S.C. § 3352

Sec. 302.   Commencing of Action for Relief

(a) Filing of Petition.—

(1) In General.—A petition requesting action under this part for the purpose of adjusting to the obligations of the United States under the Agreement may be filed with the International Trade Commission by an entity, including a trade association, firm, certified or recognized union, or group of workers, that is representative of an industry. The International Trade Commission shall transmit a copy of any petition filed under this subsection to the Trade Representative.

(2) Provisional Relief.—An entity filing a petition under this subsection may request that provisional relief be provided as if the petition had been filed under section 202(a) of the Trade Act of 1974.

(3) Critical Circumstances.—An allegation that critical circumstances exist must be included in the petition or made on or before the 90th day after the date on which the investigation is initiated under subsection (b).

(b) Investigation and Determination.—Upon the filing of a petition under subsection (a), the International Trade Commission, unless subsection (d) applies, shall promptly initiate an investigation to determine whether, as a result of the reduction or elimination of a duty provided for under the Agreement, a Canadian article or a Mexican article, as the case may be, is being imported into the United States in such increased quantities (in absolute terms) and under such conditions so that imports of the article, alone, constitute a substantial cause of—

(1) serious injury; or

(2) except in the case of a Canadian article, a threat of serious injury;

to the domestic industry producing an article that is like, or directly competitive with, the imported article.

* * *

19 U.S.C. § 3353

Sec. 303.   International Trade Commission Action on Petition

(a) Determination.—By no later than 120 days after the date on which an investigation is initiated under section 302(b) with respect to a petition, the International Trade Commission shall—

(1) make the determination required under that section; and

(2) if the determination referred to in paragraph (1) is affirmative and an allegation regarding critical circumstances was made under section 302(a), make a determination regarding that allegation.

(b) Additional Finding and Recommendation if Determination Affirmative.—If the determination made by the International Trade Commission under subsection (a) with respect to imports of an article is affirmative, the International Trade Commission shall find, and recommend to the President in the report required under subsection (c), the amount of import relief that is necessary to remedy or, except in the case of imports of a Canadian article, prevent the injury found by the International Trade Commission in the determination. The import relief recommended by the International Trade Commission under this subsection shall be limited to that described in section 304(c).

(c) Report to President.—No later than the date that is 30 days after the date on which a determination is made under subsection (a) with respect to an investigation, the International Trade Commission shall submit to the President a report that shall include—

(1) a statement of the basis for the determination;

(2) dissenting and separate views; and

(3) any finding made under subsection (b) regarding import relief.

* * *

19 U.S.C. § 3354

Sec. 304. Provision of Relief

(a) In General.—No later than the date that is 30 days after the date on which the President receives the report of the International Trade Commission containing an affirmative determination of the International Trade Commission under section 303(a), the President, subject to subsection (b), shall provide relief from imports of the article that is the subject of such determination to the extent that the President determines necessary to remedy or, except in the case of imports of a Canadian article, prevent the injury found by the International Trade Commission.

(b) Exception.—The President is not required to provide import relief under this section if the President determines that the provision of the import relief will not provide greater economic and social benefits than costs.

(c) Nature of Relief.—The import relief (including provisional relief) that the President is authorized to provide under this part is as follows:

(1) In the case of imports of a Canadian article—

(A) the suspension of any further reduction provided for under Annex 401.2 of the United States-Canada Free-Trade Agreement in the duty imposed on such article;

(B) an increase in the rate of duty imposed on such article to a level that does not exceed the lesser of—

(i) the column 1 general rate of duty imposed under the HTS on like articles at the time the import relief is provided, or

(ii) the column 1 general rate of duty imposed on like articles on December 31, 1988; or

(C) in the case of a duty applied on a seasonal basis to such article, an increase in the rate of duty imposed on the article to a level that does not exceed the column 1 general rate of duty imposed on the article for the corresponding season occurring immediately before January 1, 1989.

(2) In the case of imports of a Mexican article—

(A) the suspension of any further reduction provided for under the United States Schedule to Annex 302.2 of the Agreement in the duty imposed on such article;

(B) an increase in the rate of duty imposed on such article to a level that does not exceed the lesser of—

(i) the column 1 general rate of duty imposed under the HTS on like articles at the time the import relief is provided, or

(ii) the column 1 general rate of duty imposed under the HTS on like articles on the day before the date on which the Agreement enters into force; or

(C) in the case of a duty applied on a seasonal basis to such article, an increase in the rate of duty imposed on the article to a level that does not exceed the column 1 general rate of duty imposed under the HTS on the article for the corresponding season immediately occurring before the date on which the Agreement enters into force.

(d) Period of Relief.—The import relief that the President is authorized to provide under this section may not exceed 3 years, except that, if a Canadian article or Mexican article which is the subject of the action—

(1) is provided for in an item for which the transition period of tariff elimination set out in the United States Schedule to Annex 302.2 of the Agreement is greater than 10 years; and

(2) the President determines that the affected industry has undertaken adjustment and requires an extension of the period of the import relief;

the President, after obtaining the advice of the International Trade Commission, may extend the period of the import relief for not more than 1 year, if the duty applied during the initial period of the relief is substantially reduced at the beginning of the extension period.

(e) Rate on Mexican Articles After Termination of Import Relief.—When import relief under this part is terminated with respect to a Mexican article—

(1) the rate of duty on that article after such termination and on or before December 31 of the year in which termination occurs shall be the rate that, according to the United States Schedule to Annex 302.2 of the Agreement for the staged elimination of the tariff, would have been in effect 1 year after the initiation of the import relief action under section 302; and

(2) the tariff treatment for that article after December 31 of the year in which termination occurs shall be, at the discretion of the President, either—

(A) the rate of duty conforming to the applicable rate set out in the United States Schedule to Annex 302.2; or

(B) the rate of duty resulting from the elimination of the tariff in equal annual stages ending on the date set out in the United States Schedule to Annex 302.2 for the elimination of the tariff.

19 U.S.C. § 3355

Sec. 305. Termination of Relief Authority

(a) General Rule.—Except as provided in subsection (b), no import relief may be provided under this part—

(1) in the case of a Canadian article, after December 31, 1998; or

(2) in the case of a Mexican article, after the date that is 10 years after the date on which the Agreement enters into force;

unless the article against which the action is taken is an item for which the transition period for tariff elimination set out in the United States Schedule to Annex 302.2 of the Agreement is greater than 10 years, in which case the period during which relief may be granted shall be the period of staged tariff elimination for that article.

(b) Exception.—Import relief may be provided under this part in the case of a Canadian article or Mexican article after the date on which such relief would, but for this subsection, terminate under subsection (a), but only if the Government of Canada or Mexico, as the case may be, consents to such provision.

19 U.S.C. § 3356

* * *

PART 2—RELIEF FROM IMPORTS FROM ALL COUNTRIES
19 U.S.C. § 3371

Sec. 311. NAFTA Article Impact in Import Relief Cases Under the Trade Act of 1974

(a) In General.—If, in any investigation initiated under chapter 1 of title II of the Trade Act of 1974, the International Trade Commission makes an affirmative determination (or a determination which the President may treat as an affirmative determination under such chapter by reason of section 330(d) of the Tariff Act of 1930), the International Trade Commission shall also find (and report to the President at the time such injury determination is submitted to the President) whether—

(1) imports of the article from a NAFTA country, considered individually, account for a substantial share of total imports; and

(2) imports of the article from a NAFTA country, considered individually or, in exceptional circumstances, imports from NAFTA countries considered collectively, contribute importantly to the serious injury, or threat thereof, caused by imports.

(b) Factors.—

(1) Substantial Import Share.—In determining whether imports from a NAFTA country, considered individually, account for a substantial share of total imports, such imports normally shall not be considered to account for a substantial share of total imports if that country is not among the top 5 suppliers of the article subject to the investigation, measured in terms of import share during the most recent 3-year period.

(2) Application of "Contribute Importantly" Standard.—In determining whether imports from a NAFTA country or countries contribute importantly to the serious injury, or threat thereof, the International Trade Commission shall consider such factors as the change in the import share of the NAFTA country or countries, and the level and change in the level of imports of such country or countries. In applying the preceding sentence, imports from a NAFTA country or countries normally shall not be considered to contribute importantly to serious injury, or the threat thereof, if the growth rate of imports from such country or countries during the period in which an injurious increase in imports occurred is appreciably lower than the growth rate of total imports from all sources over the same period.

(c) Definition.—For purposes of this section and section 312(a), the term "contribute importantly" refers to an important cause, but not necessarily the most important cause.

19 U.S.C. § 3372

Sec. 312.   Presidential Action Regarding NAFTA Imports

(a) In General.—In determining whether to take action under chapter 1 of title II of the Trade Act of 1974 with respect to imports from a NAFTA country, the President shall determine whether—

(1) imports from such country, considered individually, account for a substantial share of total imports; or

(2) imports from a NAFTA country, considered individually, or in exceptional circumstances imports from NAFTA countries considered collectively, contribute importantly to the serious injury, or threat thereof, found by the International Trade Commission.

(b) Exclusion of NAFTA Imports.—In determining the nature and extent of action to be taken under chapter 1 of title II of the Trade Act of 1974, the President shall exclude from such action imports from a NAFTA country if the President makes a negative determination under subsection (a)(1) or (2) with respect to imports from such country.

(c) Action After Exclusion of NAFTA Country Imports.—

(1) In General.—If the President, under subsection (b), excludes imports from a NAFTA country or countries from action under chapter 1 of title II of the Trade Act of 1974 but thereafter determines that a surge in imports from that country or countries is undermining the effectiveness of the action—

(A) the President may take appropriate action under such chapter 1 to include those imports in the action; and

(B) any entity that is representative of an industry for which such action is being taken may request the International Trade Commission to conduct an investigation of the surge in such imports.

(2) Investigation.—Upon receiving a request under paragraph (1)(B), the International Trade Commission shall conduct an investigation to determine whether a surge in such imports undermines the effectiveness of the action. The International Trade Commission shall submit the findings of its investigation to the President no later than 30 days after the request is received by the International Trade Commission.

(3) Definition.—For purposes of this subsection, the term "surge" means a significant increase in imports over the trend for a recent representative base period.

(d) Condition Applicable to Quantitative Restrictions.—Any action taken under this section proclaiming a quantitative restriction shall permit the importation of a quantity or value of the article which is not less than the quantity or value of such article imported into the United States during the most recent period that is representative of imports of such article, with allowance for reasonable growth.

TITLE IV—DISPUTE SETTLEMENT IN ANTIDUMPING AND COUNTERVAILING DUTY CASES

Subtitle A—Organizational, Administrative, and Procedural Provisions Regarding the Implementation of Chapter 19 of the Agreement

* * *

19 U.S.C. § 3432

Sec. 402. Organizational and Administrative Provisions

(a) Criteria for Selection of Individuals to Serve on Panels and Committees.—

(1) In General.—The selection of individuals under this section for—

(A) placement on lists prepared by the interagency group under subsection (c)(2)(B)(i) and (ii);

(B) placement on preliminary candidate lists under subsection (c)(3)(A);

(C) placement on final candidate lists under subsection (c)(4)(A);

(D) placement by the Trade Representative on the rosters described in paragraph 1 of Annex 1901.2 and paragraph 1 of Annex 1904.13; and

(E) appointment by the Trade Representative for service on the panels and committees convened under chapter 19;

shall be made on the basis of the criteria provided in paragraph 1 of Annex 1901.2 and paragraph 1 of Annex 1904.13 and shall be made without regard to political affiliation.

(2) Additional Criteria for Roster Placements and Appointments Under Paragraph 1 of Annex 1901.2.—Rosters described in paragraph 1 of Annex 1901.2 shall include, to the fullest extent practicable, judges and former judges who meet the criteria referred to in paragraph (1). The Trade Representative shall, subject to subsection (b), appoint judges to binational panels convened under chapter 19, extraordinary challenge committees convened under chapter 19, and special committees established under article 1905, where such judges offer and are available to serve and such service is authorized by the chief judge of the court on which they sit.

(b) Selection of Certain Judges to Serve on Panels and Committees.—

(1) Applicability.—This subsection applies only with respect to the selection of individuals for binational panels convened under chapter 19, extraordinary challenge committees convened under chapter 19, and special committees established under article 1905, who are judges of courts created under article III of the Constitution of the United States.

(2) Consultation with Chief Judges.—The Trade Representative shall consult, from time to time, with the chief judges of the Federal judicial circuits regarding the interest in, and availability for, participation in binational panels, extraordinary challenge committees, and special committees, of judges within their respective circuits. If the chief judge of a Federal judicial circuit determines that it is appropriate for one or more judges within that circuit to be included on a roster described in subsection (a)(1)(D), the chief judge shall identify all such judges for the Chief Justice of the United States who may, upon his or her approval, submit the names of such judges to the Trade Representative. The Trade Representative shall include the names of such judges on the roster.

(3) Submission of Lists to Congress.—The Trade Representative shall submit to the Committee on the Judiciary and the Committee on

Ways and Means of the House of Representatives and to the Committee
on Finance and the Committee on the Judiciary of the Senate a list of all
judges included on a roster under paragraph (2). Such list shall be
submitted at the same time as the final candidate lists are submitted
under subsection (c)(4)(A) and the final forms of amendments are
submitted under subsection (c)(4)(C)(iv).

(4) Appointment of Judges to Panels or Committees.—At such time
as the Trade Representative proposes to appoint a judge described in
paragraph (1) to a binational panel, an extraordinary challenge committee, or a special committee, the Trade Representative shall consult with
that judge in order to ascertain whether the judge is available for such
appointment.

(c) Selection of Other Candidates.—

(1) Applicability.—This subsection applies only with respect to the
selection of individuals for binational panels convened under chapter 19,
extraordinary challenge committees convened under chapter 19, and
special committees established under article 1905, other than those
individuals to whom subsection (b) applies.

(2) Interagency Group.—

(A) Establishment.—There is established within the interagency
organization established under section 242 of the Trade Expansion
Act of 1962 (19 U.S.C. § 1872) an interagency group which shall—

(i) be chaired by the Trade Representative; and

(ii) consist of such officers (or the designees thereof) of the
United States Government as the Trade Representative considers appropriate.

(B) Functions.—The interagency group established under subparagraph (A) shall, in a manner consistent with chapter 19—

(i) prepare by January 3 of each calendar year—

(I) a list of individuals who are qualified to serve as
members of binational panels convened under chapter 19;
and

(II) a list of individuals who are qualified to serve on
extraordinary challenge committees convened under chapter 19 and special committees established under article
1905;

(ii) if the Trade Representative makes a request under
paragraph (4)(C)(i) with respect to a final candidate list during
any calendar year, prepare by July 1 of such calendar year a list
of those individuals who are qualified to be added to that final
candidate list;

(iii) exercise oversight of the administration of the United
States Section that is authorized to be established under section
105; and

(iv) make recommendations to the Trade Representative regarding the convening of extraordinary challenge committees and special committees under chapter 19.

(3) Preliminary Candidate Lists.—

(A) In General.—The Trade Representative shall select individuals from the respective lists prepared by the interagency group under paragraph (2)(B)(i) for placement on—

(i) a preliminary candidate list of individuals eligible to serve as members of binational panels under Annex 1901.2; and

(ii) a preliminary candidate list of individuals eligible for selection as members of extraordinary challenge committees under Annex 1904.13 and special committees under article 1905.

(B) Submission of Lists to Congressional Committees.—

(i) In General.—No later than January 3 of each calendar year, the Trade Representative shall submit to the Committee on Finance of the Senate and the Committee on Ways and Means of the House of Representatives (hereafter in this section referred to as the "appropriate Congressional Committees") the preliminary candidate lists of those individuals selected by the Trade Representative under subparagraph (A) to be candidates eligible to serve on panels or committees convened pursuant to chapter 19 during the 1-year period beginning on April 1 of such calendar year.

(ii) Additional Information.—At the time the candidate lists are submitted under clause (i), the Trade Representative shall submit for each individual on the list a statement of professional qualifications.

(C) Consultation.—Upon submission of the preliminary candidate lists under subparagraph (B) to the appropriate Congressional Committees, the Trade Representative shall consult with such Committees with regard to the individuals included on the preliminary candidate lists.

(D) Revision of Lists.—The Trade Representative may add and delete individuals from the preliminary candidate lists submitted under subparagraph (B) after consultation with the appropriate Congressional Committees regarding the additions and deletions. The Trade Representative shall provide to the appropriate Congressional Committees written notice of any addition or deletion of an individual from the preliminary candidate lists, along with the information described in subparagraph (B)(ii) with respect to any proposed addition.

(4) Final Candidate Lists.—

(A) Submission of Lists to Congressional Committees.—No later than March 31 of each calendar year, the Trade Representative shall

submit to the appropriate Congressional Committees the final candidate lists of those individuals selected by the Trade Representative to be candidates eligible to serve on panels and committees convened under chapter 19 during the 1-year period beginning on April 1 of such calendar year. An individual may be included on a final candidate list only if such individual was included in the preliminary candidate list or if written notice of the addition of such individual to the preliminary candidate list was submitted to the appropriate Congressional Committees at least 15 days before the date on which that final candidate list is submitted to such Committees under this subparagraph.

(B) Finality of Lists.—Except as provided in subparagraph (C), no additions may be made to the final candidate lists after the final candidate lists are submitted to the appropriate Congressional Committees under subparagraph (A).

(C) Amendment of Lists.—

(i) In General.—If, after the Trade Representative has submitted the final candidate lists to the appropriate Congressional Committees under subparagraph (A) for a calendar year and before July 1 of such calendar year, the Trade Representative determines that additional individuals need to be added to a final candidate list, the Trade Representative shall—

(I) request the interagency group established under paragraph (2)(A) to prepare a list of individuals who are qualified to be added to such candidate list;

(II) select individuals from the list prepared by the interagency group under paragraph (2)(B)(ii) to be included in a proposed amendment to such final candidate list; and

(III) by no later than July 1 of such calendar year, submit to the appropriate Congressional Committees the proposed amendments to such final candidate list developed by the Trade Representative under subclause (II), along with the information described in paragraph (3)(B)(ii).

(ii) Consultation with Congressional Committees. Upon submission of a proposed amendment under clause (i)(III) to the appropriate Congressional Committees, the Trade Representative shall consult with the appropriate Congressional Committees with regard to the individuals included in the proposed amendment.

(iii) Adjustment of Proposed Amendment.—The Trade Representative may add and delete individuals from any proposed amendment submitted under clause (i)(III) after consulting with the appropriate Congressional Committees with regard to the additions and deletions. The Trade Representative shall provide to the appropriate Congressional Committees written notice of any addition or deletion of an individual from the proposed amendment.

(iv) Final Amendment.—

(I) In General.—If the Trade Representative submits under clause (i)(III) in any calendar year a proposed amendment to a final candidate list, the Trade Representative shall, no later than September 30 of such calendar year, submit to the appropriate Congressional Committees the final form of such amendment. On October 1 of such calendar year, such amendment shall take effect and, subject to subclause (II), the individuals included in the final form of such amendment shall be added to the final candidate list.

(II) Inclusion of Individuals.—An individual may be included in the final form of an amendment submitted under subclause (I) only if such individual was included in the proposed form of such amendment or if written notice of the addition of such individual to the proposed form of such amendment was submitted to the appropriate Congressional Committees at least 15 days before the date on which the final form of such amendment is submitted to such Committees under subclause (I).

(III) Eligibility for Service.—Individuals added to a final candidate list under subclause (I) shall be eligible to serve on panels or committees convened under chapter 19 during the 6-month period beginning on October 1 of the calendar year in which such addition occurs.

(IV) Finality of Amendment.—No additions may be made to the final form of an amendment described in subclause (I) after the final form of such amendment is submitted to the appropriate Congressional Committees under subclause (I).

(5) Treatment of Responses.—For purposes of applying section 1001 of title 18, United States Code, the written or oral responses of individuals to inquiries of the interagency group established under paragraph (2)(A) or of the Trade Representative regarding their personal and professional qualifications, and financial and other relevant interests, that bear on their suitability for the placements and appointments described in subsection (a)(1), shall be treated as matters within the jurisdiction of an agency of the United States.

(d) Selection and Appointment.—

(1) Authority of Trade Representative.—The Trade Representative is the only officer of the United States Government authorized to act on behalf of the United States Government in making any selection or appointment of an individual to—

(A) the rosters described in paragraph 1 of Annex 1901.2 and paragraph 1 of Annex 1904.13; or

(B) the panels or committees convened under chapter 19;

that is to be made solely or jointly by the United States Government under the terms of the Agreement.

(2) Restrictions on Selection and Appointment.—Except as provided in paragraph (3)—

(A) the Trade Representative may—

(i) select an individual for placement on the rosters described in paragraph 1 of Annex 1901.2 and paragraph 1 of Annex 1904.13 during the 1-year period beginning on April 1 of any calendar year;

(ii) appoint an individual to serve as one of those members of any panel or committee convened under chapter 19 during such 1-year period who, under the terms of the Agreement, are to be appointed solely by the United States Government; or

(iii) act to make a joint appointment with the Government of a NAFTA country, under the terms of the Agreement, of any individual who is a citizen or national of the United States to serve as any other member of such a panel or committee;

only if such individual is on the appropriate final candidate list that was submitted to the appropriate Congressional Committees under subsection (c)(4)(A) during such calendar year or on such list as it may be amended under subsection (c)(4)(C)(iv)(I), or on the list submitted under subsection (b)(3) to the congressional committees referred to in such subsection; and

(B) no individual may—

(i) be selected by the United States Government for placement on the rosters described in paragraph 1 of Annex 1901.2 and paragraph 1 of Annex 1904.13; or

(ii) be appointed solely or jointly by the United States Government to serve as a member of a panel or committee convened under chapter 19;

during the 1-year period beginning on April 1 of any calendar year for which the Trade Representative has not met the requirements of subsection (a), and of subsection (b) or (c) (as the case may be).

(3) Exceptions.—Notwithstanding subsection (c)(3) (other than subparagraph (B)), (c)(4), or paragraph (2)(A) of this subsection, individuals included on the preliminary candidate lists submitted to the appropriate Congressional Committees under subsection (c)(3)(B) may—

(A) be selected by the Trade Representative for placement on the rosters described in paragraph 1 of Annex 1901.2 and paragraph 1 of Annex 1904.13 during the 3-month period beginning on the date on which the Agreement enters into force with respect to the United States; and

(B) be appointed solely or jointly by the Trade Representative under the terms of the Agreement to serve as members of panels or committees that are convened under chapter 19 during such 3-month period.

(e) Transition.—If the Agreement enters into force between the United States and a NAFTA country after January 3, 1994, the provisions of subsection (c) shall be applied with respect to the calendar year in which such entering into force occurs—

(1) by substituting "the date that is 30 days after the date on which the Agreement enters into force with respect to the United States" for "January 3 of each calendar year" in subsections (c)(2)(B)(i) and (c)(3)(B)(i); and

(2) by substituting "the date that is 3 months after the date on which the Agreement enters into force with respect to the United States" for "March 31 of each calendar year" in subsection (c)(4)(A).

(f) Immunity.—With the exception of acts described in section 777(f)(3) of the Tariff Act of 1930 (19 U.S.C. § 1677f(f)(3)), individuals serving on panels or committees convened pursuant to chapter 19, and individuals designated to assist the individuals serving on such panels or committees, shall be immune from suit and legal process relating to acts performed by such individuals in their official capacity and within the scope of their functions as such panelists or committee members or assistants to such panelists or committee members.

(g) Regulations.—The administering authority under title VII of the Tariff Act of 1930, the International Trade Commission, and the Trade Representative may promulgate such regulations as are necessary or appropriate to carry out actions in order to implement their respective responsibilities under chapter 19. Initial regulations to carry out such functions shall be issued before the date on which the Agreement enters into force with respect to the United States.

(h) Report to Congress.—At such time as the final candidate lists are submitted under subsection (c)(4)(A) and the final forms of amendments are submitted under subsection (c)(4)(C)(iv), the Trade Representative shall submit to the Committee on the Judiciary and the Committee on Ways and Means of the House of Representatives, and to the Committee on Finance and the Committee on the Judiciary of the Senate, a report regarding the efforts made to secure the participation of judges and former judges on binational panels, extraordinary challenge committees, and special committees established under chapter 19.

19 U.S.C. § 3433

Sec. 403. Testimony and Production of Papers in Extraordinary Challenges

(a) Authority of Extraordinary Challenge Committee to Obtain Information.—If an extraordinary challenge committee (hereafter in this section referred to as the "committee") is convened under paragraph 13 of article 1904, and the allegations before the committee include a matter referred to in paragraph 13(a)(i) of article 1904, for the purposes of carrying out its functions and duties under Annex 1904.13, the committee—

(1) shall have access to, and the right to copy, any document, paper, or record pertinent to the subject matter under consideration, in the possession of any individual, partnership, corporation, association, organization, or other entity;

(2) may summon witnesses, take testimony, and administer oaths;

(3) may require any individual, partnership, corporation, association, organization, or other entity to produce documents, books, or records relating to the matter in question; and

(4) may require any individual, partnership, corporation, association, organization, or other entity to furnish in writing, in such detail and in such form as the committee may prescribe, information in its possession pertaining to the matter.

Any member of the committee may sign subpoenas, and members of the committee, when authorized by the committee, may administer oaths and affirmations, examine witnesses, take testimony, and receive evidence.

(b) Witnesses and Evidence.—The attendance of witnesses who are authorized to be summoned, and the production of documentary evidence authorized to be ordered, under subsection (a) may be required from any place in the United States at any designated place of hearing. In the case of disobedience to a subpoena authorized under subsection (a), the committee may request the Attorney General of the United States to invoke the aid of any district or territorial court of the United States in requiring the attendance and testimony of witnesses and the production of documentary evidence. Such court, within the jurisdiction of which such inquiry is carried on, may, in case of contumacy or refusal to obey a subpoena issued to any individual, partnership, corporation, association, organization, or other entity, issue an order requiring such individual or entity to appear before the committee, or to produce documentary evidence if so ordered or to give evidence concerning the matter in question. Any failure to obey such order of the court may be punished by such court as a contempt thereof.

(c) Mandamus.—Any court referred to in subsection (b) shall have jurisdiction to issue writs of mandamus commanding compliance with the provisions of this section or any order of the committee made in pursuance thereof.

(d) Depositions.—The committee may order testimony to be taken by deposition at any stage of the committee review. Such deposition may be taken before any person designated by the committee and having power to administer oaths. Such testimony shall be reduced to writing by the person taking the deposition, or under the direction of such person, and shall then be subscribed by the deponent. Any individual, partnership, corporation, association, organization, or other entity may be compelled to appear and be deposed and to produce documentary evidence in the same manner as witnesses may be compelled to appear and testify and produce documentary evidence before the committee, as provided in this section.

19 U.S.C. § 3434

Sec. 404.   Requests for Review of Determinations by Competent Investigating Authorities of NAFTA Countries

(a) Definitions.—As used in this section:

(1) Competent Investigating Authority.—The term "competent investigating authority" means the competent investigating authority, as defined in article 1911, of a NAFTA country.

(2) United States Secretary.—The term "United States Secretary" means that officer of the United States referred to in article 1908.

(b) Requests for Review by the United States.—In the case of a final determination of a competent investigating authority, requests by the United States for binational panel review of such determination under article 1904 shall be made by the United States Secretary.

(c) Requests for Review by a Person.—In the case of a final determination of a competent investigating authority, a person, within the meaning of paragraph 5 of article 1904, may request a binational panel review of such determination by filing such a request with the United States Secretary within the time limit provided for in paragraph 4 of article 1904. The receipt of such request by the United States Secretary shall be deemed to be a request for binational panel review within the meaning of article 1904. The request for such panel review shall be without prejudice to any challenge before a binational panel of the basis for a particular request for review.

(d) Service of Request for Review.—Whenever binational panel review of a final determination made by a competent investigating authority is requested under this section, the United States Secretary shall serve a copy of the request on all persons who would otherwise be entitled under the law of the importing country to commence proceedings for judicial review of the determination.

19 U.S.C. § 3435

Sec. 405.   Rules of Procedure for Panels and Committees

(a) Rules of Procedure for Binational Panels.—The administering authority shall prescribe rules, negotiated in accordance with paragraph 14 of article 1904, governing, with respect to binational panel reviews—

* * *

(b) Rules of Procedure for Extraordinary Challenge Committees.—The administering authority shall prescribe rules, negotiated in accordance with paragraph 2 of Annex 1904.13, governing the procedures for reviews by extraordinary challenge committees.

(c) Rules of Procedure for Safeguarding the Panel Review System.—The administering authority shall prescribe rules, negotiated in accordance with Annex 1905.6, governing the procedures for special committees described in such Annex.

* * *

19 U.S.C. § 3436

Sec. 406.   Subsidy Negotiations

In the case of any trade agreement which may be entered into by the President with a NAFTA country, the negotiating objectives of the United States with respect to subsidies shall include—

(1) achievement of increased discipline on domestic subsidies provided by a foreign government, including—

(A) the provision of capital, loans, or loan guarantees on terms inconsistent with commercial considerations;

(B) the provision of goods or services at preferential rates;

(C) the granting of funds or forgiveness of debt to cover operating losses sustained by a specific industry; and

(D) the assumption of any costs or expenses of manufacture, production, or distribution;

(2) achievement of increased discipline on export subsidies provided by a foreign government, particularly with respect to agricultural products; and

(3) maintenance of effective remedies against subsidized imports, including, where appropriate, countervailing duties.

19 U.S.C. § 3437

Sec. 407.   Identification of Industries Facing Subsidized Imports

(a) Petitions.—Any entity, including a trade association, firm, certified or recognized union, or group of workers, that is representative of a United States industry and has reason to believe—

(1) that—

(A) as a result of implementation of provisions of the Agreement, the industry is likely to face increased competition from subsidized imports, from a NAFTA country, with which it directly competes; or

(B) the industry is likely to face increased competition from subsidized imports with which it directly competes from any other country designated by the President, following consultations with the Congress, as benefiting from a reduction of tariffs or other trade barriers under a trade agreement that enters into force with respect to the United States after January 1, 1994; and

(2) that the industry is likely to experience a deterioration of its competitive position before more effective rules and disciplines relating to the use of government subsidies have been developed with respect to the country concerned;

may file with the Trade Representative a petition that such industry be identified under this section.

(b) Identification of Industry.—Within 90 days after receipt of a petition under subsection (a), the Trade Representative, in consultation with the Secretary of Commerce, shall decide whether to identify the industry on the basis that there is a reasonable likelihood that the industry may face both the subsidization described in subsection (a)(1) and the deterioration described in subsection (a)(2).

(c) Action After Identification.—At the request of an entity that is representative of an industry identified under subsection (b), the Trade Representative shall—

(1) compile and make available to the industry information under section 308 of the Trade Act of 1974;

(2) recommend to the President that an investigation by the International Trade Commission be requested under section 332 of the Tariff Act of 1930; or

(3) take actions described in both paragraphs (1) and (2).

The industry may request the Trade Representative to take appropriate action to update (as often as annually) any information obtained under paragraph (1) or (2), or both, as the case may be, until an agreement on more effective rules and disciplines relating to government subsidies is reached between the United States and the NAFTA countries.

(d) Initiation of Action Under Other Law.—

(1) In General.—The Trade Representative and the Secretary of Commerce shall review information obtained under subsection (c) and consult with the industry identified under subsection (b) with a view to deciding whether any action is appropriate—

(A) under section 301 of the Trade Act of 1974, including the initiation of an investigation under section 302(c) of that Act (in the case of the Trade Representative); or

(B) under subtitle A of title VII of the Tariff Act of 1930, including the initiation of an investigation under section 702(a) of that Act (in the case of the Secretary of Commerce).

(2) Criteria for Initiation.—In determining whether to initiate any investigation under section 301 of the Trade Act of 1974 or any other

trade law, other than title VII of the Tariff Act of 1930, the Trade Representative, after consultation with the Secretary of Commerce—

(A) shall seek the advice of the advisory committees established under section 135 of the Trade Act of 1974;

(B) shall consult with the Committee on Finance of the Senate and the Committee on Ways and Means of the House of Representatives;

(C) shall coordinate with the interagency organization established under section 242 of the Trade Expansion Act of 1962; and

(D) may ask the President to request advice from the International Trade Commission.

(3) Title III Actions.—In the event an investigation is initiated under section 302(c) of the Trade Act of 1974 as a result of a review under this subsection and the Trade Representative, following such investigation (including any applicable dispute settlement proceedings under the Agreement or any other trade agreement), determines to take action under section 301(a) of such Act, the Trade Representative shall give preference to actions that most directly affect the products that benefit from governmental subsidies and were the subject of the investigation, unless there are no significant imports of such products or the Trade Representative otherwise determines that application of the action to other products would be more effective.

(e) Effect of Decisions.—Any decision, whether positive or negative, or any action by the Trade Representative or the Secretary of Commerce under this section shall not in any way—

(1) prejudice the right of any industry to file a petition under any trade law;

(2) prejudice, affect, or substitute for, any proceeding, investigation, determination, or action by the Secretary of Commerce, the International Trade Commission, or the Trade Representative pursuant to such a petition, or

(3) prejudice, affect, substitute for, or obviate any proceeding, investigation, or determination under section 301 of the Trade Act of 1974, title VII of the Tariff Act of 1930, or any other trade law.

(f) Standing.—Nothing in this section may be construed to alter in any manner the requirements in effect before the date of the enactment of this Act for standing under any law of the United States or to add any additional requirements for standing under any law of the United States.

19 U.S.C. § 3438

Sec. 408. Treatment of Amendments to Antidumping and Countervailing Duty Law

Any amendment enacted after the Agreement enters into force with respect to the United States that is made to—

(1) section 303 of title VII of the Tariff Act of 1930, or any successor statute, or

(2) any other statute which—

(A) provides for judicial review of final determinations under such section, title, or successor statute, or

(B) indicates the standard of review to be applied,

shall apply to goods from a NAFTA country only to the extent specified in the amendment.

TITLE V—NAFTA TRANSITIONAL ADJUSTMENT ASSISTANCE AND OTHER PROVISIONS

Subtitle D—Implementation of NAFTA Supplemental Agreements

PART 1—AGREEMENTS RELATING TO LABOR AND ENVIRONMENT

19 U.S.C. § 3471

Sec. 531. Agreement on Labor Cooperation

(a) Commission for Labor Cooperation

(1) Membership

The United States is authorized to participate in the Commission for Labor Cooperation in accordance with the North American Agreement on Labor Cooperation.

* * *

(b) Definitions

As used in this section—

(1) the term "Commission for Labor Cooperation" means the commission established by Part Three of the North American Agreement on Labor Cooperation; and

(2) the term "North American Agreement on Labor Cooperation" means the North American Agreement on Labor Cooperation Between the Government of the United States of America, the Government of Canada, and the Government of the United Mexican States (signed at Mexico City, Washington, and Ottawa on September 8, 9, 12, and 14, 1993).

19 U.S.C. § 3472

Sec. 532. Agreement on Environmental Cooperation

(a) Commission for Environmental Cooperation.—

(1) Membership.—The United States is authorized to participate in the Commission for Environmental Cooperation in accordance with the North American Agreement on Environmental Cooperation.

19 U.S.C. § 3473

Sec. 533. Agreement on Border Environment Cooperation Commission

(a) Border Environment Cooperation Commission

(1) Membership

The United States is authorized to participate in the Border Environment Cooperation Commission in accordance with the Border Environment Cooperation Agreement.

* * *

DOCUMENT 13

CUBAN LIBERTY AND DEMOCRATIC SOLIDARITY (LIBERTAD) ACT OF 1996

(Helms-Burton Act)
(Selected Provisions)

Pub.L. 104–114, 110 Stat. 785, 22 U.S.C. §§ 6021–6091

Table of Contents

---

§ 6023. Definitions

As used in this Act, the following terms have the following meanings:

(1) Agency or Instrumentality of a Foreign State.—The term "agency or instrumentality of a foreign state" has the meaning given that term in section 1603(b) of title 28, United States Code.

* * *

(3) Commercial Activity.—The term "commercial activity" has the meaning given that term in section 1603(d) of title 28, United States Code.[a]

a. These are the definitions in the Foreign Sovereign immunities Act.

571

(4) Confiscated.—As used in titles I and III, the term "confiscated" refers to—

(A) the nationalization, expropriation, or other seizure by the Cuban Government of ownership or control of property, on or after January 1, 1959—

(i) without the property having been returned or adequate and effective compensation provided; or

(ii) without the claim to the property having been settled pursuant to an international claims settlement agreement or other mutually accepted settlement procedure; and

(B) the repudiation by the Cuban Government of, the default by the Cuban Government on, or the failure of the Cuban Government to pay, on or after January 1, 1959—

(i) a debt of any enterprise which has been nationalized, expropriated, or otherwise taken by the Cuban Government;

(ii) a debt which is a charge on property nationalized, expropriated, or otherwise taken by the Cuban Government; or

(iii) a debt which was incurred by the Cuban Government in satisfaction or settlement of a confiscated property claim.

* * *

(9) Knowingly.—The term "knowingly" means with knowledge or having reason to know.

* * *

(12) Property.—(A) The term "property" means any property (including patents, copyrights, trademarks, and any other form of intellectual property), whether real, personal, or mixed, and any present, future, or contingent right, security, or other interest therein, including any leasehold interest.

(B) For purposes of title III of this Act, the term "property" does not include real property used for residential purposes unless, as of the date of the enactment of this Act—

(i) the claim to the property is held by a United States national and the claim has been certified under title V of the International Claims Settlement Act of 1949; or

(ii) the property is occupied by an official of the Cuban Government or the ruling political party in Cuba.

(13) Traffics.—(A) As used in title III, and except as provided in subparagraph (B), a person "traffics" in confiscated property if that person knowingly and intentionally—

(i) sells, transfers, distributes, dispenses, brokers, manages, or otherwise disposes of confiscated property, or purchases, leases, receives, possesses, obtains control of, manages, uses, or otherwise acquires or holds an interest in confiscated property,

(ii) engages in a commercial activity using or otherwise benefiting from confiscated property, or

(iii) causes, directs, participates in, or profits from, trafficking (as described in clause (i) or (ii)) by another person, or otherwise engages in trafficking (as described in clause (i) or (ii)) through another person,

without the authorization of any United States national who holds a claim to the property.

* * *

TITLE I—STRENGTHENING INTERNATIONAL SANCTIONS AGAINST THE CASTRO GOVERNMENT

§ 6032. Enforcement of the Economic Embargo of Cuba

(a) Policy.—

(1) Restrictions by other countries.—The Congress hereby reaffirms section 1704(a) of the Cuban Democracy Act of 1992, which states that the President should encourage foreign countries to restrict trade and credit relations with Cuba in a manner consistent with the purposes of that Act.

(2) Sanctions on other countries.—The Congress further urges the President to take immediate steps to apply the sanctions described in section 1704(b)(1) of that Act against countries assisting Cuba.

(b) Diplomatic Efforts.—The Secretary of State should ensure that United States diplomatic personnel abroad understand and, in their contacts with foreign officials, are communicating the reasons for the United States economic embargo of Cuba, and are urging foreign governments to cooperate more effectively with the embargo.

(c) Existing Regulations.—The President shall instruct the Secretary of the Treasury and the Attorney General to enforce fully the Cuban Assets Control Regulations set forth in part 515 of title 31, Code of Federal Regulations.

* * *

(h) Codification of Economic Embargo.—The economic embargo of Cuba, as in effect on March 1, 1996, including all restrictions under part 515 of title 31, Code of Federal Regulations, shall be in effect upon the enactment of this Act, and shall remain in effect, subject to section 204 [22 U.S.C. § 6064] of this Act.

* * *

§ 6040. Importation Safeguard Against Certain Cuban Products

(a) Prohibition on Import of and Dealings in Cuban Products.—The Congress notes that section 515.204 of title 31, Code of Federal Regulations, prohibits the entry of, and dealings outside the United States in, merchandise that—

(1) is of Cuban origin;

(2) is or has been located in or transported from or through Cuba; or

(3) is made or derived in whole or in part of any article which is the growth, produce, or manufacture of Cuba.

(b) Effect of NAFTA.—The Congress notes that United States accession to the North American Free Trade Agreement does not modify or alter the United States sanctions against Cuba. The statement of administrative action accompanying that trade agreement specifically states the following:

(1) "The NAFTA rules of origin will not in any way diminish the Cuban sanctions program.... Nothing in the NAFTA would operate to override this prohibition." .

(2) "Article 309(3) [of the NAFTA] permits the United States to ensure that Cuban products or goods made from Cuban materials are not imported into the United States from Mexico or Canada and that United States products are not exported to Cuba through those countries." .

(c) Restriction of Sugar Imports.—The Congress notes that section 902(c) of the Food Security Act of 1985 (Public Law 99–198) requires the President not to allocate any of the sugar import quota to a country that is a net importer of sugar unless appropriate officials of that country verify to the President that the country does not import for reexport to the United States any sugar produced in Cuba.

(d) Assurances Regarding Sugar Products.—Protection of essential security interests of the United States requires assurances that sugar products that are entered, or withdrawn from warehouse for consumption, into the customs territory of the United States are not products of Cuba.

* * *

TITLE II—ASSISTANCE TO A FREE AND INDEPENDENT CUBA

* * *

TITLE III—PROTECTION OF PROPERTY RIGHTS OF UNITED STATES NATIONALS

* * *

TITLE IV—EXCLUSION OF CERTAIN ALIENS

§ 6091. Exclusion From the United States of Aliens who have Confiscated Property of United States Nationals or who Traffic in Such Property

(a) Grounds for Exclusion.—The Secretary of State shall deny a visa to, and the Attorney General shall exclude from the United States, any alien who the Secretary of State determines is a person who, after the date of the enactment of this Act—

(1) has confiscated, or has directed or overseen the confiscation of, property a claim to which is owned by a United States national, or converts or has converted for personal gain confiscated property, a claim to which is owned by a United States national;

(2) traffics in confiscated property, a claim to which is owned by a United States national;

(3) is a corporate officer, principal, or shareholder with a controlling interest of an entity which has been involved in the confiscation of property or trafficking in confiscated property, a claim to which is owned by a United States national; or

(4) is a spouse, minor child, or agent of a person excludable under paragraph (1), (2), or (3).

* * *

(b) Definitions.—

* * *

(2) Traffics.—(A) ... a person "traffics" in confiscated property if that person knowingly and intentionally—

(i)(I) transfers, distributes, dispenses, brokers, or otherwise disposes of confiscated property,

(II) purchases, receives, obtains control of, or otherwise acquires confiscated property, or

(III) improves (other than for routine maintenance), invests in (by contribution of funds or anything of value, other than for routine maintenance), or begins after the date of the enactment of this Act to manage, lease, possess, use, or hold an interest in confiscated property,

(ii) enters into a commercial arrangement using or otherwise benefiting from confiscated property, or

(iii) causes, directs, participates in, or profits from, trafficking (as described in clause (i) or (ii)) by another person, or otherwise engages in trafficking (as described in clause (i) or (ii)) through another person,

without the authorization of any United States national who holds a claim to the property.

* * *

F. MISCELLANEOUS DOCUMENTS

DOCUMENT 14

ABA MODEL RULE FOR THE LICENSING OF LEGAL CONSULTANTS

§ 1. General Regulation as to Licensing

In its discretion, the [name of court] may license to practice in this State as a legal consultant, without examination, an applicant who:

(a) is a member in good standing of a recognized legal profession in a foreign country, the members of which are admitted to practice as attorneys or counselors at law or the equivalent and are subject to effective regulation and discipline by a duly constituted professional body or a public authority;

(b) for at least five of the seven years immediately preceding his or her application has been a member in good standing of such legal profession and has actually been engaged in the practice of law in the said foreign country or elsewhere substantially involving or relating to the rendering of advice or the provision of legal services concerning the law of the said foreign country;*

(c) possesses the good moral character and general fitness requisite for a member of the bar of this State;

(d) is at least twenty-six years of age;** and

(e) intends to practice as a legal consultant in this State and to maintain an office in this State for that purpose.

§ 2. Proof Required

An applicant under this Rule shall file with the clerk of the [name of court]:

(a) a certificate from the professional body or public authority in such foreign country having final jurisdiction over professional discipline, certifying as to the applicant's admission to practice and the date thereof, and as to his or her good standing as such attorney or counselor at law or the equivalent;

(b) a letter of recommendation from one of the members of the executive body of such professional body or public authority or from

---

* Section 1(b) is optional; it may be included as written, modified through the substitution of shorter periods than five and seven years, respectively, or omitted entirely.

** Section 1(d) is optional; it may be included as written, modified through the substitution of a lesser age than twenty-six years, or omitted entirely.

one of the judges of the highest law court or court of original jurisdiction of such foreign country;

(c) a duly authenticated English translation of such certificate and such letter if, in either case, it is not in English; and

(d) such other evidence as to the applicant's educational and professional qualifications, good moral character and general fitness, and compliance with the requirements of Section 1 of this Rule as the [name of court] may require.

§ 3. Reciprocal Treatment of Members of the Bar of this State

In considering whether to license an applicant to practice as a legal consultant, the [name of court] may in its discretion take into account whether a member of the bar of this State would have a reasonable and practical opportunity to establish an office for the giving of legal advice to clients in the applicant's country of admission. Any member of the bar who is seeking or has sought to establish an office in that country may request the court to consider the matter, or the [name of court] may do so sua sponte.

§ 4. Scope of Practice

A person licensed to practice as a legal consultant under this Rule may render legal services in this State subject, however, to the limitations that he or she shall not:

(a) appear for a person other than himself or herself as attorney in any court, or before any magistrate or other judicial officer, in this State (other than upon admission pro hac vice pursuant to [citation of applicable rule]);

(b) prepare any instrument effecting the transfer or registration of title to real estate located in the United States of America;

(c) prepare:

(i) any will or trust instrument effecting the disposition on death of any property located in the United States of America and owned by a resident thereof, or

(ii) any instrument relating to the administration of a decedent's estate in the United States of America;

(d) Prepare any instrument in respect of the marital or parental relations, rights or duties of a resident of the United States of America, or the custody or care of the children of such a sesident;

(e) render professional legal advice on the law of this State or of the United States of America (whether rendered incident to the preparation of legal instruments or otherwise) except on the basis of advice from a person duly qualified an entitled (otherwise than by virtue of having been licensed under this Rule) to render professional legal advice in this State;

(f) be, or in any way hold himself or herself out as, a member of the bar of this State; or

(g) carry on his or her practice under, or utilize in connection with such practice, any name, title or designation other than one or more of the following:

(i) his or her own name:

(ii) the name of the law firm with which he or she is affiliated;

(iii) his or her authorized title in the foreign country of his or her admission to practice, which may be used in conjunction with the name of such country; and

(iv) the title "legal consultant," which may be used in conjunction with the words "admitted to the practice of law in [name of the foreign country of his or her admission to practice]".

§ 5. Rights and Obligations

Subject to the limitations set forth in Section 4 of this Rule, a person licensed as a legal consultant under this Rule shall be considered a lawyer affiliated with the bar of this State and shall be entitled and subject to:

(a) the rights and obligations set forth in the [Rules] [Code] of Professional [Conduct] [Responsibility] of [citation] or arising from the other conditions and requirements that apply to a member of the bar of this State under the [rules of court governing members of the bar]; and

(b) the rights and obligations of a member of the bar of this State with respect to:

(i) affiliation in the same law firm with one or more members of the bar of this State, including by:

(A) employing one or more members of the bar of this State;

(B) being employed by one or more members of the bar of this State or by any partnership [or professional corporation] which includes members of the bar of this State or which maintains an office in this State; and

(C) being a partner in any partnership [or shareholder in any professional corporation] which includes members of the bar of this State or which maintains an office in this State; and

(ii) attorney-client privilege, work-product privilege and similar professional privileges.

§ 6. Disciplinary Provisions

A person licensed to practice as a legal consultant under this Rule shall be subject to professional discipline in the same manner and to the same extent as members of the bar of this State and to this end:

(a) Every person licensed to practice as a legal consultant under these Rules:

(i) shall be subject to control by the [name of court] and to censure, suspension, removal or revocation of his or her license to practice by the [name of court] and shall otherwise be governed by [citation of applicable statutory provisions]; and

(ii) shall execute and file with the [name of court], in such form and manner as such court may prescribe:

(A) his or her commitment to observe the [Rules] [Code] of Professional [Conduct] [Responsibility] of [citation] and the [rules of court governing members of the bar] to the extent applicable to the legal services authorized under Section 4 of this Rule;

(B) an undertaking or appropriate evidence of professional liability insurance, in such amount as the court may prescribe, to assure his or her proper professional conduct and responsibility;

(C) a written undertaking to notify the court of any change in such person's good standing as a member of the foreign legal profession referred to in Section 1(a) of this Rule and of any final action of the professional body or public authority referred to in Section 2(a) of this Rule imposing any disciplinary censure, suspension, or other sanction upon such person; and

(D) a duly acknowledged instrument, in writing, setting forth his or her address in this State and designating the clerk of such court as his or her agent upon whom process may be served, with like effect as if served personally upon him or her, in any action or proceeding thereafter brought against him or her and arising out of or based upon any legal services rendered or offered to be rendered by him or her within or to residents of this State, whenever after due diligence service cannot be made upon him or her at such address or at such new address in this State as he or she shall have filed in the office of such clerk by means of a duly acknowledged supplemental instrument in writing.

(b) Service of process on such clerk, pursuant to the designation filed as aforesaid, shall be made by personally delivering to and leaving with such clerk, or with a deputy or assistant authorized by him or her to receive such service, at his or her office, duplicate copies of such process together with a fee of $10. Service of process shall be complete when such clerk has been so served. Such clerk shall promptly send one of such copies to the legal consultant to whom the process is directed, by certified mail, return receipt requested, addressed to such legal consultant at the address specified by him or her as aforesaid.

§ 7. Application and Renewal Fees

An applicant for a license as a legal consultant under this Rule shall pay an application fee which shall be equal to the fee required to be paid by a person applying for admission as a member of the bar of this State under [rules of court governing admission without examination of persons admitted to practice in other States]. A person licensed as a legal consultant shall pay renewal fees which shall be equal to the fees required to be paid by a member of the bar of this State for renewal of his or her license to engage in the practice of law in this State.

8. Revocation of License

In the event that the [name of court] determines that a person licensed as a legal consultant under this Rule no longer meets the requirements for licensure set forth in Section 1(a) or Section 1(c) of this Rule, it shall revoke the license granted to such person hereunder.

9. Admission to Bar

In the event that a person licensed as a legal consultant under this Rule is subsequently admitted as a member of the bar of this State under the provisions of the Rules governing such admission, the license granted to such person hereunder shall be deemed superseded by the license granted to such person to practice law as a member of the bar of this State.

§ 10. Application for Waiver of Provisions

The [name of court], upon application, may in its discretion vary the application of or waive any provision of this Rule where strict compliance will cause undue hardship to the applicant. Such application shall be in the form of a verified petition setting forth the applicant's name, age and residence address, the facts relied upon and a prayer for relief.

DOCUMENT 15

FLORIDA FOREIGN LEGAL CONSULTANCY RULE

Rules Regulating the Florida Bar Title 15, Chapter 16 (1998)

TITLE 15   RULES REGULATING THE FLORIDA BAR

CHAPTER 16.   FOREIGN LEGAL CONSULTANCY RULE

RULE 16-1.1   PURPOSE

The purpose of this chapter is to permit a person who is admitted to practice in a foreign country as an attorney, counselor at law, or the equivalent to act as a foreign legal consultant in the state of Florida. This chapter authorizes an attorney licensed to practice law in 1 or more foreign countries to be certified by the Supreme Court of Florida, without examination, to render services in this state as a legal consultant regarding the laws of the country in which the attorney is admitted to practice.

RULE 16-1.2   DEFINITIONS

A foreign legal consultant is any person who:

(a) has been admitted to practice in a foreign country as an attorney, counselor at law, or the equivalent for a period of not less than 5 of the 7 years immediately preceding the application for certification under this chapter;

(b) has engaged in the practice of law of such foreign country for a period of not less than 5 of the 7 years immediately preceding the application for certification under this chapter and has remained in good standing as an attorney, counselor at law, or the equivalent throughout said period;

(c) is admitted to practice in a foreign country whose professional disciplinary system for attorneys is generally consistent with that of The Florida Bar;

(d) has not been disciplined for professional misconduct by the bar or courts of any jurisdiction within 10 years immediately preceding the application for certification under this chapter and is not the subject of any such disciplinary proceeding or investigation pending at the date of application for certification under this chapter;

(e) has not been denied admission to practice before the courts of any jurisdiction based upon character or fitness during the 15-year period preceding application for certification under this chapter;

(f) has submitted, pursuant to requirements determined by the Supreme Court of Florida, an application for certification under this chapter and the appropriate fees;

(g) agrees to abide by the applicable Rules Regulating The Florida Bar and submit to the jurisdiction of the Supreme Court of Florida for disciplinary purposes;

(h) is over 26 years of age;

(i) maintains an office in the state of Florida for the rendering of services as a foreign legal consultant; and

(j) has satisfied, in all respects, the provisions of rule 16–1.4.

RULE 16–1.3 ACTIVITIES

(a) Rendering Legal Advice. A person certified as a foreign legal consultant under this chapter may render legal services in the state of Florida; provided, however, that such services shall:

(1) be limited to those regarding the laws of the foreign country in which such person is admitted to practice as an attorney, counselor at law, or the equivalent;

(2) not include any activity or any service constituting the practice of the laws of the United States, the state of Florida, or any other state, commonwealth, or territory of the United States or the District of Columbia including, but not limited to, the restrictions that such person shall not:

(A) appear for another person as attorney in any court or before any magistrate or other judicial officer or before any federal, state, county, or municipal governmental agency, quasi-judicial, or quasi-governmental authority in the state of Florida, or prepare pleadings or any other papers in any action or proceedings brought in any such court, or before any such judicial officer, except as authorized in any rule of procedure relating to admission pro hac vice, or pursuant to administrative rule;

(B) prepare any deed, mortgage, assignment, discharge, lease, agreement of sale, or any other instrument affecting title to real property located in the United States, or personal property located in the United States, except where the instrument affecting title to such property is governed by the law of a jurisdiction in which the foreign legal consultant is admitted to practice as an attorney, counselor at law, or the equivalent;

(C) prepare any will or trust instrument affecting the disposition of any property located in the United States and owned by a resident thereof nor prepare any instrument relating to the administration of a decedent's estate in the United States;

(D) prepare any instrument with respect to the marital relations, rights, or duties of a resident of the United States or the custody or care of the children of such a resident;

(E) render professional legal advice on the law of the State of Florida, the United States, or any other state, subdivision, commonwealth, or territory of the United States, or the District of Columbia (whether rendered incident to the preparation of a legal instrument or otherwise); or

(F) render any legal services without utilizing a written retainer agreement that shall specify in bold type that the foreign legal consultant is not admitted to practice law in the state of Florida nor licensed to advise on the laws of the United States or any other state, commonwealth, territory, or the District of Columbia, unless so licensed, and that the practice of the foreign legal consultant is limited to the laws of the foreign country where such person is admitted to practice as an attorney, counselor at law, or the equivalent.

(b) Representing Status as Member of The Florida Bar. Foreign legal consultants certified to render services under this chapter shall not represent that they are admitted to The Florida Bar or licensed as an attorney or foreign legal consultant in another state, commonwealth, territory, or the District of Columbia, or as an attorney, counselor at law, or the equivalent in a foreign country, unless so licensed. Persons certified under this chapter shall not use any title other than "Foreign Legal Consultant, Not Admitted to Practice Law in Florida," although such person's authorized title and firm name in the foreign country in which the person is admitted to practice as an attorney, counselor at law, or the equivalent may be used if the title, firm name, and the name of the foreign country are stated together with the above-mentioned designation.

Foreign legal consultants certified under this chapter must provide clients with a letter disclosing the extent of professional liability insurance coverage maintained by the foreign legal consultant, if any, as well as an affirmative statement advising the client that any client aggrieved by the foreign legal consultant will not have access to the Clients' Security Fund of The Florida Bar. The letter must further include the list of activities that the foreign legal consultant certified under this chapter is prohibited from engaging in, as set out in rule 16-1.3(a)(2)(A)-(F).

RULE 16–1.4 CERTIFICATION

(a) Commencement of Permission to Perform Services. Permission for a foreign legal consultant to render legal services under this chapter shall become effective upon the filing of an application and certification, with respect to an applicant, by the International Law Section of The Florida Bar, of the requirements of rules 16-1.2(a) through (j) and 16-1.3(a) and (b) herein. In addition to any other evidence that The Florida Bar, in its discretion, may require, the application shall include the filing and approval of:

(1) a duly authenticated certificate from the entity governing the practice of law in the foreign country in which the applicant is licensed to practice, which shall be accompanied by the official seal, if any, of such entity, and which shall certify:

(A) the entity's jurisdiction in such matters;

(B) the applicant's admission to practice in such foreign country and the date thereof;

(C) the applicant's good standing as an attorney, counselor at law, or the equivalent; and

(D) whether any charge or complaint has ever been filed against the applicant with such entity, and if so, the substance of each such charge or complaint and the adjudication or disposition thereof;

(2) a letter of recommendation signed by and with the official seal, if any, of 1 of the members of the executive body of such entity or from 1 of the judges of the highest court of law of such foreign country, certifying to the applicant's professional qualifications;

(3) a letter of recommendation from at least 2 attorneys, counselors at law, or the equivalent admitted in and practicing in such foreign country, setting forth the length of time, when, and under what circumstances they have known the applicant and their appraisal of the applicant's moral character;

(4) a letter of recommendation from at least 2 members in good standing of The Florida Bar, setting forth the length of time, when, and under what circumstances they have known the applicant and their appraisal of the applicant's moral character;

(5) a sworn statement by the applicant that the applicant:

(A) has read and is familiar with the Rules of Professional Conduct as adopted by the Supreme Court of Florida and will abide by, and be subject to, the provisions thereof;

(B) submits to the jurisdiction of the Supreme Court of Florida for disciplinary purposes, as defined in chapter 3 of these rules and rule 16–1.6. The statement by the applicant must also authorize notification to the entity governing the practice of law in the foreign country in which the applicant is licensed to practice of any disciplinary action taken against the applicant in Florida; and

(C) shall comply with the requirements of rule 16-1.3(b) regarding disclosure;

(6) a written commitment to notify the court of any resignation or revocation of the foreign legal consultant's admission to practice in the foreign country of admission, or in any other state or

jurisdiction in which said consultant has been licensed as an attorney, counselor at law, or equivalent or as a foreign legal consultant, or of any censure, suspension, or expulsion in respect of such admission; and

(7) a duly acknowledged instrument setting forth the applicant's address within the state of Florida and designating the secretary of state as such person's agent upon whom process may be served, pursuant to applicable Florida law, with like effect as if served personally upon such applicant, in any action or proceeding thereafter brought against the applicant arising out of or based upon any legal services rendered or offered to be rendered by such applicant within or to the residents of the state of Florida, whenever after due diligence service cannot be made upon such applicant at such address.

(b) Annual Sworn Statement. A person certified under this chapter as a foreign legal consultant shall submit to The Florida Bar, on an annual basis, a sworn statement attesting to the foreign legal consultant's good standing as an attorney, counselor at law, or the equivalent in the foreign country in which such person is licensed to practice and shall also include with such statement an annual renewal fee equivalent to annual dues paid by members of The Florida Bar, in good standing, and such other evidence as The Florida Bar shall deem necessary to determine the continuing qualifications of the foreign legal consultant under this chapter.

RULE 16–1.5 WITHDRAWAL OR TERMINATION OF CERTIFICATION

Permission to perform services under this chapter shall cease immediately upon the earliest of the following events:

(a) The filing of a notice by the Supreme Court of Florida, in its discretion, at any time, stating that permission to perform services under this chapter has been revoked. A copy of such notice shall be mailed by the clerk of the court to The Florida Bar and to the foreign legal consultant involved. The foreign legal consultant shall have 15 days to request reinstatement for good cause.

(b) The foreign country in which the foreign legal consultant is admitted to practice discontinues having a professional disciplinary system for attorneys that is generally consistent with that of The Florida Bar.

(c) The failure of the foreign legal consultant to comply with any applicable provisions of this chapter.

RULE 16–1.6 DISCIPLINE

(a) Discipline by Florida Courts. Each person licensed to practice as a foreign legal consultant under this chapter is expressly subject to the Rules of Professional Conduct and to continuing review of such consultant's qualifications to retain any license granted hereunder, and shall be subject to the disciplinary jurisdiction of the Supreme Court of Florida and the other courts of this state.

(b) Withdrawal of Certification. In addition to any appropriate proceedings and discipline that may be imposed by The Florida Bar or the Supreme Court of Florida under chapter 3 of the Rules Regulating The Florida Bar, the Supreme Court of Florida may, at any time, with or without cause, withdraw certification hereunder.

(c) Notification of Other Jurisdictions. The Florida Bar shall be authorized to notify each entity governing the practice of law in the foreign country in which the foreign legal consultant is licensed to practice law of any disciplinary action taken against the foreign legal consultant.